Strange Places, Questionable People

JOHN SIMPSON was born in 1944 and educated at St Paul's School, London and Magdalene College, Cambridge. He has worked for the BBC since 1966 and has filled many of its main news positions, from foreign correspondent to diplomatic editor, political editor and presenter of the *Nine O'Clock News* and *Newsnight*. He conducts a weekly programme on foreign affairs, *Simpson's World*, which is broadcast on News 24 and BBC World. From 1990 to 1996, he was associate editor of the *Spectator*, and is now a columnist of the *Sunday Telegraph*.

John Simpson was appointed CBE in the Gulf War Honours List in June 1991, and was the Royal Television Society's Journalist of the Year in the same year. He has won two major BAFTA awards and the Columnist of the Year Award for his magazine writing in 1994. He is the author of nine books on current affairs and literature and lives in Dublin with his wife, Dee Krüger.

D1113179

Strange Places, Questionable People

JOHN SIMPSON

PAN BOOKS

To my wife, Dee, *prima et semper*;

to everyone who has loved and helped me
during the past turbulent half-century;

to my granddaughter Isobel, born as I began this book;

and to Martha Gellhorn, who died just as it was finished

First published 1998 by Macmillan

This edition published 1999 by Pan Books
an imprint of Pan Macmillan Ltd
Pan Macmillan, 20 New Wharf Road, London N1 9RR
Basingstoke and Oxford
Associated companies throughout the world
www.panmacmillan.com

ISBN 0 330 35566 X

29 28

A CIP catalogue record for this book is available from
the British Library.

Phototypeset by Intype London Ltd
Printed and bound in Great Britain by
Mackays of Chatham plc, Chatham, Kent

Contents

List of Illustrations

Photos not credited are from John Simpson's own collection.

SECTION ONE

Roy Simpson in 1962.

My mother and me in 1946.

The house at Dunwich.

Me at the age of six.

Brian Brooks. *(Courtesy of Brian Brooks)*

Cambridge companions: John Argent, Prince Richard of Gloucester, Simon Platt, John Simpson, Bernard Hunt, Andrew Holmes, Nicholas Snowman, Jeremy Griggs, John Thompson, Michael Binyon, Ridley Burnet.

The BBC Radio newsroom.

With Diane, Eleanor and Julia in California, 1973.

The Provisional IRA press conference, Ireland, July 1973.

Ayatollah Khomeini, Tehran 1979. *(Bill Handford)*

Colonel Gadhafi, 1979. *(Bill Nichol)*

Andrei Sakharov and his wife, Yelena Bonner, 1978.

Publicity photographs from 1981 of John Humphrys and me on the *Nine O'Clock News* set.

Chancellor Helmut Kohl. *(Don Legget and Don Nesbitt)*

Tira Shubert.

Margaret Thatcher. *(Derek Collier)*

Mikhail Gorbachev, 1988.

Peter Jouvenal and Chris Hooke in 1989.

The safe house in Kabul. *(Peter Jouvenal)*

Tiananmen Square, 4 June 1989. *(Ingo Prosser)*

SECTION TWO

Introduction

This book is not intended to be an autobiography. It is partly an explanation for the curious life I lead, and partly an account of the way the world has changed in the thirty years I have been observing it professionally. Mostly, though, it is a collection of stories, often with a light dusting of fiction over them. That is essential, given that most of the people who appear in these pages are still alive and might not want me to describe my dealings with them too fully. Nevertheless, my account of things is as truthful as I can make it, and I haven't knowingly bent any facts in order to fit them in. Above all, I haven't tried to glamorize my own involvement; on the contrary, I have done my best to be painfully honest. Even so, I notice as I read through the pages which follow that wherever I go I always seem to arrive at a key moment. Can this really be correct? You will have to make up your own mind about that, I'm afraid.

I have dealt before with several of the episodes that appear in this book, especially the big set-pieces: the revolution in Iran, Tiananmen Square, the Berlin Wall, the revolutions in Czechoslovakia and Romania, the collapse of Communism in Russia, the Gulf War. But in each case I have tried to go into the kind of detail I have never previously felt able to give.

A great many things seem to have happened to me over the years, and there is not room enough here to cover even the more interesting of them. Since this is only the first of two books, I have put off all sorts of things until the second one, from my disappearance in Lebanon at the time of the hostage-taking to meetings with cocaine barons in Peru and Colombia, and encounters with Fidel Castro and Emperor Bokassa and the Emperor of Japan. Together I have given the two books the title 'Out To The Undiscovered Ends', which comes from some lines by Hilaire Belloc:

> From quiet homes and first beginning,
>> Out to the undiscovered ends,
> There's nothing worth the wear of winning,
>> Save laughter, and the love of friends.

Many friends of mine have played an important part in my life, yet their names won't necessarily appear here. This is not the result of ingratitude or lack of interest; it is merely that the telling of stories requires the stripping out of much detail. Just because their names don't appear, it doesn't mean I have forgotten their importance to me.

Several people have helped in compiling this *apologia pro mea vita*. The BBC has been generous in all sorts of ways, from permissions to quote from past broadcasts to the kindly latitude I received from Richard Sambrooke and Adrian Van Klaveren, who have not only allowed me to go my own way but didn't turn a hair when I announced I was going to leave London and live in Dublin. My editors at the *Sunday Telegraph*, Dominic Lawson and Con Coughlin, were also most generous. My assistant at the BBC, Farne Sinclair, has helped me in hosts of ways, faxing information to me in the most unlikely parts of the world and digging out everything from the details of antique broadcasts to advice and quotations and management of the manuscript. Considerable thanks are also due to Dan Roan, who worked for me (for nothing, of course: this being the BBC's way) even while he was preparing for his finals at Cambridge.

This book had its origins in a dinner with my agent, Julian Alexander, who has been the godparent of the entire enterprise; and my association with him has not only been highly profitable in every way, it has also been extremely enjoyable. To my wife Dee I owe even more: from the precision of her judgement to the love with which she has surrounded me.

As I say, this isn't intended to be an account of current affairs, past and present. I have tried to speak a little of myself: not the broadcaster and writer, the faintly familiar face from the television, the half-remembered by-line from magazines and newspapers, but the persona behind these things. Perhaps I have said too little; perhaps too much. I haven't always been able to prevent myself from settling a few ancient scores, but I have tried to be truthful.

Dalkey, County Dublin, May 1998

1

A Peculiar Way to Earn a Living

BELGRADE, MARCH 1999

I GOT INTO THE LIFT. This entire hotel is empty, I thought: I can take any room I want. I pressed the button for the second floor, where there was a suite I had rather liked. At a time like this, cost scarcely mattered. Who knew if I'd even be around to pay the bill, anyway?

I put my suitcase down and turned to look self-critically in the mirror, as you do when you're alone. *Eheu fugaces, Postume, Postume*: a big, lumbering middle-aged fellow stared out at me, a touch paunchy, bags under the eyes, the hair turning from grey to white, fifty-four and looking every day of it. Not through bad living, particularly, but careless living: never bothering about what I eat, how much I sleep, where I go. It wears you down. And now, most careless of all, I'd ended up here all on my own. Crazy.

As the lift headed upwards I peered closer for signs of lunacy or fear, but all I could detect was relief, liberation, a weird kind of triumph. I winked jovially at this new, freer self. We were on our own now, in a big way.

The doors opened. No one around, of course; even the hotel staff seemed to have been scared away. I walked down the empty corridor to the far end, reaching in my pocket for the keys. We had been using this suite for broadcasting on the satellite phone: it still stood in the corner, a sheet of incomprehensible instructions lying beside it on the floor.

I dropped onto the bed and looked at the ceiling. I had either done the stupidest thing in my life, in which case I would pay a heavy price for it, or else I had pulled as great a stroke as anything in my convoluted career. Which was it to be? I didn't know, and I found I didn't care much. I felt obscurely good about it: I had done something I knew I should, for its own sake, without worrying about the consequences.

> What would ye, ladies? It was ever thus.
> Men are unwise, and curiously planned.

It had been a day of panic. The night before, Wednesday 24 March, NATO had begun the bombing of Yugoslavia. Massacre and ethnic cleansing had started on a big scale down in Kosovo, and here in Belgrade dangerous forces had been unleashed. A battle was going on between the more civilized figures in President Slobodan Milosević's administration and the savage nationalistic faction headed by Vojislav Seslj, vice-premier in the Serbian government, whose supporters had carried out appalling atrocities in Croatia and Bosnia some years earlier. At midday the large international press corps, three hundred or so strong, had trooped into a press conference held by the former opposition leader Vuk Draskovic, now a member of Milosević's government himself.

'You are all welcome to stay,' he told us grandly, looking more like Tsar Nicholas II than ever, his cheeks flushed with the first *slivovic* of the day. Directly we arrived back at the Hyatt Hotel, where most of the foreign journalists were staying, we were told that the communications minister, a sinister and bloodless young acolyte of Seslj's, had ordered everyone working for news organizations from the NATO countries to leave Belgrade at once. It was clear who had the real power, and it wasn't Draskovic.

That morning Christiane Amanpour, the CNN correspondent, white-faced with nervousness, had been marched out of the hotel by a group of security men from a neutral embassy, put in a car and driven straight to the Hungarian border for her own safety. Arkan, the para-military leader who was charged with war-crimes as the war began, had established himself in the Hyatt's coffee-shop in order to keep a personal eye on the Western journalists. His thugs, men and women dressed entirely in black, hung around the lobby. Reuters Television and the European Broadcasting Union had been closed down around noon by units of the secret police. They slapped some people around, and robbed a BBC cameraman and producer of a £30,000 camera.

I wanted to stay in Belgrade, and yet I wanted to get out with all the others. There were eight of us in the BBC team, not counting our Yugoslav producers, and we had a meeting. It quickly became clear that everyone else wanted to leave. I argued briefly for staying; but I didn't want to be entirely on my own here with such lawlessness going on around me. *Vorrei, e non vorrei.* We went off to pack.

By the time we had finished it was almost dark. I lugged my two suitcases downstairs and put them in one of the vehicles that was to take us to safety. It felt like a re-run of the Gulf War in 1991, only shorter. Then I had been hustled out of Iraq with the other Western journalists after the first five days of bombing; now I was leaving Belgrade after only twenty-four hours. It didn't feel right.

'I've just got to hand over the sat phone,' said one of the producers.

'What do you mean, hand it over? Who to?'

'There's an Australian chap who's staying.'

'Staying?'

It was Greg Wildsmith, a correspondent for the ABC whom I knew from Baghdad and other places, and always liked. He wandered calmly across the lobby now to meet us. It was true: he and his team weren't getting out like the rest of us.

'Unless I've missed it in the newspapers,' he drawled, 'Australia isn't a member of NATO. So I assume we don't have to go.'

That made up my mind for me: if there was someone else here to share the risk, then I would stay as well. It didn't matter that I came from a NATO country, and Greg didn't. Maybe I could talk my way out of that. I have a great belief in my ability to talk my way out of trouble.

'I'm going to get my stuff out of the car,' I said; thereby changing everything in my life for months and perhaps years to come.

So now here I was, settled into my very pleasant suite, almost but not quite alone in the hotel. I rang my wife Dee to explain (as a television journalist she understood) and then rang the BBC to tell them that, after all, I would be staying (they seemed hugely relieved). Then I settled back on the bed, poured myself a generous slug of Laphroaig and lit an Upmann's Number 2. Life began to seem almost bearable: for the moment, at any rate. As for the future, that could look after itself. I had selected a CD with some care, and it was playing now.

> There may be trouble ahead,
> But while there's moonlight, and music, and love and romance
> Let's face the music and dance.

Outside, a familiar wailing began: the air-raid siren. I took my Laphroaig and my cigar over to the window and looked out at the anti-aircraft fire which was already arcing up, red and white, into the night sky.

« »

Like a clumsy waiter, I've left behind me a little trail of smashed relationships. Being the BBC's foreign affairs editor – world affairs editor, as I'm called now out of consideration for all those people we broadcast to around the world who don't regard themselves as foreign – has not been noticeably good for my private life. Perhaps I ought to cite Lord Reith as co-respondent. The existence I lead may seem glamorous, and sometimes it is. More often, though, it has an obsessive, slightly dodgy quality to it. I am always trying to get to places where I'm not wanted, and convincing people to do things they don't want to do; it's like selling double-glazing. I have (at a certain age one begins to count up these things) reported from 103 countries, interviewed 122 emperors, monarchs, presidents, dictators, prime ministers and other assorted despots and loonies, and witnessed thirty wars, uprisings and revolutions. That's a lot of collective grief, and I suppose it has left its mark.

By now my contemporaries from Cambridge have mostly reached the culmination of their careers: the fair-round-belly-with-good-capon-lined stage, where a knighthood or a seat in the House of Lords no longer seems absurd and pompous but is starting to assume the attraction of a just reward. One of my closest university friends runs Glyndebourne. One is a judge. One, I discovered recently by chance, is in the top ranks of MI6. Others are publishers, architects, archaeologists, writers of novels or of thoughtful editorials, bankers, senior academics, government ministers past or present. Some have vanished without trace, died, or are serving prison sentences. One is an ambassador in a major capital; others soon will be.

All these people take risks, but rarely with their lives. Why should I, at an age where sensible men and women are starting to think about winding down and finding a little place in the country, want to keep on behaving like this? Why am I still standing on foreign pavements, arguing the toss with gunmen and rioters and secret policemen?

Not, certainly, because I have to. Nowadays I am the titular head of all the BBC's foreign reporting, and within reason I can do pretty much what I want. I have a pleasant office at Television Centre, filled with congenial producers and correspondents who are personal friends. The World Affairs Unit which I set up in 1988 and am nominally in charge of, is a rather distinguished kind of place, a bit like a fellows' common-room at a university. When I'm there, which is rarely, it is a pleasant place to hang out.

I could perfectly well exist on a professional diet of international summit meetings, conferences and elections. I could stay at decent hotels, eat at reasonable hours, plan my social life properly, and never again set foot in what we used to called the Third World. I could also go mad. That kind of life, safe and predictable and easy, would bore me to death; or at least to early retirement, which would probably soon become the same thing.

From time to time I am rung up by one of the newspapers and asked for an interview. I usually agree, but I don't expect to like it. On the basis of an acquaintance of perhaps an hour and a quarter, interviewers seem to feel a need to explain me. Their research often consists solely of reading other newspaper interviews I have done, or looking through the cuttings about me. So a phrase originally invented by the *Daily Mail's* gossip columnist and put in the mouth of one of my colleagues, that I was pompous and arrogant, gets regularly repeated. It's not necessarily that I'm *not* pompous and arrogant, you understand; merely that these people don't always discover it for themselves. The idea is passed from interviewer to interview like a mild infection.

So we end up going over the same half-dozen often incorrectly understood facts. The interviewer sits across the table from me at some pleasant restaurant, notebook at the ready, red light on the tape recorder unwinking, puzzlement in the eyes, hoping for something to come up which will make sense of this weird phenomenon sitting opposite.

Is it because I was raised as a Christian Scientist (even though I stopped being one decades ago)? Is it because, at the age of seven, I had to choose whether to live with my mother or my father, and chose

my father? Is it going to a public school in the fifties, and university
in the sixties? Is it my complex private life? Is it—? But by this stage I
know we will not reach an understanding. We do not have lift-off. We
merely have a reshuffling of the six known facts, which will be handed
down to yet another generation of the idle.

And yet I can perfectly well understand the need for some kind of
explanation. Why, after all, should I have stayed on in Belgrade when
most perfectly sensible people were getting out? Mine is indeed a
peculiar way to earn a living. Maybe that has a certain limited interest
in itself, just as other peculiar ways of earning a living – rat-catching,
say, or maintaining the sewers, or being a media tycoon – have an
interest. And yet there are so many far better things to write about
than that: for instance the extraordinary changes that have taken place
in the thirty years I have been reporting on the world's affairs, and
what really happened in the great events I have been privileged to see.

« »

It is often the things you do in a hurry, I have found, which have the
greatest effect. Three days after I had decided to remain behind in
Belgrade, still alone and having slept a total of seven hours since the
war began, and with every programme of an organization as many-
headed as an old bramble-bush demanding reports from me, I had to
write my weekly column for the *Sunday Telegraph*. It was five-thirty
in the morning. I described the situation as best I could, then paused
for a moment and looked at the television screens across the room.
BBC World, Sky and CNN were all showing an immense flood of
refugees crossing the Macedonian border from Kosovo: and yet protecting these people was surely the major purpose of the NATO
bombing – that, and encouraging people in Serbia itself to turn against
President Slobodan Milosević.

Well, I thought, it isn't working yet. Most of the people in Belgrade
who had once been against Milosević now seemed to have rallied to
his support: I had already had some of them shouting at me. And the
ethnic Albanians of Kosovo certainly weren't exactly being protected.
I went back to my word-processor: *If that was the purpose of the
bombing*, I wrote, *then it isn't working yet*. I added a few more
paragraphs, then hurriedly faxed the article to London before the next

wave of demands from BBC programmes I had never heard of could break over me.

The *Sunday Telegraph* ran it rather big the next day, under the imposing but embarrassing headline, 'I'm sorry, but this war isn't working.' Tony Blair read it – or at least read the headline – and was reported to be furious. Yet he knew it was true. The aim had been to carry out a swift series of air attacks which would force President Milosević to surrender; that was probably what he wanted to do anyway. But the NATO onslaught had been much too feeble, and much too circumscribed. The centre of Belgrade and the other towns and cities of Serbia had not been touched; President Clinton, as worried as ever about domestic opinion, had promised that there would be no ground war; and – significantly for the future of the war – an American Stealth aircraft had crashed, or just possibly been shot down, outside Belgrade. After four days of war it suddenly looked as though it might not be a such walkover for NATO after all.

Milosević couldn't make a quick climb-down in the face of NATO's overwhelming force now: his own public opinion, intoxicated by its unexpected success, wouldn't accept it. And anyway the force didn't seem quite so overwhelming, and Serbia didn't seem quite so feeble, any longer. NATO was in for a long campaign, and therefore there was a clear possibility that the alliance might fall apart over the next few weeks.

And so the machinery of the British government went into action to deal with the problem. Not the real problem, of course: merely the little local difficulty that someone had pointed out that things weren't going to plan. Whichever party is in power, Downing Street always likes to start its campaigns with an attack from a pliant and ambitious backbench MP, to see if that will do the trick. Ben Bradshaw, a Labour backbencher who had once worked for the BBC (there is no heresy-hunter as eager as the recent convert) started complaining publicly about my reporting and the fact that I didn't restrict it to the BBC's airwaves but carried it over into the press as well. He also suggested that my work wasn't up to much, and that my colleagues knew it.

Not long afterwards I decided to go out onto the Belgrade streets to sample opinion. Foreign camera crews had had a very difficult time of it, and the cameraman and I, together with our Serbian producer, were distinctly nervous. People crowded round and jostled us to scream their anger against NATO. These, we found, weren't supporters of Seslj and Arkan; most of them had previously taken part in the big anti-Milosević demonstrations two years earlier. But in the face of the bombing they felt they had no alternative but to regard themselves first and foremost as Serbs, and that meant giving him their support.

Not, you might think, such an extraordinary development; wars always tend to unite people. There was no doubt about the intensity of feeling: the men and women who gathered round us were on the very edge of violence. Before we started we had asked a couple of passing policemen if they would give us some protection. 'Fuck off,' one of them said, and they walked off laughing.

After our report was broadcast on that night's *Nine O'Clock News*, the government in London suggested – off the record, of course – that the people we had interviewed were obviously afraid of President Milosević's secret police, and had said only what they had been instructed to tell us. They might even have been planted by the authorities for us to interview. It was strange, the anonymous voices said, that someone as experienced as I should have failed to realize any of this.

Soon afterwards American pilots hit a convoy of ethnic Albanian refugees heading for the safety of the border. NATO put forward all sorts of suggestions about what had happened, and insisted that the convoy had been escorted by the Serbian military: thus making it a legitimate target. An American general suggested that after the NATO jets attacked that the Serbian soldiers travelling with the convoy had leaped out of their vehicles and in a fit of rage had massacred the civilians.

It wasn't necessarily all that far-fetched; both before and afterwards, Serbian soldiers and paramilitaries carried out the most disgusting reprisals against innocent ethnic Albanian civilians. But it wasn't true in this case. It later turned out that British pilots had recognized the convoy as a refugee one, and warned the Americans not to attack.

In a studio interview for that night's *Nine O'Clock News* I was asked who might have been responsible for the deaths of the refugees. I replied that if it had been the Serbs, they would try to hush it up quickly. But if it had been NATO, then the Serbian authorities would probably take us to the site of the disaster and show us. This had happened several times already, on occasions when the facts bore out the Serbian version.

The following day the military press centre in Belgrade duly provided a coach, and the foreign journalists were taken down to see the site. The Serbs had left the bodies where they lay so the cameramen could get good pictures of them; such pictures made excellent propaganda. It was perfectly clear that NATO bombs had been responsible for the deaths, and eventually NATO was obliged to own up and apologize.

But Downing Street was worried that disasters like this would turn public opinion against the war. As the person who had suggested that the Serbian version might conceivably be true, I became the direct target of the British government's public relations machine. Mr Blair had staked everything on the success of NATO's war against Milošević, and it wasn't going well. So he did precisely what the Thatcher government had done in 1982 when things looked bad in the Falklands War, and what it did in 1986 when the Americans bombed Tripoli from British bases, and what the Major government did in 1991 when civilian casualties began to mount in Iraq during the Gulf War: he attacked the BBC's reporting. When British governments have their backs to the wall, it's a knee-jerk reaction.

I'd been expecting it. Things always go wrong in war, and it's important that people should know about it when it happens, just as they should know when things are going well. That's why I had tried so hard to get to Belgrade in the first place, and why I was so determined to stay there when everyone else left. No doubt arrogantly (and of course pompously) I reckoned that over the years I had built up some credibility with the BBC's audiences, so that people wouldn't automatically believe it if they were told that I was swallowing the official Serbian line or deliberately trying to undermine NATO's war effort. I did my utmost to report fairly and openly; and then I sat back and waited for the sky to fall in.

It happened on 14 April, twenty-two days into the war. I started getting calls that afternoon from friends at Westminster that the Prime Minister's spokesman, Alistair Campbell, had criticized my reporting in the lobby. Alistair Campbell, Tony Blair's chief spokesman, briefed the lobby at Westminster about my lack of objectivity; anonymous officials at the Ministry of Defence whispered that I was blatantly pro-

Serbian. Over the next few days and weeks Robin Cook, the foreign
secretary, called on me to leave Belgrade; Claire Short, in charge of
overseas development but a leading convert to the smart bomb and
the cruise missile, suggested that my reporting from Belgrade was akin
to helping Hitler in the Second World War. Only George Robertson,
the defence secretary and a wiser person, kept quiet.

Soon Tony Blair himself was complaining to the House of
Commons that I was reporting 'under the instruction and guidance
of the Serbian authorities'. If he had said that outside Parliament, it
would have been actionable. It was absolutely and categorically untrue:
I was neither instructed nor guided by the Serbs in what I said, and in
fact my reports were more frequently censored by the Serbian authorities than those of any other correspondent working in Belgrade
throughout this period. Not only that, but our cameraman was given
twenty-four hours to leave the country at the very time these accusations were being made, in order to punish the BBC for its 'anti-
Serbian reporting' (as the official who was responsible put it). I myself
was also thrown out of the country at the end of the war.

Thanks to the political editor of *The Times*, Philip Webster, the
accusations against me ceased to be something whispered to consenting
adults in the lobby and by anonymous officials at the Ministry of
Defence. He wrote a story which *The Times* carried on its front page
on 15 April, reporting that the British government was accusing me of
pro-Serbian bias.

The result was extraordinary. Each of the main broadsheet newspapers carried an editorial criticizing the government for its attacks on
the BBC, and several of the tabloids made it clear they didn't approve
either; even the *Sun* and the *Daily Mail*, neither of which is particularly
BBC-friendly. (In the case of the *Mail*, it had its own correspondent in
Belgrade, Dave Williams, who together with a photographer had also
stayed behind when everyone else left, and did some excellent and
courageous reporting. This may have helped.)

MPs from all sides of the House, and various members of the
Lords, spoke up on my behalf. My friend and former colleague, Martin
Bell, wrote a fierce defence of me in the press. So did John Humphrys,
the BBC presenter, who will appear frequently in this book. I was
deluged with friendly messages from members of the public. As for the
BBC itself, which, if you read these pages further, you will see has not

always rallied round when its staff have come under attack from politicians, it gave me outspoken and unequivocal backing of a kind I had never witnessed before. I had calls of support from the head of news, the Director-General, and the Chairman. It felt like Christmas.

Downing Street, ever sensitive to the public mood, immediately backed away. No one, officials said blandly, had any criticism whatever about my reporting; far from it. When I wrote a letter of complaint to Alistair Campbell, I got back not an apology, certainly – governments don't do that kind of thing – but an assurance that my professional abilities had not been called into question. And that, as far as Whitehall was concerned, was the end of it. With luck, the next time a British government gets into difficulties during a war and is tempted to attack the BBC, a warning light will come on in the cockpit before any missiles are actually launched.

Still, the predictable suggestion that there was some kind of similarity between the bombing of Serbia and the Second World War clearly struck a chord with some people. I started to get shoals of angry and often insulting letters, mostly from the elderly. This example, in a spidery hand from Anglesey, was typical:

> Dear Mr John Simpson,
>   When your country is at war and when our young men are putting their lives at risk on a daily basis, it is only a fool that would say or write anything to undermine their bravery. I do not know what your age is, but what I do know is that in Hitler's day you would be put in a safe place. Where you probably belong.

In fact, as George Orwell noted, it was typical of the British character that people throughout the Second World War should have been free to publish and say anything about the conduct of the fighting, from attacks on the competence of Churchill and his generals to advocating immediate peace with the Nazis. That is how we have always run our society, and that is what makes it stronger and ultimately tougher than Hitler's Germany – let alone Saddam Hussein's Iraq or Slobodan Milosević's Serbia.

A splendid old BBC character called R. T. Clark, then head of news, called his staff together when war broke out in September 1939 and spoke to them about the job they would have to do. 'The only way to strengthen the morale of the people whose morale is worth strengthening,' he said, 'is to tell them the truth, even if the truth is horrible.'

No doubt all sorts of people with spidery writing, from Anglesey and elsewhere, wanted 'R.T.' to be put in a safe place during the Second World War; but he stayed in his job right through to 1945, and his philosophy of telling people what was really going on, as opposed to what the government preferred them to know, became one of the most admirable things about Britain's entire conduct of the war. It's still the basis of the BBC's worldwide reputation, sixty years later.

But of course the air campaign against Serbia in 1999 was nothing like the Second World War. There was no conceivable threat to Britain's democracy, nor to its existence as a nation. In this case the only danger was to NATO's cohesion, and to the reputation of Tony Blair's government. The problem is, as Mrs Thatcher showed, that politicians have a habit of identifying their own fate with that of the country as a whole.

Unfortunately for Britain's reputation in the world, the attacks on me attracted a great deal of attention around the world. I was interviewed for French, German, Italian, Dutch, Turkish, Swedish, Russian, Japanese and American television and newspapers, all of whom saw it as a clear attempt by the British government to censor the BBC. There was a certain whiff of Schadenfreude about this, I felt; most of the journalists seemed to feel that the British were boringly sanctimonious about the freedom of their press, and had now been shown up as hypocrites. I found myself defending Tony Blair, and did my best to explain the intricacies of the relationship between the BBC and government; but like most British constitutional arrangements it probably sounded pretty unconvincing in the ears of a non-believer.

In Belgrade, where the story was given huge attention, I took on the wholly unwanted and embarrassing status of an ally: I was, after all, the man whom the British government had tried to silence for being pro-Serbian. People would stop me in the street to congratulate me. A natural irritability made me answer that I wasn't at all pro-Serbian; if anything, the contrary. But there were occasional advantages. 'If you weren't Simpson, we wouldn't allow you down here,' said a harsh elderly woman in an air-raid shelter where we wanted to film.

The Serbian press and television loved the whole business, of course: it seemed to put the BBC on the same basis as themselves, totally controlled by the state. I refused on principle to be interviewed by any Serbian journalist, especially from state television, and gave any of them who asked a little homily about the difference between a free press and the kind of obedient pro-government reporting that President Milosević liked. None was quick-witted enough to reply that Tony Blair might have liked it too.

Sometimes the arguments grew heated. 'You're not a proper journalist,' I yelled at a leading correspondent from Serbian television during one such argument, 'you're a bloody politician.' We had bumped into each other outside the ruins of a building NATO had just bombed in Belgrade. This woman was a close friend and ally of Milosević's wife, and drew a lot of water in that town: a word from her could get me arrested, beaten up, or thrown out of the country. But I knew it didn't matter; now I could get away with almost anything. Thanks to Tony Blair, I had become fire-proof.

2

A Different World

I JOINED THE BBC when I was twenty-two.

Looking back, it seems to be another existence altogether: simpler, safer, less knowing, less guilty, more peaceable. And now it is as dead and gone as the world which ran by steam or horses or wind-power, the world of the great European empires, the world which built the Gothic cathedrals, the world of Byzantium, of Abbasid Baghdad, of Angkor Wat, of the Pyramids. It is hard enough for someone in his fifties to come to terms with the speed with which his hair has whitened, his face has lined and his frame has thickened; to grasp how utterly almost everything on earth has changed in only thirty years is a great deal harder still.

Thinking about the recent past is like looking through a telescope. There is an unnatural actuality about it, a false clarity. You feel you could speak to the people you can see walking along, even though they may be half a mile away. In much the same way people from the past continue to seem utterly real, a living, continuing presence, even though they may have grown old and died in the meantime, and the very places where you once knew them may have changed or disappeared entirely.

The mind condenses time in much the same way as the telescope condenses space, so that the gaps when nothing much happened dwindle away to nothing. Events take on a pattern, an apparent relationship with one another, which they rarely had at the time. When you look through your lens at people as they walk, unaware, down the street, they can never realize that their love affairs, their illnesses, their business dealings, will one day seem to an outsider observer to be part of a clear pattern of success or failure, ability or incapacity. The woman who has been getting warning letters about her overdraft thinks it won't be long before she's in the black; we, looking at her through the lens of the future, know differently. The man whose girlfriend left him last night thinks he has just had a bit of bad luck; we can see that all his relationships are going to be like that.

If, on a morning in the mid-sixties – let us say for the sake of argument Thursday, 1 September 1966 – you had crossed the Thames by train and arrived at Charing Cross, you would have seen a cityscape reasonably similar to that of the present; and yet Lutyens or Waterhouse or even Wren would have recognized entire sections of it. The great redevelopment, the vandalizing of the sixties and seventies, had not yet started in earnest. Aside from the Post Office Tower, the newest and biggest structure on the London skyline was the Hilton Hotel at the foot of Park Lane: nowadays just another unremarkable example of an outmoded architectural fashion, yet many people of my generation cannot enter it without feeling that they have come to a place which is especially vulgar and obtrusive. There were only about a quarter of today's cars in the streets, the great majority of them made by British companies whose very names have been forgotten. The crowds were almost exclusively white.

What we call the sixties had scarcely started, even though the decade was more than half over. Most women wore hats, and tight skirts down to the knee; many of the men wore bowlers and waistcoats and carried tightly rolled umbrellas. In the street, in the Underground station, on the tube train, almost every man wore a tie. There was a neatness about everything which a later generation would find positively Singaporean: no litter, no graffiti. Looking back from the complexity of the present, 1966 seems a lot more straight, and a lot easier.

« »

It had been a cloudy morning, but shortly before ten the sun shone briefly down into the narrow streets. Pushing his way through the crowd heading northwards along Upper Regent Street from Oxford Circus tube station, a tall, skinny, brown-haired young man was hurrying nervously along. He was wearing his best suit (a three-piece effort in green tweed, which had cost him £12.12s.6d a year before), a white shirt, striped tie, and brown brogues. In his right hand was an old leather briefcase containing an apple, a wrapped ham-and-cheese sandwich prepared by his thoughtful wife, and a Penguin paperback of Fielding's *Tom Jones* in case time hung heavy on his hands. He was earnest, high-minded, and almost completely innocent of the world and its ways. Characteristically, he was cutting things fine, having left home later than he should. If you had watched him through a good lens you would have noticed that he was sweating slightly. At twenty-two (his birthday had been three weeks earlier) he was just starting the first day of his working career.

I have a certain affection for this earnest, innocent, sweaty young man; also distinct feelings of amusement and contempt. He is of course myself.

The first of September was the effective start of my existence as an adult, and I knew it. As a result everything around me seemed to be an omen of some kind about the rest of my life. Because the sun was shining; because I reached the end of the platform before the 9.38 train drew in; because a non-smoking compartment stopped directly opposite me; because the ticket-collector at Charing Cross station winked as he took my oblong of green pasteboard; because the headline in someone else's evening newspaper was positive (' "Thank God He's Safe" Says 17-Year-Old Air Crash Victim's Mum'); because I had started out late and was still almost on time; for all these reasons and a dozen others, I was coming to the conclusion that the rest of my life was likely to work out well.

Now that much of the rest of my life has happened, I have long since realized that omens are merely outward indications of what we hope or fear will happen anyway. If at twenty-two I was buoyed up by the feeling that my life would be a success, at fifty-three I am a great deal more sceptical about omens, careers, success, and hope itself. Nowadays I feel a bit like Chou En-lai, Mao Zedong's charming, subtle-minded and long-suffering prime minister, when he was asked what the results of the French Revolution had been. 'Too soon to be certain,' he said, after a long pause for thought.

That morning, as the sun came through the clouds and shone on the buses and Sunbeam Talbots and bowler hats, I could see Broadcasting House rearing up ahead of me like a liner above a skiff, with

Eric Gill's sculpture of Prospero and Ariel where the figurehead would be. That building would contain my future; it still does.

The square Art Deco clock on the upper works of the building, which now seems so stylish and then seemed so dated, showed a couple of minutes past ten: it might still be possible to give the impression that I had arrived on time. I was aware now of other people hurrying towards the bows of the liner alongside me, slightly older versions of myself: tweedy, brief-cased, polite, earnest, conscientious, middle-class, slightly arty, non-conformist yet distinctly conformist as well. In front of me one of the pleasant-faced men in sports jackets, passing in, held the narrow, heavy door open for me.

'Oh, sorry,' I said, speeding up to take it over from him and hold it open for someone else.

'Sorry,' he said simultaneously.

I took the weight of the door on my arm. It felt as heavy as push-starting a car with a flat battery. The BBC might have given me a job, but it still didn't make it easy to get in to do it. The BBC didn't make anything easy, then or ever.

Being of a self-consciously literary turn of mind, I couldn't pass through these doors at a time like this without a quotation:

> And tear our pleasures with rough strife
> Thorough the iron gates of life

Not particularly apt, of course, since the doors of Broadcasting House were made of brass, and there was rarely much pleasure involved in tearing through them: certainly not on the way in, anyway. Even so, in all the years since then I don't think I have once opened them without thinking of that first morning, and remembering the quotation.

« »

My recruitment had seemed like a long seduction, though who was the seducer and who the seduced was hard to work out. I had appeared before three selection boards, during which the same questions had been asked over and over again. I began to feel they were looking for excuses not to take me. Why did I want to be a sub-editor in Radio News? Wouldn't I rather be in television (a trick question, as I perceived even then)? Might I not be tempted after a while to go into politics (another trick question)? Wasn't I over-qualified? Wasn't I under-qualified? And if under-qualified, would I be prepared to accept the job at half the pay? This last question was raised at the third board, and it was the true voice of a public corporation. Recognizing it dimly, I said yes – as long as it wasn't for too long.

It wasn't until eleven years later, when I shared an office in Brussels with one of the people who had interviewed me that day, that I found I had got into the BBC under completely false pretences.

'Oh, you Cambridge double-firsts, you're too quick for me,' he said.

I laughed. 'Don't get me mixed up with the double-firsts. I got a bad second; lucky not to get a third. I was doing so many other things at Cambridge,' I added hastily. It is one thing to get a bad second because you didn't work; another altogether to get one because you aren't very bright.

He looked shocked. 'But we had a letter from your college saying you were expected to get a first.'

'So why didn't you ask me about it at the board?'

'You're lucky we didn't.'

'This is luck?' I said, looking out at the grey Brussels skyline.

But it was, of course.

I had had two job offers already. One was from the Thomson Newspapers training scheme, to be a reporter on the *Reading Post*; it was the best position newspaper journalism had to offer a graduate trainee, and would probably lead to a staff job on the *Sunday Times*; then regarded as the best newspaper in London. The other offer was from a shadowy branch of the Foreign Office which specialized in black propaganda. No one actually told me that it was connected with intelligence, but I guessed that a name as bland as 'Information and Research Department' probably covered something much more questionable. I hadn't read Ian Fleming and Len Deighton for nothing.

The recruiting officer and I sat facing each other across an entirely empty desk at the IRD's bland headquarters beside the Thames, with the river flowing fast and muddy below us. Finally I brought myself to the point of asking exactly what work they did here. When my voice stopped there was a silence. The recruiting officer looked out at the river. In the outer office a secretary was saying, 'So I said to her, "Well," I said, "it's no use you coming here and—" '

There was a noise like a distant sheep's cough from across the desk. The recruiting officer was starting to concede that, yes, the job could be said to be connected, in a certain sense, though only peripherally, or rather tangentially, as it were, and in the widest possible interpretation of the word, if I saw what he meant, with intelligence.

'So is it dangerous? Will I have to carry a gun?' I tried to sound amused and sophisticated, but merely sounded nervous.

'My dear fellow, of course not,' said the interviewer, laughing indulgently at the absurd notions of the young and ignorant. That put him back in charge again. 'You will merely have to write reports about other countries. Rhodesia, for example.'

I see now he was trying (peripherally, or rather tangentially, as it were) to be honest with me, but I was too innocent and obtuse to realize that he was referring to the Wilson government's enemies, about whom I would be expected to spread nasty stories to the media.

'And what about the salary?' The words came out more crudely than I had intended.

The man behind the desk riffled through a set of papers with an interested air, as though no one had ever raised this particular one before and it would be an amusing exercise to find out. He did a few calculations on the blotting paper in front of him, then looked up with an encouraging smile.

'Six hundred and forty pounds per annum.' He nodded slightly as he said it, as if encouraging me to nod too, and accept.

Twelve pounds, six shillings a week; my rent was seven pounds a week, living costs were a fiver. My wife and I would just about scrape by, but it wouldn't be easy.

'Thank you very much,' I said obsequiously, putting on my grateful young intellectual face. But I was thinking, 'If only those swine at the BBC would hurry up and tell me if they've accepted me, I could turn this lot down right away.'

The swine at the BBC were in no hurry whatever. Dealing with them was, and is, like being a viceroy in Lima, in urgent need of instructions from Philip II in Spain. Weeks went by, and still no answer came from Broadcasting House. Thomson Newspapers were getting restless; even the Information and Research Department would want an answer soon. So did I.

And then at nine-thirty one morning in mid-July at our flat in Cambridge I made my usual trip down three flights of stairs and along two corridors to check the letterbox. I was still in my striped pink and green pyjamas, and my bare white feet squeaked on the lino. I eased guiltily past the open door of our doctor-landlord's waiting room, where early-rising Miss Howe, the receptionist, sat in her crisp white coat, ready for the first patient of the day.

On the doormat lay a long white envelope with the three magic initials in its bottom left-hand corner. I scooped it up and ran back past Miss Howe, gripping the letter with one hand and the front opening of my pyjama trousers with the other, my feet squeaking louder than ever. Upstairs in our delightful sitting room with its central upright pillar, where we had had so many parties and entertained so many friends, I ripped open the envelope. At this critical moment, my memory seems to go into freeze-frame: the torn envelope falling to the floor, the open letter in my hand, the sun pouring through the windows, Dido and Aeneas playing on the cheap record player, my American wife Diane holding two mugs of Lapsang Souchong and leaning against the pillar in her pink and yellow housecoat, feet bare, ready to condole or celebrate, eyes following mine, her emotions changing from sentence to sentence as I read out loud from the letter which contained her future as well as mine.

'Thank you for coming . . . After careful consideration . . . Lack of practical experience . . . Not substantive job . . . Nevertheless in circumstances . . . OFFER OF £1050.0s.0d PER YEAR . . .!!!'

We danced around the pillar hand in hand, stubbing our bare toes and making the floorboards creak above Miss Howe's tidy, tolerant head.

'We have got the magic thou.,' I sang, to the tune of 'Anyone Who Had A Heart': a doleful pop song of the time. There would be no nonsense about working in the boondocks, or dishing the dirt on Harold Wilson's enemies for a pittance: I would be a broadcaster, and I would earn eighty-seven pounds, ten shillings a month. Nowadays, after three decades of high inflation, I suppose you'd have to multiply that by about fifteen to get some idea how much it was worth in those extraordinarily different days.

'Riches,' I cackled in my miser's voice, lying on the worn brown carpet with my bare feet in the air and holding the letter over my head so I could read the wonderful words again and again.

'Let's see 'em,' said Diane, worldlier and more adult than I was.

A month later, on the strength of the letter, we left Cambridge with our seven hundred books, our eighty records, our drawing by Rowlandson, and the sets of china and glass and silverware and linen which friends had given us as wedding-presents, and took an unfurnished flat with a wig-cupboard in a Queen Anne house in Greenwich. We moved in on 1 September; which was also my first day at the BBC.

« »

And so here I was, pushing open the heavy brass doors of Broadcasting House with rough strife. Inside, the entrance hall opened up in front of me like a vast cavern.

HOC TEMPLO ARTIUM ET MUSARUM . . .

The paralysingly pompous inscription in letters the size of my head covered much of the upper part of the wall opposite. Only the BBC would have the gall to confide to the world that it was a temple of the arts and muses, and not realize that this was laying it on a bit thick. Lord Reith's name cropped up somewhere in the depths of the inscription, of course, and his gloomy influence seemed to infuse the whole place. He'd been gone twenty-six years, but it seemed like only yesterday.

'The Newsroom, please,' I said to a commissionaire sitting behind a desk the size of a church organ. He was as old and intimidating and war-marked as Reith himself. Then, never able to stand a silence, I confided, 'I'll be working there.'

'Ho, the Newsroom,' he said scornfully, as though lunatics and impostors often came in here claiming that sort of thing. 'I'll just check that, *if* you don't mind.'

It seemed to come as a personal disappointment to him when he found my name on his list after all.

'Take the lift to the Third Floor. Where you will be Met.' He made it sound like a Masonic induction ceremony.

A sombre secretary, sexlessly dressed, was waiting for me when the lift doors opened. She nodded to me and made a noise that was probably meant to be welcoming. Then she turned, and I followed her along a narrow corridor, past doors belonging to the kind of programmes I'd listened to all my life: *The Critics, Lift Up Your Hearts, Radio Newsreel*. Mine had been a radio childhood. Like most middle-class parents of the 1950s, my father believed that television was bad for you. He has, I suppose, been proven absolutely right.

At the very end of the corridor, down a dark defile, the Newsroom opened up: a large, low-ceilinged, open place, noisy and confusingly active, where the overhead lights were never switched off, day or night. People hammered away on typewriters, or dictated to secretaries, or hurried around with fresh batches of copy newly garnered from the wire-machines. There was a preponderance of grey hair and cardigans, and a distinct scarcity of women.

I was introduced to a variety of people whose names I couldn't remember, and whose functions I couldn't comprehend. A young, dark, gloomy character with aristocratic hair, atrabilarian eyes and an up-turned nose was appointed to show me how things were done.

'Long haul here,' he confided, sighing a little.

I sat beside him all morning, watching him work. He gathered together the various pieces of agency copy on a particular news story and read through it with an intensity I hadn't seen since the University Library at Cambridge, his nose close to the smudgy lines of words. Paper edged in yellow or maroon or brown or green, representing respectively British United Press (which, he said, I should never trust), Agence France Presse (which I should trust only rarely) and Associated Press (which I should trust reluctantly) and Reuters (which I should trust implicitly), lay piled on his desk, the key passages underlined in pencil. It seemed to me, when I read them carefully, that the four agencies might have been describing four different incidents. This was, I think, the first moment when I understood faintly that journalism was an art and not a science.

'Vietnam,' confided the lugubrious aristocrat. 'Bloody Yanks have bombed another friendly village. They really are a shower.'

He wrote something down with a 2B pencil on a pad of paper, crossed it out, wrote something else, then screwed up the paper and threw it away. His fine, almost feminine hands were never at rest even when he was staring gloomily out of the window. After a few moments he gave a quiet groan and suggested that we should go and get a cup of coffee, so we sidled out of the Newsroom. He glanced nervously at the editor's desk as we passed, like a shoplifter keeping an eye on a lounging security guard.

'Have to be careful about going out too often. Chief Sub,' he added meaningfully.

I nodded, as though I understood.

'Oh, God,' he burst out with a sudden rush of emotion as we reached the safety of the empty corridor, 'I simply can't stand this awful place any more.' Then, 'Oh, I say, sorry. Not very tactful, I suppose.'

'How do you mean?'

'Well, your first day.'

I didn't know how to reply, so I grinned weakly and hunched my shoulders with embarrassment, hands in my pockets digging fingernails into my palms. I hadn't, you see, got over the delight of being in the place at all; what it might turn out to be, now that I was in, scarcely mattered to me yet.

Ahead of us lay the trolley, where a jolly, mountainous woman was dispensing coffee and jokey personal remarks.

'Came here really in order to write some novels in my spare time. Trouble is, I don't do it. Just lie on my bed looking at the ceiling and waiting for my shift to start again. Two white coffees, Margaret, if you please,' he said in a completely different voice, his gloom turning at once to expansiveness. 'This is John. He's going to be one of your best customers. Doughnut?'

''E needs summink to fill 'im out,' said Margaret, and she laughed, her whole vast figure shaking, dewlaps and bosom and upper arms quivering in different directions and at different speeds. It was a pleasurable, satisfying sight, like walking into a kitchen where a seven-course meal was being prepared. I blushed, of course.

Back in the Newsroom my guide finally constructed his story and dictated it out loud to one of the typists. I marvelled at his precision and coherence, and wondered if I would ever be able to do anything like it. When it was finished he looked at it for a long while, reading it over and over in a low voice, then set it in front of the Chief Sub like a ritual sacrifice.

Which is what it proved to be. The crossings-out he had made on his early drafts were a moon-cast shadow to what the Chief Sub did to it now. His pencil must have been a 6B at least, and he used it like a US infantryman used his automatic rifle in a Vietnamese village.

'No, no, no, no, no,' he rumbled to himself, the cleft between his black eyebrows deepening. His pencil laid waste entire sentences. There were few survivors.

'Oh, Christ,' muttered their author, as I sat beside him watching.

The piece of foolscap was handed back, devastated with thick black lines. The Chief Sub had written an entirely new version in capital letters underneath. Why employ people like us, I wondered innocently? Why not just do it all himself?

'Rewrite, I'm afraid, Doris my dear,' the aristocratic young man told the typist at the desk beside him, switching once again from the deepest gloom to a courtly chirpiness. He peered at the capital letters and dictated from them in a loud, unembarrassed voice: 'A spokesman at the American military headquarters in the Vietnamese capital dash dash Saigon dash dash has admitted that—'

By twelve-forty the tempo in the Newsroom had become animated. People walked faster, spoke louder, crossed out words on scripts with even greater ferocity: clearly something was up. The newsreader of the day finished reading through his scripts and shuffled them into shape. He was a handsome, saturnine figure in his late fifties, and had been one of the voices of freedom and sanity for the entire population of Britain throughout the Second World War: a hero, therefore, even though some deeply unromantic medical condition, often speculated on – flat feet, perhaps, or chronic piles – had kept him out of the forces. During the Blitz a bomb had landed near Broadcasting House as he was reading the headlines and he had said with monumental calm, 'I'm sorry – I'll just repeat that.' Nowadays, though, he read the radio news to a dwindling domestic audience which, judging from the letters we received, was more concerned with the stress in 'controversy' and the flat, northern vowels of some BBC reporters than with the news we gave them.

At five minutes to one the Chief Sub laid down his gory pencil, the Duty Editor stood up, the saturnine newsreader gathered up his scripts and handed them to the Chief Sub, who seemed to be the only person trusted to carry them. They processed in stately fashion down the corridor towards the studio. There was a sense of mission, of being on business of national importance. Those of us who were left behind turned our chairs reverently towards the loudspeakers, as though we were at a prayer meeting. The pips went, signalling one o'clock. 'This

is the BBC Home Service,' said a sepulchral voice. The newsreader
delivered the headlines in the familiar plummy tones that had once
kept morale high during the War:

> It's now feared that ninety people - probably all British
> - died in the Britannia airliner crash in Yugoslavia.
>
> The Cabinet, at its first meeting for three weeks, has
> discussed Rhodesia and the economic situation.
>
> President de Gaulle has said the Americans must withdraw
> from South Vietnam before there can be a settlement.
>
> Hundreds of police officers from all over London lined the
> funeral route this morning at the service for their three
> murdered colleagues.
>
> The weather: Cloudy in most places with rain at times,
> but there may be some sunshine in south-western
> districts.
>
> Later in the programme, Sir Alec Douglas-Home will be
> talking about Harold Macmillan's Memoirs.

It was, as I say, a different world. There had been no shortage of
remarkable news during the summer of 1966; the three policemen had
been murdered by a ferocious thug called Harry Roberts a few days
earlier, and in the months immediately before that we had had a general
election and a World Cup which England had managed to win. Winston
Churchill had died only eight months earlier. The Beatles were already
more famous, as John Lennon would later claim, than Jesus Christ.
The Vietnam War was beginning to intrude into everyone's consciousness. Yet there was no hint of the subjects which came to dominate
the news for the next quarter-century: in other words, for most of my
career.

There was, for instance, no mention of Northern Ireland; the big
civil rights demonstrations and the start of the IRA campaign were still
two or three years into the future. Stormont, 'a Protestant parliament
for a Protestant people', ruled the province, and the B-Specials patrolled
the streets when necessary to ensure that Catholics knew their place.
Nor was there any mention of Europe: the European Economic
Community still only had its original six members, while the European

Free Trade Area, which Britain had created as a spoiler, had seven. France's veto on British membership of the EEC four years earlier remained.

In domestic politics, economic affairs dominated everything; and yet by comparison with the decades which were to follow 1966 now seems remarkably ordered and benign: inflation somewhere around 2 per cent, unemployment 3.5 per cent. No British newspaper would dream of printing details about the private life of prominent people. As for the royal family, their privacy was virtually sacrosanct.

The price of oil was markedly low, and most of the countries which produced it slumbered in their post-colonial torpor. Americans were slowly beginning to get over the murder of John F. Kennedy, and opposition to the Vietnam War was mostly restricted to left-wing academics and writers. The civil rights of black people (who still by and large preferred the expression 'coloured', and would have abhorred 'African-American') were still noticeably restricted; plenty of schools and restaurants and bars remained segregated, and it was still dangerous for a black man to register as a voter or go out with a white woman. The first black golfer would not be allowed to play in the Augusta Masters' Tournament for another nine years, and even then he would have to be escorted round the course by four armed policemen. France was governed sternly but for the time being quietly by General de Gaulle. Greece was a monarchy; Spain was a dictatorship under Franco, and Portugal under Salazar. The King of Jordan ruled the old city of Jerusalem, and Israel was a tiny country, twenty miles or so across at its slenderest part, constantly under threat from every side and supported instinctively by most European socialists.

Countries like Iran and Afghanistan, which we have become accustomed to think of as permanently closed to us, were then open; countries which are open, such as Russia, China, and Albania, then seemed irrevocably closed. Latin America, now almost entirely composed of democracies, was then the natural home of the military dictatorship. Mao Tse-tung, as his name was still spelt in the West, had scarcely started the insane experiment called the Cultural Revolution.

Britain was still the world's main colonial power; Swaziland, Bechuanaland, British Honduras, Jamaica, Hong Kong and Kuwait were all governed from London, and her biggest international problem was the rebellion by white settlers in Rhodesia. On the day I started at the BBC,

Hendrik Verwoerd, the main architect of South Africa's policy of apartheid, had another week to live before being murdered, and Nelson Mandela had been in prison for only three years.

There were 240 pennies to the pound, each of them bigger and heavier than the largest coin in anyone's pocket today, and a pound was worth $2.40, so that a penny equalled a cent. You regularly found coins of George V's and Edward VII's reigns in your change, and sometimes those of Queen Victoria. The cost of goods in the shops was higher than it had been a hundred years before, but not that much higher. If Diane and I spent £5.0s.0d. a week on our living costs, Samuel Pepys (who like me was educated at St Paul's and Magdalene College, Cambridge) had spent £7.0s.0d. a month. We were still within touching distance of the past.

'Swinging London' was a phrase as yet unexcavated from a *Time* magazine sub-editor's imagination. London was, my father used to tell me, irrevocably provincial. 150,000 tourists had visited it in 1965 (as against seven million in 1995). Carnaby Street was mostly occupied by small ironmongers, grocers and rag-traders. 'Biba' was a small, dark, crowded clothes shop south of High Street Kensington, models were often in their thirties, and the Beatles and the Animals wore dark suits and ties on stage. The world's two most popular film stars were Marilyn Monroe and John Wayne.

The *Queen Elizabeth*, the *Queen Mary*, the *France* (launched only six years earlier) and a dozen other less famous names still plied the North Atlantic route, though the arrival in service of the Boeing 707 in 1960 had been the beginning of the end for the age of the great liners: a million passengers made the sea crossing in 1959, but by 1966 the figure was around 400,000. Aberfan, My Lai, Lockerbie and Dunblane were just small dots on the map, Chernobyl was no more than the Russian word for a type of herb. Many people seriously doubted if man would ever really land on the moon or fly the Atlantic in a supersonic airliner.

Dr Mengele and Klaus Barbie lived quietly in South America. Everyone thought Kurt Waldheim was just another boring, decent Austrian politician. A majority of men and women still smoked cigarettes, even though the link with cancer, which had been made public three years earlier, had led to a slight drop in the habit. Cancer itself was universally regarded as a death sentence. AIDS and mad cow disease were unthought of.

The first practical electronic calculator would not be invented for three more years, and computers, vastly inefficient, filled entire rooms. No country in the world had colour television. The Walkman lay fourteen years in the future. Records were made of vinyl and went round at 78, 45 or 33 revolutions per minute. Japan manufactured motorcycles but not cars, and people still associated Japanese workmanship with imitation and shoddy work. 'Empire Made' on a piece of cutlery or a toy meant it came from Hong Kong and was likely to discolour, bend or break soon. Stockbrokers were fiftyish and wore tailcoats. More than ninety per cent of the populations of Britain, Germany, the Netherlands and Sweden had been born in their own country, of parents who had themselves been born there. (The percentage was a little lower in France because of the recent influx of pieds noirs from Algeria.) Kenya and Uganda still had their large Asian populations so the corner supermarket scarcely existed in Britain, and Patel hadn't yet become a familiar British name. No one went out at night for a curry and lager, and no restaurant anywhere in Britain served Tandoori, Balti, Thai, Mexican, Szechuan or Iranian food. In the United States McDonald's was a regional company known, if at all, only for its 17 cent hamburger. There were two fewer known planets in the solar system, and it was still thought that Venus had a solid surface you could walk on.

Words and entire concepts had not yet entered the popular vocabulary: 'escalation', 'syndrome', 're-negotiate', 'counter-sue', 'gazump', 'dysfunctional', 'quantum leap'. Perhaps these were things for which the world of the early sixties felt no need. Cocaine and marijuana were both much less used than later. No one put ' – gate' onto the end of a word to denote a scandal. The summer of 1966 went on a long time and was often quite hot, yet although crime was noticeably high no one called it 'a long, hot summer', any more than they called the following winter with all its strikes 'a winter of discontent'. And if something altered, no one further imitated Shakespeare by talking about a 'sea-change'.

Among the preternaturally polite British it was starting to become necessary to elaborate in order to avoid rudeness. You could no longer say 'Close the door' or even 'Please close the door', because that would sound brusque; and so you found yourself using vast circumlocutions like 'I wonder if you would mind closing the door.' In something of the same way it was still slightly ill-mannered to address a letter to 'Mr James Smith' rather than 'James Smith, Esq.', and in the absence of the fax, which would not be available for twenty more years, the only way to get it to him was either to post it (at tuppence-ha'penny, which is a concept you have to be over forty nowadays to understand) or else deliver it in person.

No one in Britain said 'Hi!', and no one in America said 'You have GOT to be joking,' or even 'Have a nice day,' except by accident. A billion meant a million million, and scarcely anyone was aware that in America it meant a thousand times less. Anyway, few people except astronomers had any use for the word: there were no billionaires, and even governments reckoned only in hundreds of millions. Software meant things you put on the bed or the floor. Gay meant happy. Only a few years before, the newspapers had speculated whether the star of *My Fair Lady* should be allowed to use the word 'bloody' at a gala performance attended by Princess Margaret. The word 'fuck' had never been intentionally broadcast on radio or television anywhere in the English-speaking world.

Class was still a real force in British life, though it was fading fast. The elderly upper-class still spoke of 'gels' and 'goff', 'orf' and 'crorss'. A few even put the accent on the middle syllable of 'balcony'; thirty years later, there's probably no one left alive who does that. There were a few old people whose grandfathers had been born in the eighteenth century, and plenty of others whose fathers had fought in the Crimea and the Indian Mutiny, or who had themselves shaken the hand of someone who remembered Pitt the Younger or Napoleon. Survivors of the Boer War were numbered in their thousands, and of the First World War in their hundreds of thousands. As for the Second World War, it was only a couple of decades back: every adult remembered it. Even the young – the upper middle-class young, at any rate – spoke differently. Their vowels were rounder, their consonants more noticeable. They didn't say 'I'm, like' when they meant 'I thought' or 'I said'. Only one person in eighteen went to university; now it is one in three.

Almost everything would start to change very soon now, and many things were changing already. But on Thursday 1 September 1966, the day my world effectively began, there seemed to be a distinct stasis. It was just about the last moment in history when you could be forgiven for expecting that the future would carry on pretty much like the past.

3

Father of the Man

LIKE TRISTRAM SHANDY, I was troubled in my mother's womb. In my case, it was Reichsmarschall Hermann Goering who was responsible.

On two different occasions during the spring of 1944, as if searching us out, his bombers dropped their loads close to the house where my mother was living during her pregnancy. We escaped unhurt both times. But the bombers seemed to be homing in. One night in July my father was home on leave from the Army. As they – we – were lying together in bed, ignoring the air-raid sirens, a bomb fell on the house next door and the ceiling collapsed all over us. My father leaped out of bed with the immense anger that used to well up inside him at the most unsuitable times. He shook his fist at the bare rafters, and shouted at my mother, who was eight-and-a-half months gone and was still lying in bed, mountainous and plaster-white like an Alp, that the life of his son (he was sure I would be a son) was in danger. She had to get out of London at once.

The following morning, still in the grip of his rage against Goering, he took her to King's Cross station and bought her a one-way ticket to the farthest place he had the cash for at the time. It turned out to be Blackpool. The journey was interminable, as the train, packed with soldiers, wound its way by spurs and side tracks through the wastes of bomb-damaged England. My mother told me later that the soldiers on board were kind and respectful, and had always ensured that she had a seat, and a certain degree of privacy, and water whenever she wanted it. The journey lasted thirty hours, but she managed to hold onto me, and when she arrived in Blackpool she made her way to the Queen's Hydro in Cleveleys, a rather grander resort a few miles up the coast.

A week later my father followed her. The weather was pleasantly hot, and he decided to take a swim in the sea. Looking back at the Hydro, the waves breaking round him, he saw a nurse standing at the window of my mother's room and holding up something white. This something was me. Each time I fill in the column which says 'Place of birth' on a visa application or a form at a hotel reception desk, the circumstances of my arrival in the world come back to me. Rather than hankering after the security and comfort of the womb, I may have spent my life hankering after the Blitz instead.

My parents were not even slightly suited to each other: she was quiet, discouraged, gentle; he was assertive, outgoing, passionate. My father, in one of those introspective moments which so disturb children, once explained to me that he had married my mother because he felt sorry for her; she had been left a widow with two children to care for.

On my mother's side my family background was impossibly romantic. Her grandmother Leila was the daughter of John Blackburn Davis, a big London horse-dealer who owned a stables behind the Royal Court Theatre in Sloane Square. Early in the 1870s he took Leila with him to the United States in a search for new and better breeds of horse. In Chicago, the centre of the cattle trade, he came across a young cowboy called Samuel Franklin Cowdery who escorted the herds northwards from his native Texas to the Chicago stockyards each year. Cowdery was captivated by Leila's sophisticated beauty and high spirits, and when John Blackburn Davis asked Cowdery to escort the horses he had bought back to England, Cowdery agreed at once.

His life had already been extraordinary. His parents' farm in Birdville, Texas, had been attacked by Indians, but he had escaped and joined a group of cowboys. As the youngest member of the team, he spent much of his time with the elderly Chinese cook. After the evening meal had been eaten and cleared away, the cook would entertain Sam by showing him how to make and fly kites; and it was this interest which, years later, on a different continent and under a different name, was to make him famous.

Cowdery brought John Blackburn Davis's horses to England, and became a familiar sight in Sloane Square and Belgravia as he rode through the streets in his buckskins and high-heeled cowboy boots, his long hair hanging down his back. The attraction which had existed from the start between him and Davis' daughter turned into a love affair. The trouble was, both of them were already married. They decided to run off to America, taking Leila's two children with them. Cowdery planned to start a travelling cowboy show with Leila, who was a fearless rider. She and her children took to their new life with enthusiasm. Dressed in leather and cowboy hats, they rode around the ring, firing and being fired at, throwing themselves and their horses down in the sawdust, jumping over fiery obstacles, rescuing each other from fates worse than death.

The Cowderys' roadshow took them across America from east to west, with moderate but never overwhelming success. By dropping a couple of consonants and a vowel he turned himself into Sam Cody: thereby illicitly siphoning off a little of the glamour and reputation of Buffalo Bill Cody, whose travelling circus was known throughout America and Europe.

The shows depended on Cody's remarkable skills as a rider and marksman, on Leila's beauty and courage, and on the abilities of her elder son Leon. He was young and fair-haired, and soon attracted as much attention as his mother and stepfather. Leon was the hero, Leila the heroine, and Cody the villain: sometimes a ferocious Indian chief, sometimes a crooked sheriff. In 'The Klondyke Nugget', Cody's ludicrous but highly enjoyable melodrama, the climax came when he tied Leila to a barrel of exploding powder and lit the fuse. Leon had to race round the arena on horseback, reach down, cut the ropes and pull her onto the saddle in front of him all in one movement, and ride off a second or so before the barrel exploded. The risks were real, and the audience knew it.

At their riding and shooting displays Leila, wearing a tiny black satin costume covered with sequins (I still have it somewhere, packed in a trunk), would stand in front of an iron screen with small glass bulbs fixed into it, around the outline of her body. Cody would shoot out the bulbs while his horse bucked and reared theatrically under him. Once it bucked too much, and Cody hit Leila in the thigh. She stood there, still smiling, until the act was over; her husband's reputation as a marksman was more important to her than the pain.

By the 1890s he began experimenting with kites. The British army thought they would be useful for reconnaissance, and Cody, deeply patriotic towards his adoptive country, volunteered for the post of kite designer and instructor to the military. From kites he moved on to dirigible balloons, and eventually to powered aircraft.

In October 1908 Cody made the first powered flight in the British Empire, travelling ten feet or so off the ground for a distance of more than a thousand yards. For the next five years he was in the front rank of international aviators. Twenty years older than most of his competitors, he earned the affectionate nickname 'Papa' Cody.

And then one day in 1913 Cody, by now fifty-three, was trying out a new aircraft he had designed. As he performed a turn over Laffan's Plain, outside Aldershot, a gust of wind caught them and flipped the aircraft upside down. Both pilot and passenger fell to the ground and were killed instantly.

With Cody gone, the colour went out of the family. He had left behind him an echo, a resonance, which none of them could ever replace in their lives. By the time my mother met my father she too was widowed, left with two children, a sad, intelligent, unfulfilled woman. Marrying my father did nothing to help.

« »

His family was the complete opposite of my mother's: stolidly upper-middle class, they had come from humble origins and never wanted to be reminded of the fact. The Simpsons had been country people, carters and farm-labourers for the most part, living in the open, flat, gentle countryside around Bury St Edmunds in Suffolk. (My father used to say to me that this was where the Simpsons climbed *into* the gutter.) In villages like Denston, Wickhambrook and Stansfield their names feature on the gravestones and in the parish registers, but never in any out-of-the-ordinary way. They worshipped and obeyed those in authority, they married and gave birth and paid their taxes and died, always in exemplary and uncomplaining fashion. The last thing they wanted was to attract attention to themselves.

Except, that is, in Stansfield in the 1770s, where a tall and remark-ably beautiful young woman called Elizabeth Simpson grew up with the belief that life must hold something better. At the age of seventeen she ran away, walking the hundred miles to London and living on raw turnips from the fields. She became an actress, taking the name of her shadowy, ineffectual husband, and soon the theatre had, in Mrs

Inchbald, an actress of sufficient stature to take the place vacated by the great Mrs Siddons. Later in life she turned to writing plays and novels; her best known book, *A Simple Story*, is a homiletic yet rather charming account of a high-minded, beautiful young woman who rises above her humble origins and meets – well, you get the picture. It's still in print today.

In the late 1840s a sickly young man called George Simpson left Suffolk for London, propelled by his bossy, ambitious wife Charlotte. He went into the building trade and set up business in South Norwood, where he and my great-grandfather proceeded to build great swathes of ugly suburban two-up-and-two-down houses in grey brick, each with its arched doorway, its outside lavatory, and its table-cloth-sized front garden hedged with privet. Every time I travel to or from Gatwick airport by train I look out at the wasteland between Norwood and Croydon which my great-great-grandfather and his cultured, sensitive son helped to create, and cringe in my seat.

My grandparents were a glamorous couple, but their marriage was doomed. My grandfather eventually built up such bad debts that he had to jump out of a window when the bailiffs came, and legged it across the fields like a character in a P. G. Wodehouse novel. He escaped to Ireland and only returned as an old man.

As for my father, he was born in 1914. He turned out to be difficult, self-reliant, anarchistic and inclined to be extreme in his views. At sixteen he ran away to sea. The P & O took him on as a steward, and he sailed round the world for five years. He told me endless stories: about lying in his bunk in the Red Sea, burning with prickly heat, about mountainous seas which terrified the passengers and kept them below, about the time when a meat-ball rolled off a plate he was carrying to the dining room and was trodden on by a blind man who was walking the deck; he told me about the colour of the flowers in Australia and watching the dawn over Rio and the way the beggars dived for pennies in the South Seas or chanted 'Give it *pice*' in Bombay.

He came back from sea in 1937 a convinced Communist, and his weekly diversion in London was to march in the East End and involve himself in fights with fascist supporters at Mosley's rallies. He volunteered to fight for the Anarchist Brigade in the Spanish Civil War, but changed his mind as the train was pulling out of Victoria station and jumped off. (Fifty years later, encouraged by too much red wine, I told this story over dinner at an Anarchists' convention in Venice which I was covering for the BBC. At first there was silence; then a Frenchman down the far end of the table shouted 'The true Anarchist never follows the crowd.' After that everyone toasted the son of the Anarchist who hadn't followed the crowd.)

In 1945, having served in the Army with little distinction, he was demobbed and at a loose end. His politics were starting that slow move from left to right which so many people of his generation have followed in the second half of this century. By 1950 he was a Liberal, on the grounds that scarcely anyone else was, and I remember him listening head in hands to the radio as the results came in from that year's election, groaning each time the announcer said, 'The Liberal candidate loses his deposit'.

Even in those days I could see how dashing and handsome he was – he may of course have explained this to me himself – in his sports jackets and his demob suits, his feet turned out as he walked, his thick hair brushed back, his eyes bright and aware. Falling in with a rather jolly group of people from the stage, he joined them in becoming a Christian Scientist. He liked it because it rejected all the boring old orthodoxies of religion and medicine, because it was American in origin, and because it taught that you can sort out the world, and particularly your health, through the way you think about it. My mother disliked it intensely. She disliked the actresses even more.

« »

During this period thousands of marriages contracted during the difficult, heightened period of the war were starting to break up: my parents' among them. Their relationship became angrier and more difficult, and rows proliferated. My very first memory, apart from the smell of wallflowers, was of my mother standing at the mirror that hung over the fireplace, putting on her lipstick while the tears rolled down her cheeks. She explained to me, her voice breaking, that we were going to leave my father and live with her family in Epsom, but that everything would be all right and we would be very happy. I was somewhere between eighteen months and two years old. My second memory is of sitting at the front of a bus and staring out at Epsom, with my mother quietly crying beside me. It seems to me, too, that she said, 'He's just impossible'; though that may have come later. Either way, she was right: he was impossible.

After that they sometimes came back together and sometimes parted, and I was attached to one or other of them like a suitcase. They were both very nice to me, so that once the immediate anxiety was settled I felt moderately comfortable.

My father treated me exactly as though I were an adult, which I enjoyed greatly. When I was six, we went together to the Marx Brothers' season at the Everyman cinema in Hampstead, and worked our way through each one of the films right through to the debased Hollywood cuteness of the last period. During *Horse Feathers*, when Groucho sang

> It doesn't matter what they say,
> It makes no difference anyway,
> Whatever it is, I'm against it.
> No matter what it is or who commenced it,
> I'm against it.

my father nudged me excitedly.

'That's exactly how you should be,' he hissed in my ear.

On the way home, or maybe it was another time altogether, I asked him what the rusted old machine on the wall of the underground station was. He answered matter-of-factly enough, and yet his words were profoundly important to me. They gave a glimpse of another and better world.

'Before the War, you put a penny in the slot and pulled that handle and out came a bar of chocolate.'

Chocolate: I was given a little of it each Christmas, together with a couple of tangerines and some even more exotic fruit, like a pineapple or a pomegranate; but sweet-rationing was so heavy that chocolate was a profound rarity. And yet it now seemed that Before-the-War (the phrase was to take on a mythic quality for me, like 'the Golden Age' or 'the reign of King Arthur', or merely 'in olden times') all you needed was a penny and the strength to pull the handle. The past must indeed have been an age of wonders, I thought; and gradually all these things, chocolate for the asking and my father's experiences at sea and the time when people in dinner jackets and long dresses danced all night at parties like in Marx Brothers films and my family had money and my parents were happy together (because I was never sure precisely what came Before-the-War and what came after) grouped together in my mind as a true Golden Age, far superior to this dull grey age of austerity and rationing and gloom which was all I had ever experienced. I felt irrevocably left outside the warmth and glamour and happiness of this time of wonders, which I knew would never return. I was an outsider – the true position for a journalist, I think – right from the start.

« »

One day in 1951, when I was seven, my father took me to the Festival of Britain, where I saw the Skylon, and put on red and green plastic spectacles to watch a film in 3-D, and listened to a recording of the accents of England and someone saying in a Cockney accent, 'Come on kettle, boil up.' We came home and found my mother packing her suitcase. When she had finished the three of us stood on the doorstep in the chilly evening light: my mother in long bottle-green coat and slanting Robin Hood-like hat with a rakish feather, my father in a tweed sports jacket, I in a light brown coat with a velvet collar as worn by Prince Charles. My mother said she would be taking me with her.

'Don't you think it should be up to the boy to decide where he wants to go and what he wants to do?' my father asked; more, probably, because it was a way of winning a debating point than because he actually wanted me to stay.

'All right,' said my mother.

They both turned to me.

I looked up at the curiously shaped knocker on the open front door with a bearded face on it, and thought. It took me a little time. My father stared up the road to the shops, my mother put down her suitcase. I went on thinking. She had two children by her first marriage; my father had none. Fairness and balance seemed to dictate that I should stay with my father. My mother burst into tears when I explained this. I couldn't understand the expression on my father's face, but I think now that surprise must have mingled with alarm: I had handed him a life sentence. To my mother it must have seemed like a terrible betrayal. For the remaining thirty years of her life I don't think either she or I could deal with the degree of guilt that was generated by the scene on the doorstep that day. I watched her, a tall, elegant figure in dark green moving down the street, her head bowed, the suitcase in her hand.

And so my father and I were on our own: difficult for him, and not without its problems for me too. I quickly learned to spot the acquisitive look in the eyes of his women friends as they locked onto us. Sometimes they wanted to mother me, sometimes they wanted me out of the way; I couldn't see why we needed them, or why he was so keen to have them around. Sometimes, because I was studious, bookish and solitary, they patronized me.

'As a matter of fact, I think I do,' I remember saying in reply to a large blonde.

'Oh, "as a matter of fact", eh? That's a clever expression for a little boy.'

In the settled, conventional atmosphere of the early 1950s children usually had two parents, and if by some mischance (usually connected with the War) they had only one, it was invariably a mother. So it became necessary to invent one, in order to be like all the other kids I was at school with. I used to introduce my fictitious mother unnecessarily into my conversation to such an extent that I sometimes wondered if the other children suspected anything. I must have sounded like the young Proust.

The school I went to was a small private one, and my father, who had to find work as and where he could in the difficult post-war period, managed to scrape together just enough to pay the fees. Whether he chose the Crispin School because it was almost next door to the grand house where my Simpson great-grandparents had raised their large, quarrelsome family, or whether this was merely a coincidence, it is too late to find out now. Either way, it was yet another powerful reminder of that golden age, Before-the-War. Like someone growing up in post-Alaric Rome, the glories of the past and the privations of the present were all around me.

Going to the Crispin School was a great trial. Not that anyone there was unpleasant: the headmistress was a gentle, bosomy woman called Isobel Jones, and the teachers (apart from the toad-faced Miss Tedman) were undemanding. The only problem was Mrs Jones's taste in colours. I had to walk the two miles to and from school every day through hostile territory wearing a bright purple blazer and cap, and a purple and silver tie. They shone out like beacons. In the gloomy, working-class streets of Norwood I felt, as Raymond Chandler has it, about as inconspicuous as a tarantula on a slice of angel food.

Like the slow purging of some ancestral blood-guilt, my way took me past some of the terraces jerry-built by the Simpson family. Rough kids would occasionally issue out to mock or throw stones at me. The territory of one particularly ferocious clan, who all had cropped, dark, round heads and never seemed to go to school, lay across my route home. This was the most dangerous part of my day; on one occasion the members of the clan captured me and shut me up in a tiny prison made from planks and broken doors on a bombed site. I was terrified and started yelling, and eventually they let me go.

It made me entirely streetwise by the age of eight. I varied my route home like a spy, and would get into conversation with women pushing prams up the long hill while we passed through the danger areas. It became something of a pleasure to watch the rough kids looking balefully out at me and to make faces at them, careful that my surrogate mother didn't cross the road or vanish into a shop while my head was turned.

The walk built up my imagination too. I would stare nosily into the windows of the houses I passed, reconstructing the lives of the people inside from the evidence of the things I could see. I watched the way the leaves on the trees flourished and fell, and the pattern they made on the paving stones when the frost had fixed them there, and the way the rainwater swirled like liquid rope as it went down the drains. I made up stories to myself about how the names of the streets I passed might have originated: Stembridge Road, Marlow Road, Wheatstone Road. There were several child-molesters around – I had trouble with one a few years later – but the streets nevertheless seemed relatively safe. Anyway I was less scared of adults than I was of rough kids.

Every autumn or winter there would be an old-fashioned peasouper, a fog so laced with the sulphurous fumes from industrial pollution and the winter's coal fires that people were forced to lead each other hand in hand through its yellow-brown, billowing waves. The sun would show through the fog as small and hard as a white ball, and by afternoon the waves of thick vapour would roll around the streets, darker than ever, turning the driveways into mysterious caves, catching me by the throat, seeping into houses, killing people with breathing difficulties. The bus conductors had to walk in front of their vehicles waving tightly rolled-up newspapers so the drivers could see where to go. Sometimes they had to light them and hold them up, walking along like Statues of Liberty.

I felt liberated whenever there was a bad fog. No rough kids could spot me now. It was impossible to see my hand clearly, even if I held it straight out in front of me. And so I could give my imagination free rein: I was an explorer, a diver in the depths of the sea, an escaped prisoner, a hunter in the jungle, a wild beast looking for its prey, the prey itself. In order to anchor myself to what was left of reality I would hug each dark-green lamp-post, thick as a sequoia, as I passed. I revelled in the strange distinction between the haziness of things a couple of feet away and their sharp clarity close up. I watched the emergence of the feeble yellow glow-worms which turned out to be car headlights, and the nervous way the drivers and passengers would stare out at the workaday suburban landscape which had suddenly turned so mysterious and alarming.

Our lives slowly began to improve. I mean my father's and mine, though it was true of just about everyone in the entire country as the post-war austerity receded. In our case, though, it was due to the arrival of a man who had a great influence on me, more than on my father, perhaps. Brian Brooks was young, gentle and scholarly, a notary public by profession, who represented a direct link with the upper middle-class world which my great-grandfather's business collapse had cut us off from. He came to live with us as a lodger, and stayed as a friend and ally and a pervading influence.

For one thing, he brought large quantities of books with him. (My father read a good deal, and encouraged me to read as well, but he had little money; his library had been restricted to a few volumes of Dickens, a large red-bound dictionary, several back copies of the short-story magazine *Argosy*, and a proto-Christian Science book called *Your Mind Can Heal You*.) We moved to a large flat near the site of the old Crystal Palace, which had burned down in 1936 and was probably the final example in my life of the grand days Before-the-War, and Brian moved in with us.

So did his books. For the first time, as I looked through them and found Edward Lear and G. A. Henty and P. G. Wodehouse, I discovered that there was more to reading than just *The Children's Newspaper*, *The Eagle*, the *Beano* and *Dandy*: that even books which looked grown-up and scholarly and boring could be interesting. I used to sit on the floor in front of Brian's bookcases and pull out anything with a cover or a title that interested me.

Brian's influence told against the Crispin School too; I needed to be in a place with good educational standards, he said, not just a little dame school. So the long walk home ended, and there was no more urban terror from the rough kids: I now went every day by bus to and from the smart and rather expensive Dulwich College Preparatory School, where various members of my family had gone in the days when there was money around. Gratefully, I exchanged my purple blazer for something much darker and tougher and less bullyable.

« »

The masters were the usual mixed bunch: old, resigned, sports-jacketed ones who smoked pipes, young, eager ones who still believed in themselves and rode motorcycles, hard-horse disciplinarians, and weaklings in whose lessons you could do anything or nothing at all. One, a former Royal Marine officer who was rumoured to have been tortured by the Germans, broke down one day under the strain of keeping thirty ten-year-olds in check and stood on the landing screaming the kind of words which we were only now starting to learn. Another master was so savage that we merely called him 'Satan', and crept away when he showed up in the playground. There were several paederasts on the staff, all of them mild and antique. They always volunteered to oversee the changing rooms but didn't seem to do much. We knew there was something dodgy about it, but we never told our parents what went on at the school they were paying so much for us to attend.

Then there was Captain Fleming, a heavily built old boy with a hook nose, a glass eye and a limp, who had served on the North-West Frontier of India. If you failed to translate a passage of Latin correctly, or made some grammatical solecism, Captain Fleming would roar 'Shake him up!'; and the boy sitting next to you would have to grab you by the hair and start to pull your head around. He had no respect for any of the other masters.

'Scrubs, the whole lot of 'em. Know what a scrub is, boy? A scrub's the fella who makes a run for it when the enemy attacks. Don't trust 'em, is my advice to you.'

Captain Fleming had cast a number of little cannon in brass and used to make gunpowder and tiny lead cannonballs for them, and he would invite a select group round to fire them. His flat was an untidy marvel of hangings, ornamental weaponry and sepia photographs, and as he ground the gunpowder or pointed his battery of miniature cannon out of the window he would tell us stories of Pathans and *jezails* and fakirs, of tribesmen from the hills who were fair-haired and blue-eyed and were descended from Alexander the Great's hoplites, of women whose bodies were entirely tattooed, breasts and all (that made an impact), of marksmen who could hit a sparrow's egg at four hundred yards and a British subaltern's heart at half a mile. He himself never managed to hit anything with the cannonballs he fired from his window with such a delightful roar of flame and blast of noise; not even the neighbour's cat. Perhaps he missed on purpose.

There was a definite hint about him of mess funds plundered, a brother-officer's wife seduced, a fortress sold to the enemy. But he was funny and generous and completely non-paederastic, and his stories took me into a world which was still only starting to die in the mid-1950s: a world of excitement and colonial endeavour, of brave deeds, bloodshed and heroic self-sacrifice among peoples and climates I could scarcely imagine.

This was a time when people could still say, without the slightest irony, that home-produced goods were 'British and best'. There was another expression you often heard too: 'Don't panic, remember you're British.' And yet within a few years the very mention of the word 'British' on *The Goon Show*, the Light Programme radio show which was the most anarchic and subversive influence of the post-War period, would make us double up with laughter at the pomposity it satirized. Major Bloodnok, played by Peter Sellers, had all the possible failings of Captain Fleming personified: cowardice, bluster, crookedness, lasciviousness. Harry Secombe's Neddy Seagoon was all of us as we had once been, pathetically believing in the decency of our government and our national institutions, and always coming off worse as a result. Spike Milligan's Bluebottle, cowardly and feeble, was the way we were now. But in 1955, though *The Goon Show* had been on the air for some time, it didn't have quite the same edge. Most people still shared Neddy Seagoon's innocence: 'British and best'.

It was understandable. Only four years before, Britain had been the biggest exporter of motor vehicles in the world. Even now it was still the second or third largest manufacturing power, and certainly the second greatest economic power. Our classroom maps showed the vast extent of the British Empire. We were virtually all royalists: republicans were just cranks, like vegetarians or nudists. On the day after King George VI died in 1952 the conductor and all the passengers on my bus wore black arm-bands, and people spoke in quiet, reverent voices. The morning of Coronation Day in 1953, when the news came through that 'a Briton' (actually a New Zealander, but there wasn't much difference then) had climbed Mount Everest, was the proudest moment of most people's lives since VJ Day.

Britain had been responsible for most of the main scientific advances of the twentieth century: radio, television, radar, penicillin, the computer, the jet engine. The Comet was the first jet airliner in service.

And yet things were already starting to go wrong. The Comet crashed, and had to be withdrawn from service. Sabotage, we said darkly, but it turned out to be metal fatigue. Britain was slipping in the world. Countries were breaking away from the Sterling Area and aligning themselves with the dollar. There were strikes at home and uprisings abroad in places like Cyprus, Kenya and Malaya, and all sorts of colonies were beginning to clamour for independence. Foreign things started appearing in the shops: Italian shoes, German tools, French kitchenware. 'Who won the war, anyway?' people would say, as goods which were British and best seemed mysteriously not to be so good after all; it didn't seem fair. When Colonel Nasser threatened our control of the Suez Canal, it was necessary to teach him a lesson.

'These Gippos only understand one thing,' Captain Fleming told us during a Latin class, and we all nodded eagerly; though we weren't quite sure what the one thing was which they understood.

And then, one dark afternoon in November 1956, the whole world seemed to change, melting like ice under our feet. Our elderly English master, who had retired from a big London public school and was humane enough to read us ghost stories rather than bother our heads with grammar, had just started E. F. Benson's *The Room in the Tower*.

'I have given you the room in the Tow—' he was intoning in a ghostly manner, when one of the older boys, his voice crackling and breaking, burst excitedly into the room.

'The Headmaster's compliments, sir, and I'm to tell you we're at war with Egypt.'

The class erupted in cheers. That was the stuff to give the old Gippos. They had it coming to them, cheeky buggers. They only understood one thing. British and best.

And yet, extraordinarily enough, it turned out that not everyone thought the same way. Some of the boys came to school the next day full of their fathers' opposition to the whole business. My own father, always so forthright about everything, seemed suddenly unsure.

Within days it was clear that things had gone very wrong. The invasion and the parachute drop had been complete tactical successes, but the Americans were against it all. We weren't a super-power after all. When they ordered us to withdraw we did, and our disconsolate French allies came with us. Anthony Eden, the Prime Minister, had a nervous breakdown and resigned. Of the three great national humiliations in my lifetime, Suez, France's veto on our joining the European Community and the application to the IMF for a loan in 1976, this was by far the worst. Our pretensions as a nation were revealed to the world as empty. It wasn't merely wrong to have attacked Egypt, it was stupid. In the meantime the Russians took advantage of the distraction to crush the Hungarian Uprising in the most brutal way possible.

After it was all over, no one seemed to think we led the world in science. No one said 'British and best' or 'Don't panic – remember you're British'. It was the start of thirty years or more of intense national self-denigration. Instead of worshipping our own way of doing things and trying to insist that large parts of the world should copy us, we came to feel ashamed of it all: the Establishment, the old boy network, the class system, the Empire. It was a long time before we even started to be comfortable with ourselves again, and by then everything had changed for ever.

A few months after Suez, in September 1957, my life changed for ever too. I stopped being a kid in short trousers, a playground hanger-out, a collector of cigarette cards and Dinky toys and bus tickets with special numbers; instead I started to turn into an increasingly individuated sophisticate who wore long trousers, went occasionally to the theatre, despised all sorts of things he didn't understand, sampled Chinese and Indian food and argued about politics and ethics. That is to say, I passed an exam and went to St Paul's School in London.

« »

St Paul's wasn't like other big public schools of the time; it was more like a grammar school. Most of us were day-boys, and came from families which had made money in business: suburban, upper middle-class, readers of the *Daily Telegraph*, endlessly complaining about teddy-boys and juke-boxes and the Americanization of everything. My father, by contrast, was now in favour of the Americanization of everything, though he objected to John F. Kennedy's election in the US in 1960 because he was a Catholic. Having been to an Anglican school where he was badly treated, he loathed all the old-established religions and refused to distinguish between them.

There was a sizeable proportion of Jewish boys, which seemed to give St Paul's a particular intellectual edge, and a surprising number from foreign countries: France, Germany, North America, India, Pakistan, Iran. We were inclined to be competitive, sharp-witted and worldly-wise, and snappy dressers too. Not, however, at first: it took me some time to come to terms with a world of stiff collars and studs, and cadet corps uniform every Monday.

And with discipline. I was too timid to be a proper rebel, but I found it hard to subjugate myself completely to the rules of this new place. As my first year progressed, I started to look around at the extraordinary and wonderful building I found myself in. It had been built by Alfred Waterhouse in the early 1880s, and was a red-brick neo-Gothic cathedral, with soaring windows filled with the brilliance of stained glass, and wide staircases, and corridors so long that you couldn't recognize someone walking towards you from the far end.

I wandered around gazing at the stained-glass coats of arms in the windows and the names of former pupils and masters back to the school's foundation in 1509. Now, accompanied by my two closest friends, I found myself wandering these corridors and trying the handles of obscure doors, exploring the farthest and deepest recesses of Alfred Waterhouse's masterpiece.

'There's a door up here,' one of the others said as we reached the end of a small corridor on the top floor. 'It must be the roof.'

I tried the door. The handle turned.

It wasn't the roof. It was the entrance to the attic, an enormous, empty, pyramidal space in the centre of the building which stretched for its entire width. At the front and the back were two enormous clocks, eight feet high. One faced out onto the Hammersmith Road, the other onto the playing fields at the back.

We stood in silence, the dust settling again around our feet, the sunbeams slanting down to the floor, the clocks ticking majestically in the silence, the pigeons faintly rustling on the sloping slates above our heads. Around us were hundreds of white plaster heads, bearded, serious, imperial. Once these busts had decorated the corridors. It was frightening, and magical, and exhilarating. I have had other, far greater experiences since then: walking through the drenching spray at Victoria Falls, climbing in the Himalayas, travelling along a tributary of the Amazon under the stars. But this was the first sense I had ever had of the nobility and grandeur of discovery. I don't suppose Howard Carter, peering through the hole in the door of Tutankhamun's tomb, felt a greater sense of wonder and achievement.

'Christ!' I said reverently.

We were all scared, and yet we couldn't stop talking about it. Every day after that, at lunch-time and in the evenings after school, we would try to return.

In a society as rigidly policed as a school our explorations were quickly discovered. There followed the usual lecture about foolishness and danger, and we were caned. It was intended to be a deterrent, and it proved so for one of our trio. But the two of us who remained carried on exploring and clambering over the narrow ladders and walkways which stretched up the steep sides of the roof; and we were caned for that as well. Gradually my friend's enthusiasm waned. He was more adult than I, though neither of us was yet fifteen, and he felt the humiliation more keenly. He began to mock my exploratory instincts as something childish, which I should grow out of. He was right; yet it didn't stop me. In the winter's darkness I no longer felt scared; I knew the busts by sight, and the noises, and could identify each of them. I would wander around between the busts, clambering over the heaps of abandoned papers, the boxes of unused William Morris tiles, the off-cuts, the unwanted detritus of a large community. For a time these adventures made me the most beaten boy in the school. I was ashamed of it, and never told my father. I even tried to keep it quiet from the other boys.

By now I was exploring the area round the school, and making discoveries there too: an ancient chalice in the foundations of a bombed church (it turned out to be the base of a Victorian oil lamp) and a genuine Roman marble head from the second century AD, which I spotted lying on a burned out sofa on another bomb-site close by.

I had become a thorough-going outsider. Not only did I not have a doctor, because I was a Christian Scientist, but I didn't even say quite the same words to the Lord's Prayer which everyone muttered compulsorily every morning. The Lord's Prayer I could get away with by muttering even more quietly than everyone else, but the medical business was more difficult. Of course, I hated being different from everyone else. The mother business was bad enough, though I had long been adept at disguising that. Dealing with inquisitive, judgmental masters about illness was harder. They didn't agree at all that physical problems are caused and can therefore be healed by the mind.

I have long since severed my connections with Christian Science, but I still believe profoundly that the way you think about yourself, your body, and your life determines your health and the way you are. Instead I have gravitated to the Church of England, and nowadays sing all the same old hymns and say all the same old prayers and collects familiar to me from the past – a specifically English past, in which I can feel most at home.

The school chaplain had nothing to do with this later metamorphosis, though. He was a muscular Christian, tall and rangy and enthusiastic and (even a fifteen-year-old could spot it) sadly innocent. Sitting in the classroom where he taught us once a week, it never occurred to me that the Church of England might one day be for me. He was in a permanent state of unhappiness about the direction the modern world was taking. The day after the court judgement in favour of Penguin Books and *Lady Chatterley's Lover* in 1960 he was a worried man.

'How can they say it's not obscene? It reeks of obscenity. Listen.' He read out a mildly embarrassing passage about someone entwining flowers in someone else's pubic hair.

We giggled, or looked down at the floor with reddening faces.

'Would any of you want to do or say something like that?'

'Not half,' said the class wit in a loud whisper.

We dissolved into laughter, and the chaplain started talking hastily about Lent.

He tried his best at other times to persuade us that masturbation was wrong (too much and you went mad, apparently, which made us roll our eyes and let our tongues loll out). He also explained to us that if you had sex with a girl and she didn't have a baby, this would do terrible things to her psyche. It was all part of a cycle; did we want to do terrible things to a girl's psyche? Actually, of course, we did if only the opportunity had arisen. It certainly didn't with me, and I suspect that if it had with anyone else in the fifth form at St Paul's we would have heard all about it. On reflection, though, maybe not: I lost my virginity at sixteen, and the circumstances seemed so shaming at the time that I kept it a deep secret from everyone.

Like a lot of teenage boys I had a deep well of energy which at times amounted to violence. At the age of fourteen I discovered both boxing and rugby, and went in for both with considerable enthusiasm. At the same time I disliked the organization of it all. I felt that sense of alienation, of being the outsider, and always heard the voice of Groucho Marx somewhere at the back of my head:

> No matter what it is or who commenced it,
> I'm against it.

At this time sports were still at least as important in the school as academic work, because they were supposed to build character. I couldn't stand the masters who were in charge of the school teams, and I only occasionally liked the enthusiasts who wanted to belong to them. I preferred the intellectuals in the school who regarded sport of all kinds as childish and ludicrous; and yet in the true Groucho Marxian spirit I didn't approve entirely of them either, and chose to box and play rugby. By the age of seventeen, though I had never represented the school at any sport, the unthinkable happened and I was made the head of my house. Even though my house (we called them, for some reason, 'clubs') was the least sporty in the school we won the rugby championship in my first term as captain; largely because the vice-captain, who later became the foremost Western expert on Italian history, shared my publicly expressed contempt for the heavies who played for the other houses. The bookish, unworldly characters who inhabited the club were easily inspired by the subversive doctrine that brains were more important than brawn. It was an early lesson in how character counts, and we beat the rest hollow.

As one high master gave way to another and the national change in sensibilities seeped into St Paul's, boxing and caning and compulsory morning prayers and the cadet corps all came under threat; and few of us missed them when they finally went. They were the last knockings of Victorianism. And by now, as head of the debating society and editor of the school newspaper, I passed for an intellectual.

« »

At home things had changed too. Norwood was far in the past: my father and Brian Brooks and I lived in a charming Edwardian house in Putney. My holidays were taken up with following their genealogical enthusiasms, and we went from village church to county archive to cathedral vault searching for records of births, marriages and deaths and transcribing flaking inscriptions on gravestones.

When I was fifteen my father, having discovered the full extent of the Simpsons' Suffolk roots, insisted that we should look for a country house there. We spent a wintry week driving from one depressing place to another and talking to lonely farmers' wives whose ideal in life was to leave their fourteenth-century thatched manor-houses and move to a semi near the shops. We had almost given up one evening and were setting out on the road to London when I spotted a brief mention at the end of an estate agent's list of a rambling place on a clifftop overlooking the sea at Dunwich. The others agreed to have a look at it.

From the moment I saw it I knew I would never be happy until I lived there. No one could call Greyfriars handsome. It was the left-hand end of an enormous 1884 mock-Elizabethan pile which had been split up into three separate sections at the end of the war. Our part had around eight bedrooms and five bathrooms; God knows how large the other two remaining sections must have been. It was always absurdly unsuitable for all of us: four hours' drive from London, and nowhere near shops or anything else. Its eleven acres of land were slowly being swallowed up by the ravenous North Sea, and it cost a small fortune to keep warm and habitable. None of that mattered; Brian and my father shared my delight in the place, and they bought it for £3,000.

The village of Dunwich immediately formed another element of that sense of past, faded glory which had haunted so much of my life. In the early Middle Ages it had been the greatest port in England, sending ships and men and hundreds of barrels of herrings to the Kings of England, and possessing a bishopric and forty churches and monasteries. But it was built on cliffs of sand, and the storms of each winter undermined it and silted up the port. In the twelfth century, and again in the thirteenth, large parts of the town collapsed into the sea. Today only the outermost street of the mediaeval town still exists. Our land ran down to the cliff edge, and we watched it shrink as the years went by.

The stories about hearing bells under the sea were always just fantasy, but Dunwich was certainly a place of ghosts. A headless horseman was said to drive a phantom coach and four along one of the roads nearby. A little farther off a black sailor called Toby, hanged for the rape and murder of a young girl even though it was clear he was not guilty, still ran a ghostly race with the London to Yarmouth stagecoach in a pathetic attempt to prove his innocence. In the grounds of our house two Bronze Age long-barrows stood among the later trees, and when the moon shone hard and silver down onto the house, and the thin clouds spread across the sky, and a single owl shrieked from the bare branches of the dead holm-oak outside my bedroom window, it was more than I could do to get out of bed and look out at them. I would think of those cold bones and the savage gold ornaments around them, and shiver myself to sleep.

Along the cliff-top, in the direction of the seaside town of South-wold, lay a ruined fifteenth-century monastery surrounded by a flintstone wall; and between that and the cliff's edge grew a small and somehow frightening wood hunched over by the ferocious offshore wind. At one time it must have been the boundary of the burial ground of All Saints' church, almost the last of the forty churches, which fell into the sea at the turn of the century. A few gravestones still stood crookedly under the shelter of the wood, and one, to John Brinkley Easy occupied a little patch of open ground on the cliff edge. It was the most easterly grave in Britain, and the name seemed rather suitable. My father's Norwich terriers hated the misshapen little wood, and yelped and dug their paws into the sandy ground if we insisted. Then, if they saw we were implacable, they would try to get through it fast, panting and laying their ears back against their heads.

One winter's afternoon, after I had been to post a letter in the main street of Dunwich, I was walking back along the cliff-top when something made me look back. Behind me was a black figure dressed in a cloak and hood. I was on my own: not even a dog for company. I was too embarrassed to run, and perhaps I felt that it wouldn't do any good if I did. The figure followed me for half a mile, in this most M. R. Jamesian of landscapes. Each time I turned round it was still the same distance behind me. I crossed the old dike which marked the outer edge of mediaeval Dunwich and reached the corner of the wood. From here on this was our land; and the notion of ownership emboldened me sufficiently to turn round again. The black figure had stopped, and seemed to be watching me. Then, when I turned round again, it had disappeared. I certainly don't believe in ghosts, but all this happened precisely as I have described. Maybe it was a kind of extrusion of the atmosphere of Dunwich.

« »

The winter of 1962 was the worst since 1947, and that was the worst since the 1660s, people said. The snow fell in early December and dug in like an invading army, its huge drifts slowly turning the colour and general consistency of rusty scrap iron. In our vast, uneconomic house at Dunwich the wind came off the North Sea with the ferocity of a guillotine blade and the exposed pipes duly froze hard. The Aga stood in the corner of the kitchen like an icy coffin. My father and I were on our own: Brian Brooks was spending Christmas with his family. We wandered round the house in overcoats, with scarves tied round our heads like the old women at Saxmundham market. None of the lavatories worked.

My father had one of his bright ideas.

'You go into the tower,' he said. 'That can be your bog. Spread this out on the floor and – you know. Just mind the carpet.'

He handed me the latest *East Anglian Daily Times*.

'Oh, Dad,' I whined.

I could hear him chortling and whistling two floors below me as I followed his instructions. When I brought my distasteful little parcel down with me, I found him pulling out boxes and bags from Harrods,

Fortnum & Mason and Peter Jones. He never threw anything like that away, always maintaining that they would come in handy some time. They came in handy now.

'Stick yours in there,' he said, holding a Fortnum's box towards my *Daily Times*, his face averted. He put the lid on and tied it up in string. 'Now let's get going.'

'But where to? Dad?' I had been calling him 'Dad' now for a couple of years, ever since I stopped using 'Daddy'. But for the most part I preferred not to call him anything: it was embarrassing.

'Not Southwold, anyway; too bloody honest in Southwold. We'll go to Ipswich.'

We drove in my father's jungle-green Triumph convertible past the white fields to Ipswich, where leather-hard snow lay heaped up in the streets and you had to walk the slick pavements with the care of an old age pensioner. My father parked in one of the main streets.

'Don't lock the door, Johnny boy,' he called as we got out.

'Don't call me "Johnny boy" ', I hissed. Then, 'Why not?'

'Just don't.'

I noticed he left the Fortnum's box on my seat. We went off and had a cup of coffee. When we came back half an hour later the Fortnum's box was gone.

'Much more satisfying than flushing,' my father said, and we laughed so much on the way back through the white fields that we almost crashed.

It became our favourite afternoon activity until the supply of expensive bags and boxes finally ran out. Then my father announced it was time to go somewhere warm. As a kind of *sortes Vergilianae* he opened a new and as yet unsullied copy of the *East Anglian Daily Times* at random. *Casablanca* was showing at the Rex.

'Marvellous film,' he said. 'Seen it loads of times. That's where we'll go.'

He didn't mean the Rex.

Nowadays Casablanca is a big, featureless industrial city. In 1962 it hadn't changed much from the days of Vichy and Claude Rains. Our DC-9 skidded across the runway where, in theory, Bogart had watched as Ingrid Bergman went off with Paul Henreid. After the weeks of snow and ice in England I had forgotten what gentle sunshine felt like. The smell of burning camel dung, which the Tuareg used as fuel, hung in the air. I pulled out my brand-new passport, the first I'd ever possessed, and a man in a tatty uniform examined it in a way I found flattering. Another man in an even tattier uniform made a chalk squiggle on our suitcases. Then we walked out of the airport building.

Outside in the sudden sunshine there was an explosion of noise. Cars hooted, porters screamed at us, their faces close to ours, and hands grabbed at us, our clothes, our suitcases.

'Bloody Arabs,' my father shouted, lashing out. I suddenly realized he was scared. It had never occurred to me that he could be frightened by anything.

'I just didn't like it when they crowded round us like that,' he said defensively as we settled into an ancient black Citroen taxi.

I stared out of the window at the shabby buildings which were the same colour as the desert, at the alleyways in whose dark cave-mouths I caught glimpses of laden donkeys, cripples, street vendors. Little lamplit shops sold heaped up melons and pomegranates, or long chains of bright, meretricious gold. Heavily veiled women made their way through crowds of men in long white robes. I caught sight of someone in the window of a tea-house, smoking a hookah.

'Didn't I tell you?' he said enthusiastically.

His mood had changed completely. It was one of his main themes that England was boring and provincial, and that the real world was full of colour and excitement. We were in the real world now. As if to confirm it, a fan circled slowly overhead in my room at the Hotel du Midi, ruffling the mosquito net which was draped elaborately over the brass bedstead.

On New Year's Eve we went to the best restaurant in town. For some reason it was a Norwegian one.

« »

The band, three men in fezzes, ended their indefinably Arabic rendering of 'As Time Goes By'. The dancers on the floor separated and clapped their hands a few times.

'Have you seen that extraordinary woman over there? Dad?'

The striking blonde in pink chiffon sitting on the far side of the restaurant had been swaying in time to the music. Now she ruffled the curly black hair of the man she was with. Even at this distance I could see he was about half her age. My father looked at her for the first time.

'Ladies and gentlemen,' announced the manager, walking out onto the dance floor and speaking into the microphone like a crooner. His English had a heavy accent; Germanic, not Arab. 'Welcome to New Year's Eve at the Ski Chalet.'

Everyone applauded. Especially the blonde in pink: she clapped her hands over her head.

'Good God,' my father said, 'that's Zsa Zsa Gabor.'

They made eye contact.

'Tonight,' pursued the manager, 'we offer you a special Norwegian delicacy: the snow goose, which only flies across the Arctic Circle once a year, at Christmas.'

'How extraordinary,' I chattered, 'to come all the way to Morocco and eat a bird from Norway.'

'Absolutely,' my father answered. He wasn't listening. He was still looking at Zsa Zsa Gabor, and Zsa Zsa Gabor was looking at him. She shook her head crossly when the young man with the curly black hair said something. Then she raised an eyebrow in the direction of the dance floor.

'Mind if I have a quick dance, old chap?'

'I didn't know you danced, Dad.'

There was a lot I didn't know.

There was some close work and a certain amount of laughter, high and frothy, or studied and baritone, from their part of the dance floor. After a few minutes they came back, panting a little. Zsa Zsa Gabor's hand, when I shook it, was warm and strong, and she brought with her an invisible, delicately perfumed cloud. I don't think it had ever crossed my mind before that a women of her age could be attractive.

'I just had to come over and say hello,' she said, sitting down in what seemed to me a little girl manner.

When my father talked to her his voice sounded unnaturally deep and rounded; he only spoke like that, I noticed with the unsympathetic sharpness of the young, in the company of people he wanted to impress. I tried to see him through her eyes: tough, tanned, barrel-chested. Sitting down, you couldn't see he was only five-foot-eight, six inches shorter than me; he was sensitive about his height.

I looked across the restaurant. Zsa Zsa Gabor's companion, young and dark and scowling, was still there. She caught my look.

'Poor Julien,' she said, in a voice as charming and unnatural as my father's. 'I'll tell him to go home.'

She drifted off, leaving a little of the perfumed cloud behind her. My father watched. I wanted to say how beautiful she was, but blurted out something altogether different instead.

'The Oxford scholarship exams are in a week's time. Maybe I ought to go back and do them.'

The idea had been weighing on my mind for some time, but I hadn't known how to break it to him. He'd set his heart on my going to Cambridge; he thought it wrong to leave East Anglia.

'Not now, old chap.'

His eyes were on Zsa Zsa Gabor. Her companion stood up morosely, and Zsa Zsa kissed him playfully on the ear, watching my father as she did it.

'You wouldn't mind if I went back?'

'Do what you like, dear old boy. This isn't quite the—'

The perfumed cloud was back.

The next morning, over croissants and coffee on the balcony of his room, my father looked tired. One eye was swollen.

'Bit of a late night after you left,' he explained.

Not knowing how to broach the topic of Zsa Zsa Gabor, I reminded him clumsily that I wanted to leave. Would he mind?

'Of course not. Why should I mind?' He stared at his untouched cup.

The next couple of days passed slowly. We wandered round the souk and came across a snake-charmer and a man with a dancing monkey. The monkey reached out its minuscule fez and collected money when the performance was over. Strange transvestite groups paraded and sang in falsetto voices, their faces heavily made up, red and purple skirts twirling in the dusty sunlight. A dancer, older than the rest, blew me a kiss. I went red, and everyone laughed.

The next morning I packed my suitcase.

'Will Zsa Zsa—' I began.

'No.'

Standing in the hotel lobby he looked lonely and old. I couldn't think of a way to phrase the offer to stay if he wanted me to; instead, I shook his hand.

'Sorry,' I mumbled.

He drew himself up to his full five-foot-eight, and smiled. Suddenly he was his old self again.

'Might be a good idea for you to disappear from Casablanca for a while.'

It was years before I realized he had been quoting from the film. And by then it was too late to tell him.

« »

I didn't get a scholarship at Oxford, though I wrote an essay which was good enough to get me interviews at five different colleges. Anyway, by then I realized that my father was right, and Cambridge was where I wanted to be; and although I failed to get either a scholarship or an exhibition there too, Magdalene College offered me a place unconditionally. The architecture of Magdalene – gentle fifteenth-century red brick, a touch of something faintly akin to Wren, and an undistinguished block by Lutyens – appealed to me greatly. So did Cambridge as a whole.

There were six months ahead of me before I started there. I left St Paul's without much nostalgia and took a temporary job at the head office of Northern Assurance, a dreary, outmoded old insurance company near the Bank of England in the City. Each day I watched Mr Barking and Miss Rodgers, a Dickensian pairing, manoeuvre closer to their inevitable affair, and each day Mr Barking docked my pay to take account of the various cheques (at twopence each) which I had filled out incorrectly. I loathed the job, but stuck at it. I had set myself the task of making the £150 which would (I hoped) keep me for four months in the United States.

And so, one evening at the end of May 1963, I walked up the gangplank of the *Queen Mary* at Southampton. With me, to see me off, were my father and Brian Brooks, together with my current girlfriend and her rather overbearing mother. Our farewells were embarrassing, and as the ship headed down the river to the sea I felt immensely liberated.

I wasn't exactly travelling in comfort. My fourth-class berth was more decks below the surface than I could have believed, and I shared it with two West Indians and a strange American who stared at the underside of the bunk above him for hours at a time, singing a song about wanting a long-legged girl. The West Indians gave me a great deal of unwanted detail about their sister, who was a night-club hostess in New York. Like my girlfriend's mother, they seemed to think we might have a future together. I also got to know the *Queen Mary*.

I roamed all over her with the interest and dedication I had once put into exploring St Paul's. I found out how to get into the first-class lavatories without being caught, and used the second-class bathrooms until one of the stewards caught me coming out with my hair and towel wet. I had tea each afternoon in the first-class lounge because I had tipped the head waiter five shillings on the second afternoon of the voyage: the first time, I think, I had ever tipped anyone in my life. The tea came out of beautiful white square-shaped teapots with no spouts, and the walnut panelling vibrated in sympathy with the ship's superb engines while the orchestra played selections from Fred Astaire films.

My favourite place, though, was on deck, close to the bow. I would stand there hour after hour, pinned in my place against a convenient mast by the ferocious headwind, watching the ship carve her way through the green waves and trying to distinguish the likely outlines of my future. I was nineteen, but by today's standards I had the experience and understanding of a fourteen-year-old.

> New York [P. G. Wodehouse wrote] is a large city conveniently situated on the edge of America, so that you step off the liner right on to it without an effort. You can't lose your way. You go out of a barn and down some stairs, and there you are, right in amongst it.

The gangplank was lowered at seven a.m., and we – passengers from the steerage and from first-class alike – were directed into the barn. This was the customs shed, and it was full of tables and rather grim-looking characters in uniforms, looking for smuggled goods. You put your suitcase on the table, and one of the grim-looking characters rifled through the contents. With both hands.

'Whaddya want two of these things for?' he asked, holding my hairbrushes in his large upraised fists.

'One has two hands,' I said loftily. I must have been a real prat in those days. 'As you have shown.'

'How do we know one ain't planning to sell one of 'em here?'

In the end I convinced him. Even before I had been loosed into America I was finding it an assault on everything I was or wanted to be. But it was to do me an enormous amount of good.

I was met by a strange elderly couple, distant Simpson relatives. Not having the least idea what to do with a teenager from England, they had booked a room in a cheap hotel in Queens for me and dropped me off there. It was the last I ever saw of them. That night I lay on my mattress, the sweat dripping off me, in heat I had never thought possible. On one side, through the thin walls, an old man coughed the night away. I thought the couple on the other side must be fighting; which shows how ignorant of the world I was.

As I lay there I took stock of the position. My £150 was worth $420 at the current rate of exchange. The hotel cost $18 a night and my evening hamburger and soft drink had been $1.50, so I had enough money for approximately nineteen more days; and since my return passage on the *Queen Mary* had been booked for 30 September that was about three and a half months less than I needed.

It hadn't occurred to me that living could cost so much. I knew nothing about America; scarcely anyone I knew had been there, not even my father. This was before the days of cheap travel and package holidays. The rich boys at my school went to the South of France or Switzerland for their holidays; students went to Spain. As for America, it was *terra incognita*.

Sweating, I opened my suitcase. Two detachable collars, lying limply on top of everything else, infuriated me. I threw them into the corner and they lay there like banana skins. Then I rifled through the rest of the contents with the ferocity of a New York customs officer, and found at last an envelope with an address inside it. The mother of another girlfriend had given me the name of some people she knew, in case I got into trouble. I hadn't anticipated getting into trouble on the first day. Still, just to look at the name and telephone number was a relief. The old man was still coughing and the couple were still going hard at it, but I fell asleep.

The Collins were American archetypes: deeply hospitable and generous, wealthy, devout. The extended family must have included about twenty people, but Buster and Lil were the centre of it. I rang Lil's number nervously from the lobby of the hotel, and she invited me to stay immediately.

'Take the bus to Red Bank, New Jersey,' she said, 'and ring us from the station before you leave. I'll be there to pick you up.'

She was: a big, handsome, generous woman, whose face showed signs of her American–Indian ancestry. Her husband Buster, small and bald, was half Irish and half German, and neither half liked Britain or the British. He had a way of sidling up and telling me I smelled bad; he had heard we didn't use deodorant, and he was right. Most men in Britain thought things that smelled of flowers or cologne were effeminate. Even after I had smothered myself with the stuff, though, he still told me I smelled. I detected a prejudice, and felt a little less of a leper.

It seems to have been my fortune to have seen the *ancien régimes* in all sorts of places, just before they disappeared for ever: in Britain itself, Eastern Europe, Russia, Zimbabwe, South Africa, Iran, Afghanistan, Latin America. And America itself. This was still recognizably the country of Eisenhower, the richest, most self-confident and most successful nation in human history. Now it had its first president born in the twentieth century, the young, handsome and deeply charismatic Kennedy. As a country it was quite sensationally self-satisfied, no doubt with some justification. By comparison Britain seemed old, tired and played out, with the Profumo Affair as the last depressing sigh of the traditional ruling class. Americans didn't have sex scandals, and they didn't have traitors who betrayed their country for cash, or for ideological reasons; nor could they understand a country which did.

What they had was wealth and progress. I had never seen anything like the goods in the supermarkets or the gadgets, from eye-level grills to nail-clippers. America was an economic free-for-all, in a way which seemed shocking to someone from welfare-state Britain. There were more beggars on the streets of New York than I had seen in Casablanca; back home I'd never seen a single one. As for unemployment, it would never, I told myself, be allowed to rise so high in Britain; there we still believed that governments could sort these things out if they chose.

And yet things in America were just about to change. Kennedy was only four months away from visiting Dallas, and Vietnam was already turning into an American war instead of being merely a colonial police action inherited from the French. Racial segregation was staging its last big stand in Arkansas. The poor, and the black, would not stay quiet much longer. Nor would the young. A new generation would soon break out, wearing unthinkable clothes, behaving unthinkably, doing unthinkable things to the American flag and American ideals.

For now, though, there were no signs of a coming revolution. Intellectually, my American contemporaries seemed dull and empty. I spent a few days at Princeton, reading in the library and talking to the students; they seemed more juvenile than I was, and much less well informed; and I hadn't even started at Cambridge yet. Of course, I wanted this to be the case; my self-esteem had taken quite a knock in America, and I was always on the look-out for opportunities to think things were better at home. There didn't seem to be many of them.

During the months I was in America, word started to reach the middle-class about the Beatles – their hair, their songs, their general behaviour. They were due to arrive in New York soon. An old *grande dame* who turned up at the Collins' house heard there was a young Englishman there, and sought me out.

'Don't think,' she said, 'that our young people are like yours. They aren't degenerate here, you know; they don't want these Beatles of yours.'

'Take no notice of her,' the Collins' eldest daughter, Carol, said soothingly afterwards, when I confided in her. She seemed to be sitting very close to me. 'I'm sure England's a great place. You mustn't worry about it.' She gripped my hand in her own warm, brown hand.

Carol was thirty-six, and had two children; but even at nineteen I found her remarkably attractive. When she asked me to stay with them, I felt a definite tug. Carol's husband Bud was more than enough to neutralize it, though. A huge brooding man of Swedish extraction, it was clear that he suspected me of being up to no good, though whether with his wife or his sixteen-year-old daughter I could never decide. There was, as it happens, nothing at all for him to worry about in either case, but it was a big worry for me. Bud ran a forestry business, and brought his hatchets and circular saws home with him. It was time to move on.

Rescue came in the Neanderthal shape of Lil's brother, a long-distance truck driver and ne'er-do-well called Connie. He was looking for a companion on a journey across the country. When I first met him, Connie was a bit of a shock. He could have modelled for

Australopithecan Man: his brow-ridges were extraordinarily developed, his eyes were small, his head poked forward, his arms hung down lower than you might expect. He looked cunning and menacing, in equal proportions. As he stood beside the pool with his sister you could see they were related, but the features which gave her a fierce beauty made him look almost hominoid. Connie didn't like Buster, and he was wary of Carol. But he loved Lil.

'Glad to know you, English,' he said, crushing the bones of my hand in his enormous paw.

'His name's John,' said his sister.

'He ain't John. John's an American name. He's "English".'

I was English.

'Bet ya never been in a rig like this,' Connie shouted over the noise of the engine a few days later.

He was right. I had never travelled in the cab of a cross-country truck before. Sitting twelve feet above the road I was shaken and vibrated to a degree I would have thought could give us brain damage, and a funnel just outside the side window from my head pumped out fumes as strong as the *Queen Mary*'s.

We were strange fellow travellers. Connie liked to tell me about the people he had whacked as an officer of the Teamsters' Union, and I tried to explain to him how people in a civilized society should behave. He would listen politely, then go on about whacking.

'Ain't no other way to run a union.'

'You could do it by persuasion.'

'Yeah – only ya use a baseball to do the persuadin' wit'.'

His knowledge of the road, and of the conditions that made driving a rig hazardous, was extraordinarily complex and interesting.

'Now this bridge here, this'd be OK in temp'raters low as say two degree. Go one, two degree lower, the frost builds up on that side the road, and she'd kill ya at this speed now.'

Everyone knew Connie at the roadhouses.

'How ya doin', beautiful?' he would say to each of the waitresses. He never varied the phrase, even if the waitresses were standing in a line together. The other drivers he knew by name, by rig, by history, by Teamsters' subscription. They treated him like royalty. He would grin, showing his brown, broken teeth.

'Nice of ya, boys.'

Behind our seats in the cab there was a bed, and a picture of a very naked girl tacked onto the back wall to keep him company. He saw me looking at it.

'Always get you one of them. These cookies . . .' He pointed his thumb back in the general direction of the last roadhouse.

I looked down.

'OK, English,' he said. 'It ain't compulsory.'

His view of Britain, and perhaps of me, was formed by two films: *Little Lord Fauntleroy* and *Mrs Miniver.* Otherwise the country seemed not to have crossed his consciousness. He wasn't hostile; there was none of Buster Collins' snideness about him. He just assumed that we lived in nineteenth-century fashion because we spoke that way. And he seemed to think that conditions in Britain must still be wartime ones; which, by comparison with America, they sometimes seemed to be.

We sang all the songs we could remember, and drove through the dusty towns leaning out of the windows shouting the choruses. He posed for my little camera with his arms round the waitresses in the roadhouses we passed, and nuzzled their necks for my benefit. It looked like King Kong and Faye Wray.

'Julie here's a great gal,' he said, making her squeal with laughter. 'Goes all night. You gotta try American gals, English: ain't none better. That right, Julie?'

Julie was too far gone to answer.

We had switched by now to his vast powder-blue Buick, and drove on to Yellowstone National Park. For several days we camped there, and in the end a bear got in and started chewing the pressure cooker. Connie had put the meat inside it. He ran out with his arms flailing, and the bear loped away. We lay down and laughed till we were tired.

After that we drove back. But something had changed. The further east we got, the more Connie talked disparagingly about blacks. The civil rights movement was important to me, and I couldn't bear it.

'I'm sick of listening to you,' I shouted. 'Haven't you got anything else to talk about?'

Connie's mouth stayed open. He looked out of the side window, then at me. He was genuinely hurt. The browridges contracted, the dark eyes almost disappeared.

We drove on for hour after hour, without exchanging a word about 'niggers'. It was past nine at night when we reached the outskirts of Philadelphia in the pouring rain. I broke the silence, my voice sounding unnaturally harsh.

'Please find the bus station.'

'I can easy take ya to Boston, English.' His voice was gentle, placatory.

'Here'll do,' I said, not looking at him.

'Remember this?' he said as we pulled up outside the Greyhound station. He turned his head to one side and pretended to gnaw something, his eyes searching mine for some softening.

I opened the Buick door. It was raining so hard I was soaked even as I got out. Connie's hairy hand emerged from the depths of the car.

'Hey, English.' He punched my arm.

I murmured something placatory, but the noise of the rain and the buses drowned it. Then as the Buick pulled away and he waved, I shouted at him to stop. I wanted him to take me to Boston after all, not because it was raining but for the company. But it was too dark and wet; he couldn't hear me. I walked into the bus terminal.

« »

Boston is the Mecca, the Rome, the Salt Lake City of Christian Science. Once it had been delightful, the home of Henry and William James and a dozen other nineteenth-century American intellectual worthies; Mary Baker Eddy, the founder of the Christian Science movement, among them. But by the time I got there the city fathers were in the process of wrecking it with underpasses, overpasses, motorways, and large quantities of concrete and steel. As a believer, I duly paid my visit to the Mother Church, and then went on to enroll for the conference. I felt good. Close by, there was an exhibition of Christian Science activities which I decided to go to. Maybe, I thought, I'll meet someone there.

Standing looking at a set of photographs straight ahead of me was a group of girls; among them a blonde in a red mackintosh. She seemed so alive and free that I stood where I was in the middle of the room and stared at her; and eventually she caught my look and returned it. That instant fixed the pattern of my life for the next twenty years.

I was, I suppose, tongue-tied. But after the unfailing first question that every American asks every other American, and every other stray like me, 'Where are you from?', we started talking. Routine stuff, about being in Boston and going to university and plans for the future; but underneath, even at that stage, I knew there was another set of questions and responses going altogether. When I found she had seen Eisenstein's *Ivan the Terrible*, and could remember the boyars' song from it, it seemed like a sign.

'How about a coffee?' To my own ears I sounded remarkably debonair, considering I was so nervous.

We had to take another girl with us, darker and not nearly so good-looking, who was inclined to give me the Buster Collins line on the British: outmoded, class-ridden and smelly. I was probably living evidence of the accuracy of all of this, but the girl in red didn't seem to agree. She was different from the very start: gentler, more aware that there was a world outside America, supportive, and – I thought – extremely beautiful with her large eyes and tip-tilted nose. I ignored the dark girl as much as I could.

We settled down in a coffee-shop somewhere, and the girl took her red coat off. She looked very good in her pale green mohair sweater; so good that in my gawky way I couldn't keep my eyes off her. The dark girl grew more and more frosty.

These were simpler days, and thanks to Christian Science both of us were more innocent than people of the same age. After it had dawned on the dark girl that she wasn't essential to the gathering, the two of us did nothing more than wander around in the late evening, holding hands.

Her name was Diane, and she came from southern California. I found this desperately attractive, and she clearly found there was an attraction in someone who lived in a lonely house on the edge of the known world and was about to go to Cambridge University. Neither of us felt entirely suited to our own very different worlds; Diane was an outsider in hers, just as I was in mine, and there was something compelling for us both in the notion of discovering other worlds. After a couple of days, no more, I had to leave for England. We left each other in a cloud of high romance. Each of us knew that some day soon we would be married.

« »

At nine o'clock one rainy October evening in 1963 I set down my cases outside the porter's lodge in the gateway of Magdalene College and looked about me. My father and Brian Brooks had driven me across from the Suffolk coast in my father's old Triumph and given me dinner at a comfortable, slightly down-at-heel old hotel called the Blue Boar.

Now I was on my own: in Cambridge, in my life. I shivered in the autumn cold. Across the road, in a pub that looked as ancient as the college, a group of convivial older undergraduates were making a racket. They knew each other; I knew no one. I knocked timidly at the lodge door, and turned the handle.

'And what, sir, may I do for you?' A large – a very large – porter stood behind the counter. It was hot in there, and his big face shone.

I explained.

'Simpson, Simpson, Simpson,' he said, running his finger down the list. 'No Simpson.'

A group of young men, older than myself, came in. A little of the cold and rain came in with them.

'Maybe it's in my full name, Fidler-Simpson.' I tried to murmur it.

'Oh, FIDLER-Simpson.'

The undergraduates nudged each other and laughed. I had always loathed that name.

The porter swept my cases up in his huge arms and set out into the rainy night: through the ancient lead-coloured wooden gates, across the road, through another mediaeval gate and into what seemed almost like a village: a strange mixture of Tudor houses and little low whitewashed modern buildings. There were old-fashioned street lamps which threw yellow light onto the slanting rain as I hurried after the giant porter. I was wracked with anxiety: should I give him five shillings for carrying my bags or not? And where, anyway, were my rooms to be?

'Number two Mallory Court, sir.'

He looked up at my name painted over the doorway: 'Fidler-Simpson, J. C.'

'I expect you'll be wanting that changed, sir,' he said meaningfully.

'Absolutely, yes. Oh,' I said, and dug out the two halfcrowns.

His gloom vanished, and he said a massive goodbye.

I went in. There were two bare rooms, a sitting room and a

bedroom, with a gas fire, low ceilings, and two deeply recessed windows which seemed to look out onto a garden. I had a small gas-ring, a kettle, knives, forks, plates, cups, a toasting-fork, two rumpsprung armchairs and an ancient, stained settee, and a cupboard. Next door there was a narrow bed with an obvious sag, and a wardrobe with a door that swung outwards. And a chamber-pot under the bed. The bathrooms and lavatories were right down at the end of a freezing corridor, to be used only in the greatest extremity.

From outside somewhere came raucous laughter and the noise of things smashing. The bloods, for which Magdalene was famous, were back.

> Like many of the upper class,
> He liked the sound of broken glass.

I felt distinctly bourgeois. Maybe, like some feeble plebeian out of Evelyn Waugh, I would be hunted through the courts of the college and debagged in one of the fountains. But it didn't really trouble me in here. Behind the door of 2 Mallory Court I was safe. I sat down in one of the armchairs and laughed aloud. I was here at last. Launched. A person in my own right. That night, huddled under the blankets to combat the damp chill of the place, I fell asleep with the smell of college polish in my nostrils and the sound of falling rain in my ears. I was supremely happy.

The next morning, still uncertain what to do with the sleeves of my strange black gown, I found myself sitting on a bench in Magdalene's dining hall with all the other freshmen. Terrific characters, graduates and patrons and fellows, stared out at us from the paintings. There was Samuel Pepys, of course, and Charles Kingsley, and T. S. Eliot. After that it was a bit like trying to name ten famous Swiss: Magdalene had never been altogether famous for its scholarship.

Someone called us out by name, and we had to walk up in front of everyone else and shake hands with the Master, a grey-haired ancient who had once been a Cabinet minister for something. Magdalene was still predominantly a public school college, and a succession of former pupils of schools far grander than mine made their way up to be looked over by the college authorities. They had, fortunately, got me down under 'Simpson'; and I had no sooner shaken hands with the Master and sat down in alphabetical order when the voice called out

'Snowman', and everyone giggled as they would have giggled at me if I had been listed under 'Fidler-Simpson'. Nicholas Snowman came and sat next to me, slight and dark; he clearly didn't like the sound of broken glass either.

'This is a weird place,' he whispered to me; and a life-long friendship began between us.

Over the course of the next week we formed ourselves into a group: Nicholas, who became the head of Glyndebourne, Prince Richard of Gloucester, Ridley Burnet, an immensely witty and talented man who went into publishing, Michael Binyon, who became diplomatic editor of *The Times*, Bernard Hunt and John Thompson, friends since childhood who later founded an architectural practice, and Jeremy Griggs, who became a judge.

Ours wasn't, in retrospect, one of the great moments in Cambridge history, either socially or intellectually. There was no one of much significance in undergraduate politics, for instance: later political power seemed to skip our generation, perhaps because Britain's national politics at that particular stage seemed so empty. Nicholas and I went to the Union in the early weeks of our first term and listened to a debate. The President was Norman Lamont, who became Chancellor of the Exchequer a quarter of a century later and behaved with a petulance unusual even at Westminster when things went wrong for him. That night, as we sat watching him from the gallery, he struck us both as being so pompous and empty that we walked out before the debate was over and never went back for the rest of our time at Cambridge.

Nicholas and I were both reading English, and in our second year we shared a grand set of rooms in the mediaeval First Court of the college. We each had our own bedroom, and the sitting room was so big that we could give enormous parties by night and play a version of cricket there by day.

One morning in 1965, over toast and lapsang souchong, Nicholas said carefully, 'If Matthew Arnold were teaching down the road, we'd go to him just for the experience, wouldn't we?'

I nodded, not understanding.

'So what about Leavis? He's just down the road too.'

He was. F. R. Leavis was an outsider, more now by choice than by the wishes of the university English faculty. He was a literary self-creation, the living embodiment of a character out of D. H. Lawrence, brown and weather-beaten, perennially tie-less. At this stage, too, he was pretty eccentric; and his wife, the critic Queenie Leavis, was more eccentric still. When the two of us walked round to see him, Queenie started calling out to him from the hallway. She thought we had been sent by the university Establishment to kidnap him.

Leavis himself was still a superb teacher, and his sensibility as a reader and dissecter of poetry and prose was untouched by his years of bitterness and his age. His principles, or rather his likes and dislikes, were as intemperate as they always had been, though; having an interest in James Joyce's work, I ventured one morning to ask Leavis about him.

'It seems to me little more than random cuttings from newspapers, pasted together,' he said.

He raved against T. S. Eliot at every seminar Nicholas and I attended. As we were heading off one morning to see him, the radio news reported that Eliot had died. The first time Leavis mentioned him he pulled himself up short.

'One mustn't of course speak uncharitably about the dead,' he interjected. But within another minute he was attacking him again; and by the end of the session he was as uncharitable as he had always been. And yet to his pupils he was courteous, even gentle.

Once I blurted out an answer to a question of his which was so wrong that it seemed clear I would be blasted into outer darkness. Instead, Leavis spent several minutes explaining why my answer, though far from correct, was an intelligent one. Sometimes, too, he showed a gentler side to himself, as when he told us how he had found a sovereign which his father must have dropped six decades earlier. Afterwards he wiped away a tear. Perhaps it was merely a case of an old man's emotional liability, but it was charming as well.

His influence on his most intense followers, though, could be malign. He attracted outsiders like himself, young men and women who hated the old school tie, conformist atmosphere of Cambridge. They tended to take him literally, when he simply wanted to redress the balance of influences on them. Examinations were an arid waste of time, destructive of literary creativity, he told us. At the end of the next term, in our Part One exams, I found myself sitting close to one of the Leavis-worshippers. Halfway through the first paper he threw his pen down.

'An arid waste of time,' he shouted. 'Destructive of literary creativity.'

He stormed out. The rest of us, mostly lacking literary creativity anyway, scribbled on. The Leavis-worshipper was the only one who didn't come back for our third year.

Fortunately, Magdalene held a man who, though almost as much of an outsider as Leavis, was generally regarded as the best individual teacher of English in the university: better than Leavis himself. Arthur Sale had no official honours, and held no college position. At the time those of us who were taught by him regarded this as a typical Establishment outrage, and only later understood that it was at least half by his own choosing.

Magdalene, though it seemed to us to be a fuddy-duddy, pass-the-port kind of place, in fact possessed a genuine respect for intellect and placed it above everything else, including conformity. It appointed people from the most unlikely backgrounds to senior positions, and would have done the same with Arthur, if he had wanted it. He didn't want it. He was a puritan, who preferred to walk the three miles from his home at Girton rather than take the bus or buy a car. He was also a pacifist, and his views on warfare made a profound impression on me for the rest of my life.

An hour with Arthur Sale in the fifteenth-century oak-beamed room he taught in at that time was revelatory. He seemed to have read and remembered everything that had been written in English; and in later life, as a searcher-out of little known writers myself (with an ambition to be one, my critics might say) I never came across anyone whom Arthur didn't seem to know better. He was almost as ferocious to us about the debased nature of contemporary popular culture as Leavis was about Joyce and Eliot; and yet a surprising number of his pupils went on to become leading media luminaries. He taught the writer and broadcaster Bamber Gascoigne, the drama critic Benedict Nightingale, Michael Binyon of *The Times*, and Alan Rusbridger, editor of the *Guardian*, the novelist Nicholas Shakespeare, and many others. Perhaps it was his character as an outsider which pushed us towards a career where being an outsider is a positive advantage. Perhaps it was merely because his influence told against accepting the obvious, the official version, the accepted view, and encouraged us to examine things for ourselves.

And perhaps it was because he was so demanding about style. Years later, after I had come back from a frightening and physically exhausting tour of duty covering the war in Afghanistan, I went to see him. My report had gone out a few days earlier. The high point of it was a piece to camera with fighting going on all round me. Arthur had seen it. He always seemed to see the things one hoped he wouldn't.

'You split two infinitives when the guns were going off,' he said.

« »

One day, in the University Library, I happened to pass the large and affable figure of Reg Gadney, then an action painter and later a successful writer. (At that time Reg's painting style involved taking fat tubes of oil paint and squirting them at a canvas. He sold one of his paintings to the young and progressive owner of one of the stateliest houses in England, who came down a few mornings later and found that the paint had emigrated from the canvas and was halfway down the eighteenth-century Chinese silk wallpaper. The resultant court case, which dragged on for a long time, turned on whether the canvas still constituted a painting, regardless of where the paint happened to be. The result was a kind of legal draw.)

Gadney, standing at the top of the main stairs in the Library, called me over.

'He'll do,' he said, gripping my arm. He was talking to a well-known English don, Jeremy Prynne.

'Do for what?' I asked, distinctly flattered. Reg was a serious figure.

'Oh, editor of *Granta*. Want it? It's hard work.'

I did want it. I wanted it very badly. *Granta* wasn't what it later became, a London-based publication with proper money behind it, but it had a long history of famous editors and contributors, from A. A. Milne and Cecil Beaton to Mark Boxer and David Frost.

I involved my friends, of course – that was what Cambridge taught you to do – and so Nicholas Snowman shared the editing with me, Ridley Burnet ran the business side and Norman Hammond, who is now a distinguished archaeologist and roots round the Central American jungle like an intelligent Indiana Jones, was sales manager.

Our fortunes were mixed. Germaine Greer, who was older than us and a dominant spirit in Cambridge at the time, announced that *Granta* had become crap. She advised a wonderfully talented, self-destructive art editor we had, Richard Yeend, to leave. (It was Richard Yeend who, by encouraging me to put an engraving by Aubrey Beardsley on the front cover of my first *Granta*, was long afterwards credited by two different art historians with having brought about the rebirth of international interest in Beardsley and the Yellow Book.) Fortunately he stayed.

Clive James, who was also older and equally dominant, was much more supportive. I published some of his poems, including a charming little aubade which caught the contemporary Cambridge spirit of narrow beds and snooping officialdom exactly. Part of it went, I remember, like this:

> Together, sleeping sideways,
> There's not much they demand:
> A knee between her knees,
> A place to put his hand.

From America Allen Ginsberg sent us a poem about making love too, but it was much too graphic for the printers and they refused to set it because they were afraid of being sued for obscenity.

Granta's big problem was financial. Its debts had begun, so the magazine tradition had it, with a trip which David Frost had taken to London for lunch when he was editor in the fifties. We used to repeat the scandalous story to each other: he had taken a taxi there and back, and had kept it waiting outside the restaurant. My small-time bourgeois instincts were appalled by this. Much of my time as editor, therefore, was taken up with organizing a fund to put the magazine on a better footing.

With the help of Nicholas Snowman and the others we put together a fund, with all sorts of luminaries from *Granta*'s past on it – Frost himself, Mark Boxer, Nicholas Tomalin and others from whom I later hoped to get a job – and slowly turned the finances round. We staged an art exhibition, of which a newly discovered Rubens was the centre-piece, and that edition of *Granta* acted as the catalogue; we put on an opera, and that edition was the programme. We even produced an anthology of *Granta*, published in 1966 by Secker and Warburg. Occasionally, rooting through a second-hand bookshop, I come across a copy. I always buy it: it has a real value nowadays.

One edition of the magazine was a terrible failure. I had

commissioned a feature on racial minorities in Cambridge (not a subject people were much aware of in those days) and selected a photograph of a Chinese cook standing outside his restaurant, the Pagoda, for the cover. I cut the photo narrow, so that only the letters 'GOD' showed above the cook's head; maybe I thought I was being clever. I wasn't. Such was the secular temper of the time that only a few hundred copies of the issue sold instead of the usual 6,000, even though it had some excellent writing in it.

At one o'clock in the morning a fortnight after it appeared, the sales manager Norman Hammond slipped out of his college, and met me in the proctor-haunted streets. He stood with me on Magdalene Bridge and we dropped five thousand unsold copies into the River Cam beneath us. Each bundle made a plangent and rather satisfying splash, then sank for ever. We shook hands when it was all over, and went our separate ways to bed.

Granta was, however, saved, but only for the time being. After struggling along for years, the title (which dated back to the 1880s) was taken over and it was turned into an international literary magazine under the editorship of a brilliant and ferocious American called Bill Buford.

In August 1965, five days after my twenty-first birthday, I married Diane. The pressure of living an ocean and a continent apart had become too great. Either we got together, or we went our different ways. I had travelled four more times to California, at great cost to my poor father, and I knew I wanted to be with her. If it had been acceptable then for couples to live together without marrying, we would probably have done that. But it wasn't; not just for God-fearing Christian Scientists, but for most people.

My family all turned out: not just my mother, who had to be brought forward continually, and my father, who dominated the proceedings, but also his brother Alan, who had fought the Japanese in the jungles of Burma, and my half-sister Pat, tall and intelligent and good-looking. It was a delightful business, starting at Cambridge register office since Magdalene College chapel wasn't licensed for weddings, going on to a service of blessing in the chapel, and finishing up with a reception in one of the college halls. Diane looked gorgeous, and you couldn't see that she had skinned both her knees when she fell over that morning. When she knelt on the altar steps they bled onto her dress, which was on loan from Alan's wife Diana. But I had never been so happy, and I spent the entire day with an enormous grin of pleasure on my face.

Married life in Cambridge was an unmitigated joy. All the loneliness and sense of separation was over, and the flat I had found for us at 40 Green Street in the centre of the city – closer than Magdalene was itself – helped us create the very essence of *la vie bohèmienne*. It was the old unreconstructed Cambridge still, dominated nine to one by males, with its May Balls, its dining clubs, and its river-life. Whenever we could, we punted on the river or wandered around the colleges seeing friends. Contributors would come to the flat with their articles and poems. Neither of us could walk down the street without bumping into someone we knew.

Diane was becoming a talented portrait artist, and the university allowed her, exceptionally, to attend its fine arts lectures. In the evenings, if we weren't out at a party or at the Arts Cinema round the corner, she would draw and I would read to her: the poetry of Keats or Matthew Arnold or Edward Thomas, the novels of Fielding or Dickens, the essays of Johnson or Lamb. We didn't have a television: too expensive, and unnecessary.

Looking back across this immense gulf of time, I can see us in our little panelled sitting room, with its ancient upright central beam from crooked floor to low ceiling. It is late at night and we huddle in armchairs with blankets over our shoulders, the feeble electric fire making the atmosphere a few degrees closer to tolerable. Outside, perhaps, there is the noise of a group of students passing in the frosty street. Inside, Diane's pencil scratches away with a faint susurrus, her feet tucked up underneath her, looking up at me from time to time as she works out the correct angles and planes of my face. I turn a page, trying not to move, and read.

> The sculptur'd dead, on each side, seem to freeze,
> Emprison'd in black, purgatorial rails:
> Knights, ladies, praying in dumb orat'ries,
> He passeth by; and his weak spirit fails
> To think how they may ache in icy hoods and mails.

'Now I really feel cold,' she says, looking across at the inch-wide gap between the bottom of the door and its frame. 'Why don't we finish the poem in bed?'

« »

In June 1966 we watched the last of our friends leave, and spent a lonely summer in Cambridge waiting for job offers. By August the BBC had finally made up its mind to take me. Then we too prepared to leave. We packed up everything and put it in the jungle green convertible Triumph my father had lent me. There was a sprinkling of rain, but we put the roof down to fit all our paintings and books and clothes in. I shut the door of 40 Green Street for the last time, without a thought for the significance of what I was doing, and climbed into the driving seat. Life lay ahead of us. I changed into fourth gear and headed for the A11.

'We're on our way,' I said.

4

Down the Word-Mine

TO SAY I WAS NOT a success in the BBC Radio Newsroom would be a litotes. I hated the place. The place didn't think much of me either.

I had assumed, in my ignorance, that journalists were pretty much the same species, like doctors or airline pilots or morticians. But as I came to know the news business from the inside, I gradually realized that two entirely different sub-species are contained within the basic genus. By this I don't mean egg-heads from television, radio and the broadsheet newspapers as opposed to the people from the tabloids. These are merely varieties of habitat; the differentiation goes far deeper than that. It is a matter of character.

One type of journalist is precise, accurate, undemonstrative and inclined to be resentful; the other is brash, noisy, disrespectful, careless, quick-witted and impatient. This first sub-species is composed essentially of sub-editors: careful, unadventurous people who wear cardigans, work at desks, make adequate financial provision for themselves and their families, drive safely, and mate for life like swans. Reporters occupy a completely different ecological niche, and as a result have completely different characteristics. They are slap-happy and take risks; they wear rumpled suits and stained ties; they always mean to check the terms of their insurance policies but never get round to it; they drive fast, and are subject to multiple divorces.

Sub-editors are the people who ring reporters with complaints:

'According to your despatch, forty-five people were injured; Reuters are saying it was forty-six. Would you check this?'

Reporters characteristically explode in a shower of fury and self-pity:

'Look, I got up at four in the morning to be here, my shoes are ruined, I was lucky not to be injured myself. It looked to me as though there were forty-five. Who's counting? Maybe there were more, and I didn't see them. It happens.'

Sub-editors don't want to hear that kind of thing. For them, news is what comes off the agency wires in handy bite-sized pieces, not a formless, meaningless event. What's more, news is immutably accurate: if not, the foundations of the universe itself would be in question. Reporters learn early that they shouldn't tell a sub-editor they have made a guess at something, that they weren't sure, that there were twenty different versions of what happened and they chose the one that seemed most likely. It unsettles the sub-editor too much. Above all, they have a different approach to life. Reporters relish the feeling that by tomorrow morning they could be in Rio de Janeiro without having had time to pack a suitcase; sub-editors like to check their shift-patterns and see if they will be working on Christmas Day next year.

I was born to be a reporter. I was not born to be a sub-editor.

« »

Little had altered in the BBC Radio Newsroom since 1945. One of the pigeon-holes for agency copy on the main Home Service news desk still bore a hand-written sign which said 'Empire'. The newsreaders might no longer have to wear dinner-jackets to read the evening news, but most of them looked as though they wanted to.

For the sub-editors who inhabited the Newsroom, change was about as welcome as the sound of pneumatic drills from the street outside. The Newsroom couldn't see the point of it. As for television, the Newsroom regarded that like a silent film star regarded the talkies. From the 1920s to the beginning of the 1950s radio had been the dominant medium, and it was therefore only in the previous ten or twelve years that television had dislodged it. Radio remained the senior service, and the news bulletins were more serious, more intelligent, and covered a far wider range of world events. (At around this time the satirical magazine *Private Eye*, in a take-off of BBC television, wrote '8.50 News: Richard Baker with pictures of some of today's fires.')

As part of the tribute which the newcomers paid to the establishment, the editor of the day in Television was obliged to ring the editor of the day on the Home Service bulletins each morning to find out what news items Radio was planning to run. Years later I discovered that Television regarded this as an antique ritual which had to be observed in order not to hurt Radio's feelings; but we in Radio regarded it as evidence that Television couldn't make its mind up about anything and needed us to tell it what to do.

As for me, I was endured rather than welcomed. A twenty-two-year-old half-price trainee sub fresh from Cambridge was, as far as the rest of the Newsroom was concerned, part of the unwelcome process of change. There were several Oxbridge graduates there, but they had always proved their worth somewhere else; they had never turned up with their inabilities fresh upon them.

Fortunately there were several understanding, gentle souls in the Newsroom who were kind and welcoming, and their names are grate-fully fixed in my memory. Others regarded it as part of their life's work to explain to me in detail why a degree was not merely unnecessary for a journalist, but a positive disadvantage. To be a graduate from the university of life, to have stood in the rain outside a funeral in Barnsley and got every single mourner's name exactly right: now that was the thing. Had I done this? No. Therefore my life's experience was deeply inadequate. I was rather inclined to agree.

And so I became the juniormost and least trusted sub-editor, allowed only to write the fifteen-second items about the weather which rounded off the bulletins. Even then I was much corrected.

'The forecasters say—'

'No, no, no, laddie: how do you know that's what they're saying? Did you hear them say it? Of course not. Put "The forecast for tomorrow is—" '

'This isn't any good, son. Where's the imagination, where's the flair? Try something a bit different, like "The forecasters say—" '

At lunchtime, when everyone else went to the canteen or the pub, I would wander off on my own through the little streets to the north of Oxford Street. There were still junk-shops and old bookshops in them which had survived from a different age, and many times I found interesting and valuable things there: first editions of Thackeray and Richard Jefferies, or late Victorian detective stories, or Edwardian science fiction. In those days you could still amass an interesting and worthwhile collection of books cheaply.

Nowadays, I mostly buy books from antiquarian dealers at prices

I would then have regarded as criminally wasteful: there may be pleasure in the acquisition, but there is none at all in the hunt. In fact there is no longer any hunt. Yet in 1966, in the dark and dusty shops of Fitzrovia and Soho I came to sense precisely where one might expect to find, say, a charmingly bound 1900s thriller by Guy Boothby, or an early edition of a Walter Scott novel.

The act of searching became a pleasure in itself, as I chatted to the strange characters who ran these places: in one, a wizened old man with a skull-cap; in another, a former actor who claimed to have been on the stage with Tree and Irving; in a third, in an alley near the British Museum, an ancient but ferocious hermit who went into a rage if you touched the books without telling him precisely what it was you were interested in; and who then turned out to be courtesy itself, a positive fountain of book-lore and reminiscences of long-forgotten authors.

'Ernest Bramah? He used to come in here a lot. It wasn't his full name, you know: he was really called Smith. But Bramah was his middle name. He used to say to me, "Who would ever buy a book by a man called Smith, eh?" When he wrote those Kai Lung books he knew nothing about China, of course: had to look it all up. He probably didn't know any blind people, either, but he had a blind hero all the same. Max Carrados: you wouldn't have heard of him.'

And if I said I had, and could prove it, he would give me a discount on whatever I wanted to buy.

I would take my finds back to the Newsroom afterwards like a child bringing back a curious shell from the beach, and show them to one of the other sub-editors: an older man, who was a bookbinder and collector himself.

'I think you could take the risk of running a damp cloth over that,' he would say, examining the cover. 'It'll bring out the tones.'

There were several people in the Newsroom like Neil: quiet, thoughtful, literary, pleasant. But I had the impression that not many of them throve there.

One evening a few weeks after I arrived, I was preparing to leave, having spent the day on the Third Programme news desk and written one brief story about the sale of a painting, which had been dropped as uninteresting hours before. It was the time when one began to think about having a last cup of coffee, and slipping out in time to catch the 10.08 from Charing Cross.

Over by the agency wire machines there was a clatter of bells. A messenger ripped off a short despatch with a flourish and ran across with it. The editor of the bulletin read it as though it was a personal communique from Lord Reith. Then he looked round. Everybody was working hard, except me.

'Well, well, laddie, I suppose I'll have to ask you to do this one. Anyway, you're young. You'll know about these things.'

He passed over the piece of paper. It was a 'snap' from the Press Association: the death of an old children's broadcaster had been announced. I had listened to Uncle Dick's programme for years and years. The editor explained to me that I should ring up Auntie Gladys, Uncle Dick's partner on the programme for years, and ask her for her reaction.

'But have a care, laddie. These old folk are apt to fall off their perches if you give them a shock, so break it to her carefully. Don't say he's dead at first; just ease her into it. Here's the number to ring. Think you can do it?'

The phone rang for a long time. Finally an ancient, gin-sodden voice answered.

'Well? Who is it?'

I meant to have a care, to break it to her carefully, to ease her into it. But I was excited, and the words came rushing out in spite of me.

'Sorry to have to tell you this, but Uncle Dick's dead. I mean passed on.'

There was a long silence at the other end. Oh God, I thought, I've given her a shock and she's fallen off her perch.

But at last the gin-sodden voice started to croak and wheeze again. It was a moment or two before I realized she was laughing.

'That evil old bastard,' she said at last. 'I hope he died in agony.'

I noted this down faithfully, though I felt even then that it wasn't the kind of thing you often heard on the radio. Then she started pouring out the story to me. Week after week, children from all over the country would win competitions to visit the BBC and meet Uncle Dick. He would welcome them, show them round, give them lunch, then take them to the Gents and interfere with them. If their parents complained afterwards, she said, the Director-General's office would write and say the nation wouldn't understand such an accusation against a much loved figure.

Finally the croaking died away. I stopped writing, thanked her, and put down the phone.

'It's an amazing business,' I said to the editor, and started to tell him.

He heard me out in silence.

'You stupid, unthinking, ignorant, destructive young idiot,' he said quietly.

Then he turned to a typist and started dictating without notes.

'Uncle Dick's partner for many years, dash dash Auntie Gladys dash dash, told the BBC tonight that she was deeply saddened by his death stop. She said, open quotes, He had a wonderful way with children, close quotes stop. That's how you do an obit,' he added, glaring at me from under his bushy eyebrows.

I was learning in other ways too. A few months after my arrival the Americans bombed yet another Vietnamese village, and this time I was asked to write the story.

'An American military spokesman in Saigon has admitted that US planes have accidentally bombed the village of Phuoc Me, close to the North Vietnamese border.'

'No, no, no,' said the chief sub, circling the name with his 6B pencil and putting a large question-mark beside it. 'Look here, you can't expect a news reader to say something disgusting like that on the air.'

We had a conference about it. The news reader agreed with the chief sub: it was filthy, and he had never before been asked to say such a thing. It would make him a laughing-stock. The news editor, a small bald man called Donald who looked like the Mekon, the extra-terrestrial mastermind in my boyhood comics, heard us out.

As the youngest person there by about a century, I kept quiet. In the end, though, I felt I had to say something.

'But it really is the name of the village. Shouldn't that be what we call it?'

'Maybe,' said someone else slowly, 'you could try pronouncing it differently.'

'And how, may I ask, might one do something like that?' asked the news reader.

'Fwoc My?' suggested Donald. 'Fwec May? Fooc Moy?'

The news reader looked up at the ceiling in a marked sort of way. No one else said anything.

'All right, sonny, bring me the atlas.'

He located Phuoc Me and pointed his finger at the next village.

'Call it that.'

I peered at it.

'It's called Ban Me Tuat.'

'Well, all right, not that one. The next place.'

I found the next place, and we called it that instead. Decency and plausibility were what counted. The people of Phuoc Me probably didn't care much; they had other things to worry about.

Some of the sharper young subs like Will Wyatt, the future head of BBC Television, were promoted out of the Newsroom altogether. Others, even younger and less regarded than myself, took their place. One of them was Stewart Purvis, who would one day be the editor of ITN. He had a worse time than I did, and eventually left for somewhere more congenial. As for me, I learned (to my shame) one of the chief rules of the place: always blame someone even more junior and power-less than yourself when things go wrong.

'Look here, laddie, Reuters are saying a hundred thousand people demonstrated in the streets of Hong Kong and you're saying it was ten thousand. How did you come to overlook a thing like that?'

'Sorry, the typist must have left a nought out.'

Eventually even I could no longer continue blaming the typists; after all, the responsibility for checking what had been typed was entirely mine. Something inside me that had been buried and half-forgotten during my time in the Newsroom finally surfaced.

'I'm afraid I didn't notice. I'm sorry.'

Maybe it was my imagination, but I thought I detected a flicker of uneasiness all round me. You didn't voluntarily admit guilt in the Newsroom: it might be used against you somehow, somewhere. We didn't know who or what it was we were afraid of, but it was better to be safe and make sure someone else had the trouble. Fear stalked the corridors.

Slowly, my stories ceased to be automatically the last and most expendable in the news bulletin; on one or two occasions they blos-somed out unexpectedly during the day and became the lead. Eventually, too, I was allowed to be a copy-taster: that strange function carried out, like in a mediaeval banquet, to ensure that the editor of the day received only choice, worthwhile morsels unpoisoned by uncertainty or inaccuracy. It was a step up, but it was also more dangerous. I was now in moment-by-moment contact with the editor, who could spot my inadequacies with greater precision and might put in a bad annual report on me.

And my inadequacies were certainly considerable. For a start, I had little idea what a good story was. I like to think now that I was more interested in signs that American special forces were losing ground in the Central Highlands of Vietnam because the villagers had turned against them, than in a meeting between the Vietnamese president and yet another American senator; but to be honest, I doubt it. I knew very little about news, and had the instincts of a jackdaw. Copy-tasting was therefore very good for me. My job was to select interesting agency despatches, fold them up, and put them into the box of pigeon-holes (including the one with the 'Empire' label) that lay flat on the desk between the copy-taster and the editor.

And because I found it genuinely hard to know what the editor would find interesting, I used to stuff so many stories into the pigeon-holes that he or she soon gave up looking at them. As for the stories which even I could see were important, I handed them straight across. If the editor asked me for something, the chances were that I'd already put it in one of the pigeon-holes, so I would merely fish it out and hand it over. You were meant to impale the stories you had discarded onto the copy-taker's spike, a dangerous-looking implement like a long upright nail. But with a certain low cunning I quickly realized that would never do. The tell-tale hole in the middle of the paper would show up my lack of judgement irreparably.

One morning, when I had filled the pigeon-holes and was sifting through the huge pile of copy in front of me, I heard a conversation between two sub-editors on a different desk behind me.

'Bloody fool ploughed straight onto the reef. Some foreign skipper, I suppose. You know, Paraguayan or something.'

Sub-editors only talk about big news stories, I thought; what could this one be? Rooting through the pile of discards, I found an item I had seen twenty minutes earlier from Lloyd's Register of Shipping: a foreign-registered tanker called the *Torrey Canyon* had gone aground off the British coast. As I searched, the greatest environmental disaster in British history was beginning. I had just excavated the piece of paper when I heard the acidulous voice of the editor.

'Do you think you might conceivably have seen a story about a tanker going aground? I really would quite like to see it, if you think you can manage it.'

Oh God, I thought, she mustn't see me putting the paper into the pigeon-hole.

'Someone over there told me about it,' I said, pointing to the far corner of the room. She turned her head to look, and I slipped the story into one of the boxes.

'I think you'll find it's in the pigeon-hole,' I said.

She looked at me hard. It was a close call, but I had managed not to show the instant of weakness that marked you down for ever as an inadequate in that unforgiving place.

Nowadays when I go into the Radio Newsroom it's all different. No cardigans, no 6B pencils, no one to tell you that it must be done this way because it's always been done like that, no one to explain that your university degree is valueless. Probably things when I was there were nothing like as bad and repressive as I have made them out to be; and later, as a foreign correspondent, I came to like many of the people who had once seemed so aloof and judgmental. Nevertheless the mythos generated by my unhappy start at the BBC stayed with me for years, much as Dickens suffered from his secret memories of the Covent Garden polish-bottling factory where he worked as a child. Until the late 1980s I couldn't even bring myself to walk through the Newsroom on the way to the editorial offices which lay beyond it on the third floor of Broadcasting House. I would take the lift to the fourth floor, walk along the corridor above the Newsroom, go down the back stairs, and get to the offices that way. And for years I convinced myself that I did all this because it was quicker.

« »

No one missed me when I finally got out of the Newsroom in May 1968 and became a producer in radio current affairs; they were probably relieved. As for me, I felt as though I had dug myself out of Stalag Luft VII.

The times were changing. Crowds of students were out on the streets in Paris every day, attacking the police and demanding the resignation of President de Gaulle. There were demonstrations against the Vietnam war from Grosvenor Square in London to Tokyo. In Prague people were openly condemning the old, conservative Soviet-installed government and demanding something better and freer. America was unrecognizable from the starchy, patriotic society I had encountered only five years before. Even in China there was a distorted, nightmarish version of the youth culture in the rest of the world, as pupils denounced their teachers and handed over their parents to the thought police. Everywhere, whatever was young and fresh became admirable, and whatever was old was condemned. Except of course in the Radio Newsroom.

Since my wife and I were twenty-three, we thought it was all wonderful. Diane looked particularly good in mini-skirts, with her blonde hair bobbed in the way we all believed looked so stylish then. We watched *Rowan and Martin's Laugh-In* on television, and listened to *Sergeant Pepper*, and read the *Guardian*, and books by Hermann Hesse, and *Lord of the Rings*, and clapped at the violent end of *If . . .*, and tried to find patchouli oil, without success.

London was suddenly the capital of the fashionable universe, and I reinvented myself to fit in with the new times. My tweed suits and sports jackets were given to the Salvation Army. Instead I bought some yellow cords and a pair of desert boots, and tied a red scarf round my neck. I also tried to grow a moustache, but no one noticed so after a few weeks I shaved it off. I whistled the tunes from the Incredible String Band's latest record (not an easy task) and fancied myself as something of a revolutionary. And slowly my self-confidence came back. Now young people were supposed to have much better ideas than older ones (a principle I didn't necessarily believe even then) so I tried to have some good ideas at work. They were listened to by serious characters who knew much more about broadcasting than I did, with an interest neither I nor my ideas deserved. Life must have been very difficult then for men and women in their forties and fifties. For me it was like being a Red Guard.

My professional life was blossoming at last. I was a producer now, in charge of entire programmes: including our ageing flagship, *Radio Newsreel*, with its delightfully bombastic theme music, 'Imperial Echoes'. On night-shifts, which I sometimes shared with Michael Cole, who later became the head of public relations for the owner of Harrods,

Mohammed Al-Fayed, and with Robert Fox, who would one day be the diplomatic editor of the *Daily Telegraph*, I would be in sole charge of the programme on the World Service. Once, after I had carelessly cut short an item about East Africa on the grounds that no one could possibly be listening at this time of night, we had complaints from the presidential offices of both Kenya and Tanzania.

We were allowed a couple of hours' sleep at the Langham, just across the road from Broadcasting House: a BBC office building which in the 1870s had been the grandest hotel in the world, where maharajahs stayed and the Victorian novelist Ouida died. The grand rooms had been partitioned without thought for architecture or visual beauty, and like many people at that stage I despaired of the way great Victorian buildings like that were being destroyed. And yet by the early 1990s the Langham had been turned back into a hotel again, and its rooms restored to their former size.

There was an ancient commissionaire in charge of the Langham at night, who always fell asleep instead of giving you a wake-up call at the time you wanted. If you were sensible you took your own alarm clock; if you were lucky you woke up of your own accord; if you didn't and weren't, it could be a disaster. Whenever the commissionaire overslept I would leap down the stairs two at a time, and give him a reproachful look.

'Did 'e call you all right?' he would ask, as though ''e', the one who had failed to wake me, was someone else altogether.

For the first time I was enjoying my work. At my suggestion politicians and academics were brought into the studio for interview. I could commission reports from some of the great figures of radio news whose names and voices I had heard since childhood: Hardiman Scott, Christopher Serpell, F. D. Walker, Anthony Lawrence. They were very grand, and very clever; but they were always courteous.

Not that everyone believed in the old doctrine of BBC impartiality, even then. Freddie Forsythe, a languid and rather superior assistant diplomatic correspondent, had been sent to Nigeria to cover the war with the breakaway region of Biafra. He became convinced of the rightness of the Biafran cause and began to slant his reporting in the rebels' favour. This gradually became more and more obvious, until one day he sent us a despatch which suggested that in a single battle the Biafran air force had shot down two more fighters than the Federal air force even possessed. I looked up the figures in *Jane's All the World's Aircraft*, and with a self-confidence I had rarely felt before refused to broadcast the report. When one of my bosses asked me why, I told him.

There was no greater offence than deliberately falsifying the news, so in the end Freddie Forsythe was invited to hand in his BBC watch (or 'wristlet stop-watch', as the bureaucrats called it) and leave. For us it was the ultimate disgrace; but it was, of course, the making of him. He went off to a garret in Paris and wrote a novel which publisher after publisher rejected, until one day a relatively junior editor actually read it and saw how good it was. Decades later people in Groucho's Club still pointed him out as the editor who had first spotted *The Day of the Jackal*.

Nervously (because of course I wasn't a revolutionary at all, merely a liberal who hankered after a bit of change) I went to the big anti-Vietnam demonstration in Grosvenor Square in October 1968. No one knew what might happen: there might be worse violence than there had been at the previous demonstration a few months earlier; the crowds might break through the police lines and storm the American embassy; they might even try to overthrow the state.

I stood in the front row, jammed up against the police, and watched the anarchists throw marbles under the feet of the police horses. The police, for their part, were not the patient, sensible characters I had always taken them for. As the crowd grew angrier they lost control of themselves. Some of them screamed obscenities. A sergeant grabbed a young woman standing close beside me by her long red hair and pulled her to the ground by it, for no reason that I could see.

And yet, as has happened on so many similar occasions in British history, the ferocity quickly ebbed on both sides. Soon the demonstrators were saying sorry if they trod on a policeman's toes, and the police were grinning if their helmets were tipped awry. By late afternoon we streamed away, with all sides moderately satisfied. The anarchists had had a fight; the left had shown their anger at US policy in Vietnam; the police line had not been broken; the American embassy was protected from attack; the state remained untoppled.

Still, I had experienced at first hand the excitement of a little action. I wrote an account of the demonstration for the *Christian Science Monitor*, for which I was now a regular contributor; but the London editor, an elderly Englishman whose pleasant appearance overlaid a pretty ferocious dislike of the young, the new fashions, demonstrations of any kind and (above all) the Labour Government, decided it wasn't right for the paper. I didn't mind too much; I had at last written something a little meatier than my usual whimsical accounts of London life, and found it to my liking.

Yet the Grosvenor Square demonstration was the only one of the great events of 1968 which I saw with my own eyes; and it was by far the least important. The others – the Prague Spring, the May uprising in Paris, the Tet Offensive in Vietnam, the Soviet-led invasion of Czechoslovakia, the murders of Bobby Kennedy and Martin Luther King, the Democratic Convention in Chicago – I merely read about or watched on television. I longed to go to Vietnam or Prague, or even to Paris, but felt myself weighed down by the reality of daily life. I had a wife to support, a pleasant flat in Greenwich, and a job that I was too insecure to give up.

Within a few months of these events Diane was pregnant with our first child: this was no time, I told myself, to do anything foolish. Still, there was a restlessness in me which had to find an outlet of some kind. I talked her into agreeing that we should buy a little yellow MG Sprite, and we raced around the countryside in that. When our daughter Julia was born in December 1969, a delightfully gentle blonde child, the pleasures of fatherhood overwhelmed me. So far, a sense of my responsibilities had triumphed over the desire to see for myself some of the more significant things of my time. I was rarely to be quite so sensible ever again.

« »

I managed, for a few months, to get myself transferred to a local radio news programme called *South-East* as a hybrid producer-reporter. For the most part the stories I dealt with weren't particularly elevated: strikes, traffic jams, what cabbies thought about the new taxis which dispensed with the old, romantic darkened back window. My first broadcast report was on the introduction of plastic joints for people with arthritic fingers.

One of my early assignments, however, had strange repercussions. There was a small item in one of the newspapers about King Freddie of Buganda, a British-educated monarch who had been in nominal charge of part of Uganda. The Ugandan president, a tough and unscrupulous man called Milton Obote, chased King Freddie out of the country, and he took refuge in Britain. He had no money, but his friends were generous. Eventually, however, he had been forced to accept an offer of a free flat in the East End of London, in a privately run estate for the poor. I saw a report about this, and decided to go and interview him.

The flat was in Bermondsey, in a pretty depressing turn-of-the-century block which has now been demolished. I climbed up the evil-smelling stairs and rang the bell of King Freddie's flat. He turned out to be charming and rather diffident, a youngish man in elderly but well-cut tweeds who spoke with a slightly absurd upper-class accent. Meeting him was like walking into a short story about Jeeves and Wooster.

'Come in, come in, my dear fellow,' he said, and showed me to an armchair. I could feel the springs beneath me. On his mantelpiece, apparently without any satirical intent, stood little busts of Queen Victoria and Gordon of Khartoum. Old pictures of Uganda hung on the walls.

'Drink?'

I shook my head. In those days, as a Christian Scientist, I didn't drink alcohol.

'I've pretty much given up too. Used to drink far too much. Bad for your health, you know.'

I nodded, as though I hadn't heard that one before. We talked a while, and then I produced my Uher tape recorder and started interviewing him. There was a kind of unembarrassed honesty about King Freddie which made him both impressive and pitiful. He spoke with gratitude about the friends who had helped him.

'And what about the government of President Obote?' I asked.

He frowned. 'Rather not talk about that, old chap, if you don't mind. Bit delicate. Between you and me, I've got problems where he's concerned.'

I switched off the tape recorder, and we chatted a little more. Then I said my goodbyes. Could I, I asked, come and see him again?

'Absolutely delighted, my dear fellow. Please do. Drop in any time. I'm here quite a lot, you know.' He sighed.

The next day the radio news announced the death of the exiled King Freddie of Buganda. The cause was alcoholic poisoning.

I couldn't believe it. He must have died about eight hours – say at the most twelve – after I had seen him; and at that stage he was neither depressed nor in the early stages of a terminal drinking bout. I rang the police in Bermondsey, who told me that when his body was found he had had several times the legal limit of alcohol in his bloodstream.

'But, sergeant,' I said, 'I was with him last night. I didn't leave till gone seven, and he was entirely sober then. Something very strange must have happened.'

'Are you trying to tell us our job, sir?' the sergeant asked nastily.

I said I wasn't, but offered to make a statement.

'If we need a statement, sir, we'll contact you.'

They didn't, of course. Afterwards Bugandans in London who had supported King Freddie were certain he had been killed on President Obote's orders. They claimed he had been held down and the contents of two bottles of vodka had been poured down his throat. Maybe he was just depressed, and drank it himself. Somehow, I doubted it.

« »

The head of reporters wasn't at all the usual kind of BBC executive. He was rough and scornful, and came from Fleet Street. He didn't think much of the namby-pambies who were sitting alongside him on today's selection board.

'We're here to appoint a group of men who'll be asked to do a real job, go to dangerous places,' he said. 'In other words, reporters. The ones we choose have got to be up to it. So when each candidate comes in, I want you to think to yourself, "Is this the kind of man who would walk into a brothel?" '

I only heard about this unusual criterion years later, from someone who had been with him on the selection board that day. I was glad I hadn't known it at the time. I wasn't at all that kind of man, not least because I wouldn't have had the nerve: which is presumably why he wanted brothel-frequenters. This was April 1970, and life was still pretty unreconstructed, even inside the BBC. There were, of course, no women candidates; the head of reporters wouldn't have considered a woman capable of doing the job. Women, at best, did social reporting; they certainly didn't do hard news.

Even without knowing that only Casanovas were required, I didn't
have much hope of success. A few weeks earlier I had been to see the
new editor of *Radio News*, a former Fleet Street man, and told him it
was my great ambition to be a reporter. I had had plenty of experience
on *South-East*, I said. He wasn't impressed.

'You've never worked on a proper newspaper, have you?'

That annoyed me: he knew perfectly well that I wrote for the
Christian Science Monitor, which I considered to be better than anything he had worked on. I said nothing. Maybe that in turn annoyed
him.

'You don't stand an earthly,' he said, grinning at me. 'Stick to
producing.'

The board rejected me, of course; I was insufficiently likely to walk
into a brothel. But a few days later they found they needed one reporter
more than they had anticipated, and mine had been at the top of the
list of those rejected: the editor had to give me a reporting job after
all. I started on 1 May 1970, still a little punch-drunk.

My new colleagues weren't welcoming.

'John here is joining you, so I want you to treat him well,' said the
editor at a formal meeting of introduction, from motives I can only
speculate about.

'Do you mean we're not allowed to stamp on his lily-white fingers?'
asked one of the old lags. Everyone else laughed, and I tried to join in.

They all seemed outmoded and discontented to me. I had arrived
at a time of tremendous reorganization. The BBC reporters formed one
large group, working for both television and radio. Now the plan was
to divide them up, and it was clear that those who weren't so good
would end up in radio: finally relegated to the role of junior partner.
And yet radio was more interesting than it had ever been. A whole
range of new current affairs programmes was being launched or
reshaped – *The World At One* and *P.M.*, for example – and the best
of the reporting talent which was left in radio went there. Not me: I
stayed with the news.

For the first few days, though, there was nothing to do. I sat around
and waited, like a batsman padded up in the pavilion. The other
reporters came in and did occasional jobs, but my phone didn't ring.
I began to wonder if I would ever get out of the building. Then on the
fourth morning the news editor wandered into the reporters' office,

where I was sitting on my own. He was a new arrival, just as I was, and since he had come from the Overseas Service at Bush House he was almost as innocent as I was about domestic reporting.

All that week the newspapers had been full of carefully planted hints that the prime minister, Harold Wilson, was about to call a snap election.

'Apparently he's going to be at Euston this morning, catching a train to Huyton,' said the news editor. Huyton was Wilson's constituency. 'Downing Street are offering a photocall. Why don't you try to get a word with him? Ask him if he really is going to call an election.'

Since I didn't know any better, and nor did he, I was flattered. My first assignment, and I was covering the prime minister.

Platform 7 at Euston was already crowded with photographers, cameramen and reporters when I arrived. They were drawn up obediently opposite the entrance to Wilson's compartment. The whole thing, as so often in the Wilson years, was totally staged. There was nothing remotely spontaneous or genuine about it: we were there merely to do the bidding of the Downing Street machine.

With so many journalists crowded together I couldn't find anywhere to stand with my trusty tape recorder, so I had to hover in front of them. I had only just arrived in time: very soon the stills cameras started flashing and the television cameras whirred as Wilson arrived accompanied by his officials and security men and walked down the platform towards us. Surrounded by officials and security men and all the panoply of power, he walked down the platform looking like a pudgy god in a cloud of angels.

Harold Wilson was expected to win the election, even though he was politically a burned-out case. His credibility (as we learned to call it in those days) had long since evaporated. President Johnson, asked privately to explain why Wilson accepted his Vietnam policy so meekly, had answered, 'I've got his pecker in my pocket'; and the phrase had gone round the world.

Wilson had come to power six years earlier on a wave of hyperbole, promising to pull Britain kicking and screaming into the twentieth century and to subject it to the white-hot technological revolution which seemed to be going on elsewhere. He had been witty and cool, the political correspondents had liked him, and at first he had seemed to be a relief from the rapidly decomposing Conservative government of 1962–4. But it didn't last. He had few discernible principles beyond trying to stay in power, his nerve failed quickly, and government (or 'governance', as he later called it) seemed to consist mostly for him in playing off his colleagues against one another, or undermining them in private and in public. Wilson was a manipulator, the first person I had heard using the word 'pragmatic' with approval. Temporary appearance, merely getting by, was what counted for him; long-term reality scarcely seemed to matter.

Still, the reporters waiting for him on Platform 7 smiled ingratiatingly, as they tend to when the great ones of the earth pass their way. I glanced round at them and realized that smiling was all they planned to do. No one was going to ask him anything. So be it, I thought; I'll do it myself.

I stepped forward into his path, microphone in the fixed-bayonet position, tape recorder running.

'Excuse me, prime minister.'

My entire world exploded. Wilson grabbed the shaft of the microphone with his left hand and tried to break it out of my grasp. With his right he punched me hard in the stomach. He was saying things to me, but I couldn't give them my undivided attention because I was too busy bending over and gasping. Wilson might not have much in the way of principle, but he certainly packed a punch.

Then he let go of my microphone and swept past. His press secretary, Gerald Kaufman, hissed something threatening in my ear. They both climbed on board the train and sat down, looking straight ahead of them in case they might have to look out at me. After a long minute or two the train began to move, and Wilson, still looking stonily ahead and puffing on his pipe, was taken out of our sight.

The journalists gathered round laughing.

'You can't just doorstep the PM like that, sonny,' said one of the older reporters, patting me comfortingly on the shoulder.

'You should have seen your face when he hit you,' said the reporter from BBC television news.

'You'll be in trouble now,' said his cameraman, irritated because I had got in the way of his shot.

I walked slowly back down the platform, struggling to come to terms with what had happened. It was only five past eleven on my first working day, and I had been physically assaulted by the prime minister. My career was finished before it had begun.

The news editor was as worried as I was when I went back and confessed, though to his credit he blamed himself rather than me. I still couldn't quite see what I had done that was so terrible: yet Wilson's reaction showed that I must have committed a crime among crimes. Lunch-time came and went, and Wilson reached Huyton. There was no call of complaint. Maybe Wilson had had second thoughts; maybe his staff had talked him out of ringing the Director-General. I still had a job after all.

As I say, it was a different world. Every newspaper in Fleet Street, and every television and newsreel organization must have had pictures of the prime minister punching me, yet none appeared. In 1970 that kind of thing would never have been published or broadcast. Senior politicians could, it seemed, still get away with – if not murder – then certainly assault and battery.

When the tape was transcribed, I gave copies of it to my friends. By then I had given up regarding the episode as a major personal tragedy, and the bruises were fading.

Transcript of interview, 4.5.70

Speakers: John Simpson (staff), the Rt Hon Harold Wilson PC MP (Prime Minister) (non-staff), Gerald Kaufman (non-staff)

JS: Excuse me, Prime Minister.

HW: How dare you do this? Who are you? Are you BBC? Your director-general knows I never do these things.

[Microphone noise]

JS: But—

HW: I shall put in the strongest complaint about your disgraceful behaviour the moment we get to Huyton.

[Microphone noise]

GK: You'll hear more of this.

JS: Argghh.

Life soon became less angst-ridden. After a year in which I did little of any moment I was transferred to a delightful new programme called *Newsdesk*, which concentrated on foreign news. It was the first proper chance I had had to try my hand at reporting on events in the outside world, and even though I never travelled anywhere and merely assembled my reports from interviews recorded on the telephone, or with the help of experts in London, it gave me a great sense of satisfaction. I knew for certain now that this was the work I most enjoyed.

Occasionally, though, there were pleasant enough domestic stories to be done. When, for instance, Le Gavroche restaurant opened in London, it was said that the prices charged were unthinkably high – the highest ever recorded, apparently, in the United Kingdom. A producer and I managed to persuade the editor of the programme that we should try it out. The meal was superb, and it came to £14 per head.

Or, as we should have said then, £14.0s.0d. These were the last days of the old non-decimal currency, and although I was no mathematician and therefore found the business of calculating twelve pennies to the shilling and twenty shillings to the pound pretty daunting, I was sufficiently conservative to dislike the new system intensely. I missed the farthings and ha'pennies and threepenny bits and sixpences and shillings and half-crowns of my childhood and youth. Only the pennies (but in a very different size) and the florins (by a very different name) were left to us.

Now we have coins which have no nicknames, and indeed no identity apart from their numerical value. Occasionally, I still find myself asking for change in 'two-shilling pieces', and am made to feel like a monetary Rip Van Winkle; and it still annoys me that the concept of the penny should so far have disappeared from our consciousness that even the Chancellor of the Exchequer can talk in his budget speech of 'one pence'. People complain now about the single European currency, which is called with a deeply depressing lack of imagination the 'Euro'; but it seems to me that our real national currency disappeared long ago, in 1971.

5

Troubles

I PICKED UP the telephone, not quite certain how I was going to explain what had happened. Diane answered, in her quiet, pleasantly modulated Californian accent. I could imagine her sitting in our large early-Victorian drawing-room, looking out at Greenwich Park, with everything around her so pleasant and ordered: the books in the shelves, the paintings on the walls, the photographs of family and friends standing in their frames on the antique piano. I could hear our two-year-old, Julia, singing in the background. As for the baby, whose name was Eleanor and who had been born only a couple of months before, she seemed to be sitting on Diane's lap. It was a picture of great contentment, and I was just about to throw a hand-grenade into the middle of it all.

A couple of weeks before, at the end of 1971, my boss had sent a note round saying that since events in Ireland were building up to such a pitch it had been decided to send a full-time correspondent to Dublin. Anyone interested in the job should let him know. There was plenty of enthusiasm in the office. Dublin had become an important news centre: the IRA operated from there, the government was increasingly beleaguered, and every now and then someone would explode a car bomb in the streets. I knew that at least three people would automatically be chosen for the job before me, but I put my name down for it anyway; volunteering never did anyone any harm in the BBC. I didn't bother to tell Diane since it was obvious that I would never be chosen. And then the three men on the list ahead of me (or more probably their wives) all turned the offer down. That just left me.

I explained all this, and waited for the answer. A great deal, I now realize, depended on the words she would say next.

'Well, I suppose we'd better go,' she said, shifting the baby on her lap. 'Sounds exciting.'

And so at five o'clock on a grey February morning, a few days after the Bloody Sunday shootings in Londonderry, I packed up some of our best things and put them in a large old station-wagon the BBC had hired for us, and drove off to catch the ferry from Fishguard to Rosslare. I was going ahead to prepare the flat I had already found for us in Dublin.

Nearly two years before, Edward Heath had unexpectedly won the election whose date Harold Wilson had been so reluctant to announce to me at Euston Station. Immediately after the result I was invited round to Heath's preternaturally tidy and impersonal flat in the Albany, off Piccadilly, where even the pictures had the air of being bought in a job lot from Asprey's, and interviewed him about his plans. These seemed at the time to be indistinguishable from those of his future enemy, Margaret Thatcher: a return to market forces, a tough line with union militancy, a phasing-out of government subsidies for ageing industries. Quite soon, of course, he abandoned them all; as prime minister he possessed all the resolute farsightedness of Harold Wilson. Between the two of them, the seventies were a pretty glum time in Britain.

His most immediate problem, apart from the economy, was Northern Ireland. Heath's approach seemed to be radically different from that of the Wilson government, which had always had a certain sympathy with the Catholic minority and political links with the Social Democratic and Labour Party. Under Labour, though, the situation had become serious. There was rioting in the streets almost every day, and the Republican movement had split between its Marxist wing (called, because it still had control of the movement's structure, the Official IRA) and the nationalists who, as the breakaway group, were called the Provisional IRA. The Conservatives' links were with the Unionists, a party still dominated by great land-owners and big businessmen who preferred not to know about the thuggery that some of their rank-and-file followers used on behalf of the union with Britain; and the Unionists' argument, that terrorist suspects should be rounded up and interned, eventually carried the day with Heath. On 9 August 1971 internment was introduced.

It was a grotesque mistake. Many of the wrong people were picked up, and when they were belatedly released they told terrible stories of being subjected to sustained torture: kept awake for days on end, having buckets placed over their heads which then were beaten with truncheons, being subjected to 'white noise' which sent them nearly mad. It seemed as though all the lunatics and extremists in the armed forces were suddenly being allowed to do what they wanted. Looking back from the perspective of a quarter-century, this too seems like part of a different world. A British government was behaving like a Latin American dictatorship, and its soldiers were treating British citizens as though they were a subject people. There was a guerrilla war on British soil, and it was being lost before our eyes.

« »

I had first gone to Northern Ireland in March 1971. Three British soldiers out for a night's drinking had been murdered at Ligoniel, near Belfast, and I caught the 7.30 plane from London the next morning, feeling extremely nervous. Major James Chichester-Clark, the current prime minister of Northern Ireland, was sitting in the front row of seats on the plane, looking as worried as I felt. One of the worst things about working for radio is that you have to operate alone. In television at least you usually have the company of a cameraman, which forces you to make jokes and hide your anxieties. As I ate my shuttle-service breakfast that morning there was no one to hide anything from.

I drove in towards the city in my hired Ford Cortina, and passed Ligoniel on the way. There was nothing much to show for what had happened a few short hours before: an unprepossessing little alleyway behind a pub, with half a dozen RUC men standing around. It was the first time I had been close to something like this, and I found it impossible to visualize the sordid little scene that had gone on here: three Scottish teenagers in uniform lured into a bar by a couple of girls, who had then slipped away and summoned an IRA executioner. The three teenagers had been shot in the back of the neck as they were urinating in the alleyway outside the bar. If I had ever made the mistake of thinking that there was something even faintly romantic about the IRA, it evaporated at that moment and has never returned.

I got into my car and drove on. The road reached the edge of the mountainside and Belfast lay spread out beneath, ugly, gloomy and poor in the grey morning light, the smoke and grime hanging over it as thick as guilt and hatred. Later, as I spent more time there, I came to love Belfast and sympathize deeply with its different groups of inhabitants. Now, though, I was too scared to feel anything for it. I rolled up the window against the raw cold and shivered. I was twenty-six, and I missed my comfortable home and my wife and baby daughter.

I checked in at the Midland Hotel near the main railway station (the Europa, which became the great press hang-out, wasn't yet built) and rang the BBC newsroom in Belfast. There was, it seemed, to be an IRA funeral at Glasnevin Cemetery that afternoon. Nervously, I drove as close to the cemetery as I could, parked my hired Cortina, and followed the stream of people heading for the big event. I didn't exactly merge in with the crowd: the tide of sixties fashion had ebbed for me, and I was back in sports jacket, dark trousers and brogues. In my pocket I carried a small cassette tape recorder, one of the first to be issued in the BBC.

Working my way closer to the open grave, I linked up with the other journalists and felt a little safer. But someone had advised me not to say who I worked for, because the IRA hated the BBC. (So did the Protestant extremist groups, and the Unionists, and the Conservative Party back in Britain: we had achieved a pretty clean sweep at that time.) So I kept my microphone out of sight, and stood there waiting for something to happen. I didn't have long to wait. The funeral was that of a Provisional IRA volunteer who had been shot by the British Army as he was trying to shoot at them. He was being given the full works: honour party, Irish tricolour over the coffin, a volley to be fired over the grave.

Now, with the benefit of twenty-seven years of standing around in awkward places, I can see that I must have stood out like an explorer at a cannibal feast. But the problem wasn't that I looked English; that wasn't in itself something to arouse the anger of the IRA. It was that I looked like an Army spy. And acted like one: the big challenge of the time was to get the sound of IRA shots being fired, so I surreptitiously drew the microphone out of my pocket when I saw the hooded IRA volunteers raise their rifles and prepare to fire in the air.

I slipped it back, feeling really good with myself. Here I was, on my first day in Belfast, and I had got the sound of shots on tape. When the funeral was over, the crowd moved off towards the cemetery gates and the British journalists moved with them. I was following them when a hand gripped my arm. I turned and saw a red-haired man of about my age with an angry blotched face standing over me.

'It's a fockin' Army spy,' he called out to a group of the nastiest people I had ever seen in my life. They gathered round.

'No I'm not,' I answered desperately. 'I'm a BBC reporter.'

'So show us yer BBC i/d.'

It so happened that I didn't have it with me. I have never been very good about carrying identification, and this has often given me problems. Now it seemed likely to cost me my life. While we were standing there, I could see a photographer (from the *Daily Mirror*, I later found out) being stopped like me and dragged over to the edge of the cemetery. There he was given such a beating he had to be air-lifted back to London. By now I could hear his screams as the boots went in. The Provisionals had accused him of taking the wrong kind of picture.

'Give the focker one up the nostril,' said the red-haired man to his friends, still holding onto my arm. He meant they should shoot me then and there.

At that point an unmistakably English voice broke in on us. It was that of Derek Humphries, a *Sunday Times* reporter who later became famous for advocating euthanasia for the terminally sick. Now, though, he was helping the terminally frightened.

'Ah, John, I wondered where you'd got to,' he said conversationally; we had been talking just before the funeral began, and as he was leaving the cemetery he had spotted what was happening to me. 'This is Mr Simpson from the BBC,' he said to the red-haired man. 'Has there been some misunderstanding?'

He was so self-assured that the group opened up to let me past. I couldn't stop prattling my thanks all the way out of the cemetery, and when I left him my hands were shaking so hard I could scarcely get the key in the lock of my Cortina. A group of IRA supporters, led by the red-haired man, followed me at a distance to see what I did; and in the rear-view mirror I saw him writing down the number of my car as I drove off.

Back in my room at the Midland Hotel I sat down on the bed, still shaking.

'It's no good,' I said out loud, 'I'm not cut out for this kind of work. I'm too sensitive for it.'

I comforted myself with the thought that I would go back to London the next morning, and tell the editor that I wouldn't go to Northern Ireland any more. But by the time I'd had a steak from room service, and watched a little television, and congratulated myself on obtaining genuine actuality of an IRA honour party firing a salute, I began to feel better. Maybe, I thought, I would wait out my fortnight in Belfast before doing anything too precipitate.

That night, though, I dreamed I was standing in an alleyway outside a bar, and a red-haired girl was saying, 'Give the focker one up the nostril.'

« »

By the time I went to Dublin as the BBC correspondent at the beginning of 1972, with Diane and the children following, I already thought of myself as something of an Irish specialist. I had been through plenty of awkward moments: pinned down in gun-battles many times, attacked by angry mobs, coming much too close to a couple of bomb-explosions. And once a pipe-bomb (a home-made grenade taped around with six-inch nails) went off underneath an army troop-carrier as I was walking past it, and although the nails missed me the pressure on my lungs made it hard to breathe properly for some time afterwards.

I knew most of the cast of characters in the unfolding story, from Bernadette Devlin and Gerry Fitt to Ian Paisley and Brian Faulkner; not to mention any number of people from the alphabet soup of Northern Ireland: the UDA, the UVF, the UFF and the rest of them. I tended to specialize in reporting on Londonderry; so it was a great disappointment to me when I couldn't cover the big demonstration there on Sunday 30 January 1972: the day which became known as 'Bloody Sunday'. Thirteen people were shot down in the area of the Rossville Flats in the Bogside by troops of the Parachute Regiment under the overall command of General Robert Ford. A fourteenth person died later, and at least fifteen others were wounded.

Eighteen months later the Provisional Sinn Fein handed me a copy of a tape which they claimed had been recorded that day by tapping a telephone call between two British army officers. The voices sounded perfectly genuine to me, though there were indications that the recording had been edited. The Provisionals had apparently waited so long because they didn't want to reveal the extent of their surveillance system.

> First Voice: I think it's gone badly wrong in the Rossville. The doctors have been at the hospital and they're pulling stiffs out of there as fast as they can get them out.
>
> Second Voice: There's nothing wrong with that, Alan.
>
> First Voice: Well, there is, because they're the wrong people . . . But he was lapping it up.
>
> Second Voice: Who was?
>
> First Voice: Ford.
>
> Second Voice: Was he?
>
> First Voice: Yes. Said it was the best thing he'd seen for a long time.

The day after the shootings I wrote a report on the incident for the *Newsdesk* programme; and because I had become reasonably well read in modern Irish history I spoke about 'a new Bloody Sunday'. It wasn't startlingly original, but it seems to have been the first use of the reference.

Two days later I was summoned to the office of one of the top men in the BBC. He was pleasant, easy-going and erudite, but his incisive intelligence could neither make up for nor hide the fact that he was completely lacking in backbone. It seemed to have been extracted, if not at birth, then at some key moment in his early career: a phenomenon which is not, unfortunately, uncommon in any big organization. The result was to make him capable of taking all sorts of cowardly and even unprincipled actions, which he could argue for with considerable intellectual distinction.

On the desk, as I sat nervously in his office, which was delightfully panelled in light oak, and overlooked Upper Regent Street, lay a letter written on House of Commons notepaper. It proved to be from a

Conservative back-bencher I had never heard of, and maintained that my reference to the shooting dead of fourteen people as 'Bloody Sunday' had been a deliberate and probably treasonable attempt to give aid and comfort to the IRA. I was to find out over the years that when things became difficult politicians in particular liked to cast around for someone to blame; and the BBC, so often afraid of defending itself robustly, presented an easy target. Hard though it is to have much respect for politicians who behave like that, it is harder to have any for people who work for an organization but are too scared to defend it.

The BBC executive hadn't heard of this particular MP any more than I had, but the mere letters 'MP' seemed to be enough to make him want to hide under his pleasant light oak desk.

'Would you care to see the reply I've drafted?' he asked; he was really being very nice to me, I thought.

I read it. It apologized unconditionally for the use of the expression 'Bloody Sunday', even though this had appeared by now in several newspapers, and it ended up with the words 'Simpson has been told of his mistake.'

'I don't think—' I started to say, my voice thick with nervousness, 'I don't think I could, well, carry on working here if you sent that.'

I sat back, terrified: these were resigning words.

'Really?' said the head of news, as though this were some unexpected twist to an already fascinating story. 'What is it you don't like about it?'

I told him. He scribbled something down on a pad and read it out to me. It wasn't quite an apology any longer, and it didn't use the word 'mistake'; it just said I had been told about the MP's complaint. I thought it still sounded pathetic and cowardly, and an invitation to hit the BBC again; but I accepted the new version with relief. I suppose that by doing so I showed a lack of backbone too: this was the day I was appointed to my new job in Dublin and I was scared of losing it.

Exactly a year after Bloody Sunday, on 30 January 1973, I was sitting in a hired car outside the old City Hotel in Derry (later blown up by the IRA) with a close friend of mine, John Sergeant. Nowadays John is the BBC's chief political correspondent but then he was a reporter who covered Northern Ireland a good deal. I was in the driver's seat and we were just about to get out when my door opened and someone pushed his way into the seat, forcing John and me to bunch together against the passenger door.

'I've got a fockin' gun,' the man shouted.

At first, as so often happens, I thought it was a practical joke: until I smelled the man's feet and looked at his face: very young, very spotty, and very nervous. He was a typical IRA volunteer. After switching on the engine he screamed away in first gear at 20 miles an hour.

John Sergeant tried to calm him down by talking to him, but sitting jammed up next to him I could see he was too worked up with fear and adrenalin even to listen. I had two fears: firstly that a British army patrol would take us for hijackers and shoot us all; secondly, as we raced towards the Rossville Flats, that this was some kind of dreadful remembrance ritual and two Englishmen were to be sacrificed on the anniversary of Bloody Sunday. It seemed a long drive.

'Can we at least take our recording equipment out of the boot?' John asked.

I thought this was no time to worry about BBC recorders, but the IRA volunteer nodded. He was less crazed with fear now that we were away from the army patrols. We got out, collected our equipment, and trudged back across the barren landscape of the flats where the shootings had taken place a year before.

My time in Ireland was, with hindsight, one of the best and most enjoyable episodes in my career. We lived there for three years, during the worst and most troubled times, and enjoyed ourselves immensely. Ever since, it has been my maxim that a foreign correspondent who loves the country where he or she is based and wants to explain it to everyone is likely to be a good and effective correspondent. And it was a good place to be. Even at the worst times, no one was unpleasant to us merely because I worked for the BBC: no one, that is, except American supporters of the IRA. I loved it; and now that I have gone back to Ireland to live, I love it more than ever.

Julia and Eleanor grew into gentle, intelligent little girls. We sang and read to them at night-time, and in the day they endured with stoicism all the changes in their lives which my career imposed on them. What, I asked Eleanor some years later, was the worst thing about moving from place to place every couple of years? 'Being in a new class and having all the other kids look at you when the teacher introduced you,' she answered. We tried to counter this by making our home life as stable and unchanging as possible; so we kept the same furniture and pictures and even arranged them the same way. We took the same cat, an Abyssinian called Minos, around the world to our different bases at great personal expense. And I read a series of books to them which gave them almost as much pleasure as it gave me.

We started with Edward Lear, A. A. Milne and Kenneth Grahame, but moved to a stronger diet as soon as they could digest it: the Narnia books of C. S. Lewis by the time they were six and four, *The Hobbit* and *Treasure Island* at seven and five, *Lord of the Rings* at eight and six, and the Jeeves stories and Jane Austen immediately after that. It created a bond between us which my later wanderings could never quite dissolve; and even now that they are tall and successful and (of course) beautiful young women in their late twenties with degrees from Oxford and Bristol, we still sometimes talk in the voices I gave the characters in the books, from Gollum or Mole to Isabella in *Northanger Abbey*.

« »

In 1972 the Republic of Ireland was in a state of violent ferment, worse than anything the country had experienced since the fighting of 1919–22. Sometimes during the next few months I wondered if it might be coming close to outright revolution. Nowadays, having seen several revolutions at close hand, I can see that I was wrong; but at the time the whole structure of the country seemed to shake beneath our feet.

On the night I arrived, my rented station-wagon weighed down with books and paintings and toys and bedding, I drove through Merrion Square on my way to the flat I had rented in the suburb of Rathgar. A few nights before I had stood here at the heart of a wild crowd of angry, yelling people, enraged by the killings on Bloody Sunday, and watched them setting fire to the British embassy, a charming large terraced house from the mid-eighteenth century on the south side of the square. The entire square and its gardens were full of people, and just about everyone knew what was going to happen. After the speeches and the shouting of slogans, a big phalanx of young men and women with upturned, excited faces broke through the sweating ranks of gardai with a savage cry of triumph. Some began throwing

Molotov cocktails through the windows and into the hallway. It was impossible for the fire brigade to get close enough until the fire had completely taken hold. As for me, I disapproved deeply of the massacre, but I didn't like seeing a beautiful building being destroyed by a mob of people who just wanted some symbol to hit out at as an act of vengeance.

Now, as I climbed out of my car and walked across in the cold February night to look at it, it was a miserable sight: the lovely eighteenth-century front door smashed and hanging off its hinges, ashes fluttering in the cold night breeze, charred beams leaning at crazy angles. I had come into this place several times to see the British diplomats who worked here, and had admired its marble fireplaces and intricate ceilings. The stars shone through the burned-out roof, and the stench of fire still hung about the place. It all seemed so pointless: Merrion Square was one of the glories of Irish architecture, and the house didn't even belong to the British government but was rented from an Irishwoman. Setting fire to it had been a self-inflicted injury. I said this to the policeman who was standing patiently outside the wrecked house, stamping his feet and rubbing his hands together for warmth.

'Ye're probably right,' he said. 'But it could have been people they took it out on.'

I got back into my car and drove on to Rathgar. Supposing, I thought, they did decide to take it out on people, and chose another symbol of Britishness: the BBC correspondent? Hauling out our things and lugging them up the front steps of the grand, silent, empty house, I felt very isolated and vulnerable. Maybe I was bringing my family to a place that was dangerous after all. That night, alone in the place, I wrapped myself in blankets on the sheetless bed and tried to sleep; but all I could think of was a crowd gathering outside and throwing petrol bombs through the windows.

The next morning things seemed very different. The sun shone thinly as I went the rounds of the government ministries. Everyone seemed very welcoming and friendly: they liked the idea of having a full-time BBC correspondent in Dublin, someone they could present their case to. They might be angry about Bloody Sunday, but no one I met, either then or later, took it out on me. On the contrary, everyone from politicians and civil servants to the people I met in my everyday life seemed glad I was there. After the long years of being regarded by the British as a primitive appendage, a good source of jokes but not a place to be taken seriously in any way, the Republic of Ireland was now seen by the BBC as being worthy of its proper attention. Maybe the people I met were disappointed that they had only been sent a twenty-seven-year-old without real experience, but at least it was a start.

I found myself part of a very small group. There were only two full-time correspondents in Dublin from the London broadsheet press: Denis Taylor of *The Times* and Dominick Coyle of the *Financial Times*. Both of them became friends as well as close colleagues.

I had decided to take my new job seriously right from the beginning. Before I left London I went the rounds of programmes like *Today* and *The World At One*, making it clear to them that I was going to Dublin to report on the political and security situation; if they wanted stories about giant potatoes or leprechaun sightings they should ask someone else. As it happened, *Today* did try several times to get me to do reports like this (these were the days when no one accused it of 'dumbing down', because it was pretty dumbed-down anyway), but I always refused. I didn't care if it sounded pompous. The quicker the British got over their irritatingly patronizing approach to Ireland, the quicker they would understand that the Irish had a part to play in solving the problem. Some British officials were starting to realize this as early as 1972.

In the immediate aftermath of Bloody Sunday, only six months after the equally disastrous introduction of internment which created a far higher degree of the kind of violence it was supposed to have dealt with, there was nothing but despair on either side of the Irish Sea. The Northern Ireland government and the British army had between them become the best recruiting officers the IRA could have wished for. And yet the British government and civil service had learned two important things from these twin disasters.

The first was that no form of local government would be possible in Northern Ireland for a long time to come, because it couldn't be trusted not to be sectarian; and the second was that no military solution was possible. Early on in my time in Dublin a senior British civil servant, superior but highly intelligent and one of my best sources, explained these things to me at length over lunch at the Shelbourne

Hotel; quietly, since he regarded himself, probably rightly, as something of a target.

'Our idiotic army think this is a war, and they can win it by shooting down the enemy. Bloody fools: they're as bad as the Yanks in Vietnam. It's not a war, it's a police action, and they're in for a long haul. We all are.'

'How long?' I asked, fork poised over my Dublin Bay prawns.

'That's just the kind of question journalists always ask. If I said at least ten years, would that satisfy you? But I promise you this: no matter how many stupid mistakes we make, the bastards won't be able to beat us.'

Sinn Fein finally reached agreement with the British and Irish governments, and even with the Unionists, having realized that the IRA's campaign of violence was never going to succeed. My lunch companion was right in everything except the time it would take: not ten years, but at least twenty-five.

« »

There were two IRAs and two Sinn Feins when I arrived in Dublin, and all of them were based there. The division began in the late 1960s, when the leadership of the Republican movement was taken over by a group of Marxists. The prevailing ideology suddenly changed. Until now it had mostly been a traditional green Catholic nationalism, a gut-level resentment against the British presence in Ireland. Now, suddenly, the talk was of class struggle. The enemy weren't just the British any more, they were the big financial interests which were taking over. The working-class Unionists of Northern Ireland, far from being the enemy, were the fellow-dupes of international capitalism. From now on the struggle wouldn't be an armed one, it would be purely political: public meetings, leafleting, the infiltration of organizations and trade unions. The green nationalists of Sinn Fein were consistently outvoted by the new Marxists in the movement's councils, and they dropped away from it, baffled and angry.

By 1968 it seemed as though Sinn Fein's new approach was exactly right. There were civil rights movements across the world, from the United States to Czechoslovakia; Northern Ireland, where the Catholic minority had been discriminated against savagely for centuries, was ripe for a civil rights campaign of its own. Sinn Fein would be in the forefront of it, determinedly non-violent but politically certain. As for the IRA, that was scarcely needed now. The battles to come would be fought out ideologically.

They reckoned without the Reverend Ian Paisley and his hardline working-class Unionist followers. Infuriated that Catholics should dare to challenge the authority of a Protestant government, they threw themselves on the civil rights marchers with a ferocity that many of us thought had long since died out of modern life. Paisley led an ambush of one march in which his followers beat the women, in particular, with sticks which had six-inch nails protruding from them; and the Royal Ulster Constabulary did nothing to stop them.

By 1969, despite the presence of British troops, mobs of Protestants went through the little enclaves in Belfast and Londonderry where Catholics lived, burning and looting. We didn't know the expression 'ethnic cleansing' then, but the job was done so effectively that soon no Catholics lived in Protestant areas at all, and there were barricades in Belfast as impregnable as those of the divided city of Berlin. The Catholics had no means of self-defence, and no one to help them: certainly not the IRA. A new slogan appeared on the walls of Ardoyne and the Bogside: 'IRA = I Ran Away'.

It was the moment the nationalists had warned of. No one could say now that their brand of politics was outmoded. The breaking-point came in December 1969, over the IRA's Army Convention's vote by a three to one majority to accept the division of Ireland and recognize the governments in London, Dublin and Stormont: the aim was to contest elections to all three parliaments. On 11 January 1970, in the unlikely surroundings of the Intercontinental Hotel in Dublin about eighty dissidents walked out of Sinn Fein's annual conference.

Under the leadership of people like Ruairi O Bradaigh, Daithi O Conail and Joe Cahill a rival structure was set up, calling itself the 'Provisional' Sinn Fein and IRA. The Provisionals got their weapons from a group of wealthy politicians and businessmen in the Republic, with the help of Irish military intelligence. The Republic's finance minister, Charles Haughey, was later cleared of channelling public funds to the Provisionals to buy weapons, but he was in political disgrace. In the 1980s, of course, he rose from his political grave to become taoiseach or prime minister; and then in 1997 he was further disgraced and shown to have accepted huge amounts of secret money from a leading Dublin businessman. With Haughey, more than most, what went around came around. As for the Provisional IRA's campaign of violence and terror, it lasted almost exactly for the remaining period of his political life.

The Official movement declined sharply after the split. The Official IRA, ineptly advised and poorly led, carried out a disastrous campaign which included blowing up a building at the British army camp in Aldershot and killing or injuring only civilian workers, and murdering a Derry man who was on leave from the army, visiting his parents. The murder of Ranger William Best revolted many people in Derry, and persuaded the Official IRA to call an indefinite cease-fire which became permanent. As for its political wing, the Official Sinn Fein, it had never seemed happy with the IRA's violence, and the leading figures in it gradually moved one by one towards more conventional left-wing politics.

The Provisional movement was far more formidable. One morning a few days after my family had arrived in Dublin I got in my car and drove to Kevin Street, a seedy road close to St Stephens Green. This was working-class Dublin, only a few hundred yards from the ministries and the Georgian grandeur of the city centre. Parking outside Number 2, which was a dry cleaners, I pushed open a yellow-painted door at the side marked '2A'. It had a cheap, do-it-yourself look to it, and the stairs inside creaked as I walked up. These were the public offices of the Provisional Sinn Fein, and I was uncertain what kind of reception I might get. On the first floor were a couple of untidy rooms filled with leaflets, piles of back copies of *An Phoblacht*, the Provisional Sinn Fein's newspaper, and inflammatory posters on the walls. A large man in late middle age with a few long teeth the colour of 2A's front door sat at the desk, wearing a loud tweed jacket.

'And what might you be wantin'?' he asked. His tone was bantering rather than aggressive.

I explained who I was.

'Well, Sean, ye're very welcome.' He shook my hand in his great horny grasp. 'Me name's Tony Ruane, and I'm, like, the keeper of this beautiful office ye see here.'

It was the start of a curious relationship with the Provisionals. I never had the slightest sympathy with their aims, and even less with their methods; but there were several figures involved in the movement whom I came to regard with actual affection. Tony Ruane was one of them. So were Ruari O Bradaigh and his brother Sean: dark, quiet men with sharp eyes. Ruairi was perhaps a little warmer than Sean, but both of them were recognizably schoolmasters who shared a political passion. Each was usually prepared to talk to me if I wanted information, and they seemed to accept my good faith as a journalist: that I wasn't a propagandist or a spy, and that I would report as honestly as I could on their opinions and position. Whatever the intensity of their political views, they were civilized men.

The Dublin-based leaders always seemed to be more rational and less bitter than those in Northern Ireland. When I was working in Derry I had come to fear Martin McGuinness, who was a leading figure in the IRA there; 'the butcher's boy', people called him, and not merely because of his early apprenticeship. Later I felt something of the same feeling towards Gerry Adams, who became the IRA's commander in Belfast. Both of them gave orders which resulted in murder and torture: so much so that it angered even some of Adams' own men. In July 1973, when he and more than a dozen others were picked up by the security forces in Belfast, a Provisional IRA investigation was held into the reasons for the arrests. Someone in the movement leaked the findings to me. The investigators had decided that Adams and the others had been turned in by fellow-republicans who were disgusted by the IRA's new tactic against people it didn't like: shooting them through the knee-caps. Soon this kind of punishment became common practice; but it seems to have begun around the time Adams took command in Belfast, and several Provisionals there and in Dublin thought he had introduced it.

At this stage men like the O Bradaighs supported the actions of Adams and McGuinness; but I never felt they were interested in killing for its own sake, and certainly not in this kind of barbarity. And yet, as it turned out, Ruari O Bradaigh was the die-hard, and Adams and McGuinness were the ones who had the courage to persuade the Republican movement to accept that its campaign of bombing and murder had failed, and should be abandoned for political means. O Bradaigh and his supporters were voted off the movement's leadership, and Adams replaced him as President of Sinn Fein. Nowadays O Bradaigh is a figure in the wilderness, continuing to argue that the movement has taken a wrong turn; while Adams appears at state functions in Dublin and Washington. But whereas I should be happy to have a cup of tea with O Bradaigh and should enjoy his company, I wouldn't cross the road to shake the hand of Gerry Adams. I admire his determination and foresight, but I remember too well what it is like to watch a teenager who has been shot through the kneecaps writhing on the ground.

One of the main themes of my first year in Dublin was the slow, subtle action taken by Jack Lynch, the taoiseach, against the IRA. Lynch was a pleasant and intelligent man, but not particularly impressive in person. Yet he understood the strength of his weakness perfectly, and used it to remarkable effect: warning the British of the backlash that would follow if he moved too fast against the IRA, and confessing to the backsliders in his own government the degree of British pressure on him to do more. It was Jack Lynch who gave the young and aggressive Desmond O'Malley the job of Justice Minister and encouraged him to stamp down hard on the Republican movement. Between them, Lynch and O'Malley protected the Irish state from instability at a critical time. The British consistently underestimated Lynch's strength. Because he was quiet and undemonstrative and rather apologetic they thought he was weak. But Irish firmness of purpose comes in different forms from British firmness of purpose, and shouldn't necessarily be judged by the same outward indications.

Lynch was tested to the utmost by the arrest and trial of Sean Mac Stiofain, the chief of staff of the Provisional IRA, in November 1972. Mac Stiofain was a strange, angry, pugnacious little man who turned out to have no recognizable drop of Irish blood in him; his name had originally been John Stephenson. He had plenty of enemies within the Republican movement, but after the Special Branch had picked him up he seemed to be shaping up as the latest in a long series of Irish nationalist martyrs. I had the feeling at the time that the demonstrations which followed might threaten the Irish state itself. Nowadays, having seen a good few revolutions, I realize I was wrong. But I certainly wasn't the only one to think that way. All sorts of prominent people ranged themselves alongside the Provisionals to demand his release, and some of them should have known better. More than one minister in Jack Lynch's cabinet seemed to be shaping up to change sides if the Republicans won the contest of wills. A couple of quite senior civil servants I spoke to seemed to me to be losing their nerve. Mac Stiofain's trial was a melodramatic business. He announced in court that he was going on a hunger and thirst strike, which would have killed him within a few days. When he was found guilty, it looked as though he would die in gaol.

And then Jack Lynch's luck began to turn. A prison warder who had noticed that Mac Stiofain seemed to be taking a lot of showers peered in and saw him, head raised, drinking the water from the shower-head. The news was leaked to the press: Mac Stiofain's thirst strike to the death was no such thing after all. He could endure for weeks.

Mac Stiofain had never been popular within the Republican movement. His Englishness, his unyielding harshness, his unwillingness to entertain new strategies all combined to weaken his position. He stood accused of failing to become an Irish martyr, and that was the end. Mac Stiofain was destroyed by it, and the pressure on the government evaporated completely. It was a remarkable victory for Jack Lynch's nerve.

Mac Stiofain's place in the limelight was taken by Daithi O Conail, a tall, sallow, lantern-jawed man with deep-set blue eyes, who was cleverer and better informed than Mac Stiofain, and much less bigoted. He had taken part in the IRA's famous Brookeborough raid in 1957, and had staged a daring escape with Ruari O Bradaigh from internment in the Republic in 1958. I saw quite a lot of O Conail in the months that followed.

'I want you to know,' he said once, gripping my elbow painfully, 'that no night is complete for me unless I have listened to the BBC World Service news.'

He was the kind of revolutionary whom the British had become used to during the long period of decolonization: a man who hated Britain's involvement in his own country, yet seemed to have a certain respect for the values which the British claimed as their own. After he had met the British Secretary of State for Northern Ireland, William Whitelaw, at a house in Chelsea in July 1973, O Conail said to me, 'I found him to be the best type of British gentleman.'

He wasn't always friendly or forthcoming. Sometimes, after a report of mine had been broadcast on the BBC, I would get a call from one of his minions.

'Dave didn't like what you was sayin' there,' he would say, and then ring off.

At first I was rather worried; then, after talking to my colleagues Denis Taylor and Dominick Coyle, both much more experienced, I realized that this was merely an intimidating tactic: no one would do anything to me; or so I hoped.

The Dublin leadership was always at odds with the men and women who ran the real risks of the campaign, and O Conail was no better at earning the respect of the active service units than the other southerners. He had a certain flair, though, and enjoyed the excitement of the revolutionary life. As a result he led a strange cloak-and-dagger life, meeting all sorts of arms dealers and (no doubt) double agents.

One afternoon, when I wanted to record an interview with him, I went round to his small, unassuming house in North Dublin; he had given me the address some weeks before. I decided not to ring beforehand, assuming that the Irish Special Branch had the line tapped. His wife, a quiet, gentle woman, opened the door and showed me into the sitting room. My arrival had obviously flustered her.

'Dave's upstairs with a visitor just now,' she said, and offered me a cup of tea.

With the pink cup and saucer poised in my hand I looked around me at the profoundly conventional furnishings of the revolutionary's house: the lacy doilies, the pictures of shepherdesses and the Irish landscapes. Mrs O Conail went out again, and in the silence I heard a man's footsteps on the stairs outside the door. There was a telephone in the hall, and I could hear him dialling a number. When he got through, he started to speak. His accent was impeccably upper-class English.

'Yes, everything has arrived satisfactorily,' he said into the mouthpiece. 'I don't think you have any reason to worry. I'd just accept the situation if I were you.'

At this moment Daithi O Conail came into the room. He realized I could hear the man on the phone, and started talking in an unusually loud voice about the situation in Northern Ireland. Eventually the Englishman put the phone down and let himself out without saying goodbye. I was never able to decide whether he was a British arms dealer, or perhaps some agent of British intelligence who had managed to make contact with O Conail. Hardly possible, you might think; and yet in the early seventies there was still a considerable degree of naivety on both sides.

O Conail was certainly interested in buying weapons. He travelled to Amsterdam in order to negotiate with the Czechoslovak arms agency and took with him a young and attractive Provisional volunteer from Northern Ireland, Maria Maguire. Eventually MI6, which tracked their progress, leaked the news to the papers that O Conail and Maguire had been having an affair. Given that the Republican movement was filled with devout Catholics, that was the end of him. Maria Maguire resigned from the Provisional movement the following year, because, she said, the IRA's bombing campaign had become an end in itself. She therefore struck two powerful blows against the Provisionals, and there were those in the movement who wondered afterwards whether she had been working for the British all along. As for O Conail, he was forced to resign, and died some years later, still an outcast from the movement.

« »

As it happened, a close relation of mine was working for British army intelligence in the strongly IRA town of Dundalk close to the Northern Ireland border throughout most of my first year in Dublin; though I had absolutely no idea what he was doing. Paul was my second cousin, a man in his early forties, sturdy and good-looking with a mane of blond hair. He had served in the army, was then ordained in the Church of England and took up a benefice in Dorset. But however willing the spirit, the flesh was weak: spectacularly so in Paul's case. One of his parishioners became pregnant by him at the time when his own wife was expecting a baby. As these things tend to do, it reached the papers; the *News of the World* ran a big story on him in traditional 'naughty vicar' terms, and Paul had to resign his living immediately. He had no money, a resentful wife, and a variety of children to care for.

After a few months he was telephoned by the colonel of his old regiment.

'Sorry about what's happened, Paul – these newspaper people are filthy liars, aren't they? Nothing in it, I'm sure. I just thought you might like to know that the regiment has funds to help former officers who are down on their luck. Interested?'

'Absolutely,' said Paul. It must have seemed as though his prayers had been answered.

'In your case, for instance, we could set you up in a nice little hay and straw business, if you were interested.'

Paul had grown up on a farm, and he jumped at the chance.

'Where is it? Somewhere round here?' He lived in Dorset.

'Actually,' the colonel said, 'it's in Ireland. Little town called Dundalk, just on the sea. Quite picturesque, I'm told.'

It took Paul a while to realize the significance of Dundalk, and that he was being asked to spy on the IRA there. But he needed the money desperately, so he agreed.

He was given a flat in a house adjoining the Imperial Hotel in Dundalk, which was the hang-out for some of the most dangerous IRA men from Northern Ireland. Stories about the goings-on at the Imperial had reached the Dublin press: a group of Provos were watching a race meeting on television, for instance, and one of them shot the set with his revolver when his horse lost.

My cousin Paul operated from his little flat next door, driving a tractor around the nearby villages and picking up loads of hay and straw for sale to the local farmers. He made no attempt to disguise the fact that he was English, but because he was so bluff and pleasant the locals accepted him apparently without question. And all the time he was listening to the conversation of the men in the saloon bar at the Imperial, and watching them when they left on operations.

He had been there for about a year when I arrived in Dublin, and he lasted most of another year. I noticed he never seemed keen that I should come and visit him in Dundalk, but he used to stop off sometimes at our flat in Rathgar for tea. I assume now that he must have come down to Dublin to report to his controller from military intelligence.

And then, late one Friday afternoon, he rang to say he was passing through Dublin on his way to London.

'Come over for tea, then.'

'Not possible, I'm afraid. You see, I'm at the airport.'

'Oh well, maybe when you come back.'

'I don't think I will be coming back.'

'So what's happening to the business?'

'The business? Oh, the hay and straw. I had to leave it.'

'But isn't it harvest-time?'

'Yes, I suppose so.'

'And there's no chance of seeing you for a cup of tea now?'

'Sorry, old chap, my plane's just been called.'

I could hear the sound of an airport announcement in the background.

The IRA must have been on to him. This was in May 1973, and a few days earlier, after an unprecedented build-up of IRA men in the town, half a dozen of the leading figures were arrested. Another group had been spotted at night-time, armed and heading for the border. They too were arrested. Perhaps Paul had had a hand in all this. He was probably lucky to have escaped with his life; other British agents in Ireland, such as Captain Robert Nairac, paid a high price for their work. I never saw Paul again, and he never told me about his real activities in Dundalk. A couple of years later he was diagnosed as having terminal cancer.

My father was always very close to him; I used to think that he would have preferred Paul to me if he had had to choose between us. They spent long hours together in the hospital where Paul lay dying, and bit by bit he told my father the whole story.

'I want you to know,' he told my father, 'that I never did anything bad – killed anyone, or anything like that. I just watched them and listened to them, that's all.'

He was only forty-seven when he died.

« »

On the night of Friday, 1 December 1972 the Dail debated a government motion to introduce tougher measures against the IRA. The opposition Fine Gael party seemed certain to vote against it, and that was expected to bring the government down. But as we sat listening to the debate the windows of Leinster House were rattled by two loud explosions. A couple of car bombs had exploded close by, though no one was badly hurt. Immediately Fine Gael changed its mind 'at this critical moment in our nation's history', as one speaker put it. Lynch survived, and the anti-IRA legislation was passed. Later Lynch told me he had always suspected the hand of British intelligence behind the bombs: the timing seemed to him to show great sophistication. It was never clear who had carried out the attacks, though Northern Ireland loyalists were also suspected.

Three weeks later, on 21 December, a team of Special Branch detectives went to the Burlington Hotel in Dublin and arrested a man called John Wyman, who gave an address in Chelsea. Another group picked up a Garda sergeant who worked as a filing-clerk at C3, the anti-IRA department of the Special Branch. Wyman later admitted that he worked for the Ministry of Defence in London, and the sergeant, whose name was Patrick Crinnion, said he had been recruited by the British after he had contacted a British official to complain that much of the information about IRA men which crossed his desk was ignored by the Lynch government. There were strong suggestions that the arrests were in revenge for the bombs which went off in Dublin on the night of 1 December.

On 23 December, a couple of days later, there was another development in Bow Street Magistrates' Court in London. A routine extradition hearing was interrupted by the solicitor for the two men in the dock. They were wanted for robbing a bank in Dublin, but the solicitor said that in the light of some new information, his clients would like to make a statement. They said the man arrested in Dublin under the name of John Wyman had recruited them to British intelligence and had ordered them to carry out the bank robbery for which the Irish government wanted to extradite them.

The two men were brothers, Kenneth and Keith Littlejohn from Torquay. When they were tried in Dublin the following summer, Kenneth told the court a complex story. He had been in the British army, but after carrying out a payroll robbery he escaped to Ireland. There someone showed him a Kalashnikov rifle: part of a consignment for the IRA which was landed from a submarine. A patriot of a kind, he contacted the Ministry of Defence when he returned to London, and had been invited to meet the army minister, Geoffrey Johnson-Smith. The British agent John Wyman became his controller. In October 1972 the Littlejohn brothers returned to Ireland and led a group of IRA men in an attack on a bank. They netted £62,000: at that time it was the biggest robbery ever carried out in the Republic.

By the time the Littlejohns had been extradited and their case came to trial, the government in Dublin had changed, and Jack Lynch had been replaced by a Fine Gael-Labour coalition headed by Liam

Cosgrave. It contained two of the most talented politicians I have met: Garret Fitzgerald, who later became taoiseach in his own right, and Conor Cruise O'Brien, the former UN pro-consul in the Congo, who was then one of the leading figures in the Irish Labour Party. Fitzgerald had expected to be made finance minister, but was given the post of minister of foreign affairs instead. O'Brien, an avowed enemy of the IRA and even in those days mildly sympathetic to some aspects of Unionist opinion in Northern Ireland, was mistrusted by his own party and by the newspapers; and he was given the job of minister of posts and telegraphs.

After the Littlejohns had made their statement in the Dublin court, I rang Conor Cruise O'Brien and asked him if he could tell me anything about the case.

'Come round this evening,' he said.

After office hours that night Denis Taylor and I went round to the gloomy headquarters of the Posts and Telecommunications ministry. Photographs of incomprehensible communications equipment hung on the walls, year-books filled the shelves, files covered the top of a nearby table in his office.

O'Brien held up a couple of pieces of paper to show us, and then started reading out loud from them. They were memoranda from the British government to Jack Lynch, warning him that the Littlejohn brothers, originally hired by MI6, had gone off the rails and were carrying out robberies in the Republic. Lynch's later complaints to London about the case were shown to have been completely disingenuous.

We composed our reports that evening without making it clear who the source was, and both appeared the following morning. But whereas *The Times* ran Denis's story low down on the front page the BBC's radio news bulletins led on mine. That gave it even greater prominence. Immediately the news was off the air my telephone started ringing. Some of the calls were from other journalists, trying to find out where we had obtained the story. There were several from people who believed this was some trick by the British government to undermine the Irish government. Not everyone gave their name, and one or two of the calls sounded more like threats than complaints.

As the morning wore on, RTE's news programmes quoted more and more of Jack Lynch's colleagues who had come out in his defence.

A spokesman for the Fianna Fail party denied the whole thing in categoric terms, which looked bad for me. I put together a report for the BBC's 1 p.m. news, reflecting all these things but trying to reinforce my confidence in the basic information. Just as I was writing it, with the deadline coming uncomfortably close, the phone rang again. This time it was my boss, speaking from London.

'This story of yours about Jack Lynch.'

'Yes?'

'Better be right.'

He hung up.

I was to have plenty of dealings with him over the next ten years, but any respect I had for him evaporated that day. He was just another executive worried about his own job, and unable to keep his worries to himself.

The next day the *Irish Press* carried the accusation that the British government's tame broadcasting organization had been used to sow dissension in Ireland, and Lynch's Attorney-General was quoted as denying any knowledge of a message from the British government. But by the evening Lynch, who was at his holiday home in County Cork, had been contacted; and he blandly agreed that he had been tipped off about the case by the British. Conor Cruise O'Brien then published the documents he had shown us in his office. The whole episode was over. It had been a brief but revealing footnote to history. Kenneth and Keith Littlejohn were sentenced to twenty and fifteen years imprisonment respectively, but soon afterwards staged a remarkable escape. Many people in Dublin wondered if their British minders had helped. John Wyman, their controller, was sentenced to three months together with his associate, Sergeant Patrick Crinnion.

« »

One evening around this time I had a call from a man I knew only as Michael, who was on the fringes of the IRA in Belfast. I never understood why he used to come to me with his stories. It certainly wasn't for money, since I never paid for anything more than a drink or two for him. It wasn't to spread disinformation either, since most of the things he told me turned out to be true. Maybe he represented one particular group or tendency within the Republican movement which wanted to make its viewpoint heard. This afternoon he asked me to meet him at an hotel on one of the quays in Dublin.

The place was dingy and run-down, with a scuffed old brown carpet and walls yellowed by decades of tobacco smoke. The door of the saloon bar creaked as I pushed it open, and his head came up nervously. He always wore a cloth cap with oil stains on it: I used to think that if I had them analyzed I would know exactly where he came from. Now the cap was turned towards me.

'Hello, Sean; how's the boy?' His greeting never varied.

I bought him a Guinness, though he wasn't really a drinking man; most Provos weren't. He waited till the old man behind the bar had shuffled off to wash some glasses.

'Big changes in Belfast,' he said. He had a way of speaking by opening his mouth like a slot, but never moving his lips. Maybe he learned it in prison.

'What changes?'

'Ah, sure, I couldn't tell you that.'

This preliminary fencing between us was commonplace. I only had to wait a little before he would start to tell me what he had all along planned to say.

It turned out after a few minutes that there had been something of a coup inside the Belfast command of the IRA, and Gerry Adams had taken control. There was, it seemed, friction between Belfast and the IRA leadership in Dublin as a result.

'Don't go tellin' anyone this, now,' Michael said.

'That's why you told me, I suppose – to keep it secret,' I said.

He laughed, and hit me playfully on the chest with his rolled-up newspaper. I knew he always wanted me to report the things he told me. When I got back home, though, I rang around my other contacts and tried to stand the story up. I failed; and when I tried writing it, it sounded flimsy and questionable. In the end I left it alone.

Michael called the following morning, complaining that I hadn't reported what he had told me. I tried to explain, but he rang off irritably. The second call I received was from the BBC in London. Another BBC correspondent was reporting that a new leader had emerged in the Belfast IRA; could I add anything to this? I could, I said, and produced as much as I could of Michael's information without revealing anything about its origins. The report was used on the lunch-time news. By about twenty past one I was getting my first 'Dave didn't like what you said' call, and by the evening I had had several other calls, two of them open threats. I had the impression that it wasn't the information itself they were complaining about, but the fact that I knew it. At two o'clock the following morning the phone rang beside my bed.

'John? Is that really you?' It was Denis Taylor, sounding nervous and relieved at the same time.

'Why shouldn't it be me?'

'We've just had a call to say your body has been found by the roadside in Andersonstown.'

The following morning I told the BBC, and they brought all four of us – Diane, the two children and me – over to London within a couple of hours, and put us up in a flat near Sloane Square. We decided that we wouldn't live in Rathgar any more, since every part of the two Republican movements knew where we were, and often put their statements through the door.

'We'll go and live beside the sea,' I said, and they all clapped and cheered. As for the BBC, it decided after a week that it was costing too much to keep us in London, so we had to go back. Very comforting, I thought as I climbed on the plane.

« »

We did go and live beside the sea. Each night we could hear the waves slapping against the rocks, and would walk down and see the boatmen who worked there. A friend of mine, Derek Davies, took me out in his boat a couple of times. He was a big, yellow-haired Ulsterman who worked with me as a sound recordist when I did occasional reports for television. He had been a bouncer at a Belfast night-club, so no one came near us. But his real talent didn't lie in recording sound or in protecting people: he was always quick-witted and funny, and eventually he talked his way into becoming a chat-show host on Irish television. Now that I live in Ireland, and have gone back to Bullock Harbour, I often switch on Derek's programme and watch him moving the microphone around his audience, as big and funny as ever.

Another friend of mine, Tom McGurk, also had a boat in the harbour. Tom used to go out mackerel fishing, accompanied by his Irish setter – a beautiful dog, but highly strung. He would usually stop by afterwards and give us a couple of mackerel, and once or twice if we were out he would hang them over the front door-knob. It was thoughtful of him and we were always grateful: until the time when we went to Crete for a three-week holiday and came back to find the ancient remains of a couple of fish on the doormat. The smell stayed for the rest of our time in Ireland.

Life became pleasanter and more relaxed as a result of the greater measure of safety which my family now enjoyed. I rented a tiny room, Number 353, in the best of the Dublin hotels, the Royal Hibernian in Dawson Street. Some vandal has long since pulled down the late eighteenth-century structure of the Hibernian and turned the site into a shopping mall; but then it was a thriving place with a high standard of service and an excellent restaurant. I liked it too because, in spite of the number of threats it received, it always refused to relinquish the 'royal' in its title or take down the Union Jack.

One sunny Sunday morning in June 1974, when Dawson Street was empty of traffic, a charming little scene was enacted on the front steps of the hotel. The Earl and Countess of Donoughmore, a fragile-looking Anglo-Irish couple in their mid-seventies, were brought there by the Dublin police and the hotel staff set them side by side on a couple of spindly chairs for the press to take their photograph. A few days earlier a group of IRA men had broken into their house not far from Dublin and kidnapped them. The reason seemed to be that the Earl had served in the British army in the Second World War; and in the contorted imaginations of the IRA that made him a justifiable target. The Earl's shirt and sports-jacket were spattered with blood – not only his, but that of a couple of his attackers: he had put up a spirited fight. Eventually the IRA men had let them go.

Now they sat, side by side, a handsome elderly couple blinking in the early sunlight. The photographers pressed round them, snapping away: Fleet Street had sent some of its finest.

'Go on, darlin', give 'im a cuddle,' shouted the man from the *Mirror*.

The Countess of Donoughmore laid one blue-veined hand on her husband's arm, and smiled winningly at the photographer.

'I think that will suffice,' she said.

During my time at the Royal Hibernian, the largest art theft in history took place, at the home of Sir Alfred Beit. (The leader of the gang turned out, to the delight of the London tabloids, to be a British woman called Dr Rose Dugdale, who came from an upper-class background but had turned into an enthusiastic follower of the Provisional IRA. The IRA itself never trusted her, and disapproved of her exploit, which was a complete failure. All the paintings were recovered.) Then there was a sensational escape from Mountjoy gaol in Dublin when the IRA hijacked a helicopter and forced it to land in the main exercise yard; several leading Provisional prisoners got away. While I was at the Hibernian the *Claudia*, a ship carrying a cargo of arms destined for the IRA from Libya, was captured; during an otherwise dull afternoon's evidence in the somnolent atmosphere of the Special Criminal Court soon afterwards, someone let slip the fact that a British submarine had followed the *Claudia* all the way to the point where she was stopped by the Irish authorities off the coast of County Cork.

One Friday afternoon in May 1974 I had decided that nothing more was likely to happen, and I would head off home to the seaside. I had just said goodbye to the doorman at the Royal Hibernian and was looking at my watch – it was 5.29 – when a terrible explosion shook the area. A column of black smoke was already starting to rise from the direction of Nassau Street, only a couple of hundred yards away, and all the burglar alarms around were jangling. As I was running down towards Nassau Street there was another explosion, slightly further away.

I have seen many terrible sights since that pleasant summer afternoon in Dublin, but this one stays with me and refuses to be exorcized: an old man sitting calmly looking at the remains of his smashed leg, which was pumping blood, and ended with a piece of protruding shinbone; a woman standing and trying to walk, and falling over with a shriek of pain; the body of another woman lying on her back, apparently eviscerated. The injuries were too unpleasant to describe when I finally got to a phone and called the BBC in London.

Transcript of 6.00 News report, Radio 4, 17.5.74

The bomb went off about ten minutes ago, a short way from where I'm phoning. At the scene of the explosion the car which presumably contained the bomb is still on fire, and people are still gathered round the area, dazed by what

```
happened. I saw a woman's body lying on the pavement,
covered with a coat. Close by an old man was being
attended to; his leg was injured fairly badly . . .
Small pools of blood up to fifty yards from the car bomb
indicated that there must be other injuries.
```

The bombing had presumably been carried out by loyalists from Northern Ireland, who had deliberately chosen the start of the evening rush-hour as the time for the explosion. There was a third bomb in the Republic that evening, in County Monaghan close to the Northern Ireland border. Altogether thirty people died: the largest loss of life through violence in the British Isles since the Second World War.

It was by no means the first car bomb I had seen; a few months earlier I had been lucky to escape from one which was detonated outside Broadcasting House in Belfast, and for a long time I kept a large piece of shrapnel which had missed me by approximately an inch. But in Northern Ireland the explosions were well choreographed: warnings were usually telephoned through, and although they were often vague and sometimes deliberately confusing not many people were killed by bombs there now. In Dublin, as in mainland Britain, it was a different matter altogether: the bombers wanted to kill as many people as possible. The Dublin bombings, like the Aldershot, Guildford, Birmingham and other bombings, were atrocities: crimes against humanity.

The bombings created a kind of paranoia in Britain which required scapegoats; the atmosphere after the Guildford and Birmingham bombs was the ugliest kind of lynch-law, which the British government (to its shame) did nothing to lessen. In Dublin, by contrast, there was nothing of the kind. No one was arrested merely in order to appease public opinion; no confessions were beaten out of innocent people by the police. Ireland suffered heavily that day, but it had nothing to feel ashamed of afterwards.

Nowadays when I walk down Nassau Street I invariably find myself looking for the slightly lighter patch on the stonework of the Trinity College wall which took part of the explosion's force; I look up at the building where a sheet of plate-glass, loosened by the blast, fell to the ground beside me; and I always reflect on the way the Irish took the

whole event in their stride, without damaging themselves in their own
and other people's eyes.

« »

My time in Ireland was the making of my professional career. In
particular it taught me how governments work. Very early in my time
I found myself reporting on the way in which the British government
was signalling its intentions both to the Irish government and to the
Provisional IRA: a practice which, before I went to Dublin, I never
understood. By watching the way both governments made their statements, repeating old familiar passages but slipping in a phrase or a
sentence that was new, I was able to see how policy progressed and
retreated.

I got to know successive British secretaries of state for Northern
Ireland too, and watched how seasoned performers like William
Whitelaw or Merlin Rees dealt with their civil servants (not all of
whom they felt they could trust) and with journalists (none of whom
they felt they could trust). I watched them shift their approach by
inches and then by yards, so that things which had once been unthinkable became perfectly acceptable.

Talking to the Provisionals, for instance. It happened on two
occasions during my time in Ireland, and each time I found out about
it from British rather than IRA sources. Once it was William Whitelaw
who met them; the other time they met Harold Wilson himself, when
he was leader of the opposition. The meeting with Wilson was ludicrous. He had clearly not been briefed properly about the nature of
the people he was meeting, and assumed perhaps that they would be
tough, thuggish characters. As a result, directly they all sat down
together he called loudly for beer (although he didn't actually like beer
much) and started using words like 'bugger' and 'shit' because he
thought he would impress them with his down-to-earth qualities. By
contrast the Provisionals sitting opposite him, Ruairi O Bradaigh and
Daithi O Conail among them, didn't swear or drink; and O Bradaigh
in particular was strongly Catholic. The meeting was a total failure.

I learned, too, not to accept everything civil servants said at face
value. Once when I had a meeting with a senior IRA man – this was
in 1973, when the Conservatives were still in power – I asked what
his view of a possible Labour government was. The IRA man said he

wasn't worried about that; he had evidence that Labour was soft on the Northern Ireland issue. Perhaps I sounded a little too disbelieving. He reached into his jacket pocket and pulled out a typewritten letter on House of Commons notepaper and signed by Merlin Rees, the shadow Northern Ireland Secretary. It was addressed to a woman with an Irish surname, living in Britain, and was obviously a reply to some letter of complaint from here about Labour Party policy. In the circumstances of the time, Merlin Rees's reply was unguarded and not very wise: 'Frankly we have not the faintest desire to stay in Ireland, and the quicker we are out the better.' The IRA man pointed out to me, correctly, that this was entirely different from Conservative policy, which was that Northern Ireland was an inalienable part of the United Kingdom. Then he put the letter back in his pocket.

There seemed to be no point in writing a report on it: Labour weren't in power, and at this stage didn't seem likely to be. But within a few months the snap election of February 1974 brought them back into government with a tiny majority, and Merlin Rees was Secretary of State. As part of a wider report I put together a piece for the *Six O'Clock News* about why the IRA thought they had probed a weak point of the new government. The editor of the day rang the Northern Ireland Office before broadcasting my report, and the Northern Ireland Office said it had checked its files and couldn't find any such letter. It must, said one of the officials, be a forgery, and I had been duped. The editor accordingly cut out my reference to the letter. I was angry, but could do nothing about it.

A couple of weeks later, when Merlin Rees came to Dublin, the Provisional Sinn Fein handed out photocopies of the letter to the waiting journalists. This time the Northern Ireland Office couldn't pretend the original didn't exist. Instead, an official said that Merlin Rees had indeed written it, but that he couldn't see what all the fuss was about: it didn't amount to anything much. The incident was trivial enough, but it taught me what governments and civil servants do when inconvenient matters come up; and I never quite took official denials or acknowledgements at their face value again.

When I arrived in Ireland in 1972, in the last months before it, like Britain and Denmark, joined what was then the European Economic Community, it was still a quiet little place. Britain and the United States were the filters through which Ireland saw just about everything in the outside world. Divorce, contraception and abortion were all illegal; the population was more than 95 per cent Catholic. What the Catholic bishops said, went. Economically, culturally and educationally too Ireland was a charming and pleasant backwater. Rural villages hadn't changed much since the nineteenth century; small towns hadn't changed since the 1930s.

After 1973 everything began to be different. The government of Liam Cosgrave, containing figures of European stature such as Garret Fitzgerald and Conor Cruise O'Brien, impressed even the superior British. So did some of the civil servants which Ireland produced. Europe was a new stage for the Irish to perform on, and they did so with enthusiasm. Money from the EEC's Regional Fund began the process of redressing the balance of poverty in Ireland to such an extent that the road system, for instance, is as good as that in France or Italy. Irish hotels, which had once been famously uncomfortable, blossomed. So did Irish cooking, which had once been mostly dependent on good beef and good vegetables. Society opened out and left its narrow Catholicism behind. It also left Sinn Fein and the IRA behind. As Northern Ireland became poorer, first in relative and then in absolute terms, the Republic's interest in it waned.

Above all, the British government began to take the Irish government seriously. The change became noticeable first at the Sunningdale conference of 1974, when the Irish government consistently produced better and clearer ideas than the British, and could no longer be steamrollered by London into agreeing with what the British wanted. In the end the Sunningdale agreement on power-sharing between the Catholic minority and Protestant majority was stronger in all sorts of ways than the British government had wanted; but it all collapsed a few months later when the new government of Harold Wilson lacked the courage to stand up to a Loyalist strike. Power-sharing became impossible; and so did Garret Fitzgerald's creative idea of a system by which anyone in Northern Ireland could choose for themselves whether they wanted to be an Irish or a British citizen.

And yet nowadays power is effectively shared in Northern Ireland, and people are free to regard themselves as being what they choose. Many of the old fears and narrow resentments are fading. The Republic of Ireland is free of British influence in a way that seemed impossible when I was based there; and no one seems scared of showing a Union Jack or offering holidays in Britain.

Diane and the two girls wept as we closed the door of our house by the sea for the last time, and drove along the harbour road in the direction of the airport and our new life in Brussels. I thought about it often, but rarely returned.

And then, twenty-three years later and married for the second time, I drove past the harbour with my new wife. We had decided to come and live full-time in Ireland. A little way past my old house we saw a 'to let' sign outside a property that hadn't even been built when I lived there before. We took it. The wheel had made yet another full turn.

6

Mercenary Activities

BRUSSELS, KINSHASA AND LUANDA, 1975–76

'YOU'VE DONE WELL in Dublin,' said the head of foreign correspondents.

I made modest noises and shifted in my seat. I knew he was going to offer me another posting, but I couldn't work out what it might be.

'You probably wonder what we've got in mind for you next.'

More modest noises, designed to indicate such a thing had never entered my head.

'We see you in Brussels,' he beamed.

I'll see you in hell, I thought. Paris is where I want to be. Paris: not somewhere they eat chips all day long and tell the rest of us how many eggs should fit into a box. Was this all I got for risking my neck in Ireland?

'Fantastic,' I said out loud, trying to twist my face into an enthusiastic expression. If the BBC offered you a foreign posting, they didn't like it if you turned it down. They remembered it against you. Holding out for a better job never seemed to work: they liked to make examples of people from time to time.

And Brussels was certainly a good job to have. Not interesting, God knows. But it was politically difficult, in something of the way Ireland had been. The Labour government which came to power in 1974 was riven with hostility over Europe in exactly the way the Conservative Party was divided over it in the 1990s, and reporting it properly was of considerable importance to the BBC.

Harold Wilson had announced that he was going to renegotiate the admittedly unfavourable terms of Britain's membership of the

European Economic Community, as it still was, and would present the results of this renegotiation to the British people in a referendum.

It was all deeply phoney, and done primarily to keep the Parliamentary Labour Party quiet. Wilson and his foreign secretary James Callaghan selected only those areas of Britain's terms of membership which they were certain could be improved, and ignored the areas they could do nothing about: then, while pretending to be completely unbiased, they ended up by the summer of 1975 recommending the result of their renegotiation to the British electorate. Not surprisingly, they got a 'yes' vote of two to one. If you like your politics contorted and lacking in detectable principle, Wilson was your man.

I was to start in Brussels in January 1975: the moment when the renegotiation process began in earnest. The referendum was still seven months away, and in the meantime everyone with a mouth, an idea or a typewriter in Britain seemed to be taking up a position for or against the European Community; and none of them seemed to realize what a stitch-up the whole business was.

Of all the subjects in British public life, Europe is the one that attracts the most number of obsessives and bores; and, as is usual with the more extreme British obsessives and bores, they automatically assumed that the BBC was ranged against them. As a result the correspondents who reported on European affairs had to be extremely careful. To make a mistake even on the finest of technical points was to invite accusations that the BBC was biased. It would, my predecessor in the job told me comfortingly, be like defusing a ticking bomb in the dark with gardening gloves on.

Unfortunately the danger didn't make the subject matter any more interesting. Milk and beef quotas, the Common Agricultural Policy, trade relations with African, Caribbean and Pacific countries, set-aside, the Green Pound, monetary compensation amounts: though undoubtedly important to somebody, they lacked the allure of the subjects I had been dealing with in Dublin. Sometimes the journalists who covered them had problems remembering that there was an outside world unconnected with European minutiae. Once a friend of mine, who worked for Reuters, told me that one of the junior reporters in his office had begun a story with the words, 'Relations between Britain and Germany fell to an all-time low today over potato quotas.' It had to be pointed out to him that relations between Britain and Germany weren't particularly high on the First Day on the Somme, or during the Blitz, or the destruction of Dresden.

And yet underneath the jargon and the initials and the intense flow of detail in Brussels, real national interests were grinding against one another with the implacability of tectonic plates; and that always makes a fascinating spectator-sport. Once again, too, I would be dealing with the ministers, and sometimes the leaders, of all the countries in the Community.

Sometimes you saw them at their rawest. At four in the morning, after sixteen hours' hard arguing, not everyone was at their best. George Brown's days as Foreign Secretary weren't after all that far in the past; he was the one who, at a formal dinner, leant over the Spanish foreign minister's wife as she sat next to him and boomed out through a fog of alcohol, 'That's a nice pair of tits. Fish 'em out and let's have a look at 'em.' He, sadly, was gone; but some British ministers still drank too much, or flirted with the women reporters.

That I could forgive. Others were merely bad-tempered. The two heavyweights of Wilson's Cabinet, Denis Healey the Chancellor of the Exchequer and James Callaghan, turned up almost every month for the big renegotiation meetings; and both, though pleasant enough when things went well, quickly turned into threatening bullies when they didn't.

Once, after a particularly gruelling ministerial session in Luxembourg, I spent twenty minutes talking to Garret Fitzgerald. He was as open as ever about what had gone on: Callaghan had been in a minority of one, and had missed several chances to win the others over because he had been so unnecessarily combative. Presumably, said Garret, he thought this was the kind of thing that went down well back at Westminster. After saying goodbye I bumped into the Dutch foreign minister, who was just about to get into his official car. He agreed with everything Garret had said.

An hour or so later I was sitting beside Callaghan in an echoing ante-room, a couple of his aides perched nervously on tables behind us, my tape recorder on the desk and my microphone pointing towards Callaghan.

Transcript of interview for 07.00 Radio 4 News, 10.4.75

Speakers: John Simpson (staff), Rt. Hon. James Callaghan PC MP (Foreign Secretary) (non-staff)

```
JS: Other foreign ministers I've spoken to after the
meeting said you'd been unnecessarily tough: that you
could have got more of what you wanted if you'd been a
little more conciliatory.

JC: That isn't true at all. I don't believe you do speak
to other ministers. I think you just sit in the bar
talking to other journalists.
```

Nowadays I wouldn't take that from a politician, but at the time I thought I'd better let it go. There was a moment's silence, and then I switched to another subject; which is precisely what Callaghan had wanted. He knew it wouldn't sound good if I traded accusations with the Foreign Secretary.

Like one of the better-known theatres in the provinces, we in Brussels would have sneak previews of new ministers sent out from London. New leaders of the opposition, too. Margaret Thatcher's first foreign trip after being chosen to head the Conservative Party in 1975 was to meet the Conservative MEPs: Heathians almost to a man. Several of them also held seats at Westminster, and it was through a couple of them that I first heard of the mistake which had led to Mrs Thatcher's election.

Only a few MPs at Westminster, the far right-wingers, had really wanted her to be the party's leader; the great majority were willing to let Edward Heath continue in the job after the two election defeats of 1974, but they wanted to teach him a lesson by a little tactical voting. It was only as they talked to each other afterwards that they realized they had managed to give Mrs Thatcher an outright victory.

'Terrible foul-up,' one of the MEPs said to me. 'God knows what we've done to the party as a result.'

'What about the country?'

'Oh, she'll be out on her ear before the election. She's absolutely hopeless. Doesn't know a thing. Just a housewife, really.'

And so I had my first sight of the housewife who was to change British life for better and for worse. In the years to come I would follow her around the world, sometimes admiring her, sometimes loathing her, but never neutral. Now, at Strasbourg, I watched her coming unsteadily down the steps of a small aircraft, an unexpectedly attractive blonde woman swathed in blue, holding her hat on with one hand and gripping her outsized handbag with the other.

She charged across the windy tarmac towards the welcoming committee in a way I was to become very used to: head stuck out and pointing forward, almost overbalancing in her hurry, handbag gripped at the angle of a bayonet. It was as though each minute contained fewer seconds than she needed, and she had to make up the shortfall. No doubt one day Margaret Thatcher will assume the romantic afterglow of a Gloriana; but for most of us who watched her closely, her undoubted magnificence was spoiled by an unbecoming smallness of mind. As Noel Coward said of Churchill, or Churchill said of de Gaulle, or maybe someone else said of someone entirely different, she was a great person, but with more Achilles' heels than are usual in a biped.

On the day she turned up in Strasbourg, blown along by the chilly breeze, she was flustered and deeply unimpressive. She clearly knew nothing serious about Europe, and wasn't interested in anyone else's opinions. After meeting the MEPs and lecturing them sharply, she gave a press conference. Her voice was unpleasantly high-pitched in those days – she was to take elocution lessons to blunt its sharper edges – and it rose higher as the questioning grew in hostility.

The inadequacy of her preparation was embarrassing, and soon she was answering long and complex questions with a single angry 'yes' or 'no'. The journalists there, all of whom knew more about Europe than she did, sat and shook their heads; and when a gloomy silence showed that no one else wanted to ask her anything she stood up, gripped the handbag and stalked out of the room in a marked way. She scarcely even bothered to say goodbye to her hosts, the Tory MEPs; she lumped them and us together as pro-Europeans and enemies.

'It's obvious she'll never be prime minister,' I said to the journalist sitting next to me, which showed how much I knew.

« »

For the first time in my life, Brussels had turned me into a commuter. It could have been worse: my morning journey took me through a forest and a park, and was spent singing and joking with my daughters as I drove them to school. After that, since it was still early, I would go to one of the small, steamed-up cafés in the old centre of the city, read my morning paper and drink my morning coffee.

There were aspects of Belgian life I still found infuriating; Eleanor, who was turning into an imaginative, quirky child, once came home from her French-speaking school with a drawing she had done of a snowman. She had coloured it yellow, and the teacher had marked it 0/10: snowmen were by definition white. After that we sent her to an English-speaking school, though Julia, who was more inclined to abide by the rules as understood by Belgian school-teachers, opted to stay with them.

But sitting in the café, with the morning light grey outside and the condensation running down the windows, I would look around me at the various characters in their *bleu de travail* as they drank their glasses of something powerful or lingered over their coffees, wiping their luxuriant blond moustaches; and I would savour the life of the place with quiet appreciation.

The Belgians you saw in their Mercedes, their furs or their green loden coats might look as bad-tempered with one another as they were with the foreigners who had taken over their city like an occupying army, but they had a rich cultural and social life which we outsiders almost never saw. I felt like a foot-soldier in this army of occupation. We might patrol the streets, we might visit the main areas of the city, but we only caught occasional glimpses of the underground opposition, to which the entire local population belonged: a few incomprehensible slogans on a wall, a shouted word from a passer-by.

Foreigners could live in Brussels for years and still not understand anything they read in the Belgian press; if, that is, they even looked at the Belgian press. It was the custom to complain endlessly at parties about the Bruxellois, and to wish that the European Commission and NATO were based somewhere a little more glamorous; and yet it was only afterwards that I understood how enjoyable and rich our life in Brussels had been, and I came to regard the Grand' Place and the Galérie de la Reine and the Musée du Cinéma and the hundreds of excellent restaurants with immense nostalgia.

My office, too, was pleasant. The head of it, Noel Harvey, had been on the selection board which first hired me, back in 1966. I used to sit and talk to him in his office with its view over the old centre of Brussels for long periods of time. He had been in the colonial service in Nyasaland, and when he was recruited in the mid-1950s he had asked whether the British Empire in Africa might not be wound up soon. 'My dear chap,' said one of the senior people at the table, 'I can assure you we will still be in Nyasaland by the end of the century.' In less than ten years Nyasaland had become the independent state of Malawi.

Sue Bonner, who ran the office, knew a lot about Brussels and its life, and made life there easier for us. I would find myself leaning up against the doorpost and talking to Clifford Smith, a Canadian who was Brussels correspondent for the BBC World Service: an expert on obscure operas and obscure Belgian beers, and a dry wit in his own right.

Then down the same corridor was the office of Malcolm Downing, the correspondent for Australian Broadcasting, and I would sit in his armchair with my feet on his coffee-table, joking and laughing while the Berlaymont, the glass-fronted building which housed the European Commission, seemed to hover outside his window a few yards away, like a gigantic spacecraft in a sci-fi film. I worked even harder in Brussels than I had in Dublin, but it was a different kind of work: you sat there while the information poured in, and merely had to sift it in order to provide a constant stream of reports to London. In Dublin I had had to fight hard for every story.

At this time the European Community was still very much a Francophone affair. The first English-speaking nations, Britain and Ireland, had only joined in 1973, and France was without any doubt the dominant power. It was hard to love the EC too much: introverted and fixed in its ways, it seemed a collection of countries united in their own selfishness. And yet it was equally difficult to have any sympathy with the British position. Whatever one might think about it, the European Economic Community was based on noble principles: forgiveness, reconciliation and understanding.

And the British, with a patronizing approach which will not surprise anyone who has had dealings with the British civil service, did their best to wreck it. We had undermined it as much as we could in the 1950s, and then set up a rival organization, the European Free Trade Area. And when the EEC flourished and became too powerful to ignore, we deserted EFTA and joined the EEC instead.

But by this time the French had set the tone. There was a Cartesian quality to the EEC which permeated the Berlaymont and all the other institutions: a reliance on written rules and clear guidelines, a sense that planning was all. When the British with their empirical instincts joined in, they found themselves still outsiders. If it wasn't in the rule-book, it couldn't be done; and the rule-book had been written without Britain in mind. Even for a Francophile like me, there was something irksome and unnecessary about the way the Community operated.

It came down, often, to a linguistic battle. I found myself swiftly intimidated by the aggressive *bilangues* who inhabited the place. At this time my French was still quite slow, but I developed strategies for dealing with the superbly educated secretaries who seemed to run the place, and would interrupt my efforts to speak French with their fast, accurate English.

'*Est-ce que je peux parler avec M. Un Tel, s'il vous—?*'

'Sorry, he's out at the moment.'

Infuriated, I learned to lapse into the most impenetrable English argot.

'Well, when old Flookumpush finally rocks up, could you get him to give me a tinkle on the dog and bone?'

[Pause] 'I'm sorry?'

'Perhaps' [this in the most deliberately execrable French imaginable] 'it would be easier for you if I spoke French.'

Our office in Brussels was in the International Press Centre, just across the road from the Berlaymont. I found it difficult not to think of all those Napoleonic missives going the rounds about the necessity for unified measures of weight and distance, straight bananas and round apples; but if you could forget the Berlaymont, it had a pleasant outlook and a good deal of space. The characteristic motion of the BBC, in my experience, has always been the alternation between systole and diastole: between over-expansion and over-contraction. At the start of 1975 the Corporation was in rather grand mood, and occupied the entire end of the IPC building. In later years we cut back and rented out half the office on a long lease, just in time for a new expansion which required us to rent other offices elsewhere.

When I arrived you could still see the marks where one of my loonier predecessors had kicked the door in. He was annoyed to find it locked one morning when he needed to get in to file an early report. It happened to be the day the King of the Belgians was due to open the IPC, and the BBC office was on the visiting route. A BBC official had to stand in front of the splintered wood to ensure that the royal eyes wouldn't be shocked by the reality of everyday broadcasting violence. The official bowed and shook hands, and remained nobly at his post while the King was shown around.

« »

The presiding figure of the BBC office was Charles Wheeler, one of the best reporters who has ever worked for the BBC. Even today, when he is in his mid-seventies, his reporting is sharper and clearer and more radical than anyone else's, and his mind has lost not a fraction of its sharpness, nor of its acidity. He was present (though as a young Royal Marine officer rather than as a correspondent) on D-Day: the moment when our modern world may be said to have begun. He served as producer or reporter in Berlin immediately after the War, was in Budapest when the Hungarian Uprising took place, and covered all the great moments of American history in the 1960s.

Even in recent times he has produced some of the best reporting we have seen. In 1991 he endured the terrible cold and exposure of the northern Iraqi mountains to show the plight of the Kurdish refugees, and he revealed the extent to which some Kuwaiti surgeons had been involved in torturing Palestinians whom they accused, often wrongly, of siding with the Iraqi troops during Saddam Hussein's occupation of the country. In traditional fashion, Charles even got his foot in the door of the hospital ward where the torture was going on.

I was the radio correspondent and Charles was the television correspondent in Brussels, recalled from Washington (so it was always said; I never knew the truth of the matter) at Edward Heath's request so that Europe could be reported as well and as fully by the BBC as the United States was.

But although Charles brought his restless intelligence to the complexities of the European Community, it was clear they bored him. He had been used to sharper flavours, brighter textures, crisper air. So when a good old-fashioned news story came our way, he grabbed at it enthusiastically. So did I.

After the Portuguese pulled abruptly out of Angola in 1975, a three-way civil war began. On one side was the MPLA: strongly Marxist, Soviet-backed, supported by troops from Cuba. The anti-

Communist forces were divided into two. UNITA, operating mostly in the east and south of Angola and headed by Jonas Savimbi, had the support of France and South Africa.

The third group, called the FNLA, was little more than the creation of the CIA. Its leader was Holden Roberto, a tall, rangy character with strong American links. From its base in Congo, across Angola's northern border, the FNLA invaded the top third of Angola and at one time seemed to be on the point of capturing Luanda, the capital. But the MPLA held on; and by the beginning of 1976 it was beginning to look as though the Marxists, with their Cuban forces and Soviet advisers, were getting the upper hand.

At this point the British were unwise enough to get involved. MI6, presumably to do a favour to the CIA, began hiring former soldiers to go to Angola as mercenaries for the FNLA. Their recruiters went around the pubs of Aldershot, concentrating in particular on former members of the Parachute Regiment who had left the army but couldn't quite break away from the military atmosphere. The group they gathered together contained plenty of specialists as well as ordinary foot-soldiers, though the total lack of officers was eventually to lead to disaster.

An operation like this couldn't be kept secret. Soon Fleet Street was alerted; and the enlisted soldiers talked. Perhaps MI6 always knew they would, and wanted to scare the Angolans and their Cuban and Russian friends with the news that a sizeable detachment of well-trained British soldiers was coming their way. Anyway, there was little real security about the enterprise; even after the news had seeped out, several large groups were brought out via Brussels to fly to Kinshasa, the capital of what was then called Zaire.

And so Charles and I became involved. I went out with him and his television crew to the airport, and it wasn't exactly hard to spot the British mercenaries: fifty or so men in their late twenties or early thirties, mostly big, muscular and tattooed with close-shaven heads, and kitbags over their shoulders. Other television crews were there, but somehow Charles and his team got closer pictures and more words out of the hapless soldiers. I acted as sheepdog, herding them into corners of the departure lounge where they couldn't escape without showing their faces or saying something.

'What are the Cubans, when we've got the best of British here?'

one small man with an aggressive, twisted face said loudly into the microphones.

Most of them were more laconic:

'If I ever see your face again, I'll fuckin' smash it.'

'I'll kill you, you fucker.'

'I'm not going to forget you,' said a particularly unpleasant thin character in a grey anorak, his eyes set too close together.

Now, twenty years later, I feel rather sorry for them: being hunted down by journalists is a frustrating experience. Then I merely felt relieved that I wouldn't have to see them again.

Charles and I drove back to the office, along the motorway that leads into the centre of Brussels. At first we were silent, but as we were passing the NATO headquarters I couldn't keep quiet any more.

'I wish I could see what happens to those characters. You know, follow them, be their war correspondent.'

It was true, but only in theoretical terms. Their anger and violence was too strong for me to want to see them ever again.

Charles, however, seized on the idea immediately. I had voiced my thoughts to the wrong man: he had done these things himself, and enjoyed them.

'You must,' he said. 'These things are always really worth it. You'll do yourself a lot of good if you do it. I'll have a word with Larry.'

Larry was the foreign editor. Fine, I thought; he'll be far too sensible to let me risk my life going on a crazy jaunt like this. It was true that I would like to know what was going to happen to the mercenaries, but I wanted someone else to go. Someone braver.

But when Charles got through he found that Larry was away. His deputy was a charming, witty, Empire-building kind of man with superbly combed-down iron grey hair called Donald Milner, whose greatest moment had been to ride on the bonnet of Mad Mike Hoare's jeep into Elisabethville during the Congo troubles of 1961. He was either holding a Union Jack, or a UN flag: it depended how Donald felt when he was telling the story. Now he could relive the experience through me. I had become the receptacle of everybody else's gung-ho feelings. A moment's irreflection had locked me in to a seriously dangerous assignment in a famously nasty country, complete with savage white mercenaries. Each one of whom I had personally offended.

'I can't wait to go,' I said glumly to Donald Milner down the tie-line to London. 'I don't suppose there'll be another plane for some days, though. When does Larry get—?'

'No, no, no, you're in luck,' he said excitedly at the other end of the line. 'I've got the airline timetable in front of me. Most useful thing you can have, you know. That and a flag for when the victory parade happens, eh? Ha, ha, ha! Yes, thought so, there's a flight tonight. Eleven-fifteen Brussels/Kinshasa non-stop. God, I envy you.'

'Thanks, Donald.'

'Don't thank me, my dear fellow, thank your lucky stars. I'd kill for a chance like this.'

You probably will, I thought: me. I'd never seen so much transferred enthusiasm in my entire life.

I packed that night as though for the scaffold. Diane was worried but supportive, and the children were restless as I sat on their beds and read them a page or two from our current book. When I kissed them goodnight, I thought it might be the last time I ever saw them. Diane insisted on carrying my suitcase down to the taxi.

She stood in the road waving, until the taxi was out of sight. I turned in my seat, and settled down. Now that I had said my goodbyes, I could direct my thoughts to the business in hand. Not for the last time in my life, I reflected that I was little more than a dead man; and somehow, instead of being a frightening or a gloomy thought, I found it distinctly liberating. If I didn't have to worry about my personal survival, I could address myself to the job wholeheartedly. And something inside me started to murmur, with an increasingly Milner-like excitement, that I was going to the darkest and most savage part of Africa.

But by the time the plane landed at Kinshasa airport the following morning, I had got everything clear in my mind. It would be insanity to go ahead with all this. The British mercenaries were violent men who would certainly want to avenge the humiliation I had helped to give them on their way through Brussels. All I needed was an easy way out; and the lack of a visa offered it to me. When the immigration official looked at my passport and pointed out that there was no visa in it, I wouldn't offer him the $20 which I had been told was the usual fee: I would simply turn round and board the Sabena plane back to Brussels. Maybe it would be a little embarrassing meeting the eyes of

Charles Wheeler and the others in the Brussels office, but I owed it to myself and my family not to go ahead with something so irresponsible. For the first time in eighteen hours I felt a little more relaxed.

By this time I was standing in the queue for the passport control desk. The airport was a decaying piece of Belgian colonial architecture, once no doubt rather smart and white-painted, but now old and stained and dilapidated. The atmosphere wrapped round my face like a hot towel at the barber's, and there was a rich, rank smell of decay everywhere: old paint, old papers, old foliage, old excrement.

Ahead of me the businessman at the front of the queue was fishing in his pocket for a twenty-dollar bill. While the passport official was searching for the right stamp to use, I turned to my right and looked out through the main entrance of the airport. Three palm-trees were framed in the open entrance. Out there, I thought, is equatorial Africa. I have never been to equatorial Africa in my life. Who knows when I'll be here again?

'Where is your visa?' asked the official.

'I don't have one,' I said. And then, without having framed the words or the ideas in my mind beforehand, I added, 'I'm a British mercenary. I got separated from the main group who arrived here last night.'

The official grunted, and called something over his shoulder. A smiling character came forward.

'Welcome,' he said, and shook my hand. 'I am from the FNLA. We wondered if there might be any late-comers.'

By now, common sense had kicked in and I wanted to make it clear what had happened. I'm really a journalist, I started to say; but the smiling FNLA official thought I was thanking him for his help.

'No, no, not all,' he said. 'Just give me your passport. We will be responsible for you. You can pick it up any time you want from our headquarters in the centre of Kinshasa. Go there now and register. Goodbye – and good luck.'

I gave up. A taxi drove me down the highway towards the city. A mile or so down the road a soldier at a barricade made of orange boxes waved us down. Experimentally, like a surgeon introducing an instrument into a patient's body, he inserted the barrel of his rifle through the small opening I had left in the taxi window. The muzzle came to rest against my temple.

'He wants cigarettes,' the driver explained.

'But I don't smoke.'

'It's for you to make that clear,' said the driver. He probably hoped there wouldn't be too much blood on his cushions.

I made it clear: it took a dollar bill.

The lobby of the InterContinental Hotel was full of men and women in uniform. The men's uniforms were camouflage fatigues in different patterns. The women's were tight skirts, bare stomachs, half-opened blouses. A lot of business was being transacted here.

As I checked in, a tall, angular white man with wavy fair hair and a pleasantly crooked smile wandered over to me.

'You must be John Simpson from the BBC?' The accent was Australian but the inflexion was unmistakably American.

I admitted that I must be.

'Name's Neil Davis. NBC. They said we should work together.'

It was hard to believe. Neil Davis was the most famous cameraman of the Vietnam War. Just before I left I had had a message from Television Centre to say that an NBC cameraman would try to meet up with me. This was like going on a blind date and finding Princess Diana waiting for you.

'Weird place,' I said, looking round at the mercenaries and the hookers in the lobby.

'This is the nicest part of it,' Neil Davis replied.

We arranged to meet later. In the meantime, I had to go to the FNLA headquarters in the centre of Kinshasa.

Even the taxi-driver looked worried when I told him where I wanted to go, and he dropped me some way from the entrance. President Mobutu had given the FNLA an old military barracks which took up an entire city block. Its walls were twelve feet high, and made of mud-brick which had once been painted white and green. As I walked closer I could hear the sound of rifle fire. FNLA soldiers did their target practice and executed offenders here. Sometimes they did both at the same time. President Mobutu had given the FNLA complete power to do what it wanted in his capital; and as the movement's fortunes deteriorated in the Angolan war, so more and more executions were carried out.

I was about twenty yards from the big double gates when a smaller door opened, and three or four men stepped through it. I knew the face of the first one only too well: it was the thin mercenary whom I had last seen the previous morning. In spite of the heat he was still wearing his grey anorak. His unpleasantly close-set eyes locked onto mine.

'That's that fucker from What's-'is-name,' he shouted, and broke into a run, reaching into his anorak. The others streamed after him.

My fear outpaced his desire for revenge. I dodged between the parked cars in the street outside, burst through a group of nervous locals, and caught up with my taxi as it drove away. The driver's frightened eyes watched me in the rear-view mirror as I fell onto his back seat, and we drove off. Something inside me couldn't resist giving the thin mercenary a two-fingered sign as we passed him at speed.

Back at the hotel, sitting in the bar beside the swimming pool which I came to know so well, I told Neil Davis everything that had happened. There was something very calming about him, and he seemed to have a genuine sympathy for me. His fair hair was carefully coifed, even in the thick, damp, enveloping heat of Kinshasa, but a lock of it always seemed to hang carelessly down over his forehead. He looked like a 1950s film-star closing in on the female lead. And indeed Neil was an insatiable lover of women, with a famous technique which, as we spent more and more time in each other's company, he explained to me in detail.

'You sit opposite her somewhere where you won't be interrupted, like the far corner of some bar, and you look very deep in her eyes, till she starts to get uncomfortable. Then, just before she says anything you say something like, "I think I'm falling in love with you," and give her a card with your phone number on it. Works every time, mate. Only you've got to mean it, a bit at least. And this way you don't have to mention bedrooms: they'll do that themselves, believe me.'

As the afternoon wore on, his conversation turned to the terrible events in Cambodia. Neil had spent a lot of time there and in Vietnam. He showed me one of the shrapnel wounds he had collected in his leg, and pointed out the scar on the side of his face. Although he was forty-one at this time and I was ten years younger, I felt a sudden pang of fatherly pity for him: his leg looked so thin and fragile, and was so badly damaged. He had done and seen extraordinary things; less than a year before, in April 1975, he had been one of the few Westerners who had dared to stay in Saigon when the Americans pulled out and the Communists took over. He filmed the lead Viet Cong tank as it smashed its way through the gates of the presidential palace in Saigon; and he went on filming even when a Viet Cong soldier jammed a rifle in his stomach and ordered him to stop.

Soon Neil started talking about Cambodia: the gentleness of the people he had known and worked with there, and the terrible savagery of the way many of them had died after the country had been taken over by the Khmer Rouge. I found the tears running unchecked down my face. Neil wasn't doing it for effect, he scarcely looked at me or listened to me, in the thick, gathering African twilight. His eyes were far away, focused on a distant country which had disappeared into a cloud of pain and suffering.

« »

It wasn't until the next day that I realized who some of our fellow guests in the hotel were. As I was standing at the reception desk a tall man in his late thirties came up and stood beside me.

'You're a reporter,' he said almost conversationally, his English accent classless and regionless. 'If you say anything I don't like, I'll know all about it immediately. And I'll know what to do. You'll be dead meat here.'

He strode away across the lobby.

I went to the pool to have lunch. A strange-looking character with heavy reddish features, a thick pair of lips and a Northern Ireland accent – Belfast, Protestant, I thought, though there were some unexpected vowel sounds – sat down at the table and, unasked, started explaining to me the various organizations which the people round us worked for; MI6, the CIA, French intelligence, the KGB. A short olive-skinned man was sitting on his own reading the dreadful local newspaper.

'And that one? Who's he with?'

'Mossad.'

'How can you be sure?'

'I can't,' he said. 'I made it up.'

I was just warming to him when his taxi driver came in and explained that he had been waiting outside now for an hour and half, and would like to be paid. My companion listened to him, drawing on his cigarette. Then he beckoned to the driver to bend down and listen to something private. The driver bent down. The man with the Northern Ireland accent jabbed the red-hot end of the cigarette into the man's eye. The sound it made, and the driver's screams, stayed with me a long time.

'What did you do that for? You owed him money.'

'Teach him to come pestering me when I'm eating.'

No one, of course, complained about the incident. The waiters went on serving food, and the other guests didn't even look round. Violence was as normal as room-service at the InterContinental.

Then there was the tall, skinny American in jeans and a big white floppy hat and the look of a psychopath. He cornered Neil and me in the bar one evening, boasting about the way he slipped poison into people's drinks. He did a particularly good imitation of their death-rattle. We called him the Cyanide Kid.

Not every mercenary seemed like a crazed killer. On my second afternoon in Kinshasa I was sitting beside the swimming-pool, waiting for a message from the FNLA that they would take Neil and me to the front line in Angola.

'May I join you?' The voice was educated and pleasant, with a distinct French accent, and the face was thin and tanned. He wore a wrinkled set of olive-green fatigues.

Max worked for French military intelligence and was attached to UNITA as an adviser.

'They tell me you are a reporter,' he said. 'Perhaps you would like to hear what my group has been doing recently.'

I nodded, and ordered him a Ricard. He began a long story of attacks by night, of ambushes, of Russian and Cuban technicians killed, of heads and ears cut off as proof of achievement. Perhaps I looked sceptical; he reached into his pocket and produced a series of photographs, each with a date and time on them, some showing lines of heads and piles of ears and others showing bodies neatly laid out on the ground. Some wore what I took to be Russian insignia; others had Spanish rather than Portuguese names on their identification tags.

I went straight up to my room and wrote a report for the BBC about what he had told me; though I was careful not to state anything as absolute, hard-and-fast fact, and even more careful not to identify Max too closely. That evening he listened to my despatch as it was broadcast on the BBC World Service and sought me out to shake my hand.

'I didn't tell you before,' he said, 'but I went to an English public school.' He named it. 'We public schoolboys must stick together. This is a bad place, this hotel. If you have any problems, let me know.' He patted his revolver meaningfully.

By now the FNLA had accepted me as a bona fide journalist, and the British mercenaries had left Kinshasa for the front. The barracks in the centre of the city was a safer place for me to go to. Meanwhile another journalist had arrived in town: an attractive American woman in her late twenties who, curiously enough, worked for my old paper, the *Christian Science Monitor.*

Robin Wright's arrival upset the uneasy balance we had established in the hotel and with the FNLA. Max was much more interested in talking to her than to Neil or me, and Holden Roberto, the FNLA leader, was keener on taking her in his private helicopter to the front line than he was in taking a couple of men. The next day, when Neil and I went to the FNLA headquarters, we found they had already flown south.

'I was right not to make a play for her,' Neil said, as though it was something that required an explanation. 'Women and work never go together.'

We stayed in Kinshasa, waiting for something to happen. It was frustrating, but it enabled me to hear more and more of Neil's stories; I had very few of my own to tell. We would sit for hour after hour, laughing and yarning, allies against the unpleasant figures who peopled our hotel.

When I came down to breakfast in the morning, or walked into the bar after filing my latest story, his face would crinkle with pleasure and he would say, 'Now that Simpson's here, the fun can begin. Garçon! [The word was always pronounced in deliberately abominable fashion.] Bring Mr Simpson the finest fruit juices that Zaire's trees and forests can offer.'

He represented the life I had always wanted, and hadn't so far experienced. Twice he quoted a couplet by an eighteenth-century poet, Thomas Mordaunt. It seems trite enough on paper, but it glowed with significance when Neil said it:

> One crowded hour of glorious life
> Is worth an age without a name.

Neil maintained that he didn't have a death wish, and never took stupid risks. He always thought everything out beforehand, he said.

'Tell you one thing, though: I don't put up with coming second. I want to be the best, and I'll do a great deal to make sure I am.'

He was the only man I had ever met who was cameraman, sound recordist and reporter all in one: a one-man-band. It's common enough nowadays, but Neil was the first to do it. He didn't have to trust anyone else; and maybe he didn't have to share the glory with anyone else either.

'If I stuck a broom up me jacksie I could sweep the floor as well,' he said.

It was a delight to watch him assemble his reports for NBC, resting the camera on a wall or on his tripod and running round to talk into the lens. But if I suggested holding it for him he grew irritable. He was a loner, and the presence of anyone else annoyed him and made him feel restless and impeded.

'Don't need help. This is the way I do it.'

He had all sorts of theories, which he expounded at great length. One was that crowds of people in the Third World behaved wildly and violently because they hadn't eaten enough protein in their early lives. When we went to the FNLA barracks in the centre of town and saw people fighting or crowding together excitedly he would look at me drolly and say, 'Protein deficiency.'

Sometimes he would start to expound on the ethics of television reporting; and although I had scarcely done any by that stage I listened intently and determined to adopt his ideas for myself.

'One thing you never, ever do is ask a soldier to fire off his weapon at random, just so you can get the kind of shot the editors back home cream their jeans over. For one thing you never know who may be on the receiving end. There could be some dear old lady half a mile away drinking a cup of tea when a bloody great round comes through the wall and gets her.

'And then again, I once saw a Yank cameraman asking an ARViN [South Vietnamese] soldier to get up and loose off at nothing when the firing had died down because he'd been lying at the bottom of the trench the whole time and hadn't shot a foot of film. And when he did, a sniper we didn't know about got him right here.' He pointed to the side of his head.

'Bloody Yank said it wasn't his fault – how could he know? I told him he was a bloody murderer. You never stage anything like that. It's bad for business.'

I swore to myself that if I worked for television I would stick to his advice; and I always have. I also appropriated his expression about being bad for business. Even now when I use it, I get a quick mental image of Neil sitting there in his usual seat in the Kinshasa bar, thin and tall, his fair hair combed back or falling over his forehead, resting his desert boots on the chair opposite, his fatigues crumpled and open at the neck to show his dog-tag.

Three nights after Robin left I was sitting on my own in the bar, waiting for something to happen, when three men in British army fatigues, their heads cropped and their faces unshaven, came in. The place was almost empty and the lamps hung low over the tables and gave little light, but I could see even from the nervous way they walked in that they were frightened. One of them, the largest, came up to me. His name was Douglas.

As he talked, I gradually realized that these men, ex-squaddies from Aldershot, were looking for an officer-figure to tell them what to do. At first they would only say that terrible things had been happening, but that I mustn't ask them for details.

Douglas, his head almost completely shaven and covered in fear-some scars, rambled on for some time about how they had been tricked into coming to Africa, and how badly planned everything had been, and how evil the FNLA was.

'But there were others worse than that,' he said quietly, as he sat down beside me on the high bar-stool.

'Callan,' said the man on his far side. The others nudged him nervously.

'Look,' I said, 'it's no good telling me that bad things have been happening and leaving it at that. You've got to give me the full details.'

The three looked at each other in the dim light, and nodded.

The story Douglas started to tell me soon became known throughout the entire world. Even now, twenty years later, people often remember something of it when they have long forgotten other, greater events that happened since.

Callan, he said, was a devil. He came originally from Cyprus, and his name was Costas Georgiou. After being an NCO in the British army, he had been recruited as a mercenary. But Callan, who took his *nom de guerre* nickname from a popular 1970s television series about a British agent, was seriously deranged. He fell into wild rages when things went wrong, and no one with him was safe. He had already shot several people, the mercenaries said, when they took over a place called Makela in northern Angola. The four of them had been part of the garrison there.

They all wanted to get away, but they were too frightened of Callan, and too worried about the dangers of the African bush, to do it. Most of the men were sick of working for the FNLA. There was a general feeling of desertion and mutiny in the air.

One evening a young recruit, still in his teens, fired off a rocket by mistake while he was on guard duty. The next morning Callan ordered the entire guard, fourteen men in all, to take part in a special punishment parade. First he called out the teenager who had fired the rocket, and shot him in the knee. Then as he lay screaming on the ground he put a bullet in his head.

After that he ordered his deputy, a sadist called Sammy Copeland, to drive the remaining thirteen men out of Makela and shoot them. Together with a man the others knew only as 'Charlie', Copeland set up a machine gun and ordered the thirteen to strip. They had to jump out of the truck and run for it across the plain. Copeland and Charlie shot them down as they ran, and then went round killing the wounded. They took their time about it.

The thirteen were all former British soldiers, some of whom I had seen and filmed at Brussels airport: not bad men, just a little weak and nostalgic for army life.

The massacre had brought everything to a halt. The rest of the men at Makela deserted *en masse*, and some of them, like the ones I met in the bar, made their way back to Kinshasa. They were terrified of Callan and Copeland, and expected them to turn up in the hotel at any moment.

'They's coming tonight,' said Douglas. Now he had talked openly about the massacre he seemed a little better.

'It doesn't matter,' I said, 'there's nothing they can do in a big place like this. Tomorrow I'll take you to the British embassy, where they'll look after you and send you back to England.'

I didn't feel nearly as confident as I sounded; I'd had too much experience of British officialdom even in those days. But I could see these men, all of them tougher and more experienced and older than I was, needed comfort and guidance.

We made a curious little group as we walked across the hotel lobby to the lifts: I was in the lead, and they followed sheepishly after me, in single file. When we got to my room I gave them all the spare clothes I had, shirts, trousers and underwear, and suggested that they changed out of their army fatigues. Their boots I could do nothing about; but at least they looked fractionally less like mercenaries on the run.

'Now,' I said, 'you can sleep here. I'll stay down the corridor with a friend of mine, Neil Davis. Room 435. When I come back I'll give three knocks on the door, then another. Don't forget.'

But I was the one who forgot something. A few minutes later I was back, and gave the three knocks, and then a fourth. As I opened the door (I'd kept the key, just in case) the three mercenaries threw themselves onto the floor, and one tried to hide under the bed; they thought it was Callan coming for them with a machine-gun.

Neil was sitting with Robin Wright when I went to his room. She had just got back from Angola, and had told him everything.

'You know what's happened?' he asked.

I told them about the detail the three men in the bar had given me. Robin confirmed it all. She had been at another place in northern Angola, and had had adventures of her own, but she had met several other mercenaries who knew the whole business. We sat in Neil's room talking until Robin decided to go to bed. Then as I lay on Neil's couch with the light out I started talking to him about the practicalities of reporting the story.

'You should get back to Europe so that we make sure the story is out safely,' Neil said. 'That way, if anything happens to me here you can get help to me immediately.'

'But if you're going to stay, I ought to as well. I can't leave you here to face the music.'

'No, listen, I've had a lot of experience of this kind of thing, and I know how to handle myself. I'll wait until you've broken the story in Europe, then I can add my material on the spot here. It'll be safer for me that way: I won't have to take the heat.'

'And what about Robin?'

'She's out of it, working for a newspaper. And who reads the *Monitor* anyway? No, directly I've heard that you've broken the story I'll file for NBC. The BBC's our ally, so we'll be keeping it in the family.'

I couldn't decide whether or not to tell him the other problem I had; it had been working on me ever since I had heard about the disaster that had come upon the FNLA. I blurted it out anyway.

'The FNLA's got my passport, down at their headquarters. I'll have to get it in order to leave the country. But once I'm inside that building they'll know that I've heard everything. They'll never give me my passport back. They're much more likely to shoot me.'

It wasn't just my nervousness speaking. In the last couple of days the executions in the barracks in Kinshasa had greatly increased in number. For me to go in there was like an elaborate way of committing suicide.

There was a silence. I thought Neil must be asleep. Then his voice, as charming and ironic as ever, floated across to me in the darkness.

'No worries, mate. Your uncle Neil'll go in there with you. They won't touch us if we're together.'

I fell asleep feeling much better about it all.

« »

The next morning I rang the British embassy and told one of the people there what had happened. He sounded as though it was a serious personal inconvenience, but promised to meet them. When I banged on the door of my room again there was the same sound of panic-stricken scrambling inside, but they were glad to hear about the embassy.

'I'm catching the afternoon plane to Brussels,' I said. 'As long as you're under the protection of the embassy when all this comes out, you'll be fine. The man there says you should go along at five o'clock.'

They shook my hand and thanked me, looking distinctly uncomfortable in my clothes. They were much too big for them.

I packed what was left, and Neil and I took a taxi to the FNLA headquarters. I was badly frightened. The FNLA had never been much more than an American-financed front, and once the news of the massacre came out the Americans would cut their funding. If I were allowed to leave the country with the story, it would mean the end of a great deal of money for people like Holden Roberto.

'You don't have to come in with me,' I said to Neil as the taxi stopped outside. 'It'd probably be better if there was someone outside who knew what had happened.'

'Think I'd let you face the music on your own?' He laughed. 'We've had some good times here. Of course I'll go in with you.'

It was the ultimate act of friendship. I felt almost happy as we walked into the compound side by side.

Things rarely go either as well or as badly as you expect. Without realizing it, we had arrived at lunch-time and the place was deserted. Inside the main office, where we had spent so many hours over the previous week, there was no one behind the desk except a nervous office-boy. I already knew where my passport was, because I had seen it put away in a drawer a few days earlier. The boy made a half-hearted attempt to refuse when I asked him for it, but I was so ferocious that he reached into the drawer and handed it over. Neil and I walked out quietly side by side until we reached the gate. Then we exploded with the kind of laughter that has a distinctly hysterical tinge to it, and shook hands. I still couldn't believe he'd walked with me into a trap like that just out of friendship.

'Good luck,' Neil said, 'and watch out for yourself at the airport: they could try something there. When you get back to civilization give NBC a call and tell them what to expect from me. This is going to be the biggest story of your life, my boy.'

I'll never forget the way he looked then. His mouth seemed to get smaller when he smiled, and so did his eyes. It was as if he was putting his entire character and personality and experience into that one expression. The taxi started up, and he stood in the road waving until I was out of sight.

I was through passport control and sitting in the dirty, uncomfortable departure lounge when the trouble started.

'*On appelle M. Simpson de la BBC de Londres.*'

The loudspeaker had made the announcement twice in quick succession before I decided what to do. I got up as casually as I could and wandered over to the men's lavatory. It stank, but at least there were separate cubicles, each with a door. I went into the farthest one and sat down: not something for the fastidious. Almost but not quite closing the door, I drew my feet up onto the filthy seat. While I waited I folded up all my notes about the massacre and put them inside my shoes. Meanwhile my name was called twice more.

After a few minutes the outer door of the lavatory was punched open and I heard the sound of footsteps: two men, perhaps three, with soft civilian shoes. Not the army, then: these must be the FNLA officials at the airport. They walked halfway down the row of cubicles, then stopped. I could imagine from the faint grunting that one or maybe two of them were down on their knees looking under the partitions.

'*Rien*,' said a thick voice. The footsteps sounded irresolute, then came the banging of the door again.

The announcement was made again, but I stayed where I was, feet drawn up, nose blocked against the stench.

'*Dernier appel pour le vol Sabena numéro un zéro deux à Bruxelles.*'

Would they be waiting outside? There was no alternative now. I pushed my way through the door and hurried out, the stench clinging perceptibly to my clothes. A couple of men I didn't recognize were standing by the gate, watching everyone. But there were plenty of white people in the queue, and I got the impression the two watchers didn't have the kind of authority to push aside the woman in her Sabena uniform and check the passengers themselves.

I handed her my boarding pass with the name upside down so the watchers wouldn't be able to read it, accepted a small stump of it in return, avoided making eye-contact with anyone, and went on board. I only started breathing freely when the plane lifted off at the end of the runway; and even then I thought that the faces of a couple of men sitting side-by-side behind me were familiar from the FNLA head-quarters. I was miserable and frightened for the long journey back to Brussels.

When I emerged into the arrivals hall I immediately spotted Noel Harvey. He listened calmly to my story about being followed by the men on the plane, much as one does to a child's fears.

'I can see you've had a hard time, but the office want you to go straight on to London first thing in the morning. A whole group of

British mercenaries have been killing one other in Zaire. They think you may have heard something about it while you were there.'

'Heard something? It was my story. What do you mean? How do you know about it?'

'Apparently there was someone in Kinshasa, working for NBC. He's been reporting it all day long.'

'But it was mine – I got it first. We had an agreement. I gave the mercenaries my trousers and shirts.'

I could see he thought I was raving again.

'When did all this hit the wires?'

Noel paused to consider. 'This afternoon, some time.'

I looked at my watch: it was after midnight.

'He must have done it directly I left,' I said as Noel took me to the office in his car. 'How could he do a thing like that? He said he'd wait till I got back. And what about the three blokes in my room? What's happened to them? I thought he liked me.'

'It sounds rather as though he wanted to get you out of the way,' said Noel Harvey, but I still couldn't believe it.

Reporting it was a difficult business. The mercenary organization which had hired Callan and the others was denying Neil's report angrily, and the anger redoubled when I added my version of it all. One of the main figures in the organization, John Banks, claimed that Callan and everyone he was said to have murdered were alive and well. It didn't help that my notes, which Noel had to send on to me because I left them in the Brussels office, contained no surnames of any of the victims: the three men I had spoken to in the InterContinental bar had known them only by their nicknames.

The BBC broadcast my reports extensively, but I could tell from the way the editors treated them, and me, that they were nervous about it. After all, how did I know it was true? Had I seen the massacre for myself? Since I didn't even know the names of the victims, how could I be so certain? It was two anxious days before Harold Wilson, the prime minister, made a statement in the House of Commons confirming the entire affair.

When it was all over I sent an angry telex to Neil Davis. His reply reached me some weeks later. It was long and sometimes contradictory, but it reinforced what I had come to believe: that he had deliberately got me out of the way so he could report the story first.

Kinshasa, Zaire. 22 Feb. 1976

Dear John,

What a naughty cable you sent me! I can well understand
your anguish, but I'm afraid you misinterpreted my (and
Robin's) intentions. We didn't mean you to believe we
definitely would not file the story. What we did say was
that - at that time - we had no intention of filing.

Then followed a lengthy justification of what had happened. Robin
Wright explained to me afterwards that Neil had told her he was going
to file the story almost immediately he came back from the airport.
Since she knew much more about it than either of us, she decided to
do the same; but as Neil had realized, writing it for the *Christian
Science Monitor* was unlikely to make as much of a splash as broadcasting it on a major US television network. Neil's exclusive was pretty
safe. His letter went on:

I hope this eases your mind somewhat. Your short stay
here wasn't crowned with great success - but then it's
sometimes necessary to hang in - as I've found over the
years in similar situations.

Take care, and drop me a line sometime.
all the best,
cheers,
Neil.
(Neil Davis).

He was right about hanging in, of course. Like the business of not
getting soldiers to fire for the camera, it was a lesson I never forgot –
no matter how painfully it was learned. But the most painful thing of
all was that his letter never referred once to the friendship I thought
we had forged.

Neil was wrong about one thing, though: my lack of success in
Kinshasa. Even if I had been badly beaten by him, I broadcast so much
about the subject and was interviewed by so many of the newspapers
that I seemed with hindsight to have done rather well. On the strength
of it I was earmarked for the plum job of Southern Africa correspondent, based in Johannesburg. My life changed as a result: I lost a

lot of my old self-doubt, and became a much more effective, confident operator.

Towards the end of my time in Southern Africa – it must, I suppose, have been early in 1978 – I was on a plane from Jo'burg to Maputo in Mozambique, sitting as I prefer to do in an aisle seat. The seat-belt sign was switched off, and a tall figure came and loomed over me.

'S'pose you're going to yell at me,' said Neil Davis, with his familiar smile.

I thought about it for a moment.

'Oh,' I said, 'what the hell.' And reached up and shook his hand.

That night we sat in a little restaurant in the centre of Maputo, eating enormous grilled prawns *peri-peri* at a street-side table under the stars. Cars drove past hooting, beggars hovered to ask us for money, the waiters started piling up the chairs, but for three hours or so we were back where we had been in Kinshasa; except that I was no longer so gauche and inexperienced. Yet if I had become a different person, Neil hadn't. He was funny, charming, and only slightly apologetic. But he was the one who paid.

'This must be the kind of charm you use to get girls into bed with you, Davis,' I said, as we stood up to go.

'Never had to put so much effort into it with any of them, mate.'

We stood up, and as the waiters moved forward with relief to clear away our table we shook hands for the last time. Maybe something had been settled, maybe not. It no longer mattered to me, and I don't suppose it had ever mattered to him. But – another lesson – you have to take people as you find them; they always disappoint you if you expect more of them than they are capable of delivering. I watched him as he headed off down the street to his hotel, tall, slightly stooping, with a lope which he had probably picked up back in his native Tasmania, and a faint limp which he certainly got in Cambodia. He didn't look round, and I didn't watch him for long. We never came across each other again.

Eight years later, on 10 September 1985, I was sitting in the courtyard of the American Colony Hotel in Jerusalem, drinking my breakfast orange juice and reading the *Jerusalem Post* in the early morning sunshine. My eye was caught by a brief story about an attempted coup in Bangkok the previous day. The last paragraph said that an Australian cameraman well-known for his Vietnam War coverage, Neil Davis, had been killed in a brief outbreak of fighting before order was restored.

It was some time before I heard the details. He had gone on filming from inadequate cover while several tanks poured fire quite pointlessly in his general direction. A round hit him and his sound recordist Bill Latch. Latch was mortally wounded, and Neil died on the spot. His camera, which continued running for minutes afterwards, recorded the entire incident. The coup attempt was so insignificant that no one would have remembered it afterwards if it hadn't cost the life of the best combat cameraman in the world. Neil Davis's one crowded hour of glorious life had finally come to an end. According to the paper, he was fifty-one. I expect he looked forty.

« »

In the summer of 1976 the MPLA government in Angola put 'Colonel Callan' and the twelve other British and American mercenaries it had captured on trial. I flew out to cover it with a posse of Fleet Street's finest who had mostly reported on the British end of the story. I had never watched the hack-pack at close quarters before, and I was shocked at the way they paired off, each with his closest rival, neither of them allowing the other out of their sight, always making sure they both had access to the basic facts.

BBC Television had sent Martin Bell to cover the trial. I had never really got to know him before, and scarcely succeeded now: he was a quiet, deeply self-contained man. Unlike me, Martin was a genuine Cambridge double first (he read English). He was a man of great personal probity, who nevertheless managed to court public attention while appearing to dislike it.

'You and that Martin Bell,' a viewer I had annoyed wrote to me with some accuracy, 'both like to back into the limelight.' In the 1997 election Martin did the unthinkable, and crossed the floor from the intermittent limelight of journalism to the permanent limelight of politics. Having left the business, he believed that the best journalism was not the balanced, objective kind he had practised throughout his career, but 'the journalism of commitment': an opinion the old Martin Bell would once have rejected with contempt.

MPs come and MPs go, but there aren't many television reporters like Martin Bell. Yet he obviously felt he had come to the end of the road as far as his career with the BBC was concerned. He left my World Affairs Unit with probable relief, and certainly without a word of goodbye; and soon, as a Member of Parliament, he was on his feet criticizing the BBC. Other people who have left the BBC for Parliament have done the same: perhaps they feel they have to make a sacrificial bonfire of their old loyalties, to prove they have adopted new ones.

In Angola in 1976, I understood for the first time why everyone said Martin was such a superb television operator. On an important assignment like this you must establish yourself at the heart of events, so that all the main actors come to see you and tell you what is going on; and nothing happens without your knowledge and agreement. In the hands of a manipulator or a liar – and there are prominent examples of both in British television – , this could be dangerous. In the hands of a Martin Bell, it merely ensures the best television coverage possible.

In particular he established himself as the principal adviser to Callan's sister, a striking blonde who came out to Luanda to be present at her brother's trial. In return she gave him several interviews in which she presented herself and her brother in as favourable a light as possible. Fleet Street thrashed around, baffled and angry. Martin didn't pay a penny for the exclusive interviews she gave him. It was simply that she knew she could trust him.

Robin Wright, now working for the *Washington Post*, was covering the trial too. She explained to me how Neil Davis, having got rid of me in Kinshasa, had also managed to wrong-foot her as well. It didn't surprise either of us that he didn't turn up for the trial.

Robin had a particular personal interest in it. One of the accused men, called Marchant, had been captured by the Cuban army in the little port of San Salvador. He was in San Salvador with the three men who had later sought me out at the InterContinental Hotel in Kinshasa. Douglas, the mercenary who told me the full details of Callan's massacre, described what life had been like in San Salvador. The four of them had had to administer the town as well as try to defend it against the advancing Cubans. They had been forced to organize the supply of fuel, detail the men of the town to dig trenches and lay crude traps for the enemy, even carry out operations in the local hospital. They had done their best, like characters from a Kipling short story, but the responsibility had simply overwhelmed them.

When Robin Wright arrived in San Salvador, flown down there in

Holden Roberto's plane, they gave up the best of the rooms they slept in and used up some of their precious time looking after her. But the men they were trying to train to defend the town were no match whatever for the Cubans, and the traps they had laid at the entrance to the town were crushed under the tracks of the enemy tanks. The four men withdrew to the waterfront in good order, firing at the tanks as they went. They ran down to the boat they had prepared there, only to realize that it wasn't big enough to take Robin as well. Marchant gave up his seat for her, and stayed on the quayside. It is a powerful image: the boat moving fast out of the harbour, the Cubans running towards him, and Marchant waiting there either to be captured or killed.

In the end it turned out to be both. For no reason that I could see the prosecution in the mercenaries' trial demanded the death penalty for Marchant, as well as for Callan and two others. It looked as though the Angolan authorities had decided beforehand how many would die and how many would be sentenced to long or short prison terms. Since Marchant had been a medic, and had been captured only because he had given up his chance of escape for a woman, it is hard to see why his offence was so grave.

I watched his face as he stood in the dock, wearing the humiliating orange pyjamas which all the accused men were issued with. When the verdict was announced he winced. The next second his face was expressionless again. According to reports Callan died bravely; I heard nothing more about Marchant.

After the trial and before the verdicts were announced, I looked around for something else to do outside Luanda. There was little or no competition; Fleet Street was staying put. As I was sitting in my hotel room there was a knock at the door, and a woman called June Goodwin, Robin Wright's replacement on the *Christian Science Monitor*, was standing there.

I knew her a little: she had been at university in the United States with my wife. June was tiny, scarcely four feet nine inches tall, but she had a remarkable eye for a story and had won many prizes for her African coverage. Now she was suggesting a trip to the northern Angolan enclave of Cabinda, which produced large amounts of oil. No Westerner had been there for at least six months, and we had been getting reports of heavy military activity in the area.

June was a brave and determined woman, but she didn't want to make the journey alone. I agreed to go with her: it sounded exactly the kind of trip I wanted to make. We worked out a way of getting the necessary passes, and two days later, around dawn, I slipped out of our hotel before the spies from DISA, the national security agency, were awake, and took a car with June to the airport.

Cabinda Town was small, run-down, and a great deal freer than Luanda. Because the local authorities weren't expecting Western visitors, there were no security policemen at the hotel where we checked in. The place was filthy: when I pulled back the top sheet on my bed, I found a kind of conglomerate human image on the bottom sheet, like the Shroud of Turin. A great many unwashed people had lain there and sweated on it over the previous few months.

June and I toured the enclave by taxi, and found that the fighting between the MPLA and the local resistance movement, FLEC, had died down for the time being. The FLEC was a rather engaging organization which had only two objectives: self-determination for Cabinda, and a share-out of the oil revenues between the citizens. Each Cabindan would get $2,600 per year.

Yet it was clear why the FLEC had gone quiet. The roads in Cabinda were full of Soviet military hardware, driven by Russian and Cuban soldiers. Back in Luanda we had seen nothing of this: while the mercenary trial was going on in Luanda, the military had been ordered to stay off the streets. The MPLA and their Soviet allies were anxious that the international group of journalists there shouldn't see the reality of life in Angola. But since no one expected any foreign journalists to go to Cabinda, there were no restrictions there. All sorts of new equipment was being driven around: armoured personnel carriers, tanks, and tank transporters not previously seen outside Russia. June Goodwin snapped away with her camera; I made notes for my radio reports.

We spent an uncomfortable night in Cabinda: June was kept awake by the stench in her room, and I slept on the floor with the cockroaches rather than add my imprint to the Turin Shroud. In the morning we found that the military were even more active than before. Soviet propaganda liked to depict the Angolan war as being between Western-supplied groups like the FNLA and UNITA, which had to hire British,

French and American mercenaries, and the Angolans themselves, who had a little assistance from Cuban volunteers.

What was more, both Cuba and the Soviet Union had given undertakings the previous year that the Cuban troops would be withdrawn from Angola. Yet this didn't seem to be happening. It was clear from what we saw by looking out of June's window on the first floor of the hotel that the Soviet Union was pouring in equipment of advanced types into the country. The tanks ground their way past, six at a time, and June snapped away. Next came the transporters, then dozens of Cuban soldiers in open lorries. The pictures were splendid; I even took a few myself.

The last truck-load of soldiers slowed down outside our hotel. June was so pleased with the pictures that she became careless. As the truck came to a halt, the officer in charge happened to look up and saw June standing in the window, pointing her camera at him. He shouted something and pointed.

'Throw everything in a bag,' I hissed at June. 'Don't leave anything. We've got about fifteen seconds.'

That turned out to be optimistic. We ran out of the room and slammed the door behind us, and I could already hear the Cuban officer and half a dozen of his men thundering up the stairs. Without thinking I thrust June behind me and stood in a corner of the staircase as they ran past me, the officer with his revolver drawn. But the figure he had seen in the room belonged to a woman: he scarcely even bothered to register me as he passed, and he can't have noticed June hiding behind me because she was so small.

As we ran downstairs I could hear the officer shoulder-charging the door to June's room, even though we hadn't had time to lock it. The proprietor was standing open-mouthed in his dirty vest in the hallway. I threw him a fifty-dollar bill (far too much for his disgusting hotel), put my finger to my lips and winked. To my surprise, he winked back: perhaps he supported the FLEC.

Upstairs I could still hear the Cuban officer shouting orders, but we jumped into a taxi and headed for a restaurant on the edge of town. There we sat and drank three Coca-Colas each in quick succession – there was nothing else in the fridge and it was very hot – and waited until the plane to Luanda was due to leave. From time to time Cuban soldiers and Angolan police would tour round in their jeeps, but they still seemed to be looking for a lone white woman. They certainly took no notice of us.

At the airport we sat and waited, and I started writing up my notes on all the military equipment we had seen. No other Western journalists had witnessed this build-up. June and I had a big story on our hands.

The departure lounge was crowded, and a white man a little older than me sat down next to me. On his far side sat an attractive Angolan woman, rather well dressed.

'What are you writing?' the man asked. Though he had a pronounced German accent, he spoke English well. He had, I thought, a pleasant, open face, and his clothes were clean and neatly pressed. He looked like someone you could trust.

Usually it annoys me when people look over my shoulder, but there was something rather gentle and unassuming about this man.

'I'm a journalist,' I said. 'I'm jotting down the details of what I've seen in Cabinda.'

That started him off. He was a doctor from West Germany, a committed Communist with strong links in Eastern Europe, who had volunteered to come to Angola to help the MPLA's medical efforts. He had risen to the position of co-ordinator of medical services for the whole country.

Soon, though, he had realized that the Russians weren't interested in helping the Angolan people: they had come, and brought the Cubans with them, in order to further Moscow's geo-political aims; and they weren't planning to leave. The health of the Angolan people was the last thing they cared about.

'These Russians are racists,' he said. I noticed that the attractive woman sitting beside him was listening to everything he said, and writing it down in a little note-book.

'I feel I've got to tell you some of the things I've seen here,' he said. He began a long account of the military disposition of the Russians and Cubans: their numbers (which he put even higher than the Americans had), their tactics, and their attitude to the local people. As for the country's hospitals, he maintained that they were disgusting. Scarcely any of the money which the Russians claimed to be putting into medical care in Angola was spent on drugs or equipment; most of it went into the pockets of MPLA officials, or else was used for military purposes.

Methodically, he went through his book. He had assembled figures for all these things.

'Can I write this down?' I asked.

'Of course. That's why I'm telling you all these things.'

After a while the attractive woman stopped making notes, and walked over to a phone box. I could see her turning round as she talked and looking at us, or else reading out her notes. When I pointed this out to the German doctor, he glanced over as if it meant nothing to him.

'She is my translator, from DISA. She is telephoning the Correctional Committee in Luanda.'

'But what'll happen to you?'

'I'll be arrested. It doesn't matter; it'll be a relief. I had to tell someone.'

'And after you're arrested?'

'Sometimes they shoot people.'

The woman from DISA came back and sat next to him as though nothing had happened.

I whispered to June something of what he had been telling me. As we got onto the plane we managed it so that she sat next to the DISA woman and I sat next to the German doctor.

He went over the figures with me again: there were between twenty and twenty-five thousand Cuban troops and advisers in Angola. Four thousand had been killed or wounded in the fighting. Instead of withdrawing 200 Cubans per week as had been promised, the Russians were entrenching them in positions of strategic importance throughout Angola, from DISA to ports, airports, prisons, food supply offices, and centres of communication.

The doctor gave me the names of many of these installations, and told me the address of an apartment block in Luanda where the families of Cuban officers had been brought to live. When I went there the next day and checked, several people confirmed that they were from Cuba. The doctor told me, too, that the Angolan President, Agostinho Neto, was trying his best to stay independent of the Russians and Cubans, but that the minister in charge of DISA, Nito Alves, was likely to stage a coup against him soon, with Soviet support. Some months after this, Alves did indeed attempt a coup, but it was smashed.

'They'll pick me up when we get to Luanda,' the German doctor said to me. 'But don't worry: they won't touch you. Just report these things as I've told you. I won't see you again. Don't let me down.'

I promised him I wouldn't; yet even then I found it all hard to believe.

As we came through the airport his DISA translator ran ahead of him and went over to a group of tough-looking men standing at the barrier.

'They're from the Correctional Committee,' he said.

The men came up to him and took his arms, pushing me away.

The German doctor twisted round and looked at me. 'I want you to remember everything I've said to you,' he said, with a little smile.

He had given me his address and telephone number in West Berlin, and from time to time I would try to call him up. There was never any answer. Two years later when I was in Germany I went to the house where he lived. His name was gone from the doorbell, and a neighbour said he had gone abroad and never come back. She thought it was somewhere in Africa, but she couldn't remember where.

'Angola?'

'*Ja, ich glaub' es.*'

Finally, I applied to the West German foreign ministry: a place in Bonn that looks like a secondary school. There was a department there which specialized in missing citizens, and I asked them for details about the doctor.

'Someone else was asking about him,' someone told me a few days later. 'He went to Africa and our embassies in Zaire and Angola haven't heard anything about him. I'm sorry to say it, but he could have died, you know.'

'And if he was executed by the Angolan government?'

'We know nothing about that,' she said, and put the phone down.

7

No Room for Ranting

SOUTH AFRICA was a different world. The skies were blue, the climate was wonderful, and there was a real story to be done. Within a couple of months of my arriving there as the BBC correspondent, I had shed the excess weight which three good Belgian meals a day had put on me. In the free and easy colonial air I felt utterly liberated.

Not, though, by the political and social system. Apartheid was at its height in 1977, and the penultimate phase as devised by its originators, Dr D. F. Malan and his colleagues, and implemented by Dr Hendrik Verwoerd, had already begun: the creation of 'homelands' for the black population of South Africa. The idea was that soon the blacks would be moved out of white areas altogether and the separation of the races would be total.

Now that the entire system has collapsed and power has been handed over to the majority of South Africans regardless of their colour, it seems barking mad: the creation of a few intense, embittered, nationalistic academics with a limited understanding of the way the world works.

And yet of course plenty of governments in black Africa as well as all the major Western countries took the apartheid state for granted and worked with it. On a pleasant summer afternoon in the mid-1980s I went to lunch with President Kenneth Kaunda of Zambia at his palace in Lusaka. He was a man I came to have a good deal of respect for, and as we sat out on the beautiful clipped lawn, with the brilliance of the table-cloth dazzling our eyes, I listened to a long, rational, good-tempered complaint about Britain's unwillingness to impose sanctions against South Africa.

'Excuse me, sir,' said the waiter, and learned over me to refill my wineglass.

The crisp white cloth fell away from the bottle as he poured, and revealed the distinctive label of one of the best South African vineyards. Kaunda felt strongly about sanctions, but not so strongly that he wanted to give up providing his guests with South African wine.

India, one of South Africa's greatest critics abroad and an advocate of moral foreign policies, also managed to be one of its biggest trading partners, buying large quantities of South African gold. The Soviet Union, which led the international attack on apartheid, was discovered (by a one-time colleague of mine, John Osman) to be operating a secret cartel for gold and diamonds in the closest co-operation with the South Africans.

So there was an enormous amount of hypocrisy in the outside world towards South Africa. A great deal of convenient forgetfulness too: for instance, the legal system of apartheid owed a great deal to the legislation originally passed when South Africa was under full British control. As I came to know more about South Africa I realized that apartheid was based not so much on race hatred as race fear, and on a foolish belief that the clock could be stopped in South Africa even though it continued to tick everywhere else in the world. Apartheid was essentially a monstrous form of nostalgia for a way of life which had already died out elsewhere.

This was a job like no other; there was a moral dimension to working in South Africa which scarcely existed elsewhere. Yet I was uncertain how the BBC wanted me to do it. Might there be some secret deal, some under-the-counter understanding, between the BBC and South Africa? I hoped not, but I wanted to know; I could always turn the job down *in extremis*. I made an appointment to see the head of news and current affairs, a wily old Ulsterman called Waldo Maguire, and put the question to him. If there were some hidden agenda, I would be able to tell from his answers. As the head of news in Belfast, Waldo had given me and many of my London-based colleagues a hard time over what he saw as unsubstantiated criticisms of the government and the armed forces; for instance, when we first started getting indications that British troops had mistreated and tortured the people who had been picked up for internment, Waldo had tried to hold us back until the evidence became overwhelming. We saw it as timidity; he saw it as wisdom.

But although I had fallen out with him then, I admired his judgement. Sitting in his office now, with a cup of BBC tea and a couple of digestive biscuits in front of me, I told him that I was worried about what was expected of me in Johannesburg, and wanted some advice. He listened to me, and then got up without speaking and walked over to his filing cabinet. Pulling open a drawer, he took out a single piece of flimsy copying paper and handed it to me. It was an ancient minute which the BBC's Board of Governors had sent to the Director-General at the beginning of the Second World War. The BBC's broadcasters should, it said in its smudged old type, address even German listeners as if they were having a conversation with them in a neutral café. 'Above all,' it concluded, 'there can be no room for ranting.'

'Those are your instructions for South Africa, my boy,' Waldo said. The afternoon sunshine fell across his desk, and I could scarcely make out his features against the light: just the white hair.

'Of course I want you to stay there and not to get expelled through carelessness,' he went on, 'but in a place like that there are bound to be stories which you can't report without the risk of getting thrown out. Make yourself a scale of importance from one to ten. Up to six or seven you should just report the story without even thinking about it. From eight to ten, give me a bit of warning first. But if it's that important you've got a duty to report it. Remember: you're not a politician, you're a journalist; and it isn't the business of a journalist to worry about the consequences of what you write. Your job is just to do the story properly. And don't forget what it says there: no room for ranting.'

When we actually got to South Africa, of course, it was all a great deal easier than I had expected. The facts spoke for themselves: here was a system which was openly designed to protect the interests of some people and keep others down economically, socially and politically. Merely to recite the agreed, publicly available facts was a clear indictment of it. When, for instance, my children went to the local white primary school their books were paid for by the government; when my black housekeeper's children went to their infinitely poorer school, she had to pay for their books herself, on an income which was a small fraction of my own.

If I wanted to take a black businessman or politician to lunch there were only two restaurants in the whole of Johannesburg I could choose; and I would have to ring up the day before and ask the manager's permission. In the expensive suburb where we lived the public lavatories and even the park benches were still segregated. Political prisoners who died in the country's gaols were officially declared to have committed suicide with absurd frequency.

And yet because white South Africa was recognizably part of the Western world still, the notions of freedom of speech and the rule of law still operated strongly in theory, even if in practice they were under threat. South Africa wasn't remotely like the dictatorships I later visited: there were many people and many organizations dedicated to the difficult task of turning the country into an open democracy like any other, and mixing with them and reporting on their activities provided the kind of oxygen which would otherwise have been denied to me.

I had no doubts on this score at all. The greatest of the BBC's postwar director-generals, Sir Hugh Greene, had declared when I first joined the Corporation that the BBC's duty to be balanced and fair didn't mean it was required to be even-handed between good and evil; and he specifically quoted the case of apartheid in South Africa. Greene had been eased out at Harold Wilson's insistence because he was too liberal, but I and many others of my generation inside the BBC regarded him as our true inspiration. For us, Greene remained the king over the water.

« »

We found a delightful, sprawling house set in a lovely garden blossoming with hibiscus, bougainvillea, jacaranda and flowers with names like Yesterday, Today and Tomorrow. In the tall pines which flourished round the edges, *Piet-my-vrouw* birds sang their characteristic songs. Here every prospect pleased and only man, in the shape of our landlord, was vile. Dr Goll was a post-war immigrant from Austria, a deeply unprepossessing character who was always trying to get the children to kiss him or come over to his flat for a piece of cake. When we first arrived, and he showed us round, he tried to stop us looking at the servants' quarters. With some reason, since they turned out to be disgusting.

'You'll have to paint these rooms properly,' Diane told him.

'Why? These people are just animals. They'll make it filthy here,' said Dr Goll calmly. I thought Diane was going to punch him.

There were plenty of people, especially among the newer immigrants, who were unquestionably racist. Yet I quickly learned to avoid generalizing about anyone in South Africa. It was, and remains, a country of extraordinary variety and individualism. Nelson Mandela's chief gaoler became his main sympathizer; the police chief in Soweto turned out to be an enthusiast for the BBC; the writer Breyten Breytenbach, who was gaoled for challenging apartheid, had a brother who was a colonel in the South African Defence Force. You had to take each person by his or her own character and beliefs in a way that wasn't so necessary elsewhere in the world.

As soon as I could after arriving, I visited Soweto. It wasn't easy: in principle whites weren't allowed there, especially after the Uprising the previous year. I had to get a permit from an office called the West Rand Bantu Administration Board, hidden away in the old centre of Johannesburg. There an ancient clerk perched on a high chair pulled out a yellowing form and filled in the details: who I was, what organization I represented, why I wanted to go. When I suggested 'reporting' he sniffed disapprovingly: Western journalists were regarded by many white South Africans as serious enemies. But he put an official stamp on the document all the same.

I wasn't altogether certain how to get to Soweto, since even though it was one of the biggest cities in Africa it wasn't marked on any map. Nor were there any signposts. Because Soweto wasn't supposed to exist politically, it didn't exist geographically. According to the theology of apartheid it was in the process of withering away, like the state under pure Communism. And even though Soweto showed a distinct reluctance to wither, official white South Africa refused to acknowledge its existence. It was unofficial and unintended. Soon it would be phased out, and the inhabitants shipped off to their respective homelands.

Eventually I decided that since the name stood for 'South-West Township' I should head out of town in that general direction. I had to stop off at Uncle Charlie's Roadhouse, a marvellous South African institution, and ask the way. The black man at the petrol pump pointed to a side-road on the other side of the highway: that was it.

It was late afternoon by the time I drove along the poorly

maintained road in a haze of red dust. Soon I saw Soweto spread out below me, thousands of chimneys pouring smoke into the clear air, and I smelt the characteristic sulphurous smell of the place. The houses were small and box-like, but they were better than I had seen in other parts of black Africa. Many were kept with remarkable neatness, and had pleasant little gardens round them: each a small victory for the human spirit in the most unpromising surroundings.

Some of the houses had generators, but for the most part they were lit by paraffin lamps or candles: there was no electricity in Soweto, except for the towering arc-lamps which illumined some of the big open areas. Nor were there any shops, apart from occasional bottle stores and small groceries, because the white shopkeepers of Johannesburg wanted the Sowetans' business. And yet commuting to Johannesburg to work or shop was a long and dreary business. It was commonplace for people to leave home at 3.30 a.m. in order to be at their places of work by 7.00; and they were rarely home until 7.00 at night.

It probably wasn't a good idea for me to be here on my own. The riots of the previous June, which had shaken the South African government to its foundations, had faded away; but there was always an element of danger for lone whites driving around the streets of the township, and police patrols were few and far between. I headed back to the road which led to Uncle Charlie's Roadhouse. If I had only realized it, I was seeing the last full manifestation of a major part of the old South Africa.

The future didn't belong with the poor urban peasants who occupied the little boxes of brown brick strung along the sides of the road; it belonged to the black middle class which scarcely existed at this time, but which within ten years would make the running of South Africa impossible without them. The architects of apartheid were obsessed with the past: they couldn't understand that society would grow and expand to the point where even black people shared in the wealth, and where white people could no longer run things alone.

Diane and I had decided not to have a servant, on the grounds that this would mean taking advantage of the unfair economic stranglehold apartheid maintained on black people; until a tactful woman working for an impeccably liberal human rights organization, the Black Sash, explained patiently that the only way white people could put money into the black people's economy was to employ them. How else could blacks afford to educate their children, or improve their own conditions?

As a result we went to a 'servants wanted' noticeboard in a nearby shopping centre, and hired the first pleasant, well-dressed woman who came along. And because we wanted to put as much money as possible into the black people's economy, I offered her double the going rate. As a result the poor housekeeper thought we had no conception of the value of money, so she robbed us blind until we were forced to sack her.

After that we hired a gentle Tswana woman called Caroline, and were careful to raise her money at set intervals and pay her costs for her, rather than giving her a sudden increase. I kept in touch with her until her early death from cancer fifteen years later. One of her British employers, she told me, cut back her pay by a third. With such people around, it wasn't surprising that many white South Africans felt there was something deeply hypocritical about the attitude of Europeans towards their country.

According to the provisions of the Group Areas Act, which was a cornerstone of the apartheid system, Caroline was allowed to live with us but her husband and children were not. Women working for unsympathetic white families who enforced this were lucky to see their husbands and children more than three or four times a year. There were, nevertheless, very many white families, Afrikaans-speakers as well as English-speakers, who encouraged their servants to bring their families to live with them in defiance of the law, as we did. Liberal-minded people encouraged their children to play together, and so perhaps helped to prepare for the miracle which took place in 1994.

Even so, there were problems for black men and children living in white areas. Any neighbour or passer-by who saw them could be pretty certain that they were there illegally, and there were some who were prepared to inform on them to the police. Early one morning when Caroline's husband left our house for work he was picked up by the police and charged under the hated Pass Laws. Diane found out where he was due to appear in court, and waited there for hours while dozens of prisoners were fined or imprisoned. Eventually the magistrate and his clerk could no longer contain their curiosity at the presence of a white woman in the court, and asked her why she was there. When she told them, they pulled Caroline's husband out of the cells, dismissed the case, and released him on the spot.

South Africa was a strange place: the rule of law, and respect for the law, were paramount, and yet the laws themselves were wickedly perverse and wrong. Time and again while I was there political activists, black and white, were beaten to death by the police. I could never drive past the unexceptionally ugly complex of police buildings in Johannesburg called John Vorster Square without being reminded of the evil things that went on behind the barred windows there.

Nelson Mandela, who had been gaoled for life thirteen years before, was almost a forgotten man. In Soweto and the other townships you rarely saw his picture or heard his name: the young activists there were attracted to other, newer organizations like the Black Consciousness Movement, and the ANC seemed to them to be an old-fashioned irrelevance. Mandela's wife Winnie was however still a powerful image of the resistance to apartheid. She had been 'banned' and exiled to the remote town of Brandfort in the Orange Free State, where she spoke neither the language of the local whites nor that of the local blacks.

I decided I would like to interview her, and contacted her lawyer in Johannesburg. He explained that it was an offence under her banning order to make an arrangement to see her, or to meet her when she was with another person, since gatherings of three or more were forbidden to 'banned' people. In principle, he said, Winnie was interested in being interviewed by the international media, and felt that whatever punishment might be inflicted on her afterwards was worth it. I disliked the idea that she might be punished for speaking to me, and said so.

'I think you'll find she can put up with that,' said her lawyer, putting his fingers together judicially and grinning.

In the end I travelled to Brandfort with a team from BBC television news. It was a neat, white-painted, clean little town, pleasant to look at and terminally conventional: the kind of place where they only sell net curtains in order to give the inhabitants something to twitch aside when they spy on their neighbours. The lawyer had told us that every afternoon at around four o'clock Winnie Mandela drove her maroon Volkswagen Beetle from the black township where she lived to the post office in the centre of Brandfort to check her mail. We should, he said, call out to her from a distance and see if she would agree to be interviewed.

'What if she doesn't?' I asked, thinking of the long drive from Johannesburg to Brandfort.

'She will,' said the lawyer.

And she did. Her shiny maroon Beetle looked remarkably smart as she drove up and parked beside the dusty pick-up trucks of the local white farmers; and when she got out, she looked like a queen among the dowdy farmers' wives, her hair done up in a turban and her magnificent figure swathed in purple and red. She was already forty, but she looked at least ten years younger. The farmers' wives gathered disapprovingly to watch as I called out to her.

There was no real problem in my recording a radio interview, since her daughter Zinzie, who had driven up with her, stayed in the car and I stood with Winnie by the roadside: a gathering, therefore, of only two people. Even the terms of her banning order didn't make that an offence. Interviewing her for television was a little more difficult: the camera crew had to film her from the other side of the street. In the clear golden evening light she looked particularly regal, dismissing the restrictions to which she was subjected with an aristocratic hauteur which I found magnificent.

```
Transcript of interview for 13.00 Radio 4 News, 12.5.77

Speaker: Mrs Winnie Mandela (non-staff)

WM: These people mean nothing to me, and they can do
nothing to affect my struggle. They may be able to inflict
their conditions on me, but they cannot prevent me from
resisting them and their injustices. I have nothing but
contempt for them.
```

Nowadays Winnie Mandela cuts a very different figure: cruel, brutal, domineering. She has significant amounts of blood on her hands, and was the only prominent black leader who in the township troubles of the mid-1980s gave public approval and encouragement to 'necklacing': the practice of burning suspected police informers to death with flaming tyres. The years of separation from Nelson Mandela and the intense worship she attracted as 'the mother of the nation' seem to have eaten away at her character until all that was left of the old magnificence was just the contempt for her enemies and the flashing eyes. But then she seemed like a queen: the Mother of the Nation indeed. At the end we didn't shake hands, for fear of compromising her further. She turned away and walked into the post office, while the white farmers' wives clucked their teeth and watched her, and us, with intense dislike.

On the way back to Johannesburg we were arrested for speeding and taken to a nearby police station. Word had already filtered through that we had been interviewing Winnie, and the atmosphere was distinctly threatening. The desk sergeant, in particular, looked like a killer: SS blonde hair, a neck that flowed over his collar, and thick butcher's hands with fingers the size of pork sausages. Yet because we were kept there for so long the sergeant was gradually drawn into conversation with us.

'So you're from England,' he said in his heavy Free State accent. I nodded.

'Have you ever been to Canterbury Cathedral?'

I nodded again, but this time more curiously. What on earth could this monster know about Canterbury?

'My wife and I have always wanted to visit Canterbury Cathedral. It has the best mediaeval stained glass in the world. My wife and I make stained glass, and it is my greatest ambition to go to Canterbury and help with the restoration of the stained glass there.'

I thought I must be hallucinating. We talked about mediaeval reds and blues, the long-term effects of lead on glass, and the characters of Edward III and the Black Prince for some time, as though they were tactics in a rugby match or the finer details of the Immorality Act. Then the word came through from someone higher up that we could go. I shook the sergeant's hand, and winced at the strength of his grip.

'Be careful how you handle the glass when you get to Canterbury,' I said. He looked blank for a moment, then grinned slowly.

« »

One afternoon in September 1977 I came into the facilities house we used for television editing. I was late for a satellite feed.

'Have you heard?' asked the picture editor. He looked really nervous. 'They've killed Steve Biko.'

I had been long enough in South Africa not to need to ask who 'they' were. I shared his nervousness: if the security police could murder someone as prominent as Biko, they could murder anyone.

Over the next day or so the details began leaking out. Biko was being interrogated in the security police offices in the Sanlam Building in Port Elizabeth when he was fatally injured. The official version said he had lunged out at his questioners and struck his head. It became clear much later that one of the policemen had hit him on the forehead with a walkie-talkie, and had done irreparable damage to his brain. With extraordinary callousness, they loaded him into the back of an open truck and drove him for seven hours in the chill of a winter's night to the main prison in Pretoria. He was dead on arrival. In making the announcement, the justice minister, Jimmie Krüger, remarked smirkingly that Biko's death left him cold.

I had never managed to meet Steve Biko. I had made an appointment to see him, then cancelled it because an urgent news story came up. Before I could make another appointment he was arrested. He was certainly the most interesting black activist working in South Africa during my time, and his Black Consciousness movement was a new political departure. While it wasn't necessarily intended to be anti-white, it stressed that black people should work for their own liberation, without needing white support.

Biko was a highly intelligent and thoughtful man, whose white friends included the newspaper editor Donald Woods. Woods wrote a series of articles and then a book about Biko which presented him in a very favourable light. Some years later Woods' book was turned into a sentimentalized film by Sir Richard Attenborough, who cast an American as Biko rather than use any of the excellent black actors from South Africa itself, and effectively made Woods the hero of the story. Much as I liked Donald Woods, Biko was the real hero. And now he was dead.

The morning after the news came through I went to the small hut on a remote green hillside outside King William's Town where Steve Biko had lived. I was the only journalist his wife allowed inside. Steve had disliked most newspaper journalists, she said, but he had always listened to the BBC. She spoke so quietly I could scarcely hear her, as the cold rain lashed down on us in the doorway. The greenness, the rain and the poverty made it look like rural Ireland a century before. Biko's wife, quiet and gentle and unsophisticated, stood aside to let me enter.

The room was low and full of smoke from the fire. Biko's coffin lay open in front of it, resting on a table. His mother sat on another chair looking at his face and scarcely registering my presence. He was their star, witty, intelligent, educated: and now he was dead. I stood beside her, stooping slightly because of the low roof. The face was pale yellow and peaceful, almost smiling, in the light of the paraffin lamp. The once-expressive eyes were closed, the dreadful wound to the forehead swelled out above them. A group of women filed quietly into the room through another door and started singing a quiet dirge, but Biko's mother still paid no attention. No one called for vengeance, no one wept. Their loss was total. It outweighed every other emotion.

I was still there when it was time for the undertakers to nail down the heavy, carved coffin-lid of yellow wood, closing for ever on the face and the evidence of what had been done to him. The dull sounds of mallets filled the little smoky room; Biko's wife and mother continued to sit and watch in silence. Then a group of family and friends carried the coffin out into the rain and made their way over the green hillside to the burial ground. The scarves and coats of the choir flew in the sharp wind like flags as they followed, continuing their dirge from a distance.

The inquest on Steve Biko, held at the Old Synagogue court in Pretoria, was one of the most important events of my life. It seemed to me that no neutrality was possible, as the evidence came out all that week of the way in which the security police had taunted and tortured the helpless man chained up at their mercy. The interests they represented – apartheid power against black resistance – seemed less important to me than the vulnerability of a lone prisoner against the arrogance and force of his captors. When the court broke for lunch on the first day of the inquest I encouraged the photographers and cameramen to follow me to the room beside the courthouse where, I had discovered, the security police witnesses were being given lunch.

It was of no value to me professionally, since I was working for radio; I just felt a savage desire to get even with these men who had behaved with such cowardice and brutality. The photographers and cameramen waded in, getting their close-ups of the police thugs, and there was nothing anyone could do to stop us. They were gathered together outside the lunch-room, furious at being hunted down like this. Some had the ugliness of Hieronymus Bosch torturers; others had

pleasant, even features which showed nothing of the lives they lived
and the crimes they had committed.

The coroner who presided at the inquest was beyond contempt,
ultimately delivering a predictable and cowardly verdict in the face of
the evidence, while the weakness of the prison doctor who had ignored
Steve Biko's condition was disgusting. By contrast Sidney Kentridge,
the lawyer who had been hired by the Biko family, seemed to represent
all the moral qualities one most wanted to see displayed: anger and
the highest moral disapproval of the powers of the security police.

One by one the men who were involved in Biko's murder stood in
the witness box and were shrivelled by his scorn. But it was their
commanding officer, Colonel Goosen, craggy and clever, who provided
us with the defining moment of the inquest. Kentridge knew that
Goosen had overstepped even the unreasonably large authority which
the South African security police possessed by ordering that the dying
Biko should be chained for his long road journey to Pretoria, and he
pressed him again and again on the point.

'Where does it say in your statutes that you can keep a prisoner in
chains?'

'I have authority to do whatever is needed to ensure that a prisoner
doesn't escape.'

'But where does it say in your statutes that you can keep someone
in chains?'

Goosen twisted and turned for minutes on end, but even the little
coroner didn't protect him and he was finally obliged to answer.

'We don't operate according to statutes.'

There was utter silence in the courtroom. You could hear the cars
going past in the streets outside.

'Thank you, colonel,' said Kentridge. 'That is what we have always
suspected.'

The crowd of black people sitting at the back of the court erupted
in cheers, and my colleagues and I in the press box sat back and
grinned at each other. Something had been established here, an ineradi-
cable point had been made. Afterwards it seemed to me that Biko's
death, the outrage expressed across the world, and the revelations of
the inquest, marked the point at which the political tide turned in
South Africa. Plenty more prisoners were murdered by the security
police, and the mad system of creating homelands – 'Bantustans' –

continued as planned. There was no big public upheaval as a result of Biko's death, and the proceedings of the inquest weren't even particularly widely reported by the South African press.

And yet looking back years later it seems to me that the heart started to go out of the apartheid system after the inquest in the Old Synogogue court. The rule of law, which had so often been trodden underfoot during the apartheid years, had been shown to have an uncrushable force. For those of us who had come to love South Africa and had caught glimpses of a decency which underlay the arrogance of government and political power, it was a profoundly optimistic moment.

The inquest closed, and the lawyers and activists were shaking hands with each other in celebration of what had in effect been their victory, the juniors were collecting together their books and shuffling papers, and the journalists were comparing notes or chatting about the outcome. I looked across at Biko's wife. She was still sitting in the seat she had occupied throughout the four days the inquest had lasted, sometimes smiling politely when people spoke to her, but mostly just looking in front of her, her eyes on the splintered floorboards. What did she care about moral victories, famous cross-examinations, historic moments? She had lost the only thing that made life worth living.

« »

My reign as the BBC's sole correspondent in Southern Africa quickly came to an end. John Humphrys, who had been based in Washington and who was one of the two youngest foreign correspondents the BBC had ever had (I was the other, if you counted Dublin as a foreign posting), came to Johannesburg. We were almost the same age and it was a difficult moment for us both.

Humphrys denies it now, but he must have thought I was another dilettante who had had an unfairly easy path in life. His own background had certainly been a good deal less comfortable than mine, and he had left school early and gone into journalism in his native South Wales at a time when I was still at Cambridge. Once inside the BBC, though, I had had a rather harder time than he had. John had been singled out for success early on, and Washington had been his reward. He was often prickly, and sometimes downright irritable; so, often, was I. We ought to have disliked each other at first sight, and perhaps we did.

Still, life would have been very difficult if we had been at logger-heads, and both of us realized that. And anyway the more I got to know him the more I liked him. We shared various things: a remarkably similar sense of humour, and a dislike of the same kind of people both within the BBC and in South Africa. Twenty years later the friendship endures, if anything stronger than before. There have been all sorts of parallels in our lives, which helps. We are almost the same age, our hair went grey at around the same time, we began reading the *Nine O'Clock News* together, the low points in our careers and our eventual successes more or less coincided.

He is shorter than I am, and I am fatter than he is, but otherwise the only real difference between us nowadays seems to be that Humphrys is clearly much richer. From time to time people in the street still mistake him for me and me for him, while in the past our detractors called us the two grey men. That was nothing to what we called them.

The regular trips we both had to make to Rhodesia in 1977 and '78 reinforced this friendship. Together with the BBC camera crew, François Marais and Carol Clark, we used to cover most of the same events, staying in Meikles' Hotel in Salisbury. In the evening, when the day's reporting was finished, we would call for room service and play Kalabriasz, a card game which our colleague Michael Cole had taught François and which he had himself learned on the Golan Heights from some quick-minded Israeli soldier during the 1973 war. Our games stretched on for month after month, and the scores mounted into the tens of thousands.

Rhodesia was a strange but rather likeable society, a fragment of English outer suburbia circa 1928 which had been lured into a time-warp by some not very intelligent local politicians. Driving into Salis-bury was like coming across a little piece of Croydon which had been towed out to the African bush and left there. The streets were wide and dusty, with names like Baker Avenue and Jameson Street, and the shops still had those colonnades of cast-iron pillars which are one of the surest marks of British colonialism the world over.

It was fashionable to be snobbish about white Rhodesians and to quote the dreary little post-war saw about officers settling in Kenya and the other ranks in Rhodesia, but there was much greater freedom of spirit there than there was in South Africa, even when the bush war was at its height. There was also far less racial antagonism. The whites treated the blacks with a genial 1920s contempt, and the blacks treated the whites with an exaggerated 1920s respect.

The Rhodesia Front government simply wasn't up to the job, however. Its members had come to realize perfectly well that the bush war was unwinnable – they would talk to you about it frankly if you asked them – but having driven out the more sensible politicians who wanted to prepare white opinion for the certainty of change, they lacked the ability and perhaps the language to change course; until, that is, they were forced to. Everything that happened was always someone else's fault, and in the end they put the blame on the British Foreign Secretary Lord Carrington; whom they called 'Lord Carry-on-selling-the-white-man-down-the-river'. They were perfectly harmless, except to the people they governed: tens of thousands of people died in a completely unnecessary war, which brought to power one of the least attractive leaders in modern Africa, Robert Mugabe.

Few of us who were in Rhodesia to report on the war saw any actual fighting. The most that would usually happen was that we would be taken in ancient Mustang aircraft, some of the last which were still operational anywhere in the world, and flown to the site of some terrible small-scale massacre: a white farmer, his family and servants butchered, or the inhabitants of a black village too scared to help a band of ZANU lying eviscerated and burned among their huts. When the Rhodesian special forces carried out some act of savagery we would only hear about it days later, and would almost never be allowed anywhere near it.

Nevertheless I came to know several members of the two main special forces regiments, the Selous Scouts and Grey's Scouts, and was always rather impressed by the quality of the men and by the general truthfulness of the stories they told me. Both regiments certainly carried out actions which, if committed by ZANU, would have been condemned by the Rhodesian government as atrocities. They were fully integrated across the colour-line, and extremely well trained.

Most Rhodesians listened to and trusted the BBC, even though Harold Wilson, as prime minister, had tried to force the BBC to broadcast anti-Rhodesian propaganda. Nevertheless the Rhodesia Front government carried out a campaign against the BBC, and the Dracula-like information minister, P. J. Van Der Byl, managed to give many white Rhodesians the impression that BBC reporters put coins in rubbish containers and filmed black children digging them out. Many of them also believed after something he said that the BBC had shown pictures of black workers taking an afternoon nap in Cecil Square in the middle of Salisbury, and had reported that they had been shot by the police. Neither was true, of course, but interestingly they are allegations which surface again and again in completely different parts of the world; though nowadays the culprits are usually said to be Italian or French reporters.

In fact there was remarkably little anti-British feeling, though a good deal of contempt existed for what the Rhodesians believed the British had become. Towards the end of 1977 I made an expedition of very questionable safety along Rhodesia's border with Mozambique, driving a beautiful yellow Land-Rover armoured against land mines. There had been a great many deaths from mines in this part of Rhodesia. I stayed at a stunning little hotel in the clear cool air of the Chimanimani Mountains, and was the first guest there for several months. The owner had kept the place going because, she told me, she couldn't bear to sack the staff. Each night when I had dinner, two magnificent characters in white uniforms crossed with red sashes and wearing fezes did everything except put the food into my mouth and turn the pages of the book that was propped up in front of me.

At the owner's suggestion I went to spend a couple of nights with a nearby farmer; 'nearby' meaning about seventy miles away. His wife was charming and very welcoming, even though I had only managed to find a bottle of Rhodesian wine as a gift, but the farmer himself was inclined to fall into gloomy reveries about the decay in British values since the war. These seemed mostly to be directed at me: perhaps he thought his wife was being a little too welcoming. The next day the farmer drove me in his old car, armoured only by its coating and mud and rust, along the wire fence which marked the Mozambican border, complaining all the way about the welfare state in Britain and the degeneration of the national character which had resulted.

'Driving a bloody stupid yellow Land-Rover all this way,' he said. It became clear that I personally represented the degeneration. 'What on earth did you think you were doing? Armoured? That wouldn't do

Above left: My father, Roy Simpson, at the time we went to Casablanca in 1962.

Above right: My mother and me in 1946, shortly after finding him impossible.

Left: The house at Dunwich, nerve-wracking and magical.

Below left: Me at the age of six, wearing my homing-beacon school tie.

Below: Brian Brooks, when he first came into our lives.

Cambridge companions: John Argent, Prince Richard of Gloucester, Simon Platt, me, Bernard Hunt, Andrew Holmes, Nicholas Snowman, Jeremy Griggs, John Thompson, Michael Binyon, Ridley Burnet.

The BBC Radio newsroom shortly before I began my sentence. Perhaps the sub-editor, centre, is dreaming of freedom.

With Diane, Eleanor and Julia in California, 1973.

The Provisional IRA gives a press conference at an hotel in Dalkey, south of Dublin, July 1973. Left to right: me, Gerry O'Hare of the Belfast Brigade, Daithi O Conail, Eamonn Mac Thomais of Sinn Fein. A Dublin newspaper included me in this photograph when it was published, partly in order to excuse its own presence there (the press conference was illegal under Irish law), and partly to get the BBC into trouble with the Irish authorities. It worked on both counts.

Ayatollah Khomeini lands in Tehran, 1979. The BBC had told me not to accompany him; but how often do you catch a charter flight to a revolution?

Colonel Gadhafi during our interview in his tent in 1979. We edited out his manic laughter, but you can still detect the ghost of a smile.

Above: Andrei Sakharov and his wife, Yelena Bonner, after our interview in 1978. The Russians wouldn't let me back for a long time afterwards, but just taking this photograph made it worthwhile.

Left: Publicity photographs from 1981 of John Humphrys and me on the *Nine O'Clock News* set. It looks almost as sophisticated as Albanian TV.

Chancellor Helmut Kohl takes a direct hit from an egg. I am just out of shot, both in camera and egg terms.

Tira Shubart at the time I first met her.

Margaret Thatcher in full flow during one of our interviews.

Mikhail Gorbachev ditto, in Dubrovnik, 1988 with Raisa by his shoulders.
The cameraman, Ray Gibbon, managed to keep the picture steady and in focus,
despite being wrestled round the neck by a KGB man throughout the entire
course of the interview. The Gorbachevs appeared not to find this strange.

Peter Jouvenal and Chris Hooke in Afghan gear during our expedition in 1989. They are rescuing packets of American army rations which the mujaheddin, not appreciating pork and beans, had used to fill in a hole in the road.

At our safe house in Kabul, two Harakat-e-Islami bomb-makers assembling the rocket which they fired at the secret police headquarters an hour or so later. Predictably, it missed.

Tiananmen Square on the night of the massacre on 4 June 1989: the crowd is attacking an armoured personnel carrier. These are not students, who remained entirely non-violent; they are ordinary people who took the opportunity that night to hit back at the system which had brutalized them for fifty years.

you any good, sonny. They put mines all along here. If I get killed or get my legs blown off, at least it's cheap. You'll get just as dead in that silly yellow contraption—'

'And it'll be no good running to you for help?'

He gave me a sour look. 'No guts nowadays, the British.'

I let him rave on. Ahead of me in the red earth of the dirt road I had spotted something. It was coming towards us very fast: a little tamped-down mound in the crown of the road, with something circular almost visible in the heart of it.

'Complain about everything. Chicken, that's their trouble.'

We were so close I could see the finger-marks in the tamped-down red earth. Also the metal ring, a few inches across, just visible at the top.

'No bloody backbone. Frightened of their own shadows. Look at 'em—'

Should I shout out to him? He wasn't looking at the road ahead, he was glaring angrily at the wire fence. But suppose I shouted and it wasn't a mine at all? He'd never forget it. To my shame and horror, I didn't have the courage to ask him to stop. No bloody backbone, I suppose.

'—pasty-faced and feeble. All this television and sex.'

I gritted my teeth and shut my eyes. The front off-side wheel hit something hard, and then the back off-side wheel went over it as well, and then we were past it. The sun still shone, the birds still shouted at us from the thorn-bushes, the car still jolted over the uneven red road.

'Socialist government, that's what's done it. Hasn't worked. Big Brother Is Watching You.'

I nodded weakly. What did I care now?

'And you BBC people are the most feeble of the lot.'

He was right: I was too feeble even now to tell him we had driven over a land mine, in case it turned out not to be one.

'Bloody pathetic BBC type,' I could imagine him saying. 'Wetted his pants because he thought a bump in the road was a mine.'

And all the other bronzed, sun-wrinkled, hairy-armed Rhodies would roar over their pints, and shake their heads with pleasure.

« »

The South African Broadcasting Corporation was structured originally along BBC lines, but by the mid-1970s it had become an embarrassing stooge of the government and the apartheid system. Nothing that might upset the National Party was allowed on the airwaves, and each morning Radio South Africa broadcast an editorial reflecting the latest bee in the government's bonnet. It wouldn't have been so bad if the newsreaders and announcers hadn't all sounded as though they came from the BBC: it gave the junk they read out a kind of verisimilitude which would otherwise have been lacking.

One of the leading television newsreaders actually was from the BBC: Michael De Morgan, a genial character for whom I had once written radio news summaries at Broadcasting House, had made the degrading move from freedom to intense control. Later, indeed, De Morgan came back to London as head of the press department at the South African embassy, with the job of deciding which British journalists were 'objective' enough to be allowed to travel to South Africa to report on the country's affairs.

This business of objectivity was very important to the SABC and its political masters; and like so many people and governments who use the word, they meant 'favourable to us'. The thought police of the National Party didn't demand a ringing endorsement from the foreign broadcasters who worked there, but anything which showed an aspect of South African life which was inconvenient to the authorities was regarded as lacking in objectivity. One foreign television correspondent, cleverer and perhaps less scrupulous than others, realized that the judgement which really counted was made in Pretoria on the basis of transcripts sent back by the embassy in London. In other words, the decision about a television correspondent's merits was taken merely on the basis of his or her words, not on the pictures contained in the report.

This particular correspondent, when dealing with the trouble that was erupting in the townships (which, incidentally, he scarcely ever visited at times of violence) learned to put an elaborate commentary over the action of the crowds – 'They picked up stones and threw them at the police, while some of the more militant threw petrol bombs' – but said nothing at all over the shocking pictures of the police using whips and sometimes guns on demonstrators who were mostly unarmed; merely introducing this sequence with a brief sentence like 'Then the police moved in.'

He was right, in a way: good television pictures don't require a commentary. But this wasn't a matter of style, so much as tactics. I suppose one should praise him for his cunning and quick-mindedness, but somehow it all seemed just a little too calculating: he was sleeping with the enemy.

There was one senior figure at the SABC who was a continual trouble to me. I'll call him Kosie, for reasons which anyone who understands Afrikaans will understand. Kosie was a heavily built, slack-featured character who seemed to have a particular dislike for the BBC. He listened regularly to my broadcasts, and would complain to me about the expressions I used or the facts I chose to report. He also regarded me as having responsibility for the failings (or, as I often thought, the virtues) of BBC programmes about South Africa, and would haul me in to lecture me about my, or the Corporation's, lack of objectivity. At first I thought it was my unpleasant duty to listen to his lectures about a quality he clearly didn't understand; but at last I decided to fight back.

Kosie was sitting back in his chair as I was shown in, and a couple of grim-faced characters sat to the right and left of him. A rather small, low chair had been placed in front of them. I sat down. Kosie started his usual list of complaints: I wasn't objective in my reporting, and had been unflattering about the creation of one of the new Bantustans. He especially disliked my use of the word 'Bantustan', which was unobjective. Then, he said, clearing his throat, there was the matter of a recent *Panorama* about South Africa, much of which had been filmed without official permission. As a result of this, my own position as BBC correspondent would have to be reconsidered.

In the normal way I would, I suppose, have reacted angrily. This, though, seemed altogether too sensitive a moment. Instead, I tried a tactic I had sometimes thought of but had never yet employed.

'Sorry, Kosie,' I said, smiling with obvious falsity, 'but I think I'm going to have to make a report about all this. Tell me again what you didn't like about my reporting.'

Poor old Kosie: he wasn't very articulate in English, and to have to go back on what he had said ten minutes earlier was a trial for him. Especially when I kept interrupting to ask him to repeat himself.

I suppose I was remembering Stephen Potter's *OneUpManship*: 'Break the flow.' It certainly worked. By the end of the hearing Kosie came close to apologizing to me for not being able to remember the precise words he had used earlier.

My position wasn't reconsidered after all. Instead, after only a year, the BBC offered me Martin Bell's job as diplomatic correspondent for television news in London; Martin was going to be the Washington correspondent. I left South Africa, and radio news, with a considerable amount of regret and nostalgia, and took up the job which I have done, essentially, ever since. We packed up our furniture, our books, our cat and our car all over again, and one March morning we drove to Jan Smuts airport and got onto the plane for London. As the plane lifted off, I felt a wholly spontaneous sigh of relief welling up inside me: I had got the family out unscathed, and had escaped alive and well myself.

Ten years later, in 1988, I went back to South Africa to fill in over Christmas. John Birt, who was then the BBC's newly appointed head of news and current affairs and was shortly to become director-general, came out to see the BBC operation there and to visit the SABC. I went with him. Kosie stood up to greet us; he had always sat for me a decade earlier. His face sagged even more with worry. Times were changing in South Africa, and those like Kosie with the wit to see which way the wind was blowing were getting nervous about their jobs.

'Tell us, Mr Birt,' he said. 'We know we aren't doing things right here, but we need to know how we can do better.'

I had the words all ready. 'You could start by trying to be a bit objective, Kosie old pal. Remember "objective"? Remember how you sat me down in this office and lectured me about it?'

I didn't, of course. Kosie was too broken down, too depressed. And what would be the point, anyway? A man like that wouldn't know objectivity if he trod in it. And so I smiled sympathetically and nodded, and let John Birt read him the objectivity lecture instead. It was enough of a revenge to watch Kosie writhe.

It would be nice to think that all this died out when power changed hands in South Africa. It didn't. The SABC is still the voice of the South African government; it's just that the government has changed.

'There has been widespread condemnation of the crimes of Winnie Madikadzele-Mandela, the former wife of South Africa's adored leader Nelson Mandela,' intoned a report I heard recently.

At the SABC, the spirit of Kosie lives on.

8

Dissidents

IT WASN'T AS GOOD to be back home as I'd expected. There was a perceptible gloom about the Britain of 1978; it was ruled by a government which had lost its way, and was being fought over by different economic interest groups. After the wide skies of southern Africa, I felt shut in again by the low cloud levels of home.

And yet with hindsight Britain was a gentler, easier, less violent place than it was soon to become. The newspapers might have their political agendas, but the *Sun* wasn't yet owned by the Murdoch group, and there was less savagery of opinion and less intrusion into private life than there is today. We didn't realize it, but we were living in the last days of the Welfare State as it had been constituted after 1945. Almost everyone except a tiny group on the right wing of the Conservative Party still believed that society could and should bear the burden of poverty and illness. No one had yet invented that most cynical of 1980s catch-phrases, 'care in the community'. The weakest and most vulnerable people still lived in homes and hospitals. There were virtually no beggars, and no one slept in cardboard boxes in doorways and underpasses. Britain's industrial base was almost double what it was to become. We thought rising crime was a problem, not realizing how lucky we were.

Like 1966, when I started at the BBC, 1978 was the prelude to another period of sudden, immense change. Within a year Margaret Thatcher was in power, and the big switch from manufacturing to service industries, from public ownership to private ownership, from high income tax to high indirect tax, from public to private, from union strength to employer strength had started. Soon we would have yuppies and the Big Bang and Channel Four and mobile phones and computers and faxes and electronic devices of all kinds.

But not quite yet. BBC television, when I arrived there, still firmly based itself on paper. The offices rang with the sound of typewriters, the in-trays were loaded high with letters and memos. If I wrote an article for a newspaper or magazine I had to drive across London to deliver it in person: it was either that or posting it.

As for television news, it was still in the film age. Electronic cameras existed – I had first seen one in Luxembourg in 1976, the huge recorder lugged around by an unfortunate character bowed under its weight – but the BBC's first experiment with electronic news gathering would not take place for another year. For the time being we were still restricted to rolls of film that lasted less than twenty minutes and were highly vulnerable to the vagaries of local processing: which could, if it wasn't done properly, make every face green or purple, or deliver scratches lasting the full length of the film.

It was possible to send reports back to London by satellite, but the cost was so high that we did it only on the most important occasions. Otherwise we would tape the film up in one of those familiar round cans, and find a 'pigeon': an airline passenger who was prepared to hand-carry the parcel and deliver it to someone from the BBC at the airport in London. The late seventies was a time of aircraft hijackings and bombings, so finding pigeons was difficult.

'This is undeveloped film, so you mustn't open it or let anyone from security open it,' you had to tell them. They didn't like that part at all. Nor did the security people.

Because it had to be shipped, film from anywhere outside Europe usually reached London the day after it had been shot. So a television news bulletin was a curious hybrid: the domestic news would be today's, but the foreign news would mostly be yesterday's, dressed up carefully to make it seem like today's.

I much preferred the atmosphere at Television Centre: there was far less of the backbiting I had grown so used to in Radio. At the morning meetings an editor might say, 'I led with the political story last night, but with hindsight I think I ought to have led on Europe.' In Radio no one would have dreamed of showing such weakness; the editors there went to their morning meetings armed with telexes and memos proving that he or she had been right, and everything that had gone wrong had been someone else's fault.

And yet it was a bad time at Television News. We knew instinctively when a big story occurred that we would come out second best to ITN. We were slower-moving and seemed to have much less competitive edge. Worse, our morale had been shot to pieces by two disasters in the mid-seventies. In 1974, when the Turks were about to invade Cyprus, the journalists were all certain that the main attack would come by sea. At a given moment everyone headed off in a convoy down to the coast. Part of the way along the road ITN's car broke down. As the ITN team sat disconsolately by their car, they heard a droning sound above them, and soon the air was thick with Turkish aircraft, dropping paratroopers. The invasion wasn't coming by sea at all, and the main landing-area was close to the spot where the ITN car had broken down. So they had the pictures. And since they were close to the television station they were able to satellite their reports every evening. The BBC, caught behind Turkish lines, had to send their pictures by sea. They always arrived too late for that night's news bulletin.

The following year, when the Americans staged their chaotic withdrawal from Saigon, the ITN reporter and crew were flown out on a US helicopter. The BBC reporter and his crew were split up by a ferocious American master-sergeant, who made the crew catch another helicopter. The BBC reporter was flown to a US aircraft carrier which went to Hong Kong; his crew were taken to Singapore. In these days of swift communications and easy access to news agency pictures there would be no real problem: the reporter would simply be told by the desk in London what the available pictures showed, and would send his script through by satellite telephone. But in the days of film you had to have your own pictures or you had nothing; and if you weren't with the cameraman you had no real idea what pictures to write to.

These twin disasters, in 1974 and 75, set a gloomy tone for the rest of the decade. We knew that ITN was better managed, and we suspected that the quality of the staff was higher. ITN had always tended to hire rather grand men and women to appear on screen: characters in their own right, raffish, experienced. Sandy Gall, Reginald Bosanquet, Julian Havilland, the novelists Gerald Seymour and Geoffrey Archer, the founder of the new *Spectator* Alexander

Chancellor, and so on: they seemed distinctly superior to us. They also seemed to have much more money to spend on their news coverage. During the revolution in Iran in 1978 and '79 I was forbidden to hire a translator, and the crew and I stumbled round in ignorance of the complex events happening in front of our eyes. The ITN team had two translators, and a hotel suite to work from.

The BBC certainly wasn't a force in international television news in those days. Its name was known because of its record during the Second World War, but we were merely local players. It was the Americans who dominated everything. ABC, NBC and CBS broadcast very little international news in their programmes, even then; but they had vast amounts of money to spend, and they all worked on the premise that they had to have pictures of every important event. Producers and reporters could be peremptorily sacked for missing a news event which the other networks had covered, even if none of the networks actually broadcast anything about it. So all the networks covered everything, just in case. The BBC was in alliance with NBC, but it didn't help us much in the field. It was too expensive and difficult to copy their film, and the Americans used a different technical system from ours anyway.

Altogether, then, BBC Television News, small, poorly funded, low in morale, was very far from being a first-rate organization. The best things about it were its technical staff, its camera crews, and its output editors – 'assistant editors', in Beeb-speak, who were in day-to-day charge of its news bulletins. They were highly intelligent and well-educated, and often possessed precisely the kind of character and idiosyncrasy which ITN's reporters displayed.

One wore a black eye-patch and was famous for his caustic wit. Another was an academic who regarded his television work as a kind of absurd hobby. A third always wore a kind of uniform – white shirt, black pullover, black tie – because he said he had so many choices to make during the day that he didn't want to make extra ones in the morning. A fourth was a well-known novelist, admired by Graham Greene. Yet because these men didn't appear on screen, their abilities and intellect scarcely showed in our output. For the most part we were frumpy and unsuccessful. We regularly came second in a field of two, and we knew it.

« »

I went through the gates at Television Centre on the morning of 28 March 1978 with a certain nervousness. This was not my world: I had only been in the place a few times before, and had always been uncomfortable. For a start, I had been used in the past to the busy streets, the wide range of restaurants and the intriguing shops of the area round Oxford Circus. White City was a desert. 'The nearest London gets to East Berlin,' Michael Cole, one of my new colleagues, said sardonically the day I arrived, 'only here there's a significant crime rate.'

I also disliked the self-regard of television, and the notion that Television Centre was somehow the centre of the universe. So although I badly wanted the job of television diplomatic correspondent I wasn't altogether looking forward to working in this new atmosphere.

Not without justification. A couple of years before, I had applied for the job of television reporter and was summoned to a selection board in the editor's office. This editor was an extraordinary character, brilliant and dissolute. Dark-faced, detested by most of his staff, he peered suspiciously out at the world through thick tinted glasses. He found it hard to disguise the contempt he felt for the people he managed. Altogether he was much too much of an outsider, and perhaps too clever, for a straight organization like television news.

Clever – and weird. A year or so earlier a uniformed commissionaire was standing at the main gates which I had just entered when a shot echoed round the forecourt of Television Centre and he was hit by something which turned out to be a pellet from an airgun. Over the next few weeks more pellets were fired at the commissionaires. Eventually the shots were traced. They came from the office of the editor of television news. There was an embarrassing meeting, and the editor was asked not to bring his air rifle to work with him any more. He agreed.

But he wasn't warned to give up being weird. At my selection board there were five or six people sitting round his large office, waiting to interview me, but the editor himself didn't seem to be there. His big chair was turned away from me, and it was only gradually that I realized he was sitting in it, looking out of the window from which he had done his Lee Harvey Oswald impression.

One by one the others asked me questions, but they all seemed nervous and constrained. Finally the man from Personnel asked the editor if he had any questions for me. From the depths of his chair, still turned away from me, there came the sound of a large raspberry.

'Well,' I said, 'I think I can probably guess the meaning of that.'

'No, no, no,' said the man from Personnel earnestly, 'he's done that to every candidate this morning.'

I still didn't get the job.

Things got worse. He turned up at the flat from which we were filming the siege of a building in London which a group of IRA men had taken over. He was drunk, and insulted the owner. She turned out to have loaned the place to the BBC for nothing because she was related to someone on the Board of Governors. We had a new editor by the following morning.

And now I was working for Television News after all. As diplomatic correspondent, I was determined to widen out the job from merely covering the Foreign Office beat. I wanted to become in effect the foreign affairs correspondent, travelling everywhere I could. There was a great deal of travelling to be done.

Radio News had almost all the foreign correspondents' posts. Television News, by contrast, had traditionally had only three: Washington, the Middle East and Hong Kong. Now it also had John Humphrys in Johannesburg, but the rest of the world was largely uncovered. The acting foreign editor was a reporter who had once been demoted for driving his car at another BBC commissionaire and breaking his leg; commissionaires had had a rough time of it from my new department.

Three years earlier, when I left Ireland, I had been to only six countries in my life. Being based in Brussels and Johannesburg had enabled me to extend the list considerably, but there were still vast areas of the globe I knew nothing about. Now, though, that changed. Within three months I had visited three continents, interviewed a dozen presidents and prime ministers, and worn out an almost new passport. At last I was doing what I had always wanted.

As I started work at Television Centre May Day was only a few weeks away, and I was determined to use the occasion to visit Moscow to report on the celebrations. The Soviet Union was a difficult place to operate in, and Television News had never sent a correspondent there; but I persuaded the assistant editors that it would be worth it. I had to go alone, since the Soviet authorities refused to allow the BBC to send in a camera crew.

Now that the Soviet Union no longer exists, it is tempting to be nostalgic about it. Life may have been restrictive and sometimes cruel, but at least things worked and Russians felt proud of their society and what it had achieved. In 1978, though, it was still very much the KGB state. Any suggestion of dissent was dealt with harshly, and the labour camps did good business. Leonid Brezhnev was moving in and out of the early stages of senile dementia, and later these years would come to be known as the Period of Stagnation.

Yet internationally the Soviet Union was more successful than it had been for years. It had effectively taken over Angola, Somalia and Ethiopia, and seemed to be threatening Zaire. Soon it would invade Afghanistan. Only thirteen years later the entire Soviet system would have collapsed into ashes, but the possibility that this might happen hadn't occurred to anyone in 1978, except perhaps a handful of anti-Communist fanatics. The rest of us assumed the Soviet Union was there to stay.

There were few passengers on board the four-hour Aeroflot flight from London, and we were not made to feel at home. A stumpy stewardess marched down the aisle offering glasses of water. I asked if we would also be getting a meal.

'*Ne mozhne*,' she said crossly: not possible.

Then she headed off to the middle of the plane and shut the red curtains which sheltered the cabin crew from the vulgar gaze of the passengers. A party began in there. You could hear laughter and the clink of glasses; but when one of the stewardesses opened the curtains and plodded down the aisle to the lavatory her face was stern and none of us met her gaze.

Everything about travelling to Moscow was inclined to make you feel like an enemy. Even on the plane I felt that I was deeply mistrusted: at best a bourgeois reactionary, at worst a rightist deviationist, a Trots-kyist or a saboteur. It got worse when we arrived at Sheremetyevo airport, which was then brand new but already showed signs of the all-pervading seediness which we then thought of as Soviet and only slowly came to realize was eternally Russian.

I lined up meekly in front of the passport control, and watched the passengers ahead of me being examined. The hall itself was dark, but from each of the booths where young KGB soldiers examined people's passports a bright light shone out onto these infiltrators who were trying to enter the Socialist Motherland. When it was my turn I stood in front of a spotty seventeen-year-old with eyes like grey pebbles. There was a height gauge on the window so that he could check I was really 1.88 metres, as my visa said, and it took him some time to make sure that the colour of my eyes (he looked at each individually) was correct as stated. Behind and above me was a mirror set at an angle, so he could see if I were standing on tiptoe or going bald or smuggling in someone else at knee-level. It took him a long time to decide that everything about me was really all right, and he stamped my visa with an air of regret.

I picked my suitcase off the creaking carousel and moved on to customs. I was more than a little nervous now: a friend of mine in London had suggested that I should bring with me the latest volume of Alexander Solzhenitsyn's *The Gulag Archipelago* in English, because someone would be bound to want it. Back in London it had seemed like an act of solidarity with the dissidents and human rights campaigners; here, it seemed like dangerous folly. Ahead of me in the queue was a small, dark man who spoke English with a German accent and seemed particularly nervous. The customs officer pointed peremptorily to a table, and the man lifted up his suitcase and opened it.

The customs officer rooted around inside it, jumbling the neatly folded clothes, pulling out things at random, leafing carefully through books. Then, with a grunt of triumph, he unearthed some kind of Jewish insignia from under a pile of shirts. I could see Hebrew characters embroidered on it. He called out, and two big thugs came out of a side office at a run and grabbed the small, dark owner of the suitcase. They took him off and in full view of all of us they told him to strip to his underwear. I called out to ask him if he was all right.

'I hope so,' he called back. And eventually, after going through everything he had, they let him go; but they kept the insignia.

Then it was my turn. The customs officer beckoned me forward. I thought of the Solzhenitsyn book, feebly camouflaged inside the dust cover of another book. The customs man only had to speak English to see what it really was. He pulled out all my books and riffled through them. Solzhenitsyn was the last one. It had a map of the Soviet Union in its end papers. The customs man saw it and looked at me.

'Russian history,' I explained, with a frank, encouraging, innocent smile. Put it down, you stupid bastard, I thought.

He put it down. Then, dismissively, he waved me on.

In the car on the way to town, I tried to come to terms with this extraordinary place. Even in the bright summer sunshine it looked crude and forbidding. Enormous trucks ground their way along the potholed roads, emitting black smoke. The apartment blocks of brown brick were huge and undifferentiated, the shops carried no name other than their function: 'Clothes', 'Restaurant', and – a cruel Stalinist joke, this, considering how little the food shops contained, – 'Gastronome'. There was nothing in most of the shop windows except placards in big Cyrillic lettering. All the fine detail, all the decoration, all the attraction of existence seemed to have been stripped away here: it was '*1984*' in real life. Over the years that followed I came to love and sympathize with Russia, and to understand more about the reasons why it had become what it was; but this first sight of it was gloomy and deeply depressing.

The block of flats where the BBC radio correspondent lived was depressing too. It was blocked off by barriers and had a permanent two-man guard on it, both to watch the inhabitants and to ensure that no Russians came in to see them. This was a little enclave of foreigners, and although every door in the building creaked, the staircases stank of cats and the lifts were dangerous, the flats were large and pleasant enough inside. Everyone explained that the block had been built by German prisoners of war, which in Moscow meant 'properly constructed'. This would be my home for the next few weeks: the correspondent had offered to put me up.

He was nervy and rather excited. Not long before he had been rung by a young woman who was desperate to meet him. Contacts like these were very tricky in the Soviet Union. The authorities would have listened to the call (if, that is, they hadn't instigated it in the first place) and were capable of staking out the meeting place and arresting you both. And if they didn't, you would wonder why not. Anyway, he had met the young woman, and they hadn't been arrested. She had heard, she said, that he was a Catholic, and she was keen on Catholicism. Oh yes, and she thought he might be interested: her father was the secretary of the Soviet Presidium.

The correspondent wasn't so much interested as horrified. Being secretary of the Presidium was the equivalent of being Cabinet secretary in Britain, and talking to his daughter could easily be made to look like espionage. But she was attractive, and the correspondent had a warm and susceptible heart. He listened, and they met again and again. She always had something interesting to tell him, but it was hard, if not impossible, to use her information. Today, for instance, she had met him somewhere and they had gone for a walk (there were no coffee-shops or fast-food restaurants in Moscow in those days). She was, he said, entirely artless: or that's how she seemed.

'My father told me last night that Brezhnev and Kosygin had a great row at yesterday's Presidium meeting – something about agriculture, I think – and Brezhnev stormed out. What do you think it means?'

That was what the correspondent wanted to know. Was this girl being instructed to tell him these things as a provocation, so that he could be thrown out if he used them in a report, or was someone inside the Kremlin trying to pass on details about high politics so that the West would understand the Soviet Union better? Anyway, there was nothing he could do about it. This material was too good to be usable. The first thing anyone would ask him was, how had he heard it; and if he tried to check the information through the forbidding press liaison department, he would never get an answer.

Some days before, she had told him that Brezhnev's car was racing along the central lane in one of the main Moscow streets (these lanes were reserved solely for Party bosses), when a policeman, newly equipped with a radar baton for checking speed, idly thought he would test it out and pointed at the Zil. An instant later one of Brezhnev's bodyguards, thinking the radar baton was a gun, leant out of a follow-up car and shot the policeman dead. It was no use: the correspondent couldn't get official confirmation of that, either.

Something occurred to me, and I asked him when this girl had first got in touch with him. When he told me, I did a quick mental calculation: it was four days after a lunch I had had with the press attaché at the Soviet embassy in London. Antonov was a sharp, cynical character whom I had nevertheless got on with rather well. It was always said he was a senior figure in the KGB. He liked to go for lunch to a Singapore Chinese restaurant in Holland Park Avenue, close to the embassy: there were large recessed booths there, rather than normal open tables at which one could be overheard.

A colleague of mine was also invited to the lunch, and Antonov asked him about the correspondent's wife: he had heard their marriage was going through a tricky patch, he said. The foreign editor answered that the couple had now split up, and she had gone back to London. I kicked him sharply under the table. The press attaché said he was sorry, and we started talking about something else.

'So do you think they set this girl onto you as a result?' I asked the correspondent.

'Certain of it,' he said.

(Later I took a dreadful revenge on poor Antonov, for having taken my hospitality at lunch and used it against the BBC. I filled his name in for a wide and enjoyable range of postal nuisances, from applications for competing insurance companies to complete ten-volume *Reader's Digest* collections of great orchestral renditions from the 1930s, 40s and 50s. And then, as time went on and there was no comeback, I grew more adventurous. I started sending him rubber incontinence pants and crutchless undies and subscriptions to sado-masochistic magazines, and finished up with a series of penis-enlargers of startling proportions. Eventually Antonov was recalled to Moscow. I used to imagine knocking on his door and asking him as he stood there, his legs slightly apart, Burt Bacharach playing in the background, how he enjoyed his leatherette thongs with leopardskin trim. But of course the ultimate satisfaction of letting him know who was responsible for his persecution was barred to me; as I was to find in Prague later, Communist secret policemen had nasty ways of getting back at people who had irritated them.)

Moscow was the kind of place where you always felt you were being followed by the KGB. Once I walked up the hill towards Dzerzhinskiy Square and the ochre yellow 1890s building which dominated it: the Lubyanka. This was the KGB's headquarters, and in the past it had been one of the most dangerous places in Russia. Even now, I noticed, people crossed the street rather than walk alongside it. The BBC stills library contained no photograph of the Lubyanka, and I was determined to take one. But I was very nervous. To stand in the street and point a camera at it was to invite arrest as a spy. Instead I decided to go into a nasty-looking little café on the other side of the square, eat something, and then take a picture as I came through the doors on my way out.

The food was terrible. Everybody stared at me as I shuffled along the counter with my tray, trying to select something that looked halfway edible. Finally I chose some sausage and a kind of rissole. The sausage was full of fat and gristle, and a horrid colourless juice ran out of it as I ate it. The rissole was so disgusting I prefer not to think about it. One or the other of them (the BBC doctor later thought the sausage, but he hadn't tasted the rissole) gave me worms. I left the larger part of both on my metal plate and blundered out with everyone watching me. In a kind of panic, my body shielding what I was doing from the other customers, I pulled out the camera, aimed it roughly at the Lubyanka fifty yards away, and pressed the shutter a couple of times. One shot cut off the entire east wing; the other was on a slant, but captured the whole thing. Back at the BBC they tut-tutted a little over the angle but cropped the picture and used it for years afterwards. So in the long run even the worms were worthwhile.

If the KGB wanted you to know they were there, they let you know. As I got to know the city better, taking the Metro to random destinations and wandering around, I was occasionally aware that I had seen the same face or hat or open-necked shirt before. Once or twice it turned out to be someone who wanted to change money illegally or try out his English. More often it was the KGB.

The correspondent's contacts with the dissident movement were excellent, which was why the Soviet authorities were so anxious to trap him. Almost every day he would slip out and meet someone, and would come back with his briefcase full of documents. One day he told me he thought he had a buyer for my copy of *The Gulag Archipelago*.

'I didn't bring it with me to sell,' I said.

'Don't worry, this man hasn't got any money anyway. He'll just want to give you something in exchange for it. And you've got to listen to his story.'

That evening, when we hoped the watchers had gone to bed, we slipped out of the building. The guard on the gate saluted politely, then made a surreptitious note in a book. There were few cars in the streets by now, but although the sun had finally gone down there were still plenty of people strolling along. We walked a little way to one of those lovely nineteenth-century avenues of which there are so many in Moscow, where the road runs in two lanes on either side of a long narrow park. Here, in the light from the early summer sky and the street lamps overhead, people were still playing games of chess or kissing on the park benches. It was warm, and the pollen from the lime trees fell like summer snow.

'There he is,' the correspondent said.

I couldn't really have missed him: a tall, thin, haggard man with a face which was noticeably pale, even in this light. He wore a ragged suit.

'Looks like a child molester.'

'You may not be altogether wrong,' the correspondent said. 'Ask him – he'll tell you.'

We shook hands. His grip was bony, and I was shocked to see how deep-set his eyes were. He had a curious twitch, which affected his face muscles and seemed to travel down to his left shoulder. We went over to a section of the park where the lights weren't working, and sat down on a bench.

'Did you bring it?' he asked, almost greedily.

I pulled the Solzhenitsyn out of my pocket, and he pulled it away from me with his bony claw and checked through it. Then he nodded.

'So what do you want for this?'

'Well, I don't really—'

The correspondent nudged me hard, and broke in. 'Tell us what you've got.'

He looked round carefully, then pulled out a grubby sheaf of newspapers and magazines. I looked at them rather blankly.

'Army newspapers from Siberia,' he said. 'Interesting.'

The correspondent explained that you couldn't get this kind of thing in Moscow, and that sometimes there were valuable details to be found in them. But a few papers weren't, he said, enough. 'What else do you have?'

Again the look around. The thin man reached into his pocket and produced three small pieces of silver. I looked at them: they were Roman denarii, two of the Emperor Domitian and one that was too badly worn to be easily identifiable. I looked questioningly into his thin, pale face. He shrugged.

'I trade. That is how I live.'

'All right,' I said. 'Done.'

It still seemed very strange to be exchanging a banned book for three Roman coins in a Moscow park.

'Now get him to tell you about himself,' Kevin said.

The thin man twitched continually as he told me his story. I began to understand the haunted, deep-set eyes and the clawlike hands.

He had been an official of the Moscow Komsomol, the Communist Youth League. I would have put him in his mid-forties, but he was still only thirty-two. He had been a good Communist, he said, and they had made him manager of the local Komsomol cinema. At first he had shown only Russian films, but the membership wanted Western ones as well. That meant he had to get in touch with the black marketeers who distributed them in Moscow. For a couple of years they showed Russian films at 7.00, then had a private viewing of Western films for a more select audience at 9.00. Eventually the older members said they were getting tired of *The French Connection* and Bond movies. They wanted something a little spicier. He got onto his suppliers, who gave him a generous selection of blue movies. They were shown to an even more select audience at 11.00 each night. It was a runaway success with the Komsomol, and more and more senior people in the Party asked him for help in getting other porn films. As for the cinema, it started making good money.

In the end, of course, someone gave them away.

'I was given seven years in a labour camp,' he said, his face muscles jerking. 'I got out three weeks ago.'

'What was it like?' I asked lamely, not being able to think of anything else to say.

'It makes you old and sick.'

After that we shook hands, and he walked off into the darkness, his shoulder still twitching perceptibly as he went. There was still something undefinably jaunty about him, now that he was inalienably an outsider, a crook, an illegal street trader. If the authorities had wrecked him, they hadn't defeated him. But his prison experience had been a variant on Einstein's theory about travelling in space and time. He had gone into the camp at twenty-five, and after his seven years there he had come out thirteen years older.

« »

Everyone was staring at me. As I stood in the noisy Metro carriage, swaying with the movement of the train, I had given up any hope of merging into the Soviet crowd. That was out of the question for most Western visitors in 1978. We were bigger, healthier, better-fed and far better turned out than Russians. I had dressed down to the best of my ability; yet even in my jeans and open-necked shirt I looked nothing like my fellow passengers. Their clothes were drab, badly cut and utilitarian, and their shoes were made of some shiny substance that was a bad substitute for leather. Life was a little better than it had been in the past, but not much.

Now, as the Metro headed out towards the far north-western suburbs of the city, the other passengers had the opportunity to look at a genuine representative of the magical world beyond the Soviet empire's borders. Some probably disapproved. Others, if the moment had been right, might have made me an offer for my clothes. The rest showed a purely passive interest. There was nothing else to look at: no advertisements, for instance. (Once, under Khrushchev, the authorities had tried to introduce socialist advertising; but after they had tried the slogan 'Fly by Aeroplane' the effort lapsed.)

Were there any KGB people among the other passengers, following me? It wasn't impossible. I was on my way to meet some refuseniks, and the appointment had been made by telephone. If anyone's phone was tapped, it would be the correspondent's: he was in contact with just about every dissident in Moscow. Refuseniks were Russian Jews who had been refused permission to emigrate to Israel. Part of the reason was a submerged official anti-Semitism; part was an often justified suspicion that many of them, highly educated at public expense, were really planning to move on to the United States.

I looked around the compartment to see who might be following me: the tall, dark-haired character in his forties at the far end, absorbed in the Soviet army newspaper? Or the smaller, younger, pastier man in the grey windcheater and shiny grey shoes, who was standing close beside me, swaying in unison with me as the train took a curve? You never could tell, I thought.

But when I reached the station whose name the refuseniks had given me, and took the steep escalator to the surface, and went out of the station into the warm summer evening, I realized you could certainly tell if they wanted you to know they were there. A large and rather expensive black Volga saloon, with as much chrome as an old American Studebaker, was waiting outside the exit. Four men in hats were sitting inside. One of them pointed at me; as I say, there was no question of my mingling with the crowd.

When I turned right and walked down the road in the direction the refuseniks had told me, the Volga kept pace with me. The few other cars on the road, guessing that it must be official, steered round it. Sometimes, to vary things, I walked faster, and sometimes slower. The Volga stayed by my left elbow. The men inside seemed to be enjoying themselves: they were grinning and joking. I was nervous. The correspondent had told me that I might expect a light beating, but nothing much more. Though he had added, 'Of course, you never know.'

I found the block of flats, and the Volga stayed outside the entrance. The lift was working, which was unusual, but it reeked of urine. And yet when I reached the flat on the twelfth floor and was admitted, I found it was a little oasis of comfort and culture. There were books on the shelves and a violin lying beside its case on the table, and there were photographs of Western cities in little wooden frames: Vienna, Paris, San Francisco. Five people lived in this two-roomed apartment: an elderly couple, their son and his wife, and their seventeen-year-old grandson.

They fed me tea and some little meatballs, and listened politely as I told them about the Volga. The seventeen-year-old rolled up his sleeve and showed me a swelling which had been caused by the latest beating the police had given him.

I pulled out the small movie-camera I had brought with me from London, and filmed interviews with all of them. They knew what they were doing: applying to emigrate from the Soviet Union was itself a declaration of defiance, an act which placed you outside the norms of everyday life. Anything could happen to you, and to have your case known about in the West as a result of recording an interview with a Western journalist conferred a certain faint protection. It was harder for the authorities to do what they wanted with you in silence after that.

At the end, the seventeen-year-old grinned and said, 'Do you really want to see your friends in the Volga again?'

'Not particularly.'

'Because there's another way out that they don't know.'

I said my goodbyes, and he took me down to the basement. Someone had knocked a hole in the wall and made a connection with the block of flats next door. He showed me up to the ground floor: the entrance was round the side, away from the place where the Volga was waiting. Then we ran across a patch of waste ground and reached the Metro station from a completely different direction.

'They'll be angry with you,' he said, still grinning with the pleasure of tweaking the KGB's tail.

'And what about you?'

'They're always angry with me.'

Later I heard they had given him another beating.

« »

Nothing was easy about working for television in Moscow. While I was there the American embassy discovered that a team of KGB operatives had been working for some time in a disused chimney in the outer wall of the embassy building, spying on the movements of the people inside and recording their conversations. There was a big diplomatic storm about it, and I managed to hire a Soviet television crew to film the outside of the embassy building. They wouldn't enter it, and refused to let me interview any of the American diplomats.

'You can at least film the chimney,' I told the cameraman.

He focused on it, and I looked through the lens: it was far too wide, and took in most of the building.

'You must show it in close-up,' I said.

He smiled. '*Ne mozhne.*'

Some days later a member of the Politburo died.

'Can I hire a film crew to cover the state funeral?' I asked the unpleasant woman who co-ordinated my requests at the international committee of Soviet television.

'But you didn't ask for this in your letter to us.'

'Of course I didn't ask for it, my dear old Commissar,' I said. 'Mr Grishin was still alive and running round the Kremlin when I wrote that letter.'

'I can't help that. You should have asked.'

When I was allowed to film inside GUM, the delightful 1890s shopping complex in Red Square opposite the Kremlin, the minder who came with me from the international committee kept finding fault with the customers I wanted to film.

'Frankly speaking, I think you have chosen this woman because she is old and ugly.'

'Listen, Igor, I chose her because she happened to be buying something at the check-out. I don't care if she is old and ugly.'

'You must film this lady instead.'

A six-foot blonde who looked like the mistress of a Party boss sashayed past.

'Fine. No problem.'

But the six-foot blonde didn't want to be filmed, and stalked off. Each time Igor and I had a disagreement the cameraman would take his camera off the tripod, the sound man would put his microphone down and the lighting man would switch off all the lights. In the end we only had four shots in the can by closing time.

'Why do you do this? It's costing the BBC a thousand dollars a day to hire the crew, and we aren't filming anything.'

'John, frankly speaking, I don't think we can cooperate with you. I hear you go out and do bad things. You are not in favour of the Soviet Union.'

And yet, in a way, I was. I detested its human rights record, but I found it completely different from the dehumanized machine-state I had expected. The fact that it was so broken down, that it was run by willpower and not much else, had a kind of attraction.

In later years I thought the most revealing anecdote about the Soviet Union concerned its Foxbat fighter, supposedly the fastest plane in the world. US Air Force intelligence specialists examined every detail they could find about it, and horrified the American defence establishment and their NATO allies by concluding that the only way a pilot could be protected at the speed and height the Foxbat could achieve would be for the plane to be made of titanium. But how could the Soviet Union have got its hands on so much titanium – one of the most expensive metals in the world?

It was some years before a Soviet pilot defected with his Foxbat to Japan, and the intelligence men could look at it. They found it was made from stainless steel. The Soviet system was cruel and repressive, and deeply careless about individual human lives; but it nevertheless contained something which was truly heroic. At first when it all collapsed I was delighted; but when I go to Russia nowadays and see the poverty and crime, I wonder if the old days were quite as bad as we used to think.

There was one last dissident for me to see, and he was the most important of all. Andrei Sakharov was a physicist who had worked on the first Soviet atomic bomb. A man of great intelligence and nobility of nature, he gradually came to see how brutal the Soviet system was. By the summer of 1978 he was the only important dissident left at liberty in the Soviet Union: the rest had either died, or been imprisoned or been deported.

'Liberty' for Andrei Sakharov was a relative term. The police had erected a small hut outside the block of flats where he lived, and he was constantly being harassed by the KGB. Nevertheless his old colleagues from academia and the nuclear programme still managed to protect him a little; so he had been allowed to live in a block reserved for leading Soviet scientists, where he had lived for years.

This time the correspondent and I didn't make the arrangement by phone. He drove us round there in the BBC Volvo himself, leaving his government-provided driver behind, and parked discreetly around the corner. The Volvo was a giveaway itself, in a city where only foreigners had foreign cars; but also had its telltale number, beginning with 'K 001'. 'K' was for 'Korrespondent', and 001 was for Britain: because the Labour government of 1922 was the first Western country to recognize the new revolutionary power in Moscow. We waited till the policemen were inside their hut, then ran across the road and pulled open the loosely hung brown-painted main door.

The Sakharovs' flat was reasonably large, and comfortably furnished; in the past, before they decided to defy the state, they hadn't been short of money. It was a donnish kind of place: books were piled everywhere, and a cheerful intellectual air of confusion reigned.

Sakharov's wife, Yelena Bonner, opened the door: bright, sharp, and for the moment rather suspicious. For some reason they had expected us later. We went down the dark corridor which smelled of old books and cooking, past the sitting room lined with bookshelves and decorated with photographs of friends and dissidents propped up against the spines of the books, and into Sakharov's bedroom.

He was lying on the bed, propped up, wearing pyjamas and reading – of all things – an old green Penguin crime story. His heart was weak, and his doctor had advised him to rest as much as possible. Courteously, he put the book down on the bed beside him.

He knew the correspondent a little, and greeted him affectionately. 'I always listen to you on the radio,' he said.

Then he turned his attention to me. It was like having a warm and pleasant light shone on me. I was so unnerved at being in the presence of a man I had admired for years that I couldn't think of anything to say. Then I told him precisely that.

Sakharov laughed, as if to say 'This business of fame is nothing.' Then he gestured to the Penguin crime novel beside him on the bed, and waved his hand at the hidden microphones which the KGB had installed in the walls and ceiling.

'As you say in England, "Everything you say here will be written down and may be used in evidence against you." '

He gave a creaky laugh which ended in a cough, and his wife moved instinctively towards him. They seemed very close to one another, and as she sat on the bed with him I asked if I could take their photograph. I'm not much of a photographer, but I thought this was one of the best portraits I had ever seen, let alone taken. Something of their character and their evident love for each other seemed to come over in it.

Then we recorded our interview. It seems hard to imagine it now, but Andrei Sakharov had never been interviewed for television before; and although the film camera I had was very primitive and my technical skills minimal, I felt a distinct excitement. The correspondent asked him most of the questions, and I added one or two others from behind the camera. On the wall was a Russian Orthodox cross – such a rarity in the Soviet Union of the 1970s that I allowed the camera to linger on it far too often, when I should have kept on Sakharov's face.

Transcript of interview with Dr Andrei Sakharov, 3.5.78

Speakers: Andrei Sakharov (non-staff), John Simpson (staff)

JS: Do you think the Soviet authorities will be able to crush the dissident movement completely?

AS: No, this will not be possible. You see, the desire, the instinct to oppose brutality and repress freedom of thought is unquenchable. Of course it can be forced to keep quiet at times, when the repression gets worse. Not everyone wants to be a martyr, and not everyone should have to be a martyr. But the instinct remains, and will

always remain. And when the circumstances become a
little more favourable, it will raise its head again.
You cannot crush this instinct, because it is part of us
- part of the human condition. The desire to be free is
one of the fundamental human desires.

I had never heard a Soviet dissident speak like this. I had heard Alexander Solzhenitsyn's Old Testament roarings, and had felt instinctively
that they were extreme and unattractive. Here, though, was a man
who had done as much as Solzhenitsyn to champion the desire for
freedom, but who was calm and unexcitable and gentle about it. He
did not hate the Soviet authorities as Solzhenitsyn did, he merely
thought they were foolish and misguided, and needed to have this
explained to them in a rational way. As I listened to his answers the
tears ran unashamedly down my cheeks. Later when I returned to
London and told my wife Diane what I felt, she showed me something
Maxim Gorky had written about Tolstoy: 'As long as this man is alive,
no man is entirely an orphan.'

I took away a typed appeal which the Sakharovs wanted to send to
the governments of Britain and the United States about the worsening
condition of a number of dissidents in Soviet gaols. The next morning
I was to catch the plane for London. I folded the message carefully
and hid it inside an astrakhan hat I bought for myself in GUM. As for
the film of our interview, I couldn't think of any way to disguise it; so
I put it in my briefcase and hoped for the best.

There were several security checks at the airport. Each time I
opened my briefcase and allowed the checkers to pull everything out
and examine it. They scarcely seemed to notice the cassette containing
Sakharov's interview: perhaps they didn't know what it was. As I sat
in the departure lounge I congratulated myself on having eluded the
best the KGB could throw at me. Then there was an announcement:
'Mr John Simpson is requested to present himself at the security desk.'

I thought of trying to ignore it, but Sheremetyevo Airport wasn't
like Kinshasa. I went over to the security desk. A smiling man in
uniform – a colonel, I thought – was sitting there. He spoke excellent
English.

'Ah, Mr Simpson. Very kind of you to come and see us. I wonder
if you would mind handing me that briefcase of yours.'

I handed it to him. He got up, and walked over to a kind of hatch in the wall, like a safe. It had a yellow and black radioactive sign on it. He opened the door and put the case in. Then he shut the door again.

'We've got to be certain,' he said jovially, and checked his watch. After a minute he opened the door again and handed me the case. 'No hard feelings, I hope,' he said.

For the entire duration of the flight I was deeply depressed. When I reached Television Centre I handed the film to the processing people, but told them I didn't think they'd find anything on it.

Two hours later, the phone rang.

'Those pictures of yours have come up very nicely,' said a voice.

I asked if he was really sure.

'Well, the first couple of feet seem to be a bit fogged, but the rest is fine.'

And so it proved. We ran the first ever television interview with Andrei Sakharov on the *Nine O'Clock News* that night.

The Soviet embassy was furious. Mr Antonov accused me of unprofessional behaviour, and Pravda spoke of the hole in the corner behaviour of BBC correspondents in Moscow, and wondered how long the authorities could put up with it.

« »

For eighteen months I had no contact whatever with the Soviet embassy. Then one morning I received an invitation to a party at the embassy to mark Soviet Army Day. I knew what it meant: my penance was over, and I was free to go back to Moscow. The Russians might do a lot of things clumsily and brutally, but they also had class.

9

Revolutionaries

EAST GERMANY, LIBYA AND IRAN, 1978–79

I MIGHT BE BARRED from Moscow, but there were plenty of other places I could go where BBC television news hadn't been before.

Now that Checkpoint Charlie is one with Nineveh and Tyre it is sometimes hard to work out exactly where the Berlin Wall used to run. But when I first crossed from the brightness of West Berlin to the East one chilly autumn evening in 1979 Berlin was still an important point of friction. A world war had seemed on the point of starting there eighteen years before, and it was still very unnerving: a dark passageway from one world to another, which you entered alone and without help.

A camera with a huge lens photographed you as you carried your luggage the thirty yards which divided East from West. After a grilling by some of the rudest customs and immigration officers in the world you walked out of a hut and found yourself in a dark, poorly lit back street, stumbling over the stones which littered the pavement. You had passed through the looking-glass.

Everything seemed utterly different this side. Instead of the brightness of the West, the lights on the Eastern side were weak and yellowish-brown. There were no taxis and no one to ask directions of, and on my first visit it took me forty minutes of stumbling round in the semi-darkness before I found my antique, inconvenient, heavily bugged hotel. And yet I found East Germany a more sympathetic society than West Germany, in some respects: much less pleased with itself, and (for a Marxist-Leninist society) relatively open: even though unpleasant things certainly went on there, and people were regarded as state property for the authorities to do what they liked with.

Yet they thought of themselves as being freer than the rest of the Soviet bloc. Here, working with an East German television crew and an East German minder, you entered into a conspiracy to see what you could get away with.

'I've filmed the Wall with Austrian television from here,' Joachim said. 'They can't see us from the watchtower over there. Anyway, they don't expect that anything will happen on this side of the Wall.'

'You're sure you won't get into trouble?'

'Pretty certain.'

It made life more difficult, in a way. I couldn't regard him as the enemy, with whom any trick was fair enough. His interests had to be taken into account as well. So although I rather liked working in East Germany, I found myself increasingly reluctant to go back there. The lines were drawn as clearly as they were in Russia, and the temptation was always to hold back. Maybe that was what Joachim and his colleagues really wanted.

All the same, I was developing a real liking for working in difficult places. It took so much more effort. Merely to get enough basic shots to build up a reasonable report was a challenge, let alone going out to find the kind of things and the kind of people the authorities wanted you to stay away from. So although, in my early time in television, I went to all the more predictable countries – France, Switzerland, West Germany, Italy – I tried to extend the agenda as much as possible. And if Television News hadn't penetrated as far as Moscow, they certainly hadn't gone to Libya.

« »

Libya was a different kind of looking-glass society, with nothing remotely rational or sane about it. Under the old regime its largest source of foreign currency had been selling the scrap-iron from the battlefields of the Second World War. By 1969, when the wild-eyed young officer Muammar al Gadhafi seized power in a coup, Libya had struck oil. The result was like a rag-and-bone man winning the lottery: crazy enterprises which bore no relation to the real world were launched, and no one had any idea of the value of money.

I arrived at Tripoli airport, in those days pleasant and recently built, together with a camera crew and a producer who had obtained absolute promises that we would have an interview with Colonel

Gadhafi. My first insight into the political life of this strange place was a large banner draped across the arrivals hall which said 'Committees Everywhere!' This was a key part of the Colonel's Third Universal Theory, as contained in his Little Green Book. The first two universal theories were Marxism and capitalism, and Gadhafi had produced a synthesis of the two which apparently sorted out all the problems of them both. Later, when I had read the Third Universal Theory in its entirety, I asked one of Gadhafi's senior advisers a question or two about it. I was, he answered, the first Western journalist to have taken the Theory seriously. I didn't feel this was altogether a compliment.

Gadhafi's idea was that unlike the political systems in the world's two main blocs, a properly constituted society was one in which every citizen could decide the course of his or her life, and could have a say in the government of the country; hence 'Committees everywhere'. Formal power would fade away. There would be no more ministers or leaders: why would they be needed, if the people were in charge of everything?

Good question – except that of course the people weren't in charge. Gadhafi might be seen less in public, but that didn't mean he and his men had given up control. They merely governed the country behind a screen of nominees on the Committees, and Gadhafi's security service, a particularly nasty one even by the standards of authoritarian Arab countries, made sure that everyone said the right thing and voted the right way at the Committees' interminable meetings.

The shops in Tripoli looked distinctly empty as we drove through the city to our hotel. The Committees, instructed by Gadhafi, had been offering to cut back on living standards because, it seemed, there had been overspending in the past; no one said by whom. For the capital of a country where there should have been so much wealth, Tripoli was a poor-looking place. The roadway in the main square, named after the 1969 revolution, had been painted green, but even there the colour was fading.

We settled down in our hotel and waited. When I tried to go for a walk I was told, politely but with finality, that it wasn't possible for the time being. We could be called at any moment to see the Leader. Nothing happened.

The next morning we came down at 5 a.m., in order to be ready to be taken to see the Leader. It was so urgent, our minder said, that if we happened to be in the lavatory when the call came, they wouldn't wait for us. At lunch-time the minder admitted that it wasn't looking so likely today, but warned us to be there at 5 a.m. the next morning. And the next. And the next.

Eventually we ignored the warnings and did some filming with our minders. And on the fourth day, not at 5.00 but at a much more civilized time, a car came to pick us up. We assumed that we were going to the palace, so I put on a suit for our interview. Instead we were taken to the Leader's private airport. And there, standing by the Leader's private aircraft, was the Leader's private pilot.

'Good Lord,' he said, 'I didn't realize we were taking the Beeb today.'

The Leader's private pilot turned out to be a former commander in the Royal Navy.

Entertaining us with anecdotes, he flew us eastwards to the road outside the town of Sirte. There, on a specially marked section of road which had already been blocked off by the police, we made our landing. Two open Land-Rovers were waiting by the side of the road. The drivers were dashing-looking Bedouin in white robes, and only their eyes showed under the folds of the cloths which they had wound round their heads to keep the sand out. I felt distinctly over-dressed in my lightweight suit, but better than the lighting man, who had elected to wear a three-piece black suit, a white shirt and striped tie, and a handkerchief in his pocket.

'Interviewees like it if you turn up looking smart,' he said. I thought he would turn up looking like a sand-covered undertaker, but merely nodded.

The desert stretched out ahead of us, as white and undulating as a film about Beau Geste. There was no road: the Bedouin drivers headed off towards a line of distant sand-dunes. We bucketed around for four hours, sometimes getting stuck in the loose sand but never once getting lost.

The Bedouin might not have been the world's greatest drivers, but they were the world's greatest navigators. After four hours, with neither map nor compass, we arrived exactly in front of a small modern town which looked like somewhere in Essex. There were overpasses and underpasses, a shopping centre, and some very dreary domestic archi-tecture indeed. It turned out to be Colonel Gadhafi's home town, in as much as he had one: it had been built in the general area where his parents, who were nomads, had pitched their tent at the time of his birth.

His mother and father still lived there. They were squatting in the corner of an open courtyard, looking rather depressed. Gadhafi had ordered that every Libyan should live in a house, and they were still waiting for theirs. After our guide had pointed them out, he explained the large multicoloured tent which had been erected in the courtyard centre.

'This is where the Leader lives,' he said.

It seemed that the Leader, much as he wanted everyone else to live in a house, preferred a tent himself. He would move from compound to compound, and it would be put up wherever he was.

'Very pleasant,' I murmured uncertainly, looking at this yellow and blue and green affair which looked like the Big Top in a circus. Someone pushed me in the small of the back and I went through the entrance flap like Bob Hope in an old 'Road' film.

Inside it was cool and pleasantly colourful: the sun's rays, shining through the garish colours of the tent, were softened and gentle. Two men sat at one end with a very large green-painted field radio. At the other, a cook was doing some encouraging work over a frying-pan, and a man was assembling a tray of mint tea. And there, on a pile of cushions in the middle of the tent, sat the Leader himself.

For a moment or two he affected not to notice that we were there; as though a group of large Europeans, three of them carrying equipment, were such a commonplace sight in his tent that you wouldn't spot them. Then he looked up. His eyes were startlingly bright, his cheeks were scored by two deep parallel crevasses, and he was wearing white robes and a white scarf on his head. He looked like one of the Rolling Stones dressed up as a lady novelist's desert hero from the 1930s.

When he got to his feet, he was surprisingly tall. In his strange way, I suppose he was also pleasant and hospitable, though there was always an oddity about his manner and the way he spoke which made you feel he was making fun of you. He waved grandly towards some cushions on the floor, and we sat down, still aching from our desert ride.

'You should eat,' he said, and everything became even more Ethel

M. Dell than ever. He snapped his fingers, and a servant brought over a silver salver on which were an array of little lamb chops and a large bowl of spaghetti. We picked at one and toyed with the other, and Gadhafi smiled at us paternally. He ate nothing himself, I noticed.

As I chewed the stringy meat I addressed a question or two to him, but I could see this would not be like other interviews. When I asked him about the training course he had been on at Sandhurst in the 1960s he laughed uproariously, and everyone around him laughed, and then he took a deep sip from a glass of water beside him. That was it: he turned to one of his assistants and murmured some instructions for a while.

Soon afterwards we set up the lights and prepared the tent for our interview. It wasn't easy: the colours looked particularly strange, but I was beginning to think this would simply match the rest of the show.

To my surprise, the question about Sandhurst seemed to trigger something in his mind, and he began talking in English that was so heavily accented I thought at first it was Arabic. I looked at the producer and the producer looked at me, and I asked Gadhafi if he would mind speaking English in our interview. There was a seismic disturbance deep in the crevasses of his cheeks, and I realized he was smiling.

'Why not?' he said.

It was obviously not going to be easy, though. Colonel Gadhafi at that time was undergoing frequent treatment at a clinic in Egypt, and the Egyptian leader, Anwar Sadat, had not long before called him 'that madman from Libya'. Every time I asked Gadhafi a question, he began every answer, no matter how serious or complex the subject, by throwing back his head and laughing long and loudly at the roof of the tent. Then he moved his head back to the usual position, and there wasn't a smile on his face. He would murmur an answer, sometimes in English and sometimes, if he forgot, in Arabic.

Transcript of interview with Colonel Muammar Al Gadhafi, 21.1.79

Speakers: Colonel Gadhafi (non-staff), John Simpson (staff)

JS: You have made it clear in the past that you have sent

money to the IRA to enable it to buy weapons. Do you still
do this?

CG [looks up and laughs loudly]: The Socialist People's
Libyan Arab Republic has never given money to any Irish
cause.

JS: With respect, you said publicly in 1973 and 74 that
you were giving money to the IRA, and a shipload of
weapons was followed from Libya to the coast of Ireland
in 1973. My question is, are you still doing this?

CG [looks up and laughs loudly]: It is not true that we
ever gave money to the IRA.
JS [getting exasperated]: So why did you say you had?

CG [looks up and laughs]: [Answer indistinct]

Not, it seems safe to say, a particularly revealing exchange of views.
Back in London it proved horribly difficult to edit, partly because of
the switches back and forth from English to Arabic, but mostly because
of the business of laughing at the roof of the tent. We felt it made the
whole business ludicrous; but we couldn't always edit out every scrap
of smile or every head movement.

After it was finished Gadhafi sat smiling as though he had won the
Nobel prize for television. He was pleasant enough: when I admired a
hooded black cloak of his, more for something to say than because I
really liked it, he gave orders that a similar one should be found for
me. It was given to me the next day; I used it long afterwards for fancy-
dress parties, sometimes going as a mad monk, and sometimes as the
Grim Reaper. When we left Gadhafi shook hands politely, then turned
his back on us and sat down. As we negotiated the tent flap I could
hear his laugh ringing out again; maybe he was thinking about one of
my questions.

The Leader might not have been fully with us, but he has managed
to survive a number of coup attempts and is still in charge of Libya,
twenty years later. He is no more conventional: the last time I saw him
he was wearing an Austin Reed ulster, a kind of caped garment people
wore to go shooting in 1890, with a startling pattern. He walked
through a room full of journalists who were expecting him to give a

press conference, smiling and shaking hands. Then he disappeared through a door at the far end of the room. In the sudden silence of bewilderment which fell, we could hear a key turning in the lock. He never reappeared, and we left disconsolately a few days later.

Still, his cheque-book is a powerful weapon. In the early 1990s, after I had told some of my Gadhafi stories on Ruby Wax's television chat show, there was an angry editorial in the following week's *Observer*, which was then owned by Tiny Rowland, denouncing the way some leading television journalists like me mocked serious international statesmen like Colonel Gadhafi. Rowland, it seems, was doing a business deal with Libya, and the editor, Donald Trelford, who always insisted hotly that his editorial judgements were entirely independent of his owner's business concerns, had simply done what he was told. Money talks; even when it is being spent by someone who marches to a different drummer.

« »

After nearly thirty years of hard travelling I still enjoy the business of getting on aeroplanes and arriving and checking into hotels as much as I ever did; you have to, I suppose. There are of course certain destinations which make the heart lift. But when a newspaper interviewer asks you for your favourite place – it's one of those questions they turn to when things are flagging – you feel something special is required: Paris and Venice aren't quite enough, somehow. So I tend to reply that Iran is my favourite country. It is certainly one of them, in terms of people, climate, landscape and culture; though it would be a little truer to say that the whole of Central and South Asia, east of the Caucasus and south of Siberia, is the area to which I feel the greatest attraction. The grandeur of the steppe, the clarity of the desert, the freedom of the hills, the dominance of Islam, the seething cities of India and Pakistan: these are the conditions in which I feel most stimulated, and most myself.

Until 1978 I had never been anywhere in this entire, vast region. As for Iran, I scarcely knew where to find it on the map; and it was something of a revelation to me to discover that it was the same as Persia. Since the beginning of that year there had been rioting in Iran, and it was getting worse. Like most people, I found the detail escaped me, but it seemed to be some kind of fundamentalist uprising against the Shah. It also sounded extremely dangerous, and in those days I was still rather apt to feel worried about that kind of thing. Iran taught me that there are rules about revolutions and civil wars, as about everything else, and that if you apply the rules properly there is no reason why the most dangerous situation shouldn't be survivable.

In August 1978, though, I found myself on a plane to Tehran, feeling very uncomfortable. The police and army had been shooting down demonstrators in the streets. I read through a vast pile of press cuttings and specialized magazine articles as we flew, trying to understand what on earth was going on there. Everyone writing about the crisis seemed confident that the Shah would survive the trouble, but there was no very clear idea what it was the protesters wanted. I saw a single reference to a particular religious leader, Ayatollah Khomeini, who lived in exile in Iraq; but beyond that it simply appeared to be a matter of Islamic unrest – 'fanatical' was a word I came across more than once – against a pro-Western, liberalizing ruler.

My excuse for going to Iran was slender. The man who was briefly the head of the Chinese Communist Party, Chairman Hua Guofeng, was making the first foray abroad of any Chinese leader in history, and I was following him around. His itinerary involved countries on the periphery of the Soviet Union which were in some way at odds with Moscow: Romania, under Ceauşescu; Yugoslavia, under Tito; and Iran under the Shah. All of them, too, were eventually to crumble under the weight of their problems, though the Chinese weren't probably farsighted enough to expect that; certainly no one else did. Anyway, Chairman Hua was about to arrive in Tehran, and I had come to report on it; though it seemed likely that I would spend more time reporting on the domestic upheavals of Iran itself.

The instant I appeared in the doorway of the aircraft and prepared to walk down the steps to the waiting coach, I knew I was going to like this place. The air was warm and had a delightful clarity, and the distant Elburz Mountains rose grandly from the plains, their topmost peaks glittering with snow even at the height of summer. There was a pungent smell in the air: the savour, I later came to realize, of Central Asia. I felt at home.

I have often been back to Iran since then. For years at a time, when I have offended the government, it has refused to let me in. But it has always relented at last, and as the fires of revolution have died down, going back has become easier. I have watched the convulsive changes there at first hand, but after twenty years it is at last a little closer to what it was that first day I arrived. It is more relaxed and freer nowadays than at any time during the past two difficult decades.

For those who know them, there is something deeply attractive about the people of Iran. The habitual, unselfish generosity which they show towards strangers is unusual even in the Islamic world. They also possess the rare ability to distinguish between individual people and the government of the country they come from. Even when the British government was being reviled daily in Iran, individual Britons were treated with kindness and respect. Maybe it comes from the Islamic tradition of treating strangers as guests; maybe it is the result of the long centuries during which individual Persians have had no voice whatever in the way they were governed, and therefore wouldn't consider blaming someone for what their government did. Yet at a time when British officials were being rude and dismissive to Iranians who had fled their country to escape persecution, and when gangs attacked and occasionally murdered innocent Iranian refugees in the streets of American cities, British and American journalists were treated with respect and kindness in Iran itself.

Once, during a time of great tension in Tehran, I was filming outside the place where Friday prayers were being held. The subject of the sermon was the iniquity of the British towards Iran, stretching back over the decades. The worshippers came boiling out into the street, chanting '*Marg bar Englistan!*' '*Marg bar Thatcher!*': Death to England! Death to Thatcher! Well, one could see their point of course, but standing out in the street filming them with a big BBC sign on our camera we felt a little exposed. Or at least the cameraman did. I had seen this before, and was less worried.

'If you stand up on this wall you can get a shot of me walking through the crowd talking to them. Put a radio mike on me and you'll be able to hear what happens.'

The cameraman was a gentle, rather paternal man not far short of retirement. 'I really don't think you ought to do this, John.'

The fact was, I had seen an American correspondent do precisely the same thing, and knew it worked. I insisted.

By now the crowd had stabilized, and had formed up in the road waving banners and beating their chests in time to their chanting. Even to someone who knew what was likely to happen, it was a little daunting.

But as I walked among them, explaining that I was from Britain, they would shake my hand and tell me I was welcome in their country. In the centre of the crowd I spotted a large and rather excitable old man with a large sprouting beard and a turban. He was getting really worked up, beating his chest with both fists and booming out the responses:

'*Marg bar Englistan! Marg bar Englistan!*'

I could see the saliva whipping out around him, and his neighbours were moving away from him to give him more room. It seemed like the ultimate test of the theory. I edged up and stood in front of him.

'Good morning. I am from Englistan and I work for the BBC.'

It was like the return of Empire. He bowed, took my hand and kissed it.

'You are very welcome in Iran, sir. I hope you like our country.'

I assured him that I did. And indeed it felt very good to be among Iranians again. It also made excellent television.

'Well, I see why you're always going on about this place,' said the cameraman when I rejoined him.

Many journalists who worked there during the revolution had reason to be grateful for the purely altruistic help of individual Iranians. A few weeks after this first visit of mine to Tehran, when the violence was even greater, a Canadian cameraman I knew was filming in a crowd when he did something which upset them: not speaking Farsi, he filmed the face of someone who was asking in Farsi not to be filmed. The crowd took this to mean that he was filming on behalf of the SAVAK – the secret police – and turned on him savagely. He broke away and ran off down the road, with the crowd streaming after him. Then, exactly as in one of those nightmares where you wake up sweating, he dodged into a side street and realized halfway down that it was a dead-end.

He backed into a doorway at the end, his camera held defensively in front of him, and waited for the crowd to catch up with him and kill him. And then the door behind him opened, and a woman pulled him in. She locked the door and piled some furniture in front of it. There was loud banging and shouting outside.

'Have you got something they want?'

'Film,' he answered, his chest heaving.

'Give it to me.'

He tore out some unexposed film that he didn't need and gave it to her. She went out onto the flat roof and shouted at the crowd, 'Look, this is what you want. Take it.'

Then she threw the film down to them. It unrolled like a New Year's Eve favour, and they grabbed at it and tore it angrily into little pieces. The woman meanwhile helped the cameraman over the roof and showed him the way to safety. She didn't want anything from him; she merely saw a stranger in trouble and, disregarding the danger to herself, felt it was her duty to look after him.

« »

I quickly lost interest in the visit of Hua Guofeng, which had been my reason for coming to Tehran. What was happening here was of extraordinary importance, and I decided to stay and cover it. (In those days of relaxed budgets and low costs it was usual to spend a fortnight or three weeks on a foreign trip, just looking for interesting stories; nowadays the office becomes restless after a few days, and wants to know when you plan to pull out.) Nevertheless it wasn't easy. The pattern of events was that groups of people hostile to the Shah's regime would gather in a mosque, and the mullahs would preach fiery sermons about the ungodly nature of the government. At the end everyone would come rushing out into the street and begin chanting slogans. The chances were, though, that someone would tip off the SAVAK, and they and the army would arrive in double-quick time and start shooting or arresting people. It happened every day, but the action would all be over within a few minutes, and unless you were actually on the spot you would miss it. We did miss it, day after day, and so did every other television team.

And then one Friday, as we were patrolling the streets of south Tehran looking for trouble, it happened. We chanced to be driving past a mosque just as everyone came pouring out. The army and the SAVAK were already waiting for them.

'Stop, stop,' I shouted to the driver.

'Are you sure we're allowed to film this?' asked the cameraman I was with. He hadn't been captivated by the magic of Iran; he thought they were all a lot of dangerous lunatics. This cameraman may not come out of this episode particularly well, but he was a good and conscientious worker, and different things worry different people. Four years later in Beirut he stood his ground with great courage in the middle of an ammunition dump which was exploding all round us, and deserved an award for his spectacular footage.

Now, though, he was distinctly reluctant. He got out of the car too slowly, and took too much time getting ready to film; and in doing so he attracted the attention of the SAVAK. One of the officers looked across and spotted us, and signed to the soldiers to arrest us. They picked us up bodily and threw us into the back of an army truck.

'This is all your fault,' the cameraman said to me. The sound recordist said nothing. He wasn't looking very well.

We stayed in the truck for hours, right through the midday heat. There was no shade, and no water. The sound recordist was starting to look really bad, and seemed to be slipping in and out of consciousness. As for the cameraman, he had taken to groaning and rubbing his hands together. One of our guards felt sorry for us and went off to buy some watermelons. After four hours of thirst they tasted wonderful, but the effect was spoiled when one of the others told us to enjoy them because they would be our last meal on earth. I didn't feel I had to explain all this to the cameraman. Nor did I tell him, when they let us wash our hands with water brought from a nearby mosque, that the soldiers were suggesting we might like to take the opportunity to go and pray in the mosque before they shot us. I hoped they were joking, but I couldn't be altogether certain.

There was a telephone box only twenty yards away, and I could see it through a gap in the canvas at the back of the truck. I pointed encouragingly to it and made ingratiating noises. One of the soldiers stuck his rifle in my stomach. Soon, though, the cameraman's hand-wringing and the sound recordist's groaning made me decide that, come what may, I had to get out and ring the British embassy. This time I pushed the gun away from my stomach and climbed out. The soldiers didn't quite know what to do, but several of them pointed their rifles at my back as I walked towards the phone.

In my life, bathos never seems far away. Directly I got there I found that it took different coins from the ones I had in my pocket. I looked round: if I walked off to get change the soldiers would probably shoot me, yet there was no one else to ask. So I went back and asked the soldiers; and like true Iranians they not only pulled out the necessary coins, but insisted I should keep them as a present. Then they pointed their guns at me again.

I got through to the diplomat on duty. He sounded disgruntled, and explained that everyone was away playing tennis. I outlined our little problem and with great reluctance he agreed to do what he could. I came away feeling much better.

An hour or so later there was a crackling on someone's walkie-talkie, a shouted instruction, and the truck's engine started up. We were driven to a SAVAK office in south Tehran. (A few months later, during the revolution proper, I looked on and filmed as a crowd sacked this very building, killing the people inside and throwing the files out of the windows. My emotions were mixed.) Now we were made to wait in the office of a fierce-looking character in plain clothes, who spent most of his time listening to someone on the other end of the phone line.

'*Bale*,' he would say, looking unpleasantly across at us.

We certainly made a mixed bunch: the cameraman inclined to rub his hands and blame me audibly, the sound recordist lapsing into semi-consciousness, and me doing an impersonation of Alec Guinness in *The Bridge On The River Kwai*, announcing that we were being treated abysmally and that I would shortly be making my second formal application for us all to be released and for medical assistance to be given to my colleague. I also said that when I next saw the Shah I would complain about this particular officer's behaviour. None of it worked, of course.

Then came another phone call.

'*Bale*,' said the officer again; but this time it sounded different. He looked at me.

'Do you know Basingstoke?' he asked in excellent English. 'My wife comes from there.'

I immediately started praising Basingstoke and the famous beauty of its women, though as a matter of fact I had never been there. But I could see things were taking a turn for the better. And a few minutes later, after a tray of tea had been brought round and we had drunk it greedily, we were given a SAVAK car and taken back to our hotel.

'Phew,' said the sound recordist as we drove away. He sat up.

'Are you all right?' I asked, rather anxiously.

"Course I am. Just put it on to fool 'em.'

'I still think you put our lives in danger unnecessarily,' said the cameraman.

I didn't care. I looked out at the dusty streets of Tehran and felt great. I didn't even mind when the superior voice on the phone line from the British embassy cut across my thanks.

'As a matter of fact I didn't do anything,' he said. 'We never do in these cases.'

« »

The situation worsened. The demonstrators called it 'doing the forty-forty': forty days after someone was shot dead by the army the custom of Shi'a Islam dictated that there should be a gathering in his or her honour. And since all such gatherings were banned, the army would turn out and more people would usually be shot. The Shah and some of his ministers thought this was the firmness they had to show; in fact it weakened their position every time it happened. When I went back to London at the end of August I put together a report which suggested that the Shah's powers might be clipped, and that he would be forced to become a constitutional monarch. With hindsight I can see that this was always a silly judgement; yet it was the first time a British journalist had suggested that the Shah's absolute power might be in danger, and the Foreign Office complained to the BBC that my report had been irresponsible and might weaken the Shah's position. At that time the British ambassador, Anthony Parsons, had great influence with the Shah, and the official British line was that the Shah would survive this ordeal as he had survived others in the past. Tony Parsons was always kind and helpful to me, and I had a considerable affection for him. But to those of us who had seen what was happening on the streets, the Shah's survival was beginning to seem less likely.

All in all, the Shah was the author of his own downfall: much more, that is, than most of us are. In January 1978, when he had seemed at the height of his power, he had ordered one of his ministers to publish a scurrilous attack on the senior cleric who, back in 1963, had headed the last bout of trouble. The Shah had survived that time, and the cleric had been forced into exile in neighbouring Iraq. His name was Ayatollah Ruhollah Khomeini. The minister's article suggested that he was a homosexual, and a British agent. Khomeini's supporters, outraged by the second accusation even more than the first, came out onto the streets and were shot down. The forty-day cycle of demon-stration/shooting/demonstration/shooting which eventually sent the Shah into exile had begun.

Now, in the autumn of 1978, the Shah was about to take the second big decision which brought him down. He put pressure on Saddam Hussein, by now the effective leader of Iraq, to force Ayatollah Khomeini out of his exile in the Shi'ite holy city of Najaf, in the south of Iraq. It was a foolish move: Najaf was almost impossible for Western journalists to get to, and Khomeini's practical influence was restricted to smuggling tape-recorded sermons across the border into Iran. Now, forced to leave Najaf, he took refuge in France. Everyone could go and see him there, and as a result his words were replayed to Iranians by radio, television and newspaper.

Soon after he had settled in the village of Neauphle-le-Château outside Paris, I went to interview him. He had taken over two houses on opposite sides of a small street. We filmed him crossing from one side to the other, and I had my first glimpse of the man whose revolu-tion was to be an important part of my professional life for years to come. I had seen his features on posters and stencils and banners back in Iran, but now, looking at those beetling brows and that ferocious frown, I thought he looked like vengeance personified.

We set up our lights in the main sitting room of the house where he lived, and settled down to wait while he prepared himself for the interview. All the Western furniture had been taken out, and the floor was thick with Persian carpets. Around the walls were the large, comfortable cushions which Iranians like to lounge against. I practised kneeling down. Then the door opened and he entered. You could feel the man's personality emanating from him: he was small, but he seemed to fill the room. He also looked extraordinarily clean: his robes were white and starched, and beautifully pressed. I wasn't quite sure what to do, so I said, 'Welcome' and put my hand out to shake his, forgetting that some of the most particular Muslims feel they have to wash after touching a non-believer.

It was potentially awkward, but he dealt with it well. Looking down, he busied himself with the folds of his robe in such a way that it seemed he hadn't noticed my outstretched hand. It was done with such tact that I couldn't feel offended. Yet he showed no real interest

in me at all: I was merely the loud-hailer through which he was about
to address a message to the Iranian people.

    Transcript of interview recorded 3.11.78 in Paris

    Speakers: Ayatollah Khomeini (non-staff), John Simpson
    (staff)

    JS: Is it your intention to lead a revolution against the
    Shah, or do you simply wish to force him to change his
    policies?

    AK: The Shah has ruled Iran as though it were his private
    estate, his property, to do with as he chooses. He has
    created a dictatorship, and has neglected his duties.
    The forces of Islam will bring this situation to an
    end. The monarchy will be eradicated.

    JS: What kind of government do you wish to see in Iran,
    and what form would an Islamic Republic take?

    AK: The Islamic Republic will be based on the will of the
    people, as expressed by universal suffrage. They will
    decide on the precise form it takes . . . But there are
    aspects of life under the present corrupt form of
    government in Iran which will have to be changed: we
    cannot allow our youth to be corrupted and our Islamic
    culture to be destroyed, and drugs such as alcoholic
    beverages will be prohibited.

Around us as we sat on the carpet were three of his aides, whose fates
would shortly be determined by the experience of working with him.
One, Abolhassan Bani-Sadr, became President and then escaped into
exile; the second, Ibrahim Yazdi, was hounded out of government and
spent his life as a dissident, in and out of gaol; and the third, Sadeq
Qotbzadeh, became foreign minister and was then executed for treason.

Now they were all enthusiastic about the prospect that Khomeini's
interview would be broadcast on the BBC, knowing it would be heard
all over Iran. Of course I understood that this kind of thing often had
a profound effect on the politics of the country in question, but a
decision not to interview Khomeini would have been as much of
a political move as the decision to interview him. In such cases I was

happy to leave it to the set of principles Waldo Maguire, my former editor, had given me before I went to South Africa: if it was of interest, if it was newsworthy, then we should report it and not bother our heads with the possible consequences.

There are Iranians in exile today who still blame me and the BBC World Service correspondent in Tehran at the time, Andrew Whitley, for creating the revolution by our reporting: as though the mood which brought the revolution about were not already fully in existence. And because strict factual accuracy isn't always one of the distinguishing characteristics of exiles, the story went round that Andrew would announce in his reports that the next big demonstration was due at such and such a time, and that as many people as possible should turn up. Foolish stuff, of course, but the Shah himself became so exercised by these suspicions that he put pressure on the British embassy to control the BBC's broadcasts, and the Foreign Office in turn complained to the BBC. A careful examination of Andrew's broadcasting carried out after the revolution showed that the accusations had been entirely false.

And yet years afterwards I was still getting anonymous letters accusing me of having received half a million dollars (the amount was always curiously specific) from Khomeini for broadcasting in a way that was favourable to the revolution. The fact that Khomeini's regime barred me from returning to Iran for seven years after the revolution didn't seem to affect any of this; but if you aren't objective and unbiased yourself, of course, you find it hard to believe that anyone else is.

Nevertheless the BBC had only its past to blame if people thought it had a political agenda in its broadcasting. The BBC Persian Service was set up by the British government in 1941 with the specific purpose of driving the Shah's father, Reza Shah, from the Persian throne for his pro-Nazi sympathies. Only forty years later, Iranians of many kinds naturally assumed that the BBC still had a political purpose in what it broadcast. The moral is, don't allow your principles to be tampered with now, and you won't suffer for it in the future.

For the moment, though, I was only concerned with ending my interview with Khomeini as politely as possible. I got to my feet slowly, and realized that although he was forty years older than I was, his knees were a great deal suppler than mine. I didn't put my hand out this time, and he permitted himself something which I realized was a faint smile. Then there was a rustling of well-starched robes and he left to go on planning his revolution.

« »

One November afternoon in 1978 the Tehran sky was dark with the smoke of fires as the demonstrators attacked public buildings and set up road blocks on every street corner. The situation was now well out of the Shah's control. I was really worried: partly because the rioters were going for anyone they thought might be British or American, and partly because I had left my camera crew in the centre of town when things seemed much quieter, and had gone back to our hotel to ring the office in London. One of the main commandments of television news is that you don't leave your colleagues on their own in nasty situations. Our driver refused to take me back to them, on the grounds that it was too dangerous, and the taxis were all off the streets. There was only one thing to do: I had to walk.

I wasn't entirely inconspicuous in my checked sports jacket, and I sang to myself to keep my spirits up as I strode along, keeping to the side-roads where I could. Whenever I came to a road-block I glared at the demonstrators, as the Victorian general Sir Charles Napier (of 'I have Sind' fame) is said to have glared at a tiger which attacked him. It worked for Napier, and it worked for me. They eyed me and they eyed my jacket, yet they fell back to allow me through as I came up to them. It was a long way to walk, but eventually I got close to the place where I had left the crew, only to realize that half a million people were thronging the previously empty streets. How could I conceivably find two men in this crowd?

But I did. In the far distance, bobbing over the uncountable heads, I spotted the absurd shape of the film magazine, shaped like Mickey Mouse ears, on top of our camera, turning as the cameraman found something new to film.

I couldn't believe my luck: still, when I reached them they were so wrapped up in the drama of what they were doing that they weren't at all surprised to see me. They had obtained some remarkable pictures, but the crowd was worked up and very volatile, and we knew that something could happen at any moment. It did. A man started shouting out that his brother had been killed by the army, and the BBC hadn't reported it: which meant that the BBC was on the side of the Shah.

Immediately people who had been perfectly pleasant to us a moment or two earlier, including one young man who had studied in Norwich and had just been telling me all about it, became caught up in the savagery of which crowds are capable at such times. They started to grab us, and I could see it would end in our being pulled to pieces. It had happened to other people that day.

Violent hands ripped at my jacket, and my own hands were trapped by my side. I could hear the others yelling and shouting, just as I was. It was getting desperate: a man was beating me in the face with a pole on which was pinned a portrait of Ayatollah Khomeini, as grim as when I had seen him at Neauphle, and blood was starting to run down my cheek.

I suppose it infuriated me that a little shrimp like this should beat me about the face simply because I couldn't defend myself. I roared with anger and dragged my arms free, and grabbed the pole out of his hands. All I could think of was hitting him back, and I got in a couple of satisfying whacks before I realized what I had to do.

'I am for Khomeini!' I shouted, waving the portrait of the old boy in the air. '*Javid* Khomeini!' The Shah wouldn't have liked it, nor would Waldo Maguire; but then no one was getting ready to pull them limb from limb. Suddenly our molesters became our greatest friends, trying to lift us onto their shoulders (I quickly stopped that) and helping us to get through the crowd to peace and safety.

'Bit of luck, that,' I said modestly, as we walked away. But the cameraman was the famous and much-missed Bernard Hesketh, who had his technical failings but possessed a fierce determination and an equally fierce sense of BBC propriety. He pulled me aside so the sound recordist wouldn't hear.

'I don't think you should have said that about Khomeini, John,' he said.

'But that's what saved us.'

'It's not right, all the same.'

'But—'

He was already striding off down the road in search of more pictures. I didn't feel particularly proud of myself, but I was very glad to have got away with just a ripped jacket and a cut on the face. I had kept the picture of Khomeini, too. It was a keepsake to remind me how I had got away from a particularly nasty death.

« »

One night a few weeks later, in January 1979, I found myself standing in the darkness, queuing up in the garden of one of Ayatollah Khomeini's houses in Neauphle-le-Château, waiting for a couple of tickets for his flight back to Tehran. The moment had come for his return, and he was willing to take a few journalists with him: but strictly on a first come, first served basis. I had been waiting almost seven hours so far, scarcely moving for fear one of the over-enthusiastic Iranian students who also wanted to go would step in and take my place. The temperature was well below freezing, and for years afterwards my right shoulder ached as a result of that day's work.

I was there in defiance of explicit orders from my foreign desk. It was too dangerous to fly with Khomeini, they said, and anyway we had a crew and a correspondent in Tehran already. Why bother? There were so many reasons for bothering that I couldn't begin to list them, but the chief one was that having covered the growing revolution for so long, I couldn't bear not to be there for the culminating moment. And I didn't think it right to let something as important as Khomeini's flight home go unreported by the BBC.

There was, of course, a terrible mêlée in the darkness when the tickets arrived. Hundred dollar bills were trampled into the mud or were caught by the freezing wind and blown away. Men wept. But no one fought harder than I. Those years of rugby playing had at last paid off. I met up with the crew in a nearby café, and we headed back to Paris. There was only a ticket for Bill Handford, the cameraman, and me. His recordist, a huge character called Dave Johnson, with a ferocious scar running down the entire side of his face, would follow on by the next commercial flight. He seemed relieved. For all his aggressive appearance, Dave was a gentle and rather discouraged man who preferred the company of his wife and cat to a life in the world's hot-spots.

'Since this may well be our last night on earth,' I said encouragingly, 'let's have a really good meal.'

We drove to the Train Bleu at the Gare de Lyons, where we were welcomed by the *maître d'hôtel*. He looked like the French ambassador at the Court of St James; we looked like tramps, and I still had mud on my clothes from the scrimmage at Neauphle. Against his better judgement, though, he led us to a table. We read the menu. Dave, who disliked too much conspicuous expenditure, even at the BBC's expense, winced.

"Ere, *garçon*,' he called out.

The *maître d'* walked over as though someone was complaining about a cockroach in the soup.

'Three pounds for a portion of peas,' Dave said. 'You must be joking.'

I soothed the *maître d'* in French, and we ate what might have been our last meal in silence. It was very good. Afterwards, since we had several hours to wait before Khomeini's charter-flight left, Bill suggested we should go somewhere for a drink.

We went into a place called '*Le Rugbyman*'; Dave thought it looked like a pub, and I couldn't stop him. Inside, it seemed to be entirely inhabited by French second-row forwards. Ears had been chewed, noses broken. Enormous hands gripped glasses of beer. There was an appreciative rumble as Dave eased his bulk through the door.

'This isn't going to end happily,' I said to Bill.

A skinny little man was playing the piano, and after a beer Dave went over to him.

"Op it, Francisco,' he said. The pianist hopped it. All round the bar, cauliflower ears pricked up: there was going to be a rumble. I hid my face. We were in enough trouble already, disobeying the BBC and facing a revolution.

But Dave eased himself onto the piano stool, and his huge fingers began playing beautiful thirties jazz. The small red eyes round the bar softened. When Dave paused, someone called out for doubles for *les anglais*.

'Great pianist,' I said chattily to a front-row forward. 'Great rugby player too.'

He gripped me by the hand so hard that tears came to my eyes.

Two hours later we said goodbye to Dave and boarded Khomeini's chartered Air France jet. An amusing gay steward explained to us that by special request there was no alcohol on board. A curtain blocked our view of the first-class section, where Khomeini and his advisers were sitting. We were back in steerage, and the students who wanted to shed their life's blood for the revolution were praying around us.

'This is a gloomy start,' Bill said as the heads went down. He was a small, wiry, bearded yachtsman in his late forties, and I had always enjoyed working with him.

There was a colleague of ours on board, a radio reporter who was usually good company. Now, though, he was badly scared by the prospect of the flight and was gloomy and depressed. He went to sleep quickly. I found it harder to sleep, partly because Khomeini's supporters were so excited. For one thing they were going home, and for another they thought there was a good chance the plane would be shot down by the Shah's airforce; which would mean they would go straight to Paradise as martyrs. This was precisely the possibility that made the correspondent so miserable.

It was light outside the plane by now, and people were starting to stir. The curtains dividing us from the first-class section parted without warning. Sadeq Qotbzadeh came through and stood on an empty seat in the front row of the tourist class section.

'I have a serious announcement to make,' he said. There was a rustle of excitement. 'We have just received a warning over the aircraft radio that the Iranian air force has orders to shoot us down directly we enter Iranian airspace.'

More rustling: it was depressingly clear that many of our fellow passengers thought this would be the best outcome imaginable. As for me, I shrugged my shoulders and drank some coffee.

> Of all the wonders that I yet have heard,
> It seems to me most strange that men should fear,
> Seeing that death, a necessary end,
> Will come when it will come.

It wasn't that I didn't care whether I lived or died: I was thirty-four, and I had a wife and two daughters, and I wanted to live very badly indeed. But it wasn't going to be up to me. It would be up to a general with a lot of gold braid somewhere down below, and a pilot with his finger on the button of a missile.

I suppose it was like being back in the Rhodesian farmer's car on the Mozambique border: if we weren't shot down, if we survived, I didn't want everybody to remember that I'd behaved embarrassingly badly. I looked across at Bill. He was sitting calmly in his seat, checking his equipment. He hadn't understood Qotbzadeh's French, but he knew exactly what was going on. Nearby sat the radio man, complaining and moaning to himself. I knew which one I wanted to be like; or perhaps, to be a little more honest, I knew which one I wanted other people to think I was like.

By now, anyway, there was something to do: which always seems to chase away the fear and introspection. Qotbzadeh beckoned us forward, and we went through the curtains and saw Khomeini sitting in the front row of first class, next to his son Ahmad. For a man who was returning from fifteen years of exile in order to start a revolution, he looked remarkably calm. I asked him that dreary, unimaginative broadcaster's question, how he felt. Deservedly, I was ignored. The grim head turned away from me and looked down. It was a few minutes later that a rather better-phrased question from a French journalist received the reply that went around the world.

'We are now over Iranian territory. What are your emotions after so many years of exile?'

'*Hichi*,' said Khomeini: nothing.

It was no good trying to explain that as a Muslim cleric he had striven to banish every emotion within himself except the love of God; that he believed the love of one's country, or hope for the future, or even the desire for revenge, were all emotions which, divorced from the worship of God, had no value or meaning. For people everywhere, even in Iran, it seemed as though this personification of vengeance had no feelings whatever for the nation he had convulsed.

Our plane wasn't shot down, of course; it merely flew round and round for a very long time, waiting for permission to land, until we were all thoroughly airsick. Down below us the greatest crowd in human history was waiting for him, and as we made our final approach I could see the vast gathering around the airport buildings and along the route Khomeini would take into Tehran. On the tarmac I recorded a long piece to camera about what had happened and what the situation was now, and we all waited for Khomeini to appear at the top of the aircraft steps. It took a long time; but when he did, a roar came from the onlookers and was taken up by the enormous, expectant crowd outside the airport buildings.

By now, though, Bill and I had ceased to play any further part in things. Having come there against instructions, our job was to hand over to the correspondent and camera crew who were already in Tehran. It was deeply anti-climactic, but we were exhausted after working hard for nearly thirty hours. And although we could hear the noise as Khomeini met and addressed a crowd of thousands of mullahs in the main part of the airport, we left that to our colleagues and slumped down exhausted on the seats in the arrivals hall. Half an hour or so later we were awakened when the doors opened and Khomeini appeared, being half-carried by a group of very worried acolytes.

No one stopped us as we followed them into a side-room. Nobody even seemed to notice we were filming as Khomeini lay down, apparently unconscious. Bill turned and looked at me, with a look on his face that seemed to say 'This could be one of the world's great exclusives.' But of course it wasn't. After a while Khomeini opened his eyes and asked for water. He had merely fainted from the heat and from nervous exhaustion; and if he ever showed such weakness again, there was no one present to see it.

The next twelve days were some of the most intense and exciting I have ever lived through. The Shah had left Iran before Khomeini arrived, but his power-structure was still more or less in place and the prime minister he left behind him, the charming and brave Shahpour Bakhtiar, was still in office. (Years later Bakhtiar would be murdered in Paris by agents sent by the government in Tehran.) But now that Khomeini was setting up his rival government it was only a matter of time before the empty structures left over from the Shah's rule collapsed and the new regime seized power.

« »

The moment came twelve days later, on 12 February. I had been up much of the night, watching and filming at a road block outside our hotel. At 6.30 I was awakened by a loud grinding noise in the street outside. A column of twenty or more tanks was heading for a confrontation with the pro-Islamic militants: the Imperial Guard was on the move.

It was an utterly bewildering day. We drove round Tehran in the direction of gun-fire, always managing to get there a little too late. Once, as we walked along a flyover we were buzzed by a pro-government helicopter which seemed about to attack us; yet we didn't even get good pictures of that. But our luck had already started to change. We found a crowd attacking the SAVAK building where I had been held prisoner by the man whose wife came from Basingstoke, and filmed them.

By this time our driver, a man called Mahmoudi whom I was to get to know very well indeed in the years that followed, had found out for us where the main action was going on and drove us there. There was no shortage of action any more. Dave Johnson, the enormous piano-playing sound recordist, had joined us by this stage, and although he did not relish the action he stayed connected up to Bill Handford's camera as we walked along a street towards the fighting, with bullets striking the walls a few feet above our heads. I was nervous enough: Dave, with his great bulk, must have felt that he offered an unfairly large target.

At the end of the street we at last understood what was going on: the crowds, and soldiers who had gone over to them, were attacking a barracks. The resistance had been strong at first, but was wearing down as we arrived. Soon a breach was made in the outer wall, and the soldiers inside began surrendering in their hundreds. For me, it was like watching the storming of the Winter Palace. I had reached the stage where filming the action was more important to me than my own safety, and I could see Bill had too. The fact that Dave stayed with us seemed to me admirable in itself. It was a dangerous time, and we were pinned down by gunfire in place after place. An American correspondent had been killed that morning, merely looking out of a window.

In North Tehran, in the foothills of the Elburz Mountains, we found a crowd gathering outside the Niavaran Palace, where the Shah and his family had lived. These were really just local people, scarcely revolutionaries at all, and their motive seemed to be a kind of militant curiosity and a desire to loot, rather than hatred for the old imperial order. Their eyes flashed with excitement as they stormed into the grounds and saw the grand style in which the Shah had lived. He seemed to have left everything behind him there. But the crowd was disappointed: the real revolutionary movement had sent some volunteers to make sure there was no theft or destruction, and the crowd obediently halted near the entrance to the palace, still avid to see the wealth of the monarch who had been overthrown. Looking through the windows, I felt a certain guilt, as though I were a looter myself.

The Shah had been no friend to the BBC, and as the originator of the plan to raise the price of oil in 1973 he was the cause of a good deal of economic pain in the Western world. I detested his record in human rights. But here at Niavaran he wasn't a monarch but a man who had been forced out of his country for ever; and there was something poignant even in the showiness and poor taste which was evident as I peered through the windows of his palace.

By the entrance stood a sheepish group of several dozen men wearing nothing but their underpants. These were the Imperial Guards, 'the Immortals', each of whom had taken a personal oath to defend the Shah with the last drop of blood in his veins. Instead the Shah had left them, and they had only defended him as far as their underwear. There was nothing grand about this revolution, any more than there was about the Russian Revolution. It was mostly absurdity and confusion.

We satellited our material from the television station at around midnight. While we were waiting for the satellite booking to start there was a wild outbreak of shooting outside. Soon hundreds of rounds were hitting the building and coming in through the windows.

'The counter-revolutionaries are getting in! They'll kill us all!', someone shouted in rather good English from the passage-way outside. From where I lay on the floor I looked around for somewhere to hide, and the only place I could see was a locker against one of the walls. I got into it for a moment or two, but felt distinctly foolish. The floor seemed a better place. In the end it turned out that there were no counter-revolutionaries anyway: it was just one group of excitable volunteers with guns shooting at one another. But a lot of people were killed or injured all the same.

As we were leaving a man with a scarf tied round his head, revolution-chic style, stuck his gun in my stomach and asked me who I was and what I was doing.

'Stop play-acting, you silly wanker,' I answered in English. I had been through a lot that day, and this seemed like the final straw. I pushed the gun-barrel away.

'I speak English,' he said grimly. 'I went to university in Manchester.'

Bad call, I thought. Then it seemed so ludicrous I grinned, and after a moment he grinned back at me. I could sense Bill Handford physically relax as he stood beside me.

'Perhaps you ought to be a bit more careful, John,' he said gently as we walked away. I agreed. My instant's irritability could have got us both killed.

In the empty streets we and a group of other television people were given a lift back to our hotel in an ambulance reeking of blood. The sides and beds were covered with it.

« »

A few days later, exhausted, we left Tehran. The blood-letting was beginning to frighten as well as sicken me; one of our team had to go to the airport every day to ship our film to London, and each time he had to deal with someone new because the others had been executed. When the British embassy organized the evacuation of Commonwealth citizens, it was agreed with the desk in London that we should film it and bring out the pictures. Someone new would have to take over.

The evacuation was carried out superbly well, headed by a young diplomat called David Reddaway who escorted a column of cars and buses filled with very nervous people through the streets of Tehran to the British embassy summer compound in the north of the city. He stood up in the lead jeep like a tank commander, cutting a tremendous figure. I disliked him on sight for being so able and good-looking, but seven years later, when I met him again, he became one of my closest friends.

We were milling around with the evacuees, filming groups of people making the best of it and keeping calm and doing all the other things British people tend to do when they're frightened, when one of the other diplomats told me in passing that a call had got through for us from London. There was, apparently, a charter plane waiting at the airport to take us out. The pilot could only wait for another forty minutes, the diplomat said languidly.

Life suddenly speeded up, like fast-forwarding a video. Within a minute I had done a curious deal with the embassy: if we were given the ambassador's car and chauffeur to take us to the airport, they said, would we agree to take someone out with us? Who it was, I didn't want to know. I imagine it was a senior figure from the Shah's regime who had worked in some way for the British, and whose life was now in danger. I agreed. We even managed to locate our luggage in one of the many trucks full of cases and packages.

The ambassador's chauffeur was a superb Pakistani, the car a rather grand Jaguar. We sped through the crowded streets with the Union Jack flying, at speeds which made me close my eyes. When there was no room in the road the chauffeur would mount the pavement and drive down that instead. It seemed to me like the last great imperial ride of the Empire. Finally, as the airport came into sight, the chauffeur looked at me proudly. Thirty-five minutes had passed since we had spoken to the languid diplomat.

The pilot was waiting for us in the deserted terminal, and we packed all our gear into the plane. Then I stood and waited in the main road for the mysterious British agent to show himself. Time passed: no vehicle appeared on the long approach to the airport. No one was coming.

The pilot came up quietly beside me and looked meaningfully at his watch. I waited a few minutes longer, then nodded my head and turned. We had kept our side of the bargain. It was time to leave.

10

Low Points

IT WAS A SUNDAY evening in March 1980, and my life was about to change for ever. The phone rang.

'Hello, sir. Are you sitting down?'

'What does it matter whether I'm standing up or sitting down? Who are you, anyway?' Oh God, I thought, I'm sounding like my father; I must stop being so irritable.

'We're from the ambulance service. I'm sorry to have to tell you your dad's had a heart attack. He died half an hour ago.'

The tears seemed to spring out of my eyes as I stood there, listening to the ambulanceman's calm, patient voice. In less than an hour I was standing by my father's body. I kissed the cold white forehead and put my hands on the thick, clever hands, and in case there might even now be some vestige of consciousness I told him aloud how sorry I was for the way I'd been. But he would have known that already.

For more than a year there had been a coolness between us. He was a difficult man, his financial affairs were collapsing around him, and a particular tax official called Windsor, a dreary little man with a drip at the end of his perpetually red nose, had made it his life's work to hunt my father down for the years of vagueness and careless accounting. A few months earlier my father had called me in that self-mocking way of his.

'I've worked it out that I've got enough money to live in comfort for the rest of my life.'

'That's good,' I said warily.

'As long as I die by Thursday.'

He had a little longer than that, but not much. He couldn't see the point in living any more.

Two days before he died he came round one evening when I was on my own in our flat in Wimbledon. We sat together in the kitchen, talking and laughing as if the old days had come back again, and there were no savage tax inspectors or unsympathetic bank managers in the world: just a gallery of funny and absurd portraits from the present and the past for us to wander through and make jokes about. He made me a cup of the rich coffee he had always used to make during my childhood, and asked me questions about my work and my opinions, which were so different from his; and when I said idly that he was never usually interested in them, he smiled. I didn't understand the significance of the smile at the time.

And then he left, and something made me call out to him that I loved him, which I probably hadn't said for a good many years, and he called out that he loved me too, and I heard the sound of his feet going downstairs and the front door closing. And that was it, for ever.

A few days after his death I had to go to his local post office and tell them to stop his mail. I had managed to arrive on the day the old age pensions were handed out, and there was a queue of sad cases, shuffling forward, supported by sticks. Well, I thought, at least my father was spared all that. He was sixty-five when he died, and he had seemed to be still at the height of his strength and powers.

I couldn't take my eyes off one poor old character in the queue, yellow-faced and bowed, who could scarcely move one foot in front of the other. And then, as though he were standing a little behind me and to my right, I heard my father's voice:

'My God, I looked better than that poor old sod after I'd been dead three days.'

It was, I suppose, a kind of objective correlative for my yearning for him, but at the time it sounded as though he was actually there beside me, and the tone was precisely that kind of gallows humour which was habitually his.

I still see him occasionally, of course, as one does: the back of his head in a crowd, the turn of his feet, a wave from across a room. And then it isn't him after all, and it's as though the level of the light has dropped a little, or the music has gone softer, or the colours are more muted again. I don't suppose a day has passed since 30 March 1980 when I haven't thought how much I miss him.

« »

My life had changed in another way that month too. Some time before my boss had announced that someone else – John Humphrys – would be reporting on the main story of the time, the Lancaster House talks on Rhodesian/Zimbabwean independence. I had been carved out of my own job. Angrily, I said I couldn't accept that and would be taking the next good position which came up. It was a superb one: the political editorship of the BBC. It had always been occupied by some tremendous grandee, and now, in my mid-thirties, I had landed it.

Yet with hindsight it was a terrible mistake. Travelling the world and reporting foreign news had become my life, and I would now have to give it all up and restrict myself to British affairs. People within the Corporation began to speak of me as the coming man, the next director-general but one, not realizing how I loathed the idea of giving up my freedom as a broadcaster in order to become an administrator.

It wasn't going to be easy. I had never set foot in the Houses of Parliament before, and had no first-hand knowledge of any domestic political issue except Northern Ireland and our membership of the European Community. But, I told myself, British politics were no different from French, or American, or Russian politics: if I could master the one I could certainly manage the other.

I knew, though, that this was a tricky time. The BBC's political editor isn't merely a journalist, he or she also has to be a diplomat. The BBC's own position is subject to political pressures, and the political editor can make an important difference in the degree of pressure which is exerted. Margaret Thatcher had become prime minister less than a year before, and although it wasn't entirely clear at that stage how far to the right she was, it was already obvious that she didn't like the BBC much and was inclined to talk about cutting it down to size.

I also didn't know whether there was some secret understanding between government and the BBC, some private channel through which instructions were passed. I had thought it might be true over South Africa, and it wasn't; but this was different. If anyone knows for certain, I thought, it will be the political editor. And when I received an invitation to go and see one of the topmost people within the BBC, himself a former political editor, I was afraid that now, at last, I was about to be inducted into the ultimate mystery.

But all he wanted to do was to give me a bit of advice.

'You've got a very difficult group of correspondents there. If I were you I'd try to get rid of—' And a name or two followed.

He was absolutely right. Pleasant and intelligent though they might be singly, together the political correspondents of whom I was now the head formed a coven which habitually united against the political editor. In my case it was worse. I was younger than any of them, had no experience whatever of reporting British politics, had come from television which they all disliked, and had been the successful candidate for a job each one of them had gone in for. On 1 March, as I made my way into the grand gothic atmosphere of Westminster for the first time in my life, I was up against it.

There were many things at Westminster I came to enjoy: being able to ring up Cabinet ministers and talk about matters of high policy or low personality; understanding the ins and outs of so many subjects that were of national importance; getting to know some of the senior civil servants who actually ran the system. I enjoyed the risk of reporting on complex subjects as candidly as I could, while knowing that if I got something wrong I might do the BBC, and myself, irreparable harm.

I loved the Palace of Westminster itself – the architecture, the smell of ancient wood and stone, the complexity of Barry's design. I never tired of walking through Westminster Hall at night, and thinking of the trials of Charles I and Robert Carr and Warren Hastings, or the lying in state of a dozen kings and queens. I couldn't pass through St Stephen's entrance without imagining the old House of Commons there in the passageway, or Pitt and Fox at the despatch box. I couldn't sit and look down from the press gallery at prime minister's questions without thinking of Gladstone and Asquith and Atlee and Churchill. But that was just about it.

Early on, someone I came to know well in the lobby assured me that if I had ever had any affinity for a particular party (though as it happened I didn't) I would soon lose it.

'The best place,' he said, 'is the Party conferences. The Nationalists are all disgusting bigots, and even if you're Scots like me you'll dislike them. Then come the Liberals.' (This was before the days of the merger with the Social Democrats.) They all turn up in their sandals talking about the whales and the importance of local government, and you'll think you've never seen a drearier or more incompetent lot in your life.

'Then you'll get the big boys. The Labour conference will be full of poison, and they're all as vicious as hell. And when you've seen the Tories with their prejudices, and you've had a look at the right-wing thugs sitting at the back, then believe me you'll never think any of them are fit to run a parish council. It's a great feeling. Like getting over being an alcoholic.'

He was right. I might think one policy was better than another, I might feel it was in the national interest that one set of politicians was bundled out of office to be replaced by another, but I would never make the mistake of imagining that there was a single correct way, or a single party which deserved to govern.

I always enjoy listening to politicians sounding off about the bias of the BBC. In the last, wretched months of the Major government in 1997 MPs and ministers were always complaining that the *Today* programme on Radio 4 was a hotbed of Labour sympathies. There was a brief pause when the Blair government took their place, and then they too were talking darkly of anti-government sympathies and deliberate wrecking tactics, when some particular Secretary of State tried to defend the indefensible against John Humphrys.

In the mid-1980s the then Chancellor of the Exchequer had made the mistake of rounding on the late Brian Redhead by saying he knew he was a Labour supporter.

'We will now have a minute's silence,' Brian said, 'while you reflect on the enormity of presuming to know how I vote in a secret ballot, and the rest of us reflect on the failure of your economic policies.'

Which, of course, is entirely what the Chancellor's outburst was designed to deflect the listeners from thinking about.

I not only disliked the political parties, I found I disliked MPs as a group. A few, indeed, became good friends of mine; but often the size of an MP's ego seemed to be in inverse proportion to his or her quality as a human being. They were inclined to orate or to quote their past speeches even over the lunch table, in a way that showed they believed it mattered. The gossip was usually enjoyable, but there was a level of pomposity which quickly became boring. Among Conservatives, the way a man (and it was always, I think, men) pronounced the key word 'Parliament' was an indicator of their tedium quotient:

'My name is Pratt, and I'm Member of Par'ment for Dullington.'

So, I found, was the wearing of bow-ties or silly waistcoats.

The warning-lights for Labour MPs were completely different. The bores in their ranks dressed down in sports jackets and old thick-soled shoes, and they were inclined to buttonhole you about Europe. In fact Europe as a whole was, and remains, a subject for Olympic-level political bores of all parties; especially if, as was the case with me, you happened to know something about it. No doubt down the decades bi-metallism, imperial preference and nationalization have attracted much the same kind of people, for and against.

I accept that I was deeply jaundiced, but I didn't like political reporters as a group much either. Being used to the free and easy, iconoclastic attitudes of foreign correspondents, I found Westminster depressing. Much political reporting was excellent, the work of some of the best and most independent minds in British journalism. The average, though, was distinctly poor.

The journalists there sometimes seemed to be as defensive of the customs of the place as any sergeant-at-arms. If you tried to go in by the wrong door, or failed to wear a tie, or sat in the wrong seat, or arrived late, they would shake their heads and someone would have a quiet word with you afterwards. Some of the reporters found it hard to distinguish between themselves and the MPs they reported on; they would adopt their language and mannerisms, and were as prickly about the rules of the place as the MPs themselves.

'I say,' said someone at a noisy group I went to early in my time at Westminster, 'order! Order!'

I felt too that the subject of their reporting tended to be the politics of personality and debating-chamber performance, rather than those of the world inhabited by ordinary men and women. Little groups would gather outside the press gallery to decide how well someone had spoken in debate, when the reality seemed to me to have been already established by civil servants and other Cabinet ministers, or by the IMF, the United States or the European Commission. You didn't hear much at Westminster about that. The outside world often scarcely seemed to exist there.

This was the way the people we came later to know as spin-doctors liked it. Everything at Westminster was designed to bolster the notion that this was the cockpit of the nation, the omphalos of the known universe. And once government or party policy had been established, the entire official machinery on all sides was geared to present it as fixed and certain; only mavericks or the insane could possibly question it. Yet if the hold of one particular party on its followers was weakened, as Labour's was from 1974 to the late eighties, or the Conservatives' was during and after John Major's prime ministership, then the political reporters gave disproportionate amounts of attention to the rebels, who gained a kind of credibility from the attention alone; even though as individuals they were sometimes quite sad cases.

But most of all I hated the lobby system. I felt like a free-range chicken which had been caught and jammed in with battery hens. Twice a day – characteristically, the times were fixed to suit the newspapers rather than radio and television, which were regarded as noisy and rather unnecessary interlopers in this cosy little world – we would troop to some place which according to the dreary mythos of the British political control system didn't exist, and where a man or woman we couldn't name or quote would tell us things which we were encouraged to present as objective fact.

The best journalists in the lobby, and there were plenty of them, used these briefings as part of their own wider enquiries and contacts, so that it wasn't necessarily true at all that Downing Street succeeded with them in setting and dominating the agenda: on the contrary. But there were many who were neither independent-minded, nor bold, nor well-connected. They were the greatest beneficiaries and the fiercest defenders of the client relationship which the lobby system inculcated: a relationship which kept them weak and at a disadvantage. They hugged their chains. The lobby system, secretive, consensual, a mystery into which you had to be inducted and in which it was necessary to believe implicitly, was a positive encouragement to the journalism of laziness; which is why it has endured so long. And the fact that lobby briefings didn't officially exist enabled the prime minister of the day to subvert the everyday reality of political life by establishing the official line first, before any alternative could be properly formulated.

There was a move by one or two of the national newspapers to boycott the institution of Downing Street briefings, and I argued in favour of the BBC's joining them. We would, I said, have to find our own stories rather than have them fed to us; it would be better for us as journalists, and better for our listeners and viewers too. It was clear, though, that there was absolutely no support for this in the BBC hierarchy, and the correspondents in the BBC's political unit were adamantly opposed to any change.

The Downing Street spokesman for most of Mrs Thatcher's time in power was Bernard Ingham. In himself he was pleasant and decent enough, but as her representative he wrapped himself in a kind of aggressive, obscurantist Englishness which I found deeply distasteful. The lobby correspondents seemed to love it, laughing deferentially at each bulldog-breed remark he came out with, noting down every crack he made against some Cabinet minister who was felt to be insufficiently loyal to Mrs Thatcher. Ingham was the kind of man who, when he went abroad, always left his watch on London time. Once, at a Commonwealth conference in Canada, a young journalist from Uganda who was sitting next to me at a British briefing stood up and with great nervousness asked a perfectly reasonable question. Ingham's response was so scathing that she sat down and started crying.

'You mustn't worry,' I whispered, putting my arm round her shoulders, 'that's how he is with everyone.'

'No, no, no,' she said, the tears pouring down her face, 'it's because I'm just a black girl. It's because I don't know anything.'

« »

No doubt a great deal of what I have said about Westminster is the sour grapes of someone who failed to make a success of his time there. As far as I can tell from watching the output in the newspapers and on television and radio the balance between journalist and politician has righted itself to a considerable extent nowadays. It helps that we no longer have a prime minister who sets out to frighten people, or who rewards mere slavish obedience with official honours. Editors who did Margaret Thatcher's work in the press could expect knighthoods, so they demanded greater Thatcherism from their political correspondents. Those who tried to keep objective had a hard time of it. Like the crowds in Iran, like the old SABC, Mrs Thatcher had a personal dictionary of political terms which contained no definition of 'objectivity'. Neutrality she regarded as mere weakness. You were either wholeheartedly for her, or she was wholeheartedly against you. I was reminded of Thucydides writing about the changes brought by the Peloponnesian War:

> What used to be described as a thoughtless act of aggression was now regarded as the courage one would expect to find in a party member; to think of the future and wait was merely another way of saying one was a coward; any idea of moderation was just another attempt to disguise one's unmanly character; ability to understand a question from all sides meant that one was totally unfitted for action.

And yet, frustrating and unsatisfying as my time at Westminster was, she made it extraordinarily interesting. Margaret Thatcher was in her first year as prime minister still, and it wasn't entirely clear how revolutionary her government would be. In those days, too, she could be charming and attractive. At a dinner in Downing Street for a number of leading businessmen early in 1980 she kicked off her shoes, jumped up on a chair to address them, and announced that she was a round peg in a Cabinet of squares.

And so she was, at first. She and her allies were in a minority within the government, and most of the older males who surrounded her were hoping desperately that her revolution would crash and burn. They would invite me to lunch, or to their offices in the evening, to tell me how dreadful things were becoming, and how damaging it all was to the country. But they never seemed to say so openly. She, for her part, used the machinery of government against them: particularly the lobby.

With hindsight, it is possible to see that Margaret Thatcher succeeded in turning round the fortunes of the country. Before she came to power, the emphasis was all on managing the national decline. No one seriously thought that this decline was a process which could be reversed. She did, and she was right.

I found myself disliking many of things she did, but admiring the woman herself. In October 1979, when I was still diplomatic correspondent, I had covered her visit to Lusaka for the Commonwealth conference. The Zambian press had been full of angry and threatening articles about her policy towards Rhodesia and South Africa, and it looked as though there would be violent demonstrations when she landed. I went to the airport with a camera crew to film her arrival, and we realized at once that everything was going to be chaotic.

It was night-time, and just as her plane touched down the lights on the airport apron failed. Lord Carrington, the Foreign Secretary wrote afterwards that he noticed her putting on some dark glasses. When he asked why, she said it was in case anyone threw acid. No one did, of course, and the mood of the crowd was curious rather than hostile. But she couldn't have known that, and she showed great courage in charging down the steps of the aircraft and right into the crowd which, thanks to the incompetence of the Zambian police, had gathered there. We had fought our way to the foot of the steps and were waiting for her. In the darkness our camera lights must have been dazzling. We moved in front of her through the crowd, and I called out to her. Even so, it was a moment or two before she realized we were a British crew. Then she answered.

```
Transcript of interview recorded 21.10.79 at Lusaka
airport

Speakers: Rt Hon Margaret Thatcher PC MP Prime Minister
(non-staff), John Simpson (staff)

Note: high level of background noise.

JS: Prime Minister, there have been many attacks on you
in the press here. Do you think you're going to have a
difficult time at the Commonwealth Conference?

MT: No, I don't. I'm just going to put our point as well
as I can, and no amount of pressure can stop that. My
goodness, it will take more than that to stop us.
```

It was a magnificent performance. Not only that, she showed that a new era had begun. In the past, as I had found on Euston Station with Harold Wilson nine years before, British prime ministers refused to speak off the cuff like this. At a stroke Mrs Thatcher had changed all that. She regarded the cameras as her allies, and used them to her own advantage; even at a difficult time like that.

Sometimes in the years to come she would say or do something foolish when the cameras were on her, but she never seemed to care. Much more often she would present herself to them in precisely the way she most wanted to appear. She was the queen of the doorstep interview, and I liked her for it. In some ways, wherever she went, it seemed to me she was back on the tarmac at Lusaka airport, charging through a hostile crowd in the dark and still managing to look good.

There was a certain element of seduction about the business of getting her to speak on camera. I learned how to position myself in order to catch her eye, and found out the kind of questions that were most likely to get a good response. It was no good shouting out something rude or aggressive; nor was there any point in starting off *in medias res* by blurting out the key question. She had first to be attracted, then to take the hook, and then be reeled in. I often waited until someone else had called out to her first and was duly ignored.

```
Transcript of interview, Luxembourg, 11.6.86

Speakers: unknown reporter, Rt Hon Margaret Thatcher PC
MP (non-staff), John Simpson (staff)

Unknown: Mrs Thatcher, surely you don't have any hope of
winning your case here today?

[Confused sounds]

JS: Good afternoon, Prime Minister.

MT: Good afternoon, John. Isn't the weather delightful?
We've only just got here, you know, and it's so much
warmer here than it was in London.

JS: Absolutely. You've got a bit of a problem on your
hands here, though, haven't you? It's going to be pretty
hard.

MT: No, I think we are going to get what we've come here
for. You see, the figures show perfectly clearly that—
```

And so on. Brevity was never one of Mrs Thatcher's more evident characteristics. Once my crew and I managed to get outside the door of some European summit meeting in Brussels and door-stepped her there. She ran through most of her brief with me, while Bernard Ingham kicked me angrily on the shin – as though it were my fault she wouldn't stop – and the assembled presidents and prime ministers inside the room shifted in their seats and tried to hear a preview of what they would shortly be subjected to in person.

'What a woman,' Jacques Chirac said once, when I came to know him. 'She never stops talking. And about such small things.'

She loved an audience. In her early years as prime minister, in particular, she could charm the most hostile of groups. At the European summit in Dublin in 1980, for instance, she gave a press conference after having demanded 'her' billion pounds as a refund from the EC budget. The journalists, from every country in the European Community and well beyond, were as always predominantly hostile. But she took each question and dealt with it so adroitly, and sometimes wittily, that at the end most of the journalists stood up and applauded her: something I had never seen before, and have never seen again. She looked good, too: a handsome, tough blonde with a charm which only later seemed to evaporate.

At the press conference she gave after the 1980 G7 summit in Venice she suddenly launched into a completely irrelevant attack on the BBC for describing the mujaheddin fighting the Russians in Afghanistan as 'guerrillas'.

'I think they're freedom-fighters,' she began to rave, 'and the BBC should be ashamed of itself for not calling them that.'

All round the briefing-room Japanese, American and French economic journalists were looking at each other and wondering what they'd stumbled into. Afterwards I went with her and her official party to the room where I was to interview her.

'Should I explain why we call them "guerrillas"?' I asked, as we walked along side by side.

She stopped, and the assorted secretaries, advisers and security men rammed into one another behind us. She put her hand on my arm and looked at me coquettishly. It was like flirting with Queen Victoria.

'My dear,' she said, 'you are sensitive. Don't you realize it's all—'

Her voice died away and she walked on again, but it was clear to me what this piece of aposiopesis meant: it was all part of the game. An important part of her constituency liked to hear the BBC attacked, and she enjoyed playing up to it.

Years later I talked at length to one of her advisers from that time, who had become one of her fiercest critics. It turned out that he had spent a couple of hours once a week with her in her first years as prime minister, discussing his particular subject. She would make him his lunch in the kitchen of the private flat at the top of 10 Downing Street while he talked. It all came to an end at the time of the Falklands War: she was of course far too busy then to receive him. And when it was over, he said, and he rang Downing Street to see when he should resume his lessons, he was informed coldly that the prime minister wouldn't have any more time for him. He was given a knighthood as a consolation prize, but it didn't help.

'After the war was over she became an empress, a dictator,' he said. 'She didn't want to see the people who had helped her before that. She'd finished with them. I wasn't the only one, you know.'

'So what happened when you saw her next time?'

'Saw her? I never saw her again. I still haven't, to this day.'

I could see what it was. Of course he was offended and hurt, but it was worse than that. He'd been in love with her, and she'd rejected him.

In public she grew better than ever at the art of being on television. When she went to Moscow in 1986 and stood up in her car outside a dreary block of flats where she had visited a highly unrepresentative family and waved at the crowd, I thought they were going to pull her to pieces in their adoration. Only minutes earlier, though, she had shown the ferocity she was beginning to be famous for. In the sitting room of the flat, I had asked her if this wasn't really all part of her campaign for the next year's general election: 'campaigning in the streets of Moscow', I said. She replied that it wasn't, and talked about Anglo-Soviet relations and the importance of Mikhail Gorbachev. But it was obviously working away at her; and when my friend and colleague John Sergeant followed up with a radio interview and asked her about her reasons for the trip, she lost her temper altogether.

'I think it's disgraceful to question the purpose of my visit,' she said, as though he was the one who had asked her about campaigning in the streets of Moscow. 'I'm here for Britain.' In her mind, she was as much the state as Louis XIV had been.

She always seemed to cut back at you in the most personal way if you offended her. In Rhodes, after the G7 summit of 1989, she was interviewed by several British television journalists, one after the other. It annoyed her that we all took so long about it, and as the BBC sound recordist put a microphone on her I made a feeble joke in an attempt to cool her down.

'Just think how long the interviews will take when there are twenty or thirty television channels.'

There was no perceptible pause before she got her retaliation in.

'I don't know why everyone says the BBC is so good,' she snapped, as though I'd just said it was. 'I think American television is the best in the world.'

I said snidely that I supposed she enjoyed all the soaps and game shows. She looked puzzled for a moment; she had no discernible sense of satire and had obviously never watched American television in her life. Her main authority on television was Rupert Murdoch, and he had probably told her that you could watch anything you wanted there, at the touch of a button. She always seemed to believe what Murdoch told her.

In many ways she grew worse, more difficult and more imperial as time went on. But she still had some vestiges of the old power to charm, when the tension of the moment eased. By election day in 1987 – her last election, as it turned out, and the moment at which, if she had had a little more humility and awareness, she might have stepped down with honour and been regarded for ever after as one of the best prime ministers of the century – the stress of the campaign was over, and it was obvious she was going to win hands down. I had covered her whole campaign, working with a cameraman who was her particular favourite. He was one of mine, too: a former naval petty officer called Derek Collier, with white hair and a rakishly broken nose. He had immense charm, especially for women of a certain age.

Now, in the car park of her constituency headquarters in Finchley, we were all standing round slightly awkwardly making polite conversation with her when Derek asked me in a whisper if he should give her his camera and let her film all of us.

'I don't think—' I started to say, but he was already off.

She loved it. He put the camera on her shoulder, and she spun round like a young girl, filming the faces of the cameramen and photographers who had followed her all through the election. I met her many times after that, but this was the last flash I saw of the woman who had once jumped on a chair in her stockinged feet and announced that she was a round peg in a Cabinet of squares. She was part Elizabeth

Tudor, part monster, part housewife with a small, suburban attitude to life. But she certainly had something; and I'm glad I was there to see it.

« »

The BBC had always had a strange attitude towards news. Originally when its news service began on radio there was a great deal of opposition from the newspapers, who sensed a potential rival and lobbied successfully for a wide range of restrictions on what the BBC could report, and how and when it could do it. Most of the formal restrictions had faded away by the end of the Second World War, during which the BBC had shown its value to the full. But the creation of a television news service brought about a revival of all the old anxieties on the part of the press, and all the BBC's old willingness to pull its punches. The first newsreaders were, for instance, instructed to look down at their scripts rather than at the camera, in case the force of their personalities leant a particular strength and force to the news items they were reading.

And they were newsreaders, rather than news presenters. ITN, which began in 1955 free of the old baggage of the past, hired experienced and qualified journalists to present its news programmes, and to emphasize the difference between them and the BBC, ITN called them newscasters; which is precisely what they were. The BBC, still nervous about the reaction of politicians and the newspapers, continued to use people who were essentially actors to read the news on television. With them, there would be no danger of slipping in an unscheduled opinion merely by the emphasis on a word or a particular look at the camera. They were purely front-men for the subeditors who wrote their scripts.

This state of affairs lasted until 1981. As it happens, the BBC's front-men were particularly impressive. Richard Baker, Robert Dougall and Kenneth Kendall looked good on camera, read superbly, and were men of intelligence and ability in their own right. But that only enhanced the essential sham. In every large television news operation, there is a team of people behind the camera to write the material which the presenter reads; but there is always the illusion that the person who presents the news is somehow the author and originator of it. Occasionally it is more than an illusion.

The main news presenter of the American network ABC, Peter Jennings, is the chief news executive, shaping the programme, examining the scripts of the reports to be broadcast, changing them where necessary, writing his own introductions, and then acting as master of ceremonies on air. (For the rest of the time he tries to work out how to spend the vast amount of money he gets for performing these functions.) But all this can only be done in a small, intimate operation like ABC News, with a single main programme per day.

Every big television news organization gives the impression, intentionally or not, that its presenters are Peter Jenningses, and many of the viewers believe they are; but the fact is that some are clever and experienced and wide-ranging and play a significant part in the construction of the news programme, and others are not.

In 1980 a new editor of television news was appointed at the BBC. He planned to change the old-fashioned newsreader system and replace it with one where leading BBC journalists wrote and shaped and presented the news themselves. At that stage television news was still an independent fiefdom of a larger independent barony, the news division. The director-general had overall control and responsibility for it, but the people in charge of the networks had none at all. Within reason, an editor of television news could do what he (there has never yet been a woman in the job) wanted.

I was desperate to be one of the news presenters. I realized by now that I had made a terrible mistake by becoming political editor, but I seemed to be trapped. Worse, people inside and outside the BBC assumed that if I were given so important a job in my mid-thirties, I was being groomed for the topmost job. It is noticeable in the BBC that people who are tipped as future director-generals very rarely make it. Their rivals combine to stymie them at some way along the line. It was one thing not to want the job in the first place; it was even worse to give up the freedom of being a broadcaster and fail to become director-general.

The only way I could avoid a career which ended with my being head of paperclips was to find something that everybody could understand was a big and worthwhile job in its own right. I knew I would infuriate the management as a whole by giving up the political editorship – they don't like it in the BBC if you duck out of the future they have in mind for you – but I gambled that my offence would eventually be forgotten. Presenting the *Nine O'Clock News* might be a clear demotion, but I knew it wouldn't seem like that to the outside world, which assumes that the presenter of the news is somehow the ring-master of the show.

So I lobbied hard, and eventually John Humphrys and I got the job. There was an awkward little session with the BBC hierarchy when I told them, but they couldn't physically stop me. I closed the door on my office at Westminster without a backward look. (The correspondents there were predictably outraged: it was bad enough that I should be put in over their heads in the first place, but to leave the job voluntarily was completely beyond their comprehension.) After some consideration the BBC appointed John Cole to be my successor, in the hope – one senior bureaucrat said to me – that his strong Ulster accent would fade after a while. I pointed out he had lived in London for a quarter of a century without losing the faintest edge to it.

And yet it was obvious that things wouldn't go smoothly. Some of the wounds were self-inflicted: the editor of television news hadn't bothered to tell the director-general that he was about to change the entire way the BBC's main news programme was presented, so there was fury in the upper levels of the Corporation. The technology we were using was on its last legs, and the system kept breaking down on air. And to cap it all, the editor believed that it would be bad for us to have any prior practice before we went on air for the first time: so Humphrys and I, neither of whom had ever sat in a television studio and read a news bulletin before, had to find out how it was done, live.

Not surprisingly, things went wrong from the start. The autocue would collapse, tapes would break down, items would be played out of order. In the first few weeks it was rare for an edition of the *Nine O'Clock News* to go smoothly. There was understandable outrage in the press about the sacking of excellent long-term BBC servants like Richard Baker and Kenneth Kendall, both of whom behaved with considerable dignity. Kendall was tricked by a newspaper into saying something bitter, and very soon afterwards fell down and broke his arm. I went to see him in hospital.

'Serves me right, dear boy,' he murmured.

Some of the newspapers were worse than others. There was one particularly spiteful critic who suggested that replacing Baker and Kendall with Humphrys and Simpson was like finding that Barry Manilow was singing in place of Pavarotti. Our own colleagues were often hostile too. One of the aims of having experienced journalists to present the news was that they should play a clear editorial role, writing stories and helping to decide what was broadcast. The team of subeditors and producers, who had long done the job themselves, didn't at all enjoy it when we altered the scripts they had written. Stories appeared in the newspapers and in *Private Eye* about us.

As a result, though, my friendship with Humphrys became firmer than ever. We stuck together, sharing a little windowless office which had once been a dressing-room, knowing that we were being sniped at continually but managing to keep going purely by making savage jokes about the large number of people – who ranged from the BBC management, our own editor and colleagues to the critics – whom we disliked. As therapy, it worked rather well.

By the spring of 1981 we were getting somewhere. The ratings were up, the criticisms were much more muted, the production values seemed to be improving, and the news was a lot sharper and better focused. The BBC had at last joined the rest of the television news world. True, I had created something of a problem at the start of the year, when President Anwar Sadat of Egypt was assassinated at a military parade in Cairo. Most of the American networks who had been covering the parade left before the shooting broke out, assuming it was just another boring military occasion. Only ABC, which was then allied to ITN, remained. There was also a cameraman there from the Visnews agency, which was part-owned by the BBC, but he had disappeared in the confusion. He had, however, booked a satellite feed to London beforehand.

In the immediate aftermath of the assassination there was total confusion. No new satellite bookings were accepted, but those which had already been booked remained. Somehow, ABC managed to get its pictures onto the Visnews satellite. I watched them as they were received in London: good under the circumstances, though understandably confused as the cameraman himself dived for cover. You could just see one or two brave souls still standing up as the gunfire ripped up the reviewing stand where Sadat had been sitting.

'What the hell are we going to do?' the editor of the day said glumly.

These pictures belonged exclusively to ABC and their partners, ITN: in the absence of any material from Visnews the BBC would have nothing at all on the most important story in the world: just a still photograph or two and some library film.

'Use them,' I said. 'After all, they came in on our satellite. We can always claim we thought there was a deal.'

Quite wrong and totally unscrupulous, of course; but it seemed to me that the ten million or so people who chose to watch the BBC rather than ITN shouldn't be robbed of the opportunity to see what had happened. Nowadays the industry is a little more sensible and a little less dog-in-the-manger: in a similar case we would ask permission to use the pictures, and credit whichever of our competitors had shot them by making an announcement on the screen. It may be hurtful to the pride, but it serves the audience better. In those days there was no agreement. Instead we ran the pictures. It was years before the resulting lawsuit was settled.

A few days later the boss of Visnews came to the BBC to ask if he could see all the rushes of the massacre. I sat in the edit suite with him. Every now and then he would ask the picture editor to freeze a particular frame, and would scan it carefully. Eventually he grunted, and pointed to someone who was standing up in the corner of the frame, even though there were bullets flying all round him.

'Brave man,' I said.

'He's a shit,' said the boss of Visnews. 'Look at that dark shape on the ground in front of him.'

I couldn't make it out. Then it was explained to me. The Visnews cameraman, an Egyptian famous for his coolness under fire, was just coming up to his sixtieth birthday. He had been at the military parade, and when the gunfire broke out he had taken an instantaneous decision. He put his video camera down on the ground – hence the dark shape – and grabbed the stills camera hanging round his neck. He knew that if he filmed the assassination for Visnews, the most he would receive would be a telex of congratulation and prizes at television festivals; if he took still photographs, he would be able to sell them for serious money.

So that's what he did. An American news magazine plastered his pictures across the cover and on four inside pages. Both he and I had had unworthy impulses, but the difference was that he enjoyed a wealthy retirement while I was blamed, rightly, for television piracy.

The *Nine O'Clock News* seemed to have outlived its bad press by the time of Argentina's invasion of the Falkland Islands in April 1982. This was the kind of occasion when television news comes into its own, and we started to build up the inevitable massive audiences. Humphrys and I powered on night after night as the crisis unfolded, and on the days when I wasn't presenting the news I would also prepare background reports – packages, as we called them – about different aspects of the Falklands War. One Friday night in May when things seemed rather quiet I decided to look back at what had happened so far, and what had led the Argentine military junta to invade the islands.

There was nothing particularly startling in my report, and a government inquiry later made all the points I did, plus plenty of others. I pointed out how the Argentines had misread signals such as the planned scrapping of HMS *Endeavour* in the South Atlantic and the Thatcher government's attempts to do a deal with Argentina over the long-term future of the islands, and regarded them as signs that Britain was no longer interested in the Falklands. The invasion, I said, had unwittingly been encouraged by British policy.

But Downing Street, already nervous about the fate of the naval task-force which had now reached the Falklands, was furious that we should have focused attention on the government's own failings at this key moment. There were angry phone calls of complaint to the BBC at various levels.

I heard nothing about it over the weekend, and came to work on Monday unaware that anything had happened. I was putting together another report on the diplomatic aspect of the war for use on that night's news when I had a call to go and see the editor. He and his deputy were sitting there looking deeply depressed. I couldn't work out what had happened first, or why they had called me in. Then the editor blurted it out: the director-general had said I was to be taken off the news.

Everyone denied it had anything to do with politics or Downing Street. Maybe they were right: there had been a disaster on air the previous week, when the programme had collapsed around me. It could have been that. It could have been helped by my resignation as political editor, which had angered the management considerably. It could have been the director-general's continuing anger at the way the editor of television news had changed everything without consulting him. Not long before there had been a meeting of the Board of Management at which the question of sacking either John Humphrys or me, or both, had been discussed; and the head of BBC 1 had said that if anyone should go it would have to be me. Whatever the reason, it was.

The BBC does these things with unparalleled brutality. The editor of television news told me my sentence: I wouldn't be allowed to resign to save face, I wouldn't be allowed to present the news again, I wouldn't even be allowed to stay in the country. In two days' time I was to go to Montevideo, the capital of Uruguay, in order to report on the diplomatic aspects of the Falklands War in Latin America. If I said anything about all this to the newspapers, I would be sacked. The deputy editor of television news was sympathetic, but the editor wasn't. I might have guessed it: it was he, all those years earlier, who had rung me in Dublin at the moment of maximum pressure after I had broadcast the story about Jack Lynch, British intelligence and the Littlejohn brothers and said, 'Better be right.'

I demanded a meeting with the director-general. If he was going to sack me, I thought, he might as well tell me the reasons to my face. The appointment was fixed for the following morning. Overnight, though, I started to reconsider my approach. It is a fine thing to shout insults at the *capo di tutti capi* and storm out of his office, but it doesn't pay the mortgage. Anyway, I liked working for the BBC: for all its faults, it was still the best broadcasting organization around. By 11.00 the next morning, as the director-general's assistant ushered me sympathetically in – she knows all about it, I thought self-pityingly – I was determined to find a new job for myself; or maybe get my old job back.

The director-general was pleasant enough, but brisk. The news wasn't working and he wanted changes, but he didn't want me to leave the BBC. He didn't say if there had been any political pressure to get rid of me, and I didn't ask. What did I want to do now? I was ready for that one.

'I'd like to be diplomatic editor,' I said, awarding myself a promotion.

'Fine,' said the director-general.

'Perhaps I ought to warn you that someone has been given the job already.' And has been promised the title, I might have added.

'I said fine.'

He was picking up the phone to the editor of television news as I left.

What goes around comes around. Within the next few years the editor of television news, a sad and disappointed man, was put out to grass in a way which was almost as humiliating as my exile from the *Nine O'Clock News*. Some years later the director-general was overthrown after a plot that was far more unpleasant than the one which had brought me down. Even the head of BBC1, who had insisted that I should be the sacrificial victim, was given the same treatment. It was like working for Stalin during the Terror, with everyone around you being taken out and shot in the back of the neck. None of these things gave me the slightest pleasure; indeed, I felt a considerable sympathy for the director-general when he was overthrown. He deserved better. We all did.

As for me, I had been publicly humiliated, and promoted, and set back on the right track in my career, all in one ferocious and bewildering move. I left the country a day later, rushed like a suspect out of court with a coat over my head, and put on a flight to Rio. I had a huge amount of BBC money in my pocket, to pay for the extraordinary costs of the television operation in the South Atlantic: the exact amount, as it happened, of my mortgage. As the plane tipped its wings and flew westwards in the clear morning air, I looked down and saw Wimbledon. I could even see the house where I had lived since returning to Britain four stressful years before. My life, I felt, was changing yet again. It was becoming a habit.

« »

I was a bit-part player in the reporting of the Falklands war. From the television point of view there were only two lead actors in it. One was Michael Nicholson of ITN; the other was Brian Hanrahan of the BBC, who would one day join the World Affairs Unit which I head as diplomatic correspondent. His coolness and understatement became legendary. He captured the attention of the entire British nation at a key moment of anxiety, and became a star. The Royal Navy particularly liked Brian and his cameraman, the splendid but sometimes difficult Bernard Hesketh.

I, by contrast, mouldered on the Uruguayan shore, watching their reports. I tried not to let self-pity get the better of me, but it was sometimes difficult. I had, for instance, been selected at first to go aboard HMS *Invincible*, the ship Hanrahan and Nicholson sailed to the Falklands with, but by a particular irony the editor of television news had blocked the idea because he said I couldn't be spared from presenting the *Nine O'Clock News* programme.

'*Inutiles regrets*,' I told myself. But as week after week passed and I stayed on at the Victoria Plaza hotel in Montevideo, it was harder than ever to come to terms with my fall from grace.

Nevertheless there was great pleasure about being there. I enjoyed eating my morning *media luna* and drinking my morning *medio y medio* at the same corner café in the square opposite the hotel. I enjoyed my morning walk to get the Buenos Aires newspapers, and stopping beside a statue of someone sitting on a horse and waving a sword to have my shoes cleaned by an ancient, courtly man in a white jacket. Most of all, I enjoyed the old-fashioned Latino grandeur about Montevideo, even though the place had clearly come down in the world.

Its splendid Art Deco buildings, twenty or thirty storeys high, encrusted with post-gothic pinnacles and gargoyles and seamed with neon signs, were mouldering and dirty. Offices were often empty, shops were short of goods, many of the cars in the streets dated back to the 1950s: the taxes on imports were immensely high. Uruguay's military junta hadn't pursued its 'dirty war' against radicals and left-wingers with anything like the cruelty and thoroughness of the military regime across the River Plate in Argentina, but there had still been a good deal of torture and some people had been murdered. The gloom created by President Gregorio Alvarez and his military colleagues had settled heavily over the country. As in Argentina, the military had become unpopular and discredited; and the bolder spirits were starting to say openly that their days were numbered.

I might not have achieved anything else worthwhile in my time in Uruguay, but I was credited later with having chased its boring, brutal and not particularly intelligent President out of office. It happened one afternoon in late May. There had been suggestions in the Buenos Aires press that the Uruguayan government was starting to shift its policy of even-handedness between Britain and Argentina in the war. Britain had found this policy extremely useful, and had secretly been using humanitarian and medical flights through Montevideo for military purposes; an inconvenient customs officer at Montevideo airport, no doubt tipped off by Argentine intelligence, had discovered a consignment of arms and ammunition on board a hospital plane.

I wanted to ask the Uruguayan government about all this, but as usual it was impossible to get anyone to comment. That afternoon the boss of the television station where the BBC was based told me quietly that President Alvarez was about to begin a televised press conference in the centre of the city. Maybe he also told me that it was for Uruguayan journalists only; if so, I paid no attention. We drove there fast.

Uruguayans are polite people, and when the cameraman, sound recordist and I appeared at the door of the building where the press conference was being held, the security men were too embarrassed to stop us. We pushed open the door of the conference room rather more noisily than we should have, and saw a group of journalists, photographers and cameramen gathered in front of a table at the far end. Sitting at the table, bathed in light, was a man in uniform. He seemed to be wearing a great many medals.

We barged our way to the front, and didn't make any friends on the way. Eventually, by a process I now prefer not to think about, we ended up right in front of General Alvarez. Close to, he was a rather neat little man with a moustache. It wasn't really that he was wearing all that many medals; it was just that his chest was rather small for the ones he had.

I waited until there was a brief gap in the proceedings, then jumped in with a question.

```
Transcript of interview recorded 23.5.82, Montevideo,
Uruguay

Speakers: General Alvarez (non-staff), John Simpson
(staff)

JS: Mr President, the Argentine press is suggesting
that Uruguay has decided to give up its policy of even-
handedness towards Britain and Argentina, and to tilt
rather more towards the Argentines. Can you tell me if
this is true?

GA: [Long pause] Pero . . . No se . . .
```

[Whisper]

Unidentified voice: His Excellency wishes to say that there is no truth in this suggestion. Thank you very much.

I still feel embarrassed about this, but not nearly as embarrassed as the President. Even as I spoke I realized that he didn't understand English, but I felt my Spanish wasn't good enough for live television. Because it was a press conference for the domestic media, there was no one on hand to translate for him. He looked at me blankly for a very long time. Then he looked down at his briefing papers. Then he turned his neat little head to the left, but there was no one there. Then he turned it to the right, where his advisers were sitting. They looked away, because none of them spoke English.

Finally someone whispered something to somebody, and a man in a beautiful double-breasted suit came out of the wings at a run and spoke to the President in a whisper. After that the man in the suit straightened up and spoke to me in superb English.

Altogether the pause between the end of my question and the reply lasted for one minute, twenty-three seconds. On live television, the difference between a gap of that length and eternity is negligible.

Since Uruguay is a country of highly educated people, where speaking English is regarded as a natural accomplishment, President Gregorio Alvarez that afternoon became its most humiliated inhabitant. Not long afterwards his military regime collapsed and was replaced by a properly elected civilian government, and Alvarez went into deep retirement from which he never emerged. People were still laughing about it years later.

I would have felt sorry for him, if it weren't for the fact that he had presided over a regime which for several years had been arresting and torturing young men and women because they were Jewish, or Protestant, or Communist. Or sometimes merely because they had studied the wrong subjects at university – subjects like sociology and psychology – and so declared themselves to be potential left-wing sympathizers.

« »

Every day BBC people would come across the River Plate from Buenos Aires, bringing video cassettes for us to satellite, or fetching television equipment, or heading back to London. Argentina had started to exert a mythic fascination for me. The understanding had been that I would go to Buenos Aires at the next handover of correspondents, but after a while the Argentine authorities announced that they would no longer accept people with British passports. From now on the only correspondents we were able to send there had to have Irish or other passports. Once again things had gone wrong for me. I waited out the rest of the war in Montevideo, watching the television pictures of the big hostile demonstrations that drove the hapless, stupid General Galtieri out of power. Montevideo remained quiet and peaceful. The plane that took me back to London stopped first at Buenos Aires; but I wasn't even allowed to get off and go into the airport terminal.

For me, Argentina was unfinished business. Directly I got back to London I quickly discovered that I was eligible for an Irish passport. I gathered together the necessary birth certificates, put in my application, and eventually took possession of a green-covered document with a golden harp on the front of it. It was to be my way into all sorts of countries which had quarrelled with Britain.

Now I was in a position to be the first British correspondent to go back to Argentina after the war. Together with a *Newsnight* producer, Jana Bennett, who was American, I worked out an elaborate cover story according to which we were working for Australian television. We kitted ourselves out with all sorts of letters of accreditation from Sydney, and got onto the plane.

We had decided to take with us the cameraman Bernard Hesketh, who had yomped across the Falklands with Brian Hanrahan and filmed the war from the British side. He too had obtained an Irish passport. His sound recordist, Neville Wong, was travelling on a passport from his native Jamaica. None of us knew what Argentina was like, and we thought that if we were discovered we could be in all sorts of trouble. One British television reporter had been kidnapped in Buenos Aires during the war, and we assumed there would still be a lot of anger against the British after Argentina's comprehensive defeat.

But the BBC is bad at keeping secrets. That night, after a long drive through the darkened streets of the city, we arrived at our hotel: the

Plaza, a delightfully old-fashioned, stately place near the pleasantest shopping street in Latin America, Florida.

'*Buenas noches*,' I said to the superb figure behind the reception desk, in the best Spanish I could rustle up. '*Mi nombre es* Simpson – John Simpson.'

'Of course, sir,' he said. 'One moment.'

Jana, Bernard, Neville and I exchanged looks. The under-manager, an even more superb figure who looked like the star of a tango movie, manifested himself behind the desk.

'Ah, yes, Mr Simpson of the BBC. We have a message for you.'

'Not the BBC,' I said, 'nothing like that. No. We're Australians. Well, Irish. And American. Also Jamaican. But we're working for Australian television. Definitely.'

'But this message is from BBC Radio News, and it says "to await the arrival of Mr Simpson of BBC London".'

'Just one of those inexplicable mistakes,' I said desperately.

'Of course. I understand entirely.' He looked down for a moment. 'Well, perhaps I can say that if you had been from the BBC, it would have been a great pleasure, and indeed an honour, to have you stay in our hotel.'

What style, I thought! What class! And what grammar, too! My love affair with Argentina started at that moment.

The defeat of the Argentine armed forces in the Falklands had shown that the military dictatorship which had run the country so corruptly and ineffectually for six years wasn't even any good at the one thing the military are supposed to be there for: fighting wars. Galtieri had long since resigned, collapsing into an alcoholic depression. His place as President had been taken by a grim character called General Bignone, whose job was to wind up the dictatorship and make way for democratic elections. Mrs Thatcher had done the Argentines a valuable favour by defeating them.

Yet she and her government also had a good deal to answer for, just as the Reagan administration in the United States did. In August 1980 Cecil Parkinson, the trade secretary, had visited Argentina when the terror and the disappearances were still at their height, and had said the most ingratiating things about the junta's performance. At one stage during a press conference he confided that Britain and Argentina were engaged in the same battle. He meant the battle against inflation,

but he must have known that the Argentine military would interpret
his words as meaning that Britain supported the junta's 'crusade against
Communism', which had already cost the lives of thousands of innocent people, many of them tortured to death, and would cost the lives
of many more before the nightmare was over.

Now that it was indeed over, I had some residual guilt about
Argentina myself. Back in 1978 I had gone to a press conference given
by Amnesty International to encourage British journalists to go to
Argentina at the time of the football World Cup finals there, in order
to look at the political situation for themselves. I toyed with the idea,
but at that stage I was so new in my job with television news that I
felt it was too difficult a thing to persuade my colleagues to let me do.
The chance slipped away.

Slowly Buenos Aires was coming back to life, waking from its
nightmare. For six years people had been afraid to go out into the
streets at night, because the unmarked Ford Falcon cars which the death
squads used were patrolling slowly, looking for victims. It hadn't
mattered who you were, or what your political opinions might be.
Plenty of supporters of the regime were arrested by accident, or carelessness, and once they had seen the reality of the disappearance process
they couldn't be allowed to live.

Case after case emerged where the killers had gone to the wrong
address by mistake, perhaps because the name of their victim was
similar to the name of someone they really wanted, sometimes because
they had written the name down wrong or their finger had slipped to
the next line in the telephone directory. On more than one occasion the
death squad pushed the wrong bell, and took away the person who
answered. Sometimes they had arrested a woman because she was
attractive, and they wanted to rape her before torturing and killing
her.

And the extraordinary thing was that all this happened in a city
which is more like Western Europe than anywhere else in Latin
America. If it had been in Honduras or Guatemala it wouldn't have
surprised anyone; but Argentina, though turbulent, had always been
wealthy and sophisticated. Between the World Wars it was regarded
as an honorary part of the British Commonwealth, and British invest-
ment in Argentina was enormous. And then a sustained campaign of
terror by several different far left-wing groups brought the country to

the pitch of paranoia, so that by the mid-1970s most people didn't care what was done as long as the terrorism was stopped. It almost was; but at an appalling cost in life and decency.

We went round on our first morning in Buenos Aires to the office of the Mothers of the Plaza de Mayo, the one group which had had the courage to demand news of the people whom the death squads had 'disappeared'. A pleasant, well-dressed woman in her fifties welcomed us; and while Jana talked to her and arranged the details of filming and interviewing I stood and looked at an entire vast wall of photographs. Thousands of people stared out at me from them: young, middle-aged, old, attractive, dull, happy, serious, proud, jokey. Some of the photographs had been taken at parties or outings: the central figure would have his or her arms draped over the shoulders of others, or be giggling, or blowing out the candles on a birthday cake. There was nothing that linked them all together except their ordinariness, and the fact that they had vanished from the face of the earth and no one except their murderers knew what had happened to them.

Now, slowly, the terrible facts were coming to light. We filmed in a corner of a cemetery where the superintendent had revealed that there was a mass grave. One night the soldiers had turned up with several trucks and a mechanical digger, and had gouged out a deep pit and thrown the bodies in. That was five years earlier. Now we filmed as the first bones were unearthed: dark brown skulls, some cruelly broken by bullets, which could have been as old as the Bronze Age yet had perhaps belonged to some of the happy or serious people on the wall of photographs.

It was so quick, from the birthday party and blowing out the candles to the torture at a holding centre and the savage death, and then to this: brown bone, eye-sockets filled with earth, jaws grinning with missing teeth, utterly stripped of identity or common humanity.

Years later I met one of the torturers, a man now tortured himself by guilt at what he had done, and unable to get rid of the images which still haunted his mind. He was a naval rating, a big strapping character, who had been recruited by one of the navy's top admirals for 'special duties'. Like many of these killers and torturers, he denied that he had ever done anything himself apart from actually arresting suspects. He would escort them back to the Naval Mechanics School in Buenos Aires, or to one of the secret houses and buildings which the killers took over, but according to his own account he was only ever an onlooker.

It was standard practice to castrate the men directly they arrived, and they and many of the women were tortured for the sexual gratification of their captors. Some of the torturers couldn't drag themselves away, and when their twelve hours of duty were over they would stay on, watching and taking part or waiting for new consignments of victims. Very quickly it became clear that they weren't the slightest bit interested in anything their victims had to say. This wasn't interrogation, it was pure sadism.

We searched for a man called Alfredo Astiz, a former naval captain now reduced to the rank of lieutenant, who had played an important part in the disappearances and murders. A young, handsome, fresh-faced man, he had infiltrated the Mothers of the Plaza on the pretext that he was looking for his brother who had disappeared. They, suitably enough, mothered him: and then one evening at a meeting of all the main figures in the movement he slipped out and came back with a killer squad. Several of the women were never seen again.

Astiz shot and injured a young Swedish girl, Dagmar Hagelin, and arrested her, perhaps mistaking her for someone else. For years the Swedish government put pressure on the Argentines about the case, but although Dagmar was seen at one of the prison camps in a wheelchair she did not survive: she knew too much. He was also involved in the disappearance of two French nuns, Sister Alicia and Sister Leonie.

Finally Astiz played his part in the Falklands War, capturing the island of South Georgia and holding it until the British arrived to repossess it. As commanding officer on the island Astiz put out a white flag of surrender, then mounted a heavy machine-gun at a point where he could mow down the British soldiers who arrived to take over. Fortunately his nerve failed him. Even so, the officer who took his surrender suspected Astiz of trying to lure them into a minefield.

Feebly, the British had handed this appalling man back to the Argentines at the end of the war, and he had gone into semi-hiding by the time we arrived. I badly wanted to find him, and we were told that he was on holiday at the Atlantic resort of Mar del Plata. We arrived there and found the part of the beach which was occupied by officers of the Argentine navy. We found his beach-hut, with the sign 'ASTIZ,

Alfredo B.' over the door, but it had been closed up for a day or two. The naval officers and their wives and children gathered round us angrily and told us that Astiz was a brave man who had served his nation well, and that we were just part of an evil witch-hunt against him. They knew nothing about any disappearances; but if people had disappeared, it was because they were terrorists. We had failed to find Astiz, but we had at least got some good material for our *Newsnight* documentary.

There were some cases of real courage to set against the darkness of the disappearances. The Mothers of the Plaza themselves were magnificent. After the organization had been smashed by Astiz in 1979 the survivors decided to hold an election to put themselves on a more formal footing. Then, in the last days of the year, they took the step which settled their future, and perhaps that of Argentina as a whole: on the first Thursday of 1980 they would resume their parade in the Plaza de Mayo, outside the presidential palace. They had been beaten and arrested there so often in the past, but this time they agreed that they would never give up their campaign there again: no matter what the government and the death squads did to them.

Fearfully, they assembled at various parts of the Plaza in their flat shoes and white headscarves. Some of them had said goodbye to their families, expecting it to be for ever. But the police hadn't expected to see them at the Plaza ever again, and were completely unprepared for them. They marched around for forty minutes, and left unmolested.

After that there were plenty of arrests and beatings, but they never again failed to hold their meetings in the Plaza; and somehow, though it may have been a coincidence, the steam gradually went out of the repression and it began to fade. There were fewer disappearances. The military men running the country were more concerned with maximizing their profits from corruption than with eradicating left-wingers. By 1982 Galtieri invaded the Falklands because he thought there was no other way he and his cronies could continue in power.

One afternoon when there was nothing else to do, Bernard Hesketh and I decided to go to see the film *Missing* at a cinema in central Buenos Aires. The military censors, who were notoriously stupid, had allowed it to be shown because it was critical of the military junta in Argentina's traditional enemy, Chile. It didn't seem to occur to them that people might spot the analogy between the two neighbouring versions of state terrorism.

We sat side by side in the uncomfortable old-fashioned cinema seats. The presentation was dreadful: the voice-over was so out of synch that eventually people were speaking on the soundtrack even though they hadn't yet appeared on screen. But none of this mattered to the audience. It was lunch-time, yet the cinema was packed. As Jack Lemmon, playing the father of a missing American girl, gradually found out the horror of what had happened with American support in Chile, the audience became more and more stirred up. Bernard and I were surrounded by relatives of people who had disappeared. The people round us were weeping and burying their heads in their hands, and sometimes they would stand up and shout incoherently at the screen.

'Where's my son? Give him back to me. What has he done? Tell me where he is.'

'You swine! You bastards! Killers! Give me back my husband!'

At the point where Jack Lemmon condemned his own government and said that as an American he had a right to know the truth, I thought the audience was going to explode with anger and grief.

Afterwards Bernard and I walked back to the hotel in silence. Talking would have been too difficult.

An American diplomat in Buenos Aires, 'Tex' Harris, catalogued no fewer than fifteen thousand disappearances, and gave visas to a number of people who were frightened that they too were about to go missing. When Jimmy Carter was President his work was much praised. Then Ronald Reagan came into office with a promise to fight Communism everywhere, and his administration decided that the military junta was fighting Communism in Argentina. At the end of his tour of duty Tex Harris was sent back to the State Department in Washington, where he stayed for years in the doldrums doing some undistinguished routine job.

In 1990 I was staying in a hotel in Cape Town when I received a call. It was Tex Harris, and he had just heard somehow that I was staying in the hotel. I had never got in touch with him again, because in the book which Jana Bennett and I had written about the disappearances I had referred several times to his enormous size. He must, I thought, have been offended. When I heard his voice I started to apologize.

'What are you saying sorry for? You saved my career.'

Someone in CBS Television had read our book, and turned Tex Harris into the hero of a documentary about the disappearances in Argentina. As a result the State Department, which had probably always had a sneaking sympathy for him, renewed his contract, promoted him, and sent him to South Africa. One of the real heroes of the episode had at last been treated as he deserved.

11

The Long Road Back

BEIRUT, PRAGUE AND LONDON, 1982–86

'WHY ARE YOU SO LATE? Everyone else arrived last month.'

I thought she was just being rude; I didn't realize this was how Israelis always were, and that she expected me to be equally disparaging in return. Even on my first day here I found I instinctively liked the country and its people, but it was never an entirely uncritical liking. And at a time like this, it couldn't be.

'I was covering the war with Argentina,' I said defensively. Well, watching it at a distance anyway.

She shrugged, as though nothing except the Middle East could ever possibly matter, and handed me my Israeli press identification. I walked out into the hot Jerusalem sunshine, a fully accredited war correspondent. It was the start of a harrowing and dangerous three months.

In July I covered the Israeli invasion of Lebanon in 1982 from the comfort of one of the huge tourist hotels along the beach in Tel Aviv. Each day my crew and I would get up at five and head northwards up the coast road to Tyre, Sidon and the outskirts of Beirut itself. We would film the Israeli tanks on the outskirts of the city, as they fired down at the huge sprawl of square white buildings against the blue sea. From this point of view it was merely a strategic game.

The tank guns roared, a target chosen on the basis of questionable intelligence and well out of visual range was presumably hit, and the gunners loaded up again. Of course you wondered what it must be like to be on the receiving end of all this, but up here in the sunshine, with the city and the sea laid out before you, it seemed completely unreal.

'Great,' I would say to the cameraman, 'they're going to fire.'

Tanks firing made good pictures, and good pictures would get us on the air in London. I don't mean to say I was morally disengaged, that I cheered the gunners on, that I thought of nothing except getting my face on the screen. It was just that in the nature of things there seemed no connection between the industrial activity up here on the mountainside and the screaming and sheared flesh which was the deliberate result a few miles away.

I had seen plenty of things which were called wars, but they had always been fleeting, surreptitious, small-scale efforts. I had never before seen late twentieth-century technology fully and deliberately applied to the maiming and killing of ordinary civilians in the name of strategy. May God forgive me for my ignorance and thoughtlessness: I would soon see enough killing and maiming to last me a lifetime.

One night during that period I had got back to Jerusalem to satellite the day's nice, bloodless, exciting pictures of soldiers firing guns into the void, to be told that Menachem Begin, the Israeli prime minister, and Ariel Sharon, the defence minister, were attending a rally in support of the invasion of Lebanon and the siege of Beirut. There is a gratifying informality about Israeli politics which makes it easy to approach senior government people without going through the official channels, so I decided to go and doorstep the pair of them that evening.

Television crews in general, and the BBC in particular, were unpopular with those Israelis who supported the invasion. As we moved through the crowd at the rally we took a lot of criticism and the occasional kick on the ankles.

'Why do you only show bad things about Israel? Why don't you show what the Palestinians do to us?'

'You distort everything about Israel.'

'You tell only lies. Why?'

'Why?'

Israelis heard from their friends and relatives in the United States and Britain about the television coverage of the war: that the main emphasis was on the damage and loss of life on the Palestinian side, that as a result there was widespread concern and anger about the way the invasion was being handled. It lost nothing in the telling. Uncertain at some level of consciousness about the rights and wrongs of the invasion, perhaps, people preferred to blame us rather than their leaders for the bad press Israel was receiving throughout the world.

Yet because Israel is a functioning democracy – that is one of the enduringly attractive things about it – there was much serious self-questioning about the invasion. Ariel Sharon was starting to come under criticism in Israel itself for having tricked the rest of the government into invading Lebanon for an indefinite period and an indefinite purpose, when the other ministers had thought they were merely agreeing to a limited incursion to stop the Palestinians rocketing kibbutzim in northern Israel. That, at any rate, was what they said afterwards. Its official name was still Operation Peace for Galilee, even though the siege of Beirut, far to the north of Galilee, had been going on for weeks.

As politely as possible, we edged our way forward until we reached the sanctuary of the area which had been set out for the Israeli media. There, at least, we were among friends. We grinned at each other ruefully.

Waiting is an essential part of my trade. The rally was a long and (for us) boring business, since both Begin and Sharon spoke mostly in Hebrew and we hadn't managed to get a translator. It was a good two hours before the rally approached its climax. Just as it was getting there, the crew and I slipped out.

Another half-hour passed as we stood in a corridor waiting for the pair of them to pass. In those simpler days, fourteen years before the murder of Yitzhak Rabin, no one thought it possible that an Israeli might want to murder an Israeli prime minister. So as long as it was clear we weren't Arabs, the security people didn't care about us.

Then they were turning the corner and walking towards us: Begin with his thick round spectacles, Sharon with his rolling sailor's walk and his gut hanging over the belt of his trousers.

I stepped forward.

Transcript of interview recorded 12.7.82 in Jerusalem

Speakers: Menachem Begin, Prime Minister (non-staff),
Ariel Sharon, defence minister (non-staff), John
Simpson (staff)

JS: Prime minister, can we have a word for the BBC?

MB: Of course.

AS: Why is the BBC interested in Israel? I thought it was only interested in Palestinians.

JS: The strategy you are using is causing a good deal of concern internationally. How much does this matter to you?

MB: We have to defend our country from the constant attacks by Palestinian terrorists. People in other countries don't have to live with the threat of attack from people who want to destroy them and the state of Israel.

JS: But there is a good deal of questioning about the justification for the invasion, and about the constitutional way it was done.

AS [pushing forward]: Listen, we are fighting a war of survival here. When you are fighting to live, you do everything you have to. If you aren't fighting to live you can't judge it. You don't know. And I would like to say that a lot of what is reported on the foreign television is lies.

JS: You mean civilians aren't dying in Beirut?

AS: We only attack military targets.

After three weeks of this I at last saw for myself what it was like to be a military target in Beirut. The city was divided into two: East Beirut was mostly Christian, and its leaders had decided to do a deal of sorts with the Israelis. They wanted to get rid of the Palestinians who had effectively run the city and much of the country since arriving from Jordan in 1970. West Beirut was mostly Moslem, and willingly or not its people had sided with the Palestinians who occupied it. West Beirut was open to the sea; East Beirut was open to Israel.

The division between the two was known as the Green Line: a succession of crossing-points which were among the most dangerous places on earth, manned by armed groups without discipline and without compunction. People trying to move from one part of the city to the other could be taken out of their cars and imprisoned or shot, on suspicion of belonging to the wrong religion or the wrong ethnic group, or merely for giving the wrong answer to a question.

Beirut was a city in the grip of total war. As a result, life meant nothing very much: not even one's own life. I was interested to see how quickly I got used to living by the new rules imposed by the war. We crawled along the corridors in the Hotel Alexandre in East Beirut because its windows were commanded by snipers, and we knelt on the floor of our editing room on the top storey of the hotel (the only place left by the time we arrived), while the picture editor reached up over his head to press the buttons on the edit machines.

'What was that?' Russ Crombie, the editor I was working with, asked absently. He was trying to do a particularly difficult sound-edit, and wasn't paying much attention to anything else.

I looked up at the window.

'It's OK,' I said, 'just a bullet hitting the blinds and the wall.'

I carried on writing my script.

I had reached East Beirut a few days earlier, from Damascus. An unwise meal in the hotel restaurant the night before I left gave me a badly unsettled stomach on the morning I left, but there was no alternative to going straight away: one of my colleagues was waiting for me to arrive before he could leave. I shared a taxi with a friend of mine, a Canadian cameraman, and we headed off in the direction of the Lebanese border and the Bekaa Valley.

Overhead Israeli jets screamed across on their way to bomb West Beirut. It happened several times: there were no air defences to stop them, no anti-aircraft batteries to shoot them down. For the Israeli pilots it was like shooting pheasants on their nests. Eventually, as we drove, the pains in my stomach became unendurable.

'Stop, stop, stop!' I shouted, and fled into a field full of the magnificent tall corn which grows in the Bekaa. There, between the stalks, I performed one of man's most basic functions, while watching the display of technological skill above my head. It seemed like a metaphor for something.

At last I threaded my way back to the taxi.

'No worry, no worry, sir,' said the taxi driver comfortingly. 'They not bomb here. You OK.'

The Canadian laughed. I tried to explain, for the sake of my self-respect, but I could see I wasn't achieving anything.

It was much worse to be in East Beirut than on the hill-top with the Israeli artillery. Here you could see from close up what was happening.

Directly I arrived at the Alexandre I went up onto the flat roof where the journalists and cameramen were watching the air raids. They had started at nine that morning, and now it was midday.

As I reached the roof another Israeli jet screeched overhead. A building three or four hundred yards away from us in West Beirut erupted in white smoke.

'Phosphorus,' someone explained. 'It burns the body for seven hours, and putting water on it only makes it worse. Even if you just breathe it in, it burns you from the inside, and you die that way.'

I stared at the building. Inside it, under the plume of white smoke, people were being slowly burned to death from the inside, while we stood here watching and commenting as though we were at the races.

The accuracy of the Israeli bombing was phenomenal: a single house would erupt in smoke and flames, while the others were left intact around it. But who knew why the inhabitants of that particular house deserved to die in one of the slowest and most painful ways possible? Who decided that everyone inside was guilty of being an enemy of Israel?

Who had taken the decision, and on what basis? What did the pilot think? What did the inventor of the phosphorus bomb think, or the people who made it, or the people who sold it?

Another wave of air attacks. As the planes went over at a couple of hundred feet you could see their markings, even see the rivetting. Then a succession of little white parachutes fell gaily over the buildings, each carrying a white coffin-like object. They floated down gently out of our sight, and there was a succession of dull explosions.

'Cluster-bombs,' said the man who knew about these things. 'Each one contains several dozen bomblets. They spring out a few feet above the ground, and when they explode everyone within forty square metres is a goner.'

We only attack military targets. That was why the Americans had supplied Israel with cluster-bombs, on the strict understanding that they would never be used against civilians, but only against military targets. It had a reassuring, manly, definite sound, that expression 'military targets'. Now, in West Beirut, military targets were old women trying to find bread, or children caught out in the open, running for shelter, or men who hated the whole tragic collapse of their city into anarchy and terrorism and wanted no part of it.

I couldn't bear to watch it any longer. To be there was one thing; to stand in the relative safety of a rooftop and watch as people were burned and died of shrapnel wounds was tantamount to cheering the bombers on. I went downstairs and found a taxi. Someone had told me there was a battle going on at the race-track, and that the cameraman I was to work with was there.

The taxi-driver had as little anxiety about taking me to the race-track as I did about going there. We were all dead men; we could die as easily on the Damascus road (many taxi-drivers did, taking people or television cassettes backwards and forwards) as in the streets of Beirut. And it seemed a little less disgusting than standing on the rooftop.

Near the Green Line the devastation was appalling. This had mostly been done by the Lebanese and Palestinians themselves, in their crazed mutual wars starting in the mid-seventies. No single building was untouched by gunfire; in fact I later started a competition to find a house in the centre of Beirut without a bullet- or shell-hole, and no one ever won it. Many were nothing more than heaps of rubble, with a few sticks of furniture sticking out of them. Entire floors of concrete building were folded down on one another, like *millefeuille* pastry. Sometimes the outer wall of a house had been stripped away, and the rooms would be left open with such furniture as remained unlooted. Occasionally the entire line of the street would have disappeared in dust and red earth and rubble, and the few cars which were operating would twist and turn around the heaps of destruction in the roadway, or climb up and down shell-holes like trawlers in a heavy sea. And above us shone the sun from a beautiful blue sky, with vapour trails to show where the latest destruction had come from.

In the street as I walked down, nothing moved. There was no sign of life in the houses, just the occasional barking of a frightened or deserted dog. A cat scuttled nervously away from something it had been chewing in the shelter of a burned-out car. The silence was more frightening than anything I had experienced yet. Or so I thought.

A violent explosion close by made me throw myself down into the dust, my arms over my head. I wasn't yet used to judging these things: it always takes a little time. Slowly, I realized what was going on: an Israeli tank was dug into the red earth of what had once been the racecourse, and was firing its big gun directly at a block of flats only two hundred yards away, across the boundary of West Beirut.

'God help the people inside there,' I thought, not knowing that very soon now the people inside there would do their best to kill me.

And then I saw the cameraman. He was standing out in the open, camera on shoulder, filming away as the tank fired, and was followed by two or three others, also dug in nearby. He made a magnificent picture.

'Garry,' I shouted.

Garry Burns was an Australian who worked for Visnews. I had known him well in Rhodesia, and a few years after this he would be lying in a Bangkok street beside his friend Neil Davis, as Davis died from shrapnel wounds fired by a tank in a battle as violent as this, and even more pointless.

'G'day, mate,' said Garry, as though it was quite usual to meet people under these circumstances. We even shook hands, though we knelt down to do it. 'Want to do a piece to camera?'

I supposed I did; although that would mean standing up again. I asked him what was happening. It turned out that a group of Palestinian fighters had taken up positions in the block of flats, and were still firing mortars at the tanks in spite of the enormous weight of shells the tanks were firing at them from close range.

'Plucky little fuckers,' said Garry.

The guns were blasting away, only twenty yards from us, but he had wired me up with a small lapel microphone, which blocked out some of the immense noise.

I stood up and, when Garry gave a little nod from behind the camera, I started shouting about what was happening. (Rule number one for pieces to camera: if you don't know the big picture, just describe what's going on around you.) But I was nervous, and stumbled over the words, not once but three times. Then at last I got it right.

'Once more for luck?' Garry called out. The man had style, I thought.

I had just started, when Garry's face looked out at me from behind the camera. His eyes were unnaturally wide. I turned to see what he was staring at, and with that simultaneous slowing down of the observations and speeding up of the thought-processes which always takes place at such moments I saw a fountain of earth going up about twenty yards behind me and thought, 'That's a mortar-shell, and it can't have gone off yet because I'm still standing here.' And as I watched, another fountain went up much closer, about eight yards away, covering me in fine dust and earth. And that one didn't go off either. 'They usually fire these things in threes,' I thought, but it seemed stupid to lie down now. The next one would land right on top of me anyway.

I waited. Nothing landed. Two duds, and that was all. That made three big strokes of luck.

'Bloody 'ell,' said Garry, and shook my hand again. By now we were crouching under the lee of a mound of earth. He took the cassette out of the camera, put it in a box, wrote something on the label, and handed it to me. Where it said 'Story Details' he had written, 'Simpson Has A Lucky Day.'

A few days later there was a temporary truce. To illustrate it, I wanted to film one of the tank crews at the race course as they played cards or dozed in the sunshine. The camera crew I was working with waited for me at a distance, while I made my way into the Israeli encampment.

'I'm from the BBC,' I said as ingratiatingly as possible. 'How about letting us film you?'

'I don't have a problem with that,' said the colonel in charge, a man in his fifties. 'I like the BBC – it's our only source of real news here. But we are Israelis; I'll have to ask the men if they agree.'

The sergeant didn't, for one. It turned into an angry argument, sometimes in Hebrew and sometimes, to make a point for my benefit, in English.

'These people hate Israel. They only come here to make their dirty films to create propaganda against us.'

'I don't agree,' the colonel said. 'They are the only way we can find out what is really going on.'

An angry burst of Hebrew from the sergeant, and an angrier reply in Hebrew from the colonel. It grew worse and worse.

'We are like Nazis here,' shouted the colonel. 'Sharon is a war criminal, and we are helping him do his dirty work. It's genocide. All of us are guilty.'

I thought the sergeant was going to have a heart attack. He screamed back in Hebrew. One of the soldiers stepped forward and whispered something to him. He stopped speaking, and stood there breathing heavily, his face as dark red as the raw earth around us.

'He just called me a traitor and said he ought to arrest me,' the colonel told me, half apologizing. 'We'll have to put it to a vote of the men.'

The men voted strongly against letting us film.

'So what can I do?' the colonel asked, with an ironic grin. 'I'm only their commanding officer. I'm sorry.'

« »

As soon as I could get the BBC's agreement I moved to West Beirut. I felt better, if more frightened, there. I stayed at the Commodore Hotel, which in those days was a small, pleasant, run-down place where everyone quickly got to know everything about you: which side you liked to be on, courtyard (which was nicer but more exposed) or street (which was ugly but safer); what you liked for breakfast and what you liked to drink in the bar; and how you liked your laundry done. That in particular, in a city which was under siege, which suffered daily artillery barrages and air raids and people died all the time of wounds and disease, seemed to me to be a sheer human triumph. I would get back from a day's filming with my clothes stained and encrusted with the reddish dust and earth of Beirut, and the next morning they would be back, clean, ironed and folded. There are expensive hotels in Paris and New York and London where they can't do that.

The Commodore offered other pleasures too: being given an egg for breakfast in the morning, when eggs were so rare; or sitting around the swimming pool in the evenings, talking and arguing over the situation or complaining about the way the office back home was dealing with the story, eating the small fried fish which people risked their lives to catch and buy; or ending up the evening in the bar, while Chris Drake's parrot crooned and chattered to itself in the half-darkness.

Chris was a BBC correspondent who had spent the worst years in Beirut based in the Commodore, and his parrot had become a fixture. Its favourite party-trick was to whistle like an incoming shell, and innocent newcomers to the bar would usually flinch or even, in some terrible cases, get down onto the floor. I am a practised flincher, but thanks God (as the Beirutis would say) it never happened to me.

One day some years later, when the Syrians had joined the long list of outsiders who decided it was a good idea to bomb the suffering people of Beirut, the Commodore was destroyed. The survivors and the locals searched long and hard for the parrot in the rubble, but never found so much as a tail feather. The hotel rose again from the ruins, grander and much more expensive; yet it afterwards lacked the charm of its old, dark, unbombed self, and the faithful staff who had cooked when there was no food and washed and ironed shirts when there was no water or power drifted away. It is still possible, though, to work out where the bar was, and where, exactly, the parrot's cage had hung.

There were times during the Israeli siege when it was hard to make oneself leave the safety of the Commodore and go out filming in the streets. Somehow, though, one always did; it was a duty one owed to the BBC, to the viewers, and to the people of the city. Without pictures, television is nothing; and what was the point of exposing yourself to the terrible dangers of being in Beirut in the first place, if you didn't report on the situation?

That, at any rate, was what I told myself; but it was still difficult. I could imagine so easily being ripped apart by a shard of steel from a cluster-bomb, or bringing up that terrible dry blackish-brown froth which was the result of inhaling phosphorus fumes. I saw it happen to other people; why shouldn't it happen to me? What was so important, so wonderful, about me, that I should be exempt from the agony of the people around me?

One morning, after a particularly heavy series of attacks by Israeli aircraft, we forced ourselves to go to the main hospital at Sabra and Chatila, the Palestinian quarter in the southern part of the city. It stank; in fact it seemed to me I could smell it even as we approached.

Inside there was ceaseless shouting and the corridors were dark, because there was no power. The operating theatres were lit with hurricane lamps, which shed a fierce yellow light on the poor victim lying on the blood-soaked table, and on the harrowed faces of the surgeons and nurses as they went about their savage business. But the worst thing was the line of young boys who stood and waited outside the doors to the operating theatre. Each trolley bringing in a new case for surgery would stop briefly before going through, and the boys would examine the bodies for large pieces of shrapnel sticking out of them like gigantic metal thorns.

Then they would pull them out with their bare hands, leaving the task of stanching the bleeding or extracting deeper pieces of shrapnel to the surgeons. I have seen many terrible things in my life, but I never saw anything worse than this, or heard anything worse than the grunt the injured person would give as the shrapnel was pulled out.

All this time, the Palestinians endured the bombing and shelling with remarkable fortitude. I went twice to Yasser Arafat's headquarters, an ordinary-looking building in a narrow street, to see him and interview him. The street itself was horribly blasted, as badly destroyed as any town I have ever been in, but somehow the Israelis had never managed to get the right building. Walking there was dangerous: some of the ordnance hadn't exploded, and there were holes in the pavement where you could break your leg. And all the time you were listening for the whine of a shell that wasn't Chris Drake's parrot, and dreading being taken to hospital.

And then, as we waited in the most damaged street in Beirut for a man who was always preternaturally late, and praying that this time at least he would hurry, Arafat suddenly appeared among us from somewhere. His eyes were red with fatigue and his baggy, bristled face was grey and sagging, but there was a sprightliness about him which surprised me. He had been so used to defeat and failure that mere endurance like this seemed something akin to victory.

Always before this moment I had shared the general Western distaste for Arafat, based I suppose on his seedy appearance and his apparently equivocal attitude to violence; but this changed my mind for good. I was to see a lot of him in the years that followed, and each time my estimate of him rose. He was nature's deal-maker, a man who perpetually found himself caught between extremists, trying to reconcile them.

He blinked a little in the sudden sunlight. Like everyone else, I had my ear cocked for the sound of aircraft, but there was nothing. The journalists gathered round, shouting the usual tunnel-vision questions. It seemed to me that they failed to understand the real significance and drama of the occasion, in their search for immediate information. What contacts had he had today with the US negotiator, Philip Habib? Was he aware of what President Reagan had said the previous evening? Was it true that he had lost forty men in Sabra that morning? When the factoids had been distributed, I seized my opportunity.

Transcript of interview with Yasser Arafat, Beirut,
14.9.82

JS: The Israelis say you are defeated, and that you will
soon surrender. Is that true?

YA: We are not, you see, defeated. We are standing up
against the Israelis and we are not surrendering. To
stay here and fight is a victory. This is our victory.
Never any soldiers have faced anywhere against such
weapons and still fighting.

JS: But Philip Habib is trying to negotiate a withdrawal
from Beirut for you. If that's agreed, won't it be a
surrender?

YA: No, it will not be a surrender. If we succeed to reach
an agreement it will be a great victory for the
Palestinians. And we will continue to fight.

JS: It's being suggested that you might go to Tunis.

YA: Who knows? Nobody knows. There are many ideas.
But we will not be defeated now. This is our victory.

Then one of his officials moved forward: they had heard that another
air attack might start soon. He took my hand in his own. It was soft
and slightly damp, and normally I would have found a touch like
this distasteful. But there was something impressive about Arafat. By
refusing to be defeated he was, in a sense, the winner.

He used the rhetoric of the habitual underdog, but you could see
what he meant. The Palestinians had indeed fought well: not many
troops could have stood up to the pounding the tanks at the race track
had given their forward positions in the block of flats where I did my
piece to camera.

Soon the Palestinian withdrawal from Beirut was negotiated. Their
fighters would be taken off by ship and sent to Tunis and other places,
and they would be allowed to keep their weapons. It wasn't really a
defeat after all.

The evening before the embarkation, I thought I would walk
around the front-line positions of the Palestinians and their Lebanese
allies and take some still photographs of the men there. It wasn't

necessarily foolhardy: a ceasefire had been declared, and seemed to be holding. The evening was golden, and at each position I came to the men seemed to be enjoying themselves, relishing the fact that they had survived and could be proud of the way they had fought.

I would climb up the outside bank of protective red earth where they could all see me, and announce in a loud voice what I wanted to do. The men would then come out and pose in front of their weapons: mostly anti-aircraft guns and Katyusha rocket launchers. They looked remarkably good in their piratical head-bands, especially the Lebanese far-left Mourabitoun, whom we called the Loony Toons because of their unpredictability and occasional moments of insane courage. Farther along I found groups of Malaysians and Indonesians, and there were occasional Nigerians. If, as had been reported, there were three black Americans, I failed to find them.

The pictures were beautiful, and I thought I would offer them to one of the big news magazines or colour supplements. There had been only one difficult moment, when a group of children who had got hold of an RPG-7 rocket launcher fired it up in the air high over my head, where it exploded spectacularly. By now I was thoroughly schooled in the ways of high explosives, and didn't even flinch; which spoiled the children's fun altogether. It is symptomatic of that extraordinarily violent time that I shouldn't even have been surprised by the fact that children should be firing RPG-7s.

I came to one last Palestinian position. The Palestinians were always more suspicious of journalists than the foreign volunteers, but I felt that I had done so well that it was worth taking one last risk. I called out, and raised my camera in the air. Immediately someone grabbed my arms from behind, and wrenched the camera away from me. I felt a gun at the side of my head: someone else had come up.

'Spy, we will kill you now.'

'I just work for the BBC. I'm not a spy. I'm taking photographs for myself.'

'Spy.'

He pushed me forward, so that I could turn and look at him. He wore a scarf round his head, and he looked crazy. His red eyes seemed to be weeping, though whether from fatigue or dust or rage I couldn't quite tell.

'Kneel down.'

Oh well, I thought, at least it wasn't phosphorus or cluster-bombs. I tried to pray and to think about my family, but the details of the ground in front of me – the empty cartridge cases, the boxes of ammunition, orange peel, the everlasting reddish dust – kept getting in the way.

There was a click. This was it: my last moment. Then I heard the unmistakable sound of the film being wrenched out of a camera, and the camera landed in front of me.

'Take it, spy.'

It didn't seem to be a trick. I took it, and stood up.

'Get away and don't look round.'

I was surprised by my lack of emotion. I wasn't even pleased or grateful. The days and nights of explosions and bloodshed and fear had blunted my feelings, I suppose, just as too much whisky dulls the palate.

The next day the Palestinians left from Beirut harbour, waving and singing and chanting as their ships put out into the Mediterranean. In their place came French and Italian troops, and American marines. Now, we thought, things were going to be a little more ordered.

« »

It was a Saturday morning in September. The Palestinian forces had left, the Israelis had stopped bombing, the streets were quiet. I slept late. When I came down to meet the crew, I found the lobby of the hotel in a ferment. Something was going on in the Palestinian quarter of Sabra and Chatila, but no one knew what. We picked up the BBC driver and headed out there.

Once the Palestinians had lived in camps, but by now Sabra and Chatila had taken on the appearance of any other poor suburb of Beirut. The one had long ago merged with the other, so there was no clear line of demarcation between them: just a long street which ran the full length of both.

This street was now jammed with people. They were terrified: too terrified to stop, and certainly too terrified to explain what had happened. They were fighting to get away. One man had a terrible neck-wound, still leaking blood through an improvised bandage, but despite that he was walking fast, pushing his way through the slower refugees.

'What happened to you?' I asked him through our driver.

'Nothing, it's nothing.'

'But you are wounded.'

'It's nothing. Please.'

It seemed cruel to detain him any longer.

No one else would say anything. Sometimes they pointed back along the road: that was all.

We drove further. The crowd thinned out, then faded away altogether. The streets were empty: just the piles of rubbish and heaped-up earth which showed where Israeli bombs had hit a house, and the savage holes in the walls where a cluster-bomb had gone off. A couple of corpses lay by the roadside, but they looked as though they had been there for a while. I got out in the heat and the eerie silence and glanced at them, but I still didn't understand; even though there was blood on the front of their clothes and a severed penis lay close by on the ground. You saw so many horrors in Lebanon at that time, it didn't seem to be anything out of the ordinary.

I got back into the car and we drove further. Outside the football stadium at the far end of the road there was a crowd of frightened people. A harassed Israeli army captain was trying to herd them into the stadium.

'What the hell are you doing?' I called out, assuming that he had something to do with whatever was terrifying the local population.

'Look,' he shouted, 'I'm getting them here for their own good – for their safety. You know what's happened?'

I shook my head; I still didn't understand.

'I can't tell you. But it's terrible. You're from the BBC? You've got to tell the world what's been happening here.'

'But where do we go?' I was almost pleading with him now.

'You'll find out in Sabra and Chatila,' he said. And like the man with the injured head, he wouldn't say any more.

We drove back, and this time we looked down the little side streets.

'Christ,' whispered the cameraman. He was a pleasant, easy-going older man called Oggie Lomas, and he and his sound recordist, Ray Gibbon, had volunteered to come to Lebanon because they thought their colleagues had borne too much of the burden.

At the far end of a street near the two bodies we had seen earlier was a great heap. From a distance you could have thought it was just rubbish and old clothes. When you looked more closely you could see that it was bodies, four or five deep. There must have been at least fifty, and they had been newly killed: the blood wasn't entirely dry, despite the heat.

Suddenly, as we were filming, there was an appalling scream. It could only have come from someone in the most intense pain.

We ran back to the main street. A woman and a couple of young boys were holding a woman in their arms, and trying to put her in the back of a car. She was wearing a dress which had been white, but blood covered the entire front of it now. It took time to put her in the back seat, and I, God forgive me, opened the door on the other side so that Oggie could get an uninterrupted shot of her before the car left. A great cross had been cut in her stomach and chest, but she was still alive and conscious. Her eyes met mine and she started to scream again, her gaze locked on mine as though screaming was a way of communicating with me.

'The car's leaving,' shouted Ray.

It was a relief to slam the door on those eyes and that screaming. I was shaking with the horror of it.

And now we found bodies everywhere: in houses, in gardens, in alleyways. A mother lay on the ground, her throat somehow pulled out, clutching her two dead children. Some bodies lay at the foot of a wall where they had been shot with a single burst of machine-gun fire, then had their throats cut. There were very few men of military age among them. The great majority were women, the old and the young. The horror was so great it was often difficult to know what to film.

We came across the mutilated body of a woman whose hands had been tied behind her back. Oggie had to go to immense trouble to avoid showing anything other than the ropes on her wrist, since it would have been unusable. Yet all the time we were afraid the murderers would come back and find us filming their handiwork. We were the only living people in the area.

I noticed several crosses painted on the walls in the blood of the victims: this had been the work of a Christian militia group working alongside the Israelis. Later it became clear that senior Israeli officers had known that the militiamen were planning to massacre the inhabitants of Sabra and Chatila, once the Palestinian forces had been evacuated and there was no one left to protect them. They had done nothing to stop it.

For the next three days, until the bodies were collected and put into mass graves, we had to go and film them. Each time we went we discovered other bodies. The September heat made it almost unbearable by the end, but neither Oggie nor Ray complained or suggested staying behind.

I saw the faces of some of the bodies in my dreams, and one night I scarcely slept at all, unable to get the screams of the young woman in white out of my mind. In later years, when I worked for the *Spectator* and then for the *Sunday Telegraph* as well as for the BBC, I found that writing about terrible things like these seemed to exorcize them. But in 1982 I didn't write for anyone, and the images stayed locked in my head. This was the biggest news story I had ever broken for television. But I would willingly have exchanged my primacy for peace of mind and the chance to sleep at night.

« »

I went back to Television Centre in October, after being away for five months. The lapse of time since my *bouleversement* the previous May hadn't made things better. People regarded me with a certain embarrassment. In a large organization a career setback like this has something of the effect on one's fellow-workers that contracting a major skin disease had on the inhabitants of a mediaeval town. They fly from me, I would quote to myself as I wandered around Television Centre, that some time did me seek.

Although I had an impressive job title, I had no perceptible function: all the areas in which I had once specialized – Eastern and Western Europe, the Soviet Union, Africa, the relationship between the superpowers – had been taken over by others. My salary was still paid at the end of each month, but I was distinctly surplus to requirements. It was going to be a long road back.

Worse, my marriage was collapsing around me, for reasons that were nobody's fault but my own. Mine wasn't a particularly easy life to stay married in, but I think I would have managed it if my father had still been alive. Somehow his death had parted the main anchor cable of my existence, and I was starting to swing around in the tide.

In May 1983 one of my colleagues, the broadcaster and novelist

Tim Sebastian, offered to stand down and let me go to Prague to report on a big international peace conference. It was good of him, and I snapped it up: anywhere, anything, was better than sitting at my desk looking out of the window.

And it had a good deal of interest for me. In those days, when Czechoslovakia was an obedient member of the Soviet bloc, an Eastern European peace conference was a propaganda weapon to be brandished in the face of NATO. Furthermore, it was the fifteenth anniversary of the Soviet invasion, which ended the Prague Spring.

On that morning in 1968 I was just twenty-four, and Czechoslovakia had become my cause: greater, even, than Vietnam. I had read with avidity everything I could find about Alexander Dubček's shift away from Soviet communism, and identified wholeheartedly with it. The invasion which smashed the efforts of the Czechs and Slovaks to find a little more freedom for themselves came totally unexpectedly on a beautiful August morning. Diane and I were driving out into the country in our yellow MG when I spotted the newspaper hoarding. I stopped the car in the road and ran into the newsagent's.

'Tanks Go Into Prague', said the headline.

I wouldn't allow myself to accept that such a thing had happened, and switched on the car radio. They were replaying the last message broadcast from Prague before the Russians stormed the transmitter:

> Don't forget us. Remember us, even when our resistance has finished, and the rest of the world has found other things to think about.

I swore to myself that I never would. And I never did, although Czechoslovakia sank into repressive gloom.

Now it was fifteen years later. On the plane journey to Prague I lectured my colleagues about the dangers which might await us. The Czechoslovak intelligence service, the StB, was one of the best in Eastern Europe, I told them, and had been entrusted by the Russians with the special task of spying on Britain. There were all sorts of ways in which this could be done, but the most common was the good old-fashioned honey trap. We should all be very careful of the women we came across.

We are none of us very good at taking our own advice. Directly we arrived at our socialist brutalist hotel I looked into the eyes of the receptionist as we filled in the forms and handed over our passports, and experienced a *coup de foudre*. Nothing was said between us; indeed, I never spoke more than a sentence or two to her during the whole of our stay. But she had registered the look.

The next ten days were enthralling. We used the conference as an excuse to carry out the most detailed reporting ever carried out for television on the repression of human rights in Communist Czechoslovakia. We were helped by a British academic whom we sent out secretly a week or so earlier, and who made contact with various dissidents on our behalf; and by a couple of delegates from the Campaign for Nuclear Disarmament, which had mandated them to attend the conference but also to meet Charter 77, the leading dissident group in Czechoslovakia. By the end of those ten days there was no significant human rights group and virtually no leading dissident at liberty whom we did not film or interview.

Each evening we had to slip out of the heavily guarded Park Hotel, get into our little hired car and lose the tail which the StB put on us; usually by overtaking a bus and then turning suddenly into a side street and switching our lights off. One night we went out as usual and found an address in the old part of the city.

The building seemed derelict, deserted. The vast nineteenth-century entrance hall smelled and was in total darkness. We found our way up the grand staircase braille-fashion, tripping over the ancient piping which someone had left there. But the flat on the first floor was a centre of light and happiness in this cold, dark, frightened city, and the Charter 77 people welcomed us in as though we were fully paid up members.

It never occurred to me in 1983, and I don't suppose it occurred to anyone else there either, that in less than seven years some of the key figures in the pleasant, book-lined room would be in the country's government, and that the brutal system which had controlled their lives not just in 1968 but for twenty years before that would simply evaporate as completely as the darkness and chill of the staircase had, once the flat door was open.

I spent one of the pleasantest evenings of my life there, while the camera crew filmed the party. Vaclav Havel was not long out of prison and would soon be back there, but he was relaxed and easy-going and unpompous. I found his company delightful that night.

```
Transcript of interview recorded in Prague, 18.5.83

Speakers: Vaclav Havel (non-staff), John Simpson
(staff)

JS: You must be nervous that the police will come and
knock on the door and arrest everyone. It could happen
at any time, couldn't it?

VH: It could happen, yes. It has happened to many of us
here. Perhaps to everyone, I don't know. But to be frank
with you, we don't care about that. It isn't important.
The police, the forces of the state, can do nothing to
us, because we are free men and women. Free inside our
minds, I mean. That is why the people you see around you
are happy. They are at peace here, in a way that other
people outside cannot be. We know the worst thing which
can happen to us,and it doesn't fear us.

JS: Frighten you?

VH: It doesn't frighten us, yes.
```

Not long afterwards there was another meeting between the CND delegates and Charter 77, in a park on the outskirts of Prague. It was both ludicrous and magnificent. When we arrived there, we found several other journalists and literally dozens of secret policemen and women had arrived. Some of them had cameras, and filmed us filming them filming us. Some were already sitting on the benches where it had been arranged that Vaclav Havel and the others would sit. Some were actually in the branches of trees. There is always something a little unnerving about the presence of secret policemen, but it is a lot harder to take them seriously when they are up trees.

The meeting duly took place, and the StB duly broke it up; and after they had pulled one of the journalists into the bushes and beaten him up, they tried to take our cassettes away from us. Fortunately it was obvious that this was going to happen, and the cameraman had switched the used tapes for blanks. Then the StB ordered us all, dissidents, journalists and CND delegation, to leave the park.

For me, this walk out of the park was an important moment. I walked between Jiři Hajek, the foreign minister during Dubček's brief

Prague Spring, a quiet, thoughtful old gentleman who could speak with sudden passion about literature and music, and an elderly woman who had been the spokesman for Charter 77 and had suffered for it. Her heavy, swollen legs moved slowly, and the three of us were soon far behind the others. A group of secret policemen and women walked with us, laughing and mocking at the old lady as she hobbled along. Somehow, it seemed much worse, coming from the policewomen. At first I was angry; then, slowly, that faded and was replaced by an intense pride that I should be walking alongside this elderly couple and suffer with them the contempt of the secret police. I thought of the words Vaclav Havel had used to me: 'The police, the forces of the state, can do nothing to us, because we are free men and women. Free inside our minds, I mean.'

The small-time place-seekers who thought they were serving their careers by mocking this old couple had got it badly wrong. In a few years' time the secret police would be out of a job, and would be embarrassed and perhaps penalized for the rest of their lives as a result of what they had been and done. It was an important lesson: nothing lasts for ever, not even cruelty and brutality. And the regime's days were already numbered, even at its time of maximum strength.

For me, though, revenge came a great deal more quickly and more directly. My colleagues were waiting patiently for me at the park gates, and when I had said goodbye to Hajek and the elderly lady, and we had packed the gear into the car and driven off, we saw what had happened to the majority of the StB people. Police cars were obviously in short supply: they were queuing up meekly in their dozens at the bus stop.

I couldn't help it. As we drove past I leaned out of the window and gave them the finger. It felt very, very good indeed. We were still laughing when we reached our hotel.

« »

For the next few days we continued to cut a swathe through the system. The international television organization Eurovision had agreed with the Czechoslovak authorities that it should handle Western television coverage of the peace conference. As part of the deal the Czechoslovak side had had to give an undertaking that they wouldn't censor or interfere with any of the foreign transmissions: not, it turned out, a wise move. Night after night the bosses of Czechoslovak television had to watch from the feedpoint as we broadcast our interviews with Havel and the other dissidents – all forbidden figures in Czechoslovakia – and showed the ludicrous and sometimes violent behaviour of the secret police. And night after night the television executives became more threatening. We knew it wouldn't be long before something happened.

One morning we managed to spirit a recently released prisoner out of his flat, past the secret policemen who were guarding it. He was a priest of the 'unofficial' Church, which refused to accept a slow death by state strangulation, and he wanted to speak to us on camera. The producer went in to get him, and the plan was to bring him out through a door at the other end of the building. I sat in the car, ready to make a break for it to the countryside where we could film him without being seen.

At that moment an enormous open car came swinging round the corner at a stately pace, with a camera on a tripod in the back of it and a cameraman filming away. I was horrified. It had always seemed likely that the authorities would try to catch us in the act and make a public show of us. This was obviously what was happening now.

But car and camera and cameraman swept past me without even pausing, and a succession of other cars came round the corner after it. Then I remembered. Miloš Forman had been given special permission to return to his original home city to film *Amadeus*. Which explained why the camera was tilted up at an unlikely angle, filming only the eighteenth-century rooftops. But I was still so shaken that I only remembered to switch on the engine when the priest and the producer came running out of the building a minute or two later.

We were caught in the end, though. After a series of muted public condemnations of our activities we thought we had better ask for an interview with a senior government minister. It was agreed; but when we arrived at the appointed room, bright lights were switched on in our faces and a couple of cameras from state television were wheeled in from side rooms. We weren't going to interview the minister, he was going to give us a public dressing down, live: it was the biter bit. I tried to make it harder for them by suggesting to my colleagues that we should laugh and talk among ourselves, but the Czech director merely ignored us and zoomed in on the minister.

Yet even this official ambush, seen right across the country, worked in our favour. For the rest of our time in Prague we were treated like heroes. Flowers appeared by our bedsides in the hotel for the first time, special treats were added to our plates at breakfast, people in the street whispered our praises as we passed.

One night at the feed-point we were enduring the anger and hostility of the bosses of Czech television as usual.

'You are a disgrace to the good name of journalism,' one of them told me.

An old man was sweeping the studio floor. He pushed his broom slowly towards me, and as he passed I felt his hand press my arm gently, in a sign of solidarity.

« »

It was only a matter of time before the Czechoslovak authorities would try to get their own back on me for all this. Some weeks later, back in London, I was going through the morning post in my office when I came across an envelope with a Prague postmark. It was a birthday card from the beautiful receptionist at the Park Hotel, and it was carefully worded to mean everything or nothing.

How on earth, I thought, could she have known it was my birthday? Then I realized: she had looked inside my passport when I handed it to her that day.

I answered in the same style. Soon the reply came, a little warmer. I replied at a similar temperature: a man approaching forty is particularly susceptible, and only too keen to persuade himself that an attractive young woman really likes him for himself, rather than for some devious purpose of her own.

The next stage wasn't a letter, but a heavily accented phone call from a Mr Blanco.

'Is this Mr John Simpson, of Park Hotel, Prague?' There was a definite nudge in the voice, a sort of 'you-naughty-dog-you' note.

I agreed that it might be.

'Because I have special envelope for you.'

He gave me his phone number and told me that he worked in import-export; and when I laughed he hung up, a touch offended.

The envelope proved to contain photographs of the receptionist:

fully clothed, but bosomy and with a definite promise of more to come. She really was very attractive.

'Please forgive bad pictures,' she wrote on the back, 'but I took it by myself alone.'

'If you look really closely you can see the reflection of someone in the glass lampshade,' said a photographer friend of mine, peering at it with a magnifier. 'She certainly didn't take this herself.'

I was nervous now. There was someone in the BBC, I knew, who had contact with MI5. I called him, and he called them. Someone came round to see me. He said he was from the Ministry of Defence.

I liked him. He had a stutter, and wore a good but rather shiny suit.

'I say,' he said, 'sh-sh-she's a bit of a st-st-stunner.'

I agreed.

'Do you think they're trying to set me up?'

He did. He told me how someone in one of the BBC's language services had been invited by a girl to meet her in Hungary – 'neutral' ground. Hungary was semi-detached from the Soviet bloc, but the KGB, the StB and other Eastern bloc intelligence services were allowed to operate their own little scams there, unhindered. The couple were in bed when her husband, or someone who said he was her husband, burst in. There was a fight, and the husband fell and hit his head. A smooth character in a suit arrived and said they would have to charge the man from the BBC with attempted murder; unless, of course, he was prepared to help them with some information: the addresses of the families of people who had escaped from countries behind the Iron Curtain to work for the BBC in London. He agreed. It was more than a year before he broke down and admitted all this to one of his colleagues.

'But I don't know any addresses,' I said obtusely.

The man from MI5 looked at me with remarkable patience.

'They w-w-want you to be an agent of influence.'

It seemed that they were trying to get me on their books: perhaps out of revenge, perhaps just because it would look good within their service. At some point they might make me broadcast something favourable to them. Or they might just ask me to carry a message to someone. You never knew, he said.

The letters from the beautiful receptionist dried up then, anyway, and I heard nothing more from MI5 until I thought I should ring them and find out what had happened. They were apologetic. Someone, I was told, would come round.

It turned out to be a rather attractive young woman, and I offered her a BBC lunch. During it she gave me back my photographs, and told me one or two things that had happened. They hadn't known about Mr Blanco, and they had deported him. They were grateful to me, she said.

'I saw in the paper a few weeks afterwards that two Czech diplomats were chucked out of the country.'

'Really?' said the attractive young woman from MI5. 'Fancy that.'

I couldn't get anything else out of her.

I thought long and hard about it all. It doesn't do journalists any good to play footsie with MI5 or the Secret Intelligence Service: they get a bad reputation. The only thing, I decided, was to set it all out in the open. That way, no one could accuse me of anything except a certain embarrassing candour. I wrote a long account of the episode for a well-known literary magazine, and the photographs were used along with the article. It was rather successful.

And that, until the collapse of Communism in Czechoslovakia, was that. Neither the StB nor MI5 ever got in contact with me again. But it did occur to me to wonder why, exactly, MI5 had chosen to send an attractive young women round to see me.

It also occurred to me to wonder, when I heard a politician or a trade union leader or a journalist writing or saying something unusually warm about the Soviet Union or its allies, whether something of the same sort hadn't happened to them: but without the happy ending.

« »

Like Mark Antony, I had not kept my square. In July 1984 I left my wife and family – not something I find it easy to write about, long years later – and went to live with an American television producer, Tira Shubart, in South Kensington. Tira had a truly metropolitan quality, which she imparted to me, curing me for ever of my suburbanism. Living in our one-roomed flat, with two of its walls entirely covered with bookshelves, we had a great deal of fun. Nowadays a lifelong, stable marriage has the kind of attraction for me which someone long faithful might secretly associate with infidelity. Still, now that I am well on in my fifties, I am on the best of terms with my two daughters and my ex-wife; and perhaps they have forgiven me. Forgiveness, acceptance and love are the things most of us yearn for, after all; and some of us seem to need them more, and more often, than others.

Slowly, very slowly, I was climbing back to the position at the BBC which I had once occupied. It took me several years, and included putting my life into a good deal of jeopardy. If I hadn't been prepared to do that, I think I might have remained in the doldrums for the rest of my life. The process included going back to Lebanon at the time of the hostage-taking there and being with Iran's Revolutionary Guards when they were attacked with poison gas by Saddam Hussein's air force; stories which will have to wait for another time to be told.

It was also greatly helped by the arrival at last of a new editor of television news: a man for whom I came to have real respect and affection. My career at the BBC has taught me the value of simply hanging on. The storm does pass eventually, no matter how long it seems to take. By 1986 no one seemed to remember the vicissitudes I had gone through a few years earlier; and a chance incident that year re-established my position for good.

We had recently been through the American bombing of Libya, a crisis which had landed the BBC in a great deal of trouble with the British government; not for the first time. Mrs Thatcher had become a far more imperial figure now, and these were her years of maximum power. Her supporters on the far right had long been urging her to privatize the BBC and a much wider group, of which she was clearly an instinctive member, believed that it was biased against the government; by which they meant that it was too independent.

She still remembered with irritation some of the phrases its leading broadcasters had used back in the Falklands War: 'if we are to believe the British version' and so on. Her view was that as the *British* Broadcasting Corporation it should follow the British government's line; even though it was perfectly plain that the reason the BBC was so respected both in Britain and abroad was that it was genuinely independent of the British government. If a Labour prime minister had tried to rail-road the BBC she would have probably seen it all in a different light; but in 1986 a Labour government – or indeed another prime minister – was unimaginable. The BBC, legally obliged by its Charter to remain independent of party political control, was one of the few great organs of state which she was not in some way able to dominate; and it made her restless.

Because the American aircraft which bombed Libya took off from bases in Britain, that made it a British issue. There was a good deal of public disquiet about it, especially since it was strongly suspected that the Reagan administration was primarily bombing Libya to teach bigger and more formidable countries, chiefly Iran, a lesson. (The pretext was a terrorist attack on a Berlin night-club used by American servicemen. Far from being the work of Libyan agents, it proved to have been carried out by a group linked to the Syrian government; but no one suggested bombing Damascus.) The level of anxiety in Britain was rather pathetic. Few people seemed to realize that Libya was a feeble if intermittently nasty little dictatorship which could never get it together to carry out a concerted campaign of terrorism. They seemed genuinely frightened that Colonel Gadhafi's agents would retaliate by blowing up their local Sainsbury's.

The real battle was a propaganda one. Colonel Gadhafi claimed his daughter had been killed in the raid, and showed her body to the journalists in Tripoli at the time. It wasn't until some time later that it became clear that he had adopted the little girl as she lay dying from her injuries. But no matter whose daughter she was, she was certainly killed by the American bombing.

The British government, though, was rattled by the hostility which sections of the public were starting to show over the bombing; and since, at times of crisis, people in Britain tend to turn to the BBC for their information, some senior ministers felt that this public opposition was the fault of the BBC and wanted it to be taught a lesson. The chairman of the Conservative Party, Norman Tebbit, announced that he would be investigating the BBC's television coverage of the raid. In a society where the government was less obsessed with controlling the broadcasters this function might reasonably have been left to the television critics; but Mr Tebbit was fiercely opposed to the BBC, and since the BBC had allowed itself to seem rattled by the threats he and the Party made, he was greatly encouraged in his approach.

One lunch-time I was sitting with a few friends in the canteen at Television Centre, toying with a curled-up piece of fish and some green peas, when the Tannoy went.

'PBX. Calling Mr John Simpson.'

I hurried over to the phone. The deputy editor of television news was on the other end.

'We've just had Tebbit's report,' he said. 'It's serious. The editor would be grateful if you could get up here.'

I finished my fish and went up. A small group of worried-looking people were sitting round in the editor's office. The editor handed me a photocopy of the document Tebbit and his researchers at Conservative Central Office had compiled. I looked through it rather nervously, anxious to see what it had to say about my own reporting of the attack. It made a few neutral comments, then one which was rather complimentary; that was all.

'That's all OK,' I blurted out, voicing my own relief. 'Nothing much there.'

The editor turned to me. I could see a faint ray of hope was glimmering for the first time.

'You think so?'

I realized that I had been speaking purely for myself. But it seemed unkind and unreasonable to destroy his only cause for optimism. He must have felt that his career was on the line.

'Oh sure. It's full of loopholes. Just go through it carefully and you'll find them all,' I said.

I hadn't read it carefully enough to know if that were true, but I have never yet read a long document that you couldn't pick holes in.

Chris Cramer, a tough character who was the news editor at the time and some years later went to CNN, agreed. Cramer and I, although different in many ways, were both affronted by the idea that in a free society the government should presume to dictate to the broadcasters and try to make them report only what the government wanted. Maybe we were both chancers too.

'John's right,' he said. 'We should go through this with a fine-tooth comb. We'll find loads of things wrong with it.'

Which is what happened. We divided the Conservative Central Office document up between us, and spent the next couple of days going through it point by point. The document compared the BBC's coverage of the raid unfavourably with ITN's, and tried to make the case that the BBC had been deliberately biased. Some of the individual points it made were reasonable enough: the news presenter on the night of the bombing had added various inaccuracies to the sub-editors' scripts. (Soon afterwards she left the BBC.)

But it was plain silly to try to pretend that there was some underlying bias. I have never yet found a senior Conservative who really believed that, though plenty have found it a useful accusation over the years, because the party rank-and-file tend to swallow it. They have, after all, had it drummed into them so often at times when the Conservative Party has been on the ropes. For years there were regular reports from something called the Glasgow Media Group which tried to prove that the BBC was equally biased against the Labour Party and the Left.

The Central Office researchers had listed all the timings of the different parts of the BBC's reportings, in an effort to show that the BBC had wilfully given less time to things that were favourable to the government and more to things that were unfavourable than ITN had.

The trouble was, the timings didn't add up to the right figure. It wasn't important, but combined with all sorts of other trivial inaccuracies it gave the impression of being a sloppy piece of politically motivated work. The fact was, of course, that it hadn't occurred to Norman Tebbit that the BBC would stand its ground. So often in the past it had fallen over itself with nervousness at the mere suggestion that the government of the day was upset with it.

Interestingly, when we issued our response there was a big wave of public support for the BBC. Partly it was because Kate Adie had established herself firmly in the public consciousness as a brave reporter, staying in Tripoli when the bombs were falling. In the past women reporters had tended to be given social affairs to report on. Here was a woman who had become a war correspondent; and although it had happened long before in newspapers it was almost unknown in British television.

But there was support also because the BBC, for all its failings, its frequent arrogance, its dopiness, and its bureaucracy, is as British an institution as any other in the country: as British as the Royal Navy or the Grand National or Marks and Spencer or milky tea, with the added advantage that 90 per cent of the population have some contact with the BBC each week. People tend not to like it when British institutions are attacked for party political reasons, and Norman Tebbit had failed to realize that. An opinion poll taken shortly afterwards indicated that Conservative voters supported the BBC on almost the same scale as voters for the other parties.

Mrs Thatcher, who even at the height of her power was a careful observer of public opinion, knew she would be calling a general election within the next year or so. She quickly distanced herself from Norman Tebbit's campaign, and gave it no support whatever. Soon afterwards the first rift between the two of them began to emerge.

On the night she won the 1987 election, she went to Conservative Central Office to celebrate with her most faithful followers. There was a particular group of young right-wingers, noisy, rough, and rather inclined to be hostile to people like me, ranged along the railings of St John's, Smith Square. Together with my camera crew I was lurking close to them, because I guessed she would go over and shake hands with them. Spotting me there, they began a chant:

> One, two, three,
> Privatize the BBC.

She saw them, and heard them, and duly charged over, head down and handbag held at the usual angle. I moved in.

```
Transcript of interview with Prime Minister, 18.6.87

Speakers: Rt Hon Margaret Thatcher, PC MP (non-staff),
John Simpson (contract)

JS: Good evening, Prime Minister. You must be feeling
pretty good tonight.

MT: Good evening, John. Yes, well, it is a magnificent
result, and a great tribute to everyone who has worked so
long and hard for this moment.

JS: The crowd here seem to want you to privatize the BBC.
Are you planning to do that?

MT: Well, I think . . . Well, you know, I must really go
and speak to them.
```

That's it, I thought as she launched herself forward and started pressing the flesh: she'll never do it now. And of course she didn't even consider it. As she'd said to me in that other moment of cautious aposiopesis in Venice seven long years before, 'don't you realize it's only . . .'. Even at the moment of her greatest triumph Margaret Thatcher knew what people would stand for, and what they wouldn't; and it was when this instinct finally deserted her that her decline and fall began. For all her autocratic promptings, she was always a crowd-pleaser.

« »

The BBC was on the point of changing out of all recognition anyway. In 1988 John Birt joined it as head of news and current affairs, on the clear understanding that when he had reformed and revitalized that particular area he would take over as director-general. Nowadays it is hard to remember how small and underfunded the news department was before Birt's arrival. We had only four television correspondents based abroad, none on the continent of Europe, and I was the only person specializing in foreign affairs in London. That meant that on consecutive days I could, and sometimes did, report on events in three different continents.

Both radio and television news and current affairs programmes operated on a shoestring, and in television terms we were of no more account than RAI in Italy or ZDF in Germany. As I write, ten years later, the BBC is the biggest newsgathering organization the world has ever seen, bar none, and its reputation is higher than it has ever been at any time since the end of the Second World War.

Suddenly there was a five-fold expansion. Entire new departments were created, where there had been only one or two correspondents before. In economics, in social affairs and in my own field of foreign affairs we were suddenly finding large numbers of new recruits. The foreign affairs unit now contained eleven people, and I was made the head of it: the only person from within the BBC who was given charge of one of these new creations. My time in the wilderness was unquestionably over.

With hindsight, the expansion came just in time. In little over a year the world itself would change, in a series of seismic upheavals which would affect every country on earth. The BBC was ready for it. So was I.

12

Undermining Marx

THE DAMP WIND sliced across the tarmac at the VIP terminal at Heathrow airport with the force of a throwing-knife. It made the red Hammer and Sickle strain and crackle on its pole alongside the Union Jack, it insinuated itself through the various layers of clothes we were wearing, it messed up the carefully plastered hair of the assembled civil service worthies who were standing in a row along the edge of a dampish length of government-issue red carpet. There was someone with a title out in front: even Buckingham Palace had been roped in for this one.

'I sincerely hope it's worth all the fuss,' I said to the cameraman, stamping my feet. Then we saw the plane coming through the low cloud for its final approach, and I stopped getting my voice on the soundtrack.

The moment I saw the man standing at the top of the aircraft steps I knew precisely what sort of Soviet official he was. I'd met several of them during my time in Russia. I thought of them as The Likely Lads: young, up-and-coming Brezhnev-era chancers, men who weren't afraid of the West as their elders were but instead found it distinctly interesting and wanted to get their share of it. No doubt Mikhail Gorbachev had ideals. He was a lawyer by training, which meant that he knew there were rules which at least had to look as though they were being obeyed. At the same time he had done his legal studies at the end of the Stalin period, which must have taught him that the rules were only there to be bent. It's not how people vote but who does the counting, Stalin once said.

Then behind the stocky, balding figure, someone else emerged from the aircraft door.

'Hey, she's not bad,' muttered the cameraman, swivelling his camera on its tripod and focusing on her. Beside us, twenty television cameramen and stills photographers were doing the same thing. From this first instant when Raisa Gorbachev made her appearance on the world stage, she was a star. Without her, none of us would have been quite so aware of how different things in the Soviet Union were becoming. And Gorbachev might not have been there in the first place.

But at that moment it was his overcoat that interested me most. It wasn't just expensive, it was characteristically Savile Row. You didn't come to the West and allow yourself to be filmed wearing one of the best coats money could buy unless you wanted to demonstrate your keenness that things should change in a big way back home.

It was November 1984. The following March a boring nonentity called Chernenko, the stop-gap General Secretary of the Soviet Communist Party, died in his sleep. There was a funeral, at which we had the first public sighting of his refrigerator-shaped wife, and an entire era went down with him into his cold grave beside the Kremlin Wall. It had been a bad era, of course, and all the old guard of Chernenko's generation bore their share of the guilt. But it had worked, and it had kept the world stable if edgy. Quite soon now the world would start to become simultaneously much safer, and much less stable. And the man who would unintentionally pull the plug on Marxism-Leninism, put the Soviet Union into liquidation, and redistribute its empire in Europe and Asia to the original owners was unanimously elected by the Politburo to take Chernenko's place. It was only four months away.

The British spotted Mikhail Gorbachev first. I was getting quiet hints from the Foreign Office about him during the summer of 1984, and they were presumably sounding him out about visiting Britain even before that. A strange combination of factors had turned him into the Soviet heir apparent. He had been the Party boss in Stavropol, a pleasant enough place in southern Russia near the Georgian border, famous for its mineral springs. Andropov, the KGB chairman, suffered from kidney trouble and was advised to take the waters there; and whenever he turned up Gorbachev and Raisa looked after him assiduously.

Andropov took to them both, and particularly to Raisa, and he was instrumental in ensuring that Gorbachev was brought to Moscow and put in charge of Soviet agriculture. It was an extremely difficult job, which Gorbachev didn't do particularly well: no one could. Still, he looked and sounded good, and managed to move on before too long. By that stage Andropov was dying, and tried to make Gorbachev his successor. The old guard preferred Chernenko, but they had run out of options even before Chernenko died of emphysema in 1985. By the time Gorbachev came to London he was a shoe-in.

He and Raisa did a great deal in their few days in London, and not all of it was on the schedule. I headed off to Highgate Cemetery with everyone else to watch him lay the obligatory wreath on Karl Marx's tomb; but after we had waited there for more than an hour a flustered team composed of the Soviet ambassador in London and several leading figures from Moscow turned up and did the job instead. There was no sign whatever of the Gorbachevs. Later that day, when I spoke to one of the British team attached to them, I found out what had happened. It was quite extraordinary.

They had been driving up Victoria Street in their official car, and Gorbachev had asked what the large mediaeval building straight ahead of them was. When he heard it was Westminster Abbey he immediately wanted to stop and go inside. His Foreign Office liaison man, sweating, pointed out that they were due in Highgate Cemetery soon. Gorbachev made it clear he didn't care about Highgate Cemetery, or Marx's tomb for that matter. He and Raisa wandered round the Abbey instead. There can't have been many times since the Revolution that any Soviet Communist that senior had voluntarily stepped inside a Christian church.

There were more shocks to come for the poor Foreign Office man. They got back into the car, swung round Parliament Square, and went down Whitehall. As they came to Downing Street Gorbachev said he would like to look at that too. Since this was in the days before the monstrous iron gates were put up at the end of the street to prevent the people of Britain getting close to the building from which they were ruled, it was merely a matter of speaking to the policeman on duty.

They drove up to the door of Number Ten. Gorbachev got out and wandered over. The policeman on duty was quick-witted enough to give his usual surreptitious knock, and the door swung open.

Gorbachev stepped inside, stood in the marble-floored hallway gazing at the pictures for a few seconds, then smiled, said thank you and walked out again. It was the photo-opportunity of a lifetime, except that the only people who would have been able to take advantage of it were seven miles away, standing in the cold in front of an ugly bust of a man with a beard and an epitaph that instructed the workers of all lands to unite.

The Foreign Office pulled out all the stops for Gorbachev. In particular they arranged a formal lunch at Hampton Court Palace, to which they invited a couple of hundred worthies: among them myself. In the reception line I spoke to Raisa in the best Russian I could muster, and she answered something rather different; which made me wonder about my pronunciation. I was late going into the great dining-hall, and as I made my way there I glanced down a little corridor into an ante-room. Inside, through the open door, I caught sight of Gorbachev doing his hair in a mirror. He was wielding the comb high over his head and patting the thinning hair on the side, his tongue protruding slightly, in exactly the way I had always associated with spivs and teddy-boys. The Likely Lad, I thought again.

Lunch was superbly memorable. The chill in Cardinal Wolsey's great hall, with its hammer-beamed roof and its vast chimneys, was only partly off-set by electric heaters ranged behind us. My feet were freezing, but the waiters and waitresses sweated as they covered the distance from the kitchens and back again with huge tureens of soup and platters of beef. I spoke a good deal to the overflowingly stout Russian on my left. He was to become one of Gorbachev's most senior advisers. (If the person in charge of the seating-plan should chance to read these words, I am profoundly grateful to him or her for putting me there; it was the start of a long and, for me, very fruitful, relationship.) Early on I asked whether Gorbachev would really be able to make a difference to the Soviet Union. He grunted, and shifted his bulk a little.

'He will have to,' he said. I noticed he didn't trouble to question my assumption that Gorbachev would get the top job.

'Why?'

'Because a great deal has to be done. Much, much more, I think, than you in the West realize.'

Then the man on his other side asked him something, and I lost my chance to ask what he meant.

During the seven years Gorbachev was in power I came to regard myself as his doorstep interview specialist, much as I did with Thatcher. It was a good deal harder with him, thanks to the language problem and the intense security with which he was always surrounded. On many occasions, though, I had a particularly useful ally: Eduard Shevardnadze, his Georgian foreign minister. I came to know Shevardnadze quite well, and when he was standing or walking close to Gorbachev I would catch his eye and ask him to point me out to the great man.

Sometimes it worked sublimely; for instance when Gorbachev went to Belgrade in 1988, and met the increasingly shaky joint leadership which Tito had bequeathed to Yugoslavia. The grey men in the home team were each speaking in turn about peace and unity, and Gorbachev was starting to look extremely bored. So I broke in and asked him about the current state of relations with the United States, which seemed at that moment to be rather rocky. Gorbachev seemed glad to be diverted from the grey men and the wonders of collective power, and launched into an immensely long account of the frustrating time he was having with the United States over nuclear weapons negotiations.

Transcript of interview recorded in Moscow, 8.5.86

Speakers: Mikhail Gorbachev, John Simpson

MK: We are engaged in creating a new relationship. Until now Soviet-American relations have been based on the principle of enmity and competition. It is our duty now to change this, and to ensure that we work together for the good of mankind.

JS: But the Americans still regard themselves as competing with you. Aren't you simply engaged in weakening the Soviet Union, as your critics say?

MG: Restructuring the economy is essential. So is the principle of openness in our internal relationships. This isn't weakness, it is strength. We are talking to the United States on the basis of a new strength.

'There is no alternative,' Margaret Thatcher would say. It was noticeable that the world's three main political leaders all used the same language. Presumably they believed it; though Gorbachev probably believed it less than the other two.

Sometimes the door-stepping tactic failed completely. When he went to the resort of Dubrovnik, on the Adriatic coast, I was determined to get another good session with him as he walked with Raisa along the main streets of the charming old town. This time his security men were there: five behind him, three on either side of him, and two appalling wreckers in front, beating their way through the crowd. These men, built along the general lines of T-72 tanks, took no prisoners. One of them hit the lens of our camera back into the eye of the cameraman; which annoyed me so much I made the tactical error of throwing a punch at the tank's chest. He reached out in a practised way, gripped my thumb and tried to break it against his knee. Fortunately his hand was sweaty, and I just managed to slip my thumb out of his grip.

'Mikhail Sergeyevich,' I called out, 'can't you stop them?'

Raisa turned and said something to him, but Gorbachev merely gave me his pleasant, ironic look and shrugged a little. Perhaps he was as much a prisoner of the security system as everyone else. By this stage, anyway, the twin tanks had rolled on. Yet it made excellent pictures. Fortunately tough characters like that don't realize, any more than crooks and secret policemen do, that to take a swing at the camera lens seems to the viewer to be a clear admission of thuggishness.

The process by which the United States slowly moved away from enmity towards a partnership with the Soviet Union was slow and delicate, and fascinating. From time to time I would go and see my large lunch-companion from Hampton Court Palace, and would be told in his slow, cautious, intelligent code how hard it was to negotiate with an American president who couldn't understand the issues and was capable of coming up with sudden, unthought-out, naive schemes such as the one he sprang on Gorbachev in Reykjavik in 1986: to give up nuclear weapons altogether, and share American *Star Wars* technology in such a way as to protect the world from nuclear attack.

I sympathized. Watching Reagan closely and from a distance throughout his eight years in office, I could never understand why he aroused such adoration among his supporters. He was obviously genial enough, but to me he never seemed to be anything more than a good front man for a team of clever speech-writers and policy people. In 1987 he spoke to the students and staff at Moscow State University: a speech about personal freedom which was so sublimely worded, and so well delivered, that many people in his audience had tears in their eyes. I was one of them.

Then the words disappeared from the prompt screens which he had been reading so well, and it was time for the real Ronald Reagan to come out from behind them. His body language changed utterly. Instead of the self-confident old man who had just proclaimed the magnificent, rolling periods which had moved us so strongly, his shoulders drooped apologetically, he rubbed his hands together, and he gave a feeble little giggle.

'Well,' he said, and even his voice sounded different now, 'I don't suppose I'll be able to answer your questions, but I'll certainly try.'

He supposed right. The students looked at each other in surprise as he stumbled through a few of the subjects he had dealt so well with, a few minutes before. Fortunately the torture didn't last long, but afterwards when I spoke to people in the audience they couldn't work out why there was this curious difference. They didn't have prompt screens in the Soviet Union.

Yet because he presided over the world's most successful economy, he ran Gorbachev off the road. The Soviet Union was falling behind at a visible rate: its roads and infrastructure were getting worse, its schools and universities were starved of money, its shops and factories and offices still operated with abacuses and typewriters. The enormous efforts of the fifties and sixties had been followed by the lethargy and indecision of the Brezhnev years. 'A great deal has to be done,' my neighbour had said to me at the Hampton Court lunch, and that proved to be a dangerous underestimate.

A short time before, Charles Wheeler had filmed a memorable sequence for *Newsnight* at a cement factory in some God-forsaken part of Russia. Next door to it, sharing a common fence, was a factory which made plastic bags for cement. But the centralizing policies of seventy years demanded that the plastic bags had to be shipped off to Moscow before they could be sent back for the cement which was being produced at the factory on the other side of the chain-link fence.

The cameraman began with a close-up of the latest supply of bags being driven off by lorry. Then he pulled out to reveal the latest supply of cement emerging. Because there were no bags to put it in, the cement was being piled up in the forecourt of the factory: little white mountains which were hardening and becoming permanent in the depressing, persistent rain.

Mikhail Gorbachev could probably never have saved the Soviet system, though he thought he could. His policy of perestroika, industrial reconstruction, was accompanied by glasnost, the policy of greater openness. The problem was that people were suddenly able to speak out about the inadequacies and stupidities and cruelties of the system, long before the advantages from perestroika could possibly have started to come through.

The situation got worse, and people were able to say so; which made it seem disastrous. If he had done what the Chinese did and provided perestroika without glasnost, he might have got away with it. But that was never an option; and once the openness had started it was forever impossible to stop it. The system would have fallen apart anyway. All Gorbachev did was to influence the direction in which it fell.

« »

1989 was to be the single most important year in the second half of the century, and I had the extraordinary good fortune to be at every one of the great events it produced: the only reporter in the entire world, I believe, who was. This sequence of events all had Mikhail Gorbachev as its common denominator. It began with the Soviet withdrawal from Afghanistan in February, continued with the demonstrations and massacre in Tiananmen Square, and went on to the breaching of the Berlin Wall and the revolutions in Czechoslovakia and Romania in November and December.

Not that it stopped there. Nelson Mandela's release from gaol (also a distant by-product of Gorbachev's revolution) took place in February 1990, and I was in South Africa for that. Perhaps not surprisingly, after a period of such exertion and so little relief, I found myself quite ill. I assumed I had caught TB from a sufferer in its final stages, with whom I had had to share a closed room for three days or more in Afghanistan; but it turned out to be exhaustion, emotional as well as merely physical. Experiencing so much joy and horror and fear and excitement in a twelve-month period had taken its toll.

And yet at the start of 1989 there was no real reason to expect that Marxism-Leninism would be on its deathbed by the end of the year. On the contrary, Gorbachev seemed to be in control, and was working behind the scenes for reformist governments to come to power in Eastern Europe. In the Soviet Union itself he was already becoming deeply unpopular, as his reforms failed to bring much in the way of results. Yet throughout the rest of the Communist world he was regarded as the great reformer, the man who could give the Marxist-Leninist system an attractive human face.

In May he went to China, to put an end to nearly twenty years of often angry, outspoken rivalry between Peking and Moscow. The future head of BBC programming, Mark Thompson, was then editor of the *Nine O'Clock News,* and he and I went to Peking to cover what we assumed would be a major diplomatic occasion. It turned out to be altogether different: the shaking of an empire, and a demonstration to the world that Marxism-Leninism was only capable of maintaining its control over the lives of the people who lived under it as long as it still had the will to use force.

But China had been in a good deal of inner political turmoil ever since the fall from office in 1987 of the former general secretary of the Communist Party, Hu Yaobang. In the frozen world of the Chinese Communist hierarchy, Hu had passed as a liberal: he had sported a dark grey Western suit when everyone else in the leadership (including the women) was still wearing Mao jackets.

Hu had finally died on 15 April 1989, still in disgrace, and university students used the occasion of his funeral to begin demanding greater democracy. There were strong suspicions within the Party hierarchy, it later emerged, that the students' demonstrations were being quietly encouraged by the leading reformer in the Party, Zhao Ziyang, as a way of getting rid of the old paramount leader Deng Xiaoping.

I knew next to nothing of all this, beyond what I had read in the newspapers. I hadn't come to Peking to report on the political situation: I was there as an observer of Gorbachev. As I drove through the city from the airport I found it utterly bewildering, and when I had unpacked after the long flight I decided to go out and take a look round. I decided to take a taxi to the Beijing Hotel, whose Chinese name I thought I could pronounce well enough so that a taxi-driver would understand me, and walk the couple of hundred yards to Tiananmen Square.

The enormous portrait of Mao Zedong which hung over the entrance to the Forbidden City showed no sign of any emotion, or of any thought-process. This was the man who killed more people than Hitler and Stalin put together, a monster of cruelty and ideological rigidity; but here he looked as bland as an egg.

Inside, I wandered from palace to palace completely baffled by the impenetrable complexity of the place. Everything, from the carved figures on the roofs to the marble reliefs on the white marble staircases, seemed so impossible to comprehend that I sometimes found myself laughing out loud. In the years to come I would strive to understand ancient Chinese culture, and even learned to translate poetry from the T'ang dynasty into English; but for now it was all completely beyond me.

Then I passed under Mao's offensively uncommunicative painting again and crossed Chang'an Avenue to Tiananmen Square. There were a few big Japanese-made cars to watch out for, the first-fruits of the corruption that was beginning to sweep the upper levels of political and industrial life in China. But for the most part the avenue was a complex river of bicycles, flowing in both directions to the incessant sound of ringing bells.

The Square virtually became my home for the next month. I came to love the students who took it over, and the thought of their death at the hands of the Chinese army still affects me, years later. But for now its vastness was mostly empty, except for a few people wandering around and taking photographs of each other. Some old men were flying little kites around its margins for the amusement of their grandchildren.

But there were plenty of police. The policeman is the dominant figure of Chinese Communism, in his green uniform with red accoutrements. In 1989, as later, the main function of the police in Tiananmen Square was to ensure that Chinese people didn't take seriously any of the official rhetoric which said that this place belonged to them. But the weakness of Deng Xiaoping's position meant that students, in particular, were prepared to claim their stake in the country. The coming visit of Mikhail Gorbachev gave them their excuse. While I was still wandering round the Forbidden City, smiling at my own inability to understand what it was all about, the students from Peking 'Beida' University were marching on Tiananmen Square. And as I stood beside the monument to the People's Heroes in the Square's centre, I saw a dozen or so red banners waving over the heads of a crowd down in Chang'an Avenue. I shall never forget the contrast between the sharp, vivid scarlet of the banners and the dull earth red of the Forbidden City's walls, nor the moment when I recognized the song the students were singing: the Internationale, the anthem of Marxism, which the students were to make their own.

The banners swung round, and I began to realize now what was happening. I was witnessing for myself the takeover of the Square, which a month later was to lead to the deaths of some, presumably, of the students who were now making purposefully for the Monument where I was standing. I got out of the way fast, while the police barked nervously into their two-way radios.

Even then, I think, I discerned some of the qualities which I later came to regard with such tenderness about the Tiananmen students: their naiveté, their gentleness and spontaneity, the delight they felt in being free of restrictions for once in their lives. They were often hopelessly ignorant of the world and its ways. They certainly had very little idea indeed of the one thing they had come here to demand: democracy. Everyone I talked to gave me a different answer. In fact what they were asking for wasn't so much democracy as a little personal freedom: the right to do what they wanted, without the fierce controls which the state imposed on everyone.

Transcript of interview recorded in Tiananmen Square, Beijing, 4.5.89

Speakers: Unknown student, John Simpson

JS: What's the purpose of coming here and taking over the Square?

Unknown: We don't want to challenge our government, we just want them to talk to us. We want to explain that we aren't patriotic, as the *People's Daily* accused us of being.

JS: In the editorial last week?

Unknown: Yes

```
JS: People say it was written by Deng Xiaoping himself.

Unknown: We think so, yes.

JS: But surely if you're coming out like this, you are
challenging the government.

Unknown: No. They should talk to us.
```

The other thing that united them was the conviction that the system, as headed by Deng Xiaoping, was irrevocably corrupt. They were right of course, and the destruction of the Tiananmen protest made it possible for the authorities to go on and become even more corrupt. The students were certainly being used, but there was more to it than that: an essential decency which gave nobility to their cause. These were not, by and large, the fiercest of Chinese students. Peking University wasn't as radical as the other universities in the city; its students had been rather more docile. Now they were trying to catch up with the others.

The fact of being together like this acted on them like a catalyst. Ideas flourished. Several of the students I came to know told me they had learned more from their time in the Square than in the rest of their university education. It wasn't just hyperbole; everywhere you went, from the tents on the side to the encampment in the middle, people were talking about politics. They argued passionately, haranguing each other, issuing documents, writing reports. Some had obviously come because they had nothing better to do. Some were there because it was said that this was the only place in China where free love was practised. But there was an earnestness about them which was very affecting. And they believed what they told themselves: that the government wasn't capable of doing anything about them.

The most effective weapon the students had was the hunger strike. Hundreds of them, wearing white scarves round their foreheads, sat quietly around the steps of the Monument under banners which read in Chinese and English 'Fast to the Death'. It was this, rather than the actual occupation of Tiananmen Square, which gave their movement its real force and validity. By threatening to starve themselves to death for their demands the demonstrators won sympathy throughout the country. China had become a society which lacked any kind of idealism, and where the leadership used the ferocious system of control in order to protect its own personal greed and corruption. By contrast the students were clean and decent and self-sacrificing.

That was genuine enough. But the hunger-strike wasn't: not, at least, according to the strict understanding of the phrase. The students who volunteered for the strike operated a rota, so that while some were fasting others were free to eat. And even the students who were formally fasting allowed themselves to snack on bars of chocolate and fruit if they became too hungry. 'Hunger-strike', for them, meant going without a proper cooked meal or two. I was reminded of Sean Mac Stiofain drinking his shower water back in Ireland.

> Transcript of interview recorded in Beijing, 6.5.89
>
> Speakers: Professor Fang Lizhe, John Simpson
>
> JS: What is the position with your students in the Square today?
>
> FL: Some of them went without their lunch, and tonight they will go without dinner as well. [Sobs].

I quickly found myself discarding the ignorant notions that so many Westerners have about the Chinese: that they are faceless automata, political clones. I realized that this was merely the picture we had drawn for ourselves from the television pictures of vast demonstrations at the time of the Cultural Revolution, when Maoism demanded that everyone should wear the same clothes and brandish the same little red book, and that children should inform on their parents.

The Chinese nation had been forced into this conformity, because to stand out against it meant imprisonment and perhaps death. But it wasn't how the Chinese people I came to know behaved when they were left to themselves. On the contrary, they were inclined to be sentimental and were given to sudden acts of generosity and impulsiveness. One day in the Square, for instance, I watched as a fat, middle-aged man grabbed a megaphone and started shouting at the students.

> Transcript of actuality from John Simpson report, Tiananmen Square, Beijing, 7.5.89
>
> I'm not afraid of dying. I saw the demonstration of the students here on 21 April, and I was deeply moved. The

next day I joined the students and I've been supporting
them ever since. You plainclothes cops, can you hear me?
My name is Wu Xiqi. I'm a worker, and my unit number is
126989799. I'm not afraid of telling you who I am . . . I
think every worker should come down here and support the
students. My heart beats with the students. Do you
support me?

[Applause and cheering]

I often wondered afterwards what became of Wu Xiqi (or at least the
man who announced his name that day; I have changed it, and his
unit number, just in case). It was still dangerous to proclaim your
identity quite so loudly. The security police might not have been able
to carry on in their usual brutal way during the Tiananmen Square
protest, because the government itself was deadlocked and no one
could decide what to do.

But they were there all right, still going about their business. As I
wandered around, either with a camera crew or on my own, I was
often aware of being filmed by men who were too old to be students.
Once I grabbed one of them and got my translator to ask him what
he was doing and who he was. The man was clearly so terrified of me
that I let him go.

'I'm a tourist,' he said.

'What are you going to do with these pictures?'

'They're for my collection.'

We all laughed at him, and he hurried away. It was some time
before I discovered what use pictures like this had been put to in the
'collections' of the security police. After the massacre the Chinese
embassy in London began distributing a videotape, very badly
assembled, which purported to show how the students had been
manipulated by sinister foreign elements.

I was one of these elements. In the video you can see me talking
to a group of students and handing one of them something. The
commentary implies strongly that it's money. Then there is a clumsy
cut, followed by pictures of a lorry-load of weapons being unloaded
by the students. The clear suggestion was that I had given them the
money to buy weapons.

As far as I could tell, the pictures came from one of those little incidents which happened all the time in Tiananmen Square. The students were always asking foreigners for their autograph, on a handbill, a piece torn from a placard, sometimes even on the material of a T-shirt.

As for the weapons on the army lorry, they arrived not long before the massacre took place, as part of a deliberate provocation by the authorities. The lorry was driven fast and erratically into the Square and the driver jumped out and ran away. When the students looked inside they saw it was full of rifles. For security they unloaded them and handed them over to the police straight away.

Eight years later, at an official dinner for my colleagues and me which was given by the Chinese foreign ministry a few months before the handover of Hong Kong in June 1997, a senior official started to criticize the undercover filming of one of the correspondents in my unit, Sue Lloyd-Roberts. It was, he said, intolerable that she should go to Tibet, which was an integral part of China, and interview enemies of the state. I stirred in my seat, and told him about the video.

'If I could get a good lawyer I could probably sue the Chinese government for a huge amount of money for defamation of character,' I said, giving him a deeply insincere smile.

The official turned back to his pork dumplings.

In fact I am certain that he, and tens of thousands of officials like him, would have supported the Tiananmen protest very strongly. It was exactly such people, Westernized, intelligent, educated, who came out day after day in support of the students. It wasn't necessarily from conscience, though it seems likely that they did hope very much that the students would win; but they joined in the vast demonstrations in Chang'an Avenue, together with judges and broadcasters and senior policemen (and even, it appeared at one stage, senior secret policemen) because it looked as though Deng Xiaoping was finished, and Zhao Ziyang would soon take his place. Zhao, the Chinese Gorbachev, would then turn the country towards much greater democracy. No one anticipated that Deng Xiaoping would have the determination, the strength, or the guts, to hold out.

As for Gorbachev himself, the demonstration completely upstaged his visit. He arrived, was driven round by a back entrance to the Great Hall of the People because of the occupation of the Square, and went through his official programme as quickly and tactfully as he could. On the morning Gorbachev arrived, I went round to the hotel where his press spokesman, Gennadi Gerasimov, was staying. I wanted to interview him for the *Today* programme.

As he opened the door in his silk dressing gown he looked like George Sanders in a 1940s film. I had known him for some time, and always liked his particular brand of cynicism. Now he was trying to make the point that all this business about demonstrations was merely something got up by the Western press.

```
Transcript of interview recorded in Beijing, 7.5.89

Speakers: Gennadi Gerasimov, John Simpson

JS: This visit is going to go ahead in a very curious
atmosphere, isn't it?

GG: I don't see why there should be a curious atmosphere.
We've waited for this visit for thirty years. The
students are just the backdrop for the media. The main
concern is the summit; and it's long overdue.
```

But the main concern wasn't the summit at all; and Gorbachev and Gennadi Gerasimov went home to Moscow a few days later with nothing clear at all. They obviously had no idea who would be running China from now on.

Nor had anyone else. The month-long occupation of the Square continued, but when the enormous demonstrations of Thursday, 18 May passed and Deng Xiaoping still hadn't resigned, the more cautious and circumspect figures began to drift away from the movement to get rid of him. Zhao Ziyang, by now completely isolated on the Standing Committee of the Politburo, was offered one last chance by his colleagues in the leadership: he must try to persuade the students to give up their hunger strike and leave the Square. If he failed, it would be the end of him.

He went down to the Square in the early hours of the morning, and climbed onto one of the buses which the hunger strikers were living on. Chinese Television went with him. He looked terrible, and started pleading with them. At times he seemed to be rambling. At the end he thanked them, and climbed down. He had achieved nothing whatever. The next day he was arrested, and has never been seen in public again. Martial law was declared.

« »

We were on our own now. Our visas had expired, but there was no one around to issue new ones or to check the old ones. We moved hotels, to be closer to Tiananmen Square, and waited for something to happen. On 20 May we became subject to Martial Law Order Number One, which read as follows:

> All foreign journalists are strictly forbidden to incite unrest or issue reports which exaggerate the situation.
>
> No foreign correspondent (including those from Hong Kong or Macau) may enter the premises of any government organization, factory, mine or university to undertake reporting or filming, without official written permission.
>
> Any foreign journalist violating these provisions renders himself or herself liable to arrest by the People's Liberation Army or the police.

Deng Xiaoping, meanwhile, was using the time to drum up support from the army commanders, and slowly the authorities were starting to get their confidence back. There were more official provocations now, and the security police were more in evidence. On the afternoon of 23 May three men from Mao Zedong's province of Hunan walked up to the entrance of the Forbidden City and threw ink at the vast portrait of Mao which hung over it. That too seemed like a provocation, to discredit the students.

An hour later, out of a clear blue sky, enormous black storm clouds had gathered and it began to rain with a wild intensity. My white tropical suit was wet through in an instant, and a pen in my inside pocket began leaking. The ferocious wind lifted the tents in Tiananmen Square and hoisted them up into the air, while the people who had been in them lay frightened and soaking on the ground. A young student who sat on the marble balustrade round the Monument bared his chest to the wind and raised his hands in a double Victory sign.

I was working with Eric Thirer, one of the best cameramen the

BBC has ever had, and his pictures of the student went around the world. It seemed like the most graphic embodiment of the spirit of the Tiananmen protest. The pictures of the storm were extraordinary, and thoroughly worth the soaking we had been given.

Soon there were only a few dozen students left in the Square, and a platoon of soldiers dressed in oilskins could have sorted out China's constitutional problem then and there. The rain came whipping laterally across at us over the empty, flat expanse of paving stones. In the distance I could see three figures battling towards us, tacking in the ferocious wind like sailing boats in a stormy bay.

As they came towards us one of the students started taking off his flimsy plastic raincoat. When he finally fought free of it he gave it to me as a gesture of thanks to someone from the outside world who had come to Peking to be with them. I couldn't accept it, of course: all he had on underneath was a thin T-shirt and shorts, and I was too wet to care anyway. In the end he took his coat back, but he knelt down on the paving stones in the rain and kissed my hand. I felt like King Lear.

At last it all came to an end. I think we all felt it was inevitable, even the students. I had come to love slipping out of the hotel in the early morning and heading off for the Square. In the first light the students would creep out of their tents, drinking tea they had brewed on their own fires. Perhaps one would play a guitar or a little flute. There was an acrid smell of cooking oil and urine and dirty clothes which became so associated in my mind with being in the Square that it ceased to offend me. My feet would crunch on the bits of bamboo and broken glass which lay everywhere ('Xiaoping' can mean 'little bottle', and for a time every demonstration involved the dropping of little bottles onto the ground to signify Deng's downfall).

I would accept a cup of thin hot tea from someone, and sit down in the hope of communicating with my few words of Chinese. The students would ask dozens of questions in their frank, affectionate way: how old my wife was, how difficult it was to have more than one child in the West, how easy it was for young people to make a living, how much pressure the British government put on me to lie about what was going on here.

When I told them I wasn't married, that young people had a hard time getting jobs, and that the British government never said anything to me about my reporting, someone would translate and they would go off into giggles of embarrassment and, perhaps, disbelief. Then I would sign a few autographs and wander over to the statue of the Goddess of Democracy which the students had erected directly opposite the portrait of Mao.

I loved the statue for its beauty and its fragility, and for the challenge it presented to the savagery and brutality of the Chinese Communist Party. But I don't think it ever occurred to me that this challenge could be successful. I was waiting for the end.

We had all been so obsessed with the students that it was hard to understand that other people were involved in the protest too. In the strange hierarchical way of the Chinese, the north-eastern part of the Square was left to the working-class people of Peking. They didn't dress any differently from the students, but they were unquestionably rougher. They also enjoyed making fun of people like me.

Eric Thirer, his Californian sound recordist Fred Scott and I had to go out late one evening soon after Gorbachev's arrival to record a piece to camera. The only way we could get above the heads of the crowd was to clamber up on little flat-bed rickshaws which we pulled together. The crowd around us quickly found out how satisfying it was to twitch one or other of the rickshaws and so force us to start all over again; especially since they saw how angry it made me. The students would never have done that. Nor would they have made the mistake which our translator overheard.

'Who's that up there?'

'Must be this character Gorbachev everyone's talking about.'

'How do you make that out?'

'Well, he's European, isn't he? And he must be important, because they're shining lights on his face and pointing that camera at him.'

'Ah well, I suppose you're right.'

I never heard anyone refer to this section of the demonstration, though on the night of the massacre it was people like this who showed the most anger. And when, on two different nights, the People's Liberation Army tried to force their way into the Square, it was the ordinary, working-class people of Peking who blocked them. I went out with a camera crew because we had heard that a huge crowd was gathering on the motorway into the centre of town, determined to stop the army getting through.

When we got there, we found an awesome sight: tens of thousands of people standing in complete silence, with a dark ferocity of purpose. It was then that I understood how I had misinterpreted the situation. The students were merely peaceable, intellectual critics of the Chinese government's repressive ways. These people had been the real victims of forty years of Marxism-Leninism. Most of the students were far too young to remember the savagery of the Cultural Revolution. Not so this crowd. They were determined, if they got the chance, to avenge the years of official cruelty and oppression, when children were encouraged to inform on their parents and the slightest sign of non-conformity was brutally punished. Now was the opportunity for these people to get their own back. You could see in their eyes that they weren't going to let it pass.

As May ended, our local staff faded away; it was like Haydn's *Disappearing Symphony*. First one of our translators failed to turn up for work, then another, then another. Then it was our transport manager, an engaging crook, who had stayed on longer than most but took all the money that was owing to him and never showed up again. They knew what was going to happen. They also knew it would do them no good at all to be associated with us.

I missed one of our translators. Mr Tang, a poet himself, first explained the principles of classical Chinese poetry to me. All our student contacts were convinced that he was a government spy, and I suppose he probably was. He certainly had a habit of writing down the things everyone said. When I asked him why, he said he was getting together the materials for a short story on his experiences with us. I didn't believe him, but I enjoyed talking about *ku-shih* and *chin-t'i-shih* and the other forms of classical Chinese poetry too much to mind.

By the night of the massacre itself we only had one local worker left, a thin, weedy little student called Wang. He was passionately committed to the students' cause, and couldn't bear to cut his links with us because he wanted to make sure we understood exactly what was going on.

I have written a good deal about the Tiananmen Square massacre, but it remains a perpetually painful subject for me. The editor of the magazine *Granta*, Bill Buford (who later became literary editor of the *New Yorker*, and therefore one of the artistic arbiters of America), asked me to write an account of it in the summer of 1989. I was flattered and agreed, not realizing how brutal Buford himself could be: as ferocious in his way as Deng Xiaoping. I wrote several drafts, but each time Buford would send them back.

'This is just shit,' he would yell down the phone, 'Unprintable shit.' Or, 'You're holding all sorts of things back from me. I know it.'

He was right. I saw a lot of unpleasant things that night, which I had buried away inside my mind.

The camera crew I was working with, Ingo Prosser and Mark McCauley, clearly shared my own view that this was one of the moments which are so important that the question of your own safety is dwarfed by the events around you. Ingo was passionate about getting as close as possible to the action, and at times that night it seemed to me he was taking insane risks.

Mark managed to retain an ironic, perceptive calm. It is often harder in dangerous circumstances to be a sound recordist than to be a cameraman, because you don't have the solace, the distraction perhaps, of staring at the action through the camera eye-piece, which shows you everything on a little screen in black and white. The sound recordist sees everything as it really is; and sometimes it requires a real sense of duty to keep from slipping away. Wang was with us that night, as intelligent, nervous and committed as ever. We also had a producer with us from *Panorama*: she and I had been assembling a much longer report on the Tiananmen Square demonstration.

It was well after midnight now, airless and intensely hot. There could be no doubt that the army was about to move in. The loud-speakers on every lamp-post around the Square were booming out an eerie, expressionless, hypnotic message:

Go home and save your lives. You will fail. You are not behaving in the correct Chinese manner. This is not the West. It is China. You should behave like good Chinese. Go home and save your lives. Go home and save your lives.

Crowds swept backwards and forwards in the darkness in front of the Gate of Heavenly Peace, while Mao looked down blandly over us, and the Goddess of Democracy held up her plaster lamp across the road from him. Then people started shouting that the army was coming, and the crowds began to haul the heavy railings set in concrete from the side of Chang'an Avenue and used them to block the roadway. We were back with the ordinary people of Peking here: the students had gathered peacefully in the Square.

Young men danced around us as we filmed, flourishing knives, coshes and home-made spears. One boy opened his coat and showed a row of Coca-Cola bottles in his belt, each one filled with petrol and corked with a rag. The uprising was coming very close now.

It wasn't a good moment to have an argument. Still, in the heat and tension the producer and I disagreed about what we should do next. It was all very trivial and unnecessary, and I should have behaved better: she wanted to do some more interviews for *Panorama*, I wanted to find a safe place from which to film the army's assault. Ingo, caught between the two of us, just wanted to get on with the business of filming what was in front of him. In a fury I left them and stormed off towards the Square in a last attempt to find a vantage-point.

My anger quickly evaporated, but I thought that before I went back to find my colleagues I would have one last stroll around the encampment in the Square. It had meant a great deal to me, and I knew now that it was about to be destroyed for ever. I threaded my way between the tents. I felt I knew each one, each smell. My feet ground for the last time on the familiar mixture of broken glass and bamboo. As I passed, the student people kept grabbing my hand, grateful that someone from the outside world was still with them: there were very few Western journalists left in the Square now, and we were the only television crew.

I had a terrible sense of foreboding. A young couple were sitting on the ground, clinging to each other, her head on his shoulder. They didn't look at me. I remember thinking that they looked like passengers at the rail of a sinking ship, looking out across the sea that would soon close over them. From the Monument came the inevitable speeches of the student leaders. As they waited for the revenge of the state, they broke into the Internationale. Plenty of irony in that, I thought.

And then it started. I heard the familiar clanking, squealing sound of an armoured personnel carrier. It was being driven at speed across the Square. Its path was marked out by petrol bombs of the kind the boy had shown me earlier, curling up into the air and smashing down onto the APC which ranged around like a maddened bull in a ring, searching for a way to get out. Finally it broke through and drove off down Chang'an Avenue, still on fire.

Directly I heard the sound of the APC I had started running. It was my worst fear to be separated from the crew when things were starting. Another APC was sent into the ring, a second sacrificial victim in order to justify the massacre which was about to begin. It flailed around wildly, then jammed up against one of the concrete blocks and stuck there. The crowd cornered it and attacked it, trying to burn the soldiers inside alive.

Now I could see the battery light on top of Ingo's camera in the darkness, and ran towards it like a maniac, pulling people out of my way and shouting. When I reached the crew, only Mark noticed me. I screamed into Ingo's ear that he was too near the APC, that it could blow up at any moment. He shook me off and carried on filming. Mark gave me a brief ironic grin. I knew what he meant: we were here for the duration.

People were swarming all over the APC now, trying to set it on fire and screaming at the soldiers who were trapped inside that they were animals who had to be killed. Then for a moment there was almost a silence. The door was opening, and we were standing right in front of it.

'They'll come out shooting,' I yelled, but Ingo was too far gone to hear. They didn't, anyway. They came out like animals to an abattoir.

Bill Buford forced me to write about it later, but I still find it hard to think about the next few minutes. Two of the soldiers were beaten to a pulp and carried away. I was so sick of bloodshed that I intervened to stop someone beating out the brains of the third soldier; though his life was really saved by the courage of the students, who drove up in a bus and rescued him. Buford wanted to know what it sounded like when the soldiers' skulls were crushed, and how the blood felt on my hand when I grabbed the brick away just as it was coming down on the head of the third. As though I could forget. I can still feel the wetness of the brick as I threw it away.

We knew we had magnificent, terrible material: the best, as it turned out, that anyone obtained that night. But the army still hadn't arrived in force, and it was obviously coming soon. Shocked and exhausted, we had to decide what to do now: to stay, even though I had failed to find a secure place to film from.

Someone suggested going to the Beijing Hotel, a little way down the road, to get some more videotapes and have something to eat; none of us had eaten for seven hours. I agreed. We had a room in the Beijing, and I could phone through a report to London from there. I allowed myself to think that we would come out again later; though at some level of consciousness I knew we wouldn't be able to. Perhaps we saved our lives that night; a Western television crew which had been discovered in the Square would have had a nasty time of it, and might well have been shot. But it felt like an act of desertion, and I regret it to this day.

Instead we took up a position on a balcony high up on the front of the Beijing Hotel. It wasn't particularly safe; a Korean photographer was shot dead only two balconies away from us on the same floor, and bullets whizzed round our rooms several times. Several Chinese people, including a well-known student leader, took refuge with us. I tried to explain to her that she would be in more danger with us than if she were on their own, but she clung to me and I didn't have the heart to turn her away.

Eventually the security police came up to stop us filming. When they hammered on the door I shouted to our translator, Wang, not to open it. Perhaps he didn't hear. They grabbed his arm and tried to pull him out of the room. I flung myself across and seized his other arm, pulling him back, and shouting the first thing that came into my head.

'If you don't let him go I'll call the British ambassador immediately!'

It must rank as the least convincing threat I have ever uttered, but it had an immediate and satisfying effect on the security police. They let go of Wang's skinny little arm and vanished down the corridor at a run. For the rest of my time in Peking Wang was my faithful friend and guide, never leaving me except at night, when he slept in the next room with the door partly open. My occult power over security policemen and British ambassadors had impressed him deeply.

From our balcony we watched and filmed everything that happened in the terrible hours which followed. Sometimes it was so dangerous to be out there that I ordered everyone else inside and the cameraman and I lay down on the balcony floor. The army's tanks and personnel carriers would grind their way towards the Square, firing randomly at the front of the big Chang'an Avenue buildings. In the Square itself we could see the tanks driving over the skimpy little tents of the students, crushing anyone they found inside. I thought about the young couple

I had seen, holding onto each other. The waters had closed over them now.

All we could see were random flashes and outbursts of firing. Someone, looking through the long lens of the camera on the balcony, shouted that the statue of the Goddess of Liberty had gone. It was only a matter of time anyway.

At around four in the morning I decided to make a break for it and get the pictures back to the other hotel, where the BBC operation was based. I went down a back staircase and ended up in the vast entrance-hall, as full of wasted space as Communist hotels always are. Everything was in darkness. There were a couple of security men at the far end, but so far away I thought I could probably get to the main entrance before they could intercept me; and once out in the night I would be away.

It worked. I ran across the marble floor and was through the door before they had even raised their heads to look at me. There was so much noise outside they probably couldn't hear anyway. I slipped out into the darkness. There was quite heavy fire along Chang'an Avenue now, from the right-hand or eastward side; it was aimed at a group of demonstrators who were trying to work their way down towards the Square. I got onto the pavement, dodging low, and half-crawling, half-creeping, got close to the cross-roads. I had to turn left, to the north, in order to reach our base.

So far I was in the shelter of some little trees, and didn't stand out against the shadows. At the corner, though, I was out on my own. The line of fire was still ten yards or so away from me to my right, and I saw two young men hit. They lay on the ground, one silent and one crying out and trying to wriggle away. There was no shelter. I lay in the gutter, my head pressed down, the cassettes gripped in my right hand. I must have stayed there for fifteen minutes, trying to work out what to do. Wait until the firing eased, I thought; and then, from the very road I had to go down there came the squealing noise of a line of armoured personnel carriers and the quick trudge of soldiers marching at the double. They would have to pass right by me; perhaps over me. I peered around: there was nowhere else to go. Ignominiously, shamed, I crept back into the shadow of the trees and headed back for the Beijing Hotel. The pictures would have to wait.

At dawn the soldiers started running around and busying

themselves with something. It proved to be an enormous curtain of black cloth, hung on frames so the Square would be hidden from us. Whatever was going on there now was secret.

The streets were still full of the noise of bullets. Every now and then one of the demonstrators who still had the courage to show themselves would be shot down and carried away by even braver friends. It was full daylight, and the pictures we filmed were destined to be just as famous as the earlier ones: among them, the sequence of the man defying the line of tanks by standing in front of them with his shopping bags. Eric Thirer shot them with his usual coolness, but the soundtrack had several exclamations from me on it:

'Fantastic! Bloody magnificent! Look at that bloke!'

He looked at me warningly, and I lapsed into a sort of silence.

I couldn't put off for much longer the moment when I would have to leave the hotel again. If the pictures were to make the plane to Hong Kong in time for the main news, I had about an hour to get them to the other hotel. There was just as much shooting going on outside, but this time it wouldn't be possible to shrink into the shadows.

There were only two cassettes. For the want of anywhere else to put them, I tucked them into my socks, then made my way down into the massive hall again. Now there were dozens of security men standing by the open door. The sound of gunfire filled the hall, and then there was silence. In that silence I walked across the marble floor, the cassettes making a plastic clanking as I walked. I knew the security men wouldn't let me out, that they would find the cassettes and take them off me, but I was committed. If I turned round they would come after me.

I had no ideas whatever: I'd made my move. I went on walking towards them. Just as I came up to them, one of the security men opened his mouth to speak to me. And at that precise instant there was a wild outburst of firing in the Avenue outside, and the security men all turned to see what it was. I slipped past quickly, and was out before they remembered to look at me. This time there was so much confusion in Chang'an Avenue that I was able to dodge between the trees and run round the corner. The pictures survived after all.

In the BBC's offices I found the redoubtable Kate Adie. She had been out in the streets all night with her camera team, and was in bad shape. A man had been killed right beside her, and her arm had been badly grazed in the incident. Together we assembled our reports. There was no time to edit words to pictures, nor even of seeing the pictures. All we could do was write our scripts, record them, and send them off to Hong Kong with the cassettes.

I sat at the computer, numbed by everything I had seen and determined not to get too emotional about it. I'd made real friends among the students in Tiananmen Square. The thought that they might now be dead or injured, that one of the best and most decent manifestations of recent times had been snuffed out in front of me was too disturbing and too painful for me to deal with it. And so I took refuge in the old BBC concepts of balance and objectivity: there wasn't an ounce of emotion in my script.

Kate's report was very different. It was full of emotion. Six months later, when I finally watched our two reports side by side, I thought that while mine was perfectly accurate it had nothing of the real feeling of what had taken place. Hers did. I suppose the two were complementary, and they were certainly used side by side on the news in Britain.

For a long time after the Tiananmen massacre, there were rumours among journalists in London that there had been something questionable about Kate's reporting of it, and that I had accused her of falsifying her story. None of this was true. Nevertheless I know how the story started.

At the Edinburgh Television Festival a couple of months later, Bill Buford turned up with copies of the story I had written for *Granta* about Tiananmen Square. For some reason he handed several copies to Germaine Greer, who was very generous about it and gave them out to people she thought would be interested. One was Kate Adie. Her reaction gave Germaine and Buford the impression that I hadn't been at Tiananmen Square at all. Buford immediately got on the phone to me.

'John,' he said, almost incomprehensible with fury, 'you sold me a crock of shit.'

It took me some time to find out what had happened, and to convince him that I had indeed been there. Tira, my girlfriend, immediately volunteered to go to Edinburgh and see what happened; and fortunately both Ingo Prosser and Mark McCauley were there anyway, and were able to confirm that things had happened as I had said. But it was a very awkward moment. I wrote Kate a harsh note about it afterwards.

The following December she and I were in Bucharest together, covering the Rumanian revolution. Conditions were difficult, and each evening we had to brave the sniper fire round the television station to get in and satellite our reports. It could be very unnerving; and one night, as Kate and I were waiting for an escort to take us in, an ITN producer showed up with a tape in his hand. His correspondent had settled into the television station immediately on arrival, and hadn't left it ever since; a sensible decision, perhaps, but one that made first-hand reporting rather difficult. I offered to take the tape in for the producer myself, to save him the risk.

'My Christmas present,' I told him.

'How do I know I can trust you?' he replied. He was that kind of person.

It was difficult and dangerous, but Kate and I finally got into the television station, and I put the tape into the hands of the ITN reporter. He and his colleagues had taken over a studio there, while we had a couple of desks outside the studio door.

Conditions were difficult for us that night, and we ended up shouting at each other. One thing led to another very quickly. Within a minute or two I had brought up the business in Edinburgh. Presumably the word 'Tiananmen' filtered through the door to the ITN room.

My bursts of anger rarely last long. Within a minute or so I suggested to Kate that we should forget about it; and she was quick to agree. We had always got along well in the past, and this ended the problem once and for all.

Or it would have done, if someone hadn't rung one of the tabloids about the row we had had. Soon afterwards, back in London, I got a call from someone on the paper asking me if it was true that I had accused Kate of inventing her report from Tiananmen. I told him angrily that it wasn't, and he in turn told me who had given him the story. Ever since I have been much more careful about the favours I do. Not everyone out there can be trusted to return them in kind.

I left for Hong Kong the day after the massacre, to edit my report for *Panorama*. Wang stayed with me to the end. First he said he would say goodbye to me at the hotel door, but when we got there he said he would travel with me as far as the city centre. Then he decided to go all the way to the airport. We drove through streets full of rubble and burned out vehicles. Every government office, every police station, every building associated with the Communist Party or the security police seemed to have been looted and burned. Twice I saw the bodies of soldiers burned to death and propped upright. Someone had put an army cap on the head of one of them as a savage joke. I think it was only then that I realized how fierce the loathing of ordinary Chinese people was for the regime that had ruled them for forty years. Having glimpsed that, I could never again believe in the long-term stability of China under anything remotely connected with the Communist system.

We reached the airport at last. Even now Wang wouldn't leave me, and bustled about getting my suitcases to the check-in desk. Finally he shook my hand very earnestly.

'What will you do?' I asked.

'I'll change my clothes, grow a moustache, and go to my home town. They don't know about my political opinions there. I'll settle down till things go quiet. Be OK.' He paused. 'You want to know a couple of lines of poetry?'

'You know I do.'

'*Gwo pwo shan he dzai,*' he quoted, looking off into the distance. '*Cheng chwun tsau mu shen.* Means, "Country destroyed, mountains and rivers remain. Spring in the city, grass and trees grow deep." It's by Du Fu.'

'I won't forget it,' I said, watching his thin little figure as he waved goodbye for the last time. I never have.

13

Falling Dominoes

IT MAY SEEM inevitable now, but it didn't look like that at the time. People had expected that something might happen in Czechoslovakia the previous year, because the eighth year of several decades this century has tended to bring great political changes there: 1918 and 1938, 1948 and 1968. But it didn't happen. 1989 was the two hundredth anniversary of the French Revolution: might that bring something? But the year dragged on, and it was November before anything moved.

Still, there had been real change. The barbed-wire fence around the countries of the Warsaw Pact had been breached by Hungary, which had now opened its borders with neutral Austria. That made it possible for people throughout Eastern Europe to get to the West easily for the first time since the Berlin Wall was erected in 1961. It was a long and roundabout route, but East Germans who were feeling the economic pinch were able to go easily to Czechoslovakia ostensibly for their summer holiday, and then on to Hungary, and through what had been the Iron Curtain into Austria. From there it was another few hours' drive to West Germany, where they could settle by law.

Soon tens of thousands of people were on the road, heading for a new future in their Trabants, the wheezing little cars which symbolized the exodus. Trabants came in four basic colours, had two-stroke engines, could manage a maximum speed of around fifty-two miles per hour, and were as unsafe and uncomfortable as they were ugly. But they came to possess a certain temporary chic, for all that.

Nobody I talked to, in Britain or in West Germany, thought the German Democratic Republic was about to come to an end.

'It's in trouble, obviously,' said one very senior figure whom it would be unfair to identify, 'but it's bound to snap out of it eventually. It's got to. The whole post-War settlement of Europe depends on it. Without East Germany, the whole bang-shoot goes.'

He was right about that, anyway.

I began work on a documentary about the new, stronger Germany which was emerging. Personally I had always had a certain affection for the two Germanies as constituted after 1945: West Germany with its modest capital in Bonn like a boring little provincial town, with its sense of embarrassment for the way its leaders had convulsed Europe throughout the twentieth century, with its Anglophilia; East Germany, with its guilt and awkwardness and the feeling you got there that the Russians were still punishing it for the past.

'The Germans,' my grandmother used to say with great hauteur, 'are always either at your throat or at your feet.'

Although she didn't actually know any Germans and had never been there, her analysis of European history stands up to a certain scrutiny. The pattern of the twentieth century was established by Bismarck in 1870, when Prussia defeated France and finally united the German states. Everything that followed – the 1914–18 war, the Bolshevik Revolution, the 1939–45 war, the Holocaust, the collapse of the great European colonial empires, the decline of Europe, the Cold War – is the direct result of 1870.

And now the kaleidoscope was about to get another shake. In November I went to Poland to cover the visit of Chancellor Kohl. Germany was flexing its considerable economic muscles and looking eastwards.

I had always had a certain regard for Helmut Kohl. I had interviewed him once, and during a particularly violent demonstration in Hamburg I had walked with him under a shower of eggs and spittle, filming him. He made a big target.

```
Transcript of interview with Chancellor Helmut Kohl,
Hamburg, 3.4.86

Speakers: Helmut Kohl, John Simpson

JS: This is a bit difficult, isn't it?
```

HK: No, it's what you have to expect sometimes in
politics. It doesn't worry me.

[Sound of egg hitting Helmut Kohl]

JS: Not even when things hit you, like that?

HK: No. It happens.

Together with the big contingent of German reporters and cameramen
we headed off to Auschwitz to report on Kohl's visit there. I had never
seen such a terrible place. In the November cold it numbed the mind
with its brooding awfulness. Even if they pulled down the whole
enormous complex, as large as a city, and planted it with flower
gardens, it would still haunt you for ever. As it is, left in more or less
the condition the Allies found it, it is unspeakably dreadful. And, in
Socialist Poland, the shortage of housing meant that dozens of families
still had to live in the building overlooking one of the main gas cham-
bers. The railway lines, the gates, the buildings, the very concrete, were
all imbued with the sense of evil: evil on a scale which only twentieth
century industry and ingenuity could have conceived.

Into this atmosphere strode the portly, confident figure of Helmut
Kohl. One of his predecessors, Willi Brandt, had gone down on his
knees here, with tears in his eyes. But Kohl represented a different
constituency: the Germany which had made good after 1945, and
didn't see why it should forever be apologizing. Not the Germany
which had worshipped Adolf Hitler, certainly, but the Germany which
could understand some of the motives for worshipping him. Not the
Germany which felt guilty, but the one which felt it deserved to enjoy
the benefits of its hard work.

Helmut Kohl didn't have tears in his eyes as he wandered round
Auschwitz. Instead, conscious of the television cameras on him, and
of the people who would be watching back home, he had a permanent
smile on his face. He spoke often to his guides, and made little jokes
to them. He hadn't come to Auschwitz to apologize. He had come to
show that his Germany had no need to apologize for anything.

Germans, after all, have suffered as well as caused suffering. After
the ceasefire in 1945 50,000 German prisoners of war died of hunger,
and in some American and French camps the level of food was kept
deliberately below starvation level. All the same, it takes a very special

kind of German politician who can go round Auschwitz with a smile on his face.

That night, as we followed Kohl's party back to Warsaw, I saw a group of his officials whispering to one another, and overheard the word '*Mauer*'.

'Something seems to have happened at the Berlin Wall,' I said to one of my colleagues. It proved to be an understatement.

Over the next few weeks all sorts of weird stories went the rounds about the way in which the Wall had been breached that evening, 9 November. Everyone who watched the live television broadcast at which the general secretary of the East German Communist Party, Günther Schabowski, had announced that the Wall was open, seemed to have a different version. Some people said an East German radio correspondent had handed him a piece of paper. A West German tabloid newspaper reported that the message had been delivered by someone nobody recognized. 'The Finger Of God', announced another. If you looked at the video, you could see that after making a series of announcements Schabowski had paused, whispered something to his neighbour, and shuffled his papers. The man next to him leant over, and a piece of paper appeared in Schabowski's hand. He read it out, slowly and hesitantly:

    Transcript of press conference by Günther Schabowski,
    East Berlin, 9.11.89

    GS: This will be interesting for you. Today the decision
    was taken to make it possible for all citizens to leave the
    country through the official border crossing-points. All
    citizens of the GDR can now be issued with visas for the
    purposes of travel or visiting relatives in the West.
    This order is to take effect at once.

It was the signal for tens of thousands of people to rush to the crossing-points at the Wall and head into the forbidden land of West Berlin, without being shot or controlled or even stopped. The nights of 9 and 10 November were two of the most exciting in modern history: the bloodless crash of an entire system, the simple joy of being free. The party continued all night, all day, all night again; and it still didn't stop, even then.

A few months later, when the fuss had died down and the two parts of Germany were coming together, I went to see Günther Schabowski. He lived in a nice flat which overlooked the Wall he had personally breached, but he clearly didn't have much money. He was writing his memoirs, and at first he didn't want to give away the key part of them: what happened on the night of 9 November. In the end, though, he agreed to tell me.

Transcript of interview with Günther Schabowski,
11.2.90

Speakers: Günther Schabowski (non-staff), John Simpson
(staff)

GS: I finished giving my information about the Central
Committee business, and then I turned to the next item on
the agenda.

JS: But it wasn't as simple as that, was it? I mean, you
had to lean over and speak to someone, and there was a long
pause.

GS: All right. [Laughs.] I'll tell you. The Politburo
decision about opening the borders was the first thing I
had planned to announce. But as I was walking into the
room I somehow got my papers mixed up. I thought I would
find it as I went, so I just started reading out the other
things first. At the end I still couldn't find it, but it
turned out to be underneath everything.

JS: And that was it? No miracle? No finger of God?

GS: No. [Laughs.] Just the finger of Schabowski.

It should have been easy enough for me to get from Warsaw to Berlin the next morning. It was only 320 miles away. But it meant travelling from one part of a still-divided Europe to the other; and the crowds fighting to get on the flights from West Germany to Berlin that evening were huge. In the end, though, I managed to get a seat on the last flight to get me there in time for the *Nine O'Clock News*. Not for the first or last time in my life, I sat down and fastened my seat-belt with a feeling of profound relief.

My colleague Richard Sambrook picked me up at the airport and drove me to the makeshift BBC studio, in a caravan in front of the Brandenburg Gate. There were Trabants everywhere, hooting their tinny horns, pumping out clouds of bluish smoke, breaking down and being pushed. People crowded round them, shaking hands and kissing everyone inside. We nearly hit another car as we went, but the driver just waved at Richard and grinned.

June 17 Street, which led to the Brandenburg Gate, was crammed with vehicles and people: a solid mass, the breath of the people rising in clouds. Above was the Gate, and the Quadriga, Victory's chariot, was green in the floodlights as it faced the Unter Den Linden. Only the day before, that had been hostile territory; now it was all Germany once again. Even at that moment of joy – and it was one of the happiest nights it has ever been my good fortune to see – it occurred to me to wonder what Germany, which had been so modest and quiet for so long, would be like when it had the pompous grandeur of Berlin as its capital again: a city built for victory marches.

We abandoned our car by the roadside and hurried on. I had more time than I had expected, so I wandered around talking to everyone and getting a sense of what was happening. And it was then that I caught sight of the great miracle of my time: hundreds of people standing and dancing on the top of the Berlin Wall, waving sparklers, kissing, jumping up and down, singing. It took me some time to make out the words:

> *Geh'n wir mal rüber, die Mauer ist weg*
> (We're going over, the Wall's gone)

It was time to stand in for my live interview with John Humphrys for the *Nine O'Clock News*. I stood there with the Brandenburg Gate behind me and the continual shouting and honking of horns in my ears, while someone clipped a microphone on me and put an earpiece in my ear so that I could hear John's voice.

'You look happy,' said the soundman. I was.

But it was a disaster, all the same. In the middle of an answer, in front of the biggest audience ever recorded at that stage for a British television news bulletin, someone from an American network pulled the plug on us, just in case New York might want the line at some stage. I fizzled out on the screen. In my ear I could hear John saying the most depressing words in live broadcasting:

'Well, we seem to have lost John Simpson there, but . . .'

I felt deeply humiliated as I unclipped the microphone and wandered away from the interview point.

But it wasn't a night to be gloomy. Someone suggested we should all go for a walk along the Wall towards the Potsdamerplatz. It took us along a little dirt path, through the woods which had grown up over the ruins of what had once been Hitler's seat of government. The division of the city had turned this area into a wasteland, and it had become overgrown, the haunt of wild animals, like the Forum in Rome. Once, near here but on the other side of the Wall, I had been filming the site of Hitler's bunker when a patrol of East German border-guards came running up with their dogs, which cornered us, barking and slavering.

Well, that wouldn't happen again, for better or worse. The little dirt path was crowded with rejoicing people, and it seemed perverse to think there could be any reason for worry, now that the two parts of Germany were being reunited.

The reunification was going on all along the Wall. There was the sound of hammering on both sides. People were beating at the Wall with pick-axes and hammers and chisels. The candles they worked by cast a golden light on the Wall itself, and threw the shadows of their picks onto the bushes, onto the other faces, onto the Wall itself. This was a very sweet revenge indeed. They worked away at the joins between the slabs of concrete, making little loopholes which were slowly getting bigger; when the crowds parted you could sometimes get a glimpse through to the no man's landscape beyond.

And there was a strange echo, which turned out not to be an echo. When the men with the pick-axes paused, the hammering continued. There was a sudden upsurge of shouting and cheering, as we realized that someone was trying to break through from the other side. At last, by alternate strokes from East and West, another wound appeared in the Wall. In the candlelight a hand came through the little gap, and waved about; and the man with the pick-axe on our side grasped it and shook it. I had never thought anything of the kind was possible. This wasn't a phony miracle, like Schabowski's announcement. It was the real thing.

« »

Now the dominoes began to fall. There were stirrings in Czechoslovakia, which by 17 November, eight days after the fall of the Berlin Wall, produced a savage response from the police. One man was said to have died, though later he turned out to be very much alive. Some very curious things went on in Prague that night, and the beginning of the Velvet Revolution may well have been planned by the KGB and my old friends the StB, Czechoslovak intelligence. Yet the real revolution was at hand anyway: this kind of thing was only an incidental.

My main worry, after my experiences in Prague six years before, was that my name would be on a black list, and that if I turned up too early I would be refused entry. And yet I couldn't bear to be there too late. I went on the 19 November, and held my breath.

As I arrived on Czech soil for the first time since 1983 I slipped on the icy tarmac at the foot of the aircraft steps and fell heavily: not an auspicious start. Perhaps, like William the Conqueror who slipped and fell on landing at Pevensey, I should have pretended I was kissing the ground. At passport control I handed over my old, worn black passport. The man with the red medal ribbon and the Hitler moustache checked it, ran his finger down a list, and found something. This is it, I thought. He looked up at me, then down at the list again. There was another pause. Then I heard the sound of a wooden stamp. I was through.

The centre of Prague was like Tiananmen Square all over again: crowds of happy, excited people drifting around with a freedom they had rarely if ever experienced before; not, certainly, since 1968. It was late afternoon, and I noticed one phenomenon at once: everyone coming away from work in the big shops and offices around Wenceslas Square seemed to be over thirty-five. Everyone moving towards the inevitable demonstrations there seemed to be under thirty-five. The destruction of the Prague Spring twenty-one years earlier had made a savage partition between the generations in Czechoslovakia.

I watched a young girl of perhaps eighteen jumping up and down as she headed for the Square with her boyfriend. They plainly took so much pleasure in each other's company, and in being alive at that moment. Before the crowd swallowed them up I saw him put his arm round her shoulder so tightly that her feet must have left the ground again.

Yet the crowds made almost no noise. There was just the steady, purposeful trudge of feet towards the evening's demonstration. And as I turned into Wenceslas Square and saw with a rush of emotion how many people were there, I knew that they would succeed this time. The Russians weren't going to send the tanks in; the StB, the police, the Czechoslovak army wouldn't make a move now. It was a long way from being over, but it was going to happen.

The BBC was wonderfully popular in Prague. For years people had listened to its services in Czech and Slovak, and their appreciation carried over to those of us who worked there for television now. When I stood in the Square doing a piece to camera with the crew a little crowd would gather round and applaud politely at the end. Each night at the Magic Lantern Theatre the Civic Forum (an organization mostly composed of former Charter 77 people) which held their nightly meetings there would allow our camera crew in when others were stopped at the door. I have always been proud to say that I worked for the BBC, but here the record of decency and straightness which its broadcasters had shown over the years made me feel particularly good.

That Friday Alexander Dubček came to Prague. Ever since 1969 he had been an internal exile in Bratislava. Once I had managed to get there on a day trip from Vienna and had found my way to his house: only to find he had gone away for the weekend. Now, for the first time, I was going to see the man for whom I had always felt such admiration and sympathy.

It was hard even for us, using the BBC's name and reputation shamelessly, to get into the Socialist Party building in Wenceslas Square where Dubček was to appear before the crowds. Seeing us get in, a group of other television cameraman managed to persuade the organizers that they should be allowed in as well. But eventually there was so much squabbling and disorder that the Civic Forum people announced that we would all have to leave. Gloomily, I told the cameraman I was with to pack his gear and come with me.

'Not the BBC,' shouted the chief organizer, exasperated by our stupidity. So we stayed.

I found myself getting nervous as the time came for Dubček to arrive. Things shouldn't work as well as this. It was too perfect, too much of a fairy-tale ending. That the man of 1968 should be there to see 1989, and that I should be there when it happened, might all turn out to be an attractive illusion projected by the Magic Lantern of this peaceable revolution.

But it was true. The door opened, and there was the old man, looking more frail and bowed than his sixty-eight years, the duck-beak nose a little bonier and the hair much more skimpy than in the photographs of twenty years before. Vaclav Havel shepherded him in, as gentle as a son with a frail father. Dubček's eyes were red and watery, and the light from our camera bothered him as he moved forward to the balcony. Perhaps this moment has come too late, I thought with a sudden pang of pain.

But it hadn't.

I watched from behind as he and Havel climbed out onto the balcony. The crowds were massed below, tens of thousands of expectant faces turned up to look at the old man who had once been the country's hero. I could see his figure outlined against them, and even inside I could feel the enormous physical warmth which reached up at him from the huge crowd. It seemed to give him the strength he had lacked a moment or two before. He gripped the microphone, and spoke the words that had once been unhoped for, unthinkable.

'Dear people of Prague, I am glad to be among you after so long a time.'

In the roar that followed I knew that it was true after all.

Not everything he said was very coherent, and sometimes it was purely practical: the speech of a man who had once been a politician before he was destroyed. But then the vagueness lifted off him just as the twenty-one wasted years had. He put his bowed shoulders back and stood a little straighter, his thin hair blowing in the breeze, the faces a vast blur below him.

'The light was here before. Why should it be dark again? We had the morning. We must act now as though the light has come again.'

They cheered him to the echo, chanting 'Svoboda! Svoboda!', 'Freedom! Freedom!', the old cry from the Prague Spring. It was one of the supreme moments of my life.

« »

No one had thought the fall of the Berlin Wall would affect Czecho-slovakia. Now no one thought the revolution in Czechoslovakia would affect Romania.

'Ceauşescu will still be there well into the 1990s,' said one of the most respected academics specializing in Eastern Europe when I interviewed him.

I was undecided. On the one hand I had seen for myself how fast things could move when there was real momentum for change. On the other, I had spent a rather difficult few days in Romania in the spring of 1989, travelling round the country with Tira and a BBC cameraman and his wife, pretending we were tourists. It hadn't taken the Romanian secret police, the Securitate, very long to spot us. For one thing, scarcely any tourists ever went to Romania. For another, I hadn't realized that a brief brush I had had with the Securitate back in 1978 – merely being held for twenty minutes and then let go – would still appear on their computer system. It did.

We were arrested, followed, threatened, heavied everywhere we went, and eventually betrayed to the Securitate by a woman we had been assured was a noble and committed democrat. At the end of the trip, as we were crossing the border in our car, the Securitate took all our tapes (including the ones Tira had hidden in her knickers) and put them through a bulk eraser. It wasn't really the Securitate's fault that we were using a brand new kind of tape which resisted that kind of thing.

As it turned out, our pictures were largely unaffected by their experience, and were perfectly broadcastable: rather like my interview with Andrei Sakharov, eleven years before. But I had been given the best glimpse possible of the ferocity of Ceauşescu's system of control, and it never occurred to me that by the end of the year it might all have collapsed. Ceauşescu thought the same thing.

'Scientific Socialism,' he told his party congress on 20 November, 'is in absolutely no danger.'

His toadying supporters, relieved, gave him forty standing ovations and re-elected him President for another five years. He had less than five weeks left to live.

Revolutions are hard things to understand; even when, as in Romania, you think you know what is going on.

On 21 December Ceauşescu, disturbed by the uprising in the western city of Timişoara in support of a Protestant clergyman, Laszlo Tokeş, was persuaded to address a public rally in Bucharest. It was a big mistake.

I later discovered that one solitary man in the crowd, Nica Leon, sick to death of Ceaușescu and the dreadful circumstances he created for everyone, started shouting in favour of the revolutionaries in Timi-șoara. The crowd around him, obedient to the last, thought that when he called out 'Long Live Timișoara!' this must be some new official slogan. They started chanting it too. It was only when he yelled, 'Down with Ceaușescu!' that they realized something wasn't quite right. Terri-fied, they tried to force a way through the rest of the crowd to get away from him, dropping the banners they had been carrying. In the crush, the wooden battens on which the banners were held began to snap underfoot, and women started screaming. It sounded like booing. Soon there really was booing.

The unthinkable was happening. Ceaușescu stood there on his balcony, ludicrously frozen in uncertainty, his mouth opening and shut-ting. Even the official camera shook with fright. Then the head of security walked swiftly across the balcony towards him and whispered, 'They're getting in.' It was clearly audible on the open microphone, and was broadcast around the country.

It wasn't true, but it was the start of the revolution. Emboldened by the sight of Ceaușescu's moment of weakness the crowds gathered in the city centre, much more angry and determined. The next morning Ceaușescu tried to address them from the balcony again, but now the crowd attacked the Central Committee building. They were swarming up the main staircase by the time Ceaușescu and his witchlike wife Elena escaped by helicopter from the roof.

I was in London when I watched Ceaușescu's first television per-formance, and decided to leave for Romania the next morning. Tira and I, accompanied by one of my favourite cameramen, Bob Prabhu, and his sound recordist Paul Francis, flew to Belgrade. By the time we got there, Ceaușescu was on the run and his system of control had collapsed. There would be nothing to stop us entering Romania now. At Belgrade airport we hired the same large Mercedes that we had used for our trip round Romania the previous spring.

Because we couldn't all fit into it, we hired a taxi as well; and when the taxi-driver, after delaying us for a couple of hours, stopped at a remote border crossing and refused to go any farther, we were fortunate enough to meet a couple of French reporters who gave us a lift. French and British journalists often seem to have an inbuilt hostility to each other, but by some stroke of good fortune I had photocopied my map of Romania for them at the airport. That made us allies.

We drove in convoy through the night. At every town and village we went through there were groups of men waving Romanian flags with the Communist insignia cut out: strange, silent groups, who would burst into song when they knew we were from the BBC and wanted to film them:

> *Olé, Olé, Olé,*
> *Ceauşescu nu mai e!*

Meaning that Ceauşescu had had it.

At about three in the morning, when we were all very tired, Bob's Mercedes hit a patch of ice on a bend in the road and nearly went into a river. We hadn't seen another vehicle for a couple of hours, and things weren't looking good. The little car the French journalists had hired certainly wasn't strong enough to pull the Mercedes out. We stood in the freezing dark and tried to think the unthinkable: that we stood a good chance of missing the Romanian revolution.

Then we heard a sound. It was some time before it appeared: a large Soviet-built truck. I stood in the road waving, and my determination not to let it go was so great that it almost went off the road as well, trying not to hit me. The driver, up in his warm cab with some young hooker he had picked up, agreed unenthusiastically to help. He had a steel cable, and attached it to the Mercedes. Within five minutes our Mercedes was back on the road and he was on his way, loaded down with chocolate and cigarettes from our supply. Things were so heavily rationed in Romania that the hooker had probably never tasted chocolate in her short life.

We reached Bucharest at dawn on Saturday 23rd, and drove into the centre of town with a column of tanks. You could hear the firing from a long way away. At the InterContinental Hotel Bob and Paul and I left Tira to look after the car and the equipment, and went running off in the direction of the gunfire. It was very bewildering; fighting in cities usually is. There were injuries, and occasional prisoners, and large numbers of men with guns, but no one seemed able to explain to us what was going on; merely that Securitate snipers were at work everywhere. I noticed one thing I had never seen before: little piles of human excrement on the pavement. People were obviously terrified, but they stayed where they were to watch what was going on.

I have rarely been in a place with so many bullets flying around. We made our way round to a building where some of the snipers were operating from. With the bullets hitting the wall a couple of feet above my head, Bob suggested that we should do a piece to camera. I wasn't enthusiastic: it usually looks slightly absurd to see a middle-aged man talking to camera with loud explosions going off close by; the middle-aged man tends to wince a bit as the bullets fly past.

'It'll be very dramatic,' Bob said.

He had wound a piece of green silk round his camera in an attempt to hide it from the snipers, who always seem to enjoy firing at that kind of thing. It was tasselled and kept slipping off, which added to the ludicrousness of the situation.

We were both right. Because it is dramatic it still gets shown occasionally; and because it is distinctly absurd I am always embarrassed to see it.

Transcript from report for 1.15 News, 23.12.89

JS: We've managed to work our way round here, and the snipers seem to be operating from the building behind me. [Shots.] The army hasn't got here yet. The firing is coming down in this direction. [More shots.] We seem to be the only ones here.

Very uncomfortable it was too. But you have to remember when you do these things that your audience will mostly be sitting quietly in the peace and comfort of their own homes, and the sound of real gunfire is as unfamiliar to them as the taste of chocolate was at that stage to most Romanians.

Later, Tira ran across two hundred yards of open ground under quite heavy fire to get these pictures of ours onto a satellite feed. Afterwards, when the BBC (whose bureaucrats aren't the most generous or appreciative of people) questioned why they should pay her and what she'd done for the money, I asked how many of them would be prepared to do the same thing in order to get a couple of minutes of video onto a news bulletin. They paid, but under protest. At that stage the BBC still had a profound distrust of freelances. Nowadays, of course, it depends on them.

We worked our way up towards the main square, called after a particularly savage predecessor of Ceauşescu's named Gheorghiu-Dej. Some of the time we had to creep along, bent double. Sometimes we lay in the gutters and kept our heads down. There was disorder and rubble and panic everywhere. Bodies lay untended in the open street. The army was blasting away with tanks and rocket-launchers and rifles, and the National Library was one of the buildings which was blazing. I grew so angry with the pointlessness of all this that I ran over and started berating the officer in charge of a group of tanks which were blasting away at the library directly in front of them.

'This is your national heritage,' I yelled, 'and you're destroying it.'

I thought he was going to shoot me. Then he turned and ordered three more shells to be fired. I really must give up behaving like this, I thought; it never does any good.

The destruction was terrible, and many people lost their lives. Even at that time it all seemed completely pointless. There certainly were some Securitate snipers operating – Bob Prabhu filmed some of them – but not enough for the army to trash the only attractive parts of the city in an attempt to kill them. But it was all, I realized from the start, being done as a show of national unity. The army had been Ceauşescu's loyal servant. By blasting away at the late nineteenth-century gems of Bucharest it was demonstrating that it had repositioned itself on the side of the revolutionaries.

If indeed it really was a revolution, after all. Some days later, when everything was safe and Tira had been relieved of her duties by someone flown in from London, a local television producer came in to our office with several cassettes he had shot during the disturbances. The new BBC arrival was so unpleasant to him that he took his cassettes away again, and was too discouraged to show them to anyone else. Several years later, when Tira and I went back to Bucharest to make a documentary about what had really happened in the Romanian revolution, we found this man and looked at his pictures. They were sensational.

While the crowd was storming up onto the roof of the Central Committee building and chasing Ceauşescu off in his helicopter, a group of very senior figures gathered in another wing of the building to decide what they should do. Our producer-cameraman wandered into this meeting, filming everything he saw. And because everything was so disorganized and the people at the meeting were so animated and busy, nobody asked him who he was or what he was doing.

All but one of the people who had gathered were all leading Communists. Most of them had fallen out with Ceaușescu at some point and been disgraced. They had formed a secret organization called the National Salvation Front about six months before, to be ready to take over power. Afterwards some of them, particularly the new president, Ion Iliescu, tried to deny that this had happened; but the evidence of the video is clear.

At one point there is an argument about what to call the new political organization which will take power. Petre Roman, a newcomer at the meeting and the only non-Communist there, objects when someone suggests the name 'National Salvation Front'.

'That sounds like hell,' he says; meaning that it has a real Communist ring to it.

Standing behind the others in his blue army uniform is a sombre figure with carefully combed white hair and deep crevices in his cheeks. The splendidly named General Nicolae Militaru had formerly been defence minister, until he had disagreed with Ceaușescu and been eased out. Now he shouts over the other voices until the camera swings round to reveal him waving his finger at the objector.

'Look, my dear fellows, the National Salvation Front has been in existence for six months.'

When the existence of this sequence on the video became known in Romania, the cameraman/producer was accused of treason for having revealed the reality of the Romanian revolution: that the spontaneous uprising was taken over by a group of plotters which was already in existence.

I went to see General Militaru to ask him about the contents of the video, and he confirmed it all. There had, he said, been a plan to stage a coup in February 1990. Ceaușescu was to be arrested at his hunting-lodge in the mountains, and his guards were to be put out of action with tranquillizer guns. But these weapons weren't to be delivered until January: a month after the uprising actually happened. The National Salvation Front was overtaken by events; but it took control of the formless uprising and turned itself into a neo-Communist government.

'If you want to call it a plot,' the sinister General Militaru said to me when we went to see him in 1994, 'that's OK by me.'

The BBC could have had the video which would have explained all this within days of the revolution in December 1989. As it was, we had to wait five years. But it was still worth it.

A few months later someone who had been prominent in Charter 77 came to the BBC with a full and carefully worked out account of how the revolution in Czechoslovakia had been engineered by the Soviet KGB and the Czechoslovak secret police, the StB. The crowds had been encouraged to come out onto the streets, and were infuriated by the killing of one of their number; which later turned out to have been completely fictitious. But public anger was so great that the old regime fell. It was a compelling account, meticulously researched, and I came to accept it completely.

The purpose was to get rid of the old, conservative, anti-Gorbachev Communist leaders like Miloš Jakeš in Czechoslovakia and Nicolae Ceaușescu in Romania, and replace them with new, more liberal-minded and malleable figures like Ion Iliescu, the chief conspirator at the meeting in the Central Committee building. In 1989 it still looked as though Mikhail Gorbachev's model of a freer, milder but still essentially Soviet empire might succeed; and to make it a possibility, the old leaders had to be cleared out. The KGB liberates Eastern Europe: it's an enthralling idea, and some years later the former Soviet minister Eduard Shevardnadze (by now the president of the independent republic of Georgia) gave me a clear nudge that something of the sort had taken place.

Transcript of interview with President Eduard
Shevardnadze, recorded in Tblisi, 21.11.94

ES: All these leaders had to go, especially Ceaușescu.
I remember the last congress of the Romanian Communist
Party, a month before the revolution there, which
Gorbachev attended. He stayed there for two days.
Gorbachev told me he talked with them until the early
hours of the morning. The discussion almost turned into
a fight, so that the security men outside had to be
alerted. Gorbachev came back with a terrible impression

```
of the place. He said Ceauşescu simply didn't
understand what was going on in the real world.

JS: And did the KGB play a part in the revolution?

ES: The KGB is a service where no one knows exactly
what's going on behind the scenes. It's possible there
was something.
```

In fact General Militaru told me he had informed the Soviet consul in the Romanian port of Constantia on 20 August 1987 that he was planning a coup against Ceauşescu. The Soviet consul was certainly a KGB officer, and the tranquillizer guns would have been supplied by the KGB. All the same, there was far more to the revolutions of 1989 than simply the machinations of the secret police. The KGB didn't really liberate Eastern Europe: the people liberated themselves, even if events were sometimes given a little nudge in the right direction.

« »

In that extraordinary year of 1989, the most extraordinary day was Christmas Day. The crew and I went out to film early in the morning. The fighting was over. Tanks and armoured personnel carriers were parked at random on the Square, and in the bitter cold their crews lay exhausted around them. Above them the skeleton of the National Library dome still smouldered, and smoke was coming out of the upper floors of the old royal palace opposite. There was a queue of about a hundred people outside the Central Committee building, so hungry that when they were given their ration of grey bread and watery soup they bolted it down there and then, not even bothering to get out of the queue and allow others to take their place. And because everyone else was so listless with hunger scarcely anyone did anything about it. The lucky ones ate fast, their faces in the metal bowls, their eyes still moving around nervously and greedily.

Near them an old woman was sweeping the ground with the branch of a fir tree, pushing everything into little piles in front of her: cartridge cases, bits of stone-work, brick dust, official documents, excrement. The people who had been camping out all night around bonfires were waking up now, and washing in pails of savagely cold water or trying to make themselves something warm to drink.

There was a sudden outburst of firing. We ran over to look inside the smashed windows in one wing of the Central Committee; the dust and plaster dislodged by the rifle fire was still billowing out into the cold grey air. By chance the soldiers had discovered a group of Securitate men hidden in a small room. Some were being taken away for questioning; others were being shot in the back of the neck in the cellars below the building. There was a revolutionary insanity in the air which justified anything.

The crew and I queued up for hours outside the main entrance to the Central Committee building, occasionally beating on the door and demanding to be let in. A red-eyed colonel inside shouted at me angrily every time I spoke to him, but it seemed to me he was weakening. I know I was; I had probably had less sleep than he had over the previous few days. Suddenly, for no apparent reason, what had been impossible on security grounds a few minutes before happened without warning. The door opened, hands reached out to pull us in and push everyone else back, and we were inside: the first Westerners who had ever been allowed into this building. The colonel grinned.

It was like the set of Eisenstein's film *Oktyabr*. The grand marble staircase was guarded by a group of soldiers armed with rifles and lying behind barricades of sandbags. There were bullet holes everywhere, and the marble was streaked in places with dried blood.

'Three men coming up with camera gear!' bellowed the colonel.

We turned the bend in the staircase and another set of soldiers started shouting.

'Three men coming up with camera gear!'

They had orders to shoot anyone who didn't match the description. Since I was first, and wasn't carrying any camera gear, I hoped they wouldn't be too literal about their orders. I smiled feebly. No one smiled back. Upstairs the guards lay behind a barricade of spindly gold furniture and rolled up carpets. Some of them had Christmas decorations on their caps, and holly leaves in their buttonholes. It had been against the law to celebrate Christmas in Ceauşescu's Romania. Now that Ceauşescu had been overthrown, Christmas ruled.

The stench of past gunfire was everywhere, and another smell which infiltrated the mouth and nose even more unpleasantly: it was, I realized eventually, the reek of burned stone-work. The locks of the doors up here had mostly been shot out, but Christmas tinsel hung from the handle of Ceauşescu's office. No one seemed to be going to stop me, so I turned it. This was the office of Ceauşescu's private secretary. We sat there for a moment or two, then someone took us into the main office.

You could have played a reasonable game of tennis in it. Now there were people with guns everywhere, some in military uniform, some in ordinary clothes. A man with a gun was screaming orders.

'Take no notice of he,' said the smooth, dark-haired, pleasant-faced young man who had escorted us into the room. 'My name is Adrian. He crazy.'

The man with the gun was a sculptor, and the experience of revolution had clearly chipped his marble. Now he was sniffing out treason. When a portrait-painter (this was an eclectic gathering) suggested that we should go into Ceauşescu's private apartments, which lay through a door at the far end of the room, the sculptor went berserk. He jammed his revolver against the portrait-painter's head, screaming that only a Securitate agent would want to go in there, and forcing him to lie face down on the floor with his hands behind his neck. The sculptor put his foot on the small of his back and looked around in an insane kind of way.

'This guy may be crazy,' said the calm voice of Adrian again. 'But he got a gun. We wait till he gets quiet.'

I had to go back to the hotel to get a couple of camera batteries and more tapes. Before I left there was another awkward moment: the sculptor had decided that a cinema stuntman and a soldier were also Securitate agents. As I left, they were standing in their underwear, hands in the air, while he waved his gun at them.

I should have been more suspicious of Adrian, of course. For a start, he was a taxi-driver, and most taxi-drivers worked for the Securitate. Secondly, his English was good; and it was always said that the best English-speakers were Securitate-trained. But he looked so pleasant, and was so helpful, that I found myself relying on him more and more. There is no doubt in my mind whatever now that he was looking for a useful means of protection and found it by chance in the BBC. Over the next few weeks he arranged everything for us, including a visit to the underground tunnels which the Securitate had used beneath the Central Committee building, and which reached for hundreds of yards in every direction.

Bob Prabhu came closest to realizing what he was, when he filmed the Securitate snipers on a rooftop near our hotel.

'One of them's Adrian,' he said to me quietly. I looked: he was right. I called Adrian in and asked him what he had been doing there with a gun, firing into the street below. He didn't pause for a second.

'We've formed a vigilante group to catch Securitate agents. I have to keep it quiet – security. I guess Bob saw me at it. Our secret, huh?'

He smiled his brilliant smile, and I found myself nodding.

It took me an hour to fetch the batteries and tapes and to get back into the Central Committee building. In that time the sculptor had been arrested and led away. This time he was the one in the underpants. Now the cinema stuntman, fully dressed again, was giving the orders, and he agreed to allow us into the Ceauşescus' flat at the back of the room. The revolutionaries kept talking about the riches that we would find on the other side of the door: far better and more valuable than anything we could have seen in the West, they said.

It was a disappointment, of course: their imaginations had been parched by decades of poverty and state control. The golden door-handles they had spoken of were made of brass. The place was dark and depressing, though far larger than the cramped places where the vast majority of Romanians lived.

Yet the Ceauşescus must have preferred it to their palaces elsewhere in the country, since this was where they spent most of their time. It was furnished indifferently, but there were large amounts of vast ornate silver everywhere, apparently confiscated from the wealthy after the Communist revolution. Enormous paintings covered the walls.

I was told later that these were the originals of works in the National Gallery; the Ceauşescus kept the real ones, and left the copies for the people. Everywhere there were gifts from the corrupt, despotic leaders of other countries: Mongolia, Ethiopia, China. The Ceauşescus were international scroungers, travelling a shrinking world exchanging objects stolen from the Romanian people for objects stolen from other subject nations.

And yet this flat made them human: a bad-tempered yet mutually affectionate couple, crooked yet honest with each other, ferocious yet tender between themselves. Their clothes, hanging in the wardrobes, were the boring fawns and greys and blacks of old age. They slept in a simple double-bed, in candy-pink sheets. Someone had laid out

Ceauşescu's brown silk pyjamas on it. If they had lived in the West the Ceauşescus' way of life would have seemed modest enough; but here, because of the repression and the ferocious austerity, their possessions seemed positively imperial.

As we were leaving, the housekeeper beckoned me into the Ceauşescus' private bathroom and sat down on the fluffy yellow lavatory seat. She seemed to have taken a liking to me. Opening a drawer, she produced a box containing a few gold items and selected something from it. It was a fat Mont Blanc pen, a bit vulgar for my taste. I handed it back to her politely, but she waved to me that I should keep it. Adrian saw the label and translated it: 'The gift of the British Labour Party'. Later, of course, the Labour Party was unable to find any record of having given Ceauşescu a fountain pen when I asked. How surprising. By now it wasn't fashionable to be a present-giver to Comrade Nicolae any more.

That evening – Christmas night – we went through the usual business of standing in the darkened roadway and forcing a car to stop and take us to the television station. (It was only the following night that I discovered the Metro had been working throughout the revolution and would take us close to the TV station for nothing.) We argued and pushed and threatened our way past the jumpy sentries, into the main television building. It was a dangerous place: a few nights earlier seven people had had their throats cut as they slept in these corridors.

The television staff hadn't slept in a bed for three nights, and they scarcely looked at the Scotch and fresh fruit we brought them. They worked magnificently hard, but they were in the last stages of exhaustion. A large woman in her fifties fell asleep as she talked to the satellite co-ordinators in Geneva about our broadcast. Because we had no editing machines and no picture-editors in Bucharest, we had to feed over our raw pictures first, then I would read my script over the line separately; a very clumsy way of proceeding.

I sat in a little glass box and wrote my account of the Ceauşescus' lifestyle. It was impossible not to be scathing. I ended up with a paragraph to say that although we knew they had been captured and were presumably still being held, nothing more had been heard of them for the past two days. Then through the glass I saw people standing up tensely. I opened the door. A television announcer was making an announcement on air:

Transcript of broadcast from Bucharest, 25.12.89

For these serious crimes committed against the Romanian people and Romania, the accused Nicolae Ceauşescu and Elena Ceauçescu, were sentenced to death and confiscation of assets. The sentences were final and were carried out.

The people at the television station began dancing round and clapping and cheering; I disliked it, but then I hadn't lived my life under one of the worst dictators in modern Europe.

I looked at my watch. There were less than ten minutes to change my script. I wrote feverishly, cutting back on the part about the Ceauşescus' bad taste; that seemed like bad taste itself now. Instead, I concentrated on the way they had stayed loyal to one another, reinforcing each other for better and for worse, corrupted absolutely by absolute power. In my mind's eye I saw that narrow, cheap double-bed, the candy-pink pillows, the brown silk pyjamas. What it was, of course, was Macbeth and Lady Macbeth; but that was a bit too literary for prime-time television, even on Christmas night.

At the end, having scribbled furiously, I finished. I looked at my watch: still a couple of minutes to go. Then, for the first time, I noticed what I had written Ceauşescu's death notice with. It was his own fountain-pen.

« »

New Year's Day 1990 was bright and sunny, and I was walking swiftly down the road to join the crew. A sharp-featured man in his late fifties came walking towards me in a blue and purple tracksuit. His hair was *en brosse*, and he was pulling along one of those embarrassing little white poodles with him, so closely clipped it was pink round the edges.

'Ah, Mr Simpson,' he said. I never found out how he knew me or my name.

The dog started a high-pitched, hysterical barking, and tried to mount my leg.

'Bobbi,' said the man warningly.

Bobbi took no notice. I tried to manoeuvre myself so he couldn't get at me.

'I have something very special to say to you,' he said. 'Could you come and have a drink with my wife and me this evening?'

I started to explain all the things I had to do. Apart from anything else, I didn't want to see Bobbi again.

'You see,' said the *en brosse*d man, lowering his voice, 'I am Securitate. Colonel. It is something important.'

Worth meeting Bobbi again for, I thought.

Mrs Colonel was a very large blonde with a massive beehive hairdo. Her clothes would have fitted a smaller woman better, especially round the bust. She was a few years younger than the Colonel, and, it turned out, was a Securitate Captain in her own right. Quite a household. You wondered what they talked about after lights out.

'And what rank is Bobbi?' I asked.

They thought that was funny. Bobbi was mounting a cushion, but it seemed only a matter of time before he would move on to my leg again.

'Bobbi is our little baby,' said the Captain, beaming.

She was an excellent cook, and produced plate after plate of delicacies. There were no food shortages here.

It turned out that the Colonel wanted to defect to Britain. The Secret Intelligence Service, MI6, was in his opinion the best there was, and he wanted to share the information he had obtained from his special department, which was liaison with international terrorism. His demands were modest enough: a million pounds sterling, a British passport, and a house in the country.

'I know nothing about this kind of thing,' I said truthfully, 'but I know someone at the British embassy who probably does.' I promised to get back to him.

As it happened, I had got to know and like the military attaché. Presumably it had always been his dream to get a colonel in the Securitate to defect.

'They'll never pay anything remotely like a million,' he said, 'but the other things are definitely possible.'

He got back to me a day or so later, rather embarrassed. London had said no to everything.

Bobbi was pleased to see me, but the Colonel was very disappointed. Could the British, maybe, pay for him to go and talk to them in London?

The military attaché came back: they were too busy.

All right, said the Colonel desperately, he would pay his own way to London if they would set some time aside to see him.

The military attaché was seriously embarrassed this time, but London couldn't even do that. The Colonel should go and talk to the French, they'd said.

It was hard breaking that one to him. I'd never thought I might feel sorry for a senior officer in the Securitate.

'But why?' he asked. 'Why?'

'My friend says they've got Warsaw Pact generals coming to them now. Heads of secret services are falling from the trees. There isn't enough time to see them and there aren't enough people to look after them. Let alone,' I added tactlessly, 'a colonel like yourself.'

The Colonel nodded and looked out of the window. Then he sighed and shook my hand. The Captain kissed me, straining at her buttons. They closed the door behind me, and I started to walk downstairs.

If even the secret services have fallen apart, I thought, that's it. No more Warsaw Pact. No more Cold War. No more of everything I've been used to all my life. Starting from now, everything will be different.

Two floors down, I could still hear Bobbi yapping.

« »

It was more than a year later, and I was so relieved to be on the plane to Moscow, I couldn't think of anything else for twenty minutes or so. Then, as the drinks trolley made the rounds and my heart rate dropped, I felt the need to write down a few thoughts. I pulled out Ceauşescu's fountain pen and the large green notebook I had just had time to buy at the airport, and started jotting down some ideas.

Mon 19 August 1991 [Heathrow-Frankfurt-Moscow]

Now it's too late, of course, they're sorry. Russia is the land of the one hundred per cent solution; anything short of that is unacceptable. Not that the Soviet Union under Mikhail Gorbachev ever came remotely near, of course. But his was the only sensible way forward, and even people who knew that rejected him with contempt. Intellectuals, who should have known better, even started to agree that life had been better under Brezhnev.

I sat in the office of a woman who had managed to get
permission to examine the secret archives of the
Communist Party. 'You can't even get tea in Moscow now,'
she said. 'It's all been a terrible disaster.' But, I
asked, what about the freedom you have to go through the
files, to find out the truth? 'Oh that,' she said, as
though I had asked her what she thought of, say, having
another television channel to watch; 'you can't eat
files, can you?'

Even at the time I remember thinking, I hope you never
have to make the choice between thinking freely and
eating better. Now they do.

That morning, lying in bed in London, I had listened to the radio news.
The military had taken power in Moscow; Mikhail Gorbachev had
been placed under arrest at his holiday home in the Crimea. There
had been a long and rather hysterical statement from Moscow:

Transcript of live broadcast from military
headquarters, Moscow, 19.8.91

Fellow countrymen! Citizens of the Soviet Union! In a
dark and critical hour for the destiny of our country
and our peoples, we address you! A mortal danger hangs
over our great homeland! The policy of reform initiated
by Mikhail Sergeyevich Gorbachev, conceived of as a
means to ensure the dynamic development of the country
and the democratization of the life of its society, has,
for a number of reasons, come to a dead end . . .

It didn't occur to me that I might be able to go to Moscow. Visas took
days to arrange, and most probably they wouldn't be issuing any in
the circumstances. And anyway I was presenting *Newsnight* that night,
and for the next couple of nights afterwards.

I was sitting at the presenter's desk in the *Newsnight* office when I
heard the editor and his deputy talking. I turned round: they were
looking at a familiar-looking piece of grey paper with a photograph
on it. The photograph was mine, and the piece of grey paper was a
Soviet visa. Weeks before, *Newsnight* had applied for a Soviet visa for
me to cover a Bush-Gorbachev summit in Moscow. For some reason I

hadn't been able to go, and this visa, unused, expired at midnight. They could always find someone else to present the programme, but there was only one visa, and I had it.

'Let's go for it,' said the editor.

I looked across at the clock: five to twelve. The last available flight left at one o'clock. There was only one problem: the passport I had in my briefcase wasn't the one the visa had been issued for. Never mind, I thought; best not to worry them with such details. I had a sporting chance of talking my way through in Moscow, if only I could catch the plane.

Someone lent me some money, and someone else offered to take me to the airport in his own car. Driving like a maniac, he got me to Heathrow at 12.37. There was time to buy the green notebook and three books: Chekhov's short stories, *The Return of the Native*, and Robertson Davies' *Deptford Trilogy*. You never know when you may have a great deal of time to kill, so you should always have some heavy reading-matter handy.

I changed planes at Frankfurt, and bought some hideously expensive clothes at the Harrods shop there. And I did a bit of forgery. Since my passport wasn't the one for which the visa had been issued, I simply wrote the number of the other passport on the front page of the one I had brought. Worth a try, I thought.

It was six-thirty London time, nine-thirty in Moscow, when the plane landed. I queued up at the immigration desk and prayed that my scheme would work. The man in the glass box studied my passport and called his superior over. His superior asked me if I realized that my visa expired in two and a half hours' time. A fellow journalist in the queue helped my stumbling efforts to explain in Russian that the Ministry of Foreign Affairs would issue me with a new visa in the morning. It wasn't true, but it kept the immigration people happy. A BBC driver met me, and we drove into town. It was dark and gloomy.

At the city limits of Moscow I spotted some light tanks parked by the side of the road, and I stopped and spoke to some of the soldiers in my rudimentary Russian. They were bored and friendly, and, I thought, slightly embarrassed. Or maybe just nervous. I had been told that they hadn't been issued with ammunition; was that true? One of the soldiers showed his yellow teeth and laughed.

'No bullets,' he said, as though it was all a big farce. Perhaps it was.

It reminded me of the Chinese army's early efforts to take over Tiananmen Square, before Deng Xiaoping found an army commander who was prepared to shoot the people down.

We drove on. The familiar shops along the way were empty of goods and customers. Few people seemed to be on the streets, but there was no sign of the general strike which Boris Yeltsin had called.

We reached the BBC office, and I started ringing round my friends and contacts. Every one of them thought that the entire reform process had come to an end. The plotters were clearly incompetent and reactionary, but they seemed to have the old Soviet system pretty firmly behind them, and some of Gorbachev's closest aides had changed sides and joined the leaders of the coup. No one I spoke to thought he would be able to reinstate himself. As for Boris Yeltsin's defiance of the coup, when he climbed up on his tank outside the White House earlier that day, most of my friends thought it was a noble but futile gesture.

'By tonight he'll be out of his head with drink,' said one. 'Boris Nikolayevich doesn't count. He's a buffoon.'

Gloomy tidings; and I reflected the position when I answered Michael Buerk's questions on the *Nine O'Clock News*.

Immediately afterwards – it was after midnight, Moscow time – I went down to the White House, the headquarters of the Russian Soviet and Parliament, which Yeltsin had turned into the centre of opposition to the coup. The new government had announced a curfew, but there were no signs of it as I headed through the darkened streets.

As we drove, I reflected on the two characters at the centre of all this: Mikhail Gorbachev, whose head had been too stuck in the clouds to realize how much suffering and discontent he had created, and Boris Yeltsin, the tough Party apparatchik who had spotted the value of the populist approach and jettisoned all his old dogmas.

I had met him and interviewed him several times, and had never been impressed. He was certainly an operator, but he seemed to me to lack any kind of principle. During the all-important Party Congress of 1988 he had been interviewed by the BBC. When he was accused of being disloyal to Gorbachev and his position was threatened, he insisted that the BBC had deliberately twisted his words. I caught him as he was leaving the Kremlin that night by the Spasskiy Gate.

Transcript of interview with Boris Yeltsin, Moscow,
12.7.88

Speakers: Boris Yeltsin, John Simpson

JS: Boris Nikolayevich, you seemed last night to be
making some criticisms of Mikhail Sergeyevich
Gorbachev. This afternoon you said you didn't say those
words.

BY: No, I didn't. A foreign broadcasting organization
twisted my words.

JS: You mean the BBC?

BY: Yes.

JS: But it was clearly recorded on videotape, and wasn't
edited in any way.

BY: I'm telling you, I didn't say these things to anyone.
It is a provocation. Now you must get out of my way. I
have to go.

This was the man, rough, unprincipled, with no very clear notion of democracy, on whom the entire future of the world seemed to depend.

I reached the White House, and found it in darkness. It was starting to rain quite heavily. The area in front of the building was filled with tanks loyal to Yeltsin: the Tamanskaya Guards regiment which operated them had gone over to Yeltsin's side.

'Why did you decide to come here?' I asked the officer who seemed to be in charge. He was clambering about on top of one of the tanks.

'We had our orders. Our general supports Boris Nikolayevich. But I'm glad. Not all soldiers are anti-democratic, you know!' He laughed, and one or two of his men joined in sycophantically. 'Not many soldiers support the coup. But they have their orders, just as we had ours.'

It was difficult to get inside the White House: some former special forces soldiers in their striped seaman-like vests, Afghan veterans who now worked for a private security firm, were blocking the door to everyone. The letters 'BBC', however, did their usual good work. Inside was a large blonde woman with a nasty-looking rash on her arms and hands. She was, she told me, Boris Yeltsin's press spokeswoman. I couldn't go and interview Boris Nikolayevich now, because he was resting. And in constant meetings.

'But is he resting, or is he in meetings?'

'Yes.'

'What will happen tomorrow?'

'I don't know, and I am afraid.'

For some reason which I have now forgotten, I asked her to write her name in my notebook: 'Lantseva Valentina, press-attasher of Verhovniya Soviet.'

Her phone kept ringing, like a shrill insect on the corner of her desk. She shouted into it. Then she turned to me.

'Gorbachev has arrived back in Moscow as a prisoner. The airport workers have just told us.'

Another call. Much nodding.

'It's not Gorbachev after all.'

The phone shrilled again, and I walked out. I couldn't tell from listening to her what was true and what wasn't.

Outside, people were getting ready for a fight. A young man with a haggard, old face shook my hand vigorously.

'I was a prisoner in the camps. I will kill anyone who comes here. No more prison.'

Upstairs I caught a glimpse of Alexander Rutskoi, Yeltsin's second in command, who two years later challenged his leader's authority and was attacked by Yeltsin's tanks in this same White House. Now he was swaggering around, allowing everyone to see that he had a gun in his belt.

'I'll stand and defend the President,' he had said on television earlier. 'Blood will flow from this.' He obviously liked the thought of that.

Outside they were building barricades out of lumps of concrete and bits of scaffolding. It was raining heavily, and blotches of water were landing on my notebook and making the ink run. Merely to look at the pages now takes me back to those nervous, dark hours, when anything seemed about to happen. The Omon, the ferocious troops of the Interior Ministry, were said to be on their way. They wouldn't take any prisoners or leave any survivors if they stormed the building. It felt like the night of the Tiananmen Square massacre all over again.

A man in a large see-through plastic raincoat which looked like a giant condom was pulling a heavy box along.

'What's inside that?'

'Bullets!' he said with a conspiratorial laugh.

Another group laboured away conspiratorially in the rain. When they heard I was from the BBC they let me see what they were doing: filling Coca-Cola bottles with petrol, just like Tiananmen.

'*Molotovskii Koktel!*' said a particularly wild-looking character proudly, holding one up and laughing. Then he added in a lower voice, 'Inside, I feel afraid. Outside, no.' It was a good summary of my own feelings.

The people in the BBC office had turned out with a will. There was even a recently married BBC picture editor who was on holiday with her husband in Moscow, and had temporarily deserted him in order to turn up for work. The office was absurdly small for the number of people who worked there, and the atmosphere wasn't good. But the great majority threw everything into the work of the moment.

I went back and wrote a gloomy report.

```
Transcript of Breakfast News report, 20.8.91

It's by no means certain that there will be violence.
The most difficult decision the members of the so-called
State Emergency Committee have to make is, what to do
about Boris Yeltsin. If they leave him alone, he's a
continuing threat to them. If they move in and arrest
him, the probable bloodshed will change everything.
But, for all the determination of the crowds round the
Parliament, they're in a small minority. Most people
seem apathetic - and that could well be the greatest
problem for Boris Yeltsin and the remaining reformers.
```

As Tuesday wore on, Yeltsin's chances seemed to shrink. The rain was his worst enemy: it meant that people were reluctant to come out and guard the White House against attack. My new jacket, bought at Frankfurt airport, was quickly ruined. So were my shoes. By 4 o'clock there were only a couple of people left to defend the place. I tried to do a piece to camera saying these things, but looked so stupid with the rain pouring down my face that I gave it up.

The rumours that the tanks were coming became stronger. Inside the White House Boris Yeltsin interrupted a phone conversation with John Major by saying he thought he could hear them outside.

I jotted down some disjointed ideas in my damp green notebook. Looking at them nowadays, I can't always work out what they meant:

> At first, quiet and uncertain. Gradually more worried.
> Silent. Now grim. Tiananmen solution? Political
> disaster to kill people. On the other hand if fail,
> collapse of coup. There's been nothing in Russian
> history since the revolution to match this. 'Down With
> The Black Junta Of Red Bandits' [placard]. Hot tea. Very
> 1917 barricade - long steel poles pointing forward.
> Accordion. Shuffling feet. Girl plays with ivory rosary,
> standing in shelter beside barricade. In drizzle people
> gather round radio. At last some chanting, shouting,
> cheering - then 'Yazov has resigned' says someone.
> Dance.

It was later denied, but there was undoubtedly trouble in the shaky, alcoholic coalition which had seized power. Back at the office I edited a report for the *Six O'Clock News*. When I had finished we started hearing reports of violence. I wanted to get out onto the streets, but was afraid that my lack of anything more than rudimentary Russian might get me into serious trouble. Sarah, a quiet, dark-haired producer in her early twenties volunteered to come with me.

We splashed through the mud, working our way closer to the barricades. I was worried that we might be too late, that some key event might have taken place already. As we reached the White House we heard the first shots. A squadron of armoured personnel carriers had been trapped by a crowd of people in the underpass close to the Arbat. The soldiers had jumped out and a couple of them had fired indiscriminately into the crowd, killing three people.

Now the rumour was that special KGB troops called Alpha Group would attack the White House at 3 a.m. These are the times that test people. Sarah announced she would stay with me; there was no sign of our local correspondent.

At the back of the crowd, which was quite large now, there was shouting.

'Shevardnadze's here!'

I saw the familiar white quiff of hair as the former foreign minister (he had resigned not long before) was shoved enthusiastically through by the crowd. He didn't look at all enthusiastic himself. But he felt it was his duty to come and stand shoulder to shoulder with Yeltsin at this critical moment. I had always liked him, and I admired him more than ever now.

Someone thrust a microphone into his hand and he started talking, his voice cracking slightly with nervousness.

'Our fate is being decided. The future of democracy and freedom is being settled. Long live the people! I salute you all!'

I gripped his hand sentimentally and asked what he was going to do.

'See Boris Nikolayevich, of course,' he answered.

I waited outside to interview him. It took him an hour or so to re-emerge.

```
Transcript of interview with Eduard Shevardnadze,
21.8.91

JS: What is Yeltsin's mood?

ES: He is in good form. He said to me, 'I'll do what a real
leader does. I'll stay here till the end, till the last
drop of blood in my body. I'll stand firm.' I was very
impressed. I'll never forget his words.
```

It was the stuff of genuine heroics, and it worked. The much-feared Alpha Group refused to attack the White House, and by disobeying orders they brought about the collapse of the coup. The conspirators surrendered, Gorbachev returned from his Black Sea captivity. But he had been fatally damaged, and by the end of the year he resigned as President. Yeltsin took his place.

In the meantime the Soviet Union itself had evaporated, and its constituent parts declared their independence. The Commonwealth of Independent States took its place. Little wars broke out in many parts of the old Soviet Union. I watched in delight as the statues of Dzerzhinsky, the first boss of the Soviet secret police, and Sverdlov, the man who ordered the murder of the Imperial family in 1918, were hoisted off their plinths by crane and taken to Gorky Park.

The old names were changed, the old habits of thought started to fade. Contrary to my expectations, there was no economic collapse. Yeltsin was never loved, but there was a certain brutal effectiveness about him and his government which saw them through the difficult times.

Some time later, I went to see Shevardnadze in Tblisi, the capital of the Georgian republic he now presided over. As he sat in his office in the presidential building, which had been much damaged in the recent civil war, I interviewed him about the way the world had changed. We started with the situation in Tblisi itself.

'We have been very successful,' he answered. 'Things are now almost entirely quiet here.'

As he paused for breath, there was a wild outburst of firing in the street outside. Shevardnadze grinned sheepishly, and it created a new sympathy between us. When the interview was over and the camera had been switched off he started reminiscing about the old days.

'I always admired Yeltsin for standing firm that night you went to see him at the White House,' I said. 'He was obviously scared, but he didn't give up.'

Shevardnadze laughed.

'He was dead drunk,' he said. 'I couldn't get him to say anything. He was lying on the floor of his office with an empty bottle beside him.'

'But what about all that business about standing firm to the last drop of his blood?'

'I had to say something at a time like that. The success of the democratic principle depended on it. What do you think would have happened if I had walked out of the White House and said to you, "Yeltsin's too drunk to talk"?'

14

Taking a Chance

A HAND PULLED AT my shoulder. For a moment I couldn't think where I was. When I opened my eyes I was strapped into an airline seat and a moon-faced stewardess was looking down at me.

'No one can remember who you are,' she said, surreally.

This kind of thing often used to happen to me, as it does to people who are on television but not memorably so. Then, somehow, I passed through a barrier. My identity and my face seem to fit together more in people's minds. I am become a name.

There are some of my colleagues to whom this is important. It's not surprising: in television, your recognizability is a marketable commodity. But to those of us who started off in radio the whole business of being famous for who you are, not for what you do, is slightly ludicrous: discreditable even. We are used to labouring away without recognition and without glamour.

It used to be different, of course. Richard Dimbleby, Howard Marshall, Wynford Vaughan-Thomas and dozens of others were household names precisely because they were the stars of radio news and current affairs. People who heard Richard Dimbleby's first report when he entered Bergen-Belsen concentration camp at the moment of its liberation never forgot it; and although he became a familiar figure on television during the 1950s, it was for this that they remembered him most.

But by the time independent television was launched, video had killed the radio star. Or, at any rate, it had siphoned off much of radio's public attention and awareness. Only now, at the end of the century, has good reporting and good writing broken surface again, so that a correspondent like Fergal Keane, who came to BBC Radio from RTE in Ireland, can find himself on the best-seller list for his volume of collected broadcasts for the Radio 4 programme *From Our Own Correspondent*, and receive recognition and awareness for that as much as for his television work. Maybe radio has found its solid base of support and appreciation once more, and can regain its full confidence as a powerful and effective medium in its own right.

Radio correspondents have long become familiar with their lack of public recognition. They can break an important news story first, then spend days, perhaps weeks, following it and nurturing it, only to find that a television correspondent comes in late and garners all the glory.

The famine in Ethiopia was probably the biggest news story BBC Television News broadcast in the 1980s, until the fall of the Berlin Wall. Yet the radio correspondent in East Africa, Mike Wooldridge, had been reporting the harrowing details for some time before Michael Buerk, the television correspondent based in Johannesburg, arrived. It didn't matter. Television as a medium grips the public attention in a way radio no longer can; and in the case of Ethiopia the decision was taken in London to give maximum impact to Buerk's reports.

As a result Buerk left the ordinary ruck of television correspondents, the people whose faces and names are faintly familiar, but only in the sense that your newsagent's or your MP's face and name are faintly familiar. He passed through the barrier and took on a special status. His name and features came into sharp focus, and the one belonged with the other.

The same process had happened to Brian Hanrahan three years earlier, during the Falklands War. He went all through the campaign from beginning to end, together with Michael Nicholson of ITN, sending back reports under difficult circumstances almost every night. But it was his broadcast on 1 May 1982 which made him a household name. He reported, famously:

> I'm not allowed to say how many planes joined the raid, but I counted them all out and I counted them all back.

It was a clever way of getting over the difficulties of military censorship. But it wasn't primarily the fact that he used an intelligent and memorable phrase which won him fame: it was the intensity of public interest in what he was saying. That day was the first time

British Harrier jets had been fully used in the war against Argentina, and no one knew what the outcome would be. When Brian produced his formula on air he had a huge audience, which was desperate to know how the British planes had fared. It was the intensity of the relief that won attention first, and his use of words encapsulated the moment. Michael Nicholson reported the same incident; but because in times of national concern like this people tend to turn to the BBC, his reports didn't have the same audience.

Brian's fame was assured, and much more was to come. His experience of climbing onto the top of the Berlin Wall on the night of 9 November 1989 and recording a piece to camera with the rejoicing crowds was unforgettable.

The third television correspondent of recent times to cross the barrier was Kate Adie, who broadcast from Libya in 1986, at another time of maximum public concern and interest. She wasn't the first woman to be a war correspondent by several decades; Martha Gellhorn and a dozen others had reported on the Spanish Civil War and the Second World War. But they did it in writing; Adie did it on camera. She had worked for several years on television, and for a time reported on the doings of the royal family. Yet it was the fact of standing out on the balcony of her hotel in Tripoli and waiting for the American bombs to fall which drew public attention to her. After that her reporting from Tiananmen Square, the Gulf and Bosnia reinforced the public perception of her. But it was Libya which plucked her out of the ranks.

The mystique of reporting can encourage charlatanism, of course. A famous broadcaster, now dead, used to give little homilies on radio in which he would refer to his past as a news correspondent. Vietnam featured occasionally in these talks, never in any specific way but always as an experience too horrendous for him to be able to talk about in detail.

'Those of us who went to Vietnam—' he would say. Listening to him, you felt he must have been through hell.

When he was still a news correspondent he and I worked together for a time, and he told me how he had gone to Vietnam. He was following some leading American politician around the Far East, and their plane stopped at Saigon airport.

'They asked us if we wanted to go into Saigon for a couple of hours, but I said no. I wasn't going to get blown up, thank you very much.' It was the only time he went there.

Martin Bell was the opposite of that kind of reporter. For decades, ever since the early 1960s, he had quietly gone about the world, from Vietnam to the Gulf, issuing his short, staccato reports of unquestioned honesty. It didn't make him particularly famous, though he was always one of the BBC's most trusted correspondents. None of the wars he covered attracted the kind of attention in Britain that the Falklands or the bombing of Tripoli generated; and he never reported on a natural disaster on the scale of the famine in Ethiopia. Having had a rather disappointing Gulf War attached to the British forces, with a lot of preliminary waiting and preparation and a very brief and unsatisfactory moment of action, he was on the look-out for something to get his teeth into. And so while other people were still recovering from the Gulf War, Martin concentrated on the unfolding disaster in the former Yugoslavia. He spent a good deal of time in Sarajevo during the siege, and eventually as he was recording a piece to camera a mortar shell landed nearby and he was injured. The cameraman filmed him as he lay on the ground.

'I'll live,' Martin said, and it seemed typical of his spare, unemotional style.

His injuries weren't serious, and the place where the incident happened became known as Martin Bell Square to the foreign press. It gave him a place in the small category of television news people whose names and faces are instantly recognizable. Later, of course, the poor man forsook it all and went off to be a politician: an even stranger way of earning a living. Others, like Jeremy Bowen, George Alagiah and Ben Brown (all former members of my World Affairs Unit) have also worked hard to earn their places on the list.

In my own case, I had – as I have already boasted in these pages – been the only reporter who was present at all the major events of 1989. It didn't do me any particular good, either in terms of public awareness or in terms of awards from the television industry. People in the streets continued to think that I was Jon Snow, or Peter Snow (depending, I suppose on how old I looked that day). Someone once thought I was Trevor McDonald, which was a greater feat of forgetfulness. As for awards, I have long understood that they are a lottery in which personal achievement and deserving are only peripherally involved. Nevertheless it can be painful to have to sit at your table in some expensive but naff hotel in Park Lane, wearing a tightish dinner jacket and applauding other people's success as they walk up to receive their perspex statuette. Since those days, others more deserving have had to do the same for me.

It was the Gulf War which plucked me out of the line. I had taken the decision to stake my efforts on going to Baghdad rather than covering the war from anywhere a little easier; yet that wasn't what did it. Nor was it the decision to stay in Baghdad when the war approached: plenty of others did that as well. It was the business of reporting from there in the first hours of the war: the time when an enormous audience in Britain had switched on their televisions, anxious to know what was going on. I wasn't even on camera: I was just reporting on a satellite phone. It didn't seem to matter. As with Brian Hanrahan, as with Kate Adie, it was the intensity with which the audience was watching which finally engraved my name and face on the national consciousness.

I don't want to seem dismissive of the processes of fame; I have benefited from them in many ways. Tables are easier to get in restaurants, cabin staff escort me from my seat at the back of the plane and upgrade me to business class, invitations arrive by every post. In the streets people smile at me as though we are personal friends. I sometimes even get a free drink in a pub. Altogether my life has been made much pleasanter by it all. I just want to put it on record that this is merely a matter of chance, and that plenty of people are labouring away on work that is often better and braver and harder than anything I have done, without getting the slightest recognition for it. It isn't just working for television that does it; it isn't just being present at some major event; it isn't even a combination of the two. It is working for television at a major event at the moment when everybody's attention is riveted to it. In other words, it is luck.

I know one famous television person who covered the walls of his sitting room with the awards and certificates he received for his coverage of a particular story. I pack mine away or use them as bookends: like the slave whispering into the ear of a Roman general at his triumph, they remind me uncomfortably how short-lived and lacking in seriousness the notion of fame is.

« »

It was guilt that took me to Baghdad in the first place.

In the early 1980s I met a smart-looking young Iranian at a reception of some kind. He was generous about my reporting of Iran, and it became clear he was looking for a job at the BBC. After that he would ring me up and tell me snippets of information about Iran. When I checked them out, they were usually correct. After that I paid him occasional amounts of money for work he did, but although I liked him I never quite trusted him enough to get him a job with the BBC. If I had, he might still be alive today.

Instead he went to the *Observer*. They obviously didn't trust him too much either, because although they printed his material from time to time they never gave him a staff post. Poor Farzad Bazoft: he always felt he had to try harder and go a little bit farther in order to impress the people he worked for.

In particular he went to Iraq. As an Iranian, whose country fought a savage war with Iraq from 1980 to 1988, it was a dangerous thing to do; especially since he had nothing more substantial than a British travel document. Between 1987 and 1989 he travelled to Iraq five times. The last time was in September 1989, and on the day he left London the news leaked out that a huge explosion had taken place the previous month at the Iraqi government's weapons manufacturing plant at Al Qa'qa near the town of Al Hilla, sixty miles south of Baghdad.

It was typical of Farzad Bazoft that nothing would prevent him from finding out what had happened. If ever there was a true martyr for the faith of investigative reporting, it was Farzad. He used his considerable charm on an attractive British nurse living in Baghdad, Daphne Parish, and persuaded her to drive him down to Al Qa'qa.

There was no question of secrecy. He asked an Iraqi minister and the information ministry for help in going there, and told the *Observer* over a heavily tapped phone line precisely what he was going to do. It was a gamble, of course; but Farzad was an habitual gambler.

They picked him up as he was leaving Baghdad airport at the end of his visit. In his luggage were some samples he had gathered from the roadside at Al Qa'qa; presumably he wanted to have them analysed back in London to reveal what type of weapon had exploded there the previous month. He was tortured, and eventually confessed to everything they wanted: in particular, to spying for the British and Israelis. Mrs Parish refused to confess, because she had done nothing wrong.

When the Iraqi authorities put them together Farzad tried to persuade her to do as he had. It would, he said, mean that she would be released.

It didn't, of course; it just meant that the Iraqis had the grounds they wanted to execute Farzad. At their trial, Farzad was sentenced to death and Mrs Parish to fifteen years. No one translated the sentence for them or told them in court what was going to happen. A British diplomat had to break the news to Farzad that he was to be hanged directly their meeting ended. He took the news as well as he could. A moment or two before he had been talking about his hopes that international pressure would work in his favour. Now he sent his love to his family and his former girlfriend, and his apologies to Mrs Parish.

'I hope the world will decide, after I'm gone, what kind of person I have really been,' he said. Minutes later he was taken out and executed. Mrs Parish was released after ten difficult months in prison.

Hanging Farzad Bazoft was Saddam Hussein's first open defiance of the Western world. Mrs Thatcher had asked for his release, and called his execution 'an act of barbarism'. If the British tabloid press hadn't been so hysterical about it – they love insulting people from a safe distance – it is possible Farzad would have been pardoned.

All this determined me to go to Baghdad for myself. Six weeks after Farzad's death I arrived there with a small BBC team and several other British journalists. There were daily demonstrations outside the British embassy complaining about the efforts which the British government was now belatedly making to stop weapons technology reaching Iraq. We were virtual prisoners in our hotel, and no one in the streets wanted to meet our eyes as we walked around with our minders. Sensible people knew that Western journalists were dangerous.

Given Farzad Bazoft's experiences, I made an unforgivable mistake. The Ministry of Information decided to impound all our video cassettes (I had said something in a broadcast about the total surveillance under which we were working, and that upset our minders) and the producer, Eamonn Matthews, wanted to stay on for a day to get them back. When I realized how determined he was, I should never have left. Anyway, the rest of us left for home but Eamonn was picked up at the airport the following day exactly as Farzad had been. He was threatened and roughly treated, and kept a virtual prisoner overnight. When he walked into the *Newsnight* office in London his face showed clear signs of the stress he had been under. As for me, I assumed I wouldn't be allowed back into Iraq. I wasn't too upset about that.

« »

On 2 August 1990 I was on holiday in southern France. Within three hours of hearing on the radio that Saddam Hussein had invaded Kuwait, I was on a plane back to London. That was the last day off I was to have for the next six months.

As the days passed, negotiation failed to dislodge the Iraqi forces and an international coalition was assembled. I tried to think where I would most want to be. There was London, of course, where I could appear in the studio each night and pull everything together: but that was much too safe and boring. There was Saudi Arabia, where the coalition forces would assemble: fine, but it was likely to be far too highly controlled. Anyway I don't really like the idea of being on our side, with our troops. I enjoy the company of the British army, and I have come to realize that it is without question the best-trained in the world, but I don't like to do my reporting in the company of friends. I prefer the principle of antagonism.

I thought back to the Falklands War, which I had covered so peripherally. There were only two places to be then: with the British forces, or in Buenos Aires. For me, that settled it. It had to be Baghdad, the epicentre of the crisis.

There were considerable problems, of course. For one thing, I had left Iraq four months earlier assuming that the authorities there would never let me back. For another, the Iraqis were already taking British and American and European expatriates hostage, and Farzad had been executed there merely for doing his job. The risk seemed to be extremely high, both personally and professionally. Put a foot wrong, and I might be strung up. Fail to get in, and I might spend the rest of the crisis at Television Centre. Yet having identified Baghdad as the place to be, I couldn't now back away from it. I decided to put everything I had on this single throw of the dice. A long career of risk-taking has taught me that gambles tend to come off; it's the failure to take the plunge which you usually regret later.

The BBC didn't like it. There was a lot of humming and hawing. Perhaps it was because of concern for me; or perhaps they were working out how much they would have to pay out if I became (a) a

The Romanian revolution, December 1989. A captured Securitate sniper is being attacked by a crowd in Bucharest, while I try ineffectually to stop them. He was executed minutes later.

The crazed sculptor, threatening the other revolutionaries in Ceauşescu's office on Christmas Day 1989, scarcely aware that he was being filmed.

An exploding missile lighting up the Baghdad skyline in the first hours of the Gulf War, January 1991: a unique picture of a cruise at the instant it strikes its target.

Recording a report to London in Baghdad during the air war.

Interviewing Radovan Karadžić in 1993, in front of a map showing his territorial pretensions. Perhaps my feelings about him show in my face.

At the old people's home in Sarajevo, December 1992. The old man is the only patient still fit enough to chop wood for the furnace; the woman, a Serb, is one of only two nurses who have remained. A couple of hours after this, the old man was shot dead by a Bosnian government sniper from close range.

Ashaninca girls putting on their bright red face paint. The one on the right is using a make-up compact. This was one of the presents and trading-goods which, together with the more traditional beads and mirrors, I took to the Amazon with me. I have never come across anyone more delightful than the Ashaninca; though given the kind of people I tend to meet that may not sound much.

Ashaninca fishermen on the Envira River in Brazil. They use bows and arrows to catch the fish.

Our first awesome glimpse of Sar-i-Sang, the mountain of lapis lazuli in Afghanistan, with the first rays of the rising sun behind it.

A group of miners show us the results of their night's work. Little has changed here in the six thousand years during which lapis has been excavated at Sar-i-Sang.

John Major on his soap-box, in the process of winning the 1992 election.

The South African election, April 1994: in Cape Town with Nigel Bateson, Dee Krüger, and Lee the Cherry-Faced Lurcher in front of some strikingly optimistic grammar: 'The Past is Tense And The Future?? Perfect'.

A piece to camera in the Algiers Casbah, June 1997: at this stage, perhaps, the most alarming place on earth. 'Killer' Kilraine and 'Moose' Campbell recording it must be hoping I won't take too long about it: a death-squad can be rustled up very quickly here, and foreign camera crews are a particular target. The eight heavily armed Algerian policeman who are protecting us prefer to stay out of sight.

I have stepped aside so Paul Simpson, my (non-related) producer, can direct the shot; though in the circumstances that may not be altogether the most suitable expression.

Happy ending: with Dee at home in Dublin.

hostage and (b) dead. All right, I suggested, but let's just see if I can get permission to go there in the first place; no point in worrying about whether I should before we know if I can. It's an argument I've often used: the powers that be feel they haven't had to take an irrevocable decision, and yet a momentum is building up which will make it more difficult for them to say no later. For me there was an added attraction: since Britain had cut its diplomatic relations with Iraq after the execution of Farzad Bazoft, applying for visas would have to be done in pleasant places like Paris, Geneva and Amman.

I went to Paris first. The Iraqi ambassador was sitting in his office watching an afternoon soap opera on television when I was shown in. He had been brutally handled in a BBC television interview the day before, and I wanted to smooth his ruffled feathers. Merely because his government and ours were at loggerheads over something didn't mean that the BBC should treat him as an enemy. I remembered Waldo Maguire's flimsy piece of typing paper: as well as saying 'there can be no room for ranting', the BBC's Board of Governors had instructed us to 'address even individual Germans as an Englishman or a Frenchman would speak to them, if they could meet in a neutral café'.

Absolutely. So we were chatting in a civilized way about this and that, when the phone rang. It was someone with information that a well-known member of the Saudi royal family had lost six million francs at the gambling table in Nice the previous night. The ambassador gave instructions that this juicy little item of black propaganda should be passed round to the Arab journalists in Paris, and beamed at me.

It seemed an auspicious moment.

'Would you help me get a visa to Baghdad?'

'Why not?' The ambassador smiled.

I was delighted, not knowing that 'Why not?' is the polite Arab response to an impossible request.

After that, with my friend Mike Davies as producer and picture editor, I processed through the Middle East reporting on the growing crisis and trying to find a way to get to Baghdad. We started in Cairo, moved on to Jerusalem, and ended up in Amman. I went to the royal palace to ask King Hussein for help, and one of his superbly suited assistants replied, 'Why not?'

I queued up outside the Iraqi embassy in Amman for hours in the hot sun. The only way to get in was to trick the guard into opening the door a crack, then pushing through. It still didn't do me any good: once I was inside the press attaché said, 'Why not?'

Just as I was about to leave for London, I heard that Tariq Aziz, the Iraqi foreign minister, was coming to Amman to give a press conference. I asked a couple of questions during the course of it, in order to imprint myself on his consciousness, then doorstepped him as he left.

'Would it be possible for the BBC to visit Baghdad?'

'Why not?' he said, as he climbed into his expensive limousine. This time, though, I had the faint sense that he meant it.

The following day the Iraqi embassy in London called. Our visas had come through.

« »

I felt like a condemned man heading off in a tumbril. It was still only a couple of weeks after Iraq's invasion of Kuwait, and we were the first European television team to be allowed into Baghdad. With me was Ray Gibbon, who had covered the Sabra and Chatila massacre with me and was now a cameraman in his own right, and a freelance cameraman who later left Baghdad when we needed him most. As the three of us left the InterContinental Hotel in Amman people shook our hands with a particular intensity. At the airport there was a camera crew from one of the television news agencies to film us leaving.

'Would you mind if I did a quick interview with you? You know, just in case.'

I did know: I'd interviewed people just in case something happened to them, too.

Another group of television people was waiting at the Iraqi Airways check-in for the Baghdad flight. They came from Cable Network News, CNN: still not very big or very important. This trip of theirs to Baghdad would establish them with the Iraqis, and as a result of their presence in Baghdad during the run-up to the war and the war itself they would pole-vault themselves way ahead of the other American television companies in terms of international awareness. I had always liked CNN because of its lack of pretension and its concentration on news, and had quite often appeared on it as an interviewee. Since the BBC had no television world service yet, there was no competition between us.

As we lined up at the check-in desk I talked to the CNN producer.

His name was Robert Wiener: a witty, quick-thinking man, more intellectually rounded than the usual run of American television news
producers, and not concerned (as so many people in this competitive
business are) to put you down in order to establish their own position.
I took to him at once – particularly when he told me he'd come across
a rather favourable review of a book I'd written. This would turn out
to be an important trip for Wiener. As a result of it he would become
the chief architect of CNN's success in Iraq over the next six or eight
months, and therefore by extension of its new importance in the world.

'So why are you going to Baghdad?' I asked. What I meant was,
the chances must be quite strong that something unpleasant will happen
to us all; why should you voluntarily put your head in the noose?

'Because it's the place to be,' he said.

I knew then that he'd been through all the same thought-processes
as I had, and had come up with the same answer. Once we had
established ourselves in Baghdad we were to slip into an atmosphere
of much greater competitiveness, which was a pity. But before the air
war began five months later he played a significant part in my decision
to stay there when other people were leaving.

'I was in Saigon when Americans pulled out in '75,' he went on.
'And I decided to leave before the Viet Cong came in. I've spent the
last fifteen years trying to make up for that. I don't want to have to
make up for anything again.'

Landing in Baghdad was disturbing and eerie. The airport was
almost entirely deserted: this was the only flight of the day, thanks to
the UN sanctions. I was the first person off the plane, and found myself
in the arrivals hall before the large group of security men expected. As
I walked in they scattered like snooker balls to the outer edges of the
hall to watch and listen. Outside, when we piled up our gear and
suitcases, the savage heat wrapped round us like a barber's heated face-
towel. It was too hot even for the flies. We took the only taxi we could
find, cramming uncomfortably into it, and had to keep the window
tightly shut. When, unable to breathe, I opened it, the hot wind burned
my face and I had to close it again.

The streets were silent and empty. It wasn't just the heat: people
were terrified of what might happen, and mostly stayed indoors with
their families. At the hotel, though, they were genuinely welcoming.

'Alas,' said a man who had taken a British Council course in English literature, 'we see regrettably few of your countrymen now.'

'Will things be very bad?' asked one of the dark, lusciously beautiful women whom Mesopotamia produces, with a touching anxiety. 'Please remember,' she added, as though I had the power to halt the coming air strikes, 'that it's not our fault.'

She glanced meaningfully at the icon of President Saddam Hussein on the wall. That was as close to political comment as you could get in Iraq without knowing someone well enough to trust them.

The same charming officials greeted me with ironic smiles. No one mentioned the confiscation of all our tapes at the end of my previous visit. They were witty and feline in turn, as though they had served their apprenticeship at the Sublime Porte rather than in one of the fiercest dictatorships around. It's easy to convince yourself that because you have good personal relations with senior people in a government like this you will be protected in some way if things go wrong. As poor Farzad Bazoft discovered, that isn't the case. In Iraq you are on your own. Your highly placed friends will shrug their shoulders and smile with ironic apology at the latest unfortunate bow-stringing. They have their own careers, their own lives, to protect.

On that first afternoon, Saddam Hussein visited some of the British hostages from Kuwait, accompanied by Iraqi television cameras, and stroked the hair of a young English boy as he talked to the parents. There was absolutely nothing wrong with that in an Arab context, but in the Anglo-Saxon world in particular it set everyone's teeth on edge. I was still meeting officials when these pictures were broadcast, and in between handshakes I tried to make out what was happening on the screen in the corner of the ministerial office. Were the hostages going to be released? What was Saddam saying? The officials were vague and unwilling to commit themselves. It was immensely frustrating, given that I was going to have to build my evening's report round the incident. Also we needed more pictures. Could Ray film from the official's window?

'Why not?'

We got a series of rather fine panoramic shots of the city skyline in the setting sun.

Going to the television station was extremely worrying. In the hot darkness soldiers patrolled the empty roadway. Our driver, the wiry and unshaven old Mr Hamid, wasn't allowed to stop anywhere near the entrance. An armoured personnel carrier sheltered in an entry, its gun pointed directly at Ray and me as we laboured along on foot, gripping our edited video-cassette and hoping to be in time for the fifteen-minute satellite booking which was due to start in only five minutes.

The soldiers inside didn't share our sense of urgency. We had no written permission to enter, and there was no answer from the office of the ferocious woman who was in charge of television news. Time passed. I paced up and down, sweating and brushing away the flies which had now come out with a sleepy intensity. Saddam Hussein looked down at me from a variety of pictures: desert sheikh, soldier, statesman. The clock ticked into our satellite time.

Finally, my patience snapped. I wrenched open the door that led to the main television complex, scarcely caring whether they shot me: all that mattered was to make the satellite. Ray came with me. There was some angry shouting, but no one quite had instructions to kill us. I looked back: the officer was resignedly waving one of his soldiers, a small moustached Saddam clone, to follow me. In the darkness of the courtyard there was the smell of sewage, and my ankle turned on the broken pavement. Feral kittens playing in an abandoned oil-drum squeaked and scattered.

The woman who had the power to broadcast our material or withhold it was handsome and dark, with hair pulled back hard on her head like Eva Perón's. She was exhausted: each day she worked sixteen or seventeen hours in the intense heat. But exhaustion had made her poisonous. When I asked her questions about the satellite she repeated my words to me mockingly; the handsomeness left her face and was replaced by a Rosa Klebb expression of contempt and anger.

Ray put the cassette into the player and ran through it to show her what we intended to transmit.

'Take that out,' she snapped, as an innocuous shot of the city skyline appeared. No good trying to tell her that a senior official at the Information Ministry had let us film it from his window: she worked for the Interior and Security ministries, which in a society like this far outranked mere Information. She took further offence at a shot of one of the giant portraits of Saddam in the city streets, at a woman carrying a bundle on her head, and at the awful monument to the war with Iran – crossed scimitars a hundred feet high, held in giant hands modelled from those of Saddam himself. I could have understood if her objection had been aesthetic. It could scarcely have been on security grounds, since pictures of the arch appeared every night on Iraqi television news. Why, then?

'No discussion,' said Rosa Klebb, and her mouth shut like a mousetrap.

What Saddam had said during his meeting with the British family was that women and children taken hostage in Kuwait would be able to leave. They were brought up by coach to Baghdad and flown out from there. Over the next week or so this was to be the staple of our reporting.

Many of the women reacted superbly. They smiled and kept calm while the cameramen sweated and shoved around them. They talked in terms of quiet affection about the husbands and sons they had been forced to leave behind, and whose fate was completely unknown. Many had no homes to go to in Britain, and no certainty about their future income. Yet they spoke about getting back to nice cups of tea and the greenness of England as though nothing had changed since the Blitz. They fought back the tears for the sake of their children, and busied themselves with their luggage so that the cameras couldn't pry into their emotions.

Others complained. Their meals were cold, they couldn't use the swimming pool in the luxurious hotel which the Iraqis had set aside for them in Baghdad, the journey from Kuwait had taken too long.

'My little boy is used to proper food – burgers, fish fingers, chips, things like that. All this rice and vegetables upsets his tummy.'

Many complained that the Foreign Office or the British embassy had failed to help them enough, and seemed to feel it was all the Government's fault, as though Saddam Hussein were an act of God like drought or flooding, and Mrs Thatcher should do something about it.

'I don't see why we should suffer because of her and President Bush,' said one affronted woman.

Another agreed. 'If she's going to call Saddam a dictator, why didn't she wait till we were safely out of Kuwait?'

A British girl of around eighteen announced proudly that she'd been forced to take the Iraqi soldiers to her father's hiding-place in

Kuwait. They wouldn't have let her leave otherwise, she explained. The Iraqis had announced that the penalty for hiding from them could be death, though in this case nothing happened to him. Perhaps they thought he was sufficiently punished by having such a daughter.

The British tabloids loved it all. They weren't allowed into Iraq, so they interviewed the women as they came through Amman. 'Journey Through Hell', was the way one headline described the trip by air-conditioned coach from Baghdad. 'Burning desert', 'torturing thirst', 'fiends', 'evil', 'sobbing', 'loved ones', 'anguish': the hacks' Roget was in constant use. There was a hint of strategically ripped clothing, of beautiful white women menaced by lustful natives.

'Thatcher Warns Evil Saddam' said the first poster I saw when I went back to London for a break. Some of us, I thought, have been writing and broadcasting about the unpleasantness of Saddam Hussein's regime for years, while the British government regarded Iraq as a good customer for weaponry of all kinds.

When the newspapers put a compulsory 'evil' in front of someone's name, you know there's a particular need for coolness and rationality. And to prove the superiority of our civilization over Saddam's, someone threw a brick through the window of the Iraqi Cultural Centre in the Tottenham Court Road.

« »

I went back to Baghdad after a week or so, and stayed on for two months, from September to November 1990. This trip, the third of six to Iraq, was the foundation stone of my entire reporting assignment in Baghdad. I got to know more and more people, both officials and private citizens, and started to find out what made the place tick. I grew to love it, and to sympathize with it too: Iraq seemed to me like a hijacked plane, being flown to an unknown destination. A man whom scarcely anyone wanted as their president was holding a gun to the pilot's head, and the passengers and the rest of the crew were terrified to say a word or stop him. The fact that British industry, with the enthusiastic encouragement of the British government, had supplied the hijacker with his gun and the bullets for it made it all the worse.

Soon I settled into a routine. We had been moved from the Sheraton to the Al-Rashid Hotel: one I had always steered clear of. The advertisement for it at the airport: 'The Al-Rashid: More Than Just A Hotel'.

How much more, I wondered? It had been built for an Arab summit conference during the Iran-Iraq War, and was equipped with slabs of concrete set at an angle above each window, to deflect any shrapnel from exploding missiles. The entrance hall of the Al-Rashid was enormous, and with its white marble and its stained-glass windows it looked like a recently built crematorium. Until the press contingent swelled to such size that every available secret policeman had to be drafted in to watch us, there would always be half a dozen of them, sitting in the lobby in their suits and Saddam moustaches, reading their newspapers and watching the comings and goings.

There were usually some peace tourists there too: well-intentioned people who hoped to prevent the war by coming to Baghdad to demonstrate with the Iraqis or try a bit of freelance negotiation. Others were attracted to trouble and media attention like bluebottles to a dustbin. Many had come to plead for the release of their fellow citizens whom Saddam Hussein was holding hostage. The most prominent of them were given an audience with the great man himself. You could see them occasionally on television, bowing over his hand. That wasn't necessarily intentional. Saddam, a man of around 5 feet 7, deliberately held his hand out quite low when they came forward to shake it, and gave them a little pull, which meant they lowered their heads automatically. His court photographers waited for that instant, and the next day's newspapers would show them inclining their heads to his greatness.

A banker friend of mine in London had advised me not to stay at the Al-Rashid. His company had loaned a large amount of money to the company which built it, and among the costs was an item for Swedish-built surveillance cameras which were fitted into the television sets in each room, so that the security people could watch you as you watched television: or did anything else, of course. It was fashionable for those who could afford it to hold their wedding receptions and honeymoons in the Al-Rashid, and shortly before I arrived there was a minor scandal when it was discovered that the security men in the hotel were selling videos of the honeymooning couples in the Bazaar. A recent bridegroom, it seemed, had recognized himself and his wife.

As far as I was concerned, there was never much for the spooks to watch: unless they liked the sight of a large man in his underwear checking through his library (as ever I brought ten or twelve books with me, large Victorian three-decker novels and collected poems mostly, in case I was taken hostage or put in prison) or playing music. I often had as many as forty CDs at a time: Shostakovich, Mozart, Stéphane Grappelli, Fred Astaire, Elgar. Then I would sit and look out at the view, and wonder what it would look like when the aerial bombardment started.

For me, the greatest pleasure was to take a car down to the Tigris River and stroll around the ancient part of the city. The Baghdad of Haroun al-Rashid, the circular city which was the most advanced in the world in the eighth and ninth centuries after Christ, was utterly destroyed by the Mongols in the thirteenth century; so there is no sign of it whatever in modern Baghdad. But along the river bank are the university and the Bazaar and other ancient buildings: often disregarded and falling apart, but recognizably of the time.

I would wander through the Bazaar, with the coppersmiths' hammers ringing in my ears and the old women calling out humorous endearments and the sellers of fruit and cloth and jewellery coming out to offer me tea and begging me just to look, no obligation, because the quality and beauty alone would steal my heart. The shopkeepers soon became familiar to me, and I learned how to bargain with them, setting aside an hour or more to look at their wares and starting the bidding, not only at prices that were absurdly low, but for objects I had no interest in. After half an hour's banter, and three or four cups of strong mint tea, I would suggest that if the merchant wanted to make a sale he should throw in whatever it was I was really interested in: a carpet from Bokhara, perhaps, or a piece of curiously carved lapis lazuli, or a British medal struck for some Mesopotamian campaign, or a collection of cups and saucers with the face of King Faisal on them. Then the shopkeeper would relax a little, and the real battle would begin.

I never scorned the quality of the goods on offer, as you are advised to do, though I would always show I had spotted the faint chip or the mended crack. Instead I would praise whatever it was I wanted to buy, and then offer a price that I thought was low but realistic. Sometimes I would have to say goodbye and leave; once I was even getting into the car before the merchant ran up and agreed the deal; but I always got what I wanted.

One merchant had a beautiful early 1920s gramophone with a

brass horn and a wind-up handle on his top shelf. I first discovered it while I was up a ladder, mountaineering for books; and it took me three visits before I could get him to agree to a price which I thought was reasonable. One Thursday evening, together with some friends, I went to pick it up.

Almost all the rest of the Bazaar had closed down. Like an illustration in an old manuscript, the yellow light from a hurricane-lamp in the shop window shone through the dark archways. Our footsteps echoed through the passages. The smells of the day's commerce, of the fruit and vegetables, the coffee, the hideous joints of meat, lingered in the darkness. The old man was still sitting in his shop, and he grinned victoriously at me: by coming I had shown I had accepted his price. With unlikely agility he swarmed up the ladder in his bare feet and fetched the whole perilous contraption for me. On the way down he paused.

'Want record?'

I nodded. He gripped a selection from a leaning pile and carried on down. I knew then that I had paid too much for the gramophone; bazaaris in Baghdad don't hand out presents unless they feel a very powerful moral obligation. I didn't care, because the thing was so lovely, with its little image of the dog, head turned, listening, and the words 'His Master's Voice' painted on it, and its beautiful brass horn. Mike Davies took it from me, and on a bench in the darkness started to reassemble the whole thing, almost by touch. Like a surgeon, he held out his hand for a record. It was too dark to read the labels, so I handed him the topmost one from the small pile I was holding. Mike placed it on with care, and wound the handle.

Then came the miracle. In the mediaeval darkness there was a hoarse, scratching sound, and the horn began to speak.

> Running wild, lost control
> Running wild, mighty bold.
> Feeling gay, reckless too,
> Carefree mind, all the time,
> Never blue.
> Always goin', don't know where.
> Always showin' I don't care.

Don't love nobody, it's not worth while.
All alone, and running wild.

The echoes of Duke Ellington and his Famous Orchestra had faded into the recesses of the ancient stonework before we started clapping.

« »

Why did the Iraqis want us there? Why should a government which had been so paranoid about foreign journalists a few months earlier now invite them to Baghdad in such large numbers that the pool of English-speaking spooks was drained by the effort of following us around? (One side-effect was that there weren't enough of them to listen in to our phone calls; realizing this, I started dictating the weekly column I was now writing for the *Spectator* by telephone. Better still, none of the snoopers the Iraqis used in London were *Spectator* readers, so the authorities in Baghdad didn't find out what I was writing. That in turn emboldened me, of course, and I found myself writing things about Saddam Hussein which would have driven the Iraqis crazy if they had known.) Now, though, there were well over a hundred journalists from the main countries, and the main news organizations, of the world; and there would be more to come.

The man who had invited them in was the chief civil servant in the Information Ministry, Najji al-Hadithi: a handsome, elegant man who had spent seven years in London as press attaché, and spoke English superbly. Somehow, he had managed to persuade his minister to approach Saddam Hussein himself with a plan: that Iraq should now regard Western journalists as useful to it's own purposes.

It worked: and having agreed to allow me in, together with the leading American networks, Iraq gradually opened the doors until every major British broadsheet newspaper, and every major American, French, German, Spanish, Italian, Canadian, and Japanese news organization, plus plenty of others, had its own representative in Baghdad. But I was the correspondent who was allowed to stay the longest.

It was because I got on so well with Najji al-Hadithi. He liked Britain and the British, and he had a British sense of humour. One evening, a couple of weeks before the air war started, I took the BBC news editor to see him. We had spent the day at the ruins of Babylon.

'I've been showing Mike here what the rest of the country is going to look like soon,' I said.

There was a silence. Oh Christ, I thought, why do I let my habit of making jokes run away with me? I was staring down at the carpet at the time, and I let my eyes stay there for a bit. Then I looked at al-Hadithi. He was rocking with silent laughter.

One evening in October he invited me to a dinner party. It was a beautiful night, with the first hint of coolness in the air after the ferocity of summer. A crescent moon hung in the black sky with a single star below it, like the Arabic letter 'B'. The table was set outside, and the terrible New Town architecture of Saddam-era Baghdad was invisible. We could have been dining in the circular city of Haroun al-Rashid.

'And how is dear old England?' asked the man on my right, a weasely fellow who seemed to be making fun of me.

Dear old England, I said, was fine.

'And where are you from?'

Suffolk, I told him.

'Ah,' he said, getting his fricatives mixed up with his sibilants, 'Suffolks – Brighton, The Old Ship Inn, Eastbourne.'

Something like that, I said.

'And how is Orpington? And Newcastle? And Edinburgh?'

When last heard of, I assured him, they were bearing up.

'When all this is over,' he said with a softening in his voice which gave me a sudden sympathy for him, 'I would love to see Edgware Road again. And High Saint Kensington.'

I didn't allow my face to change, but he knew he had made a mistake. It was as though I'd spoiled his dreams. He turned away from me at precisely the moment I felt most drawn to him.

By now, though, the conversation on my left had become interesting. Najji al-Hadithi was sitting immediately next to me, with the American journalist Carl Bernstein, of Watergate fame, on his far side.

'Kuwait is now, and always will be, a part of the motherland,' al-Hadithi said to him, dangling a set of worry-beads in some attractive semi-precious stone from an elegant hand.

'What you're telling me is that you aren't planning to withdraw,' said Carl Bernstein, pointing a stubby finger at al-Hadithi.

The beads clicked with a faint irritation.

'Why,' I broke in, 'do you allow so many foreign journalists to come to Baghdad, when you used to keep the doors so firmly shut?'

'Because we want you to see that we are human beings like yourselves. So that your readers and viewers will see it. So that if, God forbid, President Bush decides to bomb us, you will know who you are bombing. You are a form of protection for us.'

'What you're saying—' Bernstein began. But his probing finger froze in mid-air. Najji al-Hadithi was already talking to someone across the table.

It was an intelligent strategy, and in the end I think it worked. I hope it did. And if, by being a small part of Naji al-Hadithi's strategy, we helped to persuade the United States that Iraq wasn't another Vietnam or Laos or Cambodia that could be carpet-bombed because there were no Western eye-witnesses to tell the world what was happening, then I'm proud to have been there.

The Gulf War was the first (or perhaps, if you count the Falklands War, the second) since the Second World War in which it was essential not to have large-scale casualties. If Winston Churchill had promised in 1942 that German civilian casualties would be avoided where possible, he would have been howled down by a public opinion which longed for Germany to suffer just as it had made other countries suffer.

The Gulf War ended precisely when President Bush began to get nervous about the pictures of death and destruction which were coming in from the desert. Public opinion in Britain and America wanted a war fought, but it didn't want a huge body-count. And quite rightly, I believe. There are no nice, comfortable wars; but if we are still stupid enough to fight them, we might as well do it with a minimum of bloodshed. The problem was the quarter of a million deaths after the war, caused by UN sanctions and Saddam Hussein's reaction to them.

I liked Najji al-Hadithi a lot, though I must have been a real trial to him. One morning in November I received an invitation to come over to his office. In front of him on the desk lay a pile of *Spectators*, each open at my article. There must have been ten of them at least.

'Oh, John.'

I tried to explain. I was a writer; that was what I did. I couldn't not write, and it was my duty to get my material out in the best way possible.

A portrait of Saddam Hussein hung over his desk, and he glanced towards it.

'But the things you said.'

'You know it's all true, Najji.' Might as well go out frankly as try to grovel, I thought.

'It's not true at all,' he said instinctively. Then, 'You mention this elegant government official who speaks almost perfect English. Might I ask—'

'Najji, you know perfectly well it's you.'

'H'm.' There was a pause. 'Please, if you must write about our country, don't speak disrespectfully—' Another glance at the presidential portrait.

'Of course not, Najji.'

I could let up now, I thought: I'd be staying.

A few days later the Iraqi government was threatening to hang any of the foreigners in Baghdad who had taken refuge at the various Western embassies. The thought that the determinedly jolly, brown, plump men and women whom I had filmed camping out at the British embassy and splashing around like seals in the swimming pool might suffer a fate like this was quite intolerable. Yet was it so very different from the Western commentators, particularly in the United States, who were starting to talk of turning Baghdad into an empty car-lot, or back into the Stone Age, by aerial bombardment?

I thought of this as I sat in a Baghdad tea-house looking through the open window at the greasy waters of the Tigris below. The room was cooled by slow overhead fans. There was the sound of loud laughter, and of ivory dominoes being slammed victoriously down on wooden tables. A waiter with a gotch eye and a badly scarred face came over with a dirty tray of lemon-flavoured tea. Rough faces, dark and unshaven, grinned wolfishly at us from around the room. As far as I can remember, no ordinary citizen of Iraq ever once insulted or threatened me during my entire six months in the country. A cripple shuffled across to us, called each of us 'Lord' and took our shoes away to be polished.

Our driver had brought us here: an upright brown little cock-sparrow of a man who was of course working for the *Mukhabarat*, Iraq's fearsome intelligence organization, but nevertheless gave us good service. His name was Hattem.

'Mr Hattem number one driver?' he would ask.

'Absolutely, Mr Hattem,' I would reply. It was a ritual.

He was always on duty half an hour before the appointed time, and recently, with some embarrassment, he asked for the afternoon off. It turned out that his wife had given birth to their fifth child the day before, and this was his first chance to see him.

Now Mr Hattem was showing us the complexities of the Turkish versions of backgammon: *Adi, Mahbous, Gulbaha, Chesh-besh*, and another whose name I never caught. Mr Hattem threw the dice with a tremendous flourish, and went on to make a series of moves which none of us could understand, let alone copy. Out of the game, I sat back and surveyed the scene. Fat-bellied men in grubby white dishdashes knocked back tea or banged their fists on the table or laughed. Pictures of the Prophet Mohammed and of Haroun al-Rashid looked down at us from the walls. The cripple worked away on our shoes under a tree in the courtyard outside, joking with a small group of friends. This was *douceur de vie* as the poorer people of Iraq knew it. It had nothing to do with the savageries of Saddam Hussein and his government, but they would suffer equally if Iraq were indeed turned into a parking-lot. Of course, these were the kind of thoughts which his officials hoped we would have. Yet what they really amounted to was an appreciation of how pleasant Iraq could be, if only Saddam Hussein were no longer in power.

« »

In all this time I hadn't actually met the man himself. I had seen him in the flesh, had even been in a group that was allowed close to him; but I hadn't actually shaken his hand or looked him in the eyes. It was, I told myself, only a matter of time. The application was in, and the officials spoke of 'when' rather than 'if'. Then in November 1990, just as we were about to arrange the details, I suddenly couldn't get in touch with the officials any more. Somehow they were never in when I called; and when I spoke to Najji al-Hadithi about it, he went into 'Why not?' mode.

I knew why it was. Saddam Hussein couldn't allow anyone to edit his words, and I had warned the officials that we would not be able to run an hour and a half of Saddam uncut. We didn't allow that to any British politician, so we certainly couldn't allow it to the President of Iraq. It was a stand-off; and the Iraqis solved it by offering the interview to Independent Television News instead. ITN said yes at once.

I was furious, and decided to go back to London. There was a certain calculation in it as well: I was tired after ten weeks' work in Baghdad without a break. Then again, Margaret Thatcher had just resigned as prime minister, and I wanted to cover the campaign for the succession. Probably I'd have left Baghdad anyway; but I didn't tell the Iraqis that, and several of the officials were gratifyingly apologetic.

I had one last dinner with my colleagues in our favourite restaurant, and afterwards asked if anyone wanted to walk back to the hotel instead of driving. A Dutch correspondent who was with us volunteered to come with me. There seemed no reason to be worried.

We stopped on the Jomhuriya bridge across the River Tigris and looked across at Saddam Hussein's palace – one of the many – lying in darkness on the other bank. Would there really be a war?

There was the sound of a police siren. Two cars came swerving up and mounted the pavement, and four men waving guns got out and ran over to us. One of them, a man of about fifty, wore a uniform with a big unwinking eye embroidered on the shoulder-patches. When I refused to take my hands out of my pockets he screamed that he would throw me into the river. I took no notice, of course: I guessed he wouldn't go through with it. Instead he called for reinforcements.

So there we stood, on Jomhuriyah Bridge in the darkness: the poor Dutch correspondent who was more nervous than ever, me with my hands in my pockets pretending not to be worried, four police cars with flashing lights, eight policemen, and at least eight guns. The most senior of the reinforcements swaggered across to me. Baghdad isn't a town where people talk back to policemen. I cut him short directly he started shouting at me in English which was quite good.

'I work for British television,' I told him, choosing my words with as much care as a lawyer or a writer of advertising copy, 'and British television is interviewing President Saddam Hussein tomorrow morning. If I see the President tomorrow morning I shall complain to him personally about your behaviour. Please give me the names of all the policemen here.'

I can't think when I've said anything that had a more gratifying effect: it was better even than telling the Chinese security men I would report them to the British ambassador. His face went a strange prunish colour and he ran over to his car. Grabbing the two-way radio, he started yelling down it in Arabic. I could only distinguish the words 'British', 'television' and 'Saddam'; but there was no doubt a bull's-eye had been scored. Even the Dutch correspondent perked up a little. When the flow had stopped I asked the policeman what was happening. He merely held his hand up and stared out across the river as though his life was passing before him. He was a man in a career crisis.

Twenty minutes later, down the dark, empty street, came the sound of an old car. It was a beat-up Volkswagen Passat of indeterminate colour, lots of dents in the body-work, and a wire coathanger for a radio aerial. It stopped at the end of the row of flashing police cars which were ranged along the pavement like a row of fairground stalls, and a slight figure climbed slowly out. He was in his early twenties, yet the senior policeman I'd been talking to actually bowed to him. As for the others, they fell back in case he might catch sight of them.

'Hi,' he said.

His tie was loose, his expensive suit was rumpled, and he looked exhausted. Obviously he was very high up in one of Saddam Hussein's many secret police forces; even so, there was something about him I felt was rather amusing and sceptical.

'Is it true you told these men you would report them to Saddam tomorrow morning?' His English was superb.

'Something like that,' I said.

'If I drive you back to your hotel and no action is taken against you, will you agree not to say anything about it to Saddam?'

'It's a deal.'

I thought the Dutch correspondent was going to faint with relief. As for the policemen, they fawned on us as they queued up to shake hands.

We crammed into the Passat for the quick journey to the hotel. I tried to draw him into conversation about what he did, and the situation, but he grinned and shook his head.

'It's been nice knowing you,' he said.

For me, it was an eye-opener. Even failing to interview Saddam Hussein conferred a certain power.

A few hours later I was at the airport. Here, too, the security men were rather nervous. A few weeks before, their colleagues had run a scam in which one of them opened your wallet to look at your money while the other started pulling things roughly out of your hand-luggage. As you started yelling at the man with the hand-luggage, the man with the wallet palmed some money out of it. One of our people lost $300, and another a good deal more than that. I complained to the Ministry, and although they wrote me a letter saying there was no foundation whatever in my accusation one of the minders told me a couple of security men had been hanged. I felt bad about it until I reflected that they could well have been the men who arrested and beat up poor Farzad Bazoft at the airport.

Anyway, there was no repeat of the old scam now: the security men were polite and very correct. But they still wanted to know what we were taking on board. I had packed the body of my 'His Master's Voice' gramophone in my biggest suitcase, but I was carrying the brass horn with me as hand luggage.

'What's that?' asked the security man. I handed it to him.

'It's an Object,' I replied.

He took it out of its wrapping and examined it. Then he showed it to his superior.

'Murmur-murmur-murmur-object,' I heard him say.

'Object?'

The security man nodded.

'OK, no problem,' said the boss.

I took my Object on board the plane, and stayed away from Baghdad for almost a month.

« »

When I came back in mid-December, things had changed. Mr Hattem was much more subservient to our minders, and wouldn't take us anywhere without consulting them. Once we missed an entire story because of this, and in anger I turned to our second driver, the elderly, lop-sided, mildly unreliable and distinctly alcoholic (not to say unsuitably-named) Mr Ramadan.

There were other, more important changes. Saddam Hussein had ordered the release of all the foreign hostages ('You really must call them "guests", Mr Simpson,' the censor feebly insisted) who had been taken to likely targets in Baghdad and elsewhere and held prisoner there. This was a decision of considerable importance to the Coalition forces headed by the United States; public opinion at home would have been much more reluctant to support the air war if it had seemed likely that ordinary Americans, Britons, Frenchmen and others would be killed by the bombs and missiles.

The man who persuaded Saddam Hussein to give up one of the best cards in an otherwise rather empty hand was Yasser Arafat, the Palestinian leader. Poor old Yasser: he has never been loved in the West. But as I found in Beirut in 1982, he was a man with a remarkable degree of personal courage, and although he always liked to wear military uniform and at one time seemed distinctly fond of side-arms and AK-47s, he was always instinctively a man of peace and compromise. His argument had been that if Saddam Hussein let the hostages go, this would weaken the moral argument of the United States. It was a tactical mistake, and Saddam Hussein came to hate Yasser Arafat for having suggested it. But for the time being they were still friendly.

Palestinians generally had swung in Saddam's favour when, early on in the crisis, he offered to withdraw from Kuwait if Israel would withdraw from the West Bank. Yasser Arafat, whatever his private feelings, had come out publicly in support of Iraq in the crisis, and had settled in Baghdad for the duration of the crisis.

One morning, shortly before Christmas, I went round to his house to record an interview with him.

Transcript of interview with Yasser Arafat, 17.12.90

JS: Will there be a war?

YA: No. I can tell you that there will not be a war. I promise it: you will see. Something will happen: there will be an agreement. You must not think President Bush is so foolish. You must not think the Arab brothers are so foolish. War is a terrible thing. Nobody wants it. President Bush will compromise.

JS: Will there be acts of terrorism carried out by Palestinian groups?

YA: I do not think you will find this is so.

JS: You will stop them?

YA: I will ensure they do not happen.

It certainly looked at that stage as though Arafat would be right about a deal. President Bush was starting to talk of 'going the extra mile for peace', and the Iraqi press was announcing a major diplomatic victory for Saddam Hussein. As for terrorism, I was to see for myself how ferocious Arafat could be in curbing it, if he chose.

After our interview we went in to lunch, Arafat holding my hand tightly in his own. It wasn't an intimacy I would have sought: his hand was bandaged and coated with ointment, and it stuck to mine audibly. His doctor, some months earlier, had warned him that his strange habit of sleeping during the day, getting up at six or seven in the evening and working throughout the night meant that he wasn't getting enough sun. If he couldn't change his ways, the doctor had said, he must use a sun-ray lamp – but never for more than a few minutes at a time. Arafat, always tempted to overdo things, stayed under his sun-ray lamp for forty-five minutes and burned himself badly. Hence the bandages.

A dozen or so people were politely standing waiting for us in the dining-room, and sat down only when we did. Arafat's conversation was interesting and amusing, but I was fascinated by the large, dark, humble character at the foot of the table: it was Abu Abbas, the Palestinian terrorist leader who had carried out the attack on the Italian cruise ship *Achille Lauro* in 1986, and whose forces had landed on the Israeli coast in May 1990 and had been wiped out. That particular effort had infuriated Arafat, who had told him he would cut his hands off if he tried anything like it again.

'You know our Arabic expression, "cutting someone's hands off", meaning to render them incapable of action?'

'Yes,' I said.

'I told him it would not be a figure of speech in this case.' Arafat laughed hugely.

I could hear Abu Abbas with his head deep in the foodstuffs from a distance: he wasn't a discreet eater. But he was certainly a tamed man: his eyes scarcely met those of anyone else, and he never even looked in Arafat's direction.

« »

By the third week in December I started getting discreet visits from a very senior figure indeed: someone who saw Saddam Hussein on a regular basis, and for reasons that were difficult to work out told me in detail what Saddam had said and what his mood was. This man, whom I nicknamed 'Bertie', persuaded me that I should go public on Saddam Hussein's determination not to withdraw from Kuwait before the deadline imposed by the United Nations. Like the United States and British governments, I was inclined to think that Iraq would pull back at the last moment and leave the Coalition forces embarrassingly exposed. 'Bertie' was absolutely certain this wouldn't happen, and he was right. Thanks to him, so was I. This, for instance, is what I told one interviewer over the line from London.

```
Transcript of Radio 4 interview, 2.1.91

Q: So what's your estimate now? Do you think Saddam will
pull back from Kuwait?

JS: I think we can be certain that he won't. People
who have seen him in the past day or so have told me that
he is determined to stand and fight. He told one visitor
that if he pulled his forces back now,there would be
an uprising against him in the army and he might not be
able to cope with it. If he feels it's essential to his
own survival in power to face a war, he'll certainly
do it.
```

I could hear the scepticism in the interviewers' voices, but 'Bertie' had convinced me not only that what he told me was accurate, but that it was important to make it public. Of course the possibility existed that Saddam Hussein knew 'Bertie' was talking to me – the Al-Rashid hotel wasn't exactly the most secure place to have a conversation – and was feeding him this line in order to strengthen the Coalition powers' belief that he meant what he said. Somehow, though, I didn't believe that. Not wanting to identify him, I pretended when I first wrote about this period that I had gathered my information from a range of people who met Saddam Hussein. The reality was a lot easier than that; and my colleagues became used to seeing the distinguished-looking 'Bertie' coming to look for me and going off with me into the next room for a talk.

In report after report I pressed the same line until it became an act of faith for me; and when, on the day when James Baker, the US secretary of state, met the Iraqi foreign minister Tariq Aziz in Geneva and ITN reported that Tariq Aziz was bringing with him an offer of conditional withdrawal, I wondered if I had got it terribly wrong. But he had brought no such thing; and the meeting broke up without the possibility of a diplomatic settlement. That evening I saw 'Bertie' again.

```
Extract from notes of meeting with 'Bertie',
7.30pm, 13.1.91

Acc[ording] to B, S[addam] was in his hardest and most
aggressive mood today. S[ai]d Iraq wd only have to face
2 waves of air-strikes, and B[agh]dad wd be so destroyed
and loss of life so huge that international opinion wd
be revolted and wd force the US, Br & others to stop.
Result: diplomatic victory for S.

Wdn't S be killed? No, because his bunker is
impenetrable. He will survive, even if tens of
thousands die.

Where is bunker? B too nervous to say. He is driven in
with curtains on car windows closed.

Cd he open the curtains a touch and see? B: They wd want
to know why I shd do a thing like that.

But does he think it's near here? B, looking round room:
Subject not a good one to discuss.
```

In fact we had a pretty good idea on 11 January where the bunker was. Saddam Hussein was due to appear at an international Islamic conference at the government centre immediately opposite the Al-Rashid Hotel. Our minders by now were so unnerved by the prospect of the approaching war that their control over us was becoming increasingly lax. As a result we and the television organizations we worked with were able to station camera crews at every entrance to the conference centre, in the hope of getting something more than the official pictures of Saddam Hussein. We might even get a word from him, we thought.

« »

I sat in the hotel, watching Iraqi television's live coverage of the meeting. On cue the great man appeared on stage, holding out his arm in the affected way which is his trade-mark, while the audience went wild. I looked forward to the pictures the camera crews must be getting. But when they came back, each of them said that Saddam hadn't come past him. That convinced me. We had long heard rumours that his command complex was based under our hotel: this indicated that there were underground roads and passages from the complex to enable him to reach the various important government buildings in the area.

(More evidence came soon after the air war had begun. For some reason I looked out of my hotel window in the early hours of the morning, and saw a team of men in black clothes, black gloves and black balaclavas drive in on a flat-bed lorry and take up position in an empty yard below the hotel. On the back of the truck was a remarkably sophisticated air defence system, a battery of missiles which twitched and turned all the time as their radar systems picked up the faintest of signals from the sky.

That night there were no attacks on the centre of the city, and the men in black left shortly before dawn. But I couldn't think of any reason why they would want to defend a building site or the back of our hotel: unless Saddam Hussein was underneath. He was. A large village existed underground, with its own sophisticated communications and power systems, manned – according to 'Bertie' – by a number of former Soviet officers.)

So there we were, living and working a hundred feet or so above Saddam Hussein's head. We were his protection. And if he knew it, the Coalition forces did as well: the European company which had built much of the bunker had handed over all the blueprints to them. The outlook wasn't good. The American embassy in Baghdad, before it closed down, had warned everyone who stayed that they could expect to be killed by the bombing. President Bush himself had phoned the editors of the big American organizations represented in Baghdad and begged them to pull them out. And since journalism in the United States is less noted for enterprise and courage now than it once was, the big organizations (with the exception of CNN) obliged.

If we were all so certain we were going to be killed, why did we stay? In my case it was a complex mixture of motives.

First, perhaps, was the sense of duty. I wanted the BBC to have proper coverage of whatever was going to happen. No one had forced me to go to Baghdad in the first place, and now that it had become dangerous it didn't seem right for me to pull out and leave the job to someone else. I remembered very strongly the experience of the CNN producer who had left Saigon before the Viet Cong takeover, and had spent the years since trying to make up for it. I didn't want to have anything to make up for.

Second, I was too interested to want to leave. What would it be like, to be under the greatest aerial bombardment in human history? I didn't want to read about it afterwards in the newspapers.

Third, I had undertaken to write a book about the crisis, and I didn't feel I could simply walk out before the final part began.

As for the desire for glory, that didn't play much of a part at all: the chances of ending up dead and forgotten were too great. It is true, though, that I found the excitement enjoyable – but I would have to survive if I were to be able to enjoy it fully.

Months later, a particularly skilful interviewer pressed me to say why I had remained in Baghdad. I went through these answers, but they weren't enough. She forced me to go a little further.

```
Transcript of Desert Island Discs interview, 10.5.91

Speakers: Sue Lawley, John Simpson

SL: But these things - I mean, it's not really enough to
risk your life to write a book, is it?

[Pause]

JS: I suppose it's just that I'm a bit of a chancer, that's
all.
```

And although I wish I had put it in more attractive terms, that's exactly what it was. I couldn't say why, but I thought I would probably survive; if I did, the benefits of seeing the war at first hand would be considerable in every way.

And if I didn't? Perhaps my upbringing has given me a rather Victorian view of life and death. I find it hard to accept the contemporary view that life of any kind, no matter how restricted and feeble, is better than no life at all. The thing doesn't seem to me to be worth clinging onto at all costs, regardless of its quality. Like an ancient

Roman, I would prefer to get out while I'm ahead; and if that involves taking my chances in an air war of extraordinary proportions, so be it. I wouldn't like to be forgotten too soon, or ignored too completely, but once the party is over, it seems to me that one should know when to leave.

Extraordinary though it seems, the usual Wednesday race-meeting took place on the afternoon of 16 January at the Baghdad Horsemanship Ground. I wanted to film it, but the Ministry of Information wouldn't give us permission: perhaps they thought it detracted from the high seriousness of the moment.

The weather was beautiful. The blue sky was streaked with pink cirrus, and the dust thrown up by the horses' hooves was turned to gold by the late afternoon sun. The punters wore flat caps and tweed sportsjackets over grubby white dishdashas, so that they looked as though they had been transported from Punchestown or Naas or some other Irish racetrack. They were as enthusiastic about the horses as ever, and crowded forward to bet at the Tote windows on Sheherezade or Lulu in the 4.10. I queued up to watch, but was reluctant to put any money down. To lose a bet would seem like a very bad omen indeed at a time like this.

'Is Ass-cot as nice as here?' someone asked me.

'Absolutely,' I answered soothingly. Maybe in Iraqi terms it was: a place where you could get away from the horrible pressures of Saddam's Iraq. They drank local beer from the can, and wiped their mouths expressionlessly as they watched the favourite lead the field to the winning-post. At the Baghdad Horsemanship Ground, as in Iraqi elections, the favourite invariably wins. The betting depends on guessing which horse will come second and third.

'There will be no war,' said a big, sweating bookie with a brick of notes in his hand. 'Nobody wants it.'

It was a good job, I thought later, that he hadn't put any money on it.

That night I produced what I intended to be the best report I had ever done. It started off with some superbly elegiac pictures of the River Tigris enshrouded in mist, it contained moving, gentle shots of a group of Iraqi schoolgirls at their morning assembly, then moved on to the empty city with a cat running through the shot to tell Tira, who liked cats, that I had been thinking of her, and went on to show the preparations ordinary Iraqis were making against air attack: taping their windows, and so on. Finally, over a sensational shot of the night-time skyline of Baghdad, there came the sound of the first air-raid sirens of the war.

'That deserves an award,' the picture-editor said, as he spooled back to the start and pressed the 'Eject' button. He was going off to satellite it to London.

I didn't really expect to live long enough to get an award. I thought it was more likely that I would be dead by the next evening, and I wanted my last report to be the best I had ever done. Back in London a few months later, having survived, I thought I would see what it looked like. When I watched it, I realized that the editor of the *Nine O'Clock News* must have decided that it was fifteen seconds too long, and some butcher of a sub-editor had chopped off the skyline and siren sequence, cobbling up my last words in the crudest possible fashion. No one had reflected, plainly, that this might be the final report of my life, or that I might have taken pride in the way it looked. I really think if I had been killed my affronted ghost would have haunted the Nine O'Clock desk for ever. Some of these people, I reflected, had as much aesthetic sensitivity as Saddam Hussein himself.

There were seven of us in the BBC team, all committed to staying on no matter what happened. I had talked to them about it at intervals during the previous few days to make sure that they really wanted to be there, and that they knew they could leave at any moment; all of them had assured me they did. The team included Eamonn Matthews, who had had such an unpleasant time on our first visit to Baghdad, and Bob Simpson, the foreign news correspondent.

That evening, 16 January, the French and American organizations with teams in the Al-Rashid Hotel got in touch with them to say they had been told that the bombing would start that evening. We heard nothing from the British side; traditionally British governments regard British journalists as an unwanted burden, so it didn't surprise me. But the BBC, too, seemed to have changed its mind about our being there, and had decided that we should leave Baghdad. One of the most senior figures in the Corporation, a good friend of mine, gave me my orders.

'You'll have to get yourself a new foreign affairs editor then,' I said, my voice sounding harsh even in my own ears.

In the end he and I worked out a compromise. If I chose to disobey the instructions of the BBC he assured me that no disciplinary action would be taken against me.

'That's great,' I replied. 'We're about to face the biggest air bombardment in human history, so it's a real relief to know that there won't be any disciplinary action against us by the BBC.'

While this conversation had been going on, though, another and rather rougher figure in the BBC hierarchy had been threatening some of the others much more effectively. They had been left with the clear impression that if they stayed on in Baghdad in direct defiance of his instructions, they would be regarded as having resigned from the Corporation. No compensation would be paid to their widows. Four of our team – including the entire technical staff, as it happened – decided that they couldn't disobey. By the time I came back into the room, they had made their minds up.

It was a serious shock. Here we were, about to face the biggest news event of my career, and our camera crew and picture editor were explaining to me that they wanted to leave the next morning. I could just about understand the reasoning of the camera crew, since they were both on the BBC staff and were both married. Yet I knew perfectly well that if the worst happened the BBC wouldn't really be able to cut their families off without a penny; opinion inside and outside the Corporation wouldn't stand for it. Anyway, the assurance I had received overrode the threats.

But I found the attitude of the picture editor quite incomprehensible. He was an Australian, young, tough and without a family, and he was a freelance, hired in specifically to be part of the team which covered the war. Nothing had changed for him, except that he had contracted the general panic.

I felt personally let down, certainly: but the real problem was that I couldn't see how we could hope to compete effectively against ITN, if all these people left us. ITN had brought in a well-known cameraman, whose reputation was formidable. Perhaps he was a bit of a poseur – he had put body-building stickers on his camera and was inclined to boast about having links with the Princess of Wales – but we would have no camera at all. What was the point of my staying, together with the television producer, Eamonn Matthews, when we would have nothing to work with? Yet there was no question about staying. I could see the same determination in the faces of Eamonn and Bob Simpson, and in some ways the defection of the others made the three of us all the more determined.

Eamonn and I hurried out to see if we could find anyone else who would work with us. We came across two disgruntled cameramen, both of whom had been badly treated by the organizations they were working for. Now, looking back, I regard them with great affection. One was a young man, Anthony Wood, who had been working for the now defunct breakfast television programme TV-AM. He had been sacked by them when, like me, he questioned his office's instructions to come home at once. His camera gear had belonged to the company and was being shipped out, but we had a small amateur video camera which he could use to get us some pictures. The other cameraman at a loose end was Nick Della Casa, who was a freelance and had been working for CBS. Poor Nick: he, his wife and brother-in-law were all murdered in northern Iraq a few months later when he was on a trip for the BBC.

Now, though, he was full of cheerfulness and a humorous resentment against CBS. They, like so many other organizations, had ordered him out, and when he had refused to leave they warned him that they would take no further responsibility for him. Nick had his own equipment, but it was designed for the American NTSC system (known without affection as 'Never The Same Colour') rather than for European PAL. Nor did he really like working with a group, to the instructions of a producer. Still, he and Anthony offered us at least the possibility of reporting on the world's most intensive bombing campaign. These considerations took up the last few hours of peace.

We had one other important advantage. I might be angry that the camera crew were going, but they had done us an enormous service, which in the end ensured the relative success of the BBC coverage of the early part of the war. When they had arrived in Baghdad, they had smuggled in a satellite telephone: strictly forbidden by the Iraqis. (The French and ITN had already imported satellite telephones legally.) The day before the war began, I had revealed the existence of our telephone at a meeting between the various English-speaking television groups and Najji al-Hadithi. It had had a gratifyingly explosive effect on everyone: ITN and CNN both thought they had a major advantage over us, and Najji must have assumed that the BBC's broadcasts would be under government control.

It was obvious, though, that CNN had done a separate deal with the Iraqis, and soon afterwards one of the main figures in the CNN group told me what had happened. (At that stage, when we were all facing an uncertain future together, there was a certain amount of mutual regard and solidarity in the air; not that it lasted long.) The CNN man explained to me that the Iraqi government had agreed to let them have use of a government communications system, a two-way telephone line called 'a four-wire', which ran in a protected culvert to the Jordanian border. It was likely to be immune to the general telecommunications jamming which the Americans were expected to carry out.

It was a Faustian pact, of course; the BBC certainly wouldn't have entertained such a thing. Nevertheless I don't believe CNN agreed to twist its reporting in any way in order to use the Iraqi four-wire. For Iraq it was enough to have an American television team operating in its capital during the war: anything Saddam Hussein wanted the outside world to know could be said via CNN, and the extent of the terrible destruction which Saddam expected could be conveyed by its broadcasts.

It would be unfair to blame CNN for much of this, since it behaved exactly as any other commercial organization would. CNN's decision to stay in Baghdad and report from there seems to me to be perfectly reasonable; I would have wanted to stay there too, and when we were allowed to return to Baghdad I was a strong advocate of it. Since with the BBC commercial interests aren't involved, I hope we wouldn't have tried to exclude CNN as CNN tried to exclude other Western news organizations. I hope, too, that we wouldn't have tried to pretend that we were the only Western news organization in Baghdad. But these are small complaints, compared with the big issues at stake.

Later, ex-President George Bush and many of the newspapers on either side of the Atlantic were deeply critical of CNN, the BBC and other broadcasters who worked in Baghdad during the war. Yet even in wartime, broadcasters in a free society are not a co-opted branch of the military; their function is not and shouldn't be to keep up morale at home, nor to spread deliberate propaganda abroad. In the Second World War the BBC, with Churchill's full agreement, broadcast as much of the truth as the proper demands of national security would allow; so that often the first news of British reverses was broadcast, not by German or Japanese or Italian radio, but by ourselves.

'We always listened to the BBC,' said one of the tens of thousands of letters the BBC received from its European well-wishers after the War was over, 'because we knew that if you were honest about the bad things that happened to you, we could trust you to tell us about your victories.'

If you are fighting in a good cause against those who wish to suppress truth and honesty, – whether they are Nazis or the Iraqi government – it is the worst thing possible to suppress truth and honesty yourself. The results of the BBC's approach in the Second World War were of course remarkable. Not only did the civil population of Germany and the occupied countries listen to the BBC in preference to their own broadcasters, but the BBC's international reputation for honesty and unbiased reporting was established for the rest of the twentieth century.

I doubt if CNN's behaviour during the Gulf War will win it that kind of praise. Yet the Gulf War was the making of CNN. Remaining in Baghdad when the world's other major organizations were forced to leave was a central – perhaps the central – part of that strategy. CNN denies strongly that it persuaded the Iraqis to throw everyone else out soon after the war began, and that it tried to stop them being invited back some time later. In the absence of any other information, we shall have to accept CNN's word for it; though CNN has also denied, rather unconvincingly, that it used the Iraqi four-wire communication system. What we do know is that by establishing its pre-eminence in Baghdad, CNN became the television news leader in America.

« »

After the long months of waiting, my war service in Baghdad was short and extremely violent. It began in the early hours of 17 January, soon after the crew had told me they were leaving and we had hired Anthony Wood and Nick Della Casa. There was a yell of anger from Bob Simpson, the BBC radio correspondent, as his telephone line to London was cut. The Americans were starting to jam Iraqi communications: whatever was going to happen was just about to start. My mouth was dry, and I found myself picking at my fingers – a habit I thought I'd stopped. Remembering Saddam's forecast that there would be two enormously destructive waves of bombing, I felt distinctly nervous; but it was only the nervousness you feel before an important match, or a stage appearance.

At my suggestion, Anthony Wood and Eamonn and I headed out into the streets to film the start of the bombing. It was 2.32 a.m. We had two flak-jackets between the three of us, and as the least useful person of the three I went without. I can't say it was much of a sacrifice. If Baghdad was about to be swallowed up in a tidal wave of high explosive, a flak-jacket was about as much good as an extra pair of socks.

We ran across the crematorial lobby of the Al-Rashid. Outside it was cold and very silent. Most of the city lights had been switched off. Anthony had hired a driver for the night, but he turned out to be one of the most cowardly and feeble of them all. The rest, good and bad, had long since disappeared. We ran to his car, jumped in and slammed the doors.

'Drive! Drive! Drive!'

But drive where? We hadn't had time to work it out. Each of us shouted suggestions. I wanted to be in the heavily populated areas on the other side of the river, but I was afraid of crossing a bridge. All the bridges, we knew, would be bombed, and if we were stuck on the wrong side without any shelter we might well be lynched as spies.

We were still shouting when the darkness and silence exploded around us. There was an extraordinary racket, as the hidden guns and missile batteries started blasting off excitedly into the air. I remembered to look at my watch: 2.37. Red tracer flashed up in patterns beside us, lighting up the frightened, sweating face of our driver, and Eamonn peering through the window trying to see where we should go, and Anthony's face screwed into the side of the camera. Sirens started up everywhere. Our ears were besieged with waves of disorienting noise.

'I'm getting this, I'm getting this,' Anthony yelled.

The car took a sharp turn into an underpass, its wheels squealing, and came out on the other side just as a battery of rockets exploded beside us.

I'm glad you are, I thought. I could see what was happening: the driver was so frightened, he was heading straight back to the hotel. We were going on a mile-long circle, with nothing to show for it but a few flashing lights in the sky and some spectacular noise. As for the bombing, it hadn't even started. This was just a display or nervousness by the Iraqi gunners. The driver, utterly consumed by panic now, screeched up to the front door of the hotel and ran in, leaving the door of the car open. We tried briefly to set up our camera in front of the main door, just as the first rumblings of aircraft – our aircraft, friendly aircraft, – became audible over the excitability of the Iraqis. We were in for it now, I thought.

But we had no chance of staying outside. The big security guards of the *Mukhabarat*, vicious bruisers many of them, hauled us inside. It was completely dark, and people were screaming. I lost touch with the others, and was forced at gunpoint down the narrow staircase that led to the underground shelter, shoved from behind into the crowd of people who were already pushing each other in an access of panic. All it needed was for one person to slip, I thought. This was disastrous: my worst nightmare. Outside, now, you could hear the first bombs and missiles falling. The whole building juddered as they landed nearby. So far, though, nothing seemed to have hit us. Far better, I had said to the others, to be on one of the upper floors than to be packed down in the basement. Especially if one of those concrete-burrowing bombs hit the hotel on its way down to find Saddam's bunker: this place would become a liquidizer, a people-blender. No, I thought, put images like that away, or you'll start shouting and pushing too. The heat and press of bodies and the darkness were horrible; and now the women, in particular, were starting to wail.

I tried to keep as calm as I could, allowing myself to be buffeted but refusing to start lashing out as some of the other men were doing. Down in the corridor, which was seething with people, there was a little emergency lighting. Fine, I thought, now you can see well enough to find Anthony. I craned over the heads of the frightened crowd, and saw him a little way ahead of me. When I caught up with him, all he was worried about was whether he'd got the pictures properly. Armageddon was going on outside, but he was worried whether his new employers would approve of his work.

We were swept past a short flight of stairs to a room, set a little higher than the corridor itself. On these steps stood the ITN correspondent and his cameraman. In this maelstrom of emotions and superb pictures, the cameraman's eyes were bright red and his camera was pointing at the ceiling. He wasn't filming anything. I needn't be worried any more about the capability of the bodybuilding hero.

'You fucking coward,' the correspondent was raging. He was a man I had good reason not to like, but there was nothing scared about him.

'I just can't,' moaned the cameraman. I thought he might start weeping, but I was swept past them before I could hear any more.

I met up with Anthony again in one of the vast underground rooms which were being used as shelters. It smelled of fear. People were gathered all round the walls in little groups, lying or sitting, terrified or weeping or trying to come to terms with what had happened to them. The old rules that applied on the surface seemed not to work down here. I saw a young woman undressing in front of everyone, and neither she nor anyone else seemed to pay any attention. Children wept or defecated; old men and women sat looking at the floor, too frightened to do anything. And all the time, it seemed, the structure of the hotel, fifty feet above our heads, shook and shivered with the bombing.

Anthony and I fought our way out at last. Neither of us could stand to be in this living tomb any longer: we needed the cold air of the surface. A guard armed with a Kalashnikov tried to stop us, but I fought my way past him in the dark. We ran up the five flights of stairs to the BBC office, catching glimpses at each landing of the extraordinary battle that was going on outside. We couldn't stop: heavy footsteps showed that someone was chasing us.

The office was in complete darkness, and it was hard to find in the anonymous corridor. It was silent inside. The others, who were hiding there, had heard us and assumed we were from the *Mukhabarat*. The familiar room looked utterly different, lit up by green and white and red flashes from outside. Up here there was less vibration, and the missiles seemed to be landing a little way away from us. I crouched in front of the window and got one of the other cameramen to record a piece to camera for me. He had to shine his battery-light on me, which was an alarming experience; any Iraqi soldier who saw it from the outside might think we were signalling to the planes, and put a heavy round through the window. It had to be done; but I was relieved to get through it just the once, without needing a retake.

The man from the *Mukhabarat* must have heard my voice, and he started banging on the door. I thought I'd have to get out, so that the others could carry on their work. I ran out, charging towards him along the beam of his torch, and dodged into a room which seemed to be empty. Once inside I locked the door, then went through several interconnecting doors till, in the light from the missiles and the anti-aircraft guns outside, I could see there was a bed. I lay down on it. Beside me was a little short-wave radio. I switched it on: whoever owned it had been listening to the BBC.

I heard the calm voice of the announcer in London telling me that the war had started, and the equally calm voice of President Bush explaining to me why it was such a good idea for so much high explosive to be dropped on my head; it's all right for you, I thought. Close by, a 2,000-lb penetration bomb dropped and burrowed its way into the earth: the whole structure shook. One of the Americans had told me that when this happened all the fillings would be shaken out of your teeth if you were within a couple of hundred yards. I ran my tongue round the fillings: they were all there still. My watch said 5.45. I fell asleep.

Eamonn woke me up three hours later, beating on the door. He had been out in the hotel grounds, putting up our satellite phone. The guards were too demoralized to stop us going out, and we brushed past them as we ran. Thank God I won't be in vision, I thought, as I smoothed my hair down and did up the buttons of my shirt.

The gardens of the hotel were completely transformed. Little groups of journalists were gathered round the white umbrella-like dishes of satellite phones: three of them in all. This was no band of brothers: we were competing more fiercely with each other than at any time in the past few months. As for CNN, they were inside with their comfortable Iraqi four-wire.

For the time being the skies were blue and empty except for occasional puffs of smoke from speculative ground-to-air missiles, and the gun-fire was sporadic. I did a first telephone report about what I had seen in the night, but felt worried that I couldn't answer questions about what state Baghdad was in this morning.

So Anthony and I went out again; dodging the exhausted guards wasn't as difficult as I'd expected. We found a driver and went off across the still undamaged bridge to the centre of the city. It was empty, quiet, and very strange. Our car was one of the very few in the streets, and there were scarcely any people to be seen: a woman trailing a weeping child, a few old men and women selling oranges. Here and there entire buildings had been snuffed out of existence – important government buildings, *Mukhabarat* centres or Ba'ath Party head-quarters – and yet those on either side of them were mostly undamaged, and sometimes still had all their glass in the windows. A local telephone exchange, a smallish building opposite an hotel, was nothing more than a heap of rubble; the hotel was still completely usable.

A couple of hours later, a friend of mine who had been caught out in the darkness told me that she had seen strange red lights playing on the target buildings. British and perhaps American special forces had penetrated the city and were guiding in the missiles with infra-red lamps; hence the extraordinary precision.

As we drove round, the driver spotted a *Mukhabarat* car.

'Allah! He see you take picture.'

The unmarked white car picked up speed, overtook us and forced us to stop. I got out.

'Morning,' I said. 'Just looking round. I'm sure you don't mind.'

He did mind. He ordered us to follow him. I could see Anthony was as determined as I was not to go. The unmarked car went ahead and we followed. We crossed the bridge as though we were going back to our hotel, but the police car signalled that it was going to take the right fork, to *Mukhabarat* headquarters: not at all a good destination.

Now, though, the sirens were wailing again, and the Defence Ministry a quarter of a mile away along the river bank vanished in a pillar of brown smoke. You couldn't hear the cruise missiles coming: you could only see the results.

'Go straight on, Ali,' I hissed at the driver. 'Don't turn. Go there.'

I tried to look ferocious: Ali had to be more frightened of me at that moment than he was of the secret police. It did the trick. The *Mukhabarat* car turned right, and we sped straight ahead, the hotel only a few hundred yards away now. The missiles were falling again and the futile sound of anti-aircraft fire was everywhere. It must have taken the secret policeman a minute or so to realize what had happened, and another minute to turn; but as we raced into the car park the white car was already entering the hotel gates. Ali was safe enough: he told the police I had threatened to cut his throat. Technically it was a lie, but he had interpreted me right.

Upstairs I found the four BBC people who had decided to leave. I guessed by now that this was what the entire war would be like: fought out with weapons so accurate that unless our hotel was targeted we would be moderately safe. I hoped my colleagues would realize this too, and change their minds about going; but I wasn't going to beg them to stay. They didn't, even though the first night had been just about as dangerous as it got for us.

One of the four, who happened to be looking out of the window, called out in amazement. He had seen a cruise missile pass along the line of the road towards the centre of the city, at about our level on the fifth floor. Some time later I saw one myself, which actually turned left at the traffic lights and followed the road which the white police car had wanted us to take. Maybe it hit the *Mukhabarat* headquarters itself; if so, it was even better that we hadn't gone there. Soon afterwards I went down to the hotel garden, where the satellite dish had been set up. I felt I'd got enough to say to the special programme which was just starting on the BBC. It must have been around nine in the morning, London time.

Transcript of interview from Baghdad, 17.1.91

Speakers: David Dimbleby, John Simpson

DD: We have our foreign affairs editor, John Simpson, on the line from Baghdad. John, what's happening there at present?

JS: I can hear quite loud sounds of gunfire or landings of rockets or missiles, I'm not quite sure what it is at the moment. The aircraft seem to be so high, and the missiles make remarkably little noise. An extraordinary thing happened, I suppose about an hour ago now. We were looking out of the window of our fifth floor room in the hotel, and a missile of some kind, a Tomahawk - I don't know, I'm not very good at these things - passed by on the line of the road on which the hotel stands, at about the level of our windows . . .

This is the first time anyone's seen a war like this. It wasn't what we expected, to be honest. I've covered quite a lot of wars in my time, but I thought this one was going to be horrendous; or at least I thought it was going to

be last night. It's turned out not to be so horrendous,
and it's the accuracy of the missiles and the bombs which
makes it less threatening than one thought.

I didn't want to become an apologist for the war. But these words of
mine were seen by both the pro- and anti-war factions as making the
case for a new type of warfare which was somehow neat and tidy and
didn't cause much bloodshed. Until the terrible bombing of the al-
Amiriyah shelter, in which hundreds of innocent women and children
died, it's true that civilian casualties were minimal. I'm sceptical now
whether it was worth fighting the Gulf War at all; though I am certain
that the greed and carelessness of a number of countries, and particularly Britain, allowed Saddam Hussein to build up an unthinkably large
arsenal of weapons before the war began.

But what is incontrovertible is that it was the first major war since
1918 in which killing ordinary people wasn't the main purpose. Those
who disliked the war didn't want to hear this. Nor did they want to
hear that when I went back to Baghdad after the war, and managed
to get around most of the city thanks to the feebleness of the minders
and the secret police, I counted only twenty-nine buildings destroyed;
though those which had been targeted had been hit time and again.

The four BBC people left, together with about twenty or thirty
others including the ITN cameraman. They even insisted on taking the
two flak-jackets which were the only protection we had, on the grounds
that having signed for them in London they might have to pay for
them if they weren't returned. No one mentioned the circumstances
under which they might not be returned.

So now there were fewer than forty of us left: a team from the
Canadian Broadcasting Corporation, plus eleven British, eight French,
three Italians, a Spaniard, an Australian, a New Zealander, a Turk, five
Americans, and a couple of Jordanians. The French and the British
were at loggerheads, and I scarcely spoke to the ITN correspondent.
As for CNN, they rejected any request to use their broadcasting line
with extraordinary ferocity.

We didn't feel safe, either. We knew now that we could survive the
level of attack that had been directed at Baghdad so far, but that was
all. On the second night the Americans told CNN that they were going
to hit the Al-Rashid Hotel. Fortunately, if that really had been the

decision, someone changed it. Even so, we all felt that we would rather die in our beds than end our lives in that terrible shelter with all those panic-stricken Iraqis. The other time I felt real fear was when I heard that Iraq had fired its Scud missiles at Israel. What if the Israelis retaliated with nuclear weapons? Yet there is a definite comfort in powerlessness. I had lost any great interest in surviving: I just wanted to see as much as I could and report it. There was absolutely nothing else I could do, so I might as well enjoy myself. I opened another tin of oysters, poured myself a glass of Laphroaig single malt whisky, read a little Evelyn Waugh by candlelight, and woke up each morning to find myself unbombed and still alive.

The Al-Rashid had ceased to function as an hotel: there was no electric light, no heat, no power, no water, no food. You could tell which rooms were occupied by the smell coming from them. I moved from empty room to empty room, using a different lavatory each night. Out in the hotel garden where we had set up the satellite phones a large pool of sewage had formed, and every time a missile struck or a bomb landed the surface of the pool shook with the vibrations. Eventually you could tell when the planes were coming, because tiny ripples appeared round the pool's edges. Day and night the raids went on, but we scarcely bothered about them now. We realized that the missiles could loop around high buildings like the Al-Rashid.

We had established a kind of pattern now. Directly the air-raid sirens went, the minders and security men would run inside for the shelter of the hotel while we would run outside to start broadcasting without interference from them. We would usually pass them on the way, but they were too frightened and embarrassed to take any notice. One afternoon the sirens went while I was in my room. I ran down the corridor towards the emergency exit in the total darkness and cannoned into the sharp corner of a wooden desk. I cracked a couple of ribs, and lay there in the dark for a while. Then I managed to get downstairs. It was very painful.

Overhead a sensational battle was being fought between the American and British aircraft and the Iraqi ground to air missiles. There were explosions all across the sky. Chaff was thrown out, bombs fell, missiles exploded. I was desperate to get on air with an eyewitness account of it all, but a voice in the studio the other end told me sharply that they had just begun a fourteen-minute report on domestic political reaction to the war and couldn't interrupt it. By the time the fourteen minutes were up and the local politicians had finished droning, the battle was over. The sky had cleared almost completely. When David Dimbleby came on the line I was in a furious temper, both as a result of the pain in my ribs and the foolish waste of a wonderful broadcasting opportunity.

```
Transcript of interview from Baghdad, 18.1.91

Speakers: David Dimbleby, John Simpson

DD: What's been happening?

JS: If you'd been able to join me a few minutes ago, I
could have given you a description of an extraordinary
overhead battle that's been going on here. As it is, it's
completely over, I'm afraid.

DD: Do you have any information about casualties?

JS: I'm the only casualty I know about. I cracked a couple
of ribs when I made contact with a rather large desk which
someone had left in a darkened hallway in the hotel.
```

Some of the newspapers in Britain decided that this was a coded message to show that I had been beaten up by the Iraqis; and so, while an entire country's economic infrastructure was being blasted away, part at least of the British press was concerning itself with a mild injury to a couple of my ribs.

The Iraqis were only occasionally aggressive towards us. Most of the minders and security men were so reluctant to be out in the open with us that they didn't seem to care what we said. In fact it is my settled belief that most of them were praying that Saddam would be killed or overthrown as a result of the war. It seemed to me that the Coalition powers had a great deal to be grateful to the Iraqis for. If Saddam's army had fought in the way he had intended, there could have been large-scale losses for the Americans, the British, the Saudis and the French. As it was, they scarcely put up a token fight, because they didn't want to support him.

Sometimes, though, the security men could be rough. Once we were ordered inside while I was still broadcasting. I pretended that I was trying to close down the satellite phone, while in fact continuing to broadcast on it. The guard came over and started getting aggressive. I asked him if he could understand how to work it; and since he couldn't speak English I was able to get a few more sentences out before I thought he would start pulling his gun. Another time, as one of the minders was shouting at me to get inside, I told him to calm down.

'There's nothing to worry about,' I said soothingly. 'There's absolutely no danger out here.'

At that moment there was a thick, spinning sound in the air, and a heavy calibre bullet landed beside me on the steps.

'Huh – what do you think that is?' the minder said, and snatched it up angrily as a souvenir. It was still warm.

That afternoon the Information Ministry told us we would have to leave Iraq. The chief minder insisted that CNN would be going too, and it was only at the last minute that we realized for certain this was a lie. I tried to persuade the hotel doctor to say that I was in too much pain with my ribs. He gave me a note which said in English:

TO WHOME IT MAY CONCERN. MR SIMPSON HAS TWO/THREE
CRACKED RIB AND MUSLE SPASME. HE CAN NOT DRIVE IN CAR
FROM IRAQ.

Underneath he wrote in Arabic: 'No problem – he can travel.' So that was the end of another good idea.

Before we left, the area round the hotel was attacked by cruise missiles. Anthony got his little camera and started filming from the window of our room. Two of the missiles went round the hotel and hit the conference centre opposite, which was one of the entrances to Saddam Hussein's bunker. Another was damaged by anti-aircraft fire and plunged into the hotel grounds. At the height of the action I recorded a quick piece to camera, with my back to the window. There was a terrible racket outside, but the people in the room were sitting there completely immobile and silent. Then Bob Simpson spoke.

'It went right behind you while you were talking. It was a cruise.'

But there was no time to talk about it. Anthony and I went charging downstairs to film the damage done by the missile which had crashed. It had ploughed into the staff quarters, which were well ablaze by the time we got there. Fortunately no one had been in the huts at the time, and there were no casualties. As we were filming, we were jumped on by four security men. We fought them for a while, but in the end one of them got hold of the camera and took the cassette out. I ran after him and almost got close enough to rugby-tackle him, but I was held back by the others and he escaped with the cassette. It didn't just contain the pictures of the crashed missile; it also had my piece to camera with the cruise passing behind my head. I felt as though I had lost a picture of the Loch Ness Monster.

At last we were forced to leave. For me, it was a long and very painful journey, not merely because of the ribs but because I was convinced that our material had not made it through to Amman, while ITN's had. I spent the ten-hour journey jolting around on terrible roads in some gloom, certain that I had been badly beaten on the most important story I had ever covered. A BBC reporter was sent out to meet me at the border, and I suggested to him that I should just slip into the hotel and go to bed. He seemed surprised.

We drove up to the Marriott Hotel in Amman, and I got out rather unsteadily. A dozen flash-bulbs went off in my face, and Tira was there to greet me together with a reception committee from the BBC and various other television organizations. I couldn't really grasp it all. It turned out that, far from being in disgrace, we had done rather well. The BBC crew who had left Baghdad had successfully managed to smuggle our pictures through, while ITN's had been confiscated from their fleeing cameraman by the Iraqis at the border. And the telephone broadcasts in which I had been in turn excited, bad-tempered, and deceptive to the security man had been broadcast to immense audiences. I hadn't just arrived in Amman; after a quarter of a century's reporting, I seemed to have arrived altogether.

15

Under Siege

WHEN I WAS THE BBC's political editor in 1980 and 1981, during the extraordinary revolution introduced by Margaret Thatcher, no one at Westminster seemed at all interested in the fact that only twenty-two miles away from the shore of Britain a country of comparable size and importance was carrying out a policy which was the exact opposite of hers.

I never once heard a British politician or a British journalist refer to the fact that President Mitterrand of France had sharply increased public expenditure, was pouring money into the state-owned industries, and was creating jobs in an imaginative way. It was precisely the model which the Labour leader, Michael Foot, believed Britain should introduce; yet neither he nor his senior party colleagues seem to have noticed it. In the long run, perhaps, it proved to be a mistake; yet if they thought so Mrs Thatcher and *her* ministers never once referred to it.

That may have been intentional. In 1989, when France celebrated the two hundredth anniversary of the French Revolution and the rest of the world lined up to congratulate her, Mrs Thatcher's lack of enthusiasm for the occasion and for France showed itself strongly. A meeting of the G7, the richest nations in the world, was held in Paris on 14 July, and the other leaders lined up to give Mitterrand presents which reflected their countries' links with France. President Bush handed over the key to the Bastille which Lafayette had taken with him to America shortly after the Revolution. Mrs Thatcher, by contrast, gave Mitterrand a first edition of *A Tale Of Two Cities* by Charles

Dickens, worth perhaps £150. It was a grudging, insular gesture typical of British attitudes in the 1980s.

« »

My involvement with British politics nowadays is quinquennial, like Parliament itself. When there is a general election, I like to follow the prime minister of the day around, and go to his or her constituency on election night, so that I can get the first reaction to the result. It is something I pride myself on. In the case of the election John Major won in 1992, I may have played a slightly more intrusive part in his campaign than I meant to, or than I should have.

As prime minister, John Major tried hard. He tried very hard. But with a party as full of anger and resentment as the Conservatives behind him, he never had a hope of succeeding as prime minister. He was a throwback to an older kind of conservatism, middle-of-the-road, not too noisy or tub-thumping, lacking in any particular conviction except that the Conservative Party was the natural governing party of Britain. You could almost call him apolitical. He reminded me of that line from Michael Flanders and Donald Swann's revue: 'We don't have politics here, we're Conservative.'

The country had been governed by such Conservatives for much of the twentieth century, and people in Britain were slow to understand how right-wing and ideological the party had become during the Thatcher years. John Major, who had posed as a Thatcherite to win his leader's notice and support, shared none of her deepest views. That was his downfall. He must have gambled that even if his backbenchers discovered his lack of right-wing conviction, the voters of Britain who traditionally dislike extremism and ideology would give him their backing.

But they didn't. They disliked divided parties even more, and they were strongly influenced by the mockery which parts of the media directed at him. A witty and effective speaker in small gatherings – I once saw him make a gathering of businessmen in Downing Street laugh uproariously and then wipe tears of genuine emotion from their eyes in the course of a single seven-minute speech – he was useless at appealing to a wider audience. In a country as obsessed with class attributes as Britain, the signals he put out were all wrong: his harsh, much-copied voice, his shabby-genteel background, his parents who had had something to do with the circus, his general air of having just come back from Homebase or Tesco's.

I was on a prime ministerial flight when one of the journalists travelling on the plane walked past Major's seat and spotted that he wore his underpants outside his shirt-tail. Big deal; but the journalist reported it to the other journalists at the back of the plane with the glee of a schoolboy revealing the social shortcomings of some hapless new arrival in the playground. The discovery too fed eventually into the public consciousness, the general level of undeserved contempt. Steve Bell, the best and most savage political cartoonist in Britain, portrayed him for ever more with his Y-fronts outside his trousers. *Spitting Image*, the television satire programme, coloured his puppet engine-grey.

In the eyes of the British press, Major was the council-school boy, the anorak, the swot, who had ended up in Whitehall. He seemed to fit into a recognizable niche within the dreary, peculiarly English system of snobbery, and was looked down on accordingly. But it wasn't just that. Eleven years of Margaret Thatcher had taught Britain to think that the only government worth having was government by the stick; and merely by trying to introduce a less confrontational system Major looked rather feeble. Many of his enemies in the Conservative Party resented the fact that Mrs Thatcher had been overthrown, and would have taken it out on anyone who succeeded her.

Major lacked her convictions, certainly. It should have been a relief. These convictions, brandished in familiar Thatcherite style, were what had made her so unpopular in the country as a whole; and if she had led the Party into the 1992 election she would have lost it. Under other circumstances John Major might well have made as good a prime minister as anyone else: but his tiny majority in Parliament after the 1992 election and the resentments that existed on his back benches wrecked any chance he might have had.

He was certainly the wrong choice to succeed Mrs Thatcher in 1990. Either Douglas Hurd or Michael Heseltine would have drawn off the party's poison, and left the leadership to Major after a few years. Major's enormous fortune in winning Mrs Thatcher's support, and therefore the leadership, turned out to have been the worst piece of luck he could have had. Or perhaps the second worst piece of luck, since no one would have blamed him if he had led the Tories to defeat in the 1992 election. Winning it was a disaster for him, and it wasn't much help to the country, since the early 1990s were as gloomy a time in Britain as the 1970s had been under Labour. And I played an unintentional part in helping him to victory.

« »

One afternoon in the spring of 1991 the phone went in the World Affairs Unit. One of the producers answered it.

'It's Downing Street. They want to know if you're at work today.'

Everybody laughed, and I picked up the phone. A woman's pleasant voice at the other end checked that it was really me, then said she had been instructed to find out if I would be prepared to accept a CBE in the Gulf Honours List. It was, the voice explained, the civil equivalent of a military medal.

I asked for a little time to consider. Under Margaret Thatcher many people felt that the honours system had become distinctly debased, rewards for services rendered. Not having rendered any services, I was wary of accepting. And yet it was perfectly clear to me what was happening: after the years in which Mrs Thatcher had deliberately ignored the BBC in the honours list, this was intended to show that things had changed. If Major was holding out a hand to the BBC, I didn't want to ignore it. I phoned back and said I would accept. It is, I feel to this day, something to be proud of. At the same time, I have always rather leaned towards Robert Burns' opinion of these things:

> For a' that, and a' that,
> His riband, star and a' that,
> The man of independent mind
> He looks and laughs at a' that.

When the award was made public, the *Guardian* gave me an entire editorial to myself. It denounced me for accepting a tainted honour, and implied strongly that no one would ever quite believe anything I said again; which presupposed that they had ever believed anything I said in the first place. It made painful reading at the time; I had always liked the *Guardian,* and had written for it from Baghdad. But I felt there was nothing I could do except make certain no one would ever have the slightest grounds for thinking that I had been, or could ever be, for sale.

The ceremony itself was surprisingly nerve-racking. I couldn't get over the memory of a passage in *Brief Lives*, by the seventeenth-century antiquary and gossip John Aubrey. He describes how some unfortunate courtier went up the steps of Queen Elizabeth I's throne on his knees and broke wind by accident as he kissed hands. Mortified, he bought a ship and sailed the ocean for seven years. When he came back he presented himself at court again. Elizabeth I greeted him warmly: 'Welcome, Sir William. We had forgot the fart.'

It seemed to me I was bound to do something embarrassing at Buckingham Palace. The room, decorated like the ballroom of a Reno hotel only with less restraint, was full of the families and friends of the people who were being decorated for their part in the Gulf War, all in their best clothes: just the kind of audience you didn't want to disgrace yourself in front of. Tira was there, and so were Julia and Eleanor. In spite of my fears the ceremony passed off quickly enough, and the cherry-red ribbon was duly placed round my neck without the need to leave the country for seven years. The band in the gallery was playing 'Annie Get Your Gun'.

We had been heavily briefed about how to bow, how to get off-stage, and what to do afterwards, but no one told me to expect the languid young man in morning-clothes who was lounging by the doorway as I came out of the little side-room where they had taken the ribbon from round my neck, folded it up and placed it, together with the blue and gilt cross, in a blue leather box. He straightened up and walked over to me. Now, with the box in my hand and a sense of huge relief that it was all over, I let my guard down.

'So what was it like, then?' asked the languid young man.

I thought he must be some kind of courtier.

'OK,' I said, 'a bit like winning best of breed at Crufts'.'

'I say, that's rather good. Better make a note.'

'But— Who do you work for?'

'Press Association, old boy. Look good, that will. Mostly they just say how honoured they are. You know.'

'I suppose you couldn't make it anonymous? Or forget it?'

''Fraid not, old boy.'

It was in the early editions of the *Evening Standard*, to the BBC's embarrassment, but Robert Maxwell disappeared off his boat that afternoon and the flippant remarks of stray journalists were no longer of interest to anyone, fortunately.

« »

John Major called an election for April 1992. My job was to cover Major's own campaign. It turned out to be one of the less pleasant assignments. On Sunday 15 March I travelled to a place called Sawley, in his constituency of Huntingdon, where John Major was to Meet The People. The words were always said with a particular reverence by his handlers, as though real people were the greatest rarities in the world, unpredictable creatures who could only be approached with extreme care.

The whole occasion was dreadful. A local Rotary Club would have done better. Major sat on a stool like Val Doonican, looking uncomfortable, and a group of specially invited, carefully screened local supporters sat equally uncomfortably in front of him. Everything had been so rehearsed that the life had long before been completely ironed out of it.

As for the Party hacks, they reminded me of Jehovah's Witnesses. They were true believers, trying their best to be patient with the sceptics. 'This isn't a press conference,' said the most senior of them that afternoon, 'it's a people conference. You'll be able to spectate at it. He's not just going to speak to the people, it's for the people to be able to ask whatever's on their minds.'

But the people were as embarrassed and shy as he seemed, perched on his stool. What was on their minds was the kind of thing they had read in the tabloids.

'Is it true,' one asked, 'that if the Socialists win, they will do lasting damage to the British economy?'

The questions were sometimes so extreme that Major, a fair-minded man, sounded less anti-Labour than they were. The best he could do was to say that nothing much was going on in the country.

Transcript of report from Sawley, Northants, 15.3.92

Speaker: Rt Hon John Major, PC, MP

JM: Back in 1979 there was a real feeling for change. I'm telling you, it ain't there now.

Afterwards, as I drove to the place where we were editing, I thought it over. Of course I could report the whole occasion without adjectives, just giving a bald account of what had happened. It would be safer and easier, but it wasn't really what I was paid for. If the overwhelming impression was of a lack of imagination and understanding, then I should say so. After all, if I had been reporting an election in France or Germany, I would tell the truth about it. Should I tell lies in my own country? I stopped beside the road and started writing.

Transcript of report for 6.25 News, 15.3.92

JS: The campaign proper began for John Major with a chance on BBC Radio to get in a brief, quotable thrust at his opponents:

JM: This fetish the opposition parties have for raising taxes seems very damaging to the economic interests of this country.

JS: But the business of meeting the people began on his own home ground: in Sawley, part of his own constituency. The people he'd come to see had been carefully invited by the local Conservative Party, and the questions weren't exactly designed to cause him problems.

[Extract from public meeting]

JS: Mr Major is no great orator, and his handlers think he's better with small groups. But it was all desperately tame today, and there are promises that his campaign may liven up a little later.

Not what you might call revolutionary stuff, and all manifestly true; but the spin-doctors from Conservative Central Office went wild with fury. They were on the phone complaining and threatening almost before the last words of my report were broadcast. The editor who had to take the flak rang me to compliment me on my report, but he wouldn't have been human if he hadn't wished that this particular cup might have passed from him.

So the tone was established right at the start. The functionaries at Conservative Central Office had identified me as a wrecker, a trouble-maker, perhaps a paid-up member of the Labour Party. One of them complained to me the next day. Would I, he asked, have said that the Labour leader, Neil Kinnock, had had a tame audience? Of course, I replied; and I would.

That morning the same man, interviewed on the *Today* programme, had said that he and his fellow spin-doctors only rang up the BBC to complain about mistakes. Where, I asked, was the factual error in saying that Major wasn't much of an orator and the occasion the previous day had been desperately tame?

'It was all a big mistake,' he said nastily.

Meanwhile, the Labour Party was doing precisely the same thing. The man in charge of the Kinnock campaign took the view that the BBC was being uniquely hostile to them:

'If the BBC believes it can operate like this because the Conservatives hate it but Labour has a sentimental attachment to it, it had better think again. If it goes on like this and Labour wins, there won't be as much sentiment around for the BBC as it believes.'

To be honest, I had never noticed that there was any particular sentiment for the BBC in the upper levels of the Labour Party; they wanted to control it just as much as the Conservatives did. The only real difference was that under Margaret Thatcher the Conservatives gave the impression they were always thinking of tampering with the BBC's structure.

Over the years, British politicians and their acolytes have been allowed to get away far too much with the habit of picking up the phone to the broadcasters as though they own them, and trying to frighten them. It's known in the trade as 'heavy breathing', and it is successful far too often; which is of course why they do it. All too often the person at the other end tries to be conciliatory, to explain that the offence wasn't intended, to promise that everyone would be more careful next time.

The mere fact of replying like that encourages the politicos to do it again. Sometimes, perhaps, a genuine mistake has been made; but in my experience that is relatively rare as an excuse for a 'heavy breathing' call. The parties most dislike it when their people have done badly in an interview, and they choose to blame the broadcasters for this. Apologizing to such people is like paying Danegeld: a thoroughly bad form of currency, especially for broadcasters.

Nowadays a new gladiator has turned up in this particular arena. I rather liked Tony Blair's press spokesman, Alistair Campbell, when I was at Westminster: he was one of the freer-thinking political correspondents. Perhaps, like me, his time at Westminster left him less than starry-eyed about the nature of the lobby. He says what he thinks, without worrying too much about the feelings of those he talks to. (Tony Blair said recently, 'Most press secretaries go round after their prime minister has been rude to someone and soothe them by saying "Don't worry, the prime minister didn't really mean it. He likes you, you know." I have to go round saying, "Don't worry, my press secretary didn't really mean it." ')

But Alistair Campbell is a man with an agenda. He wants government ministers to look and sound good on air, regardless of whether they *are* good. When interviewers of the quality of Jeremy Paxman and John Humphrys are questioning them, they don't always shine. The Paxman style of interviewing is something that can only exist on British television. He is a national asset, and someone the BBC can and should feel great pride and confidence in. Of course Alistair Campbell and all his equivalents in British politics dislike him: he is the scourge of sloppy policy-making and muddle-headed ministers. And of course he is feared by all those who have a vested interest in tame interviews and tame broadcasting.

« »

One morning John Humphrys had just walked out of the studio at the end of the *Today* programme, and picked up the phone which was ringing on a nearby desk. He listened for a while to some threatening character from one of the parties.

'Thanks for that,' he said when the phone went quiet, 'and I wonder if I could make an observation?'

'Yes, of course.'

'Eff off.'

And he put the phone down.

In many ways my complaint is less against the robustness of the politicos and more against the feebleness of the broadcasters. There is no reason on earth why, in a free society, people like Alistair Campbell shouldn't try to put pressure on the broadcasters.

But equally there is no reason why the broadcasters should pay the slightest attention, except in cases where they have broadcast something which is false or tendentious. In that case they should be forced to put it right as soon as possible. There should only be one answer to the bully, the blackmailer and the heavy breather: *le mot de Cambronne*, or in this case *le mot de John Humphrys*.

The 1992 election was altogether nastier than either those in 1987 (which, on the Conservative side, was equally badly planned) and in 1997. As for me, branded an enemy, I found that some of the creepier newspaper journalists were so unpleasant to me in order to please the Party minders that I started travelling with the photographers and television cameramen. They were so much more fun, and so much less politically committed, that I started enjoying myself again.

Not all the Conservatives were hostile. On the contrary, the higher up the scale one went, the more pleasant and relaxed they became. Sir Norman Fowler, John Major's close ally, was remarkably consoling.

'I was on *The Times* in the days when it was really independent,' he said. 'Politicians often don't understand the concept.'

They certainly didn't seem to in April 1992.

'There you are, bright-eyed and bushy-tailed,' said the warm-up man at one of John Major's rallies. 'I can always tell a Conservative at a hundred yards.'

He was rather bushy-tailed himself, clasping his hands together like an American preacher about to pounce. The audience sat round him in a circle, and he was the ring-master.

'Who on earth is this?' I asked one of the Conservative spin-doctors, as we waited for John Major to make his big entrance.

'Bill Roache from *Coronation Street*,' he answered, and there was wariness in his voice.

'Not the one who sued some newspaper for calling him the most boring man in the world, and won a packet?'

'I'm sure you'll report that fully,' he said nastily.

At that moment the music blared out and John Major's features appeared on a bank of huge television screens at the end of the tent. But the way the man had spoken remained in my mind. Where had I heard that complaining, insinuating tone before? John and Norma Major made their big entrance, Purcell broke out like an electronic coronation anthem, and it came back to me. Of course: Dr Sa'ad.

Dr Sa'ad was the television censor in Baghdad, and my least favourite government official there; which is saying something.

'Always you are putting in unpleasant things, Mr John,' he would say. 'I know you, and I know your ways.'

He also thought he understood English better than he did. My words on the soundtrack were minutely examined for hidden meanings.

'You said "the President's palace", because you are trying to imply that he owns it himself,' Dr Sa'ad once announced in triumph, as though he had caught me out at last. 'You should say "the presidential palace", because it belongs to Iraq.'

He smiled, full of his own cleverness. Useless to argue that the point was ludicrously far-fetched, that no British audience would spot such a distinction. It is very boring to have to deal with people who think you have a hidden agenda and that they know what it is.

It was no part of my job to be snide or destructive about John Major's campaign, so I didn't mention the fact that the warm-up man had been called boring. But if the prime minister of the day was conducting a boring campaign, that was certainly relevant. His television advisers had created a campaign which emphasized the very qualities which seemed to diminish him most: the mildness, the uninspired speaking style, the pen-in-the-top-pocket concern with detail.

On Wednesday 25 March John Major was in Scotland, and we flew up there with him. It was a pleasant trip for me: the playwright David Hare was writing an election diary for the *Guardian*, and I enjoyed his company greatly. I knew, though, that I had to be careful: everything I said was likely to be taken down and used in evidence against me. We settled into our plane at the end of the day, and I was starting to write up my notes, when someone came down the aisle of the aircraft and settled beside me; and a familiar voice spoke.

'Is my campaign as bad as you say?'

I was appalled. David Hare was sitting right in front of me with a notebook, and here was the prime minister looking to me for help. I neither wanted to give ammunition to the one, nor to be rude to the other.

Hare's version, published later in the year in his book *Asking Around*, managed to leave out the key passage.

```
John Major moves behind me to talk to John Simpson, and
I suddenly realize he is asking him for professional
advice. Scraps of their conversation drift across to me.

Simpson: . . . not sure about your campaign . . . not sure
you're showing yourself to best advantage . . .

Major: No, I agree, I agree.

Simpson: . . . all seems a bit pointless . . . ways in which
you could be better presented . . .

Major: I know. I know. What do you think I should do?
```

I spluttered a bit when he asked me that. It would all look dreadful in the *Guardian*, and I could hear David Hare's pencil scribbling away. It wasn't my job to give advice to politicians, I said.

'But what is it you want?'

'I don't want anything,' I said, irritated. 'But if you're asking what makes good television, I can tell you: it always looks better to see politicians with real people, not just with the believers.'

'All right, I'll do it. You wait and see.'

He walked back to the front of the plane. I looked round at David Hare.

'Got all that,' he said, grinning.

He didn't print my disclaimers, all the same.

The following Saturday we were in a particularly depressing shopping centre in Luton: the kind of place where it always seems to be raining. We were there early, and so were the Socialist Workers' Party, ready to give him a hard time. (How did they always know where he was going to be?) His blue campaign coach nosed through the narrow streets and came to a halt beside us. Major stayed on board, talking to his officials. Someone else got off and opened the luggage hatch. He pulled something out.

'Whatever's that?'

'You'll see.'

It was a wooden construction of some kind. John Major got out of the coach, and someone handed him a megaphone.

'He's going to get on a soap box,' said a photographer beside me, in an awed kind of voice. He could see himself getting a picture in the paper at last.

When was the last time anything like this had happened? No one could think. It felt like watching Gladstone's Midlothian campaign.

'Major, Major, Major, Out, Out, Out,' chanted the Socialist Workers; but the cheering and clapping seemed slightly louder.

Now Major began to orate. Something came over him, some distant memory of being a Young Conservative in the sixties, perhaps, and he grew louder and more confident, and his voice started to drown out the shouting. There was no actual violence, though somehow the unworthy thought came to mind that if he took a bottle on the head and a trickle of blood were to run decorously down those mild features, it would be worth at least ten marginals to him.

The *enragés* refused to cooperate. A steward wiped yolk out of his eye, but nothing hit the man on the soap box; and apart from the eggs the only things that flew were balled-up election leaflets.

Of course, the sight of chanting, egg-throwing lefties did wonders for John Major's standing.

'No one's going to keep me away from the people,' he proclaimed in his harsh, much imitated, amplified voice, as though anyone was trying to. 'We're going to win this election, we're going to go on winning it, we're going to have a clear majority.'

'Major in, in, in,' chanted his supporters; but everyone seemed a little shocked at seeing the prime minister perched on a soap box like a militant vegetarian or an opponent of Ayatollah Khomeini.

There was a voice at my elbow.

'You're just a tool of the Tory government, telling people no one got killed in all that bombing in Iraq. And then you got your reward, didn't you?'

He was a thin-faced, Cassius-like figure in an anorak with lank dark hair and a badge that said 'Robin Hood was a Socialist: Vote Labour.'

'You did it all just for a medal on a ribbon. They didn't even have to pay you.'

The words were hostile but the tone was light and ironic, and instead of walking away angrily I stayed and talked to him, his brother and his friend, all SWP members. There was a jaunty air to them, as though Dickens had foreseen Trotskyists and written them into

Sketches By Boz. They loathed Neil Kinnock, they said, but they loathed Tories even more; so they wanted people to vote Labour.

I gave them my line on the Gulf War, then said there was one big difference between them and me: I didn't believe that any political theology, from Thatcherism to Trotskyism via social democracy could have all the answers all the time to all our national problems.

'Wrong,' said Cassius, fingering the lapel of my overcoat; 'there's two differences between us. I'm skint and you're not.'

It was a good exit line, and he shook my hand with warmth and a touch of self-congratulation. I saw him later on, waving his clenched fist at John Major. He winked when I caught his eye.

As for Major, he found the whole experience stimulating and enjoyable. He was sweating slightly as he got down from his box, and the rain had speckled his glasses.

'So is that the kind of thing you wanted?' he asked me.

I started to say that what I wanted didn't come into it, but then I thought it was ungracious to lecture someone who had taken a big risk with his own position in order to put a bit of life into a dead campaign.

'It'll look good on television, certainly,' I said. And it did.

'You're going to see a lot more of that. I'm going to do it my way. Until 9 April, wherever I go this soap box is coming with me.'

In hoc signo vinces became his motto, and he went on to win the election. Perhaps it was because of the soap-box. Perhaps it was for reasons which were more complex and had to do with the inbuilt British preference for things to stay as they are rather than to change. Perhaps the opinion polls, which were uniformly bad for Major, failed to distinguish between people who really intended to vote Labour and people who only pretended they were going to because they were embarrassed to say they were voting Conservative. It scarcely matters. And yet it was a bad election for John Major to win, even though at the time it seemed to be a sensational personal success for him and his soap box.

The only organ in the entire British press which called the election correctly was the *Spectator*. The editor, Dominic Lawson, headlined the article I wrote for him about the final stage of the campaign 'The Curious Confidence of Mr Major', and the magazine therefore seemed to suggest that the Conservatives would pull off a surprise win. This was partly to do with a dense comparison I made in the article between John Major's election and one in an Anthony Trollope novel.

'I'm not quite sure who you're saying will win,' Lawson said when he'd read it.

'That's good.'

I had not the slightest idea myself, though it seemed likely to me that Labour would. Yet I felt that John Major's own apparent certainty was worth mentioning. As for the analogy with Trollope, it was so complex that I couldn't understand it myself. When the result started to become clear on Friday morning, the *Spectator* looked better and better as it sat on the newsagents' shelves, surrounded by newspapers and magazines forecasting a Labour win.

« »

I loved working for the *Spec*. My connection with it began in October 1989, when I was trying to sell an article about a *Panorama* documentary I had done on Afghanistan. I had written for various American newspapers and magazines in the past, but my connection with the British press was fairly tenuous. Hawking the Afghanistan article around was a painful and humiliating business. One editor at the *Independent* was openly rude. If, he said, they wanted something about Afghanistan (which they didn't, particularly) they would get it from their own correspondents; and the implication was that it would probably be a great deal better. The British press has come to depend heavily on television as a source of news and features, but it doesn't like it. I thought I would have one last try. I rang the *Spectator*.

Dominic Lawson, who was just about to take over as editor, had the reputation of being aloof and cerebral. I found him very different: funny and warm, and remarkably indulgent to someone who was by then in his mid-forties and anxious to break away from being just another television performer. I suffered from the delusion that I was a writer who happened to work for television, and Dominic indulged me in this. Perhaps in a way we were two of a kind, though he was a dozen years my junior: loners, with a determination to shine.

My article on Afghanistan was printed on 7 October 1989. After that, as events in Eastern Europe developed, I wrote more and more. Not many people seemed to go to the weird and often nasty places my BBC work took me to, and television offers you insights and opportunities that other journalists rarely enjoy. You can't stay in your hotel room making phone calls if you work for television: you have to go and see things for yourself.

The *Spectator* valued that. After I went to Iraq in the aftermath of Farzad Bazoft's execution (Dominic headlined my article about Saddam Hussein and an excursion I took to the ancient capital 'The Hanging Guardian of Babylon') I was invited to write on a regular basis for the magazine. By the time Saddam invaded Kuwait in August 1990, I was a frequent attender at the weekly editorial meetings. Soon Dominic made me an associate editor.

As Lenin said, everything comes down to the questions 'Who, whom? We or they?' Inside an organization like the BBC you either control your own life or others control it for you; and I had always wanted a degree of independence from the BBC. Three years earlier, in 1987, I had done what no senior figure in news had managed before, and convinced the management to allow me to go onto an annual contract, instead of being an established member of the staff. It meant more money, and less job security; and both were extremely good for me.

I felt liberated: for the first time in my career I was my own man. It was particularly important to me, because of something which had happened to me in the early 1980s. *Private Eye* had printed a nasty little story about me which was entirely untrue, but the BBC refused to let me write a refutation of it. My boss agreed that the story was false as far as I was concerned, but pointed out that it was true about another BBC correspondent who was mentioned in it. And since he wouldn't be able to write a letter defending himself, any letter from me would only make his silence all the more obvious. That was all there was to it: my interests were sacrificed for the greater good of the Corporation. I felt angry and baffled, and determined to get myself into a position where nothing like this could ever happen to me again.

Now I had managed it. I was a free agent, and working for the *Spectator* made my liberty plain for everyone to see. Thursday, the day of the *Spec*'s weekly meeting, quickly became my favourite day of the week. I would travel to Holborn by tube, then stroll down Grays Inn Road looking in the shops and relishing my freedom. At John Street, which changes its name halfway down and becomes Doughty Street, I would turn off, perhaps meeting some fellow *Spectator* writer on the way. Dickens had lived in Doughty Street, and his house was a museum which I would go into whenever I had the time. But Number 56 came first, and Number 56 was the *Spectator*'s office: a handsome five-storeyed house of sombre brick, where the executives and editors of the late eighteenth century would have lived, together with their large families and servants.

The door opened at the press of a bell and a faint intercom squawk. In the room at the front were a group of rather intimidatingly good-looking and intelligent women, who ran the *Spectator*'s day-to-day business. I would say my good mornings, hang my coat in the room to the rear, where the literary editor, Mark Amory, worked, and take a copy of the brand new issue from a pile on a desk. On the stairs, or if necessary in the lavatory on the first landing, I would flick through the magazine to see what use had been made of my latest article. It always seemed to me to show an unbecoming self-interest to turn to one's own work at the editorial meeting itself.

It was important not to be late. The editor's office, if large for the drawing-room of an eighteenth century town-house, didn't contain enough chair-space for the dozen or so people who crammed in for the first part of the meeting, and it was often necessary to sit on the floor. Even the chairs that did exist tended to be faulty in some way: some had springs that stuck painfully into your bottom, others encouraged you to lean back and then gave way altogether. One only had three effective legs, and needed particularly careful balance.

A fresco of the *Spectator*'s previous office decorated one wall, and the mantelpiece carried some impressive invitations to the editor, and a row of books which had once been review copies. There was one of mine among them, and this always seemed to me to be a good omen; though I had to check it out every time I turned up, just to make sure I was still in good standing.

The plaster rose in the centre of the ceiling troubled me most. From it hung a particularly heavy chandelier; and a deep crack ran around part of the rose. I would look at the crack in meeting after meeting, and it seemed to me to grow, centimetre by centimetre. Perhaps, though, I imagined it; I never could work it out.

We went through the magazine page by page. Sometimes Dominic, sitting behind a desk the size of a small fortress, would say he couldn't understand a particular cartoon and Michael Heath, the cartoon editor, would defend it. Being fond of Heath (as well as of the sound of my own voice) I would usually agree with him. The magazine looked, I used to think, splendid on its coated white paper and with a series of gorgeous advertisements which were often more like illustrations than mere sales pitches.

After the various editors of the magazine's sections had gone through their lists of subjects for the following week there would be a general exodus. Just a few of us – four or five, perhaps – would be left: effectively the editorial team. No one doubted, though, where the real power lay. Dominic Lawson's chief asset as editor, I used to think, was his delight in stirring things up. He certainly had clear-cut opinions: he was a confirmed Tory, of the kind for whom Conservatism is simply a natural instinct and everything else seems ludicrous or false. He disliked Germany, suspected France, and thought America faintly absurd. As for the European Union, he regarded it as profoundly unnatural.

Nevertheless he liked controversy more than he liked the replication of his own opinions. He knew that I was mildly favourable to the EU, that I loved France, that I supported the Commonwealth, and that I was fiercely defensive of the BBC; and he allowed me to rave on about all these subjects in ways that annoyed and sometimes enraged many of the *Spectator's* more ideologically Conservative readers.

Yet the success of his editorship, which was very considerable in terms of sales, depended on winning readers from a much wider range of opinion. Gradually all sorts of people who were neither Europhobes, nor country gentry (would-be or genuine), and certainly not Thatcherites, started reading the magazine because its opinions were lively and varied and because it was controversial. The *Spectator* played a significant part in the destruction of John Major, which worried me from time to time in case I was allowing myself to become too identified with a particular political viewpoint; and yet we carried many articles which supported him as well.

Above all, the editorial meetings themselves were remarkably friendly, amusing, and non-ideological. Simon Heffer, the deputy editor, was a noted right-winger whose support for Thatcherism had always been strong and effective; yet he and I had been on close and friendly terms ever since we had travelled round Africa together, reporting on one of Mrs Thatcher's wider-ranging trips. He was witty and sharp-minded and remarkably objective, and we hit it off immediately. There was a certain Englishness which we had in common, and a dislike of dogma.

I had to be careful about possible conflicts of loyalty. Sometimes the BBC would be pursuing some particular exclusive story, and I would have to keep quiet about it at the *Spectator*; and vice versa. And I always had to remember that although I was among friends personally in the upstairs room at 56 Doughty Street, the BBC wasn't. The *Spectator* wasn't an instinctive supporter of the BBC: on the contrary; yet in my years there it backed the BBC on several important occasions, and the BBC responded by advertising in it.

I only got into trouble with the BBC on two occasions: once when I said I had given up wearing my flak-jacket in Sarajevo because I was embarrassed to walk among the people in the streets who had no such protection against shells and snipers' bullets, and once when I said the NATO bombing of Serbian positions round Sarajevo made me feel good. That, said one of my bosses, demonstrated a little too clearly whose side I was on; and he was quite right to complain.

It was superbly useful to me to have another outlet. When the tabloid press spent four days and nights camped outside my ex-wife Diane's flat in February 1991, besieging her and trying to get her to say something unpleasant about me in the wake of my Gulf War experiences (she refused, but someone in Fleet Street twisted something from her anyway, by ringing her up to commiserate with her on the way the tabloids had treated her and claiming to be the friend of a friend, then printing her responses), it was good to be able to hit back at them in the pages of the *Spectator*.

When the Conservative Party put such pressure on me during John Major's election campaign, I was able to retaliate by writing about it for the *Spec*. I felt altogether more formidable and independent as a result; and when my face appeared, huge and bleary, on advertising hoardings to say that my work for the *Spectator* gave me greater freedom, it might have been embarrassing but it was certainly correct.

Writing did something else for me, I found: it cauterized whatever emotional wounds I suffered in my travels. When friends of mine were killed, when I watched a public hanging or the judicial chopping off of a right hand, writing about it exorcized the ghosts. Once these experiences were honestly set down on paper and the article was faxed to London, that was effectively the end of it. I would continue to feel sorrow or pity, but the memories no longer seemed to inflame the layers of my subconscious mind like a kind of mental cellulitis.

Working for the *Spectator* was like belonging to a club. I knew and liked almost everyone there, and was greeted as though I was a full member. In an existence like mine ('A wandering and disconnected life', as Thackeray calls it in *Barry Lyndon*) it was a tremendous pleasure to feel I had roots somewhere. And I soon created little secondary rituals around my Thursday morning *Spec* experience, wandering off afterwards to the area round the British Museum and buying a book or two in the antiquarian shops, then lunching pleasurably by myself in one of the Chinese *dim sum* restaurants in Gerrard Street or Rupert Street. At times like that, life seemed to be very good indeed.

It came to an end of course, as it was always bound to do. Dominic Lawson was promoted to the editorship of the *Sunday Telegraph* in 1995, and he offered me a weekly column in the foreign news pages. This meant real money, after the £100 cheques from the *Spectator*, and it meant staying with him. Anyway, I wasn't asked to stay at the *Spectator*; my face no longer fitted.

The *Sunday Telegraph*, for which I still write, offers much more scope and is seen by more people; but I have only been to its editorial offices at Canary Wharf a couple of times, and I feel shy and in the way. And there are no antiquarian bookshops there to browse in afterwards. Life is busier, more demanding and more profitable as a result of switching from the *Spectator*, but I can't say it's necessarily more enjoyable.

« »

Working for the *Spectator* lured me into all sorts of situations I could have avoided if I had merely been working for the BBC; especially when I first went to Bosnia in December 1992. I thought I would try a tactic which had worked well in the past: the night walk. I had taken long walks after dark in Tehran, Baghdad and other weird places, and written about them for the *Guardian* and *Harper's* magazine in New York. Why not Sarajevo as well? I could walk back one night from the television station where we satellited our material to the Holiday Inn where we stayed. A lot of people tried to persuade me it was a bad idea, and I almost came to agree with them; but I had promised it to Dominic by now, and felt I had to go through with it.

I was in a world of utter darkness, loneliness and cold, and it was clear to me directly the glass door of the shattered building swung laxly closed behind me that I had made a terrible mistake. There was no sound except for the grumbling of artillery on Mount Igman and Zuć Hill, a few miles away, and no light except for occasional distant magnesium flares, which gave a blueish tinge to the skyline, like the fingernails of a corpse. The besieged city was dead, and sprawled around me abandoned. Not a window glowed in the huge blocks of flats which lay along the line of the main avenue. No street lamp was left standing. The snow itself barely glimmered in the darkness.

My colleagues had headed off in our armoured vehicle, having failed to persuade me to come with them. The cameraman had even volunteered to walk with me, but I had explained that these things had to be done alone. At that stage I had still felt good about the whole thing. Now that I was alone, I didn't.

I made my way carefully down the broken front steps of the television station. This place had taken a lot of hits, and every step was difficult. I remembered where the invisible chain ran at shin-height, and stepped over it. I was in the main street. I had only seen it before from the safety of a vehicle.

Under Tito this had been named The Boulevard of something empty and pompous, but now the journalists called it Sniper Alley. Every intersection along its course was dangerous, and in the daytime those who couldn't avoid crossing did the nervous, stuttering dash for which the journalists also had a name: the Sarajevo shuffle. The snipers were holed up in buildings which lay 100 yards or so back from the southern side of Sniper Alley – the right-hand side, as I walked in the direction of the ludicrously named Holiday Inn.

Within thirty seconds the cold had worked its way through my protective clothing. Protective in a double sense: I had put on the whole armour of Messrs Tetranike, complete with the latest in ceramic plates to the chest and back. It bound my ribs and stomach like a Victorian corset. Usually I hated it. Not now; it gave me warmth, and the feeling that even if something struck me I might live. I especially didn't want to die in this loneliness and dark.

'A scrimmage in a Border Station—' I quoted to myself uncomfortably from Kipling.

> A canter down some dark defile—:
> Two thousand pounds of education
> Drops to a ten-rupee *jezail*.

A Kalashnikov rifle cost rather more than that in Sarajevo, but the principle was the same. Today's equivalents of the *jezail* were trained on every crossing along this road. A car passed at speed. It raced across the intersection which I would soon reach myself, but I couldn't tell if anyone had fired at it. There was the crack of a bullet, certainly, but the echo from the vast, smashed, empty buildings of Tito's dream deflected the sound confusingly. Yet the buildings weren't entirely empty after all. As I ground on, my boots crushing the polyhedrons of plate glass that lay everywhere, I saw a window just above my head which was lit by a candle, dark gold in the darkness. Inside there was a repeated quiet, dry coughing, like an animal rustling in fallen leaves: the sound of the last inhabitant of a dead city.

Who killed Sarajevo, I mused as I left the little flicker of life behind me. Slobodan Milosević, the President of Serbia, whose ambitious, angry nationalism had broken up the Yugoslav Federation in 1991 and led to three ferocious wars of liberation, complete with the horrors of ethnic cleansing? Radovan Karadžić, the ludicrous Bosnian Serb leader, with his mane of greying hair and the psychiatrist's diploma on his office wall? Ratko Mladić, the psychopath who could have been his patient but was his military commander instead, playing him off against Milosević? The predominantly Muslim government of Bosnia, decent enough in its way, which had insisted on holding a referendum on independence and had given the Bosnian Serbs the excuse they needed to attack? Tito, who had bottled up the vicious nationalistic passions of a century and insisted that nothing but Yugoslavism existed? The Germans, who unwisely recognized the independence of their friends the Croats and so helped to spark off the fighting? The United Nations, which ought to have imposed its moral authority on the city, but seemed to have none to impose? Britain and France, united only in their determination to avoid getting involved in a shooting war? The United States, which liked to criticize everyone else but refused to stir from its own sloth?

It doesn't really matter, I thought, as I headed towards the first sniper intersection; but people in a state of advanced despair need someone to blame, and most of the candidates were too vague or too distant to qualify. Only the United Nations, driving round the streets in the daytime in its large white vehicles, was on hand for everyone to see and revile. There was no sign of them now.

It was hard to work out in the utter darkness whether the dark patches on the faint lightness of snow were holes in the ground or pieces of debris. I launched out into the roadway: no point in hanging around. My armour hung heavily on my back, and the extra clothes I was wearing slowed me down. I broke into a shambling run, but found my feet entangled with a thick steel cable: the tramwires had been felled here by a mortar. I tried to imagine a sniper following my Sarajevo shuffle across the open intersection with his night-sight. Would he pause to speculate why someone should be out this late? Or, as I swam through the night-sight's greenish haze, would he squeeze the trigger directly I reached the crosshairs?

I waited for the terrible, shattering blow to my right side, and then I reached the pavement. It seemed like safety. But it wasn't. As I came to a line of burned and looted shops, the tatters of their curtains stirring in the icy wind, and remembered from the daytime the charred frames of desks and chairs lying inside, there was the vindictive crack of a high-velocity rifle close by: perhaps even from the vast empty block of ruined flats opposite. Something slammed into the concrete above my head, and I ran along, bent double, until there was another crack and another hammer-blow even closer to me. Two thousand pounds of education sprawled on the ground, defenceless before the *jezail*. Someone in the cold and darkness knew I was there.

Time passed. Another car drove frantically down the boulevard, its lights switched off, and no one fired at it. Had the sniper gone off duty, or grown bored? Or was he just playing with me? I moved a little: no response. I got to my knees, stood up, and began walking again. Nothing except distant artillery and the upward rush of rockets a mile away. In a minute or so I was alongside the white wall which marked the museum dedicated to Tito's largely fictive socialist revolution.

The building was burned and empty, of course, and someone had written 'Bad Boys' and 'Devil Rapers' on the walls with spray-paint.

In a city gone mad with violence, it was a little touch of verbal violence to add to it all. I knew where I was now. The Holiday Inn loomed up ahead, a mere boulevard-width away, a few of its windows showing faint brownish lights. Everyone knew the journalists lived here, and everyone hoped the Serbs wouldn't target us deliberately. My canter down the dark defile was over.

« »

I spent quite a lot of time in Sarajevo during the war, but it took me a long time to get there. Martin Bell had established himself as our resident correspondent in the former Yugoslavia, and he had done the job so assiduously that it was very hard indeed for me to set foot in the area. So I spent my time doing other things – travelling to the Amazon, for instance – while the ugly little wars between Serbia, Slovenia, Croatia and Bosnia erupted.

Christmas 1992, though, was my opportunity. I always rather enjoy working over Christmas and the New Year. The audience for the news bulletins is huge, and as they sit digesting their turkey and Christmas pudding everyone else feels distinctly guilty as they watch you reporting from some unpleasant place. On the strength of a month there, I would spend January in the West Indies and no one would even question it.

On the morning of the 25th the crew and I drove into Sarajevo in a fleet of aid lorries manned by a group of volunteers, unemployed drivers from my own county of Suffolk. It was a terrible and frightening drive: smashed tanks, wrecked cars, burned and ruined houses. It wasn't the most damaged city I had seen, but it was the most miserable. The lorries were bringing flour to the last bakery operating in Sarajevo, though what the bakers really needed was fuel. The Bosnian Serbs who were besieging the city had put a block on that, and for the time being there was no way of running the big ovens. We filmed the last loaf of bread coming off the conveyor-belt; then we filmed the bakery closing down.

We were picked up in an armoured Land-Rover which the BBC had brought into Sarajevo, and drove to the only hotel which was still operating. The Holiday Inn was a hideous construction of concrete and yellow plastic facing which stood at the end of the motorway leading to the older part of the city. It had been hit many times by shells and mortars, and the upper floors were closed. So were the rooms at the front, which looked out at the Jewish cemetery a few hundred yards away on the hillside opposite. The Jewish cemetery marked the Bosnian Serb front line.

We parked behind the hotel, to be out of sniper-view, and worked our way nervously round the outside. Most of the big plate-glass windows on the ground floor had been smashed and covered with thin clear plastic. We found a convenient hole in the glass and stepped inside. Inside, the hotel was dark and very cold. It had been built in 'atrium' style, so that there was a large open space bigger than the Centre Court at Wimbledon. The upper floors had been walled with glass, sheets of which fell whenever the hotel was hit. The reception staff huddled in a little room on the edge of the foyer around a stove which ran on bottled gas. They wore overcoats and gloves. Our rooms were on the fourth floors: the others, lower down, had all been taken.

There were four of us: myself, Vera Kordić our producer, Eddie Stephens the sound recordist, and a redoubtable South African of gigantic proportions, Nigel Bateson, who sported a red beard as large as any worn by the Bosnian Serb soldiers besieging the city. They were to prove excellent company over the next few difficult weeks.

We weren't made to feel particularly welcome. The resident journalists were a strange combination. There were a few stars here – Christiane Amanpour from CNN and John Burns from the *New York Times*, for instance – but the rest of them were mostly young and adventurous tyros who had come here early on because it was dangerous, and had been offered jobs by famous organizations who couldn't get anyone else to go there. The correspondent of *Le Monde* was one of them.

Another Frenchman was famous for a series of distinctly studied antics, which included abseiling down the atrium from the top floor. He drove around in non-armoured cars with signs painted on them: 'We who are about to die salute you' and 'You can't hit me, I'm immortal'. Eventually a sniper shot him in the arm, and he left. I would have preferred any number of English poseurs with panama hats and shooting-sticks to this kind of self-regarding stuff. He, for his part, called people like us 'tourists', and had a considerable contempt for people who merely came in and out. That I could understand rather better.

In normal times my room would have been unremarkable. Here it was memorably dreadful. For a start, the temperature inside it was indistinguishable from the temperature outside; and that, within a day or so, had dropped to minus nineteen degrees centigrade. The windows had long since been knocked out, so there was nothing between the curtains and the outside world except a single thin sheet of clear plastic. There was no electricity, and no water of any kind, hot or cold. Sometimes, at two or three in the morning, some public-spirited character would run along the dark corridors banging on the doors and shouting that the water was on. That way you could collect enough to flush the lavatory and perhaps even to wash in.

After I had been there for two or three weeks I had collected enough water to fill the bath, and then I borrowed an incredibly dangerous element, powered by a small generator, and lowered it into the water. After half an hour the water was close to boiling, and I eventually took the risk of undressing – something one did with the utmost reluctance here – and lowered myself into it for a few won-derful, agonizing minutes. Outside, meanwhile, the artillery banged away intermittently.

For days on end I would simply wear the same things. That first night it was so cold that I only took off my boots and quilted jacket before creeping into my state-of-the-art sleeping bag, covering myself with three blankets, putting on my gloves and tying a scarf around my head like an old woman going to market. And even then it was so cold that sleep took a long time coming. Guns rumbled and chattered not far from the hotel, but I didn't bother to creep out of my refuge to look through the window.

During the night of Sunday, 27 December, thirty hours after we had arrived, the first snow of the winter fell. The city lost what little colour it still had. A sky as grey as a dirty handkerchief hung over the patchy white of fields and parks from which the trees had long been stripped for firewood. The misery grew much worse. Thanks to the United Nations, no one was starving. No one, that is, that you heard about. Anything could be happening behind the broken windows and tattered curtains in the darkness of a thousand blocks of socialistic flats and Austro-Hungarian stuccoed buildings.

Life for most people in Sarajevo was so dreadful it was hard to understand how they could remain law-abiding and relatively decent to one another. A university professor I knew kept himself and his wife alive by burning his books; and he offered some to a neighbour to help him. Yet in this Hobbesian existence people didn't savage each other for scraps of food, they behaved as if there were still rules which had to be obeyed. They presented themselves at distribution centres where the UN food was parcelled out, and accepted their inadequate ration without complaint; even though the Bosnian government bureaucrats skimmed off large quantities for their own families' use.

As we ventured out into the streets, strapped up like Michelin men in our flak-jackets, we found that for most people the worst thing wasn't so much the privation as the risk of sudden death. The city was running out of space for graves faster than it was running out of everything else.

'Stop filming!' screamed a podgy-faced young man in an absurd woollen hat, as Nigel panned across a line of shivering people queuing at one of the few water-pumps in the old city centre, outside a disused brewery. The young man believed that the Bosnian Serbs would watch our pictures and know where to aim in order to cause maximum casualties; as though they couldn't see us perfectly well through binoculars from their positions on the hillsides overlooking the city. It was interesting to see how difficult it was for people to come to terms with the idea that the violence here was utterly random. There had to be a pattern, even to the suffering. The mind shies away from the contemplation of meaningless chance.

I got rid of him and looked at the raw red noses, the chapped purple hands, the broken-down shoes slithering on the ice which had formed everywhere the water-pump had splashed. There were old Muslim women in ankle-length skirts and scarves round their heads like the one I wore at night, and once-attractive young women in expensive fur coats and dark glasses. Unlike the distribution of food, which seemed to be a matter of who you knew and how much you could pay, water was something everyone had to queue for. There was no rationing here. Some people had turned up with a dozen large plastic containers, others with little more than a couple of old wine bottles or a finely shaped Turkish vase.

A peasant woman in her late forties could only carry a couple of small orange-juice containers the two miles back to her home. Her heart was bad, she said. She moved off slowly, planting her feet deliberately on the ice. Her husband was dead, her mother had died of her wounds after being shot by a sniper. What kind of soldiers, I wondered, shot old women and forced those with weak hearts to carry unreasonable burdens?

The answer, I found as I came to know the city better, was that they all did. On the morning of the first snow the crew and I went to an old people's home not far from the airport. The building lay on the Serbs' front line, and the Bosnian government line was very close at this point. It was extremely difficult to get there. We drove in the armoured vehicle, our bullet-proof helmets as well as flak-jackets on, along a narrow lane blocked off with wooden screens which hid us from the Bosnian government snipers. There was a more urgent crack of gunfire here, and a Serbian tank was parked as neatly in the hedgerow as a suburban car, its gun pointing at positions only two hundred yards away.

The old people's home had once been rather good. Two hundred and fifty patients, most of them from the old Yugoslav *haute bourgeoisie*, had been looked after here by a staff of a hundred doctors, nurses and domestics. Now the place was badly smashed. There were bullet holes in virtually all the windows, and large portions of the building had been rendered uninhabitable by shell-fire.

A UN armoured personnel carrier stood outside, and a couple of French soldiers were chopping wood. They were careful not to move beyond the shelter of the APC. Bosnian government snipers occupied a wrecked building only thirty yards away. The smell of the pea soup which the French had brought for the inhabitants of the home lay heavy on the air. Yet food wasn't the main problem; cold and the fear of bullets was. There weren't enough stoves, or fuel, or blankets, or clean sheets. Above all, there weren't enough staff. There were still 120 old people in the home, though over the previous four nights eight of them had died of cold, and only six out of the staff of 100 had remained to look after them. Their courage and decency were extraordinary.

One was a burly Serb woman, jolly and hard-working, with a distinct moustache. She and her colleague, a tiny bird-like Muslim, were overwhelmed by the work of looking after dozens of incontinent, bedridden patients. They could only heat one room per floor, and everyone who could walk there huddled inside. The rest stayed in bed, and they were slowly dying. How dreadful, I thought as I looked at one old woman, breathing harshly, slipping out of consciousness, that the last sound on earth that she might have heard was the crack of a bullet.

An alarming old character with hollow cheeks and staring blue eyes lifted himself out of bed as we came in and chanted 'Good morning! *Bonjour! Buon giorno!*' He was ninety-four, he said, and declared proudly that he had been born and raised in Sarajevo, had lived there all his life, and would now die there. He had, I reflected, been sixteen at the time the Archduke Franz Ferdinand was assassinated as he drove through the city. The concrete footsteps with which the Serbs had proudly commemorated the killer's position had only recently been ripped up by an angry crowd of Bosnian Muslims; but Gavrilo Princip, in firing his epoch-making shots from there as the imperial car crossed a little hump-backed bridge, had effectively created the modern world.

The wars his action precipitated were to kill at least a hundred million lives in one way or another, and led directly to the establishment of Marxism-Leninism and Nazism as dominant ideologies. Even this nasty little siege in Sarajevo was a distant ripple of the shots fired by Princip; and an old man who remembered the moment when it happened was waiting to die of cold and exposure as a result.

Outside, we found the French soldiers had gone. One of the few patients from the home who was still fit, an old man in his late seventies, was finishing the job of chopping the wood they had left. We interviewed him.

Transcript of report on 9.40 News, 27.12.92

JS: Without his efforts, there will be no heating for the old people's home for the rest of the day and tonight.

Old man: I like to do it. I'm the only one left here who can do it now. They need me.

An hour or so after we left, while the old man was still chopping wood, a sniper from the Bosnian government forces shot him from their position only thirty yards away. The bullet entered his head exactly between the eyes: a copybook killing. There can have been no mistake about it, no thought that he might have been a Serb soldier.

The longer I spent in Sarajevo, the more I decided that the proper distinction was not the kind of constitutional right and wrong which I had heard from my colleague Noel Malcolm at the *Spectator*, nor the instinctive pro-Bosnian and anti-Serb position which so many Western journalists took. It was the difference between people who had power and people who didn't.

I found it a shock to discover that Sarajevo had no water or power because the Bosnian government wouldn't let the UN repair the electricity sub-stations just outside the city. There were various tactical reasons behind this, not least that the repaired sub-stations would also supply power to a Bosnian Serb weapons factory. Why, the argument went, should we help our enemies make more shells and bullets which they will fire at us?

But there was more to it than that. The Bosnian government, lacking the military strength of the Serbs, regarded international opinion as their chief weapon. The more the Western press based in the Holiday Inn reported on the savage horrors of the war, the more likely the Americans, British and French would be to intervene on their side. It wasn't therefore in the interest of President Alia Izetbegović, or his Vice-President, Eyup Ganić, or his prime minister Haris Siladzić, to ease the sufferings of their fellow-citizens. On the contrary: those sufferings might just be the key to victory.

Such reflections weren't welcome at the Holiday Inn. The prevailing mood among the Western journalists was profoundly partisan. If you share the sufferings of a city under siege you instinctively side with the people in it; that's natural enough. But what many of the journalists based there did, and it has to be remembered that many of them were young and inexperienced, was to line up with the government rather than with the people.

Much of the reporting from Sarajevo was openly one-sided. By this stage many of the journalists who turned up for the morning briefings at UN headquarters regarded the UN virtually as an enemy. The Americans in particular vied with each other to attack the hapless spokesmen who had to deal with them. The UN's announcements about the way in which the Bosnian government was obstructing its efforts to man the electricity sub-stations were scarcely reported in the Western press. Nor was the announcement that UN troops had discovered a group of Serb prisoners who had been held by Bosnian government forces in a large sewage pipe for several weeks, and fed once a day by having food thrown in to them in the darkness and excrement.

Worse atrocities were carried out by Serbs against Muslims, but those were faithfully reported. There were no awards for showing that this was a conflict in which the victims of aggression could sometimes behave as badly as the aggressors themselves. This was what came to be known as 'the journalism of attachment'; a self-congratulatory phrase which meant journalism which took sides and was therefore impossible to trust.

Those of us who didn't join the claque were much criticized. I overheard one of the local translators hired by the BBC telling someone else that I was pro-Serb; not a good thing to be in Sarajevo at that time. In fact I was very far from being pro-Serb. It was perfectly clear to me that it was the Bosnian Serbs, with the support of their puppet-master Slobodan Milosević, the President of the rump Yugoslav Feder-ation, who were guilty of the war crimes we saw enacted in front of us. The Bosnian Serbs were unquestionably the aggressors, and the Bosnian government and its people were equally unquestionably the victims: unprepared for war, peaceable, non-sectarian.

Although the government became increasingly Muslim, and some-times fiercely so, it still had the support of Croats and Serbs who lived in the city. There were no witch-hunts. I came to know an elderly Serb woman who was taken in by a Muslim family because she had nowhere else to live. Sometimes, after their area had been shelled, the Serb woman would get a phone call. It would come from her son, who was manning one of the guns on the mountainside and wanted to make sure she was all right. The old woman's Muslim hosts never blamed her for what was happening.

Towards the end of the siege the French UN forces, who specialized in counter-sniping, made the extraordinary discovery that some of the sniping was carried out by Bosnian government forces, who were firing at their own citizens; perhaps in order to make sure the Serbs got the blame. This was scarcely reported at all in the Western press. Maybe the editors found it inconceivable, and assumed that the French report must have been part of some elaborate propaganda play by the UN. Yet when I reviewed the findings of the French team, they seemed clear enough; and of course there was the example of the patient at the old people's home on the front line.

There was more. In 1994 I made a film for *Panorama* about General Sir Michael Rose, who commanded the UN forces in the city. On 18 September there was the worst outbreak of violence that year: the Bosnian forces were firing mortars at the Serb troops on the hills, and the Serbs were responding. Mortars, of course, can be quickly set up and fired, and then moved on. But the British UN forces had an instrument which could pin-point the firing base-plate of a mortar with total precision, and they found that the Bosnian mortars had been set up beside the main hospital, the government buildings, and Rose's own headquarters.

Transcript of *Panorama*, 28.1.95

Speakers: General Sir Michael Rose, John Simpson

MR: By demonstrating who was firing and from where people were firing we were able to go down and see President Izetbegović and explain to him the consequences of what his army were doing: and of course one doesn't say that President Izetbegović had anything to do with this strategy, but he looked sufficiently concerned to stop the firing immediately.

JS: What was the purpose of firing out of the city like that?

MR: One can only suppose it was to try to create images of war which would help some political purpose.

JS: But the idea was to get the Serbs to fire back?

MR: I guess that would have been one of the purposes of opening fire, yes.

The fact was, Izetbegović was going to New York the next day to address the UN and ask for help. If the American television network news had been full of pictures of damage to a hospital and to government and UN buildings, that would have done his cause nothing but good. He, or his military commanders, had no problem with encouraging the enemy to fire on a hospital.

So does this mean the Bosnian government forces were also responsible for the single worst action of the siege: the firing of the mortar shell which landed in the market place in Sarajevo in February 1994 and killed sixty-six people? It certainly happened at a superbly useful moment for the Bosnian government: the United States was just considering whether to bomb Serbian positions for the first time, and the market-place massacre made it an inevitability.

I arrived in Sarajevo that night, and saw the crater the bomb had made. It was still full of blood. The market place was a relatively small affair, with forty or fifty stalls of wood and tubular steel. They sold food and clothes and small gadgets, and it was usually crowded because it was the one place where you could get fresh foodstuffs from outside the city. The television pictures of the bombing were terrible to look at: a mortar bomb, landing in a crowd of people, can do dreadful damage. The Bosnian Serbs, watching the pictures, did nothing to help their cause by claiming that the bodies which were carried away were really tailors' dummies.

But the final evidence of responsibility is lacking. Although the science of 'craterology' had grown up in Sarajevo among the UN forces, it was fairly inexact. The crater for the market-place mortar looked like a sunburst, with rays of almost equal length. The bomb had landed straight down, rather than at an angle, so there was no clear indication which direction it had come from. On the one hand the Serbs were constantly firing at the city anyway, and maybe this was just another shell. On the other hand, it is clear the Bosnian government was capable of carrying out attacks on its own people in order to further its political position.

The American television teams who poured into Sarajevo to cover the aftermath of the attack seemed to have no conception of any of this. For them it was the simplest of moral issues: so simple that one of the big networks instructed its part-time correspondent in Sarajevo not to use the expression 'Bosnian Serb', because the viewers were confused by the idea that someone could be a Bosnian and a Serb at the same time, and then went on to instruct him not to mention the Croats at all because no one could envisage a war that had three participants, rather than the normal ration.

In other words, they wanted a different kind of war: one where the issues were clear-cut, and there was a direct confrontation between good and evil. Any suggestion that this particular war might be a little more complicated than that was swiftly buried. A senior ABC producer who came over from New York discussed it with me for a while over lunch at the Holiday Inn, but he clearly thought I was just another Chamberlainite stooge, anxious to appease today's Nazis. The fact is, I had no problems about people who sided with the Bosnian government against the Bosnian Serbs. That seemed perfectly reasonable. I just didn't like it when they tried to pretend that one side was uniquely guilty while the other was uniquely innocent.

Salman Rushdie once said cuttingly that people with a religious sense had 'a God-shaped hole in their lives'. One of the strangest coalitions of modern times seemed to have a crusade-shaped hole in their lives, and Bosnia was cut and shaped to fit it. In the United States and Britain, right-wing conservatives like Lady Thatcher joined with traditional, liberals, and plutocrats like George Soros in condemning the feebleness of the Europeans and their appeasement of the Bosnian Serbs. The war was fought out at a time when the Nazi Holocaust was much in people's minds, and the Muslims of Bosnia seemed to equal the Jews of Europe. At a foreign affairs conference in 1994 I questioned the Nazi-Serb/Jew-Muslim analogy and was accused by the head of a leading Los Angeles radio station first of being an appeaser, then of being pro-Nazi, and finally of being anti-Semitic.

The UN was despicably feeble in its approach to the Bosnian Serb checkpoints around the city. It stopped trying to get fuel to Sarajevo in the middle of winter, merely because the Bosnian Serbs didn't like it. That, unquestionably, was appeasement. But to take the argument further, as the head of the Los Angeles radio station did, and say that the UN should stop feeding the people of Sarajevo because this was simply fattening them up for genocide, seemed ludicrous, and in the end was proven clearly wrong.

Yet it was British television which gave a powerful impetus to the idea that the Bosnian war was the present-day Holocaust. By some clever planning a team from ITN managed to get to the camps run by the Bosnian Serbs at Omarska and Trnopolje in August 1992. The pictures were quite unforgettable: barbed wire, skeletal figures. It could have been Dachau. The pictures went round the world, and ABC television ran them in full on their nightly news.

Somehow along the way, though, the reservations of the ITN team which had filmed them were ignored. The ITN team was careful not to make the analogy with Nazi concentration camps. Others did. The skeletal figures weren't inside the barbed wire, for instance, they were *outside* it. The wire was old and ran round a small enclosure. The cameraman got behind the wire to film the scene. There was a serious food shortage, and everyone went hungry at that time; but the most skeletal of all the prisoners, Fikrit Alić, was just as thin weeks after his release. The ITN team's reporting was accurate; but the pictures seemed to speak for themselves. They caused a sensation in the United States.

Second-rate journalism is a herd activity. Editors want from their reporters what other editors are getting from theirs. The hunt was on in Bosnia for Nazi-style atrocities, and several reporters won major awards for revealing them, even though their sources were afterwards questioned. Atrocities certainly took place, and more were carried out by the Bosnian Serbs than by anyone else. But a climate was created in which it became very hard to understand what was really going on, because everything came to be seen through the filter of the Holocaust.

And so we had stories about extermination centres and mass rape camps, as though the Bosnian Serbs were capable of a Germanic level of organization. They were believed, and as a direct result the Bosnian crisis began to monopolize the foreign policy of the major Western powers. When Rwanda exploded in mass murder in 1994, and far more people died in a genuine campaign of genocide, the Western powers scarcely did anything about it. They were still much too tied up with Bosnia, thanks in considerable part to the journalism of the herd.

I reported on the former Yugoslavia for three years, but I didn't enjoy it. To be honest, I didn't like the place at all. There was too much extremism, too much hatred, too much cruelty. I liked many individuals, but found each of the population groups – Serbs, Croats and Muslims – equally unattractive. The Serbs, overall, were the least lovable, but I found the international media's demonization of them outrageous. It was an enormous relief to read the words of my friend and colleague, Nik Gowing of BBC World:

> Some of the strongly anti-Serb reporting in Bosnia is the secret shame of journalism. There is a cancer now which is affecting journalism: it is the unspoken issue of partiality and bias in foreign reporting.

I am not alone, I thought when I read that.

There were no good guys. The abandonment of the Muslims of Srbrenica to the murderous General Mladić by the Dutch contingent of the UN was one of the most shameful incidents of my lifetime. The Ukrainian contingent sold their petrol and guns to the locals and were incapable of going on patrol. The Egyptians sometimes behaved with considerable cowardice. The French were involved in heavy-duty black-marketeering. The British, though by far the best soldiers, played a minimal part in it all. The Clinton administration, with the dreadful Madeleine Albright as its cheer-leader, blamed everybody else but did nothing because it suspected its army wasn't up to the job. When I think back to those days, it is with a sense of dull dislike.

One freezing Sarajevo evening my colleagues and I arrived at the television station to find a large, impressive-looking man in his sixties sitting hunched up and miserable, with a man beside him clutching a small video camera. Behind them on the wall someone had written 'Is that a torch in your pocket, or are you just glad to be in Sarajevo?' The impressive-looking man, who didn't look at all glad to be in Sarajevo, introduced himself.

'Marcel Ophuls,' he said. I knew him, of course. *The Sorrow And The Pity,* his account of French complicity in the Holocaust, was one of the best and most moving films I had ever seen. He was in Sarajevo to make a film about the siege, and the way it was reported. I offered him every assistance I could.

I enjoyed his company greatly over the next week or so. As we sat in the Holiday Inn dining room, eating the watery soup, the nameless tiny piece of meat and the rice, and finishing up with the inevitable match-box-sized piece of coconut and chocolate cake, we exchanged memories of old films and I listened to his reminiscences of Truffaut and of his father, Max Ophuls, and we tried to guess each other's quotations.

' "I ain't sayin' this steak's tough," ' I ventured, sticking my fork into the grey meatlike substance on my plate and holding it up, ' "I'm just sayin' I ain't seen that old horse around lately." '

'W.C. Fields,' Ophuls called out before I'd finished, and did an impersonation of Mae West in *My Little Chickadee*. We were all suffering from the most disgusting colds, which came complete with mouth-sores, so too much laughter was difficult. The waiters, some of the true heroes of the siege, looked on amused in their white jackets and black bow ties while Marcel and his cameraman filmed us and the other journalists at play.

At the end we all left together. On our way to the airport Marcel and I argued endlessly about the situation.

'It's Munich all over again,' said the harsh, combative voice with its interwoven accents of Germany, France and the United States, 'and you pretend you can't see it.'

'Bullshit,' I answered, lurching against the armour-plating as we took the turn into Sniper's Alley too fast. I had been expounding the view that a sensible government doesn't involve itself in an open-ended war unless its own security is directly threatened. 'Your trouble,' I continued, 'is that you think everything is a re-run of Munich. You only ever make films about the Holocaust,' I added nastily.

He sat there and thought about that for a bit. *The Sorrow And The Pity* and *Hotel Terminus* (about Klaus Barbie) were probably the two best documentary films made during the 1970s and 1980s.

'So what if I do only make films about the Holocaust? Not that I accept that I do, of course. I'm a Jew. To me it's the most important thing that ever happened. And, yes, I think it has lessons now.'

The Land Rover lurched on. My camera crew had long since stopped listening to our conversations. I pointed out the dangers of chiliasm: if you are always seeing Armageddon and the imminent arrival of the Emperor of the Last Days, you are likely to end up like Eden over Suez or Lyndon Johnson over Vietnam: you lose your sense of proportion and get in over your head.

'I see no need for a sense of proportion where evil is concerned,' Ophuls answered stiffly.

By now, though, I was thinking about something else. We had decided to make our way to the airport on our own, for quickness' sake. It was risky. If we had gone with a UN escort we would have had no trouble at the big Serbian checkpoint on the road to the airport, but the UN was unreliable and we hadn't wanted to wait.

All sorts of unpleasant things happened at this checkpoint: equipment was stolen, money was confiscated. Only a week before, as we came through here, a Serb officer with a pitted, primitive face had found my wallet with a great deal of BBC money in it, and had accused me of planning to buy weapons for the Muslims. He had hefted the wallet appreciatively in his hand, and his soldiers had grinned wolfishly, anticipating their share of the loot.

'You have my word of honour that this money is only for my own use,' I said.

'To me you are nothing,' he answered.

'Tell him,' I had said to our translator, Vera, 'that we are going to see Dr Radovan Karadžić, and I will give him a careful description of the way we have been treated here.'

It had worked, of course, just as it did on the Jomhuriya Bridge in Baghdad. With creeps like that it always does. The wallet was handed back, apologies were made, the pitted face split into an ingratiating smile. A dirty hand was raised to cap-level in an approximation of a salute, and we were waved deferentially on our way.

This particular checkpoint caused the city of Sarajevo to run out of drinking-water that summer, because it wouldn't allow the UN to bring oil for the pumping-station through. I had thought the previous winter that things had reached an unsurpassable depth of misery; but in the pleasant warmth of summer there was a new fear which was, if anything, worse than the cold and hunger. You could sense the fear people felt about not having enough to drink. Their – our – mouths cracked with dryness, and everybody smelled bad. Interviewing people became a burden, because their breath stank; and in our armoured vehicles we tried to keep apart from each other as much as possible. Once again the hotel was noisome; I was reminded of the Al-Rashid, where you could tell which rooms were occupied.

The checkpoint on the airport road was responsible for all this. It had no right to be there, according to the agreement the Serbs had with the UN, but the UN allowed it to continue because if the Serbs were antagonized it would be harder than ever to bring food and medicines into the city. This was weakness, and the Serbs recognized it as such.

The UN policed the siege in other ways for the Serbs, stopping people leaving the city, forcibly turning back those they caught trying to escape, preventing private individuals from bringing in food supplies.

'But this is collaboration of the kind I dealt with in *The Sorrow And The Pity*, Ophuls said, and recalled all those busy, conscientious Vichy policemen rounding up Jews and resisters.

Now we were getting close to the checkpoint. We were all nervous as we headed down the desolate, much attacked road to the airport, past the wrecked tanks and the shot-up, abandoned containers. If the Serbs chose to stop us and search us now, they could take our gear and Marcel's films from us. It happened often. We approached the bend in the road where the Serbs had protected the post with a big earthen bank.

If only, I thought, the UN had had the guts to fire a couple of tank rounds here on the day the Serbs had set up the post, how much easier things would have been for the people of Sarajevo. We drove through the chicane and saw the post ahead of us. It was empty. The soldiers who manned it hadn't even bothered to turn up, even though it was 8.30 in the morning. We clapped and shouted in our relief as we drove through at speed.

'No one tests these things,' said Marcel Ophuls. 'Everyone accepts the front these bastards put up.' He snorted. 'And you say it isn't like Munich.'

We picked up speed along the empty airport road. In a couple of hours a UN flight would take us out of all this, and we would be somewhere comfortable and decent: at best Italy, at worst Croatia. Either way there would be real food. There would even be hot water.

« »

Early one morning in 1993 we headed off to see the man who was primarily responsible for causing so much misery. The Bosnian Serbs' headquarters was a small skiing village on the outskirts of Sarajevo. During the Winter Olympics a few years earlier, Pale had been one of the main centres, and various identikit hotels were built there in a style that was half Communist and half Alpine. That made it just about suitable as the capital of a statelet as small as Republika Srpska. The hotels and boarding-houses became departments of state. It always reminded me of one of those model towns in Denmark or Sweden, where adults and children wander around, towering over the knee-high buildings.

But Pale was quiet, and there were no serious shortages of anything there.

'What are they doing to my lovely Sarajevo?' asked a dark, fierce-featured young woman.

She was President Radovan Karadžić's daughter, and one had to be careful about offending her. Still, there were limits.

'When you say "they", who exactly do you mean?'

'The Muslims, of course. They're always shelling their own people. You've been there; didn't you realize that's what they did?'

Our translator looked at me and gave the faintest shake of the head. I took the point.

'No, I hadn't heard that,' I said.

Her father came bustling into the room: a big man with hair like a badger, and a jacket with sleeves that came down to his knuckles. His fingers were badly gnawed from nervousness. Great for a consultant psychiatrist, I thought: like going to a doctor with eczema.

He was noisy and rather impersonally jolly, like a pub landlord, and he seemed to expect, like his daughter, that I would agree with him on everything. He was clearly not very bright, nor obviously evil. (His military commander, Ratko Mladić, seemed by contrast to be a monster of ferocity and anger; a strong, stocky little man with a thick neck. I once saw him reach up, grab a Sky News correspondent round the throat and force him up on tiptoe.)

I assume that Karadžić managed to live with himself by blocking off the reality of what he was doing. Like his daughter, he regarded everything as the fault of the other side. If the Muslims hadn't done this or that, his forces wouldn't have been obliged to respond. 'They started it'; it was like being in the schoolroom again.

Transcript of interview with Dr Radovan Karadžić, 8.1.93

JS: Conditions in Sarajevo are increasingly bad now. Why do you treat innocent civilians as the legitimate targets of war?

RK: But we don't, you understand. Our Serbian communities inside and outside the city are under constant attack by the Muslims, and we have to defend them. That is what we are doing.

JS: But how is firing mortars and sniping and cutting off their food and fuel and water supplies defending the Serbs?

RK: We have to respond to their attacks. Our people
are dying and being injured every day, and the
international community does nothing to help them.
We have to help ourselves.

JS: And what about the Serbs who live in Sarajevo and
support the government there?

RK: They are not acting as true Serbs.

JS: So they become legitimate targets too?

RK: If the Muslims attack us, we must defend ourselves.

The argument could go on in this circular fashion indefinitely.

Outside, against the background of the snowy hillside, I bumped into Karadžić's deputy, a small, silver-haired, tubby little man called Nikola Koljević. He had been a Shakespearean scholar at Sarajevo University, and beamed with a curious pleasantness. Tags from Shakespeare peppered his conversation, though I used to feel they were mildly misquoted. I was never able to check them, unless they were on tape.

Interview with Nikola Koljević, 8.1.93

NK: We are surrounded by enemies, and it is necessary for
us to keep our own counsel. As your great national poet
William Shakespeare says in his tragedy of *Macbeth*,
'Love, obedience and honour and groups of friends/
We cannot expect to have.'

I found it impossible to fathom how someone who had spent his life studying the works of the most humane writer who ever lived could support so inhumane a cause. People said it was because his son had been killed, apparently by Muslims; until that time he had been a gentle enough academic, but his character had been changed by the incident. Perhaps it was true. Yet even as he mouthed the verbal defences of the Bosnian Serbs, about being the innocent victims of Muslim aggression, something else seems to have been working away inside him. Eventually, when the siege of Sarajevo was in its final stages, his internal battle reached a climax and he shot himself.

'What they're doing is wrong, and they know it,' said Marcel

Ophuls; and perhaps it was this knowledge that made Koljević put a bullet in his brain.

« »

Being surrounded by so much suffering does different things to different people. There were those who took advantage of it, like the Spanish UN officer who sold passes which would allow people to leave the city: he demanded money and sexual favours in return. There were those who ignored it altogether. Others, like the Reuters people, collected money and clothes for an orphanage. John Burns of the *New York Times* spent a part of every day trying to help a range of individual people; even though he was recovering from cancer.

One morning, as we were driving through Sarajevo in our armoured vehicle, I started talking to Vera Kordić, our fixer and translator, about ways of showing the misery of ordinary people.

'Why don't we just ask any of these?' she said, pointing at the lines of harassed women waiting for water.

But I felt we needed to be inside someone's house, to see how they lived from day to day. We walked along a street, with the crack of a sniper's rifle not far away.

'Someone lives there,' said Vera.

It was a small doorway with a dark little window on either side of it: a miserable, humble place. We knocked at the door, and eventually an old woman clutching her worn dressing-gown to her came to the door. She agreed to let us in.

She lived in a single room. It was cold, but the fug of living and cooking filled the place. It took some time to get used to it.

A candle burned by her bedside. She spent most of the day in bed: it kept her warmer, and used up fewer calories. The food she was given by the UN was just enough to keep her going. One of her neighbours, a Muslim, had helped for a time, but that had stopped. Maybe it was because she herself was a Serb; maybe the neighbour had been killed.

She had a small stove, and a covered bucket was her lavatory. There was no water: she had to queue up for that, if her neighbour couldn't spare any. A few keepsakes from her past decorated the place, and a little tapestry of a young girl hung on the wall. The woman was sallow and not very clean, and her grey hair was greasy. Most people in Sarajevo lived without washing: water was too valuable to waste, and soap non-existent. In the background shells landed from time to time, and there was the crack of the sniper's rifle. The old woman flinched in fear each time there was an explosion. Sometimes, if it were close, the whole place shook. A little dust drifted down from the ceiling.

She was ashamed of the way she lived, and ashamed that we should see it; but Vera, who could charm almost anyone into doing almost anything, persuaded her that this was the only way people outside Sarajevo could understand what it was like to live there. And by the time we started to interview her, she was willing to tell us all about her life. It poured out of her.

Transcript of interview with woman in Sarajevo, 14.1.93

I was a nurse in a hospital, a trained nurse. I wasn't always poor like you see me now. I had people under me. But I am alone in the world, you see. My neighbours, they were Muslims, were very good to me even though I am Serbian. 'We must help each other,' they said, and they helped me. But now they don't. Maybe they are dead, I don't know. So many people have died here.

[Sound of shell explosion, not far away]

I am so frightened when I hear these noises, I don't know what to do. I am old, you see, and completely alone. No one cares about me. I have no family, no husband, no children. I am alone in the world. And I am very frightened.

We gave her everything we could possibly spare, of course: money, medicine, food. She wept again, and gave us a few little keepsakes: things from her old life, before the siege. I kissed her hand as we left.

Every time I went to Sarajevo after that we would take her things, and see how she was. Perhaps it made her feel a little better. But the real effect was on us. To do anything for anyone in this horror certainly made us feel a little better; and also perhaps a little less guilty that we could get out of Sarajevo any time we wanted, and leave the victims of the siege to the mercy of the guns and the shortages.

16

Forest Magic

I BALANCED ON the three-legged leather chair with the loose spring in the seat, and tried to work out if the crack in the ceiling were spreading. Dominic Lawson was sitting at his desk, reading a letter. The weekly editorial meeting was over, and the others were filing out, chatting and making arrangements for lunch. I waited for them to go, while Dominic scribbled something.

'I'm off to the Amazon on Monday,' I ventured.

It felt good to say the words so off-handedly. This, I thought, is what I exist to do: to tell editors I am leaving for impossibly romantic places.

'Tell me more.'

I told him more: I had been reading up. I told him that despite the rape of the forest, eighty per cent of it, approximately the size of the Indian sub-continent, was untouched by man. I told him how the Amazon had once been an oceanic gulf opening westwards into the Pacific, and how, a hundred million years ago, the rise of the Andes had cut it off and turned it into an inland sea which eventually broke through its eastern escarpment into the Atlantic. I told him how, as a result, sea-creatures such as sting-rays, electric eels and dolphins now swam in the fresh water of the Amazon and its vast tributaries.

I told him that there were 250 species of tree per hectare, 300 species of frog, 1600 species of bird, 3000 species of fish, and uncounted millions of species of insect. I told him that the Mebengokre tribe could classify and treat more than fifty distinct types of diarrhoea. I told him of the pit viper, the most dangerous snake in the forest, which could sense the presence of its prey by detecting differences as slight as 0.003 degrees Centigrade between their body temperature and the surrounding atmosphere. I told him of the *candirus* fish, which had an unpleasant tendency to swim up into the penis or vagina and lodge there, putting out barbs to stop itself being extracted.

When I had finished I sat quietly, embarrassed at my volubility and unsure whether I had interested or revolted him. Dominic is a product of civilization; wildness and savagery have little interest for him, except within the ranks of the Conservative Party.

'Spare us no detail,' he said at last, and I knew he was hooked. 'In particular about the insects. And the willy-fish.'

'The *candirus*?'

'*Spectator* readers will prefer "willy-fish".'

I was going to spend some weeks in the Amazon before going on to the Earth Summit of 1992 in Rio de Janeiro; and I didn't know how close my acquaintance with such things was going to be.

From a thousand feet, the forest was a dark green sea, and the waves in it were the stippled tops of uncountable trees. There wasn't a break in any direction: nowhere to glide down and land. Ours was the lightest of planes with only one engine, on which all our lives depended. Florindo the pilot, large and sweaty, had been telling us cheerfully that of the four pilots who had started with him a decade earlier, three had crashed and the other was an alcoholic who was expected to go at any moment. I looked down. The sea below us wasn't the kind you swim in.

Overhead were enormous bunched yellow and grey and white clouds, which carried the moisture which the sun's heat had drawn up from the trees then dropped it back again as rain. There was a storm to our left. Water poured down from the sky, and the sun shone through it and made a rainbow which you felt would be hard and supple and shiny like snakeskin, if only you could reach out and run your hand over it.

Now we were slowly descending, and I could see individual trees: they weren't exclusively green now, but pink and red and yellow as well. They reseeded themselves over a wide area instead of bunching together, so that no individual species can be wiped out by disease or insects. When the Brazilian government chopped down a section of the forest as large as a small country and replanted it exclusively with eucalyptus (i.e. 'something useful') the new trees were almost all dead within four years. Disease had run through them like fire.

Florindo pointed. A wide yellow-brown river parted the trees, looking ugly and inhospitable. It would be our home for the next couple of weeks. It was too late to worry now, but I was distinctly nervous that I wouldn't be able to match up to the ordeal that lay ahead of us: the heat, the insects, the willy-fish, sleeping outdoors in a hammock, catching one of fifty distinct types of diarrhoea or dysentry, hostile indians. I expected to be miserable; in fact it was the most memorable episode of my entire life.

(I spell the word 'indian' without a capital letter intentionally, by the way. Ever since Columbus, out by a matter of 8,800 miles, landed in the New World and thought he had hit India, the world has followed his mistake. I suppose I should call the aboriginal inhabitants of Amazonia 'indigenous people', which means exactly the same as 'natives' but is more politically correct. It's too much of a mouthful, though. If I call them 'indians' but write it in lower-case, it will be a reminder that it's easy but not quite right.)

We made a bumpy landing along a grassy patch cut out of the forest. A group of almost naked indians stood and smiled at us, and the doctor who was to be our guide ran forward to shake hands. I hadn't expected a young, attractive woman. Maria turned out to be from a wealthy family on the Atlantic coast, who had decided to give everything up and work here. The heat was overpowering, even at nine in the morning. All round us was the noise of flesh being slapped: I had been warned about the *pium*, the tiny midges which brought up great welts with their stings.

Three of us were going with Maria on this trip: my companions were Alex, the local field officer for Health Unlimited, the small medical charity of which I was a patron, and Mike, a freelance photographer who was doubling as a cameraman for me. The *pium* hung round our heads in a small, painful, private cloud: and not just ours as newcomers but the indians' as well. Each of these detestable little insects was the size of an inverted comma on a printed page, so everywhere we went we seemed to be in quotation marks, like clumsy jokes. I had my own cloud, like the rest, but they didn't sting me. Perhaps it was the roll-on insect repellent I used, but it might just have been the way I smelled. The others found my immunity mildly annoying.

Maria's mother, hot but indefinably glamorous with her golden earrings, was sitting in the cedarwood *fazenda* where they lived, fanning Maria's baby. Mother and daughter were both so badly bitten by the *pium* that their feet seemed to be tattooed. The house was stripped of everything: doors, windows, furniture. Only a few hammocks swung in the breeze. Butterflies the size of my opened hands showed flashes of yellow or orange like petticoats, and a bird with a wonderfully liquid warbling cry spent most of the day in the nearby banana trees.

Ants and cockroaches the size of household pets tramped the floor, but in our hammocks our only enemies were flying ones. It was too hot to do anything, even to slap yourself. The others showed me how to drape my mosquito-net – not in fact a net at all, but a sheet with holes too fine for the *pium*, or the air, to penetrate – over my hammock, turning into a narrow, white, coffin-shaped tent with a distinct sag in the middle. They also taught me to lie across the hammock, rather than down its length, so that I kept the structure taut and avoided an aching back. A pair of earplugs kept out the snores and night-noises. I lay entirely naked in the privacy of my tent, sweating copiously, and fell asleep at around ten. By three I was wakened by the chill: the temperature must have dropped by twenty degrees. I covered myself up and slept till dawn.

First light is a magical time in the Amazon. The air was pure and slightly chilly, great cobwebs jewelled with dew hung like necklaces in the long grass, and parrots flew over the *fazenda* scolding as they went. Our boat, a long dug-out canoe with an outboard engine, was waiting for us. It took a lot of stowing and shouting and disagreeing for our indian boatmen to get everything ready, and we didn't finally leave until 8.30, shouting and waving to Maria's mother and the baby and the half-dozen others who lived there.

On the river our speed made it cooler, and the *pium* and every other irritating insect were blown away. The river must have been a hundred yards wide, and the colour of a milky coffee from the BBC canteen. Dozens of trees, which had fallen into the water and been swept along until they hit submerged sandbanks, stuck their bare heads out like gigantic water-snakes, ugly and threatening and sometimes nodding grimly in the current. The water itself was warm, but I didn't trail my hand in it: it was full of sting-rays, electric eels and *piranhas*, not to mention the other 2,997 species of Amazonian fish. And for all I knew the *candirus* could find its way into my penis by climbing up my arm.

I felt extraordinarily ignorant as our telegraph-pole of a boat, three feet wide and eighteen feet long, powered its way through the warm river water. What were the huge black birds which wheeled overhead? Or the small black and white ones with red legs which picked their way across the sandbanks with an air of disapproval? Or the great red and brown dragonflies which buzzed us like helicopters? It's an important comfort, in the welter of the natural world, to be able to differentiate things, to tell them apart, to understand their separateness; so that when I asked the indians in the boat the names of the trees we passed, and they could tell me, it gave me real satisfaction.

Those with brilliant scarlet blossoms were called *mulugu*, they said, while the ones with gloriously grooved red naked trunks and broad shiny leaves were *boulateras*. Our boat was made from the *jacareube* tree, *jacare* being the word for cayman, little alligator-like creatures a few feet long which sunned themselves on the sandbanks. The *taboca* tree, looking a little like a large bamboo plant, was used for making the wooden barbs for war- and hunting-arrows, because it splits easily into extremely sharp splinters and is slightly absorbent, so that it can be coated with poison.

Occasionally as we went along the river we saw another type of tree, the largest in the forest, with delicate over-arching leaves and silver bark on its veined trunks. This was the *samauma*, and when the village shamans die the indians believe they go and live in its branches like monkeys. Sometimes you could see the monkeys who might be the souls of the shamans, larking and shrieking from tree to tree. There must have been many other animals too, but most of them kept quiet and hid when they heard our outboard motor roaring in the silence of the river. We scarcely saw anything except birds and insects. Now a hover-fly, as bright as a kingfisher and not much smaller, came and sat in the air in front of my face and stared at me before swooping off.

At a village along the river bank the chief's grandfather, a man of ninety, dressed in a T-shirt and shorts which were in the last stages of decay, was making a hat with feathers. He had a few terrible dark brown teeth like worn and broken rocks, and an amused expression. Once he had been one of the great killers of white people, in the days when the indians clashed with the rubber tappers in this area. He reminded me of an elderly friend of mine in London: his habit of holding his chin, and looking sideways at you were exactly the same. Perhaps he was sizing us up for a poisoned arrow in the neck, for old times' sake.

The indians here belonged to the Kulina tribe; though they regard the name 'Kulina' as derogatory. Their own name for themselves is Shananawa, after a beautiful little song-bird which lives in the surrounding forest.

This was my first view of an indian village, and it was a disappointment. Everyone, like the great killer of white men, wore ragged T-shirts and shorts, even the women; though a few had streaks of red paint on their faces, which came from the berries of the *mulugu* trees we had seen. The children had cat's whiskers on their upper lips and noses. Mike and I had brought gifts to exchange with the indians – beads, knives, scissors, mirrors. I gave the ninety-year-old a pair of bright, sharp scissors: an unsuitable present in the circumstances. He had never seen such things before, but he quickly learned to use them to cut material and string. As we left he spoke to Maria, and gave her something for me. Our boat was in the middle of the river before she handed it over; it was a magnificent necklace made of the teeth of monkeys and caymans.

By now I was glorying in the rich strangeness of the river and the forest. When we stopped on a sand-bank to eat some dried peccary meat, extraordinary creatures paraded around us: a long-legged spider shaped like a star which leaped with tremendous speed and caught a fly with its two front legs, like a rugby threequarter making a tackle; large dark striped wasps which moved heavily and slowly out of their nest in the fork of a dead tree with the speed and noise of bombers; ants, of course, of many sizes and several colours; a tall, languid insect with thin elegant legs that looked like a mosquito but went everywhere on foot and had a bright red head; a sluglike vegetable which lay on the ground like a squashy green speckled snake, and crushed to mere juice if you trod on it.

Once, before the Europeans came, there were three million indians in Amazonia; now there are 50,000, in 130 tribes, divided into six main language groups: Tupi, Arawak, Cario, Je, Pano, and Xiriana. There are more caymans, and far more monkeys, than humans. In an area as large as Western Europe, there were only 7,000 people. Along this part of the river, still only a few days' journey by boat from a small town, the villages were about ten miles apart and the inhabitants had plenty of goods and clothes that came from what we would think of as civilization. As a result they seemed degenerate and ugly; but Maria kept my spirits up by telling me that much farther up the river there were people who had never seen white men or their goods. She called them the Ashaninca.

The Shananawa village of Igarape was in a glorious situation, high on the bluffs overlooking the river, but it seemed particularly depressing close to. Empty tortoise shells littered the approaches, and someone was carelessly slaughtering a beautiful blue macaw to eat. Maria had come here to see a five-year-old girl who was ill. She proved to have meningitis, and Maria had to take her back down the river to the *fazenda*, where the plane that brought us could take her to hospital in the town of Rio Branco, several hundred miles away.

As she left, the village shaman, a dark, stocky man with sharp eyes and only one thumb made an announcement.

'He's going to make *dime* to help the soul of the little girl,' Alex explained. *Dime*, it turned out, was a hallucinogenic drink, made from the stem of the *ayahuasca* vine and the leaves of the *chacrona* bush.

'What does this *dime* do to you?'

'The *ayahuasca* opens the door to knowledge, and the *chacrona* gives the voices.' As though that explained anything.

'I don't think I'll be having any,' I said.

'You'll upset them if you don't.'

They were little people, I thought as I looked round, but I had to spend the night here. And after seeing what had been done to the blue macaw, I didn't want to upset them.

The shaman was a sharp, alert little man who looked at least fifty. To learn his art he had had to wander the forest for five years, taught by another shaman, eating only a few specified plants and abstaining from any contact with other people. As I watched, he crushed the two ingredients together, and was simmering them in a large pot, big enough for the entire village: the resulting fluid was greenish-brown, and a disgusting green scum floated on top. Two young girls swept an open area in the middle of the village; a boy played them a delicate little tune, scarcely audible, on his mouth-bow. The sky turned a fiery orange, and a full moon edged up suddenly over the dense forest. Just as suddenly these people stopped seeming deracinated and ugly, and took on the full mystery of their past. By the light of a candle an old man was teaching a group of children nearby, and they were repeating words after him:

· *Mahe, mahu, mahe, mapam, maboru, mabore.*

The shaman carried the pot over to the area which the girls had swept clean, and set it down. The entire village gathered round, under a full moon which was bright enough to write by. I queued up with the others. There was only one cup, a big clay beaker, and the shaman blew into it with great concentration, and touched me with it first on the left shoulder, then on the right, then on the forehead. I took it from him with feigned gratitude and raised it. It tasted dreadful: bitter, gritty and lukewarm, with an aftertaste like the most heavily stewed tea British Rail ever made. There was no hope of taking a polite sip and handing the beaker over. In the moonlight they could all see exactly what you were doing. I drank three big gulps, but managed to leave a little at the bottom of the beaker.

I looked at my watch nervously. It was 8.35. The young girls were starting to dance, laughing and joking, their mooncast shadows sharp on the ground. I certainly didn't feel any effects. Mike was filming the dance, which five older men had now joined, and half a dozen more women, two with babies at their naked breasts. It was a charming scene, as they sang their gentle song:

> *Anoyn, anoyn, anoynday,*
> *Anoyn, aaaanoyn, anoynday,*
> *Anoynday.*

I went over to shine a torch on them so Mike could film them. Alex was lying on the ground in the moonlight, clearly in the grip of the drug. I could hear him crooning to himself and laughing. Mike, like me, felt no effects whatever. Eventually he stopped filming and took out his stills camera instead, and since I had nothing more to do I went and sat down near Alex, looking out onto the grand sweep of the river below in the copper light of the moon. I had my notebook with me, in case the drug had any effects which I could describe.

And then, at 9.20, it started. The first I knew, the gigantic golden full moon slammed right down from the sky and into my face, then shot back across into its proper position as though it was on a 249,000-mile spring. While I recovered from that, I started making notes. The writing got bigger and bigger, and makes increasingly silly reading.

> Starting to see shooting stars.
> Now my head is some distance from my body.
> I just banged my pen on the ground because I thought it was a beetle.
> I am making a strange face, and red light is coming from the pen as I write this.

> The light from Mike's flash gives hallucinogenic effect to the hopheads who are sitting in a row watching the dancing.
> Now stars and colours.
> My hands are very heavy. I'm also laughing stupidly.
> Alex is talking about people being bright, lit up with radium.
> The words are taking on all sorts of meaning, and more than merely sound.

> I'm finding it incredibly hard to get the pen onto the paper.

> The trees over there look like the winged figure by the gates of Babylon.
> And just then when I closed my eyes I saw a goldfish with glasses on.
> Yet I can speak perfectly normally and remember difficult words.

> My head weighs a lot.

> Halo round moon and an ENORMOUS cloud round it.

After that the writing becomes impossible to decipher. Reading it now, I am reminded of Thomas Huxley, who woke up in the night knowing that he had just dreamed the secret of the universe. He jotted it down in a notebook which he kept beside his bed for moments like this, and went back to sleep. In the morning he reached for it eagerly, wanting to know what the great revelation had been. He had written:

> Higamus hogamus,
> Woman is monogamous,
> Hogamus higamus,
> Man is polygamous.

With which in mind, we could probably have taken the girls back to our hammocks with us if we'd wanted: the Shananawa were very relaxed about sex, and the girls would probably have thought it was an interesting experience. But we were all too married, or embarrassed, or English, even though we were completely stoned, and the three of us wandered back alone to our hut, giggling and happy.

As I lay in my hammock, thinking over the experience and preparing for sleep, I could still hear the chanting of the Shananawa girls, the people of the song-bird, as they continued dancing in the moonlight. It was one of the most magical experiences of my life.

« »

There was a certain pleasant lassitude the following morning, but no other discernible after-effects. Mike and I went to film and photograph the rising sun, which shone as small as an orange through the mist and lit the dew on the grass. A young man sat roasting a monkey over a fire, while a pet toucan with an enormous blue beak hopped around, pecking at an abandoned root vegetable and squawking angrily when a passing peccary snatched it. It turned, its vast beak slightly open in comic disappointment, and watched the peccary crunching up the vegetable. Then it hopped disconsolately away.

I ate some monkey later, because I felt I had no choice. It was horribly like eating a baby, and its charred little arms and legs had the gamy favour of an old guinea-fowl. After a couple of bites for politeness' sake I concentrated on the flavourless, gritty manioc which accompanied it, and washed it down quickly with brackish river water. Fortunately I still had some Laphroaig in my hammock, and when I had the chance I slipped away and rinsed my mouth out with it. That got rid of the taste, but I couldn't quite forget the experience.

> It is reported that in the Alps thou didst eat strange meat
> Which some did die to look upon.

Now I knew the feeling.

Parrot tasted bland, fishy and slithery, like Kentucky Fried Chicken stripped of its breaded coating. I wouldn't have known what kind of bird it was if they hadn't told me. It seemed a serious waste, though I loved seeing the indians wearing collars of parrot feathers, and I knew perfectly well that the feathers didn't simply drop off the parrots in flight.

I ate a variety of things in the forest which are better forgotten. The tails of caymans I found particularly distasteful, the meat watery and white and inclined to slip down the throat in an insinuating kind of way. Tapir-meat tasted like fatty venison, peccary like pork-flavoured cardboard, tortoise like chamois leather. The worst thing I heard of in the Amazon, but fortunately never came across, was the intestinal worms from tortoises, which are squeezed out of the guts and cooked. The indians used everything the forest gave them, wasting nothing and regarding it all without prejudice. As Woody Allen said, nature is one big restaurant.

It was still cool. As I went back and lay in my hammock, I felt there were layers of sound in the air: the bird song, the insect sounds, the light voices of the Shananawa, the grunting of pigs, the clatter of cooking, and, to wind around them all and bind them up like a delicately-coloured thread, the faint sounds of a bamboo flute playing an intricate little tune that I could never quite catch.

By now we were getting beyond the range of the white man's influence. People from the agency for indian affairs, FUNAI, had been here before, but there were no rubber-tappers and no one was logging the valuable woods which the forest contains: mahogany and cedar, for instance. The people in the occasional villages needed nothing they couldn't produce themselves, except a little salt and maybe an axe-head or two.

Ahead of us the parrots screeched with anger and fear like the headlines of tabloid newspapers, terrified by the racket of our engine along the silent river. Turtles sunned themselves on the branches of trees which stuck out above the surface of the fast-running water. What lay behind the dark frontage of trees along the river-bank? It was like driving down a suburban street and wondering who lived behind the lace curtains. I stirred myself to record a piece to camera, which Mike filmed. I sat in the farthest point of the bows, took my hat off in the blazing sun – never, the television dictum goes, wear a hat of any kind

in a piece to camera – and spoke over the noise of the engine and the
hissing river water.

Transcript of report from Brazil, recorded 23.5.92

It's hard to give a sense of the vast scale of things here.
We're a good seven days' journey by motorboat from the
nearest small town, and the people here, who number
only around 7,000 altogether, cover an area the size of
Western Europe. Apart from them, it's uninhabited
by man.

By 5.30 that afternoon the sky was a deep cornelian red, small strips
of clouds lay banded across it, and the stars were coming out. As for
the water, it had lost its beverage colour; it was glistening and exciting
and silver-grey. Bats the size of small kites jerked across the surface,
snaffling up insects. Sometimes a hatchet fish flew out of the water like
a silver rocket and took a careless fly. The noise of insects and frogs
was beginning to rival the engine for noise. *Whence*, I asked myself in
Newton's words, *comes all this beauty and order in the world?*

It was almost midnight by the time we reached the bluffs where
the Ashaninca village lay. It was called Simpatia. Yesterday's full moon,
which had slammed into my face when I was under the influence of
the *dime*, had stayed in its place tonight. Now it lit up a strange group
of robed figures on the cliff-tops. It was like being greeted by Roman
senators. We stumbled up the steep path and were inspected by them.
They bowed jerkily to us, men and women wearing coarse brown tunics
called *cushmas* which reached below their knees. In the moonlight I
could see that their faces were heavily painted with red dye. One of
them offered us his hut: a few poles supporting a roof thatched with
reeds, and a floor of split cane which yielded pleasantly under our feet.

As we tied the ropes of our hammocks to a communal pole, a hairy
brownish-purple spider as big as my hand shot angrily along the wood
and vanished. I didn't care; after twelve hours sitting in an open boat
on the river I was too tired to worry about such trivial things as deadly
poisonous spiders. A mist had gathered, and in the beam of my torch
it seemed to be composed of whirling particles. The mist gave the
moon a double ring, and a moonbow lay on the bank of mist across
the river.

I woke at 5.45, just as the darkness was starting to crumble. A cockerel crowed, and I could hear the children of the village stirring. I slipped out into the cool grey and silver world outside. A group of Ashaninca girls were already up, sitting side by side on the cliff-top in their *cushmas* and painting each others' faces with *urucum*, the red dye. To me they seemed remarkably beautiful, with features that could have been Japanese. Farther down the river *urucum* was in short supply, but it grew thickly in the forest here and they could put it on as heavily and imaginatively as they wanted. The marks they painted on each other, blocks and stripes and thin lines, were fantastical and charming.

The men sat separately, cutting fishing arrows four or five feet long, yet light and pliable, from the wood of the *pupunha* tree: a kind of palm. The flights were red, yellow and blue parrot feathers, the brown wood barbs were often a foot long and sharp enough to bring up a bead of blood on your finger if you pricked yourself with one. The bows were as big as the Ashaninca themselves, and were also made of *pupunha* wood, fibrous, light and springy.

Originally, the chief told me, the Ashininca had come from 'the high mountains'; by which he meant Peru. Spanish writers recorded that in the forests there the Ashaninca had gathered the breast feathers of humming-birds for the cloaks the great Inca lords wore, before the Conquest. The Ashaninca were faithful to them, and helped to protect Manco Inca, who escaped to the forest soon after the Conquest and established his capital there until he was murdered by renegade Spaniards.

The name 'Ashaninca' means 'the real people'. Like other tribes of indians, they worship the sun, which they call Pawa. But they also have a god named Inca, who taught them to make bows and arrows. Inca was captured by the white men, the *viracoche* or devils, who forced him to teach them his secrets; which explains the technological superiority of the invaders. One day, though, a great flood will wash Inca back down the river to the Ashaninca, and then at last they will have all the weapons and goods the white men do, and will be able to clear them out of the forest.

Not knowing any of this before I arrived, I suppose I thought the Ashaninca would be knuckle-dragging primitives little better than apes. I am ashamed of my ignorance. Instead, I found they were sharp and funny and inventive, and possessed characters which were instantly recognizable from our own experience: the hen-pecked husband, the sharp, ambitious wife, the dreamer, the calculator, the quick-witted child of slower parents. They aren't strictly monogamous, but when a man takes a second wife it can cause serious trouble in the household. No one in Simpatia had more than two wives, and most only had one.

They were as quick as any other human beings to understand new things. They had never, for instance, heard that it was possible to capture a photographic likeness; in fact most of them had never seen themselves in a mirror. Yet when Mike produced his camera and had shown them the flash in order not to frighten them, one woman adjusted her robe and her hair and looked directly and unflinchingly into the lens. And when he showed them the transparencies he had taken six months earlier of some of their distant relatives at a village several days' journey by boat, they learned immediately to hold them up to the light and soon recognized the faces.

The Ashininca here were extremely honest, unlike some of the indians in the villages we had stopped at earlier. They had very few possessions, and loved the beads and mirrors and knives we had brought; yet we could leave these things out for their inspection all day while we went off into the forest, and everything would be in place when we got back. They had a contempt for the indians farther down the river, who stole things as a matter of course. During a long walk through the forest I asked the chief of Simpatia, whose name was Irao, why they were so honest.

'Because I would be angry if they weren't, and anyway the others wouldn't like it.'

Irao himself was the only person in Simpatia who didn't wear the brown Ashaninca robe, the *cushma*. To us his T-shirt and shorts gave him a ragged, degenerate air, so that he seemed much less impressive than the rest of them. But to the people of Simpatia, his clothes represented his knowledge of the white men (he had once spent a day and a night in a little town many days' journey down the river) and his ability to get on with them.

We usually assume that people we regard as primitive must speak in a primitive way. Not at all. As society develops, language loses its complexity and becomes simpler and easier. The standard work on the grammar of the Ashaninca language is 500 pages long, and it is full of concepts such as inalienable substantives, pronominal prefixes, directional suffixes, and frustrative suffixes.

As in Turkish or Hungarian, the Ashanincas' nouns and verbs are like magnets: they attract other words as though they are iron filings. *Iitontsi* means a head, *noito* = my head, *piito* = your head, *iito* = his head, *oito* = her head, *aito* = our head.

Since the Ashaninca, like other forest tribes, are so isolated, they have no real need for the concept of big groups. Numbers, too, are very limited: *apaani* (one), *apite* (two), and *mava* (three). After that they simply say *pashine* (more) and *oshequi* (many).

Their verbs, by contrast, are sensationally complex: 'to think', for example, is *quinquithashiryaantsi* (the word is closely associated with 'to remember', 'to count' and 'to tell a story'). I think = *quinquithashiryaaca*, he thinks = *iquinquithashiryaaca*, he thinks it = *iquinquithashiryaacaro*, he thinks it of her = *iquinquithashiryaacanaro*.

The Ashaninca have no form for 'they', perhaps because they think in such individual and restricted terms; their relationships are all face to face and personal. Yet in their dealings with one another they require the most minute and sophisticated methods of differentiation.

Later that year, 1992, I was to travel to Peru and saw other Ashaninca people reduced to humiliation and beggary in the small towns carved out of the forest. I saw some who had been pressed into service by the Peruvian army, or been forced by the savage Maoist group known as The Shining Path to kill and torture their own friends and fellow-tribesmen. The Ashaninca had no real defences against the late twentieth century, for all their quick-wittedness; only the forest protected them.

But the forest is as vulnerable as they are. Not long ago a governor of Brazil's Amazonias province denounced it as a breeding-ground for termites, a useless blank on the map which had to be replaced with plants and trees which were useful to man. It is regarded as a resource, to be dug and cut and stripped, and its remoteness and difficulty are increasingly seen as challenges to be overcome rather than barriers. On our last full day at Simpatia Irao, the chief, took us into the forest to show us some of the plants and trees the Ashaninca used. With the sweat running down my face and the *pium* attacking me, I recorded this piece to camera.

Transcript of report for *Nine O'Clock News*, 2.6.92

JS: The danger isn't really that the rain-forest will completely disappear and turn into desert. That's beyond the capability even of the people who are trying their hardest to cut the forest down. The real danger is that it'll lose its rare trees and its animal life, that its rivers will become poisoned, and that the indians, the indigenous people who know it best and look after it best, will be driven out. The forest would still be here, but it'd be empty and silent.

Days later, we left at dawn. The Ashaninca lined up on the cliff-top to say goodbye to us. I had got to know them now, from the cheerful woodsman to Irao's quarrelsome elder wife. Their intelligence and gentleness had captivated me: I don't think I have ever met a community I liked and admired so much. The girls with their new red face-paint, overmarked with delicate black lines, met our eyes with a pleasant sexual frankness, the children danced around our feet.

During my trip along the Envira I had met a white man, an official for the Brazilian department of indian affairs, who lived on the river in a thatched house like theirs, with split-cane floors and tame tapirs and peccaries and macaws and a gentle little Ashaninca girl to look after him. He had, he said, seen signs of thirty groups of indians in his area who had never had any contacts with white people, and occasionally one of them would loose off an arrow at his house as a kind of protest at his invasion of their forest. How, I asked, did he feel about living in this ultimate isolation?

'It is a heaven beyond any heaven you can imagine,' he answered.

Now, I thought, I could start to imagine it. And when I waved to the Ashaninca on the bluffs for the last time, and our boat rounded a bend in the river so that they were hidden from us by the overhanging trees, I knew I would never be able to forget this place and its people. Sometimes, years later, I still go to sleep thinking of lying in my hammock in the cool of the dawn, with the gentle noises of the forest around, and the Ashaninca painting each other's faces beside the river.

« »

As we headed back, our boatmen started to tell us about the river and its fish. The *pirarucu*, they said, grew to nine feet and the indians used its huge scales as cutting and scraping tools; but it was a gentle, meek fish which didn't fight when it was caught. By contrast pirhanas took a chunk out of your hand if you weren't careful. One of the indians travelling with us held out his hand and showed the nasty half-moon scar between his thumb and forefinger. I had already seen the results of a sting-ray wound: the flesh of a man's leg had been laid open to the bone, and had healed that way.

Electric eels could shock you through at fifty yards; and although each shock lasted only for a couple of seconds the eels swam closer and closer, shocking you again and again until you sank. One of the boatmen, toothy and rather dapper with his small moustache and his cut-off shorts, claimed to have cut off the head of an eel as it moved in for the final shock.

And the *candirus* or willy-fish? Maria, the Brazilian doctor with us, said she had treated plenty of women for them, but never a man. It entered you and sucked your blood from the inside, she said, but it slipped out quickly afterwards because it had to breathe; the spines were nothing like as bad as I had been told, and the experience was only mildly painful because the *candirus* was so tiny. Even so, Maria thought it was better to keep your legs together if you fell into the water. Then I looked at the milky brown surface: who knew what was going on down there?

We found out that night. I jotted down an account in my notebook, the first part as it was happening and the rest immediately afterwards.

« »

'Claudio, the helmsman, has no real sense; Zezinho, sitting in the bows with his torch and looking for caymans to catch, rather than sunken trees and sandbanks, has none either. It is dark and cloudy: no moon yet, and no stars. We barge into things and nearly tip over more than once. But at around 8 o'clock, half an hour from the *fazenda*, Claudio gets excited and starts speeding up. The indian tries to warn him, and we know we're going wrong, but we race across the river at an angle and hit a large tree which is sticking out of the water at an angle of twenty-five degrees. Mike and I, only half-joking, have already agreed that if there's a smash he will look after the still camera case and I'll look after the movie camera.

'At first Claudio whirrs the engine and tries to get us off the tree, but it doesn't work. The boat is filling up. We begin to realize that our uncomfortable means of transport for the last nine days can no longer hold us up. Alex says the river on his side is very deep. I have grown used to the notion that it was shallow enough to walk in.

'We don't, however, panic; in fact everyone behaves with great calmness. We discuss the situation as the boat shifts, and Mike and I are left sitting on the uppermost edge. Things are going. I just manage to catch one of my excellent boots, but the arrows I bought in the Kulina village and the little carved animals slip down into the water and float off into the darkness. The small tortoise that Alex bought vanishes also, alas.

'We scramble for the long bamboo poles in the canoe, gripping and pushing in the dark swirling water. We have two torches, though mine is running out and I don't have time to get the batteries from my case. I am determined not to give up this notebook, or the audio and video tapes; Mike too. Calmly, we discuss the position. If we can tie the cases to the tree we hit, then we might be able to shift to the next submerged tree, approximately in the middle of the river. It takes Claudio and Maria a long time, but Maria is superb.

'Weirdly, I find myself amused though certainly frightened. Here we are, in almost pitch darkness, days away from rescue, in the middle of an Amazonian river with unmentionable things lurking in the water and waiting for us on the banks; if we ever make it to the banks. How can late twentieth-century man get himself in such a position? I stand outside myself and try to say intelligent, calming things. Alex and Mike are both excellent: we're living the ethic of the 1950s British war-film, very clipped and unemotional and polite.

'The indian and Zezinho don't quite know where they are; indeed, Zezinho misunderstands to the point where he clambers along the submerged end of the canoe, making it shift and sink some more. I have so often thought about all this as a possibility (though not in the darkness) that it seems ludicrous and I laugh. But now it's happening, and it's real.

'At last we start to move, in order of where we sit: Claudio, Maria, Alex, me, Mike, Zezinho. I shuffle along a branch behind the upturned side, climb down into the submerged area by the stern, grab hold of a bamboo pole and am scrabbled at, then find myself perched on a branch of the other tree like a sparrow. The trouble is, I'm worried the tree will shift under our weight, and will collapse into the water.

'I have my boots (and socks, which Zezinho politely tucked into them for me) hanging round my neck, and am wearing my cagoul. I still believe the water will be shallow enough to ford. As the heaviest one there, I decide to get off the tree and into the water, clutching onto branches beneath the surface. It's my Captain Oates complex, I suppose.

'The water is warm, higher than blood temperature, and reaches to my neck. Only now do I realize the force of the current: it pins me to the tree and rips my cagoul from me, and I only just manage to catch it. I get Claudio to hang my boots on the tree – heavy fruit – and the cagoul I wrap round a lower branch. The water isn't shallow at all: I have to stand on tiptoe on the shifting sand of the bottom to keep my head above water. I would like the protection of the cagoul and the boots, but it's plain now that we will have to swim to the shore, and they would drown me. You can just see the white sand of the shore glimmering in the utter darkness. I want to pee in the warm water, but am too afraid of the willy-fish. I keep my legs together and my buttocks clenched instead.

'Claudio, anxious to rehabilitate himself, launches out in a wild swim, and Zezinho throws himself despairingly in afterwards. Tangled together, they manage to reach shallower water and stand triumphantly. I must be forty, maybe fifty yards away: a long swim in the dark with a current this strong. Maria crosses herself and follows them. She is a weak swimmer and drifts away, but Claudio reaches her with a bamboo pole.

'Now it's my turn. Because I'm already in the water, unlike the others, I don't have the advantage of the dive down from the tree. I'm nervous about the current. It's too strong to stand up in, when I move away from the tree, and the sand is melting under my feet. Nothing for it: I look up at the stars and think how odd it is that I can listen to the BBC on my short-wave radio here, but have no way of telling anyone what has happened to me. I think of asking Mike to send a message home for me, but it sounds too sentimental. I launch out and fight the current. It swirls round and my head goes under, but Maria and Claudio are shouting 'Good, good,' and I reach the proffered pole. Mike's and Alex's delight at reaching dry land is a pleasure to see.

'It's almost a pity to get out of the warm water, because the air seems much colder. We clamber up the wide sandy beach, and Claudio and Zezinho make up for their earlier stupidity even more by taking Alex's Bic lighter, which still works, and setting fire to a little piece of wood.

'Mike, Alex and I start collecting logs for a bonfire, but now the others have all had it and just sit around doing nothing. They even use the logs we have found as pillows, and we almost have to threaten force to get Zezinho and Claudio to help us. They have no concept of the need to build up a supply of wood for the hours when it gets really cold: 3–5 a.m.

'There are, however, dangers. I pull a piece of wood from a bark bush on the forest edge and hear the rasping sound of a cricket. Then it doesn't sound like a cricket any more, but a rattlesnake. It's a fer-de-lance, the second most dangerous snake in Amazonia. I run for it.

'Maria says this is the most frightening time for her, much worse than the river, because there is no one to listen for danger from animals or wild tribesmen. The indian who is with us left the forest as a child, and the boatmen are useless.

'Five hours later Mike and I, badly bitten and unable to sleep, wander along the beach and spot the tracks of an enormous jaguar which is known to frequent this part of the forest. Maria had told us she saw it once, swimming boldly across the river in front of her boat by daylight. It is a female, and not long ago went into a village before dark, gripped a large pig by the neck, and ran back into the forest with the pig squealing as she went.

'There are five or six lines of recent pawmarks in the sand, some larger than my hand and some much smaller. They are all fresher than our own footprints when we were fetching the firewood: the jaguar seems to have brought her cub up to look at us in the night. The prints stop a few yards from the bonfire where we lay. Mike says he heard two clear splashes in the river at separate times, and assumed it was our things dropping off the tree in the middle of the river. More probably it was the jaguars coming and going.

'We debate endlessly how long it will be before we were rescued. But all these things seem to end in anti-climax. When Claudio and Zezhinho wake up they say they know there's a Kulina village nearby; and now we can hear the cocks crowing there. As the light increases, a Kulina boat comes along. We can see our boxes with the video and stills in them, still hanging safely out of the water.

« »

Someone at the *fazenda* had dreamt we were all drowned, and they were getting ready to come and search for us. Back there we ate our first meal for twenty-four hours, of tapir, beans and rice, and a lot of very sweet coffee. Maria gave us each jaguar's teeth and an affectionate kiss, and we headed off to the airstrip where Florindo was waiting with his hat on in the pilot's seat of his little one-engined plane. He had to take off in five minutes, he said, because of an approaching rain-storm. If we'd missed him, it would have been a four-day journey down-river to the nearest town, Feijo.

It was a superb old-time take-off, bumping along the ground with Mike filming and Florindo's hat flying off his head at the moment of lift-off. The forest swelled out below us. For the first time I put my hand up to my face and neck and ears, and counted eighty-eight bites. All of them came from our night on the river-bank.

The town of Feijo was a little frontier place, dusty and silent, with a dozen general shops in a state of slow decay. Horses were tied up and standing in the shadows out of the heat. Vast cumulus clouds were bunching up overhead, but the forest which had created them seemed a world away. From a phone box in a dirty restaurant in Feijo, where beef and chicken were being served on spits and dark, unshaven men sat round eating them I rang Dominic Lawson's country cottage in Gloucestershire: the first time, I should think, such a connection had ever been made. Rosa Lawson, one of my favourite people, answered. Dominic was out, and I blurted the whole story to her – the Ashaninca, the *dime*, the river, the willy-fish, the jaguar, the bites. I was anxious to give her husband an idea of the scale of it all, so he could use it as the cover story for the *Spectator* the following week.

'I'll make sure he does that.'

'And, Rosa, one last thing—'
'Yes?'
'Please tell him I'll spare no detail.'
And I certainly didn't.

17

The Mountain of Light

FOREIGN CORRESPONDENTS, like pilots and soldiers, have a tendency to superstition. They think that if they carry the right things in their pockets, or go through some private little ritual, they can protect themselves from violence, bad luck, and the wrath of their editors. If they get shot, you can't say to them, 'See, your system doesn't work,' because they just reply, 'It would've been far worse if I hadn't had my lucky coin, or worn my lucky white suit,' or whatever.

I'm not superstitious. I may carry the occasional lucky stone or go through a little ritual or two when I leave for a difficult assignment; but if I leave the stone at home, or get distracted halfway through the ritual, I don't worry. I know that none of these things matters in the slightest: thanks to a journey I made to Kabul in 1989.

One rainy morning in London, in January that year, I had a call from the editor of *Panorama* inviting me round to his office.

'Can we have a chat about Afghanistan?'

At that stage the Russians were just about to pull out of the country after ten years of a brutal war of occupation. I knew little about it, apart from what I had seen in the news bulletins. But I remembered a poem I had had to learn when I was eleven: 'The Amir's Soliloquy', written by a grand old Indian Civil Service poet of the nineteenth century, Sir Alfred Lyall. It was probably the best background material I could want. It's all about the tribal divisions of Afghanistan and the impossibility of governing the place. In his palace at the Bala Hissar in Kabul the unfortunate Amir who has to do it indulges in a gloomy soliloquy:

I look from a fort half-ruined on Kabul spreading below,
    On the near hills crowned with cannon, and the far hills
        piled with snow;
Fair are the vales well watered, and the vines on the upland
    swell,
    You might think you were reigning in Heaven – I know I am
        ruling Hell.
For there's hardly a room in my palace but a kinsman there was
    killed,
    And never a street in the city but with false fierce curs is
        filled
With a mob of priests, and fanatics, and all my mutinous host;
    They follow my steps, as the wolves do, for a prince who
        slips is lost.

A purist might complain about the scansion, but anyone who knows anything about Afghanistan could see that old Sir Alfred had got everything else dead right. The idea of going there appealed greatly to me; but as I opened the editor's door I found myself crossing my fingers. It was something I still did in those superstitious days.

Inside, sipping BBC tea from styrofoam cups, were two characters who looked like quintessential Empire-builders. They were both cameramen in their early thirties who specialized in covering Afghanistan. One of them, Chris Hooke, was a tall, rangy Australian who had first gone there in 1984. The other, Peter Jouvenal, was fair-haired, English, and had a moustache straight out of a sepia regimental photograph. After serving in the Army he had hitchhiked to Afghanistan in 1980, working first as a photographer and then as a cameraman. The two of them, together with several others of a similar kind, had based themselves in Peshawar on the Pakistani side of the Khyber Pass, and had produced the best coverage of the war. There were, of course, rogues who passed off phoney pictures as combat footage; but Peter and Chris, together with some other British cameramen and photographers whom I later came to know, Rory Peck, Vaughan Smith, Ken Guest and John Gunston, had nothing to do with them. They competed with each other to get the best.

The editor of *Panorama* handed me a document. 'The Fall of Kabul', it said. It was a programme proposal by Chris and Peter.

When the last Soviet combat unit crosses the Oxus and reaches the safety of home soil the Afghan war will enter its last phase. The Russians leave behind them a client regime, weak and divided, dependent upon a demoralized army of no more than 70,000. Set against this is a mujaheddin force, also divided, of roughly 200,000, whose morale has never been higher. Their final offensive will inevitably lead to the collapse of the Afghan army, the destruction of the Communist regime and the fall of the capital, Kabul. This film will document the mujaheddin's final offensive.

'I thought this might appeal to you,' said the editor casually, as he fiddled with a pen on his desk. He didn't look at me.

He needn't have worried. The travelling I had done over the previous few years had mostly been pretty tame stuff, and I needed something a little stronger. Afghanistan was unquestionably it.

Chris and Peter weren't making us a cheap offer: television documentaries are expensive. Pinned to the back of the synopsis was a budget summary:

Salaries – production staff	£38,400
Salaries – technical staff	£5,070
Equipment	£29,880
Video stock	£2,350
Travel and transport	£9,210
Living expenses	£4,880
Insurance	£1,450
Location admin & expenses	£1,200
Contingency 5%	£4,622
Production cost total	£97,062

It would be a good deal more than that now, and it went well over budget. But it was money well spent. The BBC won prizes and a great deal of praise for the finished documentary and sold it round the world. It became the standard work on the subject. Yet the subject proved not to be the fall of Kabul, but the reason why Kabul failed to fall.

As we sat there discussing the idea, Chris and Peter ran through the mujaheddin groups and their racial and religious origins. It would have been hard to keep all the savage-sounding names in my head without the help of Sir Alfred Lyall.

And far from the Suleiman Heights come the sounds of the
      stirring of tribes,
   Afreedi, Hazara and Ghilzai, they clamour for plunder and
      bribes;
And Herat is but held by thread, and the Uzbek has raised
      Badukshan;
   And the chief may sleep sound, in his grave, who would rule
      the unruly Afghan.

Not an awful lot had changed in Afghanistan since the 1870s, I could
see. Except of course the firepower.

It sounded highly dangerous and highly romantic, in roughly equal
proportions. I leapt at it, and a few weeks later, equipped with the best
boots, anoraks and long silk underwear money could buy, we arrived
in Peshawar, in Pakistan. There were four us: Chris and Peter, myself,
and a *Panorama* producer. It was Eamonn Matthews, who was to go
to Baghdad with me the following year.

The snow did nothing to soften the sharp edges of the Hindu Kush
as we flew in. I tried to imagine myself climbing those ridges and
working my way through the passes, but the effort was too great. Yet
merely looking up at them from the comfortable hotel I was staying
at made my heart lift inside me. This was the North-West Frontier: the
jagged lines of the landscape, the sharpness of the light, and the thin,
pure air were a powerful lift to the spirit.

It wasn't just the landscape. When I went to the bazaar in Peshawar
to buy some Afghan clothes, I found the muddy alleyways jammed
with tall, hawk-nosed, villainous-looking characters in long robes and
green and silver turbans, striding around with a characteristic rolling
walk that made them look as though they owned the place.

This was a different world. There was a fiercer reality here, a sense
of being beyond petty comforts like the rule of law, or British consul-
ates, or insurance policies, or hospitals, or BBC administrators. These
men weren't necessarily noble savages at all: there was nothing of the
Ashaninca about them. Many were treacherous thieves, and outside
the bazaar there were pathetic bundles of rags in the last stages of
opium addiction, huddled over a one-rupee opium reefer. Life here was
lived as it always had been: you were on your own, with only your
strength and cunning to help you. That, like the cruel landscape, was

where the real exhilaration lay. In contrast to the peaceable, safe life of the developed world, where most people never see a fight, let alone a dead body, I found it profoundly liberating.

Our expedition to Afghanistan was something Sir Richard Burton himself might have enjoyed. And since it was played out against a magnificent backdrop of mountains and villages that had scarcely changed since the days of *The Amir's Soliloquy* it had a remarkably historical quality, as though it were all happening in 1889 rather than a century later and we were players in the Great Game, the old competition between Russia and Britain in Central Asia. As with my trip to the Amazon, I probably enjoyed it more in retrospect than I did at the time; yet even then I knew I was experiencing one of the high points in my professional life, a period of sustained excitement and danger.

We travelled along the border between Afghanistan and Pakistan, to the high valley at Ali Mangal where many of the Afghan mujaheddin groups had their base camps. Some, especially the fanatical Hezb-i-Islami, were hostile and mistrustful, and we had to be extremely careful even going near their camp. They had murdered several journalists, including a BBC cameraman. Our plan had been to join up with Hezbi and follow its subtle, treacherous leader Gulbadeen Hekmatyar in the race for Kabul. It soon became clear, though, that they would never agree to accept us and were best avoided. It didn't matter. Hezbi might be good at murdering journalists but they weren't much good at fighting, and their forces played only a small part in the battles that lay ahead.

Other groups seemed to be rooted in exile, interested in picking up money and supplies from the Pakistani and American governments but not really in going back to take power. Others again were fawning and crafty; the BBC Pashtu and Farsi language services are listened to by just about every adult male Afghan, so there was huge kudos to be gained by any organization which took us with them in their search for power. We made our contacts with them and met their representatives, but I found it hard to know which to trust. We slept night after night in a barrack-like hut as the guests of men from a large middle-of-the-road organization: reliable enough, but not particularly noted as fighters and with no apparent interest in the race for Kabul. If there even was one.

One evening we came across a small Shi'ite Muslim organization called Harakat-e-Islami. There was something about the stocky little men who belonged to it which inspired trust. They looked very different from the usual tall, hawk-featured Pashtuns who belonged to the other groups: Harakat's people had Mongolian features, broad faces with high cheekbones, and they claimed descent from the Hazara, the thousand troops whom Genghis Khan had left behind to garrison Afghanistan as he made his way westwards, conquering and destroying everything he found.

There was a particularly impressive figure among the group we met, who was treated with great respect by the others. They called him Mahmoud. He was taller and bulkier, but he had their high cheekbones and slanted eyes. He looked at you straight, and had an open, easy laugh. I sat next to him, cross-legged, on the floor of the mud-built hut which acted as Harakat's headquarters, drinking little cups of strong, bitter tea. His English was basic but easy to understand.

'You know,' he said quietly to me, 'our people are everywhere in Kabul. They sweep the floors, they clean out the waste-paper bins. They find all the government's secrets.' He paused for a moment. Then he added in a lower voice, 'They are also inside the Khad headquarters. You know what is Khad?'

I did. Khad was the Soviet-trained secret police, which ran Kabul now that the Russians had withdrawn.

'If you come with us, we will show you everything Khad does. We will drive you through Kabul in the car which belongs to the commander of Khad. We will show you Harakat people who are in important positions in Khad. Will you come with us?'

The questions were still running through my mind as we climbed down the wooden ladder that was the only entrance to the hut. Could we trust Mahmoud? If Harakat had infiltrated Khad, couldn't Khad have infiltrated Harakat? On the other hand, how could we turn down this brilliant offer, to ride through the streets of Kabul in the Khad commander's car?

> Is it not passing brave to be a king
> And drive in triumph through Persepolis?

I had already decided that this trip would have to be undertaken in the spirit of Burton or Sir Samuel Baker. There was no point in holding back or in looking for safeguards here. Forget the mortgage, the children, the group pension scheme; if you got it wrong you would be lucky if someone scraped a hole for you in the stony ground and piled a few rocks over you. In these mountains, with these people, you had to rely on your judgement and your luck.

'I think we can trust them,' I said to Eamonn, as we walked away.

There was no possible way of checking up: to have talked about Harakat's offer with any of the other Afghan groups, each of which was in a state of ferocious rivalry with every other, would have been to invite instant betrayal. I suppose what really decided me was the tough appearance of Harakat, Genghis Khan's men, and their romantic history. The sensible, responsible journalist in me, the BBC executive, finally bowed out at this moment, and the adventurer took over entirely. It wasn't really our job to infiltrate Kabul in disguise or to investigate the claims of any particular group; we were here to make a sober assessment of the mujaheddin's chances of seizing power once the Russians had left. It was just that I guessed this would make superb television; and in the long run I was right.

In the end, sitting on the floor of our hut and eating the packs of iron rations which the Americans had donated to the mujaheddin and which they had used contemptuously to fill in the holes in the road (Peter and Chris, always thrifty, had collected up the undamaged packs) we decided to split up. Since I was willing to trust Harakat I would go with them to Kabul, and Peter Jouvenal would come with me. Eamonn Matthews and Chris Hooke would trek off through the Hindu Kush to meet the legendary Ahmad Shah Massoud, the man who had defended the Panshir Valley for more than a decade against the most determined assault of the Soviet army. Our journey seemed likely to be more risky; theirs would be much more arduous.

We drove into Afghanistan as a group, and were quite close to Kabul when, a couple of mornings later, we shook hands in the snow and split up, two and two. The others watched us climb into the little pick-up truck which Harakat had arranged for us. I turned round as we bucketed along the icy road: they were still standing there in the distance, waving. It didn't seem altogether likely that we would see each other again.

The more time I spent with Peter Jouvenal, the more I liked him. He could be taciturn and stiff-upper-lipped in an early Victorian kind of way, but he was good company too: just so long as you didn't tempt fate. If you said something careless like 'We seem to be getting on quite well now,' Peter would get furious; and directly things did go wrong it would be your fault.

I was pretty nervous anyway, because of something that had happened back in Peshawar just as we were leaving, at the very start of our expedition. I was sitting in the passenger seat of our vehicle, and the driver shoved the gear lever a little too roughly into reverse as we left the driveway of the house where we had been staying. The vehicle jerked backwards, and the glove compartment came open, shooting a book which had been inside it onto my lap. I looked down: the title of the book was *Kabul Catastrophe*. If someone were trying to give me a message, then this was undoubtedly it. I kept quiet and shoved the book back into the glove compartment, but there were moments over the next few weeks when I remembered the incident with a real feeling of discomfort.

For the time being, though, there was no catastrophe. We bundled along through the mountain passes and down into the plain that separates Kabul from the Hindu Kush. The stark black rock of the mountain ridges showed through the brilliant snow, and the road lay yellow with mud before us. Nothing had changed here since Roberts fought his way north from Kandahar; not even the houses ringed with sallow-trees and protected by high walls, all made of this same mud. They were primitive places (we stayed in a couple of them, lying on straw, and ate thin unleavened bread and dried apricots for dinner and breakfast) yet they were strong enough to withstand the violence of the late twentieth century. Russian tanks, passing this way, had often fired their big guns at the walls, but the sheer mass of packed mud absorbed the shock without cracking or crumbling.

There had been a lot of fighting. Beside every track, outside every shell-blasted house, there were little heaps of rocks surmounted by a bamboo pole with a few green and white rags fluttering from it: the graves of people who had died fighting the Russians, or perhaps just other Afghans. All very Alfred Lyall.

May he rest, the Amir Sher Ali, in his tomb by the holy shrine;
    The virtues of God are pardon and pity, they never were
        mine;

> They have never been ours, in a kingdom all stained with the
>   blood of our kin,
>   Where the brothers embrace in the war-field, and the reddest
>   sword must win.

As for people, they were few and far between: just the occasional
Pashtun wearing a turban and *shalwar kameez* with a blanket wrapped
round him and the inevitable Kalashnikov automatic rifle in his hand.
Sometimes we saw a few brightly dressed children in the villages we
passed, but never a woman, not even an old one.

Mahmoud, the Harakat leader, brought us at last to a higher,
snowier valley: Sanglakh. Our vehicle stopped, and swarms of stocky,
willing men in mujaheddin uniform gathered round us, grinning and
taking our equipment and ran up the steep side of the mountain to a
series of caves a hundred feet or so above us. It took me, in my mid-
forties, rather longer to get there. When I arrived, I found myself in
the literature of my boyhood. The main cave was full of dark, turbaned
characters sitting in a line on blankets. There were pictures of the
Prophet Mohammed and the Holy Shrine at Mecca on the walls, in
between racks of guns. The turbaned characters were leaning against
low wooden lockers which contained ammunition: tens of thousands
of rounds of it.

'*Salaam aleykum,*' I said politely, Peace be upon you, and once
again had that feeling of being a character in a Kipling short story.

'*Aleykum asalaam,*' they murmured gravely: Upon you be peace.

By the light of hurricane lamps tea was passed round in an enormous enamelled kettle, and from some unimaginable Pakistani source
there were sweet biscuits. There were also questions, which Mahmoud
translated.

'Why,' asked an old man so deep in the recesses of the cave that I
could scarcely see him, 'does England allow the Holy Prophet's name
to be insulted?'

It was said quite conversationally: there seemed to be no anger
behind it. A week earlier there had been rioting in Pakistan over Salman
Rushdie's book *The Satanic Verses*, and even here in their distant cave
in the Sanglakh Valley the Harakat leaders had heard all about it from
the BBC.

I explained as best I could the Western notion of free speech; not something your average Afghan warrior readily understands. There was a polite silence, then someone asked if I personally thought the book should be published. It was a difficult moment, but I thought they would be shrewd enough to realize if I merely soft-soaped them. So I gritted my teeth and went for it.

'A famous philosopher once said "I hate what you say but I will defend your right to say it with my life." '

The friendly features turned disapproving, frowning in the yellow lamplight.

'After all,' I added, searching for an argument they might appreciate, 'you're Shi'a Muslims. You have no reason to love Sunni Muslims, yet you fought the Russians to protect them. It doesn't mean you have become more sympathetic to Sunni Islam.'

A little murmur of surprise and pleasure went round the cave. If you talked approvingly about religion and fighting, I found, you could never go far wrong with Afghans. After that they were a little more inclined to give me the benefit of the doubt.

At four-thirty in the morning, a few days later, I was awakened with a rough shake to the shoulder, and a whisper. I hadn't slept much, and even though we were in pitch darkness I knew instantly where I was: in a house in a village outside Kabul. Now we were going to be smuggled through the outer defences and into the city itself. Feeling around, I grabbed one of the plastic bags I'd brought, and quickly stuffed some essentials in it. Peter brought the little tourist video camera he was planning to use in Kabul. We made our way silently into the street.

Kabul was entirely ringed by small Army posts, fifty or so yards apart, and all night long the sentries in them kept up a weird wailing to let the posts on either side of them know that they were still alive and hadn't gone over to the enemy. We crept forward in the darkness, Peter and I side by side with Mahmoud just in front to guide us. As we were passing between two of the posts, the wailing died away; and in that instant of silence my wretched electronic wristwatch beeped: it was exactly five o'clock. The guards seemed not to notice; the next moment they were wailing as before.

We came out onto a road, with the darkness a little less intense. By the time we reached the first police post there was enough light to check our gear. I looked down: the plastic bag I had brought with me was blue and green, and looked disturbingly familiar. 'Books from Heffers of Cambridge', it announced in large letters. There was a policeman up ahead, standing at the barrier; how could he fail to spot the bag? However could he think that Peter Jouvenal and I were Afghans? What would he do?

We walked on. To waver or turn back would be to invite a bullet in the head. I gripped the Heffers' bag tighter. We were almost level with the policeman now. Somehow I couldn't avoid looking him in the eye. But his gaze faltered and fell away from mine: a mujaheddin sympathizer, maybe.

A red Kabul taxi was waiting for us farther on, and it drove us to one of the main roads of the city. We got out there and climbed into a large and very official-looking jeep with several aerials on its roof. The driver grinned.

'Car of commander of Khad,' he said.

Peter and I looked at each other: Harakat, after all our doubts, had come up with the goods. We rattled along the road and stopped outside the British embassy, which was closed and empty, and our minder insisted that we should get out and walk up and down while Peter filmed. Then we drove on, past the Russian embassy and the defence ministry and Khad headquarters itself, and I recorded a piece to camera as we rattled over the bumpy roads. Playing the videotape of it now, I can still hear the nervousness and surprise in my voice.

Transcript of *Panorama* on Afghanistan, 2.10.89

JS: This is clear evidence of the degree to which the resistance movement has penetrated the system in Kabul. We have changed vehicles now, and the one we're in is a jeep belonging to the commander of the Afghan equivalent of the KGB, Khad. And the two men with us are both officers of Khad.

It was consummate cheek on the part of Harakat-e-Islami. They all knew they were endangering their lives by allowing us to film the jeep. But they thought it was worth it from the movement's point of view. To have the BBC show the secret power they possessed inside the enemy's capital was more important to them than their own lives.

That night we spent in a safe house, and were then moved on, again by taxi. Two men arrived and announced themselves as senior officers in Khad who were double agents for our mujaheddin group, Harakat. They wrapped their faces in their turbans and sat down to be interviewed.

Directly they had gone an older man with shifty eyes, completely different from the bold, smiling Mongolian types, arrived and announced he was going to make a rocket. There and then he started filling a big metal pipe with explosives and fiddled round with a watch which was to act as the fuse. Peter filmed away, but we both had serious doubts about the ethics of all this. And about the wisdom of it too. Suppose Khad arrived and arrested us: wouldn't we be accessories in an act of terrorism?

The trouble was, these people had no concept of the function of journalism. We weren't just observers to them, we were fellow-conspirators. To have announced that we were no longer taking part in all this might have been suicidal. Anyway, it was so extraordinary that I think neither of us would have done it.

But worse was to come: our shifty-eyed minder insisted that we must also film the firing of his rocket. Yet another taxi, driven by yet another Harakat supporter, was already waiting outside. The bomb-maker dumped his rocket in my lap and went and sat in the front seat. We drove along, jammed in together, with me nursing the rocket and feeling very much as though I didn't want to be there.

That was when our Kabul Catastrophe seemed likely to begin. First, the taxi-driver panicked and stopped right beside a patch of open ground where a soccer game was going on. Twenty-two players plus a referee saw Peter climb out with his camera and the shifty-eyed one carrying the rocket over to a group of men a hundred yards or so away, who were going to fire it. My job was to stay with Shifty-eyes and make sure he didn't try to get away. Meanwhile Peter realized that the target was to be the Khad headquarters, which loomed up at the far end of the open patch of ground where we were.

He shrugged his shoulders and started filming. The Harakat team walked across the open ground, pointed the rocket at it, and fired. Only the mujaheddin, we agreed afterwards, could have missed a five-storey building at that range; but the rocket fizzed over the top and fell harmlessly on the other side. We made a run for it.

We spent that night in another safe house. But the next morning it became clear to us that things were going badly wrong. The deadlines our guides had given for picking us up came and went. We were prisoners, and it was getting claustrophobic. Peter and I told yarns to each other and laughed a lot: another sign we were nervous. From time to time Peter would peer through a narrow gap in the curtains to gauge the height and direction of the military planes which came and went overhead. He wanted to work out where in Kabul we were.

Suddenly, late in the afternoon, things started to happen very fast. There was the sound of gunshots, and Mahmoud appeared, shouting at us to get out. It turned out that Khad had known about us all along: even before we had arrived in Kabul. Their spies along the way had told them we were coming. Finally they had heard all about the rocket incident, and they knew we were using taxis to get around the city.

Now they had discovered our safe house. A few minutes earlier a colonel from Khad had reconnoitred it and was actually raising his walkie-talkie to his mouth to give an order when Mahmoud ran up behind him and shot him in the back of the head. We had escaped just in time.

As we drove off in the inevitable taxi I felt bad about the Khad colonel, but not too bad: a secret policeman that senior must have tortured and executed a lot of people. Things looked extremely black for us now, though. If we were caught we would have absolutely no defence against the charge that we were accomplices of terrorists and murderers; the chances were that we would be quietly executed, rather than put on public trial. What had started off as an adventure had turned serious. Blood had been shed, and there could be more to come. I felt foolish and guilty: this hadn't been how it was meant to go at all. Out of the window now I could see groups of police and army stopping red taxis just like ours.

Peter was sitting bolt upright beside me.

'For God's sake,' I said irritably, 'can't you stop looking so bloody British?'

'Sorry,' he murmured, and tried to slouch down. He wasn't very good at it.

We passed the InterContinental Hotel, where the remnants of the international press corps were staying, and I yearned to tell the driver to turn in and set us down there. But they wouldn't have been able to protect us, and might not have wanted to. We were outlaws, hunted like animals. It was an ugly feeling.

And then, somehow, we had passed through the most dangerous area. The police and army road blocks became fewer and fewer. By the time we reached the edge of town, where the Pagman Mountains met the road, we were starting to feel we had a chance of escape. The winter's sun was going down redly over Kabul.

We shook hands quickly with the taxi driver, and walked fast for the hills with Mahmoud guiding us. Darkness fell quickly. We made our way through the ring of army watch-towers again, but this time one of them was unmanned. Mahmoud led us close to it so that we were out of sight of the others.

Only a few minutes later, the watch-towers erupted in a gigantic display of Véry lights and tracer bullets. It was like Guy Fawkes Night and Chinese New Year all in one. We stood on a mountain ridge and looked back at the red and white lights shooting up into the sky. A thought struck me.

'It couldn't be for our benefit, could it?' I said.

'No,' said Peter; 'the government must be celebrating some kind of victory.'

Mahmoud said nothing.

Hours later we stumbled in at the door of the Harakat headquarters in Pagman. Somehow I still had my Heffers of Cambridge bag with me. We were just drinking our first cup of tea when someone else arrived: a soldier who had just deserted from one of the watch-towers.

'Are you the ones?' he said, with respect in his voice. 'We were ordered to fire every tracer bullet we had in the air in order to see you and catch you.'

All the Harakat people crowded round to congratulate us, and in my relief I gripped their hands harder than I meant. Mahmoud winced.

'We will call you *Dast-e-gir*,' he said, 'the friend of the handshake.'

It had happened to me in the past; now I was doing it to them. I suppose I ought to have remembered Sir Alfred Lyall:

> For never did chief more sorely need Heaven for his aid and stay
>   Than the man who would reign in this country, and tame
>   Afghans for a day.

Instead, all I could think of was that our Kabul Catastrophe had turned into an extraordinary, undeserved Kabul escape. I would never, I promised myself, enter a serious undertaking so lightly again. And I would never pay attention to omens either; good or bad.

« »

In the years that followed the Soviet withdrawal, Afghans of all persuasions found it hard to understand why their country had been forgotten. Once it had been a significant piece on the international chessboard, but now the game had changed. The fighting was no longer against a super-power; it was a civil war.

When I went back to Kabul in April 1996 I found that things were much worse than they had been seven years earlier. The factions which Peter Jouvenal and Chris Hooke had wanted to follow had indeed captured Kabul, though it took them far longer than any of us had expected. Once there, they had brought their rivalries with them. Soon it had turned into outright war.

The destruction was terrible. We filmed in a mile-long stretch of road leading to the outskirts of town. There had been two universities and five schools along this road. Now there was nothing but ruins and rubble. Sarajevo, by comparison with this, had got off lightly. The mud-brick, yellowish grey in colour, had been smashed into piles of little more than dust. An occasional page from a text-book fluttered among the ruins. Everything else worth having had long since been looted, regardless of the danger from anti-personnel mines and unexploded shells.

None of this was done by the Russians. On the contrary, it had been with Russian help that the universities and schools were built up. Instead the destruction was the result of the fighting between the mujaheddin groups since the Russian withdrawal. With help and encouragement from Afghanistan's neighbours, who had no particular interest in seeing so difficult a country at peace, faction after faction had taken on the relatively moderate groups which form the government in Kabul.

Gulbeddin Hekmatyar had fought his way into the government coalition as prime minister, and then been ejected forcibly from it. His Hezb-i-Islami group had strong support from Pakistan, which fought out its proxy battles with India and Russia, backers of the Kabul government, on the territory of Afghanistan. General Dostam, with covert help from Russia, fought the government troops along this road and was responsible for the worst of the destruction. The Shi'ite groups, backed by Iran, flared up in occasional rebellion. Afghanistan had become a political black hole, without effective government, from which nothing emerged but heroin, and casualties too bad for the local hospitals to cope with.

Peter Jouvenal was with me again, but the other two were newcomers: Tom Giles from *Newsnight* and Garry Marvin, an academic who was researching for a documentary on newsgathering and occasionally acted as sound recordist. Directly we arrived in the centre of Kabul we went to the compound of the International Committee of the Red Cross. It was obvious that something was up.

'We've got to hurry,' one of the people there said, and he called for his driver and his big white Toyota Land Cruiser. ICRC delegates work in style.

It sounded like some important national ceremony, but it was in fact a public execution. I suppose I should have been horrified, but my first reaction, like the ICRC man's, was to hope we wouldn't be too late for it. Working for television can do bad things to the soul. It makes you rejoice in the concept of 'good' pictures, 'good' meaning attractive or exciting. A public hanging would come high in the ranking of 'good' pictures: a little above an earthquake or an erupting volcano, perhaps, though not as high as a political assassination on camera.

I am, of course, being satirical; yet which of us, if we were warned that something of the sort was about to be shown, would switch off the television in disgust? Why do people gather at scenes of violence and disaster, while even those who blame them for doing it take a look to see what is going on? Why do we read accounts of deaths or last words with such avidity? Because there is a terrible, slightly shameful fascination in the thought that a life which is so strong and ardent at one moment can be snuffed out the next. It could be us; in a way, it will be us eventually, and perhaps we want to know what it looks like.

At this stage – April 1996 – public executions were rare in Kabul. The relatively moderate mujaheddin coalition led by President Rabbani and Ahmad Shah Massoud was still in power, but its position was under serious threat from the Taliban. Within a few months the Taliban would put Rabbani and Massoud to flight and capture the city. Sensing the pressure from the Islamic extremists opposing them, the Rabbani government was keen to show that it, too, could behave with proper Islamic zeal.

In Saudi Arabia they behead criminals in public, but are outraged if pictures of the executions appear in the Western media. The Saudis like the essential savagery of their punishments to be a secret which is kept within the family. For the Afghans, on the other hand, the outside world scarcely exists. It is the place where weapons, foreign broadcasts, a little money and a little medical aid come from, and it is as distant to them as another galaxy. That foreigners might find a public execution degrading or unpleasant was both unimaginable and irrelevant.

We drove to the place of execution: a dreary open area in the centre of the city, where modern buildings overlooked a large patch of scrubby grass. Hours beforehand, thousands of people had gathered in almost complete silence, waiting for something to happen. The crowd was entirely male. After the victory of the mujaheddin over the Communists, women were rarely seen in the city, occasionally showing themselves in shapeless *burkhas* of dull yellow or grey, their faces hidden behind a little square mesh of cotton or lace like a grille in a cell-door, scurrying around as though they too wanted to rid the streets of themselves.

The gallows had been set up on a grassless knoll. Its shape was familiar from a thousand Westerns; yet it was still a shock to see it, like coming across a headsman sharpening his axe. The onlookers stood twenty deep at the closest point, and young boys hung in the branches of trees.

There was a sudden panic: people had climbed in such numbers onto the roof of a ruined building in front of the gallows that it seemed to be about to collapse, and men were jumping the twenty feet to the ground in fear. Some of them were injured, but no one cared: it wasn't injury they'd come here to see, but death itself.

The police, a ragged lot in old stained blue uniforms, had broken branches off the trees around the gallows and were using them to beat the legs of the men and boys in the front row to keep order. It was essential. A couple of days earlier there had been a practice-run for the executions, and the crowd had grown violent when it was clear no one was going to die. They turned on the police and the half-dozen journalists who had turned out to see what was going on, attacking them with rocks and hunting them into the nearby buildings. One way or another, it seemed, there had to be death and violence.

It was clear the crowd wouldn't be disappointed this time. Three nooses of yellow plastic rope hung loosely from the cross-tree, moving a little in the light breeze. A desk for the presiding mullah was set alongside, and a doctor with a dirty white coat over his mujaheddin fatigues checked his stethoscope nervously. I knew how he felt. I have seen people die in front of me many times, but none of them was put to death formally, by pre-arrangement, for the public good. I found myself swallowing a good deal.

For the small group of foreigners, most of them from aid agencies, it was a curiously social occasion. People like the ICRC man were greeting each other and grinning, as though they were going to watch a fireworks display. Someone ran over to me with a walkie-talkie, and a woman's voice, faintly familiar, squeaked from inside it. The voice said her name, and then I remembered: she was a rather glamorous UN official whom I had last encountered in Sarajevo.

'Look up!' squeaked the voice, and eventually I located her, waving from the fifth floor of the building opposite. She had binoculars: this was something she wasn't going to miss. Orange-sellers and vendors of unpleasant-looking meats went through the crowds, shouting their wares, but there was still very little noise.

Then came the roar and grinding of an engine, and an armoured personnel carrier ground its way up the slope in a fog of dark blue exhaust. A dozen guards and enthusiasts hung on to its upper works as it lurched up the slope to the gallows. This was the equivalent of the tumbril. A big crowd gathered round the rear of the APC as someone struggled to open the hatch at the back. Out of it, one after the other, came the three condemned men. It was the first sighting, and the crowd made a little rustle of excitement.

Blinking in the light, their hands and feet manacled, they looked like any other mujaheddin: bearded, wearing flat *pukal* caps and camouflage fatigues, young, gawky, unremarkable in every way except that they had barely ten minutes left to live. Their feet were bare, and they stood round idly on the knoll in front of the gallows while the men in charge of the hanging directed all their attention to pushing our cameraman and the two or three other photographers back. As far as I could see, none of the condemned men even looked at the ropes which had been prepared to kill them.

Their crime was a savage one. They had killed a *kouchi*, or nomad, raped his wife, injured his sons, and stolen his sheep. The four crimes seemed to rank roughly equal in the eyes of Afghan law. As they stood there, waiting for the fuss to die down and the executioners to start their work, the smallest of the three, Farid Ahmad, said loudly that he was only being hanged because he had no money. It was probably true. Anyway, it sounded more like a statement of fact than a plea for mercy; he must have known that there was no hope now. Once his outburst was over, he stood quietly enough in front of the middle noose. The man on his left, Nicmohammed, looked up at the crossbar and licked his lips. Zmarey, on the right, much taller and more bulky than the others, joked and laughed at the crowd opposite. They didn't respond; they were too curious at the spectacle of a man who would soon be beyond joking or laughing or any feeling whatever.

There was no ceremony. The whole affair was much uglier, more brutish and more careless than I had anticipated, and yet the first to die, Farid Ahmad, was strangling, disregarded, before we had realized that the noose had been tightened round his neck. It looked as though he had decided to get it over with quickly, and had put his weight into it immediately, slumping down like a sack of potatoes.

The executioner put the noose round Nicmohammed's neck. He took it quietly too, dropping down as the noose tautened but twisting round, his legs pointing and shaking dreadfully, his neck at an ugly angle, his eyes open as though he was trying to examine something very intently. As I watched, his hands and feet started to go a dull greyish blue.

Zmarey, who had played the fool, died the hardest. Although he was the tallest, he had been allotted the longest rope. His feet touched the ground and the rope throttled him slowly while the idiots in charge tried feebly to shorten it by twisting an iron bar across it, and then dug a hole under his feet. It was sickening to watch, and took a terrible amount of time before he, too, slumped, his head down on his shoulder and his feet at last pointing straight.

By comparison with a painful disease, or with what the three of them had done to the *kouchi* and his family, even Zmarey's death was mercifully fast. But what was lacking was any ceremony, any feeling that something of significance had happened here. There was no grand finale to the lives of the three murderers, none of the sense of occasion which we, who see so little of death, feel ought to accompany the irrevocable business of dying. Farid Ahmad, Nicmohammed and Zmarey should have been turned off like pirates at Execution Dock, with prayers and long-winded confessions and the sudden jolting of a cart. Instead, three bodies twisted in the cold wind and the crowd melted away, deeply dissatisfied, balked of a ceremony. The whole purpose, to teach society an Islamic lesson, had somehow been dissipated.

It took us a lot of effort to get the kind of pictures which would avoid showing the nasty reality of what we had observed. All we used when the pictures were edited were shots of the three standing in front of the gallows, but not having the nooses put round their necks; the cross-tree bending under the weight of the first and second hangings; the eager faces of the onlookers; the shadow of Nicmohammed's feet on the ground; and a distant wide shot of the three hanging there side by side. Even so, there were complaints from viewers. There always are.

The people from the aid agencies who had started off by being such enthusiastic onlookers had gone very quiet. When they left, there was none of the earlier hand-shaking and back-slapping. I had the sense that they all felt guilty and embarrassed and in some way diminished, as though they'd been carried away in some big crowd action like looting or burning someone unpopular out of their house; and now, when they thought about it, they didn't feel so good about what they had done. A Western photographer came up to us quietly afterwards and said he had a favour to ask.

'I'd be glad if you didn't show any shots of me up close, getting pictures of their faces.'

We at least hadn't done anything to be ashamed of. We'd just been doing our job, and we'd put a lot of effort into making the hangings as inoffensive as we could. Even so, we ate our dinner quietly that night at the German Club, where we were staying. For once there were no jokes, no anecdotes about the absurdities of friends and colleagues. I brought out my bottle of Laphroaig single malt, and we each drank more than we usually would. With its aid I slept heavily that night, and remembered nothing until I woke up with the thin grey light coming through the curtains. But I dreamt about it the next night, all the same.

« »

The first time I came across Taliban soldiers, I couldn't tell the difference between them and any other mujaheddin group. And perhaps there wasn't any difference: a clever mixture of bribery and good propaganda had won over dozens of local warlords to the Taliban side. They were crouched behind a makeshift wall of piled-up rocks beside the road, and we had just made the nerve-racking journey by car between the two front lines, on the outskirts of Kabul. These men had no objection whatever to being filmed. Nor did their commander, though because he was still nervous about his new masters (he had only recently changed sides) he insisted that someone else had to do the talking on camera for him.

It was only when we went south to Kandahar, the Taliban capital, that we found the real thing. They were very alarming indeed. Kandahar is famous for its homosexuality, and it was commonplace to find Taliban soldiers with mascara'd eyes, painted finger- and toenails, and high-heeled gold sandals. Also the AK-47.

'I've only seen one thing worse,' Peter said.

In Liberia, it seems, he was filming a whole gang of soldiers looting the shops when they came running down the street after him. They'd just hit a bridal shop and a lighting store, so they were wearing wedding-dresses and lampshades on their head. And they were angry.

The Taliban – the word means 'religious students' – began in the refugee camps around the Pakistani border town of Quetta and swept across into Afghanistan in 1994, in rage at the failure of the government to impose the basics of fundamentalist Islam. They weren't particularly good fighters, but they were Pashtu-speakers who had played intelligently on the linguistic divisions inside Afghanistan and had gained the support of many groups which disliked the lordly ways of the predominantly Tajik-speaking government in Kabul.

Some of the Taliban's greatest gains had been achieved through making deals, rather than on the field of battle. Now they controlled half the territory and almost half the population of Afghanistan, from Herat in the West to the border with Pakistan, and their forces were besieging the capital, Kabul, itself. The Taliban's main centres, Kandahar and Herat, were on the Pakistani telephone system, and Pakistani banks flourished in several of their towns and cities.

The Taliban were probably the most extreme Islamic fundamentalist group in the world. By comparison, Iran and even Saudi Arabia seemed positively liberal. There were even fewer women on the streets than in Kabul, and those few who appeared were covered from head to foot in the traditional *burkhas*. On either side of the road that led into the centre of the city stood two rickety steel towers. The Taliban had strung up old televisions and video-cassettes on them, hanging them with recording tape like the bodies of executed criminals from gibbets. Television was evil, because it presumed to capture the likeness of living creatures: something which, according to their interpretation of the Koran, was blasphemous.

Kandahar wasn't, therefore, the easiest place for a television team to work. An aggressive young mullah was appointed to chaperone us, and he had instructions not even to let us film the hanging television sets. Peter did it anyway, since the mullah had little idea of the scope a cameraman has for filming surreptitiously. On the flat roof of a nearby building, while our translator talked to the mullah, we recorded a piece to camera and at least got some pictures of people walking around in the streets.

> Transcript of report for the *Nine O'Clock News*,
> Kandahar, 27.4.96
>
> JS: The Taliban are probably the most extreme Islamic
> fundamentalist group in the world. By comparison with
> this place, Iran and even Saudi Arabia seem positively
> liberal. We aren't allowed to film any living creature,
> because that would constitute making a graven image of
> it. The Taliban police Kandahar very intensively, and
> those who don't necessarily support the regime here are
> too frightened to speak to us. It's hard to move here
> without being watched or stopped and questioned.

But we had one sensational piece of good luck. On the morning after we arrived Mullah Omar Akund, the one-eyed, reclusive leader of the Taliban, was to reveal the cloak of the Prophet Mohammed, donated centuries before to Kandahar, before the eyes of an expectant crowd.

The cloak was only shown publicly at moments of great significance; the last time had been more than sixty years before. Now, as the Taliban prepared to open their great onslaught against Kabul, they took it out again.

Our driver, a fat turbaned character whose young sidekick had some disgusting habits – we called him Ghastly Boy – edged the vehicle gingerly through the enormous crowd that had gathered in front of the building where the cloak was kept.

People gathered round us in large numbers, staring in through the windows. They weren't hostile; it was just that they hadn't seen Europeans before. It had happened the evening before as well, and that was quite alarming. The crowd looked particularly menacing, and men with terrible scars and one with an empty eye socket pressed their faces against the glass. It was very hot in the vehicle, and we were getting distinctly uneasy. Then Garry Marvin made the joke of the entire trip.

'Don't look now,' he said, 'but the crowd's turning ugly.'

Now, with the ceremony of the Prophet's cloak to attract their attention, scarcely anyone noticed us. Peter Jouvenal was able to get some extraordinary pictures, as Mullah Omar held up the ancient piece of pale brown material. The emotion of the crowd was intense. People wept aloud, and tore the turbans off their heads to throw them up into the air and touch the cloak. It was like watching Peter the Hermit preaching the First Crusade. The result was rather similar, too: within a few months the Taliban had captured in Kabul.

It seemed impossible to persuade any senior figure in the Taliban to record an interview with us on camera. One of them agreed to have his answers recorded, but wouldn't show any part of himself to the camera. He wouldn't even allow us to film the cup he drank tea from. Instead, the camera had to be on my face all the time, as I listened to him; tough on the audience. Some Taliban leaders, more moderate, were sympathetic to the idea, but felt their position within the organization would suffer if it were known that we had made a graven image of them.

On our last day we went to see the Taliban minister of health, Mullah Balouch. He had a fearsome reputation: a strong supporter of the punishments defined in the *Sharia*, or Islamic law, he tried to persuade the surgeons under his control to cut off the hands and feet of convicted criminals. If they refused, he did it himself. By all accounts he rather enjoyed it.

We found him in his office, surrounded by a couple of dozen petitioners. When he saw us he waved them away. With the camera running, I went over to him and asked him if he would consider giving us an interview. It never occurred to me that he might. Yet Mullah Balouch turned out to be a liberal; relatively speaking, that is.

'It is idolatry to show a person's face only, since a graven image can be made from that. But if you show me down to the waist, no graven image can be made from it.'

'Absolutely,' I said, not understanding a word of it; and we showed him, as he wanted, down to the waist.

He proved to be a frank interviewee, except on the question of his own involvement in the punishments. He absolutely denied cutting off anyone's hands or feet himself, even though what he had done was a matter of public knowledge in Kandahar. Perhaps he realized the effect it might have on a Western audience if he admitted it. But he insisted it wasn't in any way strange that a minister of health should try to persuade hospital surgeons to amputate perfectly healthy limbs. I wasn't going to disagree with him. Liberals were in short enough supply in the ranks of the Taliban without falling out with the only one we'd found.

« »

Since 1989 Peter Jouvenal is the only cameraman I have worked with in Afghanistan. In the normal way I would tell the cameraman what I wanted to do, but in Afghanistan the pattern is rather different. In nearly twenty years Peter has made dozens of expeditions there, often in the most dangerous conditions. He knows almost every part of it. When we plan a trip, therefore, I don't tell him what we will do, I ask him what he thinks. And I take his advice.

His knowledge of military things is unrivalled. If you walk with Peter through the battlefields of Afghanistan he can tell you, not simply what each piece of rusting metal is, but what kind of gun or helicopter or military aircraft it comes from. He will know at a range of twenty yards which particular factory in which particular country the AK-47 in the hands of some louche mujahid was made. In Kabul he collects and restores the *jezails* and British muskets which can still be found there in large numbers.

Peter is a loner. His background is as odd as my own. His mother is German, and they lived with Peter's guardian, an old lady with a sensational Arts and Crafts house overlooking the Thames outside Henley. Then the old lady died, and the death duties forced Peter to sell the house. He tried unsuccessfully to raise enough money from the contents, and showed me some of the things that were there. His guardian's family had never thrown anything away, so there were copies of *The Times* from the 1830s, still unopened in their wrappers, medals, swords, letters from the famous, a cocked hat with a bullet-hole in it that someone had worn at the Battle of Waterloo, endless mementoes from the Crimean War. It all went, and the house along with it.

Peter is a man who has everything carefully worked out: suppliers of goods, houses in the most unlikely places, unexpected comforts. At his house in Kabul, his cook had once been the French ambassador's chef. At the end of a long day's marching or riding, it is always Peter who pulls out the bar of chocolate, the restoring tin of bully-beef. The unexpected is his speciality. Once when we were staying at the German Club in Kabul, a large and rather pleasant compound where we could drink whisky and smoke cigars at the end of the day, he called us over to his room and pulled a couple of large metal trunks out from under his bed.

'Guess what's in there?'

We made a few wrong guesses.

'Couple of skeletons.'

He started to open one of them and show us. Skeletons were exactly what you would expect to find in metal boxes under Peter Jouvenal's bed.

For some years he had run an organization which seeks to find information about the Russian and Afghan soldiers missing after the war in Afghanistan. From time to time he discovered the body of a Russian and dug it up, in order to be able to send it back to the family. It's typical of Peter: something no one else would do, extremely philanthropic, yet somehow weird. He is a thoroughly nineteenth-century character, buccaneering and highly principled. Sir Charles Napier, Sir James Brooke, Sir Henry Lawrence would all recognize him as one of their own, and John Buchan would have written a thriller about him.

One evening in 1989, as I sat in their house in Peshawar, Peter and Chris Hooke showed me a film they had made some time before in the remotest part of Afghanistan, the mountains of the far north-east. In the Kvarjeh Mohammed range, where the Kowkcheh River runs parallel to Afghanistan's borders with Tajikistan and Pakistan, lies the world's best deposit of the dark blue semi-precious stone lapis lazuli. It may be the world's oldest continuously worked mine; lapis was being taken out of Sar-i-Sang for the jewellery of the Indus civilizations and those of Egypt and Mesopotamia as early as the fourth millennium BC. According to Peter and Chris, the methods used now had improved very little.

Over the years that followed, I often thought about going to Sar-i-Sang: especially when I saw the lapis jewellery of Ur in the British Museum, or the inlaid eyes on the funeral mask of Tutankhamun, or an illustrated mediaeval manuscript where the Virgin's cloak was coloured by the crushed lapis which the artists called 'ultramarine' because it came from beyond the seas.

> Some lump, ah God, of LAPIS LAZULI,
> Blue as a vein o'er the Madonna's breast

So wrote Robert Browning. When I bought a set of lapis worry-beads in the Grand Bazaar in Tehran, I felt a powerful desire to see the place where all this had come from.

Other mines, in Africa and South America, produce lapis lazuli of a sort. But the best quality, a deep rich blue often flecked with gold, comes today as it did before the first dynasties in Egypt and China, from this one mountain in the Hindu Kush. Lapis isn't a precious stone; it is a rock. The blueness comes from the mineral lazulite, and the golden flecks are iron pyrites – 'fool's gold'. German, Japanese and American jewellers prize lapis highly, and rich Arabs encrust their bathroom scales with it.

It was difficult to persuade anyone that this would make a particularly good news story. Still, it seemed that the mujaheddin leaders in the area financed their war from the proceeds of the lapis that was dug out there, and the big drugs dealers of Pakistan often used it to mask the profits from heroin. The BBC's initial doubts weren't so much editorial as practical: it seemed too dangerous. Sar-i-Sang was one of the hardest places in the world to get to. Robbers abounded, and the pack-horse and mule were the only reliable means of transport.

It would take at least three weeks, and it wasn't easy for me to set aside a period as long as that. Things have a disturbing habit of happening in other parts of the world when you're locked into something like this. I was investigating human rights abuses in Argentina when Mrs Gandhi was assassinated in India, and in the depths of the Peruvian jungle when sterling fell out of the European Monetary System. To be away from one's desk at such times is distinctly bad for business.

Still, it was merely a question of opening the diary at an empty page or two, and hoping that they would stay empty after I had written 'Afghanistan?' on them. It had also become markedly easier to sell the idea to my colleagues. Our trip to Afghanistan in 1996 had won various awards in Britain and the United States, and I proposed that the same team – Tom Giles, Peter Jouvenal and I (Garry Marvin had now started a new job as a university lecturer) – should come to Sar-i-Sang with me now. We also invited a dealer in gems, Guy Clutterbuck, to go with us, since he knew the place and had been there more than once on buying expeditions.

On the last day of September 1997 we flew in to the small mountain town of Faisabad, two hundred difficult miles north-east of Kabul, in a UN plane. It was already starting to be cold. Horsemen skittered bravely on the dusty roads that wound round the mountainside, and went closer than was comfortable to the edge of the road, which fell away to the rushing green river half a mile below. The Hindu Kush range has a savage name; it means 'Hindu Killer', because so many slaves captured in raids on India died as they were being brought through these high passes.

In Persian, though, it is *Uparisena*, 'the peak too high for eagles to fly over', and Alexander the Great borrowed the name and turned it in Greek: *Paropamisus*. He passed through this region in 327 BC, and the beautiful Persian woman he married, Roxane, daughter of Oxy-artes, came either from the Panshir Valley or from Tajikistan, depending on your loyalties. Somewhere around the modern air base of Bagram, north of Kabul, Alexander founded a city which he called Alexandria-in-the-Caucasus, with 7,000 local people and those of his own soldiers who were too ill, too old or too unwilling to go further east with him. These are the mountains of Kipling's *The Man Who Would Be King*, whose two ex-Army heroes come across the remains of an ancient Greek civilization.

> 'See here!' said Dravot, his thumb on the map. 'Up to Jagdallak, Peachey and me know the road. We was there with Roberts' Army. We'll have to turn off to the right at Jagdallak through Laghman territory. Then we get among the hills – fourteen thousand feet – fifteen thousand – it will be cold work there, but it don't look very far on the map.'

It was an awful long way on the ground, though. In the straggling market of Faisabad we bought everything we lacked: heavy blankets, some rotten little Chinese torches, a couple of elderly Russian sleeping bags, a gigantic ancient hand-made padlock to protect the contents of my army surplus kitbag from pilferers. A leather-worker, squatting in the roadway, sewed thick leather patches on the tough-looking but easily torn Camel bag I had bought at Harrods; a lesson in the futility of Roughing-It chic. (On the other hand, my Barbour boots and my Drizabone topcoat, which I bought at the same time, proved to be superb in the most difficult conditions. Not everything cheap is good; not everything expensive lets you down.) We also paid a tailor to run up a couple of flags with 'BBC' on them, blue on white. In a country where the BBC was so popular, and where there were so many brigands, we thought they might possibly do us a bit of good.

I was taking photographs in the market when Guy pointed out a small girl to me. She must have been about six, and had crept out with her friends to look at the extraordinary foreigners who were strutting round the market. Her hair was as gold as the brash necklaces that hung in the bazaars, her skin was lighter than mine, and her eyes were a startling blue. Directly I raised the camera to take a photograph, she and her friends ran off squealing in pleasurable terror. They came back again and again, of course, but I was never able to get a clear picture of this Roxane of the Hindu Kush.

In the meantime Tom and Peter had hired a pair of Russian-made jeeps, complete with drivers. The vehicles were brutalist in construction: the windows didn't open, and there were all sorts of flanges and unfinished edges of metal, one of which cut my leg and landed me in hospital months later, when the wound failed to heal. But they were the only vehicles tough enough for the journey. We left in the end, flags flying, waving, hooting our horns, while the children squealed and the mangy dogs barked and the old men laughed behind their hands at the spectacle we had made of ourselves and the amount of money we had parted with.

'I think we slipped out of there without anyone noticing,' I said, echoing a joke which Eamonn Matthews had made on a similar occasion in the Peruvian jungle. What, after all, is the point of a good joke if you don't recycle it occasionally?

Before the fatigue of being constantly jolted up and down and sideways began to get to us, the journey was very enjoyable. Guy Clutterbuck was a good raconteur. One of his best stories was about how he had hidden a large, valuable and distinctively-cut jewel up his backside for security when he was in a particularly difficult part of the world. After arriving in Britain and extracting it, he sold it to one of the big London jewellers. The next time he saw it, he said, was in a photograph on the cover of *Hello* magazine. Hanging round the neck of Diana, Princess of Wales.

We made a two-day detour to the front line to film the war between the Taliban and Ahmad Shah Massoud. It was just as war always is in Afghanistan, a mixture of absurd carelessness on the part of the fighters you are with, sudden sharp moments of considerable danger, and the strange lassitude which follows it. Tom and I, unused to the particular sounds which the weaponry of the mujaheddin made, tended to duck when there was outgoing fire and sometimes failed to notice when it was incoming. That caused a good deal of laughter. Years of working with Peter Jouvenal, though, had taught me that when he made for cover it was a good idea to follow.

Then it was time to begin the drive to Sar-i-Sang in earnest. It took another two days. A local warlord called Najimudeen Khan, loyal to Massoud, controlled the area, and a few days earlier we had managed to get his permission to go there.

It was given hurriedly, since a Taliban plane was coming in to dive-bomb us at the time.

'Go on, put anything in front of him and he'll sign it,' Guy said. 'Write out his will and he'll sign that.'

'Or your expenses,' said Tom, thinking perhaps of the administration that lay ahead of him when we got back to Britain.

I said nothing. I was watching the Taliban plane wheeling in the sky and coming towards us. Fortunately the pilot changed his mind.

Plenty of heavily-armed men along our way owed no loyalty to anyone, and the threat of robbery was very real. Once a group of men fired shots to make us stop and pick them up; we didn't, of course. At night, as we slept, wandering groups of shepherds made their way through our camp with their flocks of sheep and goats.

There were occasional road-blocks, and the atmosphere was tense. Other groups of mujaheddin seemed to be trying to muscle in on Najimuddin Khan's lapis lazuli. A piece of paper, scribbled by one of his junior commanders, got us through any problems, and maybe our BBC flags helped too. They certainly seemed to impress a lot of people as we drove through. But the worst part was the road itself: often nothing more than a boulder-strewn, dried-up river or a precarious track beside an abyss. Soon it was dark, but the track was too narrow for us to be able to stop and camp for the night, so the drivers decided to press on. They peered intently out into the darkness at the rocks and grey dust ahead, avoiding disaster by their instinct and the strength of their wrists. On our left was the solid grey rock wall of the mountain-side; on our right there was nothing but darkness, where the edge of the road fell away into a precipice. Somewhere down there was the Kowkcheh River. When we stopped we could hear it rushing and foaming over the boulders in its bed.

We lit fires and ate a quick meal, then lay down to sleep. I stayed awake for what seemed like hours, listening to the strange sounds of the night. Some *kouchis* seemed to be camping nearby with their animals. Once there was a crack in the sky, as a shooting star hit the earth's atmosphere. I must have slept, though; each time I looked up at them, the amazing star-patterns had shifted perceptibly.

We were on our way at five o'clock. It was Friday 3 October, and the journey I had waited eight years for was about to reach its climax. It had taken us fifteen hours to drive the last forty miles. Shortly after six our jeeps mounted the crest of a ridge and Sar-i-Sang lay in front of us. We got out and stood in the keen, cold air. It was a magical moment. Behind the mountain of lapis the rising sun's rays fanned out into the sky. 'Like the crown of a god-emperor,' I enthused a couple of days later, as I dictated my weekly column for the *Sunday Telegraph* by satellite phone. Then, thinking I had gone a bit over the top, I added, 'or the letter-heading of a dodgy insurance company'. The sub-editors, romantics despite themselves, disapproved and cut that part out.

We couldn't take our eyes off the mountain and its brilliant nimbus now.

'The Holy Grail,' said Tom, and we shook hands silently as though we were Victorian explorers. And indeed only four Westerners had reached the mine in at least the previous quarter-century. Two of them – Peter Jouvenal and Guy Clutterbuck – were here with us now.

The mountain was an isosceles triangle of yellowish granite a mile above us. The mining shift had just changed, and tiny figures ran down the steep paths, their feet throwing up clouds of dust, their backs bent under the weight of the lapis they had excavated, the overseers urging them on with sticks. They descended on a primitive village at the mountain-foot, which can't have changed in any essential for six thousand years: single-roomed huts made of piled stones, a few ill-smelling alleyways, shops selling vegetables, newly butchered goats' meat. There were no women here, and no children. Sar-i-Sang village exists solely to serve the mine, and the superstition goes that the mine is female. The presence of women here would make her jealous, and the supply of lapis would dry up.

The system of exploiting the mine is probably the same now as it always has been. Big dealers lease the workings for a month or so at a time, and the lapis that is dug out belongs to them. The miners are given wages. Long tradition allows them to pilfer a certain amount, and this is sold to small dealers who meet them on their way down from their shift; but the overseers are on hand to see that no really good quality lapis is sold like this.

While we filmed a miner sitting on a rock and playing an intricate little tune on a handmade flute, one of our drivers nudged me. The man who ran the mine for Najimudeen Khan, Commander Malik, was coming down the little street between the stone houses towards us, accompanied by his lackeys and thrusting aside the donkeys and the little fringed and tasselled horses who stood in his way. The miners moved back quickly: Malik was the real power at Sar-i-Sang.

To us he was charming, and invited us to his house for tea and a meal. We sat on the floor and leant against cushions as the tea-kettle went round. A hurricane-lamp hissed on the carpeted floor in front of us, and some very questionable meat on metal plates appeared. I ate the unleavened bread and a few gritty radishes, but declined the meat. I had seen a bloody goat's head lying in the alley close by, and assumed there was some connection.

Commander Malik had a crafty, intellectual face, with a high domed forehead and ears which stuck out under his turban. He looked as though he was always about to smile, but never quite did; and after he had said something his eyes scanned our faces to guess our reaction.

'How old do you think the mine is?' I asked.

'Well, I'm thirty-four and it was going when I was born.'

I couldn't work out whether he genuinely didn't know, or was reluctant to give us any straight information. When I asked him about the profits from the lapis, he lied blandly.

Transcript of *Newsnight* report, 5.11.97

Speaker: Commander Malik

The money earned here is for everyone in Afghanistan.
All over the country people come here to work, including
those who are very poor. None of the money we raise here
goes to the war or to the military commanders. It goes
towards building roads, mosques and clinics, and
helping the poor.

When an Afghan commander gets pious like that, you can usually guess he's lying. Still, he was hospitable enough, and invited us to climb up and see the mine for ourselves.

There are now four mines on the mountain, but only the first, Mardan-i-Yek, and the fourth, Mardan-i-Chahar, produce the best quality lapis. The fourth mine was slightly easier to get to, but I was determined to see the workings that dated back before the earliest Egyptian and Chinese dynasties.

We set off shortly before noon. The entrance to Mardan-i-Yek was visible close to the peak of the mountain, but it was a long way up: at least a mile. The two-hour climb was one of the hardest things I have ever done, and I was soon the last of the group; though the rest, the oldest of whom was a good fifteen years younger than me, had their problems too. In some places the path had been swept away by land-slides, and we had to clamber up the bare rock. On the last and steepest part I looked down at the village, with the figures of miners and horses scarcely even discernible, and tried to summon up the willpower to fight my way on. Tom leaned over from a little way above me, his face showing his anxiety.

'You are going to be able to make it, aren't you? We really need a piece to camera there.'

I didn't want to let Tom down, but I didn't want to let myself down either. To have waited eight years and then give up so close to the mine was unthinkable. I gripped a fault in the rock, put one of my Barbour boots onto a tuft of some greyish-green weed and the other on a little rivulet of small brown gravel, and pushed upwards. Hands gripped me. As is so often the way, there was a path not far from us, and directly we found ourselves on that everything was much easier.

It was a magnificent moment when the dark mouth of the mine yawned above us. We slumped down on a little platform covered with an old carpet, and one of the miners brought us tea. It was dark and bitter, but it tasted better than anything I had ever drunk. I sipped it and looked out over the superb river valley, southwards in the general direction of Kabul.

The entrance to the mine was blackened by the smoke of six thousand years. In prehistory the sharp blueness of the lapis lazuli must have been discernible on the surface of the rock, and men must have lugged wood and water all the way up here, laid the wood against the rock-face, set fire to it, and then dashed the water against the hot rock to crack it and get the lapis out. It was primitive and immensely strenuous, but it worked well enough to produce the material for Tutankhamun's funeral mask.

Until twenty years ago, the mining techniques were improving. Compressors and generators were installed, experts of different kinds came in. The war has ended all that. Nowadays the miners have a few Swedish-made drills, elderly and small, with which they make holes in the rock-face. One of the miners holds the bit in his bare hand to direct it. Then they jam explosives into the holes, light the fuses, and run like mad for safety. Peter and Tom, filming them, had no idea what was going to happen, and they ran for it too. We were just outside when a deep rumble shook the mountain, and dust drifted out of the mine entrance. But there is often a problem: if several sticks of explosive go off at once, they can't tell how many bangs there were. That means someone has to go back inside to see if all the explosives have gone off. Almost every month someone dies like this. Once they're sure, the miners race back in before the fumes have faded to grab the best chunks of lapis for themselves.

It is about as dangerous a way to earn a living as you can imagine. And these must be some of the worst-paid workers in the entire world, taking into account the value of what they produce. For a twelve-hour shift they earn £1.20; ten pence an hour. Each kilo of lapis lazuli they dig out is worth up to £12,000 when cut and polished: ten thousand times as much. The miners are essentially slaves of the mountain.

Worse, the brutal methods they use constitute a kind of rape. The lapis is fractured and spoiled by the explosives; and because it is being produced in such large quantities, and is so damaged, the international price for it is falling. To have a unique source like this, and yet to sell it off more and more cheaply, is a sign of the most foolish wastefulness.

We interviewed one of the miners, a young man called Abdul Samad. What he said had the ring of truth to it, and contradicted everything Commander Malik had told us earlier.

Transcript of interview from *Newsnight* report, 5.11.97

Speaker: Abdul Samad

AS: Najimuddin Khan sells concessions to the mine to big businessmen in Pakistan. They give him the money, and he issues the orders from his base. Commander Malik keeps a check on it all for him. The commanders who have the power make the money. We blast the mine, but the commanders take over the big rocks and the rest of us get the left-overs. The commanders spend the money on themselves.

And the roads, the mosques, the clinics? Non-existent, except for a short stretch of rough road running southwards for a few miles along the line of the Kowkcheh River to the village of Skazar. The caravans of lapis, which once went to Kabul for cutting and polishing, now go over the mountains to Pakistan.

Commander Malik was as watchfully affable as ever when we left the following morning. There was a formal exchange of presents in front of everybody: he gave us a thousand pounds' worth of lapis, and I gave him my Sony Walkman. The crowd seemed to think it was a fair exchange. Everything was very pleasant; except that Malik warned our translator privately that we must never talk about the things we had seen at Sar-i-Sang. The purpose of television broadcasting seemed rather to have eluded him.

We headed off for the village of Skazar in a pleasant, open valley at the confluence of the Kowkcheh and Monjan rivers. There we paid off our faithful drivers and their even more faithful Russian jeeps, and while I dictated my column to the *Sunday Telegraph* by satellite phone the others hired a team of horsemen at the caravanserai. On the map, the distance is short: 25 miles to the Pakistani border. But maps can be very deceptive. Some of the mountains around us rose to more than twenty thousand feet, and even the passes between them were extremely difficult.

Not, however, for the first leg of the journey. We merely headed along the river valley. My horse was rather good: a stallion which Ahmad Shah Massoud's chief of intelligence had once ridden in games of *buzkashi*, the ferocious version of polo which Afghans play with the headless body of a goat instead of a ball, while their mounts attack and bite each other. Now, though, my horse's fighting spirit seemed to have been completely crushed out of him, and he merely plodded along, carrying my fifteen stone and a good part of our equipment. We established a good relationship, though. I found a noise which seemed to comfort him, and every time I made it he would turn his head and nuzzle my foot affectionately; alarming the first time, when I remembered his *buzkashi*-playing past, but fine after that. 'Together,' as Peachy Carnehan says to Rudyard Kipling, 'we starts forward into those bitter cold mountainous parts, and never a road broader than the back of your hand.'

The landscape was superb; and in the chill of the evening, we came to a little mosque by the riverside and prepared to settle down there for the night. The drivers were simple men and very poor, and right from the start they seemed to show an unhealthy interest in the things we had: torches, gloves, penknives, food. By their standards we must have seemed unthinkably rich.

We were off by 5.30 the following morning, a penumbra of dust hanging over us in the golden morning sunlight and blurring the details like an impressionist watercolour. By eight o'clock we were climbing the mountains, and the difficult part had begun. The track curled in and out between rocks and over ridges, and whenever it got steep we had to get off our horses and walk. At this altitude the air felt fine and very thin, and we found ourselves taking thirsty gulps of it. The energy tablets I had bought at Boots before I left became very popular.

We often saw other caravans of horses or donkeys. This is the main trade route for all sorts of goods, smuggled or otherwise: lapis lazuli, emeralds, opium and heroin, guns. At midday, still without food, we came to a high plateau which served as a resting-place for travellers. There were boulders everywhere which were used to shelter small fires from the wind, and half a dozen or more groups of travellers had stopped to brew tea, smoke, gossip and rest. There was a kind of truce here. You could leave your bags of lapis or opium and go off, and no one would tamper with them.

A little further off sat a group of men with six Siberian falcons, live and hooded, which they were giving a little air and exercise to. The falcons were more valuable than any lapis or emeralds. At the markets in Peshawar they would be bought by dealers and taken to Saudi Arabia, where they would fetch £100,000 each. Hooded, they turned their heads alertly to the sound of our voices, as though they were hoping to find out what was going to happen to them.

'Of course I know it's not right,' the head of the group said. 'These are our birds – Afghanistan's. Once there used to be lions here and all sorts of other animals. Now they've all gone. They've been hunted to extinction. I don't want that to happen to the falcons. But I'm a poor man. What else can I do?'

There was a characteristic whine in his voice, yet he was right in a way. Afghanistan has become a country which plunders itself for the benefit of others, and the most that Afghans can do is to get their cut – the smallest of all.

It was dark by the time we reached the border with Pakistan and found a couple of vehicles which would take us onwards. In the confusion the drivers decided to steal some of our things: the lapis Malik had given us, and my Camel bag containing my passport, money, notebooks and my Psion organizer, which contains my entire life and is irreplaceable. Hunger, fatigue and cold drove me wild with fury. I grabbed one of the drivers by the neck and told our translator to go off and get a Kalashnikov. I'd shoot the driver with it, I said.

Maybe I didn't mean it, but the drivers thought I did. Even before the translator had started off in search of the AK, the lapis and the Camel bag had mysteriously been found. A superb golden moon climbed above the mountains and shone into the lake which lay between them. We still had twenty hours' travelling to do over the mountains into Pakistan before we reached Chitral, some of it as rough as anything we'd endured in Afghanistan. But the journey had been a success. I put my hand into my pocket and gripped the small piece of lapis I had picked up on the mountainside at Sar-i-Sang: as dark and rich as the blue of the Virgin's cloak, gently veined with a faint line of glittering gold like a vapour trail in the sky. It was true. I'd done it.

18

Journey's End

THE STREETS WERE DARK and crowded. I parked at an angle on the steep camber and handed a coin to the ragged figure whose only source of income came from waving white drivers unnecessarily into parking places. In the evening warmth, with the smell of *boerewors* on the air, it felt good to be back in Johannesburg again. It had been eighteen years since I lived here, and I was on the lookout for old haunts.

Hillbrow had been my favourite part of the city, mixed and raffish. It was one part of the old South Africa where blacks and whites could socialize without trouble from officialdom. And not only socialize, but live together in the blocks of flats that reached down every hill leading from the brow. You could get things here – music, books, clothes – that weren't available anywhere else on the continent of Africa. Hillbrow felt like being in Europe, only it had the pioneering freedom of Africa as well. It felt good just to walk its slanting pavements again.

Music was blaring from a record shop, but it wasn't the one I was looking for. That seemed to have been taken over by a fast-food joint. People sat inside, heads together, laughing. I crossed the road, climbing the camber and then walking down it: on the rare occasions when it rained here, the flow of water was fierce. It swept everything else aside.

It was harder to work out where the bookshop had been. Surely it couldn't have gone out of business? You really could find almost everything there: books by Communists, books by the ANC, serious literature, even – God help us – books about sex. Wisely, the South African thought-police left this shop alone. It was a colony of freedom in an independent state of mental repression.

But where was it now? There was the clothes boutique I remembered. There was the upstairs café where the old refugees from Nazi Central Europe used to play chess. Surely it was down here? But the place was so dark and closed, it was hard to think anything of interest had ever been here.

'What happened to Exclusive Books?' I asked in the chemist's shop opposite.

The elderly white man behind the counter peered at me curiously. Exclusive Books, it seemed, had moved out to the relative safety of the rich northern suburbs.

'You've got to be careful here,' he said in the accent of Lithuania or Poland. 'Hillbrow's very dangerous now.'

Apparently there had been a stabbing on the pavement outside only twenty minutes earlier. The old man had called the police himself. So why stay?

'At my age—'

He'd been in Theresienstadt and survived that; why move now? He pointed to a pump-action shotgun in the corner which was almost as big as he was.

'It keeps them away.'

He didn't say who 'they' were.

Outside, on the pavement, I saw the place with new eyes. It wasn't charming, raffish and mixed any longer, it was dangerous. I was the only whitey on the streets, and I didn't feel comfortable any longer. When I had lived here, the law had imposed segregation on the races. Nowadays crime performed the same function.

I had come back to Johannesburg a month before the election of May 1994, which would bring about majority rule. It was, in its way, another revolution to cover. Journalists were starting to move in in large numbers, convinced that a bloodbath was likely. Reading the British newspapers, I thought so too. Supporters of the predominantly Zulu Inkatha movement were murdering and being murdered by supporters of Nelson Mandela's ANC every day. Given the possibility of violence from the white extremist fringe, the chances of a peaceful election seemed remarkably slight.

The next morning, in the warm, clear weather no one from England ever tires of, I went on a tour of inspection, beginning with the place where I had lived with Diane, Julia and Eleanor when we were based here in the late seventies. Our lovely sprawling colonial bungalow had been knocked down now. In its place was an estate of imitation Tex-Mex town houses called Rancho something, with heavy gates and warnings about dogs and rapid armed response.

Standing looking through the bars I couldn't even work out where the house had stood, nor the studio from which I had broadcast about uprisings in Soweto and the death of Steve Biko and the creation of phoney apartheid statelets like Bophuthatswana. As for the incomparable garden where the *Piet-my-vrouw* birds called, and the jacaranda trees and the bougainvillea flowered, that had vanished under the concrete adobe: gone like apartheid, gone like Bophuthatswana.

The area seemed grander and more prosperous now, like white South Africa as a whole. More frightened, too. Almost every house had signs from security firms on them. If you pressed the alarm button which had been fitted in each room (two in the larger ones) a truckload of men would screech to a halt outside in less than four minutes. They would be equipped with sawn-off shotguns and a computer print-out which named everyone entitled to be on the premises. Anyone else could be shot without too many problems.

There used to be a sign outside one house that said, 'Is There Life After Death? Trespass Here And Find Out.' Now people no longer joked about such things; not when you could emerge from your electronically operated gates and be blown away by a group of armed thugs who had been lying in wait for you. As a result, every householder could legally hold a gun for protection; and the newspapers carried innumerable stories about children shooting themselves with their parents' guns, or fathers coming home in a bad mood and wiping out the entire family plus the dog.

As I drove round that morning, every tree by the side of the road carried an election promise: 'Vote ANC For More Jobs', 'Only The National Party Can Stop The ANC', 'The Democrats: No Murderers, No Corrupt Politicians'. And below the party signs were the newspaper placards: 'Anxiety Grows In Durban', 'Massacre Investigation Latest'. Mass murder, riot and murder had become the stock-in-trade of the newspaper reporter now. And yet I found it strangely difficult to be gloomy. It wasn't just the weather, or being back in a country I had come to love. It was the extraordinary changes which had taken place.

When I lived in South Africa the National Party existed for three reasons: to further the interests of the Afrikaner, to force English-speakers out of political life, and to keep the black, 'coloured' and Indian populations as helots. I hadn't met very many Afrikaners. I knew a few middle-class intellectuals, highly intelligent, often anglophile and usually deeply opposed to apartheid. I had met various kindly, crackbrained souls who believed that the Bible had ordered the different races to live apart, and I had come across the quiet, hospitable Boers who farmed the Karoo or the Lowveld. But the Afrikaners I had met most often were the angry policemen and small-time bureaucrats who had been empowered by decades of unbroken National Party rule to do whatever they wanted to anyone: especially anyone who challenged the power of the state. I knew little of the intelligent, liberal, educated, European-minded Afrikaners of the big cities.

I left the pleasant, wooded suburbs with their reassuringly English names (Westcliff Drive, Oxford Road, Jellicoe Street) where everything was intended to make you forget you were in Africa, and drove into Johannesburg proper. In the seventies it had had a charming touch of the frontier town: red earth was liable to boil up between the paving stones, and there were still plenty of the shaded arcades supported by elaborate white-painted Victorian steel posts. Now Africa had started to take over. The streets were littered and dirty, there were street markets on many of the corners, and the white men in suits who had once walked between their offices had all gone. You had to be very careful in the centre of Jo'burg now.

Here there were different National Party posters, directed to the new voters: the black population. 'Once We Imprisoned You Without Trial,' they said; 'Now We've Made The Change.' A few years before it would have been inconceivable: apologizing for apartheid, wooing black voters, allowing blacks to vote at all. Most National Party supporters assumed that their power would last indefinitely, and most liberal whites assumed that it would all end in bloody revolution. Blood was indeed being shed copiously in South Africa now, but this was neither revolution nor civil war: merely a frightening level of crime.

The National Party was still run by the very people who had run apartheid and banned other political parties under a law called, humourlessly, The Prevention of Political Interference Act. Yet these people had indeed made a change. They had understood that they could no longer hang on to power, and they were trying for the best deal available.

It still surprised me to see black people driving expensive cars and sitting in expensive restaurants being waited on by white people. To find that the National Party was seriously trying to win votes from the people whose interests it had deliberately injured was extraordinary.

'This whole country is changing so much, so much,' the old man in the Hillbrow pharmacy had said when I asked him what had happened to Exclusive Books. He was right, and that was a reason for hope. As I turned my car and drove back to the northern suburbs I began to think for the first time that the election might pass off without anarchy and disaster. I decided to write an article for the *Spectator* about it. The *Spec* was the one place where you could stick your neck out and make judgements on the basis of things which an organization like the BBC would be uncomfortable with: instincts, feelings, personal perceptions; especially when they seemed to go so much against the tide. Even Dominic Lawson raised an eyebrow, but he still printed my article.

I've made a lot of bad calls in my career. I predicted that Saddam Hussein would be overthrown by his generals, that Deng Xiaoping and his cronies would lose power after Tiananmen Square, that Shimon Peres would just defeat Benjamin Netanyahu in the 1996 election in Israel. At the same time, I've got some things right: that Saddam would fight a war rather than retreat from Kuwait, that John Major would win the 1992 election, that the Asian Tiger economies were riding for a fall. But the suggestion that the South African election would pass off smoothly was the one I'm most grateful for. It's like backing a horse: you think how good it looks as it walks round the paddock, and you mean to put a bit of money on it, but then you are influenced by all the money on the favourite. Can so many people really be wrong? In the case of South Africa I backed my hunch; and the horse came in first.

« »

In the depths of KwaZulu a week later, though, I thought I'd made a serious mistake. Tired of the BBC office, which was crammed with people from London, I headed out for the area where the worst of the massacres were taking place. With me were Nigel Bateson, the bearded giant who had kept me company in Sarajevo, and a charming, dissolute-looking South African sound recordist called Lee, who in his spare time played in a band called the Cherry-Faced Lurchers. The Lurchers had a serious cult following for their weird, anti-apartheid music. And to guide us around we had a small, delicate Zulu woman called Zandi, who looked as though she was scarcely out of her teens.

I wanted to go first to see Mangosuthu Buthelezi, the leader of Inkatha. It was his refusal to take part in the election which had led to much of the violence with the ANC. I had known Buthelezi in the seventies – had indeed once been walking with him when someone tried to assassinate him – and had been taught some words of Zulu by him over a very pleasant lunch. Now I wanted to get some idea from him of why he was taking his abstentionist line. We flew to the KwaZulu capital, Ulundi, in a light aircraft hired from a company with a good frontier name: Wilgo Airlines.

Below us lay the Mahlabatini plain, as green as a Welsh valley. Here in January 1879 the *amabutho*, the largest army ever fielded by the Zulu kingdom, set out to meet the British at Isandlwana. Behind them as they went they left a trail through the long grass so great that it could still be seen a year later. Our Baron aircraft tipped its wings, and I caught sight of Ulundi, Cetshwayo's capital, where in the following July Lord Chelmsford avenged the disaster at Isandlwana in a battle lasting less than an hour.

Nowadays Ulundi is a small, unremarkable provincial African town built of brick and cinderblock. On a hillside stood a grander set of buildings. In another town, on another continent, it might be the local council offices. In KwaZulu (the prefix 'Kwa' indicates 'the place of') it houses the government of a kingdom. In the days of high apartheid South African tax-payers had dug deep into their pockets so that homeland capitals like Ulundi would be taken seriously.

The airport was expensive too, though where the taxi rank ought to have been, cows cropped the grass. It was hot, the government buildings were a long way off, and we had to carry the television gear. As we emerged from the shade of the fever-trees a car stopped by the roadside. The driver, black and stoutish, wore a purple vest and a silver pectoral; he was an Anglican bishop on his way to conduct the funeral of an Inkatha supporter shot by the ANC a day or two before. The funeral procession was a few hundred yards behind, he said. I told him we would like to film it. He looked troubled, but agreed to drive us back to see it. Beside him sat his chaplain, holding a Bible. The chaplain leant over and whispered something, but the bishop shook his head.

They came round the corner at a slow trot: several blocks of jogging men, fifty or so in each block, brandishing spears and clubs. It was an *amabutho* on the march. The bishop stopped where we asked him, looking more troubled than ever. We got out and started filming.

It was a serious mistake. They gathered in front of us, screaming, brandishing their spears, streaming with sweat, eyes reddened with an anger that was suddenly directed away from the ANC and focused on us. The bishop, a true Christian, stayed with us, raising his arms beseechingly. His chaplain stayed in the car, gripping his Bible harder than ever. Zandi, our Zulu fixer, slipped away. I couldn't blame her; why should she stay and get herself killed? The large KwaZulu police sergeant who had been controlling the march wandered off too. That showed me we were in deep trouble.

The three of us, large, white, and worried, stood in front of the screaming crowd. The clubs and spears were coming very close to our faces, and one old man in particular was going mad, his spittle striking the car and running down our faces.

'No problem, no problem,' I kept saying. All three of us were trying to smile.

Nigel had taken the camera off his shoulder and was showing elaborately that he wasn't filming. If the old man had attacked us, the others would have joined in and we would have been dead in seconds. Instead a beaten-up little car drove up and Zandi shouted at us from it. She had kept her head and hadn't deserted us: she was just getting us a way of escape. We put the television gear in the new car, still smiling and saying 'No problem, no problem,' and the *amabutho* growled angrily and moved on. The bishop looked as though he needed to sit down and have a cup of tea.

The journalists who lived in South Africa, and particularly the cameramen, faced worse dangers than this every day. But it was a long time since I had last seen an angry Zulu crowd, and it was an alarming reminder of the passions that boil up in those compact, disciplined blocks of jogging, sweating men. No wonder, I thought, as we grinned at each other in our relief and thanked Zandi for her presence of mind, that these people had fought so well at Isandlwana and were now killing each other with such ferocity in Natal and on the Witwat- ersrand.

This wasn't a war like the one in Bosnia. There were no armies, no artillery. After a state of emergency was declared in March 1994 an average of eighteen people were dying each day. In Bosnia that would have constituted a lull in the fighting, but less force can have far more effect in Africa than in Europe. The death rate was roughly the same in the bush war in Rhodesia; it had still brought down white rule there.

Two days later we came across the reality of the war. We drove out of the pleasant, brash resort of Durban and headed northwards. The palm trees and the surfers and the great blocks of offices and flats gave way to garages and supermarkets, and then to smaller, poorer houses among the rank, dominating vegetation. Here the faces on the streets were no longer white. A mosque stood on one hillside, an Indian temple on another. Finally the pavement stopped altogether and we were in KwaMashu, the biggest and most troubled of the black town- ships. Almost everyone here was Zulu, but KwaMashu was fiercely divided between Inkatha and the ANC. The atmosphere was extremely tense. As we drove past the remains of previous roadblocks and old burned-out cars everyone watched us nervously.

KwaMashu was built in the bush, and swathes of tall grass sepa- rated the mean houses. Two armoured personnel carriers of the South African army stood in front of a house which had been burned out the previous night. ANC loyalists lived here. The soldiers had experienced a welcome which would once have been unthinkable a few years before, when the government in Pretoria had ordered them in as part of the state of emergency. The inhabitants of KwaMashu had danced and waved and sung with relief as the armoured vehicles rumbled through the streets.

But Inkatha insisted that they were there merely to do the bidding of the ANC, which would shortly be their new master; and Inkatha supporters I spoke to in the street told me the army had just killed a thirteen-year-old boy who had been throwing a petrol bomb. They were now the enemy too, said the Inkatha people. As I walked back to the car I could hear the wind hiss in the long grass, where the snipers and the murder squads hid and watched. But they only operated at night, when people lay awake in their unprotected little huts, listening for the sound of footsteps. That night there was more killing, and more burning of houses.

Back in my hotel on the sea front at Durban I listened to an American-accented voice on my short-wave radio droning portentously, 'As South Africa slides into chaos and bloodshed—' At the time I was looking out of the window at the surfers riding the rollers and the holidaymakers squealing as they took the corners on the chair lift high above the sea-front. There was chaos and bloodshed, but South Africa as a whole wasn't sliding into it. As a result, some of the more gung-ho characters in the international press corps – 'the epaulette brigade', as they're known – were becoming distinctly restless back in Johannes-burg. When we got back there I found a little gathering of people I knew from some of the world's less pleasant places. They were com-plaining about the way things were going.

'I didn't come here to report an *election*,' one of them said, in a voice which showed what he thought about elections; 'I came to report a civil war.'

« »

A couple of days later, on 14 April, I took part in a televised debate between Nelson Mandela and F.W. de Klerk at the Youth Theatre in the centre of Johannesburg. I seemed to be the token foreigner, invited because the debate was to be broadcast by CNN, the BBC, and various other foreign organizations.

I reached the theatre early, in the hope of meeting the two men privately. I had come across F. W. various times in the 1970s; he was the government minister you interviewed if you wanted someone to defend the continued imprisonment of Nelson Mandela. In those days, de Klerk was very strong on Mandela's criminality and his links with terrorism.

Now, when I went to see him in his dressing-room before the debate, he seemed nervous of this ordeal by broadcast. The National Party wouldn't win the forthcoming election, he conceded, but it would become the natural party of opposition to the ANC and ought to be in a good position to win the election that followed. Did he like Mandela? He parried the question. As a person, I said. He parried it again. It was obvious that he didn't, but that politics had brought them together like an arranged marriage of state, and they must pretend to be the best of friends for the good of the country.

I had never met Mandela, though I had seen him after his release from prison in 1990. Now he was affability itself, and thoroughly relaxed as he sat in front of the mirror. The BBC, he said, was one of the most honoured organizations in the world; the initials meant honesty and decency. We exchanged civilities for longer than we talked politics. I noticed how anglophile he was; as a member of a royal house himself, when he spoke about 'Her Majesty the Queen', he said the words with a kind of reverence, as though he felt himself to be her loyal subject.

An awed white make-up woman dabbed his cheeks and forehead with powder, standing back and looking at him professionally, then moving in with little embarrassed movements to cover some unfinished area of his face. He treated her in as courtly a way as he treated me, or as he would treat F. W. de Klerk; as though, after his years in gaol, he had seen a common humanity in us all and directed his attention towards that rather than to our personal importance in the world's order of things. Nelson Mandela wasn't perfect. His temper could be short, his naiveté considerable, and his willingness to overlook the crookedness of his friends and relations depressing. But he radiated jollity and forgiveness, like someone in the last chapter of a Dickens novel.

Outside, his followers were making the life of the debate's producer miserable, like a pack of Alistair Campbells. I found the producer standing on the stage, looking out into the empty seats where the audience would sit, running his hand over his neatly clipped beard in despair. His position was awkward. He was an Indian, one of the new non-white intake into the upper ranks of the SABC, whose job it was to prepare the old mouthpiece of apartheid for a new existence: the future mouthpiece, in all probability, of the ANC.

Only now something had gone wrong. The ANC publicity team had demanded that the desks of the two speakers, Mandela and de Klerk, should be set at an angle of forty-five degrees; anything less, they said, would put Mandela at a disadvantage. Though they didn't explain why, it seemed to be important to them. But the studio technicians had put the desks side by side, and now it was too late to change them. The Indian producer would have to explain that to the ANC.

'They'll go crazy,' he said to his assistant. 'And if anything goes wrong tonight, it'll all be blamed on the desks.' And him, of course.

But nothing went wrong. It wasn't a debate, it was a mime act. I asked a couple of sharp questions, and so did one or two of the South African journalists, but we were allowed no supplementaries and there was no possibility that anyone, questioner or participant, would draw blood.

The only memorable thing about the entire evening was a carefully planned gesture by Mandela. He leant across from his desk and offered his hand to de Klerk, who hadn't expected it. But he took the hand and shook it warmly. The image went around the world; and we finally understood why the ANC had wanted the desks to be at an angle of forty-five degrees. It was so that Nelson Mandela wouldn't have to stretch too far.

There were two main obstacles to peace now: the angry alienation of the far right-wing Afrikaners, and the vicious conflict that was going on between Inkatha and the ANC. Slowly, the extraordinary mood which was starting to come over South Africa affected even these intractable problems. Gen. Constand Viljoen, who had once headed the South African army and was now the leader of the Volksfront, representing right-wing Afrikaners, met Nelson Mandela secretly, and the two men got on remarkably well with one another. As a result, the Volksfront agreed to drop its opposition to the election, and to field candidates. That left only the real extremists. I went to see the *enragé* of *enragés*, Eugene Terre'blanche, whose AWB movement was holding a rally in the small town of Brits, not far from Johannesburg. It was a hallucinogenic vision of beer bellies and shaven heads, dark glasses and weaponry: *Soldier of Fortune* magazine made flesh.

Terre'blanche, a one-time actor, gave an effective speech in his flowing Afrikaans. He compared the founders of apartheid to Julius Caesar, stabbed in the back by the very people who ought to have been the greatest supporters of the principle of division by race; meaning, of course, F.W. de Klerk's National Party. It was good knock-about stuff, but the National Party and Viljoen, by deciding to take part in the election, had siphoned off all but the extreme right-wingers. On the rugby ground at Brits the single rickety stand, which could have held

600 people, was only half full. There was applause when Terre'blanche finished, but no frenzy; and whereas my colleagues and I might have expected plenty of jostling, and perhaps a beating-up in a quiet corner, we were left alone. The heart had gone out of white supremacy.

Terre'blanche's men had tried to intervene in an attempted coup in Bophuthatswana a few weeks before, and some had been killed by a single black policeman in front of the cameras. It had been a terrible shock to everyone who thought whites were inevitably dominant. After his rally I said to Terre'blanche that this incident was the single biggest reason why his support was dropping away. He denied it. Then, his pale blue eyes lighting up, he gripped my hand with his thick fingers, and I could feel the stiff hairs that grew on their backs.

'Things will happen,' he said. 'You will see.'

We did. Bombs soon went off in various parts of South Africa, and a few unfortunates were killed or injured. It made no difference. The process of reconciliation had become inevitable. Now only Inkatha refused to take part in the election. The killings in Natal grew worse.

« »

On Sunday 17 April, the day before Inkatha supporters were due to march through the centre of Johannesburg to the ANC's headquarters, in revenge for the shootings of several of their members there some weeks earlier, a number of political and religious groups held a peace rally in Durban. An enormous crowd of people, black, white and Indian, had gathered in the main rugby stadium. There was a remarkable and moving outpouring of feeling, as speaker after speaker prayed for peace. We moved through the crowd and felt the extraordinary waves of anxiety and grief washing over us.

'If you've lost a member of your family, stand up.'

Close to us, a black girl of about eighteen in a bright red dress stood up, her eyes full of tears, and raised her hand. In it she held the photograph of a young man: a brother, perhaps, or a boyfriend. Others were standing up now, and soon all over the rugby field people were standing in their dozens, then in their hundreds. A white woman put her arms round the black woman who was standing next to her; a white man went down on his knees.

'Let us now pray for the leaders of South Africa.'

There was silence as they prayed, and the intensity of it was so strong it seemed as though nothing could stand in its way.

And yet, up in the VIP lounge at the stadium, there was an empty seat. Chief Mangosuthu Buthelezi, the head of Inkatha, had come as an act of reconciliation, he told us. We had filmed him meeting one of the top figures in the ANC, Jacob Zuma, before the service. There was personal warmth between them, but when I asked him if he would call off the march his followers were planning for Johannesburg the next day, Buthelezi merely said, 'Why should we?'

And yet something was going on after all. Two days earlier an elderly Kenyan academic, Professor Washington Okumu, had flown in with a British and American team of negotiators. Okumu had known Buthelezi for twenty years. Buthelezi didn't want to meet the group, and took a flight back to Natal. It seemed like the last effective chance for peace.

And then, in mid air, the plane developed engine trouble and had to turn back. Buthelezi, a practising Christian, decided this was a sign to him to speak to Professor Okumu after all; and Okumu went a long way to persuade him to take part in the election. The service for peace at the rugby ground in Durban was the deciding factor. The day after it took place, Buthelezi called off the march through Johannesburg and announced that Inkatha would take part in the election. There were those who used the word 'grandstanding'; but I had the impression, talking to Buthelezi afterwards, that something more than mere political calculation was involved. It was, perhaps, the spirit of the moment.

Extraordinary things were starting to happen. Nelson Mandela was greeted like an emperor when he visited Natal, and F.W. de Klerk went electioneering in Soweto. That was a change of enormous proportions. At his campaign headquarters in Pretoria afterwards I asked him if it had all come about as the result of a sudden flash of inspiration: to release Mandela from prison, to negotiate a settlement with him, to hold elections which would inevitably mean handing over power to the majority?

Transcript of interview with F.W. de Klerk, 27.4.94

de K: If you mean, did I have a Damascus revelation, the answer is no. It didn't come about like that, nor could it.

```
It was a process of change in people's minds, and in my
own mind, which took place over quite a long period of
time.

JS: And now that it's coming to fruition, you don't have
any doubts?

de K: There was nothing else we could have done. And it's
working out very peacefully, very well. We have a lot to
be grateful for.
```

A telephone engineer, an Afrikaner in his early fifties, came into the BBC office to install some more phones. He was just the kind of person that had most to fear from the changes which the election would bring, and people like him were always regarded as bed-rock supporters of the old apartheid system.

'What do you think about all this?' one of my colleagues asked him.

'I feel as though a burden has been lifted off my shoulders.'

A few miles away, in a quiet, pleasantly tended garden, I talked to Mandela's former gaoler, Warrant Officer James Gregory. He had first encountered him on Robben Island, a brutal, dehumanized prison where some of the warders had treated the political prisoners abominably. Not so James Gregory. He came to realize Mandela's moral strength and protect it; and when Mandela's son died in a car crash he spent a good deal of extra time with him, allowing Mandela to talk about the boy and about everything that had happened to himself. Some years later Gregory's son also died in a car crash. Now it was Mandela who sat with him for hours on end, listening to him and quietly asking questions to draw him out.

'Some of the other warders called me *Kaffirboetie*, you know, nigger lover. But I didn't take any notice. Then eventually the minister of prisons called me in to see him. I was very worried, but he said I had opened a line of communication to Nelson, and one day that might be important. So when he moved to another prison, I was moved there too. And I stayed with him till they let him out altogether.'

Gregory pulled out a letter from Mandela, thanking him for everything he had done over the years they had been together. And on the night of the first formal banquet after Mandela had been elected president, ex-Warrant Officer James Gregory was one of the guests of honour.

'You took the sting from Mandela's bitterness towards white people,' Gregory's boss told him when he retired. But it was South Africa's great good fortune that Mandela had long given up any bitterness towards white people. James Gregory's real achievement, perhaps, was in helping some white people to realize that.

'The struggle for democracy has never,' Mandela said, later standing on the balcony of the City Hall in Cape Town, leaning in his dignified way towards the microphone, 'been a matter pursued by one race, class, colour, religion, or gender among South Africans.'

He was entirely right. Each word, enunciated with that slow, thoughtful care which his age, his years in prison and his attitude to the world combined to give him, rolled around the huge crowd packed into the square and echoed off the face of Table Mountain above us. Heads in the crowd nodded: a bearded, toothless old African, a beautiful young coloured woman, a white man in a striped shirt who might have been an accountant. Close by, an Afrikaans policeman was moved to tears by the emotion of the moment.

They, we, all wanted to believe this new myth that was being created for South Africa from the balcony of the City Hall: there was no guilt, there were no enemies, there would be no witch-hunts, no trials for retrospective thought-crime. Everyone, by association if not in person, was officially absolved from the sins of the past.

Mandela was making white South Africa out to be a nation of James Gregorys. And as I listened to the words he spoke from the City Hall balcony, echoing back from the incomparable mountain above, and glanced at the white policeman with the tears in his eyes, and saw the curt nod he gave me as he caught me looking at him, I too wanted the myth of the righteous white man to be true.

At a minute to midnight on 26 April 1994, the past became another country in South Africa. As I stood in the cold at a ceremony in the centre of Johannesburg with my Afrikaans producer, a bottle of pink champagne beside us, the old flag of South Africa, an orange, blue and white tricolour with a jumble of little provincial flags in the centre, was pulled down. The band played 'Die Stem', the beautiful old pre-apartheid words which had been absorbed into the old national anthem. Then, in the first seconds of 27 April, the new flag, a mixture of all the colours of the new South Africa, was broken out. 'Nkosi Sikekel'iAfrika', God Save Africa, the anthem of the ANC which it had once been illegal to play, sounded out in the darkness.

If there were tears, they were quickly forgotten. The African Jazz Pioneers started up the easy, lively rhythm of township music, and we danced for hours. Under the influence of the pink champagne, I found myself doing a few turns with the saxophonist.

A few hours later, at dawn, the queues started forming outside the polling-stations in extraordinary numbers. At the same time a bomb went off at the international arrivals hall of Johannesburg airport: no one was hurt, but it was the last salute of the far-right supremacists to the system which had come to an end. Otherwise the day passed off quietly: even the thieves were too busy voting to work. Late in the afternoon I went with a camera crew to one of the most dangerous areas in the whole of South Africa, and filmed the voting there.

Transcript of report for *Nine O'Clock News*, 27.4.94

JS: This is Alexandra, on the edge of Johannesburg, perhaps the most crime-ridden township in South Africa: twenty or so murders a week, a car hijacking every twenty minutes. Not today, though. In Alexandra, as in most other townships across the country, it's been entirely peaceful and quiet.

John Simpson, BBC News, Johannesburg

The result, when it was announced, seemed to have been crafted in politics heaven. The ANC received 62.7 per cent of the vote: impressive, but not quite enough to give it the two-thirds majority it needed to be able to write the new constitution entirely by itself. Mandela, more interested in the welfare of the country than in the narrow interests of his party, said he was profoundly relieved; which irritated the less reflective ANC politicians. The National Party received 20.4 per cent – far less than the 35 per cent they had been hoping for, but enough to give them control over the Western Cape.

Inkatha won KwaZulu-Natal, and Mandela accepted the result although there was widespread suspicion that there had been cheating there. Even the Volksfront of Gen. Constand Viljoen got 680,000 votes,

which ensured that the idea of an independent Afrikaner state would
be taken with a certain seriousness. As for the Pan-Africanist Congress,
which had once adopted as its slogan 'One settler, one bullet', it
received 1.25 per cent. For all the serious, reconciliation-minded parties
which had taken part, as for all the contestants in Alice in Wonderland's
caucus race, there was a suitable prize.

« »

'And the ransomed of the Lord shall return, and come unto Zion, and
sorrow and sighing shall flee away.'

The splendours of the King James version of the Bible echoed
around the Arts and Crafts splendours of Sir Herbert Baker's Anglican
cathedral in Cape Town. Archbishop Desmond Tutu was holding a
service of thanksgiving for the peaceful outcome of the election.

'Many of us in the run-up to the election were gritting our teeth
and putting on our tin hats. And then the miracle came. We have come
to say thank you to God for that incredible miracle that came to our
country. Black and white stood together and voted; and then they made
a profound scientific discovery: we're all South Africans.'

He made us stand and applaud all those political leaders who had
decided to take part in the election, and we sang 'Now Thank We All
Our God' with a greater degree of feeling than I had ever heard.

That evening the producer, the crew and I went down to the beach
at Camps Bay in Cape Town. They were all South Africans, and they
felt like celebrating. I followed them across the pale sandy beach as
the sun went down, pulling off my shoes and socks and paddling
in the bitterly cold surging water. I looked back to the road along the
beach-front. Seventeen years earlier Diane, Julia, Eleanor and I had
spent Christmas Day on this beach, and I had pointed out to them the
serious, silent coloured children who were standing on the pavement
watching them play, and not able to come onto the beach themselves.

We stood watching the sun sink slowly into the sea, then hurried
back to the nearby studio to do a live interview for the *Six O'Clock
News*. We got there so late I didn't have time to wash the sand off my
feet and put my socks and shoes back on. The studio staff loved it: I
looked fine on screen, but from my knees southwards I looked like a
beach-bum.

There was one last moment of grandeur. On 10 May Nelson

Mandela's inauguration as President took place in Pretoria. Half a million people, black and white, had come to witness it. It was one of the happiest days of my life.

There was a wonderful moment when, after the flypast by the Impala and Mirage jets of the South African air force, a squadron of helicopters passed close overhead. In 1977 I had seen people in Soweto lose control of themselves with fear when the helicopters came over. The helicopter had been the ultimate symbol of the cruelty of white rule. Now they laughed and cheered to see them fly over; the helicopters belonged to them.

I sat in an editing-suite that evening with a colleague of mine, Peter Burdin, as we compiled our account of this remarkable day: Mandela holding up F.W. de Klerk's hand in triumph, and laughing and singing in his happiness. And when he spoke of creating 'a society of which all mankind will be proud, an actual South African reality to strengthen the human soul and sustain all our hopes,' he seemed to be speaking for every one of us.

Transcript of report for *Nine O'Clock News*, 10.5.94

JS: The new President's speech was full of passion. But there were no clenched fists, no chanting of the old slogan 'Amandla!', or 'Power!', no references to 'comrades' or the armed struggle. This was the President of the whole nation speaking. He spoke at times in Afrikaans, and he reserved some of his greatest praise for his white vice-president.

Mandela: Mr de Klerk is one of the greatest reformers ever, and one of the greatest sons of our soil.

JS: It was a supremely happy day, and everyone was enjoying it.

[Jazz music; people dancing]

Man in crowd: I feel so happy and relaxed. This is a dream come true.

'We could just end it there,' I said when we'd edited that passage.

'I think it just needs something more. A bit more of you, maybe,' Peter said. 'Some final thought.'

'I've used up every final thought I've ever had over the last couple of weeks,' I replied. Then something occurred to me. 'Would you call the Pretoria police and find out how many crimes have been committed here today?'

When I lived in South Africa, half a million black people roaming the streets of Pretoria would have been most white people's definition of revolution. The idea was synonymous with violence, looting and murder. Peter came back and told me what the police had said, and over some pictures of people dancing in the streets I wrote the pay-off:

```
Tonight they were still dancing; and according to the
Pretoria police, not a single crime has been committed
here all day.

John Simpson, BBC News, Pretoria.
```

It hasn't stayed that way, of course. The crime levels have risen higher and higher, and the Afrikaners who once gladly handed over power with the feeling that they were doing something noble and decent and generous now feel that the gesture was wasted. White farmers and their families who willingly adopted the new South Africa have been murdered in their dozens; yet on the one occasion when a farmer fired off nervously at a group of interlopers crossing his land and killed a black child, it was as though the whole basis of Mandela's agreement with the whites had been undermined. The Afrikaners feel they have been tricked, and are very bitter. English-speaking whites are leaving the country at an alarming rate. Mandela, if asked about the pandemic crime which affects the life of every single person in the big cities of South Africa, blandly says it's all an exaggeration. Corruption is growing, and leading ANC supporters have very quickly got their hands into the pot. The apartheid of wealth and poverty has replaced the apartheid of black and white, and the ANC has done nothing serious to eradicate it. A civil war by other means is being fought out in South Africa. It has become dangerous to drive a car down a motorway there.

So does all this negate what was done during those days in April and May 1994? Nothing can. It genuinely was a kind of miracle, and it was a privilege to be there and watch it. There are no happy endings in real life, no point at which the characters walk off into the sunset, the music breaks out and the credits roll. The moment itself is what counts, and the moment in South Africa was wonderful; whatever may have happened later. And with a little luck, some afterglow from the original miracle will still be there to illuminate the future.

There was a miracle in my own life too. A couple of years before the 1994 election, a friend of mine, John Harrison, had been the BBC's chief political correspondent at Westminister, and he had been very unhappy. One afternoon he stopped me in the corridor at Television Centre, and asked me with some emotion if I could do anything to help him get the job of Southern Africa correspondent, based in Johannesburg. I felt really sorry for him, and agreed to put a word in. He got the job.

As the South African election drew closer, I spoke to him over the phone. He was a highly competitive man, and wasn't altogether happy that I was coming; but he said he knew he couldn't keep the story entirely to himself, and would rather I came than someone else. I explained as tactfully as I could that I would make background films about the issues while he did the main news coverage.

'I'll get you the best producer,' he said.

He kept his promise. The producer he hired had made a series of excellent documentaries for the SABC on the arts as well as on politics. Her name was Dee Krüger. Then one evening as John was driving back to the satellite point from Bophuthatswana, where he had been covering the AWB's foolish part in the coup, his car left the road and crashed. He died instantly.

I first became aware of Dee when I walked into the office where I was to work. It was empty apart from a desk and a telephone. She was one of the most beautiful women I had ever seen, and as a way of making conversation I offered to make her a cup of tea. It seemed to make an impression on her.

Over the next four weeks we worked together closely. It was she who sat next to me as the old South African flag came down, and braved the AWB at Brits, and stood with me when Archbishop Tutu held his service of thanksgiving in St George's Cathedral, and walked on the beach with me at Camps Bay, and watched beside me when Nelson Mandela lifted F.W. de Klerk's hand in triumph at the inauguration. I fell deeply in love with her.

The next few months were difficult and painful, but slowly things shaped themselves. I have been very fortunate with the women in my life, and remained on good terms with Tira as I had with Diane.

Dee came to Britain and lived for a while in Covent Garden. Then we moved to Chelsea. On 8 May 1996 we were married at Chelsea Register Office. We made it a very small occasion, but my past life was thoroughly represented: Brian Brooks, my mentor from my childhood, was there. Nicholas Snowman, my room-mate at Magdalene, was best man, and Martha Gellhorn and Dominic and Rosa Lawson were among the guests. As we came out onto the front steps in the King's Road, and the guests showered us with May blossom gathered that morning by Dee's sister Gina, an entirely new and extremely happy chapter in my life was just opening.

19

Colophon

LONDON AND BELGRADE, 1999

BUT OF COURSE I WAS married already. I don't mean my marriage with Diane, which was later dissolved; I mean the one which took place on 1 September 1966, and has so far lasted thirty-two years. I can't pretend there hasn't been a little infidelity from time to time, on both sides. But essentially we have stayed together through thick and thin, rain and shine, for richer and (in my case) for poorer. That's because I have been married to the BBC; and the BBC doesn't make you rich. What it does is make you feel grateful, against all reason, that you work for the BBC.

Maybe I am. What other set of initials would have got me so quickly into the private office of Boris Yeltsin, or the cave of a group of mujaheddin, or the château of the Emperor Bokassa, or the hotel suite of Jacques Chirac, or the plane of Ayatollah Khomeini? What other organization would impress a Colombian drugs baron sufficiently to make him risk arrest to give me an interview? Or a group of Hezbollah guerrillas, so that they decided not to kidnap me? Or a Russian policeman, so that he let me off without a bribe? Despite all the terrible foul-ups the BBC has committed, despite the fact that it can be a rotten employer, despite its pomposity and slowness and inefficiency, despite the length of its memory about trivial administrative detail and the shortness of its memory about the promises it has made, despite its slowness to pay and its speed to demand payment, despite the rotten tea and the stained brown carpets and the fact that no one ever seems to answer the phones, despite the thousand daily errors of fact and the ten thousand daily errors of pronunciation, I still love it dearly.

Now, to the surprise of us all, the BBC has become the largest news-gathering organization on earth: the biggest there has ever been. If all goes right, and we don't hit an iceberg in our hubris, the BBC will be in television what it has always been in radio: a dominant international broadcaster.

I remember sitting in the canteen at Broadcasting House in 1968 listening as an Australian-born colleague of mine, Will Baines, explained that Britain had it in its power to be the world's radio and television super-power. I thought he had been reading too much Marshall McLuhan; anyway, it seemed absurd to think that we could compete with American money and influence. But a generation later it could happen.

« »

So why, if the future is so bright we have to wear shades, are so many BBC people so depressed? 'Beeb Morale At Rock Bottom', said a headline in a trade magazine the other day. I have been reading that headline, with minor variations, throughout my entire working life. I had only been in the BBC for six months when the old radio system, Home Service, Light Programme and Third Programme, was scrapped in favour of the unimaginatively named Radios One, Two, Three and Four. 'BBC Morale Reaches Lowest Point' said, I think, the *Daily Telegraph*.

We had a staff meeting about it with Donald Edwards, the head of news at the time. Outside the sky darkened and the rain fell with astonishing force.

'And God said, I will smite Donald Edwards,' said the Newsroom wit, looking out of the window. Everyone was certain that standards would be lowered, the BBC's reputation tarnished. The expression 'dumbing-down' was still decades from being invented, but it expressed exactly what we were all sure would happen.

The collective memory is so short. There is nothing faintly new about any of the accusations which are directed at the BBC nowadays: that it's lowering its standards, that it's cowardly in the face of politicians, that it's Stalinist, that it's heading for disaster and extinction. To look back to some previous Golden Age when the BBC was great and bemoan the fall from its old high standards is either self-delusive or disingenuous. 'Oh for the days of Trethowan and Milne,' some histrionic soul wrote anonymously in the internal computer system recently, after some new accusation about political cowardice by the top management; yet in the days of Trethowan and Milne other histrionic souls dreamt of the glories of Reith: and it wasn't any truer or more false then.

The BBC has changed out of all recognition in terms of its management structures since 1966. But the people who work for it now are pretty much the same as they have always been, especially in the area of news and current affairs: hard-working, competitive, and inclined to be rather serious-minded. Their compulsion to make sure that they get the best possible material on the air is remarkable.

John Harrison, the BBC correspondent in Johannesburg, died because he wanted to get an extra sequence of pictures on the screen. Cameramen, camerawomen and sound recordists sometimes take immense risks to get coverage which is only slightly better than what everyone else is getting. Producers and picture editors wreck their marriages or their health by staying away from home too long and racing too late to the satellite-point, having added yet another unneeded bit of polish to the final production. Every television organization has people like this; there's something about the medium that encourages such behaviour. But the BBC specializes in them. And the people who are prepared to put themselves and their lives on the line *are* the BBC.

'You're just the temporary staff,' a cameraman once snarled at the head of television news. 'We're the permanent ones.'

He was right; and that kind of bolshie, obsessive approach is what makes good programmes.

The changes which John Birt began to introduce in 1988 have of course been deeply unpopular within the BBC. It's not hard to understand why. A new management culture has hit a staid, old-fashioned and not particularly well-run organization with the force of a meteor, and everyone's life has been affected by it. The BBC, never knowingly underadministered, nowadays has managers like the Austro-Hungarian navy had admirals, so many of them that it is hard to imagine how they can each have a differentiated job to do. The culture seems to get tougher and more aggressive the further down the system it travels. Men and women who have served the organization long and faithfully find themselves being hectored by people less than half their age, whose expertise is restricted to repeating the weasel words of the language of down-sizing.

Although there has been an extraordinary expansion in jobs, in services, in equipment, and in the money available for programmes, it has been achieved partly by getting people to be much more flexible about the work they do. The days when going abroad for the BBC was like taking the British Expeditionary Force to France, complete with lighting-man, sound-man, picture editor, producer and correspondent plus local fixer, are long gone, and few would want them back. Much of my work is now done alone with a lone cameraman or -woman, who lights, records sound, edits, and sometimes makes the arrangements. It is quicker, and if the technical quality isn't always quite as good, it certainly allows us to cover things more easily.

But of course old dogs – and I am one of them in many ways – dislike the prospect of having to learn new tricks. And if they are able to wrap their reluctance in some kind of moral guise, they are liable to get a lot of attention in the media. Mark Tully, who had served BBC radio in India famously for years, was at last faced with great upheavals, including the arrival of a new, much younger, television-capable correspondent. Tully denounced the Birtist management of the BBC as Stalinist.

It was a basic misunderstanding of the nature both of the BBC, and of Stalinism. Under Stalin, people did not condemn their leader and get away with it. They couldn't even tell jokes about him. The BBC is not a pyramidal organization like Stalin's Russia; it is composed of semi-independent baronies, each of which is inclined to resist outside interference. If Mark Tully had worked for a more conventional employer – a newspaper, a big industrial corporation or a government – he would have been sacked on the spot. The BBC doesn't work like that. He left the BBC Delhi office eventually, but by his own decision. And he never suffered for attacking the management. On the contrary, it made him extremely popular among all those who felt their jobs, or their programme standards, were at risk from the Birtist revolution: and that included a good many editors. Someone drew a halo over his head on a publicity photograph mounted on the main staircase at Broadcasting House.

If attacking John Birt gets you publicity and does you no harm, defending him does you absolutely no good at all. Early in 1993 someone leaked the details of his personal finances to the press. There was nothing illegal about them, but at a time when people's budgets and their very jobs were being cut back it didn't look good. Nor did the revelation that, like me, he was on a freelance contract rather than being a paid-up member of the BBC's staff.

It seemed to reinforce all the suspicions of the embattled people who had served the BBC throughout their entire lives, and who saw him as a carpet-bagger without the slightest loyalty to an organization he was convulsing. Most of the newspapers went for John Birt about it. Many felt that British public life was damaged as badly as the BBC itself by what they saw as his carpet-bagging. Others disliked the thought that, if John Birt's grand schemes came to fruition, the BBC might play too big a part in world television. It was noticeable that the Murdoch press was particularly hostile.

One evening, just as it looked as though Birt would be forced to resign, I had a call from Polly Toynbee, then the BBC's Social Affairs editor. She had drafted a letter in Birt's support, and wanted me to sign it. The other editors of the big departments in BBC News had already done so: Robin Oakley in the Political Unit and Peter Jay at Economics. That left me. I was the only long-serving BBC figure among them, and although the Gulf War period was fading I still had a certain amount of prestige left. It was plain to me as I listened to Polly that my signature, or the lack of it, would be decisive. If I signed, there was a chance that Birt's job would be saved. If I refused, it would be obvious that the sole BBC old-timer among the specialist editors had turned against him, and the letter would result in even worse damage to him.

I'd never been particularly close to John Birt. Unlike his chilly public persona, he was pleasant, rather warm and surprisingly tentative in private. But I wasn't particularly happy about many of the massive changes he was introducing into the BBC. The pain had been intense, and the gain less obvious. Nevertheless I had benefited from some of the changes myself: the enormous expansion of the BBC news and current affairs department, and its transformation from a small, cosy, purely national television news service into a first-class international one. After the years of being rather apologetic about our amateurish status, I was able to point to all the bureaux and correspondents we now had around the world. All this was the direct result of John Birt's policies.

So was the possibility that the new satellite television services, BBC World and BBC Prime, would play a big part in world broadcasting. As a believer in the public service ideal, I didn't want to see the BBC drift into genteel decline as had happened to CBC in Canada and ABC in Australia. It seemed to me that there was only one choice: between becoming bigger and more powerful, and becoming smaller and more parochial. This begs a dozen questions, but the options were few and the decision a stark one.

I agreed to sign the letter.

Directly it was published, it tipped the balance as I had guessed it would. The Murdoch campaign eased up, and the pressure slackened. But the next few weeks weren't pleasant. I lost two friends of long-standing for good, and three or more for a longish period of time. Someone kicked in the rear door of my car in the BBC news garage. I must have had fifty letters from inside and outside the Corporation, the nastiest of which were of course anonymous: 'You arse-licking toady . . .', 'I hope you die of cancer,' that kind of thing. As Helmut Kohl said when the egg hit him, it happens.

It goes without saying that I didn't gain anything from having signed the John Birt letter. No one in the higher echelons of the BBC so much as mentioned the incident to me, and as a baron among barons my position in the structure remained entirely unchanged in every way: neither better nor worse.

So the BBC held its course, and has continued on it to this day. It's something of a white-knuckle ride. No one can be entirely sure whether the money will be there to build up the kind of structures that are required, and the BBC's critics are already starting to question whether an organization which gets some of its money from commercial sources should also continue to receive a licence fee. Yet the public service ethos still seems to be as strong as ever. There are dangers, of course. What happens when the BBC's commercial interests in, say, China, conflict with its determination to report honestly what is going on in China? When that happens to Rupert Murdoch, the commercial interests naturally win. This hasn't, as far as I can tell, happened with the BBC.

A decision was taken to call off an undercover assignment to China because it was clear the BBC's coverage of the handover of Hong Kong in June 1997 would suffer as a result. Some footage of Chinese repression in Tibet, which *Newsnight* obtained, wasn't broadcast for the same reason. Neither of these were news events which were deliberately suppressed; it wasn't like ignoring a statement by a leading Chinese or Tibetan dissident, or conveniently failing to mention some particular act of brutality. In both cases it was a matter of timing, and the judgement was that the wider interests of BBC news coverage would be better served by holding off.

Nevertheless, tiptoeing round the Chinese government doesn't work, since China, a natural bully, regards compromise as weakness. In general, it seems to me that it shouldn't be for free broadcasters and journalists to worry about the reactions of repressive regimes; if anyone does the worrying, it should be the repressive regimes. As Waldo Maguire once told me, to take political considerations into account isn't the job of a journalist.

As for me, however much I may still love the BBC after our long years of marriage, I would walk out without a backward look the day it decided to trim its reporting to suit its commercial interests. It would have ceased to be the BBC then, and there would be no difference between it and any other fat international organization. But I don't somehow think it will happen.

« »

Nowadays the lines are fallen to me in pleasant places. My flat in County Dublin, overlooking the Irish Sea, is a source of great peace to my wife and me: a base from which we can move out and travel. Together we have a programme (*Simpson's World*) which I present and she produces, and which tries to do something a little different in television news: allowing the viewers to see things more for themselves, and the interviewees to talk at length instead of being interrupted and sliced up into sound-bites.

I feel more contented and at ease with myself than I have ever felt before. But I also know that everything can change in an instant; I have, after all, made a living by reporting on other people whose lives have done exactly that, for better or worse. In the charming, hot, noisy town of Fatehpur Sikri, in the Indian state of Uttar Pradesh, you can see a carved inscription in elaborate script on an otherwise unremarkable, rather tatty wall. It is an aphorism of the Moghul Emperor Akbar:

> The world is a bridge; cross it, but build no house upon it.

Make the most of it, in other words, but don't rely on it too much. If you do, you can (as my South African wife would say) come short.

This book has been written peripatetically, and in the process I have been surrounded by some very questionable people in some very strange places indeed: Afghanistan, Albania, Colombia, Abkhazia, Somalia, Iran, as well as easier ones like China, Argentina and Brazil. I even wrote part of it crossing the Atlantic on the QE2.

But I began it with a story about being in Belgrade during the war of 1999. I managed to hang on there, sometimes by the skin of my teeth, for fourteen weeks altogether; and I would have stayed longer if I had not been thrown out by the security police for 'non-objective' reporting; that is, reporting which was too objective for their taste. By that stage the war itself was over. But my part in it had become rather passive, since towards the end of May I slipped, completely unromantically, on the wet tiles beside the swimming-pool of the Hyatt Hotel, and ruptured the tendons of my thigh muscle so badly that I needed an urgent operation.

Fortunately, by that stage my wife Dee had been with me for almost a month, braving the NATO bombs and the sometimes angry crowds in order to make some *Simpson's World*'s there. She and our local producer, Dragan Petrovic, came with me in the ambulance and took me into the hospital. One of the stretcher-bearers, an unpleasant shaven-headed character, started shouting at me about Tony Blair and NATO and bombing, but even at a time like that, doubled up with pain, I retained enough of my instinctive irritability to tell him to fuck off.

I had filmed inside this hospital before. It was surrounded by potential NATO targets, and part of it had been hit. Power-cuts occurred every day here, and operations were always being affected as a result. Even so, there was nothing for it but to place myself under the care of a scalpel-wielding Serb and hope the Hippocratic oath still applied; I certainly wasn't going to leave Belgrade with the war still not finished.

That night, the operation over (it had been carried out with great care) and the spinal injection beginning to wear off, I lay in a large ward listening to the NATO planes flying overhead. Most of my war had been spent in the Hyatt Hotel, which even NATO seemed unlikely to regard as a target. The hospital was different. Every now and then there would be the sound of a heavy explosion, not far away. The patients up and down the corridor groaned or yelled out in their sleep. It was completely dark, because the power had been cut yet again.

I lay there utterly immobilized, feeling like someone who has so far only had one leg set in concrete by the Mafia. Sometimes one of the fifty or so people in the ward would call urgently for a nurse.

'Sestre!'

No one would come. The hospital tried to minimize the danger to its staff by keeping as few people on at night as possible. There were only two nurses in our part of the hospital, and neither of them seem to come our way often. What would happen, I wondered, if the ward were hit by NATO? Would they leave me till last? How could I get out, given that I couldn't even move?

'Sestre!'

No response. I drifted into a kind of sleep, troubled by the aftermath of anaesthesia, memories of the accident, the sound of bombers overhead and the shudder of explosions. In many ways, I suppose, it was unpleasant and frightening. Yet even then I saw it as something slightly different, as though I were standing outside myself and observing. It was an extraordinary experience, what journalists would call a story, and for once I was the participant as well as the onlooker. I used to hate the expression, because I thought it had too many connotations of invention, embroidery and shaping about it. But that is really what I exist to do: discover stories, and tell them to other people.

Once, perhaps, this was done round a fire, in a cave or a cottage. Now it is done remotely, with all the paraphenalia of television. In the future it will be done in ways which we can no more imagine than the cave-dwellers or the cottagers could conceive of television. But it is something which human beings seem to need, whatever their circumstances.

This is really why I do the work I do, and live the strange, rootless, insecure life I do; and even when it goes wrong I can turn it into a story. Lying in my hospital bed I fished a torch out of my bag, reached for my notebook, and started writing a despatch for From Our Own Correspondent about being in a Serbian hospital during the bombing.

I much admire Sir Richard Burton, who wrote to his friend Monckton Milnes in 1863:

> Starting in a hollowed log of wood – some thousand miles up a river, with an infinitesimal prospect of returning, I ask myself 'Why?' and the only echo is 'damned fool! . . . the Devil drives'.

I know the feeling, of course; anyone who does my job must do. But this isn't me; I don't feel driven by inner demons. Nor is it anything to do with being brought up in a strange way, or leading a wandering life, or having an unhealthy liking for danger or for going where no one else has been before me. It isn't even that I like the sound of my own voice; not totally, anyway. It's because I like finding out stories and telling them to other people. I've spent most of my life doing it.

And I hope to continue.

Index